Property

BY JAMES E. KRIER
University of Michigan

Seventeenth Edition

THOMSON

WEST

EDITORIAL OFFICES: 1 North Dearborn St., Suite 650, Chicago, IL 60602
REGIONAL OFFICES: Chicago, Dallas, Los Angeles, New York, Washington, D.C.

PROJECT EDITOR
Melissa B. Vasich, B.A., J.D.
Attorney At Law

SERIES EDITOR
Elizabeth L. Snyder, B.A., J.D.
Attorney At Law

QUALITY CONTROL EDITOR
Sanetta M. Hister

Summary of Contents

Text Correlation Chart

Gilbert Law Summary PROPERTY	Cribbet, Johnson, Findley, Smith *Property* 2002 (8th ed.)	Dukeminier, Krier, Alexander, Schill *Property* 2006 (6th ed.)	Kurtz, Hovenkamp *Cases and Materials on American Property Law* 2003 (4th ed.)	Nelson, Stoebuck, Whitman *Contemporary Property* 2002 (2nd ed.)	Singer *Property Law: Rules, Policies, and Practices* 2006 (4th ed.)
I. ACQUISITION OF PROPERTY					
A. Introduction	Page 2-78, 83-84	Page 3-17	Page 1-8	Page 2-29	Page 3-4
B. The Rule of Capture	42-49, 63-69, 88-90, 633-669	17-50	8-37, 67-82	32-37, 162-196	3-24, 76-91, 164-173, 232-237
C. Acquisition by Creation	50, 52-60, 151-159	51-93	28-31, 82-123	13-21, 1237-1283	32-53, 1087-1141, 1154-1171
D. Acquisition by Find	85-113, 132-136	95-112	37-67	37-64	92-97
E. Acquisition by Adverse Possession	136-150, 1213-1252	112-157	193-245	79-124, 883-885	179-226
F. Remedies of a Possessor	132-136	87-90, 97-98	159-165	29-32, 61-64	103-114
G. Rights of Owners	10-12, 26-37	86-93			103-124
II. PERSONAL PROPERTY					
A. Bailments	114-121, 135-136	97	175-192	64-79	101-102
B. Gifts of Personal Property	160-181	157-172	123-158		75-76
C. Bona Fide Purchasers of Personal Property	122-131	148-150, 155-156	165-175		101-102
III. POSSESSORY ESTATES					
A. Introduction	185-200	173-181	246-263	219-224	503-505
B. The Fee Simple	200-212, 225-247	181-186, 206-224	264-278	224-239	505-508, 516-526, 557-567
C. The Fee Tail	247-252	186-189	279-290	239-243	513
D. The Life Estate	212-225	189-206	290-294	243-245, 286-296	508-509, 553-557
E. The Rule Against Restraints on Alienation	284-287	179-180, 190-196, 223-224	275	284-286	450-472
F. Summary of Possessory Estates	199-200	181-224	261-264	223-224	503-505, 514-515
IV. FUTURE INTERESTS					
A. Introduction	253	225-226	261-263	246-274	503-505
B. Reversion	253	226-227		248-249, 254-255	508-509
C. Possibility of Reverter	242-243, 253, 305	207, 227	276-277	248, 255-256	506-508
D. Right of Entry	242-243, 253, 305	208, 227	277-278	248, 256-257	507-508
E. Remainder	253-262, 289-293	229-232	295-297, 301-322	249-253, 257-272	508-511

Gilbert Law Summary PROPERTY	Cribbet, Johnson, Findley, Smith *Property* 2002 (8th ed.)	Dukeminier, Krier, Alexander, Schill *Property* 2006 (6th ed.)	Kurtz, Hovenkamp *Cases and Materials on American Property Law* 2003 (4th ed.)	Nelson, Stoebuck, Whitman *Contemporary Property* 2002 (2nd ed.)	Singer *Property Law: Rules, Policies, and Practices* 2006 (4th ed.)
F. Executory Interests	274-284, 293-298	233-239	297-299	249-253, 272-274	508
G. Rules Restricting Contingent Remainders (Mostly Abolished)	262-274	240-244	322-332	264-267, 274-277	511-513
H. The Rule Against Perpetuities	284-287, 298-310	244-274	308, 332-347	277-282	529-553
I. The Trust	277-278	239-240, 249, 540-541	293, 372-373	217-218	323-328, 503, 514, 526-527
J. Summary of Future Interests	253	225-239	261-263	246-274	503-505, 514-515
V. CONCURRENT OWNERSHIP AND MARITAL RIGHTS					
A. Tenancy in Common	311-312	275-276	348-351	316-317, 355-373	570-571
B. Joint Tenancy	312-316, 337-369	276, 278-291	348-350, 360-379	312-314, 318-355, 378-383	571-573, 581-587
C. Tenancy by the Entirety	316-318, 358-361	276-277	350, 383-397	314-316, 374-378	575-576, 587-593
D. Rights and Duties of Co-Tenants	325-336	291-310	351-360	107-108, 355-373	573-581
E. Marital Rights on Divorce		321-335	395-396, 413-434	390-392	69-75, 595-596, 599-607
F. Marital Rights on Death	319-320	335-338	380-383	304-311	593-595, 598-599
G. Community Property	320-323	338-344	397-413	383-392	596-597
H. Rights of Unmarried Partners	323-324	344-359	434-457		608-624
VI. LANDLORD AND TENANT					
A. Introduction	385	363-376	458	245-246, 393-402	639-640
B. Types of Tenancies and Their Creation	385-394, 409-418	363-376	458-474, 589-595	402-415	640-642, 659-660
C. Selection of Tenants	395-404	376-384	979-1025	519-521	817-871
D. Landlord's Duty to Deliver Possession	404-409	384-388	474-483	415-421	679-680
E. Landlord's Duty Not to Interfere with Tenant's Quiet Enjoyment	423-435	421-431	490-498	420, 447-452	726-737
F. Landlord's Duty to Provide Habitable Premises	451-457	431-440, 449	488-490, 498-529, 536-555	429-479	701-720
G. Landlord's Tort Liability	451-457	440-441	529-536	484-510	738-742
H. Tenant's Duties	435-451	441-449	485-488, 595-609	421-429, 510-519, 557-569, 579-583	670-679, 692-697
I. Landlord's Remedies	458-478	403-421	571-589	479-484, 540-557, 569-579	642-670, 697-700
J. Assignment and Subletting	478-490	388-402	555-570	521-540, 592-620	680-692

Gilbert Law Summary PROPERTY	Cribbet, Johnson, Findley, Smith *Property* 2002 (8th ed.)	Dukeminier, Krier, Alexander, Schill *Property* 2006 (6th ed.)	Kurtz, Hovenkamp *Cases and Materials on American Property Law* 2003 (4th ed.)	Nelson, Stoebuck, Whitman *Contemporary Property* 2002 (2nd ed.)	Singer *Property Law: Rules, Policies, and Practices* 2006 (4th ed.)
VII. EASEMENTS AND COVENANTS					
A. Easements	492-552	668-740	612-672, 711, 721-728	715-810	207-214, 319-365
B. Real Covenants	553-569	740-746, 750-798	672-694, 711	584-660	365-394, 406-411
C. Equitable Servitudes	569-608	746-755, 773-786, 791-797	695-711, 714-721, 728-740	660-714	394-406, 411-425, 433-450
D. Common Interest Communities	369-384	798-819	1026-1035	161, 645-660	425-490
VIII. RIGHTS AGAINST NEIGHBORS					
A. Nuisance	608-626	639-666	743-788	125-160	271-284, 286-316
B. Right to Support	626-633	645-646	788-790	196-203	242-271
C. Rights in Airspace	669-690	644	747-757	153-160	284-287, 302-308
IX. PUBLIC LAND USE CONTROLS					
A. Zoning	693-706, 721-744, 816-846	821-939	887-978	1066-1236	871-949
B. Subdivision Control and Maps	706-714				
C. Eminent Domain	714-720, 745-815	941-1065	791-886	1064-1160	953-1067
X. THE SALE OF LAND					
A. The Contract for Sale of Land	849-1008	453-494, 502-513	1036-1100	812-901	743-779
B. The Deed	1009-1030, 1042-1068	513-532	1105-1126	927-952	779-780
C. Delivery of the Deed	1031-1042	532-541	1127-1145	953-969	780-781
D. Warranties of Title	1145-1168	513-514, 517-532	1149-1159	990-1000	781-783
E. Warranties of Quality	1129-1145	494-502		969-990	776
F. The Mortgage	901-928	541-558	1100-1104	336-342, 901-917	799-815
XI. TITLE ASSURANCE					
A. Recording System	1069-1127	559-614	1148-1149, 1159-1183	1000-1033	783-798
B. Title Registration	1184-1192	615-623	1206-1207	1033-1035	799
C. Title Insurance	1192-1213	623-635	1183-1206	1035-1046	798

Capsule Summary

I. ACQUISITION OF PROPERTY

A. INTRODUCTION §2
The most **fundamental rule** for determining ownership is that the **first person to take possession of a thing owns it** (**rule of capture**).

B. THE RULE OF CAPTURE

1. General Rule §3
Under the general rule, whoever is prior in time wins; *i.e.*, the first to capture resources is entitled to them.

2. Capture of Wild Animals §7
Wild animals **must be captured** to be owned; mere chase is not enough.

    a. Wounded or trapped animals §8
If a wild animal has been mortally wounded or trapped so that **capture is practically certain,** it is treated as captured. A competitor can interfere with another person's attempt to capture only if he **intends to capture** the animal. Generally, a captor must acquire physical control over the animal absent a **custom** to the contrary, *e.g.*, whalers.

    b. Wild animals with *animus revertendi* §13
Captured wild animals that develop a habit of returning to the captor's property continue to belong to the captor as they roam at large.

    c. Escaped wild animals §14
In these cases, the original captor loses possession unless a second captor has notice that the animal has escaped from someone with prior possession (*e.g.*, an elephant found in the Pennsylvania woods).

    d. Limitations §15
Congress has enacted laws to protect endangered species, and a state can regulate its natural resources under its **police power**.

3. Discovery of Caves §17
The rights to caves are generally determined by the legal maxim that a landowner owns the earth below his surface, rather than by the rule of capture.

Each surface owner is entitled to *share profits* from people visiting the portion of a cave under his property.

4. Rights to Oil and Gas §19

Applying the rule of capture to oil and gas permits a landowner to extract ("capture") all the oil and gas from a well bottomed under her land even if it drains from a neighbor's land. However, the "capture" must be *non-negligent*.

a. Limitations §21

States have enacted statutes regulating the extraction of oil and gas deposits.

5. Rights in Water §22

The rule of capture is applied to certain water rights, depending on the water's source.

a. Percolating ground water §23

Many eastern states apply the rule of capture under which a surface owner can take and use underground water as he wishes unless done negligently or maliciously.

(1) Reasonable use doctrine §24

In most western states and some eastern ones (where water is scarce), a surface owner can pump water for reasonable uses on her own land in unlimited quantities. She can transport it off her land *only* if neighbors are not harmed.

b. Surface water

(1) Capture §26

Surface water belongs to the person who captures it and can be used in any manner as long as lower owners are not harmed.

(2) Expelling §27

Frequently, a landowner will try to expel surface waters by changing the natural drainage. Liability depends on the doctrine applied:

(a) Common enemy doctrine §28

Under this theory, surface water is a common enemy and an owner can expel it. Interference with neighbors must be *reasonable*; unnecessary or disproportionate harm must be avoided.

(b) Natural servitude doctrine §29

About half the states provide that lower lands are servient to the natural flow of ground waters. An owner cannot change the flow so as to injure owners above or below his land. The modern trend is to allow reasonable changes in the flow.

c. Streams and lakes

(1) Riparian rights §30

A large majority gives an owner of land adjacent to a stream or lake riparian rights in the **quantity**, **quality**, and **velocity** of the water. This right is attached to the land and can never be transferred to a **nonriparian** owner.

(2) **Natural flow**   §33

Riparian owners are entitled to the **natural flow** of water, **without material diminution in quantity or quality**. Each owner may use the water for natural wants (*i.e.,* household uses) and even for artificial wants if the natural flow is not diminished. But an owner cannot use the water on nonriparian land and cannot deplete the quantity **even though no one is harmed**. Few states apply this doctrine to streams, preferring the reasonable use theory.

(3) **Reasonable use**   §35

The majority of courts follow the theory that a riparian owner is entitled to a reasonable use of the water. If a downstream owner is not harmed, he has no cause of action.

(a) **Preferred use**   §36

Most states give preferred status to **domestic use** regardless of the effect on the natural flow or the needs of downstream owners. An upstream owner can take water for **commercial** use **if** the taking does not interfere with the domestic uses of all owners. Use for **nonriparian** purposes is similarly permitted if no harm is suffered by riparians. In some western states, irrigation is favored over all other commercial uses.

(4) **Prior appropriation doctrine**   §40

In 10 western states, riparian water rights have been replaced by this doctrine, which is a rule of capture. Rights are determined by **prior beneficial use**. Once a water right is established, it can be **severed** from the land and sold to another (*i.e.*, water can be used on land distant from the water).

(5) **Public rights**   §42

A riparian owner may not infringe on public rights in public waters, *e.g.*, navigable waters, great lakes, and streams.

C. ACQUISITION BY CREATION

1. **General Rule**   §44

The purpose of recognizing property by creation is to reward labor. However, problems arise in defining "creation," *e.g.*, one's labor mixed with goods or labor of another.

2. **Acquisition by Accession**   §45

Accession occurs when one adds to another's property either **labor** or **labor and new materials**. A person may lose title by another's accessions, but is entitled to the unimproved value. If the improver is denied title, the owner is entitled to the added value of the property.

on the premises for a limited purpose. Objects found under the soil belong to the **landowner**. However, **treasure trove** (*i.e.,* intentionally buried gold, silver, or money) can belong to **either** the finder or the landowner, depending on the jurisdiction.

b.   **Object found in private home or public place** §69
Objects found inside someone's home or other very private place are usually awarded to the owner of the premises. Possession of objects found in **public** places is determined by deciding whether the property was **lost** (accidentally left by owner) or **mislaid** (intentionally placed somewhere and then forgotten). Lost property goes to the **finder**, while mislaid property goes to the **owner of the premises**.

3.   **Abandoned Property** §75
Property intentionally abandoned by the true owner is awarded to the finder. If there are **multiple finders**, a court may apply the rule of **equitable division** (*i.e.,* sell the property and divide the proceeds).

4.   **Statutory Changes** §77
Some states have enacted statutes abolishing the court-made distinctions in finders cases, and award the property to the finder.

E.   ACQUISITION BY ADVERSE POSSESSION

1.   **Overview** §78
If a landowner does not bring an action to eject an adverse possessor within the statutory period, the owner is thereafter **barred** from bringing an ejectment action.

a.   **Effect** §79
The running of the statute of limitations not only **bars the owner's claim** to possession, but also **creates a new title** in the adverse possessor. However, the new title **cannot be recorded** without first obtaining a **quiet title** decree.

b.   **Purpose of doctrine** §80
The doctrine of adverse possession protects title, bars stale claims, rewards productive use of land, and gives effect to expectations (a basic policy of property law).

c.   **Possessor's rights before acquiring title** §86
Before the statute of limitations runs, the adverse possessor has all the rights of a possessor, but he has **no** interest in the property valid against the true owner.

2.   **Requirements of Adverse Possession** §87
An adverse possessor must show:

a.   **Actual entry giving exclusive possession** §88
This requirement **triggers** the cause of action. There must be actual entry; if entry is on **part** of the land, the possessor is in **constructive** adverse possession.

b.   **Open and notorious possession** §91
The possessor must occupy the property in an open, notorious, and

visible manner so as to give ***reasonable notice*** to the owner that the possessor is claiming dominion adverse to the owner's rights.

c.   Adverse and under a claim of right   §97
A claim of right means that the adverse possessor is acting ***adversely*** to the owner.

   (1)   Objective test   §98
   The state of mind of the possessor is not controlling. The possessor's ***actions*** must appear to the community to be acts of an owner. The possessor need not actually claim title, but ***must*** be occupying the land ***without permission***.

   (2)   Subjective test   §99
   Some jurisdictions interpret claim of right to mean the possessor has a ***good faith belief*** that he has title.

   (3)   Color of title   §102
   A few states require an adverse possessor to have color of title (an instrument that, unknown to the possessor, is defective; *e.g.*, forged deed).

   (4)   Boundary disputes   §106
   If a neighbor occupies adjacent land, ***mistakenly*** believing it to be his, the ***majority*** holds that he is an adverse possessor. Actual intent is not determinative (***objective test***). The ***minority*** view holds that there is no adverse possession unless the neighbor has an ***actual hostile intent*** to claim the land.

      (a)   Agreement on boundaries   §112
      An oral agreement may fix a boundary line, and if one party acts in reliance thereon, the other party is ***estopped*** from denying the boundary. ***Acquiescence*** in a boundary over a long period is evidence of an agreement between the parties.

      (b)   Mistaken improver   §116
      Contrary to common law, modern courts give some relief to a ***good faith*** encroacher (*e.g.*, A erects a building, part of which is on B's land). A court may allow the encroachment to remain by ordering various remedies, *e.g.*, A pays damages to B; B is awarded the building and pays its value to A, etc.

d.   Continuous, uninterrupted possession   §119
Continuous possession requires only the ***degree of occupancy*** and use that the ***average owner*** would make of the property. An adverse use is continuous when it is made without a break in the essential ***attitude of mind*** required for adverse use.

   (1)   Seasonal use   §122
   A person can be in continuous possession when she takes possession only during a particular season, if seasonal possession is

how the average owner would use the property (*e.g.*, use of summer home only during summer).

(2) Abandonment

§123

If the possessor ***intentionally relinquishes*** the property for ***any period*** of time, continuity is broken.

(3) Tacking by successive possessors

§124

An adverse possessor can establish continuous possession by tacking onto her own period of possession any period of adverse possession by ***predecessors in interest***—if there is ***privity of estate*** (*i.e.*, a possessor ***voluntarily*** transferred to a subsequent possessor either an estate in land ***or*** physical possession).

(a) Ouster or abandonment

§126

An adverse possessor cannot tack on a prior period of possession if she has ousted the prior possessor or if the prior possessor abandoned the property.

(b) Tacking on owner's side

§129

Once adverse possession has begun to run against an owner, it runs against that owner and all his successors in interest, *i.e.*, tacking on the owner's side.

(4) Interruption by true owner

§130

If the owner interrupts the adverse possession by reentering with ***intent of regaining possession***, continuity is broken. An ***objective*** test is used (*i.e.*, ordinary acts of ownership suffice).

e. Payment of taxes

§132

In several states, payment of property taxes by the adverse possessor is necessary before her claim will prevail.

3. Disabilities of Owner

§133

If the owner is under a disability (*e.g.*, infancy, insanity) at the time of an adverse entry, the statute is ***tolled*** until the disability ends. However, only the initial ***disability at the time of entry*** tolls the statute; a different disability arising after entry does not count.

4. Extent of Land Acquired by Adverse Possession

a. Without color of title

§137

An adverse possessor who enters with no color of title takes possession only of land ***actually occupied or controlled***.

b. With color of title—constructive adverse possession

§138

A good faith claimant who actually possesses some significant portion of the land under color of title (*e.g.*, a defective deed) is in possession of the entire property described in the instrument; *i.e.*, she is in constructive adverse possession of the part of the tract she does not actually possess.

5. Interests Not Affected by Adverse Possession

a. Future interests

§140

Adverse possession does ***not*** run against the owner of a future interest (remainder) if **entry** is made when a life tenant has possession. Note that if entry had been made before the owner created the remainder, the statute would begin to run against the owner and his **successor in interest** (the owner of the remainder).

    b.   **Liens, easements, equitable servitudes**   §141

An adverse possessor does **not** destroy any lien, covenant, etc., until he interferes with it so as to give the holder of the right cause to sue the adverse possessor.

    c.   **Governmental land**   §142

With a few exceptions, public policy **exempts** government land from adverse possession.

6. **Adverse Possession of Chattels**   §143

Title to **personal property** may also be acquired through adverse possession. However, difficulty arises in determining when adverse possession of chattels begins. The majority view is that the cause of action accrues when the owner knows, or **reasonably should know through exercise of due diligence**, where the goods are.

    a.   **Stolen goods**   §146

A bona fide purchaser's claim to stolen goods is subordinate to the owner's claim unless the statute of limitations has run.

F. **REMEDIES OF A POSSESSOR**

1. **Forms of Action**   §147

At common law, a plaintiff had to bring suit in an appropriate form of action to obtain a remedy. These highly technical actions have been abolished or reformed, although their impact remains in today's concept of possession.

    a.   **Actions to recover damages**

        (1) **Trespass**   §149

Trespass required a showing that defendant intentionally or negligently acted to inflict a direct, forcible injury to the plaintiff's property or person. The basis for a trespass action is **injury to possession**. This action included **trespass to chattels** and **trespass to land**.

        (2) **Trespass on the case**   §152

Such an action would lie where one of the elements of a trespass action was missing (*e.g.*, indirect or consequential injury rather than an immediate injury).

        (3) **Trover**   §153

A suit in trover was used to recover the value of the plaintiff's **chattel** that the **defendant had converted**. Trover did not apply to trespass to land.

    b.   **Actions to recover possession**   §155

Replevin was used to recover possession of a **chattel**. **Ejectment** was used to recover possession of land.

c. **Modern law** §158
The basic difference in remedies afforded by these common law actions—the return of the thing as opposed to damages—exists today in modern codes of civil procedure.

2. **Defense of *Jus Tertii*** §159
The majority rule is that a defense of *jus tertii* (*i.e.*, only a true owner may bring suit) is not allowed. The fact that a possessor recovers **damages** from a defendant does not bar a second recovery by the true owner.

3. **Measure of Damages** §165
Courts are divided as to whether a prior possessor may recover from a subsequent possessor **permanent damages** to the entire property **or** only for the **damage to date** to his possessory interest.

a. **Life tenant** §166
The majority view permits a life tenant to recover only damages to her interest. The remainderman can bring a separate suit for damages to the remainder.

4. **Law and Equity** §169
In most jurisdictions today, law and equity courts have been merged and **legal** remedies (damages) and **equitable** remedies (*e.g.*, injunction) may be sought and applied in the same action.

G. **RIGHTS OF OWNERS** §172
An owner generally has the right to use, transfer, and **exclude** others from her land, subject to some restrictions, *e.g.*, zoning laws, mistaken improvement, civil rights laws, etc. The right to exclude others is the most fundamental right of property.

II. **PERSONAL PROPERTY**

A. **BAILMENTS**

1. **Definition** §181
A bailment is the **rightful possession** of goods by one who is **not the owner**. The person in possession is a **bailee**, who holds the goods on behalf of the **bailor**. A bailee must assume **actual physical control** with the **intent to possess**.

2. **Creation** §182
Custody without possession is not a bailment. Custody results when goods are handed over but the owner has no intention of relinquishing dominion. Thus, servants are usually not bailees. If one is **mistaken as to the contents** of a parcel, he may have possession but lacks the **intent** necessary for a bailment.

3. **Duties of Bailee**

a. **Duty to exercise care** §193
The standard of care varies with the type of bailment and usually is commensurate with who gets the **benefit** of the bailment:

(1) **Sole benefit of bailee—extraordinary care** and liable for **even slight negligence**;

(2) *Mutual benefit of bailor and bailee—ordinary care* and liable for *ordinary negligence*;

(3) *Sole benefit of bailor*—only *slight care* and liable only for *gross negligence*;

(4) *Modern trend*—a standard of *ordinary care under the circumstances*.

b. Duty to redeliver §200

A bailee is held to **strict liability** for redelivery. However, an *involuntary bailee* is liable only if *negligent* in delivering the goods to the wrong person.

4. Contractual Modification of Liability §202

Most courts permit bailees to limit their liability by contract provisions *if the bailor consents*. However, such provisions will not relieve the bailee from *gross or willful negligence*.

B. GIFTS OF PERSONAL PROPERTY

1. Definition §204

A gift is a *voluntary* transfer of property *without consideration*. There must be: (i) *intent* by the donor to make a gift; (ii) *delivery* to the donee; and (iii) *acceptance* of the chattel by the donee.

a. Gift inter vivos §205

This is a gift made *during the donor's life* when there is no threat of impending death. Such gifts are *irrevocable*.

b. Gift causa mortis §206

This is a gift made *in contemplation of immediately approaching death*. Requirements for a gift are strictly enforced in gifts causa mortis. The gift is *revoked* if the donor recovers from the illness that prompts the gift.

2. Intent §207

For a valid gift, the donor must intend to *pass title presently*, not merely to transfer possession. Absent a deed of gift, extrinsic evidence (*e.g.*, delivery) is necessary to show intent.

3. Delivery §209

Delivery requires some *act* giving up dominion and passing control to the donee. Manual transfer is not always necessary.

a. Constructive delivery §212

Constructive delivery is the handing over of the *means* of obtaining possession and control (*e.g.*, a key), or in some other way *relinquishing dominion and control*. This is permitted when actual manual delivery is *impracticable*.

(1) Donor's intent §215

Constructive delivery can include any acts that the *donor deems sufficient* to pass a present interest.

b. Symbolic delivery — §216

Symbolic delivery is the handing over of some object that represents the thing given (*e.g.*, instrument in writing). This is permitted when actual manual delivery is *impracticable*.

c. Delivery through third person — §221

If a donor makes delivery to *his agent*, no gift takes place *until* the agent makes delivery to the donee. However, if the donor makes delivery to a third party who is the *donee's agent* or an *independent agent*, the gift is effective on delivery to the third party. Most courts today uphold a gift to be delivered by a third party (not donor's agent) on the *donor's death*.

d. Revocable gifts — §224

Generally, no gift is made when a donor retains the right to revoke the gift.

4. Acceptance — §230

The donee must accept the gift, but where the gift is beneficial to the donee, acceptance is *presumed*.

C. BONA FIDE PURCHASERS OF PERSONAL PROPERTY

1. General Rule — §232

A seller can transfer *no better title than he has*.

2. Exceptions — §233

Title to *money and negotiable instruments* passes to a *bona fide purchaser* ("BFP"). Also, where a seller has *voidable* title (one the owner can void), a BFP takes title. *Estoppel* and *entrusting goods* to a merchant may also be applied to pass title to a BFP. *But note:* A BFP takes *no* title from a *thief* (void title).

3. Bona Fide Purchaser — §239

A BFP is one who takes possession *in good faith*, for *valuable consideration*, and *without notice* of any wrongful possession.

III. POSSESSORY ESTATES

A. INTRODUCTION

1. The Feudal Background — §241

The concept of estates in Anglo-American law arose out of the feudal system imposed on England by the Norman conquerors. Feudal incidents (a form of inheritance tax) were owed by every tenant to his lord. As landowners tried to avoid these "taxes," the courts developed rules (discussed *infra*) to maintain the lords' economic basis, *e.g.*, the Rule in Shelley's Case. In 1536, the Statute of Uses restored the king's feudal incidents and laid the foundation for modern conveyancing and trusts.

2. The System of Estates

a. Historic development — §244

Today, an estate is an interest in land that *is or may become possessory* and is *measured by some period of time*.

b. Types of estates

(1) Fee simple　　　　　　　　　　　　　　　　　　　§247
This estate has the potential of *enduring forever*.

(2) Fee tail　　　　　　　　　　　　　　　　　　　　§248
A fee tail estate also has the potential to endure forever, but *ends if and when* the first fee tail tenant has *no lineal descendants* to succeed him in possession.

(3) Life estate　　　　　　　　　　　　　　　　　　§249
This estate will end at the *death of a person*.

(4) Leasehold estate　　　　　　　　　　　　　　　§250
This estate lasts for a fixed time or by other agreement between a landlord and tenant.

c. Freehold and nonfreehold estates　　　　　　　　　§251
The fee simple, fee tail (where not abolished), and life estate are freehold estates, whereas leasehold estates are nonfreehold estates. Under the feudal system, a freeholder in possession was treated as having *seisin* while a leaseholder had only *possession*.

d. Hierarchy of estates　　　　　　　　　　　　　　§253
The common law ranked estates according to their potential duration, *i.e.*, fee simple, fee tail, and then life estate. All freehold estates were presumed longer than leaseholds.

e. Estates in personal property　　　　　　　　　　　§254
Possessory estates and future interests can be created in both real property (land) and personal property.

f. No new estates may be created　　　　　　　　　　§255
No new kinds of estates can be created. Language creating an estate will be construed to mean one of the four: a fee simple, a fee tail, a life estate, or a leasehold.

B. THE FEE SIMPLE

1. Fee Simple Absolute　　　　　　　　　　　　　　　§256
A fee simple absolute is absolute ownership. It is of *potentially infinite duration* with *no limitations* on its *inheritability*, and it *cannot be divested* or end on the happening of *any* event.

a. Words of purchase and words of limitation　　　　　§257
Words of purchase identify the *person* in whom the estate is created, *e.g.*, "to A." Words of limitation describe the *type of estate* created, *e.g.*, "and her heirs."

b. Creation　　　　　　　　　　　　　　　　　　　§258
At *common law*, a fee simple was created by deed only by using the words, "*and his heirs*." If these words were omitted, the grantee took only a life estate. Under *modern law*, the requirement of "and his heirs" has been abolished by most states. Either a deed or will is presumed to pass the largest estate the *grantor or testator owns*.

estate. A remainder can be **both** vested subject to open and vested subject to complete divestment (*e.g.*, "to A for life, then to the children of A, but if no child survives A, to B").

  (4) Alienability   §414
    A vested remainder is alienable inter vivos and devisable by will. It descends to heirs if not otherwise disposed of. However, it can be limited so as to be divested at death.

 b. Contingent remainders   §416
  A remainder is contingent if given to an **unascertained person**, or **subject to a condition precedent**.

  (1) Unascertained person   §417
    This means a person not yet born or one who cannot be determined until the happening of an event. A contingent remainder in fee simple always creates a **reversion** in the grantor.

  (2) Condition precedent   §422
    This is an **express** condition set forth in the instrument which must happen before the remainder becomes possessory (*e.g.*, "to A for life, then to B if B survives A"). The termination of a preceding estate is **not** a condition precedent.

  (3) Distinguish—conditions subsequent   §427
    Whether a condition is precedent or subsequent (as in a vested remainder subject to divestment) depends on the **sequence** of the words of the instrument. If the condition is incorporated into the words of a gift, it is precedent; if it later adds words divesting a gift, it is subsequent. When the language is ambiguous, **vested remainders** are preferred.

  (4) Alienability   §431
    Contingent remainders were inalienable inter vivos at common law. In most states today, however, contingent remainders are alienable, devisable, and descendible.

F. EXECUTORY INTERESTS

 1. Historical Background   §434
  At early law, executory interests grew out of **uses** recognized by **equity** courts to bypass the inflexibility of law courts.

  a. No springing interests   §444
    At law, a grantor could not create a freehold estate to **spring out** in the future (because no seisin was conveyed). **Equity** found a way around this restriction.

  b. No shifting interests   §446
    At law, a grantor could not create a future interest that would **cut short** a freehold estate. **Equity** permitted shifting uses.

 2. Statute of Uses (1536)   §452
  This converted all equitable uses into legal estates.

H. THE RULE AGAINST PERPETUITIES

1. **Purpose** §524

   The three rules discussed above (G., *supra*) were developed to prevent land dynasties but applied only to contingent remainders. Eventually the Rule Against Perpetuities was developed to curb *all contingent future interests, including executory interests* (which are indestructible).

2. **The Rule** §525

   No interest is good unless it *must vest*, if at all, not later than *21 years after some life in being at the creation of the interest*.

3. **Interests Subject to the Rule** §527

   The Rule applies to *contingent remainders* and *executory interests*. It does *not* apply to vested interests (vested remainder, reversion, possibility of reverter, and right of entry).

4. **What-Might-Happen Is Test** §528

   If there is *any possibility* that a contingent interest will vest too remotely, the interest is *void*. Courts do not wait to see what actually happens, but look at the interest at the time of creation.

5. **Lives in Being** §532

   Any person who can affect the vesting of the interest and who is alive at the *creation* of the interest can be a validating life, provided the *claimant* can prove the interest will vest or fail within 21 years of the person's death.

6. **Meaning of "Vest"** §536

   The Rule does not apply to vested interests. But note that *class gifts* do not vest in any member of the class *until* the interests of *all members* have vested. Thus, if the gift to one member of the class might vest too remotely, the whole class gift is void (all-or-nothing rule).

   a. **Executory interest** §538

   An executory interest following a fee simple determinable or divesting a fee simple vests *only* when the condition happens and *it becomes a possessory estate*.

7. **Remote Possibilities** §539

   An interest is void, under the Rule, if there is *any possibility* the interest might vest beyond the permitted period (*e.g.*, the fertile octogenarian, the unborn widow).

8. **Application to Defeasible Fees** §543

   Although a fee simple determinable followed by an executory interest is subject to the Rule, an *exception* applies to a *gift over from one charity to another charity*. Note that the Rule is *not* applicable to a fee simple determinable created by will.

9. **Application to Options** §550

   Generally, options are subject to the Rule. However, a *preemptive option* (right of first refusal) for a *condominium* and an option to *renew a lease* are excepted from the Rule. The Uniform Statutory Rule Against Perpetuities, adopted in about half the states, exempts options.

10. Wait-and-See Doctrine
§555

More than half the states have reformed the Rule. Under the wait-and-see doctrine, the interests are judged by **actual events**, not by possible events. Some states wait out the relevant lives plus 21 years, while states following the Uniform Rule (*supra*) wait for 90 years before determining the validity of a contingent interest.

11. Cy Pres Doctrine
§560

This rule reforms an invalid interest, within the Rule's limitations, to approximate most closely the intention of the creator of the interest.

12. Abolition of Rule
§562

In a number of states, application of the Rule to **interests in trusts** has been abolished. This results in perpetual trusts that, in effect, allow avoidance of estate and generation skipping transfer taxes, *i.e.*, **dynasty trusts**.

I. THE TRUST

1. Definition
§563

A trust is a fiduciary relationship in which one person (the **trustee**) holds legal title to property (**res**) subject to equitable rights in **beneficiaries**. It is basically a device whereby one person manages property for the benefit of others. A person who creates the trust is the **settlor**.

2. Creation
§564

The settlor must manifest an **intent** to create an express trust. A written instrument (*e.g.*, will or deed) is necessary for an express trust of **land**; an express trust of **personal property** may be created inter vivos by written or spoken words or by conduct. Ordinarily, a trust is created by a written instrument naming the trustee and specifying the rights of beneficiaries (and remaindermen), and the trustee's powers. Property **must** be delivered to the trustee.

a. Trustee
§565

Any person with legal capacity, including the settlor or a beneficiary, can serve as trustee.

b. Types
§567

A trust can be either testamentary or inter vivos, and can be made revocable or irrevocable.

3. Powers of Trustee
§570

A trustee usually has very broad powers and can manage the property in the same manner as an intelligent person would manage her own property.

4. Duties of Trustee
§571

A trustee is **personally liable** for breach of a fiduciary duty. She must exercise that degree of care, skill, and prudence as would a reasonably prudent person in managing her own affairs (**prudent investor rule**), *e.g.*, diversification of assets.

a **tenancy by the entirety**. In most states today, a conveyance to two or more persons (usually including spouses) creates a **tenancy in common**.

b. Overcoming presumption §606
Today, a joint tenancy can be created only by **express words** indicating such an intent.

4. Severance of Joint Tenancy §613
Modern law generally holds that severance of one of the four unities severs the joint tenancy and destroys the right of survivorship. It destroys the joint tenancy and creates a tenancy in common.

a. Conveyance by joint tenant §614
A joint tenant has the right to convey her interest, but by doing so she severs the joint tenancy with respect to that share.

b. Mortgage by joint tenant §618
In **title theory states**, a mortgage usually conveys legal title and thus severs the tenancy. In **lien theory states** (the majority), a security interest, rather than legal title, is conveyed and a mortgage does **not** sever a joint tenancy.

c. Lease by joint tenant §621
Some jurisdictions follow the common law rule that a lease by one joint tenant severs a joint tenancy and others hold that it does not.

d. Agreement among joint tenants §624
Joint tenants can agree that one tenant has the right to exclusive possession without severance. However, severance occurs if they agree to hold as tenants in common although none of the four unities is broken; **intent controls**.

e. Other situations §625
Divorce does not terminate a joint tenancy, unless the parties agree. Where one joint tenant **murders** the other, a severance occurs in most states, creating a tenancy in common. In **simultaneous death** cases, usually the property is equally divided among the estates of the joint tenants.

5. Avoidance of Probate §628
Joint tenancy avoids probate because there is no need to change title at a joint tenant's death.

6. Joint Bank Accounts §629
There is a **presumption** that opening a **joint and survivor bank account** creates survivorship rights, *i.e.*, it is a **"true"** joint account, unless it can be shown that the account was intended to be a **"convenience account."** Most states hold that during the parties' lifetimes, the account belongs to them in proportion to the net contributions of each, rather than in equal shares.

1. **Possession by One Co-Tenant** §662
   Each co-tenant is equally entitled to the possession of the entire property. The parties may agree among themselves that one co-tenant has the right to exclusive possession.

   a. **Accounting by co-tenant in possession** §664
      If one co-tenant *ousts* another, he must pay *reasonable rental value*. In a *minority* of jurisdictions, a co-tenant in possession is required to pay fair rental value to the other co-tenants even without an ouster.

      (1) **Ouster** §667
         Ouster occurs when one co-tenant deprives another co-tenant of the right to possession. An ousted co-tenant can bring suit to collect his share of reasonable rental value or to partition the property.

2. **Accounting for Rents Received from a Third Party** §672
   Such rents must be shared equally with the other co-tenants.

3. **Exploiting Natural Resources** §674
   A co-tenant is entitled to mine or drill for oil but must pay to the other co-tenants a proportionate part of the net amount received. However, because timber is visible and can be easily apportioned, some courts permit a co-tenant to cut a proportionate share with no liability for its value to other co-tenants.

4. **Actions by Co-Tenant to Protect Property**

   a. **Taxes and mortgage interest** §680
      Each co-tenant is liable for her share of taxes *except* if in *exclusive possession*, she has the duty to pay the taxes and mortgage interest up to the amount of the reasonable rental value of the property. If a co-tenant pays off the mortgage *principal*, she is subrogated to the mortgagee and has whatever rights it had, *e.g.*, a lien.

   b. **Repairs** §685
      Repairs are voluntary. At common law, a co-tenant who makes repairs *cannot compel contribution* from co-tenants, although she can offset the costs in an accounting for rents. In some states, a co-tenant can compel contribution for *necessary* repairs of which the other co-tenants had *notice*.

   c. **Improvements** §686
      No co-tenant has a duty to pay for improvements, and the cost may *not* be offset in an accounting for rents. Only upon partition may the improver be reimbursed.

5. **Co-Tenants as Fiduciaries** §687
   Co-tenants are treated as fiduciaries, holding for the benefit of all *when a confidential relationship exists* (e.g., inheritance by siblings).

   a. **Acquisition of outstanding title** §690
      If a co-tenant (held to fiduciary standards) acquires an outstanding title (*e.g.,* at a tax or foreclosure sale), she holds for the benefit of other co-tenants who contributed to the purchase price.

6. Adverse Possession   §693

A co-tenant can become an adverse possessor only upon clear *notice of repudiation of the common title* being given to the other co-tenants. Exclusive possession alone is insufficient.

7. Partition   §694

Any common or joint tenant may bring a suit in partition. A court either physically divides (partition in kind) or sells the common property, adjusts all claims of the parties, and separates them. Note that partition is not available to tenants by the entirety.

E. MARITAL RIGHTS ON DIVORCE

1. Common Law   §699

On divorce, the husband's property belonged to him and the wife's belonged to her, but the husband had a duty to support the wife for her lifetime. *Alimony* was awarded to the wife unless she had been unfaithful or forfeited the right to support.

2. Modern Law   §700

All states have enacted statutes attempting to equalize property distribution between spouses.

a. Alimony   §701

Alimony (sometimes called *rehabilitative alimony* or *support*) is now granted to a wife for a limited time, rather than for life.

b. Property division   §702

Contrary to common law, all states today authorize *equitable distribution* of marital property. The scope of property subject to this concept varies from state to state.

F. MARITAL RIGHTS ON DEATH

1. Common Law

a. Dower   §708

At common law, on a husband's death, a wife has dower in all freehold land of which her husband is *seised during marriage* and which is *inheritable by issue* born of the marriage. Dower is a *life estate* in *one-third* of each parcel of qualifying land.

(1) Scope   §709

There was no dower in land in which the husband had a life estate, a joint tenancy, or a leasehold. Neither did dower attach to personal property or an equitable interest of the husband. Dower has been *abolished* in all but five states.

b. Curtesy   §716

At common law, on a wife's death, a husband received a *life estate* in *all* of his wife's lands *if issue were born* of the marriage. Curtesy has been abolished wherever dower has been abolished. Where dower is retained, it has been extended to the husband and curtesy has been abolished.

2. **Contracts Between Unmarried Partners** §741

Some jurisdictions that do not recognize common law marriages still give certain rights to unmarried cohabitants on dissolution of the relationship under various theories: express or implied contract; partnership; or quantum meruit.

3. **Same-Sex Partners** §747

Such cohabitants can make express contracts concerning property rights, but generally are prohibited from marrying and acquiring the rights of that status. Only Massachusetts affords same-sex couples *who are residents of the state* the same rights given married persons. Another state has enacted a statute allowing same-sex partners to enter into a "civil union," which gives them the same rights as married persons under state, but not federal, law. Some states have enacted provisions barring housing or employment discrimination based on sexual orientation, and some cities grant same-sex partners certain limited rights.

VI. LANDLORD AND TENANT

A. INTRODUCTION

1. **Background** §750

Landlord-tenant law developed out of the feudal relationship between a landlord and his tenant farmer, and thus imposed few duties on the landlord. The modern trend is to adapt the law to the needs of the urban tenant. Today, a lease creates an estate in land (*i.e.*, a *chattel real*). It is *both* a *conveyance* of an estate in land and a *contract* containing promises, which until recent times were independent; if one party breached, the other was still required to perform. Traditionally, property law was dominant; upon buying an estate in land, a tenant assumed the risks of caring for the land. During recent years, contract principles have become more important.

2. **Lease Distinguished from Other Relationships** §757

A tenant has the right to *possession*; this distinguishes the lease from other relationships, *e.g.,* an easement, license, or profit.

a. **Oil and gas lease** §763

Such a lease grants a *profit or ownership of minerals* in place and does not create a leasehold.

b. **Billboard "lease"** §764

A billboard lease creates an *easement* which gives the lessee a right to *use*.

c. **Lodging agreements** §765

These may create a *license* (*e.g.*, hotel guest) or a lease (*e.g.*, when lodger furnishes the place).

B. TYPES OF TENANCIES AND THEIR CREATION

1. **Tenancy for Years** §770

A tenancy for years is an estate with a beginning and end *fixed* from the outset. Usually a *calendar period* is used (*e.g.*, one year; two months).

a. Indefinite ending §771
Where the termination date is fixed upon the happening of some event (*e.g.*, "until war ends"), courts have held that a tenancy for years is created because that is closest to the parties' intentions.

b. Termination §774
A tenancy for years differs from all other tenancies in that it has a definite ending; it expires without notice.

2. Periodic Tenancy §775
A periodic tenancy is a tenancy for a fixed period that continues for succeeding periods (*e.g.,* month to month, year to year) until either the landlord or the tenant *gives notice* of termination.

a. Creation §777
A periodic tenancy may be created by an express agreement or by operation of law.

(1) Rent agreement §779
A periodic tenancy frequently arises by implication where the lease agreement provides only for periodic payment of rent but no termination date, *e.g.*, rent due monthly, yearly, etc. Note that where the *annual rent is payable monthly*, most jurisdictions hold the period to be year to year.

(2) By operation of law §783
A periodic tenancy is created by operation of law where the tenant *holds over* after the lease expires or where he takes possession under an *invalid lease*.

b. Notice of termination §786
A periodic tenancy continues until *proper notice* is given. Notice must be *equal to the length of the period*, except *six months'* notice is required for a *year-to-year* tenancy. Notice must specify the *last day* of the period and must terminate the lease on that day. Many states have reduced the common law time requirements for notice in year-to-year tenancies to one month.

3. Tenancy at Will §792
An estate terminable *at the will* of *either* the landlord or tenant is a tenancy at will and can arise expressly or, more frequently, by operation of law.

a. Terminable by only one party §794
Such an estate is *not* a tenancy at will. A term of years, periodic tenancy, or life estate can be made *determinable* at the will of only one party. However, if the tenancy is not a term of years, periodic tenancy, or life estate and is terminable at the will of only one party, some courts will find an *implied tenancy at will*; others hold the tenant has a *determinable life estate*.

b. Termination §799
At common law, the tenancy terminated on the day notice was given.

Today, most states require some notice, usually 30 days. Note that an attempted *assignment* will also terminate a tenancy at will.

4. Statute of Frauds §801
The Statute requires a term of years, periodic tenancy, or tenancy at will to be in writing to be enforceable.

a. Short-term lease exception §802
Most states exempt short-term leases (usually one year) from the Statute of Frauds requirement of a writing. An oral lease for more than a year creates a tenancy at will.

b. Oral lease to commence in the future §804
An oral lease for a year to commence in the future is *valid* (under majority view), even though an oral contract (other than a lease) not to be performed within a year is void.

c. Entry and rent payment under invalid lease §806
Although an oral lease may be void, entry by a tenant creates a *tenancy at will*. As soon as the tenant pays rent, a *periodic tenancy* is created with the majority view finding a *year-to-year tenancy* regardless of rental payments.

5. Holdover Tenant §809
A tenant who holds over when her term expires is a *tenant at sufferance*. This situation lasts only until the landlord *evicts* the tenant *or elects* to hold the tenant to another term. Modern cases afford an innocent (unwilling) holdover tenant some relief, and many statutes have modified landlord remedies to be more proportionate to the acts of holdover. However, willful holdovers may be subjected to additional penalties, *e.g.*, double rent.

C. SELECTION OF TENANTS

1. Introduction §816
Traditionally, a seller or landlord was free to sell or rent to whomever he pleased. Today, however, statutes have regulated the *sale or rental* of property in certain respects.

2. Civil Rights Act of 1866 §817
This Act (*i.e.*, "section 1982") prohibits *racial or ethnic discrimination* in the sale or rental of *all* property.

3. Fair Housing Act of 1968 §821
This Act makes it unlawful to refuse to sell or rent a *dwelling* to any person because of race, color, religion, national origin, sex, handicap, or familial status.

a. Advertising §822
Discriminatory advertising is prohibited.

b. Exemptions §823
There are certain specified exemptions from the Act: a single-family dwelling rented by the owner; four units or less where one is occupied

by the owner ("Mrs. Murphy" exception); private clubs; and religious organizations. Note that section 1982 does **not** contain these exemptions.

c. Enforcement §827
One may sue in federal court for an injunction and damages.

4. Proving Discrimination §828
Plaintiff must first establish a prima facie case, *i.e.*, that she (i) is a member of a protected class; (ii) applied for and was qualified to rent; (iii) was denied inspection or rental of the dwelling; and (iv) the opportunity remained available for others. The burden then **shifts** to the defendant to show that the refusal to rent was based on **legitimate considerations** having **nothing** to do with the plaintiff's status. Once legitimate reasons have been proffered, the plaintiff then has the burden to show they are **pretextual**.

5. Kinds of Discrimination §829
Unlawful practices under the Fair Housing Act include those that have a **disproportionate effect** on one race or that discriminate on the basis of sex, familial status (including existence of minor children in the family unit), or physical or mental impairments.

6. State Statutes §835
Some states extend the protection given under the federal Act to prohibit discrimination on the basis of marital status, sexual orientation, or age.

7. Admission to Public Housing §837
Housing authorities can use "desirability standards" to determine eligibility, but must afford prospective tenants due process of law.

D. LANDLORD'S DUTY TO DELIVER POSSESSION

1. Legal Right to Possession §839
A landlord has the duty of delivering to the tenant the legal right to possession. If another person has **paramount title**, the landlord is in default. If the tenant is **unaware** of the paramount title **before** entry, he may **terminate** the lease. **After entry**, the tenant has **no remedy** unless he is actually evicted by paramount title.

2. Actual Possession §843
In most states, the landlord has the duty to deliver actual possession at the beginning of the lease. If a previous tenant does not get out in time, the landlord is in default ("English rule"). The minority hold that there is no duty to deliver actual possession; rather, the tenant has the burden of ejecting the holdover tenant ("American rule").

E. LANDLORD'S DUTY NOT TO INTERFERE WITH TENANT'S QUIET ENJOYMENT

1. Covenant of Quiet Enjoyment §847
A tenant has a right of quiet enjoyment of the premises without interference by the landlord. If not expressed in the lease, such a covenant is **always implied**.

2. Actual Eviction §850

If a tenant is evicted from the **entire** premises by anyone, the tenant's rent obligation terminates.

a. Partial eviction §851

If the tenant is evicted from all or **any** portion of the leased premises by the **landlord**, his rent obligation **abates entirely** until possession is restored to him. (Tenant may stay in possession without paying rent.) If the tenant is partially evicted by a third party with **paramount title**, the tenant can terminate the lease, recover damages, or receive a proportionate rent abatement.

3. Constructive Eviction §855

If a landlord **substantially interferes** with a tenant's **enjoyment** of the premises without actually evicting the tenant, the tenant can claim constructive eviction and **vacate** the premises (*e.g.*, where water floods basement office).

a. Remedy §862

A tenant's only remedy is to **move out** within a **reasonable time** and claim damages.

b. Acts of other tenants §868

A tenant cannot claim a constructive eviction because of wrongful acts of a third person, except that a landlord has a duty not to permit a **nuisance** on the premises and also a duty to control **common areas**. Also, a developing trend holds a landlord responsible for other tenants' acts if the landlord has the legal ability to correct the conditions and fails to do so.

F. LANDLORD'S DUTY TO PROVIDE HABITABLE PREMISES

1. Landlord's Duty at Inception of the Lease

a. Common law §873

At common law, there is no implied covenant by the landlord that the premises are habitable or are fit for the purposes intended (caveat lessee).

(1) Exceptions §874

The four recognized exceptions to the above rule are: a **furnished house for a short term** (*e.g.*, summer cottage); **hidden defects known** to the landlord; **common areas**; and a building under **construction**.

b. Implied covenant of habitability §880

Many recent cases imply a **covenant of initial habitability** and fitness in leases of urban buildings, including apartments. Courts are beginning to apply this covenant to some **commercial leases**, *e.g.*, office tenants.

(1) Remedies §886

For breach of the covenant, a tenant has contract remedies of damages, restitution, and rescission. Additionally, a tenant may be able to use the rent for repairs or withhold rent. Note that a tenant may *waive* minor defects, but waiver of more serious defects may be against public policy.

c. Statutory duties §889
By statute, many states have imposed a duty of habitability before the landlord leases the premises.

d. Illegal lease §890
A lease of premises which the *landlord knows* are in substantial violation of the housing code is illegal *if* the code prohibits rental of property in violation of the code. If the lease is illegal, the covenant to pay rent cannot be enforced.

2. Landlord's Duty to Repair After Entry by Tenant

a. Common law §891
At common law, the landlord has *no duty* to maintain and repair the premises. If such a duty is expressed in the lease, the covenant to repair might be *independent* of the tenant's covenant to pay rent. In that case, upon the landlord's breach the tenant must continue to pay rent and can sue for damages or specific performance, unless the landlord's acts give rise to a claim for constructive eviction (*see supra*).

b. Implied covenant of habitability §893
Many recent cases have *implied* a *continuing covenant of habitability* and repair in urban leases. Contrary to common law, a tenant's covenant to pay rent is dependent upon the landlord's performance of his covenant.

(1) Commercial leases §894
A few cases have implied the covenant where it appears that the commercial tenant has bargained for continuing maintenance (more likely for a single office than the entire building).

(2) Remedies for breach §899
The tenant may *terminate* or continue the lease and *recover damages*; or continue the lease and use *rent to repair* or *withhold rent*. Breach of the duty may also be used as a *defense* to the landlord's action for rent.

(3) Waiver by tenant §910
Clauses in a lease waiving the landlord's obligations under the implied covenant of habitability are generally not permitted.

c. Statutory duties of landlord §913
In many states, landlords have statutory duties of repair and maintenance, and tenants are given various remedies for breach (*e.g.*, repairing and deducting costs, rent withholding).

d. Retaliatory eviction §921
Some recent cases hold that a landlord cannot evict a tenant in retaliation for an exercise of statutory rights that depend upon private initiative for their enforcement.

G. LANDLORD'S TORT LIABILITY

1. Introduction §930

At common law, with a few recognized exceptions, a landlord had no duty to make the premises safe. The tenant took the premises as is, and after taking possession the tenant was responsible for tort injuries.

2. Dangerous Condition Existing at Time of Lease §932

Modern courts have tailored several exceptions to avoid the harshness of the common law rule of no landlord tort liability.

a. Concealed dangerous condition (latent defect) §933

If a landlord *knows or should know* of a dangerous condition and has reason to believe that the tenant will not discover it, she is liable for injuries caused by the condition if she did not *disclose* it to the tenant. No liability attaches *after* disclosure to the tenant.

b. Public use §935

A majority of courts hold a landlord liable for injuries even when only two or three members of the public will be on the premises at one time (*e.g.*, doctor's office) *if* (i) the landlord knew or should have known of the dangerous condition; (ii) had reason to believe the tenant would not correct it; and (iii) failed to exercise reasonable care to remedy the condition. For landlord liability, the defect must have existed at the *beginning* of the lease.

3. Defects Arising After Tenant Takes Possession §940

Generally, a landlord has no liability for personal injury from dangerous conditions that arise *after* a tenant takes possession. However, if a landlord voluntarily undertakes to make *repairs*, she has a duty to exercise reasonable care in so doing.

4. Common Areas §943

Where a landlord *retains control* of common areas, she has a *duty of reasonable care* and is liable for defects in the premises and for foreseeable tortious acts of others (*e.g.*, assault in the lobby).

5. Landlord Contracts to Repair §945

Today, a majority of states hold a landlord who contracts to repair (*e.g.*, clause in lease) liable to a tenant and his guests.

6. Landlord Under Legal Duty to Repair §947

Liability to a tenant and her guests may attach if the landlord breaches a statutory duty to repair (*e.g.*, housing code). However, breach of the *implied covenant of habitability* imposes liability only for the landlord's *negligence*.

7. Modern Trend—Landlord Liability §950

Some recent cases ignore the general rule and its exceptions and hold that a landlord must *exercise reasonable care* not to subject others to an unreasonable risk of harm (*i.e.*, general negligence).

a. **Use becomes illegal** §973

Where this occurs *after* the lease is made, sometimes a tenant may terminate the lease.

b. **Frustration of purpose** §977

A tenant may terminate the lease in case of extreme hardship if: (i) the frustrated use was *contemplated by both* the landlord and tenant; (ii) the frustration is *total or near total*; and (iii) the event was *not foreseen or foreseeable* by the parties. The *impossibility of performance* rule is similar.

c. **Destruction of the premises** §980

At common law, a tenant was still obligated to pay rent for destroyed premises. Today, most states have statutes that provide that, absent a contrary lease provision, the tenant may terminate the lease if the premises are destroyed without fault of the tenant.

d. **Eminent domain** §981

A permanent taking of *all lease property* by condemnation *extinguishes* the leasehold, and the lessee is entitled to compensation. A *temporary* taking does *not terminate* the lease. The tenant must continue to pay rent but can recover from the government the value of the occupancy taken.

7. **Rights and Duties Relating to Fixtures** §982

At common law, fixtures cannot be removed by a tenant at the end of the lease. Courts look to the nature of the article, how it is attached, and the amount of damage that would be caused by removal to determine a tenant's intention as to whether an article is a fixture.

a. **Exception** §985

A tenant is permitted to remove *trade fixtures*, *i.e.*, those installed for the purpose of carrying on a business or trade.

b. **Modern trend** §986

The modern trend is to be very liberal in permitting a tenant to remove *any* installed chattel, as long as *no substantial damage* occurs. The tenant must remove fixtures *before* the end of the lease term.

I. **LANDLORD'S REMEDIES**

1. **Means of Assuring Performance**

a. **Distress** §989

At common law, if a tenant were in arrears in rent, the landlord could enter and *seize the tenant's chattels* as security for the rent. Many states have substituted a statutory right which usually eliminates the self-help feature or requires a peaceable entry. The constitutionality of some of these distress statutes is questionable.

b. **Statutory liens** §992

Many states have enacted a landlord's lien on a tenant's goods, giving a landlord priority over other creditors. The landlord must judicially foreclose her lien if the rent is in arrears.

b. **Nonaction by landlord** §1030

The landlord may leave the premises vacant and sue for rent as it comes due. Under the older view, the landlord has **no duty to mitigate damages** by finding another tenant. (The modern, and probably majority, view is contra).

c. **Repossess and relet** §1034

A landlord can repossess and relet, but some courts hold that this **effects a surrender**. Other views hold that **no surrender** occurs if the landlord gives the tenant **notice** of reletting, or if the landlord otherwise shows **intent** not to effect a surrender.

J. ASSIGNMENT AND SUBLETTING

1. **Assignment** §1035

Unless the lease prohibits, a tenant can assign her interest in the leasehold. Thus, the assignee comes into **privity of estate** with the landlord and each can sue the other on lease covenants which run with the land.

2. **Sublease Distinguished from Assignment** §1038

Unless the lease prohibits, a tenant can sublease and thus become the landlord of the sublessee. There is **no privity of estate** between the sublessee and the original landlord.

a. **Reversion retained** §1039

At common law, a sublease occurs if the tenant retains a **reversion**; *i.e.*, the tenant is entitled to possession again before the tenant's lease expires.

b. **Right of entry retained** §1040

If a tenant retains a **right of entry** upon default in rent, some cases hold that the transfer is a sublease. This is contrary to the common law rule that holds it is an assignment because no reversion was retained. Recently, a few cases have held that the **intent** of the parties determines whether a transfer is a sublease or assignment.

3. **Duty to Pay Rent** §1045

Generally, a landlord can sue for rent any person who is either in **privity of contract or privity of estate** with him.

a. **Assignment** §1046

If there is an assignment, the landlord can sue the tenant (privity of contract) or the assignee (privity of estate). The assignee's liability ends when he reassigns to a third party.

b. **Sublease** §1055

A sublessee is **not** liable to the landlord for rent.

c. **Third-party beneficiary suits** §1056

If an assignee or sublessee **expressly assumes** the covenants of the master lease, he is directly liable to the landlord, who is a third-party beneficiary of the contract between the tenant and the assignee or sublessee.

(1) Affirmative easement §1085

Most easements are affirmative, giving a person the right to **go onto** another's land (the servient land) and do some act on the land.

(2) Negative easement §1086

The owner of a negative easement can **prevent** a servient landowner from doing some act on the servient land (*infra*).

b. Easement appurtenant §1088

Such an easement **benefits** its owner in the **use** of another tract of land. The land benefited is the **dominant tenement**; the land burdened is the **servient tenement**.

(1) Passes with dominant tenement §1089

An easement appurtenant is attached to the dominant tenement and ordinarily passes to any subsequent owner of the tenement. If the easement is **personal**, however, it will not pass to subsequent owners.

c. Easement in gross §1091

This easement does not benefit an owner in the use and enjoyment of his land, but merely gives him the **right to use** the servient land. *Note:* "In gross" means that the easement is not appurtenant; it does not mean that the easement is personal and cannot be assigned.

(1) Easement appurtenant favored §1092

In cases of ambiguity, easements appurtenant are favored over easements in gross.

d. Distinguish—profit §1094

A profit is the right to **take something off** another's land that is a part or product of the land (*e.g.*, timber). A grant of a profit implies an easement to go onto the land and remove the subject matter.

e. Distinguish—license §1095

A license is **permission** to go on another's land (*e.g.*, plumber repairing faucet). It can be written or oral and is generally **revocable** at the licensor's will unless it is coupled with an interest or estoppel applies. Confusion sometimes arises as to whether there is a license or an easement in gross. Because easements in gross clog title, courts **prefer licenses**.

2. Creation of Easements

a. Creation by express grant §1105

An easement, being an interest in land, must be in **a writing signed by the grantor** to satisfy the Statute of Frauds. If a grantor gives **oral** permission to enter land, a **license** is created. Exceptions to the Statute include fraud, part performance, and estoppel; easements by implication and prescription; and easements lasting less than one year.

(1) Construction §1108

An easement can be created for any length of time. If ambiguity exists as to whether an easement or fee simple was granted, a grant for a *limited use*, or for a *limited purpose*, or of a space *without clearly marked boundaries* indicates an easement. Some courts presume that the grantor conveys the largest interest he can convey, unless expressly limited, and favor a fee simple.

b. Creation by reservation   §1110
A grantor may convey land and reserve for *himself* an easement over the land. Early common law prohibited a reservation because there was no express grant by the new owner. To overcome this obstacle, courts invented a theory that the grantee *regranted the easement* to the grantor.

(1) Exception of an easement   §1112
A reservation is the regrant of a *new easement*. An exception is a deed provision that excludes from the grant a *preexisting easement*.

(2) Reservation for third party   §1113
The majority view follows the common law *prohibition* against reservation in favor of a third party.

c. Creation by implication   §1117
An exception to the Statute of Frauds, an easement by implication is created by *operation of law*. There are only two kinds:

(1) Easement from existing use   §1118
If, before a tract of land is divided, a use exists on the servient part that is reasonably necessary for the enjoyment of the dominant part and a court finds the parties intended the use to continue after separation, an easement may be implied.

(a) Requirements   §1119
An easement can be implied only *over land granted or reserved when the tract was divided* and *only in favor of the dominant tenement* (an easement in gross will not be implied). Additionally, the *use must exist at the time of tract division* and must have been *continuous, apparent*, and *reasonably necessary* to the enjoyment of the dominant part. In many states, a stronger showing of necessity is required for an implied reservation than for an implied grant.

(2) Easement by necessity   §1127
This usually involves a way of access and involves *strict necessity*, not merely convenience. An easement by necessity is implied only when a tract is divided; no prior existing use is required. It *terminates* when the necessity ends.

d. Creation by prescription   §1133
An easement may be created by a period of *adverse use* (prescription). The English theory that the easement was created by a *lost grant* is still used in a few American states; however, the majority permits prescription as a matter of public policy by analogy to the law of adverse possession.

(1) Elements of prescription §1136
The usual elements required for adverse possession must be shown:

(a) **Open and notorious use**;

(b) **Adverse and under a claim of right**; and

(c) **Continuous and uninterrupted use** (tacking is allowed).

(2) Public easements §1146
The majority of jurisdictions permit the public at large to acquire a public easement if the public uses **private land** in a manner that fulfills prescription requirements (*e.g.*, a roadway).

3. **Scope of Easements**

a. **General rule** §1150
The intent of the parties determines the scope.

b. **How easement was created** §1151
If an easement was **expressly created**, a court will look to the instrument's language and surrounding circumstances. An **easement of way** is favored and given a scope that meets the needs of the dominant tenement as it normally develops.

(1) Implied easements §1153
A **use existing** at the time a tract is divided into two parcels generally has the same scope as an express easement. Changes that are necessary to preserve the use or that might have been reasonably foreseen are allowed. For an **easement by necessity**, the extent of necessity determines the scope.

(2) Prescriptive easements §1155
Usually, the burden of a prescriptive easement on a servient estate cannot be increased because there is no assumption that the parties intended to accommodate future needs.

c. **Subdivision of dominant tenement** §1156
Upon subdivision of the dominant estate, each subdivided lot has a right to use easements appurtenant to the dominant estate. But the servient estate cannot be burdened more than was contemplated when the easement was created.

d. **Use for benefit of nondominant land** §1157
A dominant owner cannot increase the scope of an easement by using it to benefit a nondominant tenement. The easement may be extinguished if it is extended to a nondominant parcel and the unlawful use cannot be eliminated (*e.g.*, by injunction).

e. **Change in easement location** §1158
Mutual consent is required.

f. **Use by servient owner** §1161
The servient owner may use the servient land in ways that do not unreasonably interfere with the easement.

promise not to use his land in a certain way. (Remember an easement is a grant of an interest in land; a covenant is a promise regarding use of land.) Negative easements *cannot* arise by *prescription*.

B. REAL COVENANTS

1. Introduction
§1188

A covenant is a *promise* to do or not to do something; a real covenant is a promise relating to the *use* of land. The law of contracts applies if the *promisee* sues the promisor for breach. However, property law is applicable if a successor to the promisee or promisor is involved in the suit.

a. Remedies for breach
§1189

A suit for damages must be filed in law while a suit for an injunction or specific performance must be filed in equity.

b. Real covenant defined
§1190

A real covenant is a covenant that runs with the land *at law* so that each successor landowner may enforce or is burdened by the covenant. A real covenant gives rise to *personal liability only* and is enforceable only by an award of money damages.

(1) Distinguish—equitable servitude
§1192

This is a covenant enforceable *in equity* by or against successors to the land of the original parties.

(2) Distinguish—condition
§1193

A condition is created by language limiting the duration of an estate or cutting it short. The remedy for breach of covenant is damages; the remedy for breach of condition is *forfeiture*.

2. Creation
§1194

Although not an interest in land, a *writing* is required for a real covenant. A real covenant will not be implied nor can it arise by prescription. Usually, only the *grantor* must sign, but the grantee is also bound.

3. Enforcement By or Against Assignees
§1196

The major issue involving real covenants is whether they can be enforced by or against assignees (*i.e.*, whether the *benefit or the burden* will run to assignees). Easements run to successive owners because they are interests in land, while covenants originated only as promises concerning the use of land. Courts therefore developed different rules regarding when promises run to successors.

a. Requirements for burden to run
§1197

The burden of a covenant will run to assignees of the burdened land if: (i) the parties so *intend*; (ii) there is *privity of estate* (majority view); (iii) the covenant *touches and concerns* the burdened land; and (iv) the assignee has *notice* of the covenant before buying.

b. Requirements for benefit to run
§1198

The benefit of a covenant will run to assignees of the benefited land if: (i) the parties so *intend*; (ii) there is some form of *privity of estate* (*infra*); and (iii) the covenant *touches and concerns* the benefited land.

c. Intention of the parties §1199

Intention is usually found in the language of the deed or contract (*e.g.*, "covenants shall run with the land").

(1) Necessity of word "assigns" §1200

Abolished in a majority of states, the Rule in Spencer's Case holds that a covenant concerning a thing *not in being* will not bind assigns unless they are *expressly mentioned* (*e.g.*, "and her assigns").

d. Privity of estate

(1) Horizontal privity—burden §1202

Horizontal privity of estate is the relationship that exists between the original promisor and promisee. For the *burden* of a covenant to run to assignees, the majority rule is that the original parties to the covenant must be in privity of estate. In some jurisdictions, this means that the covenant is contained in a *conveyance* of an interest in land; in others, there must be a mutual relationship.

(2) Horizontal privity—benefit §1208

Most jurisdictions do not require horizontal privity for the running of a benefit.

(3) Vertical privity §1209

Privity of estate between the covenanting party and an assignee is required for the running of the burden and the benefit. Privity here means succession to the estate of one of the original parties. Privity of estate requires that the assignee of a *burden* succeed to the *identical estate* owned by the promisor. A *benefit* will run to assigns of the original estate *or* of a lesser estate.

(a) Restatement of Servitudes §1213

Under the Restatement, vertical privity is discarded for both the burden and the benefit. Instead the Restatement distinguishes affirmative and negative covenants. *Negative* covenants run to successors because they are interests in land. Burdens and benefits of *affirmative* covenants run to successors to an *estate of the same duration*, but not to persons who succeed to lesser estates, which are subject to special rules.

(b) Exception §1214

A *homeowners' association* may enforce the benefit even though it succeeds to no land owned by the original promisee, because it is considered an agent of the real owners.

e. Touch and concern §1215

For both benefits and burdens to run with the land, the covenant must touch and concern the affected land.

f. Notice §1216

A BFP is not bound by a covenant if he has no notice of it.

g. **Liability of original promisor after assignment** §1217
The assignor retains **no liability** on a promise **to do or not to do an act**.

C. EQUITABLE SERVITUDES

1. **Introduction** §1218
An equitable servitude is a covenant that **equity** will enforce against **assignees** of the burdened land who have **notice** of the covenant. An **injunction** is the usual remedy. An equitable servitude is an **interest** in land.

   a. **Distinguish—real covenant**

      (1) **Remedy** §1223
      If a plaintiff wants **damages**, she goes to law on a real covenant; if she wants an **injunction**, she goes to equity and asks for enforcement of an equitable servitude.

      (2) **Creation** §1225
      Although a real covenant must be in writing, many states will **imply** an equitable servitude.

      (3) **Privity of estate** §1226
      Because an interest in land (analogous to an easement) is being enforced, neither horizontal nor (generally) vertical privity are required for an equitable servitude. However, some states require **vertical privity** when a person other than the original promisee is enforcing the **benefit**.

      (4) **Similarities** §1227
      Both real covenants and equitable servitudes must touch and concern the land, and neither is enforceable against a BFP without notice. *Note:* The **Restatement of Servitudes** abolishes any distinction between real covenants and equitable servitudes.

2. **Creation** §1229
Because an equitable servitude is an interest in land, most courts require a **writing** signed by the promisor.

   a. **Exception—implied from a general plan** §1230
   Where a developer has previously sold restricted lots, many courts will imply a negative servitude on a lot subsequently conveyed even though there is no writing that creates a servitude. The developer must have had a **general plan** for an exclusively residential subdivision, **and** subsequent grantees must have had **notice** of restrictions on lots previously conveyed.

      (1) **General plan** §1232
      There must be evidence of a reasonably uniform general plan for developing all lots similarly, which existed when the first burdened lot was sold. In addition to covenants in prior deeds, evidence may

consist of a recorded restricted plat, exhibition of a map or plat showing restrictions to buyers, oral representations, and sales brochures.

    (a) Kind of servitude   **§1234**
         Where implied, the servitude is similar to a *reciprocal negative easement*.

  b. Note   **§1238**
    Real covenants will *not* be implied in any state.

3. Enforcement By or Against Assignees   **§1239**
An equitable servitude can be enforced by a successor to the promisee or against a successor to the promisor if certain requirements are met.

  a. Intent   **§1240**
    The contracting parties must intend that the servitude be enforceable by and against assignees.

  b. No privity of estate   **§1241**
    Neither horizontal nor vertical privity is required unless, in some states, the person trying to enforce does not own land owned by the original promisee.

  c. Touch and concern requirement   **§1245**
    Early cases held that the covenant must burden or benefit a party in the *physical use or enjoyment* of the land. Today, some covenants, especially negative covenants, touch and concern the land if they merely *enhance the value* of the land.

    (1) Negative covenants   **§1247**
        Negative covenants touch and concern; *e.g.*, a *covenant not to compete* restricts the use of the burdened land and enhances the commercial value of the benefited land.

    (2) Affirmative covenants   **§1250**
        Most courts permit affirmative covenants to run both in law and equity. If the act is to be performed off the burdened land, there is no touch and concern relationship.

    (3) Covenants to pay money   **§1252**
        Covenants to pay money for some improvement that enhances the promisor's land, even though the improvements are on other land, touch and concern.

    (4) Restatement of Servitudes   **§1254**
        Under the Restatement, the touch and concern requirement has been superseded by specific tests for unenforceability, including the reasonableness of the covenant.

    (5) Benefit in gross   **§1255**
        Most courts hold that the burden of a covenant will not run to assignees where the benefit is in gross because the benefit does not touch and concern the land.

Provisions for financial contributions are covenants, enforceable against assignees only if they "run with the land." Unit owners are jointly liable for injuries occurring in the common areas.

d. Restrictions on transfer §1299
Restrictions on transfer of the fee simple might be invalid unless carefully worded and reasonable (*e.g.*, no racial discrimination).

2. Cooperatives §1302
A cooperative apartment house is owned by a corporation whose stock is owned by the tenants. Thus, the residents are **both tenants** (under leases from the corporation) **and owners** of the cooperative corporation. The building has **one mortgage**; if one tenant defaults, the others must pay that share or face foreclosure. Taxes, maintenance, and repairs of the common areas are usually the responsibility of the corporation.

a. Restrictions on transfer §1306
Generally, both the lease and stock interest are subject to restrictions on transfer (*e.g.*, consent of board of directors to transfer, right of first refusal by board). Racial restrictions are **not** valid.

b. Termination of lease §1309
A tenant's lease may be terminated by the corporation if the tenant fails to pay his assessed share or violates rules of conduct established by the corporation. Rules are unenforceable if they are arbitrary or unreasonable.

VIII. RIGHTS AGAINST NEIGHBORS

A. NUISANCE

1. In General §1311
A nuisance is an unprivileged interference with a person's use and enjoyment of her land.

2. Private Nuisance §1312
A private nuisance is a **substantial** interference that is either **intentional and unreasonable** or **unintentional but negligent**, reckless, or abnormally dangerous. The plaintiff must have a **property interest** that is affected by the nuisance.

a. Intentional nuisance §1313
The **unreasonableness** of the interference determines whether the nuisance is intentional. Conduct is unreasonable if the gravity of the **harm outweighs the utility** of the actor's conduct.

(1) Gravity of harm §1314
Factors to be considered in determining the gravity include the **extent and character** of the harm, the **social value** of the use invaded, the **suitability** of the use invaded to the locality, and the **burden** to the plaintiff in avoiding the harm.

(2) Utility of conduct §1315
Courts consider the **social value** of the purpose of the invader's

conduct, the *suitability* of the conduct to the locality, and the *impracticability* of preventing the harm.

(3) Fault §1316

Fault of the defendant is not controlling, but his failure to use reasonable avoidance devices is important.

b. Unintentional act §1318

An unintentional act may give rise to a nuisance if the act is *reckless*, *negligent*, or involves *abnormally dangerous activities*.

c. Types of unreasonable interference §1319

To determine whether there is a nuisance courts consider: the character of the harm, the character of the neighborhood, the social value of the conflicting uses, and priority (whether the plaintiff has *come to the nuisance*).

d. Distinguish—trespass §1329

Trespass is invasion of *possession*; nuisance is invasion of *use and enjoyment*. Trespass requires an *unprivileged intrusion*, whereas nuisance requires unreasonable interference *and* substantial injury. Additionally, the remedies for nuisance are more flexible than for trespass.

e. Economic analysis §1331

Modern economic analysis considers neither party the sole cause of harm; both are responsible due to conflicting land uses.

(1) Coase theorem §1335

This provides that the *market* will move the right to the highest valued use if the transaction costs are low. Transaction costs include obtaining *information* about persons with whom one must deal, *negotiations, coming to terms* with the parties, and *enforcing* the bargains.

(a) Note §1337

If many neighbors are damaged, transaction costs will be high because of problems caused by holdouts, free riders, and strategies used by certain neighbors. In these cases, the right will likely stay where it was initially allocated.

(2) Initial allocation §1341

The initial allocation of the right (*i.e.*, the entitlement) can be based on economic arguments (*e.g.*, give to *highest valued user*, thus increasing society's total wealth; *first in time prevails* because of the greater investment), or on a moral basis (*e.g.*, *wealth redistribution*; *healthy environment*).

f. Remedies §1347

Whether a court grants an *injunction or damages* may depend on whether transaction costs are high. If so, a court may be more likely to grant damages (*i.e.*, a forced sale of plaintiff's right to sue for nuisance at an objectively determined price).

of sunlight. Courts would probably give more protection to solar collectors than swimming pools.

IX. PUBLIC LAND USE CONTROLS

A. ZONING

1. Theory of Zoning §1377
Zoning purports to prevent harm from incompatible uses by dividing a city into zones. Modern zoning also regulates uses to achieve public benefits or to maximize the tax base.

a. Separation of uses §1378
Single-family homes are deemed the *highest use* (least harmful), and are to be protected from lower uses such as apartments, commercial, or industrial. The principle of *cumulative uses* allows higher but not lower uses in a district. However, some noncumulative ordinances may exclude higher uses, *e.g.*, no residential or commercial use in industrial park district.

b. Density controls §1382
These indirectly control the number of people using an area (*e.g.*, height limitations, lot sizes, etc.).

2. Source of Zoning Power §1383
State statutes called *enabling acts* grant authority to local governmental units (city or county) to regulate land use.

3. Constitutional Limitations §1385
Zoning is a valid exercise of the police power. But it must be constitutional as applied to *each individual lot*.

a. Due Process Clause §1386
Zoning regulations are subject to the requirements of due process, both procedural and substantive.

(1) Procedural due process §1387
Legislative zoning actions (*e.g.*, enactment of ordinance for entire city) do not require notice to each landowner. *Administrative* actions (*e.g.*, variances) require individual notice.

(2) Substantive due process §1388
A zoning regulation must bear a *rational relationship to a permissible state objective* (*i.e.*, public health, safety, and general welfare). The only time a zoning ordinance is subject to *strict scrutiny* is when it infringes on a *fundamental right* (*e.g.*, free speech). Note that housing is *not* a fundamental right.

(3) State due process §1390
Unlike federal courts, state courts continue to recognize that state due process clauses have *considerable substantive content*. Thus, state courts strike down zoning regulations that are "arbitrary" or "unreasonable," even though *a rational means* of achieving the objective.

b. **Equal Protection Clause** §1391

The plaintiff must prove a *discriminatory purpose or intent* (discriminatory effect is *not* enough). The *rational relationship test* is used unless a suspect classification (*e.g.*, race) is involved.

c. **Takings Clause** §1394

A zoning regulation that takes property without compensation is a taking, the remedy for which is an injunction or damages. Do not confuse a taking ordinance with one that is void as violative of due process.

4. **Nonconforming Uses** §1402

A nonconforming use is one *in existence when the zoning ordinance is passed*, that is not allowed in the newly zoned area. It may remain but may be limited or terminated under certain conditions.

5. **Administration of Zoning Ordinance** §1408

Zoning must be in accordance with a *comprehensive plan*. The trend is for actual plans, but policies of the planning commission shown by documents or testimony may be a plan.

a. **Amendment of zoning ordinance** §1411

An amendment not in accordance with the comprehensive plan is *spot zoning* and is unlawful. Amendments are *presumptively valid*, but some courts shift the burden to the proponent of the amendment to show a *mistake* in the original ordinance or a *substantial change* in conditions.

b. **Variances** §1416

A variance may be granted where ordinance restrictions cause an owner *practical difficulty* or *unnecessary hardship*. A variance *runs with the land* and may have conditions attached.

c. **Special exception** §1421

A special exception (special use) is allowed when certain conditions specified in the ordinance are met. Courts usually uphold special exceptions even where standards are unclear.

d. **Discretionary or non-Euclidean zoning** §1423

Discretionary zoning has gradually been implemented to supplement the use of variances and special exceptions, which are sometimes too inflexible for effective public land planning. After initial judicial resistance, the trend is to uphold these devices.

(1) **Contract zoning** §1424

Rezoning a particular tract of land on the condition that the owner sign a contract with the city restricting the land's use grants greater flexibility to a city's land development plans.

(2) **Density zoning** §1425

Density or cluster zoning provides developers with an option to use spaces in various ways, provided a specified overall density is maintained.

(3) Floating zones §1426

A floating zone is a zone provided in the ordinance to which no land is assigned on the map until a landowner requests and is granted that classification.

(4) Planned unit development §1427

In a PUD district (usually a large tract of land), a developer can mix uses. The test as to validity is whether such rezoning is in accordance with a comprehensive plan.

e. Zoning by referendum §1428

Some zoning ordinances provide that an amendment can be made only by public referendum. Even where the effect has been exclusionary, mandatory referenda have been upheld.

6. Purposes of Zoning §1429

Recent litigation concerns zoning for purposes other than protecting the public health or safety.

a. Zoning for aesthetic purposes §1430

Although this was impermissible under the old doctrine, today many courts permit such zoning if the prohibited use is offensive to the *average person* and tends to *depress property values*.

(1) Application §1432

City boards may deny building permits for buildings out of character with the neighborhood. Commercial advertisements can be banned from residential areas. However, zoning that regulates commercial and political advertising is sensitive to First Amendment challenges.

b. Zoning against adult entertainment §1436

A zoning ordinance may disperse or limit adult entertainment to certain zones. Moreover, the Court has upheld a total ban on nude dancing as serving a substantial government interest.

c. Zoning and religious establishments §1437

The Religious Land Use and Institutionalized Persons Act of 2000 prohibits land use regulations that impose substantial burdens on (without a compelling state interest or least restrictive means), discriminate against, or totally exclude religious institutions.

d. Zoning for preservation §1438

Whether property so zoned is "taken" depends on weighing the landowner's economic loss against the reasonable need for fulfillment of a substantial public purpose.

(1) Historic preservation §1439

Historic preservation ordinances applied to historic districts are usually upheld. But courts have been reluctant to uphold legislation to preserve *individual landmarks* (equal protection and "taking" problems). The most recent Supreme Court case in this area upholds a landmark preservation law if the owner is left a reasonable return on his investment.

a. **Application**   §1459

Regulations that require a developer to put in paved streets, sewers, etc., are valid if reasonable. Requiring dedication for parks and schools is upheld in some states, but struck down in others on the ground that the need is not *specifically and uniquely attributable* to the developer's activity.

2. **Official Maps**   §1461

An official map, prohibiting building on land to be acquired by the city in the future, is *not* a taking unless the *owner applies for and is denied a building permit* and is thereby substantially damaged.

C. EMINENT DOMAIN

1. **In General**   §1463

Governments have the power to take title to property against the owner's will. The Fifth Amendment requires just compensation for a taking.

2. **What Is Public Use?**   §1464

The Fifth Amendment prohibits a taking of land "for public use" without just compensation. The Supreme Court has broadly interpreted "public use" to mean a *public purpose* (*i.e.*, it must *benefit* the public).

a. **Application**   §1466

In *urban renewal*, the government exercises eminent domain and then transfers title to a private redeveloper to develop according to an urban renewal plan. It has been upheld under a rational basis approach as being for a public purpose. However, some states apply strict scrutiny or per se standards to such government acts.

3. **What Is a "Taking"?**

a. **Condemnation action to take title**   §1468

If the government takes title to the land, it must pay for it.

b. **Physical occupation or invasion**   §1469

Any *permanent* physical occupation or invasion by the government (or by a third party with government authorization) is a *per se taking* and must be paid for.

c. **Regulatory takings**   §1472

Several tests have been developed to determine whether a governmental regulation (under its police power) that affects the *use and value* of the land, rather than involves occupation or invasion, is a taking:

(1) **Destruction of *all* economic value**   §1473

If the regulation deprives land of *all* economically beneficial uses, it is a per se taking *unless* the government is acting to *prevent a common law nuisance* (see *infra*). The fact that the regulation was *enacted before purchase* does not foreclose a takings claim. Moreover, a regulation that destroys all economic value for only a *limited time* (e.g., a development moratorium) does *not* result in a per se taking.

(a) Exception—control of common law nuisances §1476
No taking results if the government regulates to control common law nuisances or nuisance-like activity (*i.e.*, protect against a *harm*). However, if the regulation aims to extract a *benefit*, a taking has occurred and compensation must be paid.

(2) Diminution in value §1477
If a government regulation of a use that is not a common law nuisance imposes *too great a burden* on property owners, the government must provide compensation.

(a) Reciprocal advantages and disadvantages §1479
Regulations that involve reciprocal advantages and disadvantages (*e.g.*, zoning ordinances, where each of the regulated owners receives *some* advantage, although not necessarily equal) are *not* takings.

(3) Exactions and impact fees §1481
A city may impose on a property owner applying for a building permit a condition (exaction) that benefits the city, *e.g.*, provide a public path for beach access. The exaction must (i) be logically related to the specific public need that the owner's building creates (*essential nexus*), and (ii) bear a *rough proportionality* to the negative impact of the development on the public. *Impact fees* are monetary, rather than physical, exactions. The courts are split on whether the above test applies to impact fees.

d. Remedies for regulatory takings §1483
A suit for compensation usually proceeds by way of an action in *inverse condemnation*. For regulatory takings, the government may be liable for *interim and permanent damages*. If the regulation is unconstitutional, it is *void*.

e. State balancing test §1484
This test, used by some state courts, balances private loss against public gain. The trend is to look at both the *utility* of the action (economic efficiency) and its *fairness*.

4. What Is Just Compensation?

a. Market value §1485
Usually, just compensation means the fair market value—*i.e.*, price a willing buyer would pay a willing seller. Market value includes the value of possible *future expectations* as well as existing uses (including the value of an expected renewal of a lease). It does *not* include the *loss of a business* located on the land.

(1) Exception §1487
Where there is no relevant market such as for *special purpose property*, any just and equitable method may be used.

b. Partial taking §1492
If only part of a tract is taken, the owner is entitled to severance

damages. In some states, this is the difference in the value of the **entire tract** before taking and the value of the **remainder** after taking (before and after rule). Another method is to give an owner the **sum of the value** of the part taken and any **net damages** to the remainder after offsetting benefits (value plus damage rule).

X. THE SALE OF LAND

A. THE CONTRACT FOR SALE OF LAND

1. **Broker's Role** §1495

   A broker's contract gives him the exclusive right to sell the property at the price or terms in the contract **or at any other price or terms agreed on by the parties**. A broker earns a commission only **when the buyer pays the purchase price**. However, the seller is liable for the commission if she defaults.

2. **Attorney's Role** §1498

   An attorney is often employed for various tasks, *e.g.*, examining title, closing, etc. Note that an attorney may be acting unethically if she represents both the buyer and seller.

3. **Written Contract Required** §1499

   The Statute of Frauds requires that a contract for the sale of land be **in writing** and **signed by the party to be charged**. The writing can be informal, and may consist of several documents. It must, however, contain all of the **essential terms**: *i.e.*, parties' identification; property description; and terms and conditions of the sale, including price (the **price** must be in the writing if it has been agreed upon; if not, a court may imply an agreement to pay a reasonable price).

   a. **Part performance** §1506

      Equity courts may enforce an **oral** contract for the sale of land under certain circumstances.

      (1) **Acts of "unequivocal reference to a contract"** §1507

         Most courts require acts that make sense only as having been done pursuant to a contract. In most states, part performance occurs when a buyer (i) **pays** all or part of the purchase price, **and** (ii) takes **possession**, **and** (iii) **makes improvements**. Some states hold the contract enforceable based merely on possession **or** on payment or improvements; still others require more, such as **irreparable injury** if the contract is not enforced or **detrimental reliance**.

      (2) **Contracts to devise** §1511

         The part performance doctrine may be applied to oral contracts to devise land at death in exchange for services when: proof of the promise is clear and convincing, the promisee detrimentally relied, and failure to enforce would be unconscionable.

   b. **Estoppel** §1513

      In the few states where part performance is not recognized, estoppel is used to enforce oral contracts where unconscionable injury would occur to a person who detrimentally relied on the contract.

   c. **Revocation** §1514

      A written contract can be revoked by an **oral** agreement.

4. Time of Performance §1515

Unless a contract contains a *"time is of the essence"* clause, performance can take place within a reasonable time *after* the specified date.

5. Marketable Title §1517

Absent a provision to the contrary, it is implied in a contract that the seller is giving the buyer a good and marketable title. A marketable title is one reasonably free from doubt, one which a prudent purchaser would accept; a perfect title is *not* required. Marketable title can be shown by good *record title* or, in many states, by title by *adverse possession*.

a. Defects in title §1523

A title may be unmarketable because of prior defects in the chain of title. Defects may be incorrect land description, improper recordation, or prior private encumbrances (*e.g.*, mortgages, liens, covenants, and easements). A buyer may *expressly waive an encumbrance*.

(1) Zoning restrictions §1528

A zoning restriction does not make title unmarketable unless the ordinance is passed *after* the buyer signed the contract and the restrictions would frustrate the buyer's proposed use, or if the property is in violation of a zoning restriction.

6. Defects in the Premises §1530

Some states still apply the old rule that a seller need not disclose any defect unless it was fraudulently concealed (*caveat emptor*); however, exceptions are commonly applied in these states.

a. Duty to disclose §1532

Most states now require a seller to disclose to the buyer all known material defects. Generally, a broker also must disclose defects unknown and undetectable by the buyer.

7. Remedies for Breach of Contract §1535

Neither the seller nor the buyer can place the other in default unless one *tenders his own performance and demands* that the other party perform. If breach occurs, the injured party has remedies of rescission, specific performance, or damages.

a. Remedies of the buyer

(1) Rescission §1536

Upon the seller's breach, the buyer can rescind the contract and recover her down payment. However, if, as is customary, the seller is to furnish title on the closing date, a buyer *cannot rescind prior to closing*, thereby giving the seller a chance to perform (*e.g.*, obtain title, cure defects).

(2) Specific performance §1537

Because land is unique, a buyer may demand specific performance, subject however to a seller's equitable defenses (*e.g.*, undue hardship). A buyer can also take a defective title and receive an *abatement in the purchase price*.

(3) Damages §1539

A buyer can sue the seller **at law** for damages, which in most states is the **benefit of the bargain** (*i.e.*, the difference between the contract price and the market value).

(a) Exception §1541

Where a seller acts in **good faith**, a buyer can only get his out-of-pocket expenses in many states.

b. Remedies of the seller

(1) Rescission §1542

If the buyer breaches, the seller may rescind the contract.

(2) Specific performance §1543

Or, the seller may demand specific performance, even if there is an insubstantial defect in the seller's title (of course with an abatement in the purchase price).

(a) Defenses §1544

An apparent new trend denies a seller specific performance if she can easily resell and damages are adequate.

(3) Damages §1545

The seller may keep the land and sue for the difference between the contract price and the market price. She may also be entitled to keep the down payment as **liquidated damages** if there is a **reasonable relationship** between the sum and the actual damages.

8. Equitable Conversion §1547

This determines who has title during the time period between the contract of sale and the closing. Because either party can demand specific performance of the contract, the buyer is considered the **equitable owner** of the land; the seller has a security interest.

a. Devolution on death §1549

Used in both testate and intestate devolution, the doctrine states that on the buyer's death, his interest is treated as **real** property; on the seller's death, her interest is treated as **personal** property.

b. Right to possession §1551

Under the doctrine, the buyer has **equitable**, **not legal**, **title** and does **not** have the right to possession.

c. Risk of loss §1552

If the property is damaged or destroyed before closing, the **majority** view is that the risk of loss falls **on the buyer** who, by equitable conversion, owns the land (the seller has only a security interest). The seller must have **marketable title** for the risk of loss to shift.

(1) Insurance §1555

A majority of states holds that if the risk of loss is on the buyer and the seller is insured, then the seller must apply the insurance proceeds to the purchase price if he seeks specific performance of the contract.

(2) **Minority rule**   §1556
A minority of courts *implies* a condition in the contract that if a *substantial loss* occurs and the terms show that the building constituted an *important part* of the subject matter of the contract, the contract is not binding; the buyer can rescind and recover his earnest money. In other words, the *seller has the risk of loss*.

    (a) **Insubstantial damage**   §1557
In this case, the buyer can get *specific performance with abatement* for the damage.

    (b) **Buyer's insurance**   §1558
Where a buyer purchases insurance, a seller who has the risk of loss *cannot* reach the proceeds.

(3) **Party in possession**   §1559
A few states and the Uniform Vendor and Purchaser Risk Act find that the *party in possession* has the risk of loss.

d. **Options**   §1560
Equitable conversion does *not* apply to options *until* exercised because an option is not a mutually specifically enforceable contract.

9. **The Closing**   §1561
At the closing, payment and deed are transferred, any mortgage is executed, and necessary adjustments are made (utility bills, prorated taxes, etc.).

B. **THE DEED**

1. **Formalities**

a. **Statute of Frauds**   §1562
To transfer an interest in land, the Statute of Frauds requires a writing signed by the *grantor*. Acknowledgement is unnecessary but is required for *recordation* of the deed. A *spouse's signature* is necessary only to release certain rights in the property (*e.g.*, dower rights).

b. **Words of grant**   §1572
Technical words used at common law are no longer necessary; any words indicating an intent to transfer are sufficient.

c. **Consideration**   §1574
This is *not* necessary to transfer; one can *give* land away.

d. **Parts of the deed**   §1575
The usual deed contains a granting clause (parties, consideration, words of grant, land description), and the grantor's covenants, signature, and acknowledgement. The habendum clause ("to have and to hold") is superfluous in statutory deeds.

e. **Description of the grantee**   §1581
A grantee need not be actually named but must be sufficiently described so it can be determined who is intended.

(1) **Grantee's name left blank**   §1583
Older cases would hold the deed a nullity. A majority of modern

cases holds that the intended grantee is the agent of the grantor with **implied authority** to fill in the blank (even after the grantor's death).

2. Description of Land Conveyed

a. Admission of extrinsic evidence §1586
If the description in the deed furnishes any means of identification, the description is sufficient. Extrinsic evidence is usually admissible to clear up ambiguities but may not contradict the deed. Contradictory evidence is only admissible in a suit to reform because of mutual mistake.

b. Canons of construction §1589
When there is a conflicting description, preference is given in the following order: original survey monuments, natural monuments, artificial monuments, maps, courses, distances, name, and lastly, quantity.

c. Streets and railways §1596
If streets or railways are used as boundaries, there is a rebuttable presumption that the **grantee's title extends to the center** of the right of way (or to the full width if the grantor owns it).

d. Water boundaries §1597
Here, a deed is usually construed to give a grantee the land under the water so as to permit access to the water.

C. DELIVERY OF THE DEED

1. In General §1598
Delivery requires words or conduct by the grantor that show an **intent** to make an immediate transfer. Usually, this means a **manual transfer** of the deed, but manual transfer is unnecessary if other acts sufficiently show intent.

a. Presumptions §1599
Delivery is presumed if the deed is: (i) **handed** to the grantee; (ii) **acknowledged** by the grantor before a notary; or (iii) **recorded**.

(1) Deeds effective at death §1600
If a grantor executes a deed and puts it away someplace, and it can be shown the grantor intended the deed to be legally effective **before** death, it is a validly delivered deed. If not effective until death, the deed is invalid for lack of delivery.

b. Cancellation of delivery §1601
After effective delivery, **title has passed** to the grantee and cannot be revoked or passed back to the grantor without delivery of a **new deed**.

2. Conditional Delivery to Grantee

a. Written condition §1602
A deed containing a provision that it is only to take effect on the happening of a certain event may be interpreted to mean that there is **no delivery until the condition happens** (a nullity); or it may be interpreted to mean that the grantor intends the deed to be **immediately effective, but passing only an interest subject to a condition precedent** (grantee

receives a *springing executory interest*). The words of condition are crucial if the deed is not to be held invalid as a *will substitute* due to a lack of delivery.

(1) Power to revoke §1606
If the grantor retains the power to revoke the deed, the courts are split as to whether effective delivery has occurred.

b. Oral condition §1608
If delivery is made to the grantee upon an oral condition, the delivery is good and the *condition is void*.

3. Deed Given to Third Party (Escrow)

a. Donative escrow §1610
A deed delivered in escrow (but not directly to the grantee) may contain *oral or written* instructions. However, if the grantor retains a *power to revoke*, the escrow agent is considered solely the *grantor's agent* and no delivery has occurred.

b. Commercial escrow §1615
A commercial escrow agent is a fiduciary for *both* parties. Therefore, written instructions are binding on the grantor. But where the instructions are *oral*, the grantor may recall the deed while still in the agent's hands, *unless* there is a *written contract of sale*.

c. Relation-back doctrine §1619
When there is a valid delivery in escrow, on subsequent delivery to the grantee by the escrow agent ("second delivery"), the *title relates back to the first delivery* if "equity and justice require," but this doctrine is *inapplicable* against a *subsequent BFP*.

4. Estoppel of Grantor §1625
When the grantor voluntarily gives possession of a deed to the grantee (*e.g.*, to examine it), and the grantee conveys to a BFP, the grantor may be *estopped* to deny delivery on a theory of negligent entrustment. Where a grantor puts a deed into escrow and a grantee wrongfully obtains possession of the deed and then conveys to a BFP, the cases are evenly split as to whether the grantor is or is not estopped.

D. WARRANTIES OF TITLE

1. Covenants of Title §1631
Covenants of title in the deed govern the scope of a seller's liability; *no* covenants of title are implied.

a. Types of deeds

(1) General warranty deed §1633
This usually contains all six of the usual covenants (*see* below) and warrants title against defects arising *before* as well as *during* the time the grantor has title.

(2) Special warranty deed §1634

A special warranty deed contains all six of the covenants, but covers only defects arising *during* the grantor's tenure.

(3) Quitclaim deed §1635

A quitclaim deed contains no warranties.

(4) Statutory warranty deeds §1636

In many states, specific words of conveyance, *e.g.*, "grant," "convey," are statutorily presumed to connote general warranties of title.

b. Covenants for title in warranty deeds §1637

The six usual covenants are:

(1) Covenant of *seisin* (grantor is owner);

(2) Covenant of *right to convey*;

(3) Covenant *against encumbrances*;

(4) Covenant of *quiet enjoyment*;

(5) Covenant of *warranty* (*i.e.*, grantor will defend grantee against any lawful claims existing at time of transfer); and

(6) Covenant of *further assurances* (grantor will perfect grantee's title, if necessary).

c. Merger of contract into deed §1644

Once the buyer accepts a deed, the contract merges into the deed, and the buyer can sue only on the warranties in the deed. The merger doctrine is now disfavored and often is not applied where a buyer expects the seller to perform.

2. Breach of Covenants

a. Present covenants §1646

These are breached *when made*, if at all, and include the covenants of *seisin*, *right to convey*, *and against encumbrances*. The majority rule is that the covenants of seisin and against encumbrances are breached even if the grantee knew of the defect. The majority rule is that present covenants *do not run with the land* and cannot be enforced by a remote grantee.

b. Future covenants §1654

The covenants of *quiet enjoyment*, *warranty*, *and further assurances* are breached when the grantee is actually or constructively *evicted*. A future covenant *runs with the land* if there is *privity of estate* between the original grantor-covenantor and the remote grantee. This means that the covenantor conveyed either *title or possession* to his grantee, who conveyed it to the remote grantee.

c. Damages for breach §1662

In all but a few New England states, the grantee cannot recover more than the covenantor received as consideration. If the land is a *gift*, some courts allow no recovery for breach; other courts allow the grantee to recover the market value at the time the covenant is made.

(1) Covenant of seisin §1666

If title to the entire tract fails, the grantee may recover the full purchase price. If there is a ***partial breach***, the grantee may recover damages proportionate to that part of land to which title fails. Or, if the grantee receives a good title to a part that is not usable, she can rescind and recover the entire purchase price.

(2) Covenant against encumbrances §1668

If the encumbrance is not removable, damages are the difference in value of the land with and without the encumbrance. If the grantee can remove the encumbrance, damages are the cost of removal. If the grantee does not remove a removable encumbrance, she is entitled to only nominal damages unless she can prove actual loss.

(3) Future covenants §1669

For breach of a future covenant, a grantee receives her purchase price back, not the actual market loss. Courts are split on damages for a ***remote grantee***: Some give a remote grantee out-of-pocket losses; others give what the covenantor received if it is more than her out-of-pocket loss.

3. Estoppel by Deed §1671

Where a grantor purports to convey land he does not then own, and subsequently he acquires title, title passes to the grantee ***under the earlier deed***.

E. WARRANTIES OF QUALITY

1. Builder's Liability §1674

Contrary to common law, most jurisdictions now imply a ***warranty of quality*** in the sale of ***new homes***; *i.e.*, the builder warrants that the building is free from defective materials and is properly constructed. Some courts apply this warranty on a tort theory, and it runs to ***all persons*** who buy the product. Liability cannot be waived and runs from the time the defect is discovered. Other courts use a contract theory wherein the warranty runs only to those in privity of contract to the builder, and it begins to run from the date of conveyance. The implied warranty of quality has ***not*** yet been extended to the sale of commercial buildings.

2. Seller's Liability §1679

A seller of a used house who is not a builder has ***no liability*** based on the warranty of quality. However, she may be liable for ***misrepresentation or fraud***. Modern cases hold that a seller must disclose known defects not readily discoverable by the buyer.

F. THE MORTGAGE

1. Why a Mortgage Is Used §1680

A person borrows money to purchase property. The lender holds a mortgage on the property as security for the loan.

2. Nature of the Mortgage Transaction §1681

A mortgage transaction consists of: (i) the ***note***, which evidences the debt;

and (ii) a **mortgage**, which is an agreement that the land will be sold if the debt is not paid (security for lender). The note and mortgage may be one document. Usually, the mortgage is **recorded**, giving the lender priority over subsequent purchasers.

3. **Terminology**   §1682

A **mortgagor** is the borrower; a **mortgagee** is the lender. A **purchase money mortgage** secures the purchase price of land; a mortgage to secure a debt or to finance home improvements is not a purchase money mortgage. A **balloon payment mortgage** provides for periodic interest payments until the due date of the debt, when the **entire principal sum** must be paid at once. The standard home mortgage, the **amortized payment** mortgage, has even monthly payments consisting of both interest and principal that are spread out over many years (*e.g.*, 30-year mortgage). A **second mortgage** is a mortgage on the same tract of land, given after and with notice of the original mortgage. The second mortgagee's rights are **subject to** the rights of the first mortgagee; thus, because the risks are greater, second mortgages have a higher interest rate.

a. **Deed of trust**   §1691

In many states, the borrower transfers title to a third person **as trustee** for the lender to secure the debt. The major difference concerns the power to sell the land upon default. However, in many states, modern statutes have largely eliminated this difference.

b. **Installment land contract**   §1692

A buyer may agree to pay for a land purchase over a period of years. The buyer receives possession and the seller keeps title until the last payment. Modern courts have alleviated the harshness of the rule that permitted the seller to keep both the land and all payments made upon default.

4. **History of the Mortgage**   §1693

Originally, if the borrower did not pay **on the agreed date**, the land belonged to the lender. Equity intervened to give borrowers a right to redeem **at any time** after the agreed date. This created difficulties for the sale of the land upon default, so equity then gave the lender the right to **foreclose the right of redemption**. Today, foreclosing the mortgage is a judicial proceeding involving a public sale; the equity of redemption is barred, the debt is paid, and excess proceeds are given to the borrower.

a. **Equitable mortgage**   §1694

Today, some lenders use several devices to obtain a fee simple as security. Courts look to the **substance** of the transaction, and where the intent was to use land as security for a debt, a court will declare an equitable mortgage; *i.e.*, it will be **treated as a mortgage**.

b. **Statutory period of redemption**   §1695

Many states give borrowers a statutory period (*e.g.*, two years) **after judicial foreclosure** during which they can redeem the land from the foreclosure purchaser.

5. Theory of the Mortgage   §1696

Title theory states treat legal *title* as being in the mortgagee. *Lien theory* states consider that legal title remains in the mortgagor and the mortgagee merely has a *lien* on the property.

6. Transfer of the Mortgagor's Interest

a. Sale subject to the mortgage   §1698

The new buyer takes the land subject to the lien but is *not personally liable* on the debt. The original mortgagor remains personally liable. If the debt is not paid, the mortgagee may sue the mortgagor or proceed against the land by foreclosure and sale.

b. Sale with assumption of the mortgage   §1699

If the new buyer assumes the mortgage, she becomes *personally liable* on the debt although the original mortgagor remains secondarily liable. Thus, the mortgagee can sue either person on the debt; if he sues the original mortgagor, the mortgagor can then sue the new buyer or foreclose.

c. Due-on-sale clauses   §1700

A due-on-sale clause in a mortgage provides that, at the mortgagee's election, the *entire mortgage debt* is due upon sale of the mortgagor's interest. Such clauses are legally enforceable.

7. Default by the Mortgagor   §1701

Upon default, the mortgagee can sue on the debt or foreclose. A minority of states requires the mortgagee to foreclose and exhaust the security before suing on the debt. Either way, after a foreclosure sale, the mortgagee can get a *deficiency judgment* against the mortgagor for the difference between the sale proceeds and the debt amount.

a. Legislation   §1702

To protect a mortgagor in default, some states have enacted certain provisions such as fair market value requirements, no deficiency judgments on purchase money mortgages, and the statutory right of redemption.

XI. TITLE ASSURANCE

A. RECORDING SYSTEM

1. Common Law Rule—Prior in Time   §1707

A grantee who was *prior in time* prevailed over one subsequent in time.

2. Recording Acts   §1709

To discourage the fraudulent acts by a grantor that the prior in time rule permitted, all states eventually enacted statutes providing for deed recordation in each county to protect a grantee from subsequent purchasers.

3. Mechanics of Recording   §1710

Any instrument affecting title to land (*e.g.*, mortgage) can be recorded. The grantee first files a copy with the county recorder. The recorder indexes the deed; the index book is used to find the deed in subsequent title searches.

Separate index volumes are kept for **grantors and grantees** (some urban areas index by tract, *i.e.*, blocks and lots).

4. **Types of Recording Acts** §1722

There are three major types of recording acts:

a. **"Race" statutes** §1723

As between two claimants, whoever **records first** wins; actual notice of prior claims is irrelevant.

b. **"Notice" statutes** §1724

A subsequent purchaser is protected against a prior unrecorded instrument if he has **no actual or constructive notice** of a prior claim.

c. **"Race-notice" statutes** §1725

A subsequent purchaser **without notice** is protected against a prior unrecorded instrument **only** if he **records before** the prior instrument is recorded.

5. **Effect of Recordation** §1726

Recordation protects a grantee by giving notice to all the world of the contents of the recorded instrument. It raises a rebuttable **presumption** of delivery, but it will **not** validate an invalid deed. Recordation also does **not** protect a grantee against interests arising by **operation of law** (e.g., implied easement).

a. **Effect of failure to record** §1730

If a person does not record, the common law rule of **"prior in time, prior in effect"** is applicable.

6. **Requirements for Recordation** §1733

Nearly any instrument or decree affecting an interest in land can be recorded. Most states require an **acknowledgement** (some also require witnesses) for recordation.

a. **"Recordation"** §1735

To be recorded, the document must be entered in the recorder's books in accordance with the applicable statute or judicial decisions.

(1) **Failure to index** §1736

Courts are split on whether the failure to properly index an instrument protects the grantee against subsequent bona fide purchasers.

(2) **Recording unacknowledged instrument** §1740

If an unacknowledged instrument is mistakenly recorded, it does **not** give constructive notice to subsequent purchasers. Where the acknowledgement is **defective** but the defect is not apparent on the face of the instrument, recordation gives constructive notice, but there is authority to the contrary.

7. **Who Is Protected by Recording Acts**

a. **Purchasers** §1742

All **purchasers** who are **without notice** and **given valuable consideration** (BFPs) are within the protection of the recording system (under race statutes, notice is irrelevant). Purchasers include **mortgagees**.

(1) "Shelter rule"

A person who takes **from** a protected BFP stands in her shoes and is protected even though the person has notice of a prior unrecorded interest.

§1744

(2) Donees

Generally, donees are not protected.

§1745

(3) Creditors

There is considerable variation in the protection afforded creditors. Some acts protect creditors once they become judgment or lien creditors; other creditors gain protection only by purchasing the debtor-owner's interest at a judicial sale.

§1746

b. Without notice

The purchaser must be without **actual**, **record**, or **inquiry** notice of the prior claim **at the time she paid consideration**.

§1750

(1) Inquiry notice

(a) Quitclaim deed

A majority of states do not require inquiry on a quitclaim deed; others are contra.

§1754

(b) Possession

In most states, a person is required to make inquiry of a person in possession of the land; however, some states impose a lesser inquiry burden.

§1755

(c) Neighborhood

In some states, a person is put on inquiry as to possible implied negative restrictions on use of the land by the looks of the neighborhood (especially subdivisions).

§1758

(d) Unrecorded instruments

If a recorded instrument **expressly** refers to an unrecorded instrument, most states require inquiry.

§1759

c. Valuable consideration

A person is not a BFP unless she gives valuable consideration. It must be more than nominal consideration but does not have to equal the market value; love and affection are **not** enough. A person who receives a deed or mortgage as security for a **preexisting debt** has not given valuable consideration.

§1760

8. Chain of Title Problems

Where grantor and grantee indexes are used (not tract indexes), problems arise when a deed is not in the chain of title.

§1765

a. Chain of title

A purchaser in grantor-grantee index jurisdictions has constructive notice of all conveyances by her grantor **recorded after the grantor acquired the property** from his predecessor in title and **recorded before a deed is recorded conveying title from that grantor** to another, and also conveyances made by various predecessors in title.

§1766

C. TITLE INSURANCE

1. Who Is Insured §1810
Property owners or mortgagees can obtain a policy which protects only the ***person who owns the policy***.

2. Extent of Coverage §1811
The usual policy insures only a ***good record title*** and agrees to defend the record title if litigated. If the title company gives ***legal advice*** as to marketability of the title, it is liable in negligence for wrong advice.

a. Exclusions §1816
The standard title insurance policy does not cover legal liens not in public records, claims of parties in possession not in the records, boundary disputes, easements or covenants not recorded, zoning and building ordinances, or presence of hazardous wastes.

Approach to Exams

Property is basic to the social welfare. People seek it, nations war over it, and no one can do without it. The function of Property law is to determine *who* among the competing claimants gets *what, when*, and under *what conditions*. Given the complexity of the world today, that is a tall order. Just try to imagine all of the resources in this country that might be claimed. There is land, there are watches, there are cars, and cows, and coins, and so on. Indeed, there is around us a whole "supermarket" of things. But property is not limited to things you can see or feel. Property can include a copyright, a promise, airspace, a right to fish, a right to continued employment, a right to be free of racial discrimination, etc. All these the law may call property, deeming it useful to do so in the scheme of things. The law of Property is complex because it is possible and desirable to have an enormous variety of arrangements for using all of the resources in society.

But because the law of Property is complex, a law school course in property can cover a wide range of topics. Thus, it is difficult (if not impossible) to give a general approach to answering all Property questions. However, some of the general concepts that run throughout this area of law are discussed below and may help you analyze Property issues. Also, at the beginning of each chapter, a chapter approach targets the more specific considerations for topics covered in the particular chapter.

1. What Is Property?

In legal discourse, *property is what the law defines as property*. If a claim to a resource is not recognized by law, it is not property in a legal sense. Once recognized by law, a claim becomes a legal *right*. For example, if a judge declares that A can walk across Blackacre free of B's interference, A has a property right; but if a judge declares that B can exclude A, B—and not A—has a property right. Hence, a central question in the law of Property is:

— What claims *should* the courts and the legislatures recognize as property? This depends, of course, on the applicable policies, on what the lawgivers want to accomplish. Two considerations are especially important in Property law and run through most of it: *fairness* and *economic efficiency*. The lawgivers want to be fair, but at the same time they want the system to generate more wealth. But these are not the only policies in view. Life, and the distribution of the world's goods, is not so simple.

2. What Is Property Law?

Property law has been largely formulated in each state by *courts* (deciding *cases*) and *legislatures* (enacting *statutes*). (Very little Property law has been developed by the federal government.) Each state is free to develop its Property law as it desires, provided it does not contravene the United States Constitution. Even so, because of a common heritage (the common law inherited from the English), there are far more similarities than differences in Property law among the various states; Property law in Florida is likely to be based on the same principles as Property law in Massachusetts. Of course, the legislature may modify the common law (subject to the constraints of the state and federal constitutions), and if so, statutes prevail over earlier case law.

3. How Do You Analyze "Property"?

The word "property" can be used to denote the thing or resource (even the intangible object) being discussed (*e.g.*, "the property was destroyed by fire"). In this sense, all property can be divided into two types, *real* and *personal*. Generally speaking, *real property* is land and any structures built on it. *Personal property*, which is everything else, consists of *tangible* items (things that can be seen or felt, such as a watch or a book) and *intangible* items (things that cannot be seen, such as a bank account or the right not to be unfairly kicked out of law school).

In legal analysis, the word "property" often is used in another way. It denotes the *legal relationships among people* in regard to a thing. The thing may be real or personal, tangible or intangible; according to this usage, it is the legal relationship that is important. For example, if a lawyer says, "This watch is Joe's property" or "Joe owns this watch," the words "property" and "owns" do not refer directly to the watch but to the legal relationship Joe has with other persons in regard to the watch. Assume Suzy is sitting next to Joe. The statement that "Joe owns this watch" means that Joe can wear it—even smash it—without Suzy's consent; that Suzy is under a legal duty not to interfere with Joe's use, and Joe can recover damages from her if she takes it and smashes it; that Joe can recover the watch from a thief; that if Joe gives the watch to a repair shop, he is entitled to get it back. Observe that each of the foregoing statements describes a relationship between Joe and another person with respect to the watch (specifically, Joe's rights and others' duties). All of these relationships can be collected together in a bundle, and thus what Joe has is "a bundle of rights."

In other words, "property," for lawyers, is conceived of as "a bundle of rights." You will become familiar with the peculiar conceptualizations inherent in the study of property (*e.g.*, a "bundle of rights") and will begin to view commonplace items with a different perspective.

4. What Is the Rationale for the Law?

This Summary attempts to describe in brief form all of the various ways that lawyers have worked out for talking about property. One thing you will soon realize in the study of Property is that Property law is a highly analytical subject, but if you understand the terminology and the basic principles before going on to the meticulous details, this subject is not too difficult. However, understanding requires an *examination of reasons* for things. As Justice Harlan said in the *Civil Rights Cases*, 109 U.S. 3 (1883): "The letter of the law is the body; the sense and reason of the law is the soul." If you try to learn Property law by rote—by memorization and drill—weeks, even months, may pass without your ever getting the feel of what you are doing. In this Summary, as each new term is introduced—and there are a lot of them—the term is defined. As each rule is set forth, illustrations of it are given so that it can be more easily understood, *and its underlying reasons are presented.*

It is impossible to overemphasize the importance of ascertaining and *understanding the purposes behind rules.* If you do not understand the purposes, you do not really understand the rules. At the end of your course in Property, most likely your exam will contain questions asking for the application of rules to new situations not discussed in class. (This is, in essence, what the lawyer does.) But you cannot properly apply rules to new fact situations without understanding that rules are construed to give effect to, and are limited by, their purposes. Hence, always seek the reasons for a rule. If you understand the reasons, you can appropriately apply the rule to new or different fact situations.

Author's Note: This Summary cites almost all of the principal cases in the leading casebooks used in first-year Property courses. To find out about the rules of law discussed in the case, and how the case fits within those rules, look up the name of the case in the Table of Cases at the back of this Summary. Then turn to the section in the Summary where the case is cited.

Also note that the organization of this Summary more or less follows the organization of leading casebooks. But because no two casebooks follow exactly the same order, you should look up the topic you are studying in the Table of Contents and/or the Text Correlation Chart to find where it is covered in this Summary.

Chapter One:
Acquisition of Property

CONTENTS

Chapter Approach

Chapter Approach

Most Property courses begin with problems in the acquisition of property. The object is to make you think about why private property is recognized and the reasons for the rules of acquisition.

This chapter covers all the materials traditionally treated and tested under the topic of acquisition, including:

1. **First-in-Time Rule**

    A fundamental property rule is that the *first person to take possession of an unowned thing owns it.* A corollary of this rule is that *a prior possessor prevails over a subsequent possessor.* These rules implement important social policies relating to rewarding labor, protecting investment in resources, and encouraging people to bargain with each other rather than fight. It is important to apply the first-in-time rule in several factual contexts to see its reach and its limitations. The two contexts in which this rule is usually tested in property courses are "wild animals" and "finders."

    a. **Capture of wild animals**

        The most important thing to remember regarding possession of wild animals is that the law requires *capture*, rather than *pursuit*. Consider the goals of the law: Rewarding capture fosters competition and is an easier rule to administer.

    b. **Finding property**

        The fundamental issue here is when a finder should be entitled to the value of the find against other claimants, such as the owner of the thing found, the owner of the land where the thing is found, and a prior finder. This may turn on whether the property was lost, mislaid, abandoned, or treasure trove. The concept of *constructive possession*, under which a person is deemed to be in possession of things of which he is unaware, is important in analyzing some issues in this area.

2. **Adverse Possession**

    Adverse possession is a doctrine providing that possession will ripen into *ownership* if held long enough under certain conditions. This doctrine, which may strip ownership from A and give it to B, may also protect an owner who cannot prove ownership because of faulty records. The important issues of adverse possession relate to whether a possessor claiming ownership under this doctrine has satisfied *all the requirements* for adverse possession.

This chapter on acquisition of property also discusses rights in oil and gas, and in water (sometimes governed by the "prior possessor wins" rule); acquisition by creation (accession and intellectual property); remedies of a possessor; and the right of an owner of land to exclude others from entering. Thus, this chapter covers a wide range of issues largely dealing with possession and its consequences. Many casebooks and most teachers cover only some, and not all, of the topics in this chapter in exploring the way property is acquired. Use the index and text correlation chart to coordinate your studying with your teacher's coverage.

A. Introduction

1. Property Rights Defined [§1]

A property right is protection by the state of a claim to resources. A property right may be in an individual, it may be held by a particular group, or it may be held in common by people at large. How property is originally acquired and how an individual claim to common resources is recognized as private ownership are the subjects of this chapter. The object is to encourage thinking about the aims of property law and, thus, the *reasons* for the rules.

2. First-in-Time Rule [§2]

The most fundamental rule for determining ownership is that *the first person to take possession of a thing owns it.* This rule, also known as the *rule of capture,* implements important social policies relating to rewarding labor and protecting investment in resources. It is important to study the first-in-time rule in several factual contexts to see its reach and its limitations.

B. The Rule of Capture

1. General Rule [§3]

A person who first captures otherwise unowned resources is entitled to the resources. Another way of putting this rule is: Whoever is prior in time wins. This rule has been applied to many different kinds of resources.

2. Discovery of America [§4]

"In the beginning all the world was America," John Locke wrote, meaning that it was up for grabs. The European nations had a convention that discovery of America gave title to a government when its subjects made the discovery. When the Native Americans contested this, the Supreme Court, through Chief Justice Marshall, held that discovery gave title to the European nations which passed title to the states or to the United States. The Native Americans were not regarded as in prior possession of America; they were hunters who moved their villages and, unlike the Europeans, were not settlers who built permanent homes, staked out farms, and took possession of tracts of land. As an alternative to title by discovery, Marshall held that the Europeans—and subsequently the United States—acquired title by conquest. "Conquest gives a title which the Courts of the conqueror cannot deny," wrote Marshall, "whatever the private and speculative opinions of individuals may be, respecting the original justice of the claim." [**Johnson v. M'Intosh,** 21 U.S. 543 (1823)]

a. Native American right of occupancy [§5]
Although not recognized as having title or ownership, Indian tribes have a right of occupancy of their land. This right has been granted by, and remains subject to the control of, the sovereign Congress. [**Tee-Hit-Ton Indians v. United States,** 348 U.S. 272 (1955)] Congress has a trust or fiduciary obligation to protect the land occupied by the Native Americans. [**Joint Tribal Council of the Passamaquoddy Tribe v. Morton,** 388 F. Supp. 649 (D. Me. 1975)]

b. Lessons from America [§6]
Perhaps two lessons can be drawn from the above. First, "possession," a term so important in the law, is an elastic word. Its meaning is culturally determined. The European idea of possession of land was unknown to the Native Americans, who used the land but never thought of "possessing" it. Second, the determination and enforcement of property rights depends on the power of the state to impose its will. Property thus both confers and rests upon power.

3. Capture of Wild Animals [§7]
If wild animals (sometimes called animals *ferae naturae*) are captured, usually they belong to the captor. But *capture is required*; merely chasing the animal is not enough. [**Pierson v. Post,** 3 Cai. R. 175 (N.Y. 1805)]

 Example: Post and his hounds are pursuing a fox. Pierson spots the fox and shoots it, killing it. Pierson is entitled to the fox. [**Pierson v. Post,** *supra*]

---

a. Rationale
Various reasons can be found for this rule:

(1) Competition
Society's object is to capture foxes (to destroy them) or ducks (to put them on the table). To foster competition, resulting in more wild animals being captured, society does not reward the pursuer, only the captor. It is assumed that this promotes more effective means of capture.

(2) Ease of administration
Rewarding capture, an objective act, is an easier rule to administer than protecting pursuit and a prospect of capture, which is difficult to determine.

Thus, the rule of capture promotes certainty and efficient administration in a situation where the stakes (a fox, some ducks, some fish) are not high and not worth a lot of judicial time in resolving conflicting claims.

(3) But note

The rule of capture was laid down in the 19th century, when wild animals were abundant. Today, the rule of capture, promoting pursuit and killing, leads to overcapture in many instances, and to overinvestment in capture technology (Save The Whales!). Some species have become endangered by a rule that treats wild animals as unowned property available to anyone.

EXAM TIP — gilbert

Although the rule of capture can be applied to several different things (*see infra*), capture of **wild animals** is a traditional favorite of casebooks and law school exams. Therefore, it is worth remembering the rule (that capture—**not just pursuit**—is required) and the reasons behind the rule.

---

b. Wounded or trapped animals [§8]

If a wild animal has been *mortally wounded* or *trapped* so that capture is virtually certain, the animal is treated as captured. But if the animal is only in the process of being entrapped, and the door *has not snapped shut*, it has not been captured.

Example: A has driven a school of fish into a net and is in the process of encircling them, but the fish could still turn tail and escape. A has not captured the fish. Until the net has closed, another person, B, can sweep in with a net and take the fish. [**Young v. Hichens,** 6 Q.B. 606 (1844)]

---

(1) Unfair competition [§9]

Although the law wants competition to promote capture, it also wants competition to be fair so as to attract more persons into the pursuit. Protecting against unfair competition also protects against monopolies (with resulting high prices). Thus, in the **Young v. Hichens** example above, B could not sink A's boat. In fact, the actual action of B in dashing in with a smaller net to take the fish before the big net closed comes close to being unfair competition and might be so deemed today.

(2) Cage not escape-proof [§10]

To trap or net a wild animal, the animal must be confined in an enclosure, but it is not necessary that there be absolutely no possibility of escape. The captor acquires possession if he uses *reasonable precautions against escape*.

> **Example:** A tugboat crew removes fish from a net owned by another. The net has a series of smaller and smaller entrances from which escape is possible but unlikely. The fish are possessed by the owner of the net, and thus the tugboat crew is guilty of larceny. [**State v. Shaw,** 65 N.E. 875 (Ohio 1902)]

c. Interference by noncompetitor [§11]

If a person is in the process of entrapping animals, a competitor who also wants to capture the animals can interfere with the other person's activity and try to capture the animals. But a *person who does not want to capture the animal cannot interfere.* (*Remember:* Society wants the animal caught.)

> **Example:** Keeble puts out decoys on his pond to attract ducks and sets nets to catch them. Hickeringill, a neighbor, shoots off guns at the pond to scare the ducks away. Hickeringill is liable for damages. [**Keeble v. Hickeringill,** 103 Eng. Rep. 1127 (1707)]

> **Compare:** Hickeringill would be able to shoot to kill the ducks flying over his land to the pond.

(1) Conservation

This rule promotes killing; it does not promote conservation of wildlife, which may be a goal of society today. But observe how, in these wild animal cases, the rules are designed to achieve ends. They show the instrumental nature of the law.

d. Custom [§12]

While the general rule is that the captor must acquire physical control over the animal, in some hunting trades, *a custom*, which is thought more effective in getting animals killed, *may dictate a different result.* Among American whalers, *e.g.,* the custom was to award the whale to the ship that first killed the whale—even though the whale sank and was discovered several days later floating on the surface by another whaler. This custom advanced the killing of whales (society's objective at the time), because the killer ship could be off looking for other whales without waiting around for the whale to rise. This custom was recognized by the courts as giving possession. [**Ghen v. Rich,** 8 F. 159 (D. Mass. 1881)]

e. Wild animals with *animus revertendi* [§13]

Captured wild animals that develop an *animus revertendi* (habit of return) continue to belong to the captor when they roam at large. Thus, if deer are captured, then tamed, and return home after grazing, they are not available for capture by another. The reason behind this rule is that domesticated animals are valuable to society and this effort to tame wild animals is rewarded.

(1) Criticism

Notice the problem of uncertainty: How is a hunter to know that an apparently wild animal, such as a deer, is in fact domesticated and has the habit of return? A good solution to this problem would be to require that the owners of such animals make their status obvious by some reasonable means, such as attaching a bell to the animal, putting a bright ribbon around its neck, or marking it with an obvious brand.

f. Escaped wild animals [§14]

Ordinarily, if a captured wild animal that has *no animus revertendi* escapes, the captor loses possession, and the animal is again subject to capture by another. However, if the animal is not native to the area, but unusual (*e.g.*, an elephant in the Pennsylvania woods), a hunter may be put on notice that the animal has escaped and some other person has prior possession. In that case, the hunter cannot capture the animal for himself. [**E.A. Stephens & Co. v. Albers,** 256 P. 15 (Colo. 1927)]

g. Limitations on capture of wild animals [§15]

The common law, assuming wild animals were plentiful, placed no limit on the number that may be captured. Today, game may be scarce and some species endangered. Statutes have been enacted by states to change the common law and regulate hunting and fishing so as to protect the resources. Congress has enacted a statute to protect endangered species.

(1) Regulation by state [§16]

Game laws have the purpose of preventing overkill and preserving natural resources. It has sometimes been argued that these protective laws are valid because the state *owns* wild game, and therefore prevails over a person who takes *possession* of it. But this argument is entirely fictional. The better reason is that the state has the power to regulate the taking of game under its *police power*, by which it prevents conduct harmful to the public. [**Commonwealth v. Agway, Inc.,** 232 A.2d 69 (Pa. 1967)] (For more on the police power, *see* zoning, *infra*, §§1377 *et seq.*)

4. Discovery of Caves [§17]

In determining the rights to caves, the rule of capture runs into an old legal maxim, which says that a landowner owns the earth below his surface as well as the sky above. In at least one state, this maxim, rather than the rule of capture, has been applied to caves. Thus, a cave extending under two or more surface tracts does not belong to the discoverer (who is regarded as a trespasser in the earth below a neighbor's lot) or to the owner of the entrance. Whatever portion of the cave lies in a direct line between the surface and the center of the earth belongs to the surface owner. [**Edwards v. Sims,** 24 S.W.2d 619 (Ky. 1929)]

a. Profit sharing [§18]

Each surface owner over a cave is entitled to share in the profits made by the owner of the cave entrance if the public visits underneath the surface above. [**Edwards v. Lee's Administrator,** 96 S.W.2d 1028 (Ky. 1936)]

b. Criticism

If the capture rule were applied, giving ownership of the cave to the owner of the entrance, it would be more efficient and reward exploration. The resource would become available to the public at lower transaction costs than occur when surveying and profit sharing of the whole cave among many owners are required.

5. Rights to Oil and Gas [§19]

The rule of capture has been applied by courts to oil and gas. Some courts have characterized oil and gas as "fugitive" resources, analogous to wild animals, which might wander from a space under A's land to a space under B's land. The most persuasive reason for applying the rule of capture to oil and gas, however, is that it gives an incentive to produce oil and gas. A landowner can extract ("capture") all the oil and gas from a well bottomed under the landowner's land, even though the oil and gas may be drained from neighboring land. [**Barnard v. Monongahela Natural Gas Co.,** 65 A. 801 (Pa. 1907)]

a. Nonnegligent capture required [§20]

The rule of capture does not protect an owner who negligently drills a well, which blows out, catches fire, and consumes huge quantities of gas from underneath neighboring property. A negligent driller must pay damages for injuring the common reservoir and thus is penalized for negligently destroying common resources. But if the driller is not negligent, he can withdraw all of the oil from the common pool and make it his own. [**Elliff v. Texon Drilling Co.,** 210 S.W.2d 558 (Tex. 1948)]

b. Limitations on capture of oil and gas [§21]

To conserve resources, most states with oil and gas deposits have statutes regulating the number of acres required for a well and requiring apportionment of the drilling profits among the surface owners within the acreage unit. "Unitization" or "pooling" prevents landowners from racing to put down wells to capture oil and gas from their neighbors.

6. Rights in Water [§22]

The rule of capture is applied to rights in water in certain contexts. Much depends on the source of the water.

a. Percolating ground water [§23]

The English applied a rule of capture to ground water, which was deemed to be part of the soil. The surface owner has the right to pump water either for his own use or commercial use; the captured water can be sold to another. [**Acton v. Blundell,** 12 Mees. & W. 324 (1843)] This rule is followed in many eastern states where underground water is plentiful. Unless done with negligence or malicious intent, an owner can with impunity sink a well and cause a neighbor's well to go dry or cause subsidence of a neighbor's land. [**Friendswood Development Co. v. Smith-Southwest Industries, Inc.,** 576 S.W.2d 21 (Tex. 1978)]

(1) Reasonable use doctrine [§24]

In most western states and some eastern ones where water is scarce, the rule of capture is limited by the reasonable use doctrine. A surface owner may capture percolating ground water only to the extent that the use of the water is reasonable. The test of reasonable use is similar to the reasonable use doctrine applied to streams (*see infra*, §35). Generally, an overlying owner can pump water for use on his own land for reasonable uses in unlimited quantities—even if it causes a neighboring landowner harm. [**Bristor v. Cheatham**, 255 P.2d 173 (Ariz. 1953)] An overlying owner cannot, however, divert water from his well to noncontiguous land if another owner within the water basin would be harmed. In an arid climate, this limitation poses a serious obstacle for cities attempting to supplement their water supplies by purchasing land and sinking wells. [**Prather v. Eisenmann**, 261 N.W.2d 766 (Neb. 1978); **Meeker v. City of East Orange**, 74 A. 379 (N.J. 1909)]

Example: A, a dairy farmer, has a well on her property that provides water for her cattle. On one side of A's farm, B, an adjoining owner, sinks a powerful well that provides water to B's pulp mill, which is discharged back into the source basin. City Water Co. sinks pumps on the other side of A's land for a city water supply. A's well dries up. City Water Co. is liable to A (because it is diverting water to noncontiguous landowners), but B is not liable (because the water is used entirely on B's land).

b. Surface water [§25]

Diffused surface water refers to water that has no channel but passes across the surface of land. The source may be rainfall, melting snow, or seepage. The rights of the landowner depend on whether the water is beneficial and wanted, or not wanted. In the first case, the owner wants to capture the water; in the second, he wants to expel it.

(1) Capture [§26]

If a person wants to, he may capture surface water. Once captured, by a dam or in barrels, it can be diverted by the owner to any use he sees fit, on or off the land. The only limitation is that the capturing owner not unnecessarily harm owners below him.

Example: A builds an earthen dam on her farm to catch water seeping across her land for her livestock. Subsequently B, a farm owner on higher ground, builds a dam and creates a pool. This lowers the level of A's water. A has no right to the continued flow of the surface water, and B is within his rights in capturing the water.

(2) Expelling [§27]

More often the landowner will try to get rid of surface waters by changing the natural drainage. Liability to the landowner's neighbors depends on whether the state follows the "common enemy" doctrine or the "natural servitude" doctrine.

(a) Common enemy doctrine [§28]

Under the common enemy view, surface water is a common enemy, and any owner theoretically has an unqualified right to fend off surface waters by changing the drainage or building a dam. [**Argyelan v. Haviland,** 435 N.E.2d 973 (Ind. 1982)] The common enemy doctrine is rarely applied in its extreme form anymore. Almost all modern decisions applying the doctrine modify it by requiring that the interference with the neighbors be *reasonable* or at least not negligent. The landowner must avoid unnecessary or disproportionate harm to neighbors. [**Tucker v. Badoian,** 384 N.E.2d 1195 (Mass. 1978); **Armstrong v. Francis Corp.,** 120 A.2d 4 (N.J. 1956); **Pendergrast v. Aiken,** 236 S.E.2d 787 (N.C. 1977)]

(b) Natural servitude doctrine [§29]

The natural servitude doctrine, sometimes known as the "civil law doctrine," is followed in about half the states. It provides that lower lands are servient to the natural flow of surface waters. The owner cannot obstruct or change the flow so as to injure others either above (by building a dam and backing up water on the upper owner) or below (by digging a channel so as to hasten the flow of water).

1) Criticism

Although having the advantage of predictability, this doctrine limits development and improvement of land. In most states, it is being altered to permit reasonable changes in the flow from the servient land (such as channeling drainage), particularly in urban areas. Under the natural servitude doctrine, as well as under the common enemy doctrine, courts are gradually introducing a reasonableness test, and it is likely that ultimately both of these doctrines will disappear and be replaced by a reasonableness test. The same trend is taking place in riparian rights, where the reasonable use test is replacing the natural flow doctrine.

c. Streams and lakes [§30]

Rights in streams and lakes adjoining land are different from rights in percolating ground water under the owner's land and surface water on the land. In most jurisdictions, adjacent landowners have *riparian rights* in streams or lakes. A stream is a *flowing* body of water, either aboveground or underground, contained *within a definite course.* Riparian rights include rights in the *quantity, quality,* and *velocity* of the water. Riparian owners have swimming, boating, and fishing privileges, as well as the right to use or take the water onto riparian land. The extent of riparian rights depends on whether the jurisdiction follows the natural flow doctrine or reasonable use doctrine (discussed below).

(1) Riparian land defined [§31]

Riparian land is all land under a unit title contiguous to a body of water, provided the land is within the watershed of the body of water. The reason for this proviso is that water used in the watershed will return to the body of water and be available for other riparian owners. [**Stratton v. Mt. Hermon Boys' School,** 103 N.E. 87 (Mass. 1913)] In a few jurisdictions, the unit of title is the smallest tract of land that has always been contiguous to the water, but in most states, a riparian owner can buy contiguous land within the watershed and extend riparian rights to it.

(a) Use on nonriparian land [§32]

A riparian right is "attached" to the riparian land and can never be transferred to a nonriparian owner. The right runs with the land, so to speak. This is not to say, however, that water can never be used on nonriparian land by the riparian owner. Under the reasonable use theory, use of water by a riparian owner for nonriparian purposes (*e.g.,* selling it to the public as drinking water) or to irrigate nonriparian land may be permitted. (*See infra,* §38.)

(2) Natural flow doctrine [§33]

In determining the extent of riparian rights, the English courts developed the natural flow doctrine, which was well suited to an agrarian society and the early days of the Industrial Revolution when many mills were powered by water. Under this doctrine, one riparian owner can use the water but must return it to the stream in its natural condition. Each riparian owner is entitled to the *natural flow of water, without material diminution in quantity or quality.* In determining what is "natural," courts have held that each riparian owner has the privilege of using water for domestic needs. In addition, each riparian owner can use water for "artificial" or commercial needs, provided such uses do not materially affect the quantity or quality of the water.

(a) Limitations [§34]

A riparian owner is not permitted to use water on nonriparian land. Also, a riparian owner, limited to uses that do not interfere with natural flow, cannot deplete the quantity of water *even though no one is harmed.* Water storage is not permissible.

(b) Criticism

The natural flow doctrine severely limits the use of water for irrigation and commercial use. It inhibits the full use of water because, even though no one is harmed and the water would otherwise be wasted, a riparian owner cannot deplete the natural quantity of water. Because it is not utilitarian, the large majority of states refuse to apply the natural flow doctrine to streams and follow the reasonable use theory.

(3) Reasonable use doctrine [§35]

Most American courts follow a reasonable use doctrine. The riparian owner is entitled to a reasonable use of the water, and downstream owners cannot enjoin the owner or recover damages unless they are not receiving enough water for their needs or the upstream owner is substantially interfering with their needs. If the downstream owner is not harmed, he cannot enjoin the upstream owner's use. [**Harris v. Brooks,** 283 S.W.2d 129 (Ark. 1955); **Borough of Westville v. Whitney Home Builders, Inc.,** 122 A.2d 233 (N.J. 1956)]

(a) Domestic use preferred [§36]

Although in theory no one factor is controlling in determining reasonableness, in most states domestic uses are preferred over others. The upstream owner can take whatever water is necessary for domestic purposes—without regard to its effect on the natural flow or level of the water or the needs of lower riparians. For domestic use, the upstream owner has a preferred status. "Domestic use" includes water for drinking and bathing, for farm animals on a small farm, and for irrigation of a garden to supply produce to the riparian owner. [**Evans v. Merriweather,** 4 Ill. 492 (1842)]

1) Rationale

"Domestic uses" are necessary to maintain life. They usually involve taking only small quantities of water. In times of drought, nondomestic users must cut their use of water to accommodate domestic users.

EXAM TIP   gilbert

Keep in mind that because domestic use is preferred over other uses, a domestic use can be established *at any time*, even interfering with existing nondomestic uses.

(b) Commercial use [§37]

The upstream owner cannot take water for commercial purposes unless there is enough water for the domestic wants of all. To the extent that water is in excess of everyone's domestic needs, it can be used for commercial purposes. Irrigation of a large farm is deemed a commercial riparian use, not a domestic use. In some reasonable use jurisdictions, especially in the arid West, irrigation is favored over all other commercial uses and may even impair rights of lower owners for water power use.

(c) Use on nonriparian land [§38]

Some, but not all, courts adhering to the reasonable use doctrine have permitted a riparian owner to use water on nonriparian land if this does not cause harm to a reasonable use of another riparian owner. Courts that permit this are usually in states where irrigation of land is particularly important.

(d) Economic justification [§39]

Although the reasonable use doctrine favors development and use of water, any theory of reasonable use—with the resulting uncertainty of what is reasonable—has costs that a fixed definition of rights does not have. Ad hoc balancing of interests has high judicial costs and costs of legal advice and litigation. On the other hand, it is economically better if a right passes to the user who values it most (*see* Coase theorem, *infra*, §1335). A fixed definition of riparian rights, as under the natural flow doctrine, will not result in the right passing to the highest valued user because of high transaction costs. Usually there are many persons along a stream with riparian rights who would be necessary parties to a bargain. Hence, the economic justification for the reasonable use doctrine is that the court should intervene to achieve efficiency because of the high transaction costs that will prevent private parties from cutting a deal.

(4) Prior appropriation doctrine [§40]

In 10 arid western states, common law riparian rights have been rejected as unsuitable because they hinder investment in commercial irrigation and other water uses. Riparian rights have been replaced by the ***prior appropriation*** doctrine. Under this doctrine, which is a doctrine of ***capture***, water rights are determined by priority of appropriation of the water. The water can be used on land far away from the water ("nonriparian"). The prior appropriation doctrine grew out of the custom of miners in diverting water for their needs, sometimes miles away from the source. Once a right to water is established, it is an interest independent of the land—called a "water right"—and ***can be severed*** from the land and sold to another for use on other land. [**Coffin v. Left Hand Ditch Co.**, 6 Colo. 443 (1882)]

(a) Economic justification [§41]

The prior appropriation doctrine is a rule of capture and has the advantages of such a rule: It encourages development of water uses and is predictable; it is efficient in that it permits the transfer of a prior appropriation right to a user who puts a higher value on it; and transaction costs are low.

(5) Public rights [§42]

A riparian owner may not exercise his rights so as to infringe on public rights in public waters. Public waters include navigable waters of all kinds and great lakes and streams. Public rights include boating, swimming, and fishing. Such public rights may be exercised by any person *with legal access to the water.* In most jurisdictions, the state can regulate the public rights under the police power and can permit a riparian owner to impair public rights. In some states, however, the state holds public waters *in trust* for the public and cannot permit uses that violate public rights. [**Illinois Central Railroad v. Illinois,** 146 U.S. 387 (1892); **National Audubon Society v. Superior Court,** 33 Cal. 3d 419 (1983)]

(a) Federal regulation [§43]

Under the Constitution, the federal government has the power to regulate all navigation in navigable waters. Under this power, it can build dams across rivers, interfering with the natural flow of the river. A riparian owner has no right to maintenance of a river at any given level below high-water mark as against improvements of navigation. The government may raise the level of the river to high-water mark or lower it. Lands above the high-water mark are fast lands, and to flood them requires compensation. [**United States v. Willow River Power Co.,** 324 U.S. 499 (1945)]

C. Acquisition by Creation

1. General Rule [§44]

A person can acquire property by creating it, but there are a number of difficulties in defining "creation," as this section shows. The primary purpose in recognizing property by creation is to reward labor, but when one's labor is mixed with the labor or goods of another, how shall ownership be determined?

2. Acquisition by Accession [§45]

Acquisition by accession comes into play when one person adds to the property of another either *labor* or *labor and new materials.* A person whose property is taken and used by another is always entitled to the value of the property taken, but that person may lose title by the accessions ("additions") of the other. If the improver is denied title by accession, the original owner is entitled to the value added by the taker.

a. Labor added [§46]

Where A adds labor to B's raw material, the courts usually award the final product to the owner of the raw material (B), *unless* A's efforts have *sufficiently increased* its value to make it unfair to award the final product to B.

Just how much is "sufficient" is difficult to determine. In addition, most states require that for A to recover, he must show that he acted *in good faith* and not willfully.

Example: A, relying on permission that he supposes came from B, enters B's land, cuts timber, and makes hoops from the timber. The standing timber was worth $25; the hoops are worth $700. The hoops belong to A, although B can sue A for $25 in damages for trespass. [**Wetherbee v. Green,** 22 Mich. 311 (1871)]

Compare: If the timber was worth $2.87 and the value of A's labor is worth $1.87, A has not sufficiently increased the value of the timber to have his labor rewarded. [**Isle Royale Mining Co. v. Hertin,** 37 Mich. 332 (1877)]

EXAM TIP   **gilbert**

Note that A's act in the example above is a trespass, regardless of his good faith. Nonetheless, where it would be *grossly unjust* for B to appropriate A's labor to himself, A will get compensation for his labor and B will get damages for A's trespass. Be sure to discuss this if it should arise on an exam.

---

b. **Labor and materials added [§47]**

Where A, an innocent trespasser, adds labor and materials to raw material owned by B, the final product is generally awarded to the *owner of the principal material*. However, where A is not innocent (*e.g.*, a thief or one who knowingly took from a thief), most courts will award the final product to B regardless of the extent of the labor and materials that were added.

Example: A's car is stolen and stripped by thieves. The thieves dispose of the car's nearly worthless body on an empty lot. B subsequently spots the body and, incorrectly believing that its owner had abandoned it, takes the body home for restoration. B installs in the body an engine, transmission, radio, tires, glass, and upholstery. If A subsequently discovers his car body in B's hands, A will not be entitled to the car; B will only have to pay A the value of the stripped car body. [*See* **Ochoa v. Rogers,** 234 S.W. 693 (Tex. 1921); **Capitol Chevrolet Co. v. Earheart,** 627 S.W.2d 369 (Tenn. 1981)]

c. **Confusion of goods [§48]**

Confusion differs from accession in that *no labor* is added to the goods. Confusion involves an intermingling of fungible goods of different owners that can no longer be separately identified. The general rule is that each owner receives his proportionate share of the intermingled goods.

Example: A *negligently* mixes his wheat with B's wheat. Under the general rule, A and B each receive a proportionate part of the wheat.

3. Intellectual Property [§49]

Intellectual property is the "catchall" label for property in ideas. The term includes copyrights, patents, and trademarks, but it may also cover property in a persona.

a. The dilemma [§50]

The dilemma in recognizing intellectual property is how to nurture individual creativity and reward labor without going too far by creating monopolies and stifling creativity in others. After all, creativity thrives on imitation. The law of intellectual property is full of careful balances of what ideas are protected as private property and for how long and what ideas are not protected. [**Downey v. General Foods Corp.**, 31 N.Y.2d 56 (1972)]

b. The common law [§51]

To avoid monopoly and encourage competition, the common law commonly allows copying and imitation of ideas, as opposed to their expression. [**Cheney Brothers v. Doris Silk Corp.**, 35 F.2d 279 (2d Cir. 1929)] But there are exceptions, like the right of publicity. A person may not use a celebrity's name, likeness, voice, or signature for profit without the celebrity's consent. The celebrity's labor in creating a persona of value is protected against another's using it for profit.

Example: It has been held that, even though there is no intent to deceive, the use of an imitation (not a likeness) of a celebrity for commercial profit infringes her right of publicity. [**Vanna White v. Samsung Electronics America, Inc.**, 971 F.2d 1395 (9th Cir. 1992)]

c. Statutes [§52]

Copyright, trademark, and patent laws have been enacted by Congress to solve the dilemma of how much protection to give creativity. Intellectual property rights are limited in time. Moreover, copyright law includes a fair use exception and a right to parody. A person cannot copyright an *idea*, but can copyright the *expression* of it. A full explanation must await a course in copyright, but in a nutshell a person can imitate another's work to some extent, but not too much.

d. Unfair competition [§53]

Courts have sometimes protected labor and investment under the law of unfair competition (*compare supra*, §9). For example, it has been held that a news agency has a quasi-property interest in news it has gathered and can prohibit competitors from disseminating the news until its commercial value as news has passed away. [**International News Service v. Associated Press**, 248 U.S. 215 (1918)]

4. Rights in Body Products [§54]

Some body products have long been sold on the market, *e.g.,* blood, hair, sperm. But recent advances in medical science have created an unprecedented demand for body products or body parts of other types. Can these be sold? Can they be "owned"? In **Moore v. Regents of the University of California,** 51 Cal. 3d 120 (1990), the court held that a man did not have a property right in his spleen following its removal from his body by doctors who made it into a patented cell line of great commercial value. The doctors who created the cell line thus acquired original ownership. The court held that the patient had only the right to sue the doctors for failure to disclose their research and economic interest in the patient's cells. In ruling, the court was concerned about making body products property that could be sold. However, transferability in the market is not an essential characteristic of property. Although most property is freely transferable (*see infra,* §173), some property is not alienable (*e.g.,* Social Security) and some property can be given away but not sold (*e.g.,* items from endangered species such as ivory or eagle feathers). This latter type of property is sometimes called "market-inalienable." The hard question with body products or body parts is not whether they should be treated as property, but whether they should be saleable. Should the demand for body products be satisfied through the traditional market mechanism? This question is bound to arise in connection with a sale by a woman of an egg to an infertile couple for a profit.

a. Frozen embryos [§55]

When a human egg is fertilized by sperm and frozen, does it become property and, if so, who is the owner? (It seems clear that the first-in-time rule is not helpful in answering the latter question.) The Tennessee Supreme Court has held that the frozen embryo is neither a person nor property, but is entitled to "special respect" because of its potential for human life. [**Davis v. Davis,** 842 S.W.2d 588 (Tenn. 1992); *compare* **Hecht v. Superior Court,** 16 Cal. App. 4th 836 (1993)—holding that sperm deposited in a sperm bank was property of the donor and could be devised by will]

b. Surrogacy contracts [§56]

Suppose that H and W want a child, but W is infertile. They contract with A, a woman, to be fertilized by H's sperm through artificial insemination. A agrees to give up the child to H and W after it is born. Should the contract be enforced if, after the child is born, A refuses to give it up? *In re* **Baby M,** 537 A.2d 1227 (N.J. 1988), held the surrogacy contract void as against public policy. Custody disputes would have to be settled by what is in the best interests of the child. On the other hand, other courts have held that surrogacy contracts are voidable only under specified circumstances [**Surrogate Parenting Associates v. Commonwealth,** 704 S.W.2d 209 (Ky. 1986)] or that they are specifically enforceable [**Johnson v. Calvert,** 5 Cal. 4th 84 (1993)]. The issue is much litigated now and much debated.

D. Acquisition by Find

1. General Rule [§57]

An *owner* of property does not lose title by losing the property. The owner's rights persist even though the article has been lost or mislaid. [**Ganter v. Kapiloff**, 516 A.2d 611 (Md. 1986)] Thus, as a general rule, *a finder has rights superior to everyone but the true owner*, but note that there are important exceptions to this rule.

---

e.g. **Example:** Chimney Sweep finds a jewel and takes it to a jeweler to have it appraised. The jeweler refuses to give the jewel back to Chimney Sweep, saying that Chimney Sweep does not own it. Chimney Sweep is entitled to recover from the jeweler either the jewel or the full money value of the jewel. As between Chimney Sweep and the jeweler, Chimney Sweep, *the prior possessor, has the superior right.* [**Armory v. Delamirie**, 1 Strange 505 (1722)]

---

a. Prior possessor wins [§58]

The rule that a prior possessor wins over a subsequent possessor is an important and fundamental one. It applies to *both personal property* and *real property*. The reasons for the rule include:

(1) *Prior possession protects an owner* who has no indicia of ownership (title papers, etc.). *Possession* is not the same as *ownership*. *Ownership* is "title" to the property. It is usually proved by showing documents by the previous owner (or first possessor) transferring title to the present title holder. *Possession* is proved by showing physical control and the intent to exclude others. Possession is easier to prove than ownership. An owner always wins against a mere possessor.

(2) *Entrusting goods to another is an efficient practice*, facilitating all kinds of purposes that ought to be encouraged. For example, in the previous example, the jeweler is a *bailee*, who must surrender the goods to a prior possessor. Imagine a person not getting her clothes back from a dry cleaner, or a neighbor not having to return a lawn mower, unless the person or neighbor could prove ownership.

(3) *Prior possessors expect to prevail* over subsequent possessors. By giving them their expectations, the law reinforces the popular belief that the law is just.

(4) *The protection of peaceable possession is an ancient policy* in law, aimed at deterring disruptions in the public order.

(5) *Protecting a finder who reports the find rewards honesty.*

(6) *Protecting a finder rewards labor in returning a useful item to society.*

b. Relativity of title [§59]

Note that title to the jewel in the above example is relative to who the claimants are. The owner of the jewel prevails over A, the finder. A, the finder, prevails over a subsequent possessor. Suppose that A, after finding the jewel, loses it and B thereafter finds it. Would B prevail over A? No. A, the prior possessor, prevails over B, a subsequent possessor. A's rights are not lost by losing the article.

c. Prior possessor a trespasser [§60]

The "prior possessor wins" rule applies to objects acquired through theft or trespass. Thus, if A steals a jewel and hands it to B, who refuses to return it, B is liable to A. B cannot question A's title or rightful prior possession if B is merely a subsequent possessor. *Rationale:* To rule in favor of B would not likely deter crime, but it would likely immerse owners and prior possessors in costly litigation with subsequent possessors to prove that they are not thieves. [**Anderson v. Gouldberg**, 53 N.W. 636 (Minn. 1892)—"Any other rule would lead to an endless series of unlawful seizures and reprisals in every case where property had once passed out of the possession of the rightful owner"]

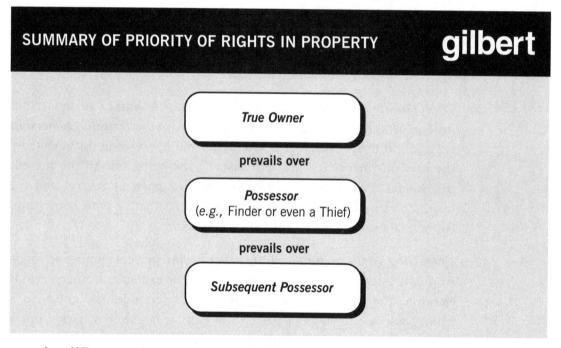

d. What constitutes possession [§61]

For the finder to become a prior possessor, the finder must—like the captor of wild animals—acquire *physical control* over the object *and* have an *intent* to assume dominion over it.

Example: Brazelton discovers a shipwreck at the bottom of the Mississippi River. The ship sank some 27 years before and was abandoned by the owners. Brazelton attaches a temporary buoy to the wreck, intending to return the next day, but Brazelton does not return. Nine months later, Eads finds the wreck and salvages it. Eads prevails over Brazelton because Brazelton has shown only an intent to take possession and has not shown sufficient acts of physical control. Brazelton must place his boat over the wreck, *with the means to raise it*, to give notice to subsequent searchers of his prior possession. The court defines the acts necessary to constitute possession in such a way as to encourage salvage of shipwrecks. Note that the court says that nothing short of placing a salvage boat over the wreck, capable of salvaging it, will constitute possession. [**Eads v. Brazelton,** 22 Ark. 499 (1861)]

EXAM TIP   **gilbert**

Keep in mind that "possession" in this context is like "capture" (*supra*)—*i.e.,* there must be **physical control** of the property **and** the **intent to assume dominion** over it. Thus, it is not enough just to notice a gold coin lying in the street; the finder must pick it up or place his foot over it before someone else does. Likewise, if the finder is absent-mindedly kicking the coin down the street, another person may be able to intercept it and take it because the finder does not have the intent to assume dominion over it. *But note:* Despite this rule requiring possession, **"constructive" possession** will sometimes substitute for actual possession (see below).

---

e. **Constructive possession [§62]**

A person is in "constructive possession" when the law treats him *as if* he is in possession although, in fact, he is not or he is unaware of it. Constructive possession is a fiction that permits judges to reach a desired result. The owner or occupant of premises may constructively possess something on the premises of which he is unaware. If so, he is entitled to the benefit of the "prior possessor wins" rule.

Example: A landowner is in constructive possession of the objects located under the surface of her land even though she is unaware of the objects. If A hires B to clean out her pool (or cesspool) and B finds a ring at the bottom of the pool, the ring belongs to A, not B, even though A was unaware that the ring was there. [**South Staffordshire Water Co. v. Sharman,** 2 Q.B. 44 (1896)]

---

2. **Finder vs. Owner of Premises [§63]**

Often the finder will claim an object; so will the owner of the premises where the object is found. (This assumes that the owner of the premises *does not own the object*; if she does, she would prevail over the finder.) The owner of the premises claims to have actual or, more usually, constructive prior possession. Some of the cases are in conflict; many are confused in their reasoning or make no attempt to relate "constructive possession" to the policies at issue.

a. **Finder is trespasser [§64]**

If the finder is a trespasser, the owner of the premises where the object is found always prevails over the finder. This rule discourages trespass and unauthorized entries on property. [**Favorite v. Miller,** 407 A.2d 974 (Conn. 1978); **Morgan v. Wiser,** 711 S.W.2d 220 (Tenn. 1985)]

b. **Finder is employee [§65]**

If the finder is an employee of the owner of the premises, some cases hold that the employee cannot keep the object. Some courts reason that an employee is *"acting for"* an employer in the course of his duties. Others emphasize that the employee has a *contractual duty* to report the object to the employer. This duty is usually imposed, *e.g.*, by hotel owners on the people who clean the rooms in order to facilitate the return of the object to the hotel guest who left it. But if the guest never claims it, why should the duty to report preclude the finder from getting it? *Remember:* Rewarding honesty is a social good, and rewarding the report of the find may encourage a report, which is the first step toward getting an object back to its owner.

c. **Finder is on premises for a limited purpose [§66]**

If the finder is on the premises for a limited purpose (*e.g.*, cleaning out a stopped sewer drain), it may be said that the owner gave permission to enter only for a limited purpose of cleaning, under the direction of the owner, and the owner of the premises is entitled to objects found. [**South Staffordshire Water Co. v. Sharman,** *supra*]

d. **Object found under the soil [§67]**

If the object is found under or embedded in the soil, it is awarded to the owner of the premises, not to the finder. [**Elwes v. Brigg Gas Co.,** [1886] 33 Ch. D. 562; **Goodard v. Winchell,** 52 N.W. 1124 (Iowa 1892)] *Rationale:* Owners of land *expect* that objects found underneath the soil belong to them; they think of these objects as part of the land itself.

(1) **Exception—treasure trove [§68]**

Treasure trove is found gold, silver, or money *intentionally buried* or concealed in the soil *with the intent of returning to claim it*. Under English law, treasure trove belongs to the crown (the state). American courts have generally rejected giving treasure trove to the state. Some give it to the finder; others give it to the landowner. [*See, e.g.,* **Schley v. Couch,** 284 S.W.2d 333 (Tex. 1955)—currency buried in the ground was "mislaid" property and belonged to the landowner] Treasure trove does not include objects buried with the dead, which do not belong to the finder. [**Charrier v. Bell,** 496 So. 2d 601 (La. 1986)]

e. **Object found in private home or other highly private place [§69]**

Objects found inside a private home or other very private place are usually awarded to the owner of the premises. *Rationale:* The locus owner has an intent to exclude everyone and to admit persons only for specific limited purposes (to deliver laundry, to eat dinner, etc.) that do not include finding property. Also, the locus owner has strong expectations that *all* objects located in a highly private place—including those of which he is unaware—are "his."

Example: Guest, who is at a party in Homeowner's home, finds a diamond ring under the sofa which no one claims to own. Homeowner is in constructive prior possession of the ring and can keep it until the true owner reclaims it.

(1) Owner not in possession [§70]

If the owner of the house has not moved into the house (has not made it his "personal space"), it has been held that the owner of the house is not in constructive possession of articles therein of which he is unaware. [**Hannah v. Peel,** 1 K.B. 509 (1945)]

> **Example:** Peel owns a large house requisitioned by the government to quarter soldiers. Peel bought the house two years earlier and never moved in. A soldier finds a brooch in the house hidden on a window ledge. The soldier prevails over Peel because Peel never moved into the house and took physical possession of it. (The fact that the house was involuntarily taken from Peel by the state for the limited purpose of quartering soldiers, thus depriving Peel of the possibility of physical possession, was ignored by the court in *Hannah, supra.* But perhaps the motivating factor was rewarding honesty.)

f. Object found in public place [§71]

In dealing with objects found in a public place, courts have generally resolved the issue by resorting to the "lost-mislaid" distinction. [**Benjamin v. Lindner Aviation, Inc.,** 534 N.W.2d 400 (Iowa 1995)]

(1) Lost-mislaid distinction [§72]

Lost property is property that the owner accidentally and casually lost (*e.g.*, a ring slips through a hole in a pocket). *Mislaid* property is property *intentionally placed* somewhere and then forgotten (*e.g.*, a purse placed on a table and forgotten).

(a) Lost property goes to the finder [§73]

Lost property goes to the *finder* rather than the owner of the premises.

(b) Mislaid property goes to owner of premises [§74]

Mislaid property goes to the *owner of the premises*.

1) Rationale

The purpose of classifying property as mislaid is to facilitate the return of the object to the true owner: Because it is assumed the object was intentionally placed where it is found, it is likely that the *true owner will remember* where she placed it and will return to the shop to claim it.

> **Example:** Adrian finds a wallet on the floor of a beauty shop and a ring on the counter in the same shop. The *wallet* is *lost* property because it is assumed that it was not intentionally placed on the floor. Thus, Adrian, the finder, prevails over the owner of the shop, and can take the wallet home to keep for the true owner (if the true owner shows up). [*See* **Bridges v. Hawkesworth,** 21 L.J.Q.B. 75

(1851)] The *ring* is *mislaid* property because, from its position, it is assumed it was intentionally placed on the counter and forgotten. The ring goes to the owner of the shop to keep until the true owner claims it. Adrian has no rights in the ring. [*See* **McAvoy v. Medina**, 93 Mass. (11 Allen) 548 (1866)]

(c) Criticism

The lost-mislaid distinction has been roundly criticized.

1) From the findings of fact, the court must infer whether the owner casually dropped the object or placed it there intentionally and forgot it. This is often a guess. In the preceding example, was the wallet casually dropped on the floor? Or was it placed on the counter and accidentally brushed to the floor by another customer? Or was it (like many purses nowadays) intentionally placed on the floor?

2) It is assumed that the true owner will retrace her steps only if the property is mislaid (and not if it is lost); therefore awarding *lost* property to the finder does not lessen the chances of return to the true owner. Experience indicates that when a person misses something, she retraces her steps whether the object was lost or mislaid.

3. Abandoned Property [§75]

Abandoned property is property intentionally abandoned by the true owner, who no longer claims any right to it (*e.g.*, items left in a garbage can). Abandoned property is awarded to the finder.

a. Multiple finders—rule of equitable division [§76]

If there are multiple finders, a court may choose to apply the *rule of equitable division—i.e.*, order the property sold and divide the proceeds among the claimants.

Example: Barry Bonds's record-setting home-run baseball was caught by Fan A, who then lost control of the ball when he was rushed by a crowd of people. Fan B picked up the ball and left the stadium with it. In a subsequent lawsuit by A, the judge ruled that the ball was abandoned by Major League Baseball and belonged to the first person to possess it. A, who had caught the ball, had just about gotten complete control of it, when the crowd interfered, so he had a prepossessory interest (resulting from the fact that the actions of the crowd kept him from perfecting his possession). B, who had picked up the ball thereafter, did nothing wrong, but nevertheless took the ball subject to A's interest. The judge decided it would be unfair to award the ball solely to A or to B. A might never have managed to get complete control, but if he had, then B would not have been able to pick up the loose ball.

	CIRCUMSTANCES	EXAMPLE	FINDER'S RIGHTS
LOST	Owner *accidentally and casually parted* with possession and does not know where to find property	O does not notice that his watch has slipped off his wrist and landed on the street	Finder entitled to possession against all the world except the true owner (*exceptions:* if finder is a trespasser, employee, guest, or licensee, or if property is found in a highly private locus or buried, owner of locus gets possessory rights)
MISLAID	Owner *intentionally* placed property in the spot where it is found and thereafter forgot it	O lays his watch on the sink in a hotel room and forgets to pick it up	Owner of premises entitled to possession against all the world except the true owner (because the owner might return to the locus looking for the item)
ABANDONED	Owner voluntarily and *intentionally relinquished ownership* with intent to give up both title and possession	O throws his old watch into a garbage can because a new battery for it would cost too much	Finder obtains both possession and title if he exercises control over the property with intent to assert ownership

Unable to resolve the matter, the judge invoked the rule of equitable division, ordered the ball sold at auction, and divided the proceeds ($450,000) between the two claimants. [*See* **Popov v. Hayashi,** No. 400545, 2002 WL 31833731 (Cal. Super. Ct. Dec. 18, 2002)]

4. Statutory Changes [§77]

In some states, statutes have been enacted abolishing the distinctions developed by the courts in finders cases. New York, *e.g.*, has abolished the distinctions between lost, mislaid, and abandoned property and treasure trove. All such property is treated as lost property and goes to the finder. Thus, under the New York statute, in **Hurley v. City of Niagara Falls,** 30 A.D.2d 89 (1968), a contractor hired to build a recreation room in a basement was held entitled to $4,900 he found under a sink in the basement. Any claim that the homeowner might have had under the common law concept of mislaid property was swept away by the statutory reform.

E. Acquisition by Adverse Possession

1. Overview

a. Theory of adverse possession [§78]

The basic theory of adverse possession is simple: If, within the number of years specified in the state *statute of limitations*, the owner of land does not take legal action to eject a possessor who claims adversely to the owner, the *owner is thereafter barred* from bringing an action in ejectment. Once the owner is barred from suing in ejectment, the adverse possessor has title to the land.

Example: Owner owns Blackacre. Imposter, pretending to be Owner, gives Grantee a deed to Blackacre, forging Owner's name. Grantee enters Blackacre in 1992 and possesses the land adversely to Owner for 10 years. Owner does nothing during the 10-year period. The state statute of limitations provides that if an owner of land does not bring an action to recover possession within 10 years after the cause of action first arises, the owner is forever barred from bringing such an action. In 2002, Owner's action in ejectment is barred and Grantee owns Blackacre.

b. Effect of adverse possession [§79]

Adverse possession is a means of acquiring *title* to property by long, uninterrupted possession. The running of the statute of limitations on the owner's action in ejectment *not only bars* the owner's claim to possession, it also extinguishes the old title of the owner and *creates a new title* by operation of law in the adverse possessor. The adverse possessor's right to possession, heretofore good against all the world except the rightful owner, is now good against the rightful owner as well. Once the adverse possessor has title, it can be transferred in the same manner as any other title to land (by a deed, will, or through intestacy to heirs). However, and this is very important, *title acquired by adverse possession cannot be recorded* in the courthouse (as can a deed or will) because it does not arise from a recordable document but rather from *operation of law*. Thus, if the adverse possessor wishes to have his title and name as owner recorded in the courthouse, he must file a *quiet title action* against the former owner barred by the statute of limitations. The decree in this lawsuit will be recorded and will declare that the adverse possessor has legal title.

EXAM TIP   **gilbert**

This is an important point to understand. Although an adverse possessor acquires title to the property, it is due to the running of the statute of limitations—the former owner is *barred from suing* to recover the property. For all intents and purposes, the adverse possessor is the owner and can improve the property, lease it, sell it, etc. The one difficulty the adverse possessor may have, however, is in selling the property. Because she has *no record title*, there may be issues of "marketable title" (*i.e.*, a purchaser may be nervous about who really has title). That is why a quiet title suit may be useful to settle the matter and provide record title. (For more about marketable title and adverse possession, see *infra*, §1522.)

---

c.   **Purpose of the doctrine [§80]**

Acquiring title by adverse possession might look at first glance like acquiring title by theft, but the doctrine serves several important purposes.

(1)   **To protect title [§81]**

Protection of possession in fact protects ownership because title may be difficult to prove (*see supra*, §58). The same policy underlies adverse possession.

Example: O owns Blackacre in 1960. In 1970, A deeds Blackacre to B, and in 1985, B deeds Blackacre to C. B is in possession from 1970 to 1985, and C is in possession after 1985. In 2001, C contracts to sell Blackacre to D. Upon searching the records, D finds no deed from O to A and alleges that C does not have title. It is possible that O gave A a deed to the property before 1970 and the deed was lost and not recorded, but in any event B and C thought they were the owners after 1970 and acted as such by taking possession. O is now barred by the statute of limitations and C can convey to D a good title based on adverse possession.

(a)   **Land records**

Land title records are kept in each county courthouse, but these records are deficient in many respects. The doctrine of adverse possession makes these records more reliable by protecting possessors whose record title is deficient in some way. It also tends to limit record searches of title to land to a reasonable period of time and not back to a sovereign, which would be very costly.

(2) To bar stale claims [§82]

A and B both may be claiming Blackacre, and B goes into possession. As time passes, witnesses die or their memories grow dim, and the evidence of the respective claims of A and B becomes less and less reliable. Thus, another purpose of the statute of limitations is to require a lawsuit to be brought to oust a possessor while the witnesses' memories are still fresh.

(3) To reward those who use land productively [§83]

Society likes to have land used for farming or housing or other productive enterprises. By rewarding the possessor who is productive, and penalizing the owner who would let the land lie unproductive, the doctrine of adverse possession encourages productivity.

(a) Criticism

The adverse possession doctrine has been criticized for its implicit rejection of the value of conserving open space and undeveloped land, but in fact the common law rules of adverse possession (as opposed to statutes in some states) do not require that an adverse possessor develop the land claimed, as long as there is some open and notorious use made of it (*see infra*, §93).

(4) To honor expectations [§84]

Persons in possession of property quite naturally, after a long time, acquire attachments to the land and expectations that they can continue to use the property as they have long done, however they came by it. *Giving effect to expectations* is a policy running throughout the law of property.

d. Length of time required [§85]

The statutory period for adverse possession varies from state to state—from five to 21 years. The modern trend is to shorten the period of adverse possession.

e. Possessor's rights before acquiring title [§86]

Before the statute of limitations bars the true owner, the adverse possessor has all the rights of a possessor described above: She can evict a subsequent possessor who takes possession away from her ("prior possessor wins," *supra*, §58). [**Brumagim v. Bradshaw**, 39 Cal. 24 (1870)] She has an interest—"possession"—which she can transfer to another (*see* "tacking," *infra*, §124). [**Howard v. Kunto**, 477 P.2d 210 (Wash. 1970)] *But* before the expiration of the statutory period, an adverse possessor has *no interest in the property valid against the true owner*. The true owner may retake possession at any time. (This is another example of relativity of title discussed *supra*, §59.)

2. Requirements of Adverse Possession [§87]

To establish title by adverse possession, the possessor must show (i) an *actual entry* giving *exclusive possession* that is (ii) *open and notorious,* (iii) *adverse and under a claim of right,* and (iv) *continuous* for the statutory period. Even if the statute of limitations does not specify these requirements, courts have, on their own, added them. Hence, adverse possession law is a blend of statutes and judicial decisions.

a. Actual entry giving exclusive possession [§88]
The primary purpose of the entry requirement is to *trigger the cause of action,* which starts the statute of limitations running. It also shows the extent of the adverse possessor's claim.

(1) Constructive possession of part [§89]
If there is an actual entry on *part* of the land described in a deed, the possessor may be deemed in constructive possession of the rest (*see* "constructive adverse possession," *infra,* §138). But an actual entry on some part of the land is required.

(2) Exclusive possession [§90]
The requirement that the adverse possessor be in exclusive possession means that she not be sharing possession with the *owner* nor with the *public generally.* If the adverse possessor were so sharing possession, the owner would probably not realize the adverse possessor was claiming ownership against him. However, it is possible for two or more persons, acting in concert and sharing only among themselves, to acquire title by adverse possession as tenants in common.

b. Open and notorious possession

(1) Definition [§91]
The adverse possessor must occupy the property in an *open, notorious,* and *visible* manner. Her acts must be such as will constitute *reasonable notice* to the owner that she is claiming dominion, so that the owner can defend his rights. Generally, open and notorious acts are those that look like typical acts of an owner of property; they are acts from which the community, observing them, would infer the actor to be claiming ownership. Obviously, the type of act required turns on the type of land involved. The acts must be *appropriate* to the condition, size, and locality of the land.

(a) Possession of farmland [§92]
Fencing, cultivating, and erecting a building on farmland are usually deemed open and notorious acts. [**Jarvis v. Gillespie,** 587 A.2d 981 (Vt. 1991)]

(b) Possession of wild, undeveloped land [§93]
Wild, undeveloped land can be adversely possessed by acts indicating a claim of dominion.

Example: O owns Blackacre, wild and undeveloped land. A erects a *hunting cabin* on the land and uses it about six times a year, including each hunting season. A *pays taxes* on the land. A *sells the timber on Blackacre* to others, and *executes a number of oil leases.* These acts are sufficient to constitute adverse possession. Fencing the land or living on it is not necessary. [**Alaska National Bank v. Linck,** 559 P.2d 1049 (Alaska 1977); **Monroe v. Rawlings,** 49 N.W.2d 55 (Mich. 1951)]

1) Comment

Presumably, A's claim should be equally strong were he simply to enclose the property and use it only for an occasional walk in the woods or, indeed, not use it at all with the hope of maintaining it in an utterly natural state—provided the enclosure is sufficiently apparent to put O on constructive notice.

(c) Possession of city land [§94]

The erection of a fence or a building may constitute adverse possession. But the totality of the acts must give a picture of a person claiming dominion. For example, the Supreme Court held that where the adverse possessor took sand and gravel from a city lot principally valuable for sand and gravel, *and granted permission* to others to take sand and gravel, *and sued in trespass* those who took sand and gravel without permission, *and paid taxes,* these acts constituted adverse possession of a lot within a city. [**Ewing's Lessee v. Burnet,** 36 U.S. 41 (1837); *and see* **Snowball Corp. v. Pope,** 580 N.E.2d 733 (Ind. 1991)]

(d) Statutory requirements [§95]

Some states have statutes that require specific kinds of acts for adverse possession. New York statutes, *e.g.,* provide that if the claimant does not enter with color of title (*see infra,* §102), adverse possession can be claimed only where the land "has been protected by a substantial inclosure" or has been "usually cultivated or improved." Hence, in New York, a person *without color of title* would have to show—in the preceding examples—that a hunting cabin is a "usual improvement" and that taking sand and gravel was a "usual cultivation" in order to win. [**Van Valkenburgh v. Lutz,** 304 N.Y. 95 (1952)]

(2) Possession of minerals [§96]

Because of the requirement of actual, open, and notorious possession, is it possible to possess minerals lying under the surface of the earth? If the same person owns both the surface estate and the mineral rights when adverse possession begins, adverse possession of the *surface* includes possession of the *minerals.* The minerals are treated as part of the adversely possessed land. On the other hand, *if the minerals have been severed* by sale to another *prior to entry* of the adverse possessor on the surface, possession of the surface does not carry possession of the minerals.

To start adverse possession running against the owner of the minerals, the adverse possessor must start removing them. Possession of the surface does not give a cause of action to the separate owner of the minerals until the minerals are disturbed.

Example: Owner, who owns Blackacre, sells the mineral rights to X. A enters Blackacre and adversely possesses the surface for 30 years, but does not disturb the minerals. A now owns Blackacre, but X still owns the minerals under Blackacre. [**Failoni v. Chicago & North Western Railway,** 195 N.E.2d 619 (Ill. 1964)]

---

c. **Adverse and under a claim of right [§97]**

To be an adverse possessor, a person must hold *adversely* to the owner and *under a claim of right.* Sometimes the word *hostile* is inserted as an element of adverse possession. It does not mean animosity; rather it means only that the possession is *without the owner's consent—it is not subordinate to the owner.* One purpose of the claim of right requirement is to help assure that the true owner is not lulled into believing an occupant will make no claim against him. The key question in determining whether a person is adverse and under a claim of right is: Does the court apply an *objective* or *subjective* test? This question has been the subject of much litigation and dispute.

(1) **Objective test [§98]**

Under the objective test, the state of mind of the possessor is not very important; what is important are the *actions of the possessor.* The possessor's actions, including statements, must *look like* they are claims of ownership. If they look that way to the community, the claim is adverse and *under a claim of right.* Under the objective test, a person can be an adverse possessor even though *he is not actually claiming title* against the true owner. The important thing is that he is *occupying* the land *without the permission* of the owner. Permission negates a claim of right. [**Peters v. Juneau-Douglas Girl Scout Council,** 519 P.2d 826 (Alaska 1974)]

Example: A enters land owned by O and occupies it for more than 20 years. A uses the land as the average owner would, but frequently asserts that he is making no claim of title and will surrender the land to the true owner when he appears. *Legally, A is making a claim of right* and is an adverse possessor. He is not occupying with the permission of the owner, and the owner *has a cause of action* in ejectment upon which the statute of limitations is running. Regardless of A's state of mind, his occupation of the land is *prima facie evidence* that he does so under a claim of title. The very nature of the act of entry and possession is the assertion of a claim of right and triggers the owner's cause of action. [**Patterson v. Reigle,** 4 Pa. 201 (1846)]

---

(2) Subjective test [§99]

Under the subjective test, a claim of right means that the adverse possessor must have a ***bona fide or good faith belief*** that he has title. If the possessor knows he has no title, and that someone else has title, his possession is not adverse. Under this view, a mere squatter (a person who enters into possession knowing that the land belongs to another) cannot be an adverse possessor. [**Carpenter v. Ruperto**, 315 N.W.2d 782 (Iowa 1982)]

Example: O tells A, "Blackacre is yours. Go and farm it." A enters Blackacre and farms it. O did not transfer title to A because the Statute of Frauds requires that title to land be transferred by a written instrument. However, A has a bona fide claim of title and is an adverse possessor.

(a) Mistaken belief [§100]

Within the group of states requiring a bona fide claim of title, a subgroup holds—at least in boundary disputes—that if the possessor ***mistakenly believes*** that he has title but, ***if he knew the truth, would not claim title,*** he is not occupying adversely. This view is treated more fully in connection with boundary disputes (*see infra,* §§106 *et seq.*).

(b) Recent cases [§101]

Although the objective test is recommended by all the commentators (American Law of Property, Powell on Real Property, Restatement) and said by them to be the majority rule, a recent study of cases since 1966 claims that courts usually do require the possessor to act in good faith. A possessor acting under an honest mistake is holding adversely, but a person who knows the land does not belong to him is not holding under a claim of right. Thus, it is alleged, willful trespassers and squatters have not prevailed unless they have strong equities in their favor. [Richard H. Helmholz, Adverse Possession and Subjective Intent, 61 Wash. U. L.Q. 331 (1983); *but see* Roger A. Cunningham, Adverse Possession and Subjective Intent: A Reply to Professor Helmholz, 64 Wash. U. L.Q. 1 (1986)—challenging conclusions; *and see* Roger A. Cunningham, More on Adverse Possession: A Rejoinder to Professor Helmholz, 64 Wash. U. L.Q. 1167 (1986) for further debate]

(3) Color of title [§102]

Color of title refers to a claim founded on a ***written instrument*** (a deed, a will) or a judgment or decree which, unknown to the claimant, is defective and invalid. *Examples:* The grantor's name is forged to the deed; the grantor does not own the land deeded; the grantor was mentally incompetent; the deed is improperly executed; the deed is a tax deed void because the owner was not given notice of the tax sale. In all of these cases, the grantee without knowledge of the defect takes possession *under color of title.* Where a person enters with color of title, no further claim of title or proof of adversity is required.

(a) Color of title not required [§103]

In most states, color of title is *not* required to be an adverse possessor. Even where a bona fide claim of title is required, color of title is not necessary. In the example (*supra, §99*) where O orally gives Blackacre to A, A has no color of title, but A—believing the oral transfer was valid—possesses under a claim of title.

1) Minority views [§104]

In a few states, entry under color of title is required for adverse possession. In a few others, the requirements for adverse possession are more lenient, or the statutory period shorter, for claimants under color of title.

2) Constructive adverse possession [§105]

Entry under color of title is an advantage in all states under the doctrine of constructive adverse possession (*infra, §138*).

EXAM TIP   **gilbert**

Do not confuse *claim of title* with *color of title*. Claim of title (or claim of right) expresses the necessary adversity, discussed *supra*, §§97-101. Color of title just means that the claim is based on a written instrument or judgment that is defective. Although color of title satisfies the adversity requirement, it usually is not required for adverse possession.

---

(4) Boundary disputes [§106]

Claim of right issues often arise between adjoining landowners where one of the parties (A) has been in open and notorious possession of a strip of land along his boundary, *mistakenly believing it to be his.* In fact, it belongs to his neighbor B. There are several views taken of adverse possession in this context.

(a) Objective test—majority view [§107]

The majority of courts apply the objective test of claim of right (*supra, §98*) to boundary disputes. Thus, the possessor's mistake is not determinative; the possessor is necessarily holding under a claim of right if his actions appear to the community to be a claim of ownership and he is not holding with permission of the owner. Under this test, if A fences in the land, or otherwise indicates the boundaries and maintains the strip, A acquires title by adverse possession when the statutory period expires.

(b) The Maine doctrine [§108]

A minority of jurisdictions hold that if the possessor is *mistaken* as to the boundary and would *not* have occupied or claimed the land *if he had known the mistake,* the possessor has *no intention* to claim title and adversity is missing. This is called the "Maine doctrine." [**Preble v. Maine Central Railroad,** 27 A. 149 (Me. 1893)]

Example: Frost, *intending* to claim only to the true boundary line, erects a fence on what he *mistakenly* believes to be the correct boundary line dividing his land from that of his neighbor Sandburg. In fact, the fence is 10 feet over onto Sandburg's land, giving Frost possession of 10 feet of Sandburg's land. The fence remains for the period of limitations. Under the majority view, Frost owns the 10 feet by adverse possession. Under the Maine doctrine, Frost's actual state of mind is relevant. If he would not have claimed title to the 10 feet had he known it belonged to Sandburg, Frost does *not* possess under a *claim of right,* and hence there is no adverse possession.

---

1) **Distinguish—bona fide claim of title [§109]**

The Maine doctrine and the view that the adverse possessor must have a bona fide claim of title are similar but not quite the same. Suppose that Frost was a greedy neighbor and has an intent to claim title to the 10 feet whether or not he is mistaken. Under the Maine doctrine, Frost would get title by adverse possession, but he would not get title if the court requires a bona fide claim of title for adverse possession.

2) **Criticism [§110]**

The Maine doctrine has been criticized on the following grounds: (i) An *action in ejectment* lies against the possessor regardless of his actual intent, and the statute bars the action after a specified period. (ii) If actual intent is determinative, the intentional *wrongdoer wins* when the good neighbor would not. (iii) The Maine doctrine *encourages* honest neighbors to *lie* on the witness stand ("I wanted it as mine in any case"). (iv) The objective test of adverse possession—evidenced by the possessor's acts and conduct—is more reliable and *cheaper to administer* than a subjective test of what was actually in the possessor's mind.

(c) **The New Jersey view [§111]**

New Jersey for a long time adhered to the Maine doctrine, but New Jersey has now joined the majority and applies the objective test with this qualification: "[W]hen the encroachment of an adjoining owner *is of a small area* and the fact of an intrusion is not clearly and self-evidently apparent to the naked eye but requires an on-site survey for certain disclosure," the encroachment is *not open and notorious.* In that case, the statute of limitations will run against the owner only if the owner has *actual knowledge* of the encroachment. [**Mannillo v. Gorski,** 255 A.2d 258 (N.J. 1969)]

(d) Agreement on boundaries [§112]

Apart from adverse possession, boundary disputes can be resolved by other doctrines that assume an agreement between the neighboring parties. An oral agreement is unenforceable because the Statute of Frauds requires a written instrument for the conveyance of land, and in the example *supra,* an agreement by A and B would in effect be conveying 10 feet of B's land to A. Nonetheless, courts have found ways of enforcing oral agreements.

1) Agreed boundaries [§113]

The doctrine of agreed boundaries provides that if there is uncertainty between neighbors as to the true boundary line, an *oral agreement* to settle such uncertainty is enforceable—*not* as a *conveyance,* which would violate the Statute of Frauds, but as a *way of locating the boundary described in the deeds.* [**Joaquin v. Shiloh Orchards,** 84 Cal. App. 3d 192 (1978)]

2) Acquiescence [§114]

The doctrine of acquiescence provides that long acquiescence—but perhaps for a shorter period of time than the statute of limitations—is evidence of an agreement between the parties fixing the boundary line.

3) Estoppel [§115]

Estoppel applies where neighbor B makes positive representations about, or conducts himself so as to indicate, the location of a common boundary, and neighbor A substantially changes his position in reliance on such representations or conduct. Neighbor B is estopped to deny the validity of his statements or acts. Estoppel has also occasionally been applied when neighbor B remains silent in the face of substantial expenditures by neighbor A.

(e) Mistaken improver [§116]

Suppose that A erects a building, or part of a building, on neighbor B's property, mistakenly believing the building is on A's own land. When B discovers this mistake, the encroachment has not existed for the period of the statute of limitations; therefore, A does not have an adverse possession claim. What are B's rights? The common law was rather harsh on A. At common law, B had the right to force A to remove the encroachment. [**Geragosian v. Union Realty Co.,** 193 N.E. 726 (Mass. 1935); **Peters v. Archambault,** 278 N.E.2d 729 (Mass. 1972); **Pile v. Pedrick,** 31 A. 646 (Pa. 1895)]

1) **Modern law [§117]**

Under modern law (sometimes by statute) a *good faith* improver of a neighbor's lot gets some relief. A court sitting in equity may let A's encroachment remain if A pays damages to B, or a court may award the building to B if B pays its value to A, or the court may give B the option of paying A the value of the house or selling A the land at fair market value. [**Madrid v. Spears,** 250 F.2d 51 (10th Cir. 1957); **Raab v. Casper,** 51 Cal. App. 3d 866 (1975); **Hardy v. Burroughs,** 232 N.W. 200 (Mich. 1930); **Somerville v. Jacobs,** 170 S.E.2d 805 (W. Va. 1969)]

2) **Intentional encroachment [§118]**

If a person knowingly encroaches on her neighbor's lot, the person must remove the encroachment if the neighbor so demands. A cannot seize B's land, but instead must bargain with B for it. Equitable relief is available only to those who act in good faith and improve the adjoining lot by mistake. [**Goulding v. Cook,** 661 N.E.2d 1322 (Mass. 1996)]

d. **Continuous, uninterrupted possession [§119]**

The fourth requirement for adverse possession is that the possession continue uninterrupted throughout the statutory period.

(1) **Continuous possession [§120]**

Continuous possession requires only the *degree of occupancy* and use that the *average owner* would make of the particular type of property. An adverse use is continuous when it is made without a break in the essential *attitude of mind* required for adverse use. A person can be in continuous possession even though there are considerable intervals during which the property is not used.

(a) **Purpose [§121]**

The purpose of the continuity requirement is to give the owner notice that the possessor is claiming ownership, and that the entries are not just a series of trespasses.

(b) **Seasonal use [§122]**

Use of a summer home only during the summer for the statutory period is continuous use. [**Howard v. Kunto,** *supra,* §86] Similarly, seasonal use of a hunting cabin during the hunting seasons, or the grazing of cattle on range lands in summer, may be sufficiently continuous possession, *if such lands are normally used this way.* [**Nome 2000 v. Fagerstrom,** 799 P.2d 304 (Alaska 1990); **Monroe v. Rawlings,** *supra,* §93]

In considering the adverse possession requirement of continuous and un-interrupted possession, be sure to analyze any intervals when the adverse possessor is *not using* the property. To determine if the use is continuous, you must first decide whether the use is *consistent with the type of property* involved. If the average owner would use the property all year, but the adverse possessor uses it only for his two-week vacation, that is probably not enough for continuous possession, even though he vacations there every year for the statutory period. If, however, the property is such that the average owner would use it only for vacationing, it might be enough.

(c) Abandonment [§123]

Abandonment is the *intentional relinquishment* of possession. If the possessor abandons the property for *any period* of time, without intent to return, continuity of adverse possession is lost. The adverse possession comes to an end, and possession returns constructively to the true owner. If the adverse possessor later returns, the statute of limitations begins to run anew.

If there are intervals when the adverse possessor is not using the property, you must also consider *his intent*. If he used the property for a period of time, but then packed up his things and headed to a job in a different state, only to return later when the job didn't work out, the adverse possession period *starts anew* when he returns because when he left, he abandoned the property (he didn't intend to return). On the other hand, if he left the property to go take care of his elderly aunt for awhile, leaving some of his possessions on the property, it is likely that he did not abandon the property, and the period continues to run. To make these determinations, the facts must be analyzed carefully.

(2) Tacking by successive adverse possessors [§124]

To establish continuous possession for the statutory period, an adverse possessor can tack onto her own period of adverse possession any period of adverse possession by *predecessors in interest*. Thus, separate periods of actual possession by those holding hostilely to the owner can be tacked together, provided there is *privity of estate* between the adverse possessors (*see* below).

Example: O owns Blackacre. In 1981, A enters adversely. In 1994, A sells her interest to B, who continues to hold adversely to O. In 1998, B dies and his interest is inherited by C, who takes possession and continues to hold adversely to O. The statutory period is 20 years. In 2001, C acquires title by adverse possession—13 years of A's possession and four years of B's possession are tacked onto three years of C's own possession. [**Brown v. Gobble,** 474 S.E.2d 489 (W. Va. 1996)]

(a) Privity of estate [§125]

To tack onto a preceding possession, there must be privity of estate between the two possessors. Privity of estate in this context means that a possessor *voluntarily* transferred to a subsequent possessor either an *estate in land* (*see infra*, §§246 *et seq.*) or *physical possession.* Where the transfer is not voluntary, as in the case of someone *ousting* the prior possessor, there is no privity of estate. [**Porter v. Posey,** 592 S.W.2d 844 (Mo. 1979)]

1) Rationale

Why is privity required? In England, it is not required. The statute of limitations runs against the true owner from the time adverse possession began, and as long as adverse possession continues unbroken, it makes no difference who continues it. The English simply penalize the owner who sleeps on his rights. In this country, courts require privity because they view title by adverse possession as something *to be gained by meritorious conduct*—an involuntary transfer by ouster or seizure is not regarded as meritorious.

Example: A owns lot 1, but by mistake builds her house on the adjoining lot 2 owned by O. Five years later, A sells "her house" to B, giving B a deed describing lot 1 and transferring to B physical possession of lot 2 (where the house is). B can tack A's possession of lot 2 onto his own. [**Belotti v. Bickhardt,** 228 N.Y. 296 (1920); **Howard v. Kunto,** *supra*, §122]

(b) Ouster by third party [§126]

When an adverse possessor (A) is ousted by a third party (X), X *cannot tack* on A's period of prior possession because of lack of privity. Privity of estate requires a *voluntary* transfer for tacking.

1) Reentry by A [§127]

Suppose that six months after A is ousted by X, A manages to reenter the property and resume possession. What effect does the ouster by X have on A's adverse possession rights? *A can tack her prior possession onto her later possession, but the statute is tolled during the period* of X's possession, because in that period O had no cause of action against A (who was out of possession). Thus, A has to stay in possession for the statutory period plus six months (the period in which X was in possession).

(c) Abandonment [§128]

Tacking is *not permitted* where one adverse possessor *abandons* the property, even though another enters immediately. The statute of limitations starts running anew on the new entry. For tacking, there must be privity of estate—a voluntary transfer between possessors.

(d) Tacking on the owner's side [§129]

Once adverse possession has begun to run against O, it runs against O and all of O's successors in interest. Hence, if A enters against O in 1990, and O conveys to C in 1995, the statute continues to run against C—from 1990. Thus, successive ownerships are tacked on the owner's side as well as on the adverse possessor's side.

EXAM TIP   **gilbert**

Tacking is a common issue on exam questions dealing with adverse possession. For tacking to be permitted, remember that there must be *privity of estate* between the possessors. All this means is that one possessor *voluntarily transferred possession* or an estate in land to a subsequent possessor. Recall too that tacking can be on the owner's side as well, but again there must be privity—a voluntary transfer. If the successor did not receive the property through a voluntary transfer (e.g., she ousted the possessor or moves in upon seeing the possessor abandon the place), there is no privity.

---

(3) Interruption by true owner [§130]

If the true owner reenters the land openly and notoriously for the *purpose of regaining possession,* an interruption has occurred. Interruption of possession by the true owner stops the statute of limitations from running.

(a) Objective test [§131]

In most states, interruption can occur without an actual intent to oust the possessor. Courts use the same sort of objective test for interruption as they use for establishing possession under a claim of right. If the owner's acts are ordinary acts of ownership and would give notice of claim to the average person, they are an interruption. There is a *presumption* that the use of land by the owner is the exercise of his *right* to use it, and therefore when the owner uses land, such use presumptively asserts ownership. [**Mendonca v. Cities Service Oil Co.**, 237 N.E.2d 16 (Mass. 1968)]

e. Payment of property taxes [§132]

In several states, principally in the west, the adverse possessor must pay taxes on the land in order to prevail. [*See, e.g.,* Cal. Civ. Proc. Code §325] This requirement is traceable to the influence of land-rich railroad companies in the western states in the 19th century. With vast tracts of land, the owners found it virtually impossible to discover potential adverse possessors by visual inspection, but the payment of taxes is recorded in the courthouse, giving notice to the owner. In all states, payment of taxes is good evidence of a claim of right.

ADVERSE POSSESSION CHECKLIST

TO ACQUIRE PROPERTY BY ADVERSE POSSESSION THERE MUST BE:

- ☑ *Actual entry* giving *exclusive possession* (*i.e.,* not sharing possession with the owner or the public);

- ☑ *Open and notorious possession* (*i.e.,* acts appropriate to the condition, size, and locality of the land to constitute reasonable notice to the owner of a claim of dominion);

- ☑ *Adverse and under a claim of right* (*i.e.,* without the owner's consent); and

- ☑ *Continuous, uninterrupted possession* (*i.e.,* degree of occupancy and use that an average owner would make of the property) *for statutory period* (tacking allowed).

---

3. **Disabilities of Owner [§133]**

Most legislatures think it unfair for a statute of limitations to run upon a person who is unable to bring a lawsuit due to a legal disability. Therefore, most statutes give an *additional period* of time to bring an action if the owner is under a disability. However, disability provisions are strictly limited in two ways: (i) only the disabilities *specified* in the statute (*e.g.,* insanity, infancy) can be considered; and (ii) usually only disabilities of the owner *at the time adverse possession begins* count. The best way to understand disability provisions, and how they work, is to look at a typical statute.

a. **Typical statute [§134]**

The following statute contains a typical disabilities provision: "An action to recover the title to or possession of real property shall be brought within 21 years after the cause of action accrued, but if a person entitled to bring the action is, *at the time the cause of action accrues,* within the *age of minority* or of *unsound mind,* the person, after the expiration of 21 years from the time the cause of action accrues, may bring the action *within 10 years after the disability is removed.*" [Ohio Rev. Code Ann. §2305.04 (Baldwin 1975), *applied in* **Ewing's Lessee v. Burnet,** *supra,* §94]

b. **Read statute carefully [§135]**

Observe that only two disabilities count (minority and insanity); that they must be disabilities at the time the adverse possessor first enters; and that in case such disabilities exist, the owner or her successor in interest has 21 years *or* 10 years after the removal of the disability (whichever period is longer) to bring an action.

🔵 *e.g.* **Example:** A enters Blackacre in 1980 when the owner (O) is two years old. The age of majority is 18. The statute of limitations is 21 years or 10 years after the disability (minority) is removed, whichever is longer. The 21-year period expires in 2001, but if O reaches her majority in 1996, she has until 2006 to bring suit. The alternative period will expire earlier if O dies under age 18; it will expire 10 years after O's death. Thus, if O dies at age 12 (1990), O's heir has until 2000 to bring suit under the alternative period—but because the period will not expire in any event until 2001, the alternative period, expiring before 2001, is not used.

4. Extent of Land Acquired by Adverse Possession [§136]

Assuming all requirements for adverse possession are satisfied, to what physical area does the adverse possessor's claim extend? There are two basic rules, depending on whether the possessor entered with or without color of title. (For explanation of "color of title," *see supra*, §102.)

a. Without color of title [§137]

If the adverse possessor did not enter under color of title, her claim extends only to such part of the land as she *actually occupied or controlled* in a manner consistent with ownership of such premises.

b. With color of title—doctrine of constructive adverse possession [§138]

If the good faith claimant goes into actual possession of some significant portion of the property under color of title (*e.g.*, defective deed), she is deemed to be in adverse possession of the entire property described in the instrument provided the tract of land described in the deed is recognized in the community as one defined parcel of land. On the theory that she intends to control all of the land described in the instrument, the adverse possessor is in *constructive adverse possession* of the part of the tract she does not actually possess.

Example: X forges the names of O and B on a deed to A. A believes the signatures are genuine. The deed describes Blackacre (owned by O) and Whiteacre (owned by B). A moves into the farmhouse on Blackacre, but does not go onto Whiteacre. A has *actual possession* of the farmhouse on Blackacre and *constructive possession* of all the rest of Blackacre, for the farmhouse is a significant part. A does not have constructive adverse possession of Whiteacre. A has not entered Whiteacre, and B has no cause of action on which the statute of limitations has run. Therefore A has neither actual nor constructive adverse possession of Whiteacre.

5. Interests Not Affected by Adverse Possession [§139]

Recall that the basic principle of adverse possession is that a statute of limitations is running on a person who has a cause of action and does not bring a suit. If a person has *no cause of action,* he is not barred by any statute of limitations running. The application of this principle can become rather tricky, particularly to future interests.

a. Future interests [§140]

A future interest is a right to possession of the property in the future (*see infra*, §§366 *et seq.*). The most common example is where O transfers land to

Child for life, and on Child's death to Grandchild. Child has a *life estate*, and Grandchild has a future interest called a *remainder*. Only the life tenant, Child, has the right to possession while Child is alive. Until Child dies, Grandchild has no right to possession. Hence, the statute of limitations does not run against a remainder *existing at the time of entry* by an adverse possessor because the holder of the remainder has no right to eject the adverse possessor from possession.

Example: O owns Whiteacre. In 1989, O conveys Whiteacre to Child for life, remainder to Grandchild. In 1990, A enters adversely. The statute of limitations is 10 years. In 2007, Child dies. Grandchild is now entitled to possession and has until 2017 (10 years from 2007) to eject A. [**Harper v. Paradise**, 210 S.E.2d 710 (Ga. 1974)]

Compare—entry prior to O's transfer: If, in the above example, A had entered Whiteacre in 1988, *before O created the remainder*, the statute would begin to run in 1988 *against O and his successors in interest*, and A would acquire title in 1998. Although Grandchild never had a chance to evict A, she is barred because she is a *successor in interest to O* in whom the cause of action originally arose. In the preceding example, the adverse possessor entered against Child, who had a cause of action, and the statute of limitations runs against Child and his successors in interest. But Grandchild is *not* a successor in interest to Child; she is a successor in possession. "Successor in interest" means one party takes his interest from the other, and Grandchild acquired her remainder interest from O, not from Child. Child gave Grandchild nothing. (For more on successors in interest, *see supra*, §§124 *et seq.*).

---

(1) Note

Given that in the above example the statute of limitations is running against Grandchild, Grandchild does have some means to protect her interest. One possibility is that she ask Child to bring an ejectment action against A before the statute runs and, if Child refuses, bring an action for waste against Child and argue that given Child's inaction, Grandchild should have the right to eject A in order to prevent waste of her remainder interest. Another possibility is that, if Child refuses, Grandchild sues for a declaratory judgment that A's adverse possession is not running against Grandchild and will not start to do so until Child dies.

b. Liens, easements, equitable servitudes [§141]

If the land is subject to outstanding liens, easements, or equitable servitudes when the adverse possessor enters, any title acquired by the adverse possessor *remains subject to such interests*. The owner of any such interest is not affected by adverse possession until he has a cause of action against the possessor.

> **Example:** O owns Greenacre, which is subject to a covenant benefiting B's land restricting Greenacre's use to residential purposes. It is also subject to an easement of way benefiting C's land. A enters adversely, does not violate the covenant, does not interfere with C's passage, and occupies the land for the period of the statute of limitations. O is barred, but B and C are not barred, for they have never had a cause of action against A.

c. Government land [§142]

Except where a statute is construed to provide otherwise, a governmental entity (federal, state, or municipal) is *exempt* from operation of statutes of limitation. Public policy forbids a private individual from acquiring title to government land by adverse possession. It is not expected that government officials will watch extensive government land as private owners are expected to do. *But note:* There are exceptions to the general rule. In some states, adverse possession of streets and roadways is permitted. Additionally, in some states, land held by a county or city in its private capacity, and not for public use, is subject to adverse possession. [**Hinkley v. State**, 234 N.Y. 309 (1922)]

6. Adverse Possession of Chattels [§143]

A person can acquire title to chattels by adverse possession just as he can acquire title to land. Once the remedy is barred, the adverse possessor has title. [**Chapin v. Freeland**, 8 N.E. 128 (Mass. 1886)] Generally, the requirements for adverse possession of chattels are the same as for land, except the period of limitations is shorter. [**Henderson v. First National Bank of Dewitt**, 494 S.W.2d 452 (Ark. 1973)] There is, however, *one great difference* between adversely possessing land and adversely possessing chattels: Adverse possession of land is open and notorious, whereas adverse possession of chattels seldom is. How should this difference be handled? Basically, there are two approaches:

a. New York rule [§144]

New York holds that the statute of limitations does not begin to run on the owner of stolen goods until the owner knows who has the goods and makes a demand for return of the goods that is rejected. If the person in possession refuses to return the goods, the three-year statute of limitations begins to run. By making it very difficult to obtain title to stolen goods by adverse possession, New York believes it will deter theft. The New York rule also puts the risk of buying stolen goods on purchasers, who can often protect themselves by making inquiries. [**Solomon R. Guggenheim Foundation v. Lubell**, 77 N.Y.2d 311 (1991)]

b. Due diligence rule [§145]

A majority of courts appear to hold that the statute of limitations does not begin to run on the owner of stolen goods as long as the owner continues to use due diligence in looking for them. The conduct of the *owner*, not the possessor, is controlling. The cause of action thus accrues when the owner first knows, *or reasonably should know through the exercise of due diligence,* where the stolen goods are. [**O'Keeffe v. Snyder,** 416 A.2d 862 (N.J. 1980)]

Example: A steals a valuable painting belonging to O. A sells the painting to B, a bona fide purchaser. O learns that B has the painting. Under the due diligence rule, adverse possession runs from the time of the theft unless O can show that she used due diligence and failed to locate the painting; if O can show due diligence, adverse possession begins to run when O locates the painting.

Compare: Under the New York rule, due diligence is irrelevant. The cause of action begins to run when O learns that B has the painting.

c. **Bona fide purchaser of stolen goods [§146]**
A bona fide purchaser of stolen goods is not protected against the claim of the owner unless the statute of limitations has run on the owner. The risk is on the purchaser. The law protects the owner over the purchaser for three reasons. First, whether the purchaser was really bona fide, and did not know the goods were stolen, is questionable in many cases. What the purchaser knew lies in the purchaser's testimony, and is hard for the owner to disprove. Second, the purchaser can lessen the risk of buying stolen goods by inquiries of the seller. Third, if the owners were not protected, owners would spend more money on protective devices to prevent theft, which is not a socially productive expenditure. (*See infra,* §§233 *et seq.*).

F. Remedies of a Possessor

1. **Forms of Action [§147]**
At common law, a plaintiff had to bring suit in an appropriate *form of action* to obtain the particular remedy desired. If the plaintiff brought the wrong form of action, he would be thrown out of court. The forms of action were unbelievably technical and have been abolished or reformed in almost all jurisdictions. However, because for so long they were an important part of our laws, and because some of them *required an allegation of prior possession,* they had an impact on what the law deems to be possession. The courts sometimes defined "possession" in such a way as to enable the plaintiff to bring a lawsuit, or to prevent him from doing so. Thus, the concept of possession occupied a central place in the procedural system. A brief sketch is in order. (*See also* Civil Procedure Summary.)

a. **Actions to recover damages [§148]**
There were several actions permissible where the plaintiff wanted to recover damages for injury to himself or the property, including the following:

(1) **Trespass [§149]**
A suit in trespass required the plaintiff to show that the defendant intentionally or negligently acted so as to inflict a direct, forcible injury to the

plaintiff's person or to property in his possession. The plaintiff had to allege his prior possession or right to possession. The gist of a trespass action is *injury to possession.* If no substantial harm could be shown, nominal damages were given. There were two kinds of trespass actions:

(a) Trespass to chattels [§150]

This action was for any *forcible carrying away* of or injury to plaintiff's chattels, or for excluding the plaintiff from possession of his chattels. The Latin name of this action was *trespass de bonis asportatis,* meaning injury "by carrying away goods."

Example: O is in possession of a cow. A seizes the cow, and gives it to her friend, B. O can sue A in trespass for damages. The measure of damages is not the value of the cow, but the injury done to O by having his possession disturbed. If O recovered the cow from B, *e.g.,* A would be liable only for the value of the cow (milk) from the time of A's seizure to the time of O's recovery.

(b) Trespass to land [§151]

This action was for any forcible interference with plaintiff's possession of land. The Latin name was *trespass quare clausum fregit* ("trespass q.c.f."), meaning "because he broke the close."

Example: O, owner of Blackacre, finds A has cut trees on Blackacre, and in doing so has damaged O's corn crop. O can sue A for money damages to his possessory interest (*i.e.,* the loss in value of Blackacre by having the trees cut and damage to the corn).

(2) Trespass on the case (known as "case") [§152]

Trespass on the case developed as an action where one of the elements of a trespass action was missing. Trespass on the case would lie when the defendant's acts were not immediately injurious but injury was indirect or consequent (*e.g.,* if A drove a nail through the hoof of O's cow, which did no immediate injury, but later caused a crippling infection, case would lie). Or case would lie when the defendant had a duty to act but failed to do so (from which the modern law of unintentional torts stems). Or case would lie where the injury was to property not in the plaintiff's possession (remember, the gist of trespass is injury to *possession*). To sue in case, the plaintiff did *not* have to allege prior possession—only that the defendant had a *duty,* that the defendant *breached* the duty, and that the breach *resulted in substantial harm to the plaintiff.* Substantial harm, not possession, is the gist of trespass on the case.

> **e.g.** **Example:** Consider the facts of **Pierson v. Post,** *supra, §7.* Post, on a horse, is pursuing a fox. Pierson sees the fox running in front of Post. Pierson shoots and kills the fox. Should Post sue Pierson in trespass or in case? Post sued in case, which does not require an allegation of injury to something in his possession (the fox), but merely alleges a tortious interference with his pursuit of the fox. For unknown reasons, the court treated the action as one in trespass, where the crucial issue is whether Post had possession of the fox.

(3) Trover [§153]

A suit in trover was a suit to recover the value of the plaintiff's chattel that *the defendant had converted* (usually by selling it to an unknown party). Originally the action lay only by an owner or prior possessor *against a person who had found the plaintiff's chattel* and refused to give it up, but in time the action was permitted against anyone who refused to deliver up the plaintiff's chattel. (Nonetheless, to bring the action, the plaintiff still had to allege that "plaintiff had casually lost and defendant had found" the chattel—a purely fictional allegation that the defendant could not deny.) In trover, the plaintiff was entitled to *full value* of the chattel at the time the conversion took place. In effect, the plaintiff waives the right to the return of the chattel and insists that the defendant be subjected to a forced purchase of it.

> **e.g.** **Example:** Chimney Sweep finds a jewel belonging to O. Chimney Sweep takes the jewel to a jeweler to have it appraised. The jeweler refuses to return it. Chimney Sweep can sue the jeweler in trover and recover the full value of the jewel. [**Armory v. Delamirie,** *supra, §57*]

(a) Trover distinguished from trespass [§154]

Trover did not apply to damage to land, only to chattels, whereas trespass q.c.f. applied to land. Trespass, not trover, applied in cases where the chattel was damaged but not converted. However, there was a good deal of overlap between these forms of action, and the plaintiff might elect the one that gave the larger recovery. Recall that the measure of damages differed (trespass—injury to possession; trover—value of chattel at time of conversion).

b. Actions to recover possession [§155]

If the plaintiff did not want damages but wanted to recover possession, the plaintiff could bring one of the following actions:

(1) Replevin of chattels [§156]

The plaintiff could bring *replevin* to recover possession of a *chattel* defendant had wrongfully distrained. (An earlier form of action, *detinue,* was absorbed by the development of replevin.) The plaintiff had to allege either that he was in prior possession or owned the chattel.

---

e.g. **Example:** Plaintiff cuts logs on land belonging to O, without O's consent. Defendant takes the logs away from Plaintiff. Plaintiff's *prior possession gained as a trespasser* is sufficient to enable him to bring replevin against Defendant. [**Anderson v. Gouldberg,** *supra,* §60; *and see* **Gissel v. State,** 727 P.2d 1153 (Idaho 1986)—can recover damages]

---

(2) Ejectment [§157]

The plaintiff could bring *ejectment* to recover possession of *land.* Although this was originally an action by a possessor (not an owner) to recover possession, it was a more expeditious remedy than that available to owners, and owners came to use this remedy to recover possession. Ultimately, it became the most common method of *trying title* to land (in such case sometimes called "ejectment to try title"). The plaintiff had to allege either prior possession or title to the land.

c. Modern law [§158]

The common law actions of trespass, case, trover, replevin, and ejectment have in most states been simplified and in many renamed. But the essential difference in remedies afforded by these actions—the return of the thing as opposed to damages—is preserved in modern codes of civil procedure.

2. Defense of *Jus Tertii* [§159]

A defense of *jus tertii* is the defense that neither the plaintiff nor the defendant, *but a third party,* is the true owner, and only the true owner can bring the lawsuit. Is this defense permitted in suits by A (a prior possessor) against B? Distinguish between suits to recover possession (replevin and ejectment) and suits to recover damages (trespass, case, and trover).

a. Actions to recover possession [§160]

In actions to recover possession, the *jus tertii* defense is *not* allowed.

---

e.g. **Example:** O owns Blackacre. A takes possession of Blackacre for a few years and then moves away. B takes possession of Blackacre. A sues B in ejectment. B defends that A is not entitled to prevail because O owns Blackacre. A prevails over B because all A has to show is prior possession. [*See* **Tapscott v. Cobbs,** 52 Va. 172 (1854)]

---

b. Actions for damages [§161]

If A sues B for *damages* rather than possession, and B has to pay A damages, B might be liable later to O (the true owner) for damages. Nonetheless, the majority rule is that B *cannot* assert the defense of *jus tertii* and must pay A damages, thus taking the risk that B will later have to pay O as well. *Rationale:*

Because title is so difficult to prove, the plaintiff is not put to such proof if the plaintiff can prove prior possession. [**Welke v. City of Davenport,** 309 N.W.2d 450 (Iowa 1981)]

(1) Minority rule [§162]

A minority of courts deem the possibility of double liability to be unfair to B and do not permit A, a prior possessor, to recover *damages* from B where B shows that O is the true owner. [**Russell v. Hill,** 34 S.E. 640 (N.C. 1899)] But in jurisdictions following this minority rule, A can recover *possession* from B. Recovery of possession does not subject B to the risk of double liability.

(2) Allegation of ownership [§163]

If A alleges in his complaint that he *owns the property,* but is able to prove only prior possession, it has been held that A's suit against B for damages must fail because A has failed to prove ownership. [**Winchester v. City of Stevens Point,** 17 N.W. 3 (Wis. 1883)] This holding makes little sense because prior possession should be sufficient for the recovery of damages. *Tactic:* Do not allege more than what must be proven or the judges may be distracted from the fundamental issue.

(3) Interpleader [§164]

Under modern statutes, B can interplead O in a suit by A against B. This will bring O into the lawsuit and avoid double recovery against B. But B, the wrongdoer, has the burden of locating O and subjecting O to the jurisdiction of the court. This may be difficult to do if O is living in Montana and the suit is brought in Florida, and O does not want to enter the lawsuit. As a practical matter, however, B can negotiate with O and buy her superior claim, thus defeating A. Thus, in modern times the possibility of double recovery is often unrealistic, especially in suits over land where owners can be ascertained by searching the public land records.

3. Measure of Damages [§165]

Where a prior possessor is permitted to sue a subsequent possessor for damages, what is the measure of damages? Is the prior possessor entitled to *permanent damages* to the entire property *or* only to *damage to date* to his possessory interest? *Remember:* The prior possessor's interest may end when the true owner asserts her rights, so the prior possessor may not be the "permanent owner." The issue is best understood by an example.

Example: O owns Blackacre. A takes possession of Blackacre. B, a neighbor, erects a dam, which floods Blackacre. Can A recover from B the permanent loss in value of Blackacre or only the loss that A has suffered to date by not being able to farm the land? The cases are split. Some courts say A can have permanent damages, leaving B with the risk of double liability if O later sues B. [**Illinois & St. Louis Railroad & Coal Co. v. Cobb,** 94 Ill. 55 (1879)] Other courts give A only damages for being deprived of possession to date. [**LaSalle County Carbon Coal Co. v. Sanitary District of Chicago,** 103 N.E. 175 (Ill. 1913)]

---

a. Life tenant as plaintiff [§166]

A similar problem of measuring damages arises when a life tenant sues a third party in tort for damage to the property. What amount can a life tenant recover in tort from a third party who damages the property?

(1) Majority view [§167]

The prevailing view is that because the life tenant is not responsible to the owners of the remainder for damages to the property that are not the life tenant's fault, the life tenant is entitled to recover only damages to her interest as life tenant. The owner of the remainder can bring a separate suit for damages to the remainder. [**Zimmerman v. Shreeve,** 59 Md. 357 (1883)] *Criticism:* The wrongdoer may escape some liability when the owners of the remainder are unborn or unascertained and cannot sue. It is hard to assess separately the damages sustained by the life estate. This view requires a multiplicity of actions.

(2) Minority view [§168]

Because the life tenant has possessory title, she, like an adverse possessor, is able to recover for all damages to the property. She holds the amount recovered as trustee for the owners of the remainder who must then sue the life tenant, not the tortfeasor. [**Rogers v. Atlantic, Gulf & Pacific Co.,** 213 N.Y. 246 (1915)] *Criticism:* This limits the owners of the remainder to the amount recovered by the life tenant (who might have hired a foolish lawyer), and requires them to rely upon the solvency of the life tenant.

4. Law and Equity

a. History [§169]

In addition to courts of law, England had a separate court of equity in which the chancellor sat. In medieval times, the courts of common law, adhering to their ancient customs and formulas, left many wrongs without redress. The chancellor, a cleric and keeper of the king's conscience, intervened to give relief. Gradually there developed a court of chancery (later known as a court of equity, meaning "fairness" or "justice"). Chancery imparted a much needed element of elasticity into the remedies available from the law courts. In America, separate courts of chancery exist in some states, but in most states, law and equity have been merged, and *legal* and *equitable remedies* may be sought and applied in the same action.

b. Remedies [§170]

The law courts offered the remedy of *damages* to an aggrieved party. Thus, if

B refused to return A's cow, A could sue B at law for the value of the cow. Equity, enforcing personal duties, offered an *injunction* as a remedy. The chancellor would order B *to do* something (such as to let A into possession) or *not to do* something (such as forbidding B from interfering with A's use of the land).

(1) Modern importance [§171]

It remains important to know whether a remedy is legal or equitable because the legal rules for granting *damages* or the equitable rules for granting an *injunction* may differ. (*See* the discussion of real covenants and equitable servitudes, *infra,* §§1188 *et seq.*)

G. Rights of Owners

1. Right to Use [§172]

The owner of property has the right to use it as she sees fit, subject to some rights in neighbors and to police power regulation. Among other things, the neighbors can sue to prevent a nuisance (*see infra,* §§1311 *et seq.*) or to prevent the owner from withdrawing support for their land by excavating her own (*see infra,* §§1358 *et seq.*). Also, the government may have zoning or environmental laws prohibiting particular uses (*see infra,* §§1377 *et seq.*).

2. Right to Transfer [§173]

An owner ordinarily has the power to transfer her property by gift, sale, inheritance, or will. The right to transfer property during life is important because it encourages people to bargain with each other and transfer the property by agreement to the person who values it most highly. In making property transferable, property law furthers a market economy. If the rules about creation of property rights are clear, so that persons know exactly with whom they must bargain to buy these rights, the objective of the market of transferring resources to the persons who value them most highly is furthered.

a. Restrictions on transfer [§174]

Restrictions on transfer of property imposed by some former owner may be held void under the rule prohibiting restraints on alienation (*see infra,* §§349 *et seq.*). The law requires a very convincing justification for making property inalienable.

3. Right to Exclude [§175]

It is generally accepted that the essence of private property is the right of the owner to exclude others—the right to exclusive possession. Courts have traditionally granted great protection to this right. The reason for this type of protection is that if A wants to enter B's land, B should bargain with A for this right and not seize it. [**Jacque v. Steenberg Homes, Inc.,** 563 N.W.2d 154 (Wis. 1997)—granting $100,000 punitive damages against a man who willfully moved a trailer across the plaintiff's land over the plaintiff's objection] However, the right to exclude has some limitations when important rights of others become involved.

a. **Mistaken improver [§176]**

When a neighbor mistakenly improves land not his own, but believing it is his, the owner of the land might not be able to remove the encroachment. But if the encroachment is knowing and willful, the improver must remove the encroachment. (*See supra,* §116 *et seq.*)

b. **Civil rights laws [§177]**

Civil rights laws may prohibit persons offering public accommodations or housing from discriminating based on race, ethnic origin, religion, or other grounds. [**United States Jaycees v. McClure**, 305 N.W.2d 764 (Minn. 1981); **Frank v. Ivy Club**, 576 A.2d 241 (N.J. 1990); *see also* the Fair Housing Act, *infra,* §821]

(1) **Common law [§178]**

Apart from civil rights statutes, there may be a common law right guaranteeing all citizens access to places of public accommodation. A common law right would protect all persons and not merely those within the enumerated classes of civil rights statutes. Thus, a sign saying, "We reserve the right to refuse service to anyone," may be only for show and without legal effect. [**Uston v. Resorts International Hotel, Inc.**, 445 A.2d 370 (N.J. 1982)—protecting the right of a blackjack "counter" to play at a casino]

c. **Shopping centers [§179]**

Shopping malls have displaced downtown business districts as a place for people to gather and intermingle. Persons may want to exercise in a mall the same rights of free speech (passing out religious tracts, protesting a war, or soliciting votes) as people have in a public business district. Their claim to free speech rights, of course, runs into the mall owner's right to exclude. The Supreme Court has held that the First Amendment to the United States Constitution does not require mall owners to allow access for such purposes. [**Lloyd Corp. v. Tanner**, 407 U.S. 551 (1972)] However, a state court may read a *state* constitutional right to free speech to include exercising that speech within a shopping mall. [**PruneYard Shopping Center v. Robins**, 447 U.S. 74 (1980)] Hence, in many states, solicitors in shopping centers are protected under a state constitutional guarantee of free speech. [**New Jersey Coalition Against War in the Middle East v. J.M.B. Realty Corp.**, 650 A.2d 757 (N.J. 1994)]

d. **Workers' rights to organize [§180]**

Under federal law, workers have a right to organize a union, and unions have a right to communicate with workers on the employer's premises seeking their votes. To secure these rights, an employer housing migrant farm workers cannot exclude union organizers from coming onto the property. [**State v. Shack**, 277 A.2d 369 (N.J. 1971)]

Chapter Two:
Personal Property

CONTENTS

Chapter Approach

Chapter Approach

All property can be divided into *real property* (land) and *personal property* (everything else). The first chapter dealt with the acquisition of both kinds of property. Here we look at some special problems peculiar to personal property.

1. **Bailments**

   Simply put, a bailment occurs when one person gives temporary possession of her property to another. Bailments arise often in ordinary life: holding another person's coat, borrowing a pencil, parking a car. The bailee has *possession* of another's goods. The major issues to focus on are *when a bailment is created* and the *duty of care* of the bailee.

2. **Gifts**

   A gift of personal property requires *intent* to make a gift and, usually, *delivery* of the object to the donee. The delivery requirement is what you are most likely to be tested on. Be sure to consider all the possibilities—including constructive or symbolic delivery, delivery to a third person, etc.

3. **Sales**

   In a sales question, the central issue is whether a purchaser can acquire title to personal property from a *possessor* who does not own the property. The general rule says "no," but there are limited exceptions for a *bona fide purchaser*. (Note that you probably won't find a sale of personal property question on your Property exam because such issues are now covered by the Uniform Commercial Code and taught in a course on Commercial Law.)

A. Bailments

1. **Definition [§181]**

   A bailment is the *rightful possession* of goods by one who is *not the owner*. The person in possession of the goods is a *bailee*; the person on whose behalf the bailee holds the goods is the *bailor*. The bailee has the duty to care for the goods and return them to the bailor as agreed or, in the case of involuntary bailments (*see infra*, §192), as determined by common law or statutory rules.

   Examples: A bailment arises when O leaves an appliance with an electrician for repair, checks a coat, has furniture moved by a moving company, or deposits mail in the post office. In each case O is a bailor. These bailments arise out of consensual arrangements of the two parties. But bailments can also arise from *involuntary* possession (*see infra*, §192).

   ---

2. Creation [§182]

To create a bailment, the alleged bailee must assume *actual physical control* with the *intent to possess*. Because a bailee has duties and liabilities, courts define "physical control" and "intent" in such a way as to carry out the expectations of the parties and to be fair. If a court thinks that liability would be unexpected or unfair, it can usually find that the defendant did not have "physical control" or "intent to possess."

a. Actual physical control [§183]

To have a bailment, the bailee must take actual physical control of the object.

(1) Parking lot cases [§184]

A frequently litigated situation involving creation of a bailment involves O leaving his car in a parking lot owned by B. Is B a bailee for O (and subject to a bailee's liability for loss or damage)? Distinguish two types of cases:

(a) Park and lock [§185]

If O parks his own car in a lot, retains the keys, and does not deliver the car to the attendant, some older cases hold that *no bailment* is created.

e.g. **Example:** O parks his car on the common airport parking lot, where he pays when he leaves. This does not create a bailment, because B has not assumed control over the car. [**Ellish v. Airport Parking Co. of America,** 42 A.D.2d 174 (1973)] *But note:* Newer cases, however, hold that a *bailment is created* in such a "park and lock" parking garage. [**Allen v. Hyatt Regency-Nashville Hotel,** 668 S.W.2d 286 (Tenn. 1984)]

(b) Attended lots [§186]

If O leaves the keys with an attendant, who gives O a ticket identifying the car for redelivery, a *bailment is created.* If O does not leave the keys, but B has attendants present parking other cars and able to exercise surveillance—thus *creating expectations* in O that B has accepted a duty of reasonable care—a bailment may be found even though the attendant has no physical control of the car.

(2) Custody distinguished [§187]

A person who has *custody* but not possession is not a bailee. Custody is where goods are handed over but the owner does not intend to relinquish the right of dominion over them. A common example is where a department store clerk hands goods to a customer for examination. The *customer has custody,* not possession, and is not a bailee.

(a) Servants [§188]

A servant entrusted with goods by his master is *not a bailee,* but rather is a custodian. The distinction is important in criminal law.

A person who feloniously takes goods from the *possession* of an owner is guilty of common law *larceny*. A person who fraudulently converts goods in his possession that belong to another is guilty of the statutory crime of *embezzlement*. Thus, if the accused *had possession* of the goods, he *cannot be convicted of larceny*. By saying that a servant has only custody, the law permits servants to be convicted of larceny of their master's chattels. [**State v. Schingen**, 20 Wis. 74 (1865)]

b. Intent [§189]

The bailee must have an *intent* to exercise physical control, and in consensual arrangements the bailor must intend to give up the right to possess the object.

(1) Mistake as to contents [§190]

If a person is mistaken as to the contents of a parcel, he may not be deemed in possession of the contents of the parcel, even though he is in possession of the parcel. Thus, suppose a statute *forbids the possession* of marijuana. O gives A a parcel which, unknown to A, is filled with marijuana. A is to deliver the parcel to B. En route to B's home, A is arrested. A has not violated the statute. The court will read into the statute the requirement of *intent* to possess marijuana because it seems unfair to convict an innocent and unknowing person.

(2) Value undisclosed to bailee [§191]

If a bailor gives an article to a bailee but does not disclose the exceptional value of the article, a bailment is created. The risk of caring for the article in its true value is put on the bailee when he accepts possession of the article.

---

e.g. **Example:** O owns a ring set with a very valuable cabochon sapphire and diamonds. O hands it to Hotel's cashier, asking her to deliver it to a particular guest. The cashier agrees to do so, not knowing that the ring is very valuable. The cashier negligently loses the ring. A bailment has been created. [**Peet v. Roth Hotel Co.**, 253 N.W. 546 (Minn. 1934)]

---

c. Involuntary bailment [§192]

The normal bailment is consensual. In a few situations, however, a bailment arises even though the bailor and bailee have not consented to the bailee's possession. In a sense, the legal consequence of a bailment is imposed on the person without his consent. Such a situation may involve a *finder*, a person who pens up *stray cattle*, or a *landlord* who resumes possession of leased premises after the tenant has vacated the premises leaving some goods behind. These are called *constructive* or *involuntary bailments*. The basic issue is whether it is reasonable to impose liability on such persons and, if so, to what extent. (*See infra,* §§198-201.)

3. Duties of Bailee

a. Duty to exercise care [§193]

Generally, all bailees are under a duty to exercise care over the bailed goods, but the standard of care varies with the type of bailment. Traditionally, the degree of care has been commensurate with *who gets the benefit* of the bailment.

(1) Bailment for sole benefit of bailee [§194]

If the bailment is for the sole benefit of the bailee (as when a person borrows a lawn mower), the bailee is required to use *extraordinary care*. The bailee is liable for even slight neglect that results in the goods being lost, damaged, or destroyed.

(2) Bailment for mutual benefit of bailor and bailee [§195]

If the bailment benefits both the bailor and bailee (as when O leaves a clock at the repair shop), the bailee must *exercise ordinary care* and is liable for *ordinary negligence*.

(a) "Mutual benefit" [§196]

A mutual benefit is clear where the bailee charges for the service. In other cases, courts have stretched the facts to find some benefit to both parties from the service rendered. Thus, if a hotel cashier accepts a ring for delivery to a guest in the hotel, the hotel gets a benefit from rendering a service to a guest (goodwill if nothing else). [**Peet v. Roth Hotel Co.**, *supra*]

(3) Bailment for sole benefit of bailor [§197]

If the bailment is for the sole benefit of the bailor (as when O asks Friend to keep his car while he is on vacation), it is a "gratuitous" bailment. A gratuitous bailee must use *only slight care* and is liable only for *gross negligence*. *But note:* Some courts, while giving lip service to the rule, in effect reject it by defining "gross negligence" as lack of reasonable care under the circumstances.

EXAM TIP	gilbert

Most exam questions on bailment concern the duty of care owed to the bailor. The first thing you need to do to answer those questions is to figure out *who is benefiting from the bailment*; is it a bailment for the sole benefit of the bailee, the sole benefit of the bailor, or the mutual benefit of both parties? Once you have determined the type of bailment, you know the duty to apply. One way to think about the different duties is to consider that the person benefiting has the greater duty/risk. In other words, when the bailment is for the *sole benefit* of the bailee, the bailee has to be very careful with the bailor's property (*extraordinary care*). If the bailee is doing a favor *for the bailor*, the bailor carries more of the risk and the bailee only has to use *slight care*. Finally, if the bailment benefits *both parties*, *ordinary care* is required.

(a) Distinguish—involuntary bailment [§198]

Where the bailment is not consensual, but the bailee has the goods thrust upon her, so to speak, the bailee *does not have to take affirmative steps* to protect the property. For example, a finder can ignore the find, and a farmer can drive lost cattle off her property. But if the finder does take possession, she is usually held to the same standard as a bailee for the sole benefit of the bailor. She must use *slight care*. For example, a landlord cannot throw a departed tenant's goods on the street, but instead must put them in some fairly safe place.

(4) Modern trend [§199]

This system of classification by benefits is not very satisfactory. In almost all bailments *some* benefit results to both parties. If Neighbor borrows O's lawn mower, *e.g.*, O benefits by goodwill. Similarly, a finder or farmer who pens stray cattle benefits at least by goodwill, maybe by a reward, and perhaps by ultimate ownership if the true owner does not show up. Nor are the distinctions between gross, ordinary, and slight negligence always easy to apply to the facts. In view of this, modern courts may well be moving away from this system to a *standard of ordinary care under the circumstances*. The bailee has the burden of proving due care.

b. Duty to redeliver [§200]

Regardless of the standard of care required of a bailee while the goods are in his custody, a bailee is held to *strict liability* when it comes to redelivery. If the bailee misdelivers the goods to the wrong person, he is stuck with liability even though he used reasonable care. Thus, if the bailee delivers the goods to A on a forged order from the bailor, the bailee is liable. This is a *harsh rule*, and one of doubtful soundness inherited from past times.

EXAM TIP   **gilbert**

Keep the duty to *redeliver* separate in your mind from the duty of *due care*. Failing to return the goods is the worst thing any type of bailee can do and the law comes down hard on him. Thus, *no matter what type of bailment* it is (who gets the benefit), the bailee is held *strictly liable* for not returning the goods to the bailor.

---

(1) Exception [§201]

An *involuntary bailee* is liable only if the bailee was *negligent* in delivering the goods to the wrong person. The courts impose strict liability on the ordinary bailee because he is in breach of contract when he misdelivers. But an involuntary bailee has no contract and has a lesser liability.

Example: Cowen and Pressprich are stockbrokers. Cowen's agent brings a bearer bond to Pressprich's office, and drops it through a letter slot in a door. Pressprich's clerk picks it up, sees it is the wrong bond, opens the door, and calls for Cowen's agent. X, who is not Cowen's agent, responds promptly and the clerk, not knowing Cowen's

SUMMARY OF BAILEE'S DUTY OF CARE

gilbert

STANDARD OF CARE	WHEN APPLIED	EXAMPLE
SLIGHT CARE/LIABILITY ONLY FOR GROSS NEGLIGENCE	Bailment is *solely for the benefit of the bailor*	X leaves her car at a gas station operated by her friend Y for a free car wash
ORDINARY CARE/LIABILITY FOR ORDINARY NEGLIGENCE	Bailment is for the *mutual benefit* of bailor and bailee, as in bailments for hire	X leaves her car with a mechanic for service
EXTRAORDINARY CARE/ LIABILITY FOR EVEN SLIGHT NEGLIGENCE	Bailment is *solely for the benefit of the bailee*	X gratuitously lends her sports car to her friend Y to drive to Y's class reunion
ABSOLUTE LIABILITY	Bailee *departs from terms* of bailment or *fails to re-deliver item* (*exceptions:* involuntary bailee, and possibly delivery to impostor holding "indispensable instrument")	X has turned the keys to her sports car over to Y's parking garage; employee drives X's car to his class reunion. (But probably no absolute liability if X loses the claim check and Y's employee, without notice, turns X's car over to a dishonest finder of the claim check)

Note: There is a modern trend away from the above classifications and toward a rule requiring *ordinary care under all circumstances*.

agent, hands the faker the bond. As an involuntary bailee, Pressprich can be liable only if negligence is shown. [**Cowen v. Pressprich,** 202 A.D. 796 (1922)]

4. Contractual Modification of Liability [§202]

Bailees often attempt to limit their liability by provision in the contract. Most courts permit such contractual limitations provided the limitations do not relieve the bailee from *gross or willful negligence.*

a. Bailor must consent [§203]

A contractual limitation on liability requires the *consent of the bailor.* (A contract requires assent of both parties.) Posting a sign is not enough unless the bailee can show that the bailor saw and accepted the sign. Putting a limited liability provision on a claim check will not work either unless the bailee can show that the bailor was, or should have been, aware of it. If the bailor thought the claim check was merely for identification purposes, no contract limiting liability results.

EXAM TIP   **gilbert**

A common fact situation on an exam will have a bailee attempt to limit liability by a writing on the back of a claim check. Recall that this will *not limit* the bailee's liability unless the facts show that the bailor was *aware* of the provision (*i.e.,* read the waiver) or *should have been aware* of it (*e.g.,* had to sign or initial the waiver before leaving the property with the bailee).

B. Gifts of Personal Property

1. Definition [§204]

A *gift* is a *voluntary* transfer of property *without any consideration.* There are three requirements for a gift of chattels:

(i)   The donor must *intend* to make a gift;

(ii) The donor must *deliver* the chattel to the donee (there are some acceptable substitutes for manual delivery); and

(iii) The donee must *accept* the chattel.

EXAM TIP   **gilbert**

Although when answering a question on gifts you need to consider all three requirements above, almost all litigation concerning gifts occurs over the second requirement, *delivery.* That requirement is also most important to understand for your exam. Be sure you know what it means and what substitutes are acceptable in place of manual delivery.

---

a. Gift inter vivos [§205]

An inter vivos gift is a gift made during the donor's life when the donor is not under any threat of impending death. The ordinary gift is an inter vivos ("during life") gift. An inter vivos gift, once made, is *irrevocable*. The donor cannot get the object back. (Of course the donee could, if she wished, give it back.)

b. Gift causa mortis [§206]

A gift causa mortis is a gift made in *contemplation of immediately approaching death*. The requirements for making an inter vivos gift and a gift causa mortis are substantially the same, although a court may be more strict in the case of a gift causa mortis, as there may be greater danger of fraudulent claims because the donor is dead and cannot speak. A gift causa mortis is *revoked if the donor recovers* from the illness that prompted the gift. In practical effect, a gift causa mortis is a substitute for a will—*i.e.*, a deathbed will where the donor, instead of making a written will, delivers the object to the donee.

Example: O, having suffered a cerebral hemorrhage, and critically ill, hands over some stock certificates to A, saying, "If anything happens to me, these stocks are yours." O dies shortly thereafter. This is a valid gift causa mortis. The words implying "if I die" do not state a condition precedent, but are merely the expression of the condition attached by law to every gift causa mortis—that it does not become irrevocable until the donor dies.

EXAM TIP	**gilbert**

An exam question may require you to distinguish between an inter vivos gift and a gift causa mortis. To do so you must analyze the facts carefully to determine the *intent of the donor:* Did the donor intend the gift to be *irrevocable,* or was it made *in contemplation of death and to be revoked* if death does not ensue? Note that it is possible to be near death and still make an ordinary inter vivos gift. For example, suppose Husband says to Wife, "Since I'm dying soon and won't be around for your birthday, I want to give you your birthday present now," and hands her a wrapped gift. The language about dying should make you think about a gift causa mortis, but if you consider these facts carefully, you will realize that it was not actually made in contemplation of his death (he would have given his wife a birthday gift anyway), and it clearly was not revocable if he does not die.

2. Intent [§207]

The donor must intend to *pass title presently*, and not merely to transfer possession. In the absence of a deed of gift, intent will always have to be shown by extrinsic evidence. The requirement of delivery sustains intent by requiring an objective act—but *intent* and *delivery* are *separate requirements*.

a. Promise compared [§208]

A promise to give property *in the future* is *not* a gift. A gift transfers title to the donee right now. A gratuitous promise (*i.e.*, a promise without consideration) is not enforceable as a gift or under the law of contracts (because there was no consideration).

3. Delivery [§209]

In the leading case of **Cochrane v. Moore**, 25 Q.B.D. 57 (1890), affirming **Irons v. Smallpiece**, 106 Eng. Rep. 467 (1819), the English court laid down a requirement that, in a parol (*i.e.*, oral) gift, *delivery* of the chattel is required. This has been the law ever since. [**Welton v. Gallagher**, 630 P.2d 1077 (Haw. 1981)]

a. Reasons for requirement [§210]

Three reasons for delivery have been suggested:

(1) Ritual

Delivery of the chattel impresses the grantor with the *legal significance* and *finality* of the act. Once she hands over the object, she realizes it belongs to another. Or, as the common phrase goes, the grantor "must feel the wrench of delivery."

(2) Evidentiary

Delivery of the chattel is reliable, *objective* evidence of the grantor's intent to give. There is no need to rely on oral testimony; reliance is placed on the objective act of delivery. Moreover, the presence of the object in the grantee's hands substantiates his claim of a gift.

(3) Protective

Requiring delivery protects the unwary or barely competent donor from making improvident oral statements.

b. Alternative methods of delivery [§211]

The requirement of delivery does not necessarily mean that the object must be "handed over" directly to the donee. It means that the donor must do an *act* that evinces an intent to be immediately bound. Several types of acts are acceptable as substitutes for "handing over." These are called *constructive* or *symbolic* delivery. Moreover, delivery can be accomplished through a third person.

(1) Constructive delivery [§212]

Where actual manual delivery is *impracticable, constructive delivery* is permitted. A constructive delivery is the handing over of the *means* of obtaining possession and control (usually a key), or in some other way *relinquishing dominion and control* over the property.

(a) Handing over a key [§213]

The typical constructive delivery case involves the handing over of a key to a locked receptacle (*e.g.*, box, trunk, room). If it is *impracticable* to manually transfer the receptacle or the articles in the receptacle, handing over the key is constructive delivery of the contents.

EXAM TIP   **gilbert**

Remember that for constructive delivery to be permitted, delivery of the object of the gift *must be impracticable*.

Example: O, lying on his deathbed, calls in his housekeeper Julia, hands her the keys to all the furniture in the house, and says she is to have everything in the house. In his bedroom bureau, which one of the keys unlocks, is an insurance policy. O has not made a gift of the insurance policy because it is in the room where O lies dying and is capable of manual delivery. Julia does, however, receive as a gift all the furniture unlocked by the keys (either a constructive or symbolic delivery) because it is impracticable to hand the furniture over manually. [**Newman v. Bost,** 29 S.E. 848 (N.C. 1898)]

---

1) **Safe deposit box [§214]**

Handing over the sole key to a safe deposit box has usually been sufficient constructive delivery of the contents. But where the donor hands over one of two keys, and keeps the other, the cases are divided as to whether this is constructive delivery. A number of courts have held that because the donor can still enter the box, the donor has not surrendered dominion and control. [**Hocks v. Jeremiah,** 759 P.2d 312 (Or. 1988)] If the facts show that the donor did not, after delivering the key, go into the box, the case is stronger for a gift.

(b) **Donor deems acts sufficient [§215]**

Constructive delivery can be broadly defined to include any acts that the donor deems sufficient to pass a present interest to the donee. This approach, deemphasizing delivery and emphasizing intent, is more concerned with whether, on the facts, the ritual and evidentiary purposes of delivery (*supra,* §210) are met. [**Elyachar v. Gerel Corp.,** 583 F. Supp. 907 (S.D.N.Y. 1984)]

Example: O, depressed from being injured in an auto accident, receives a check for $17,400 from the insurance company. O indorses the check in blank and puts it with a suicide note to her lover, giving all her possessions to him. O leaves her apartment and commits suicide. This has been held a valid constructive delivery of a gift causa mortis. [**Scherer v. Hyland,** 380 A.2d 698 (N.J. 1977)]

(2) Symbolic delivery [§216]

Where actual manual delivery is *impracticable* because the chattel is too large, or the situation of the parties will not permit it, *symbolic delivery* is permitted. A symbolic delivery is the handing over of some object that is symbolic of the thing given. The most common example of symbolic delivery is where the donor hands over an *instrument in writing* under circumstances where manual delivery is difficult or impracticable.

Example: Leopold Cohn, in the presence of his entire family, in New Jersey, on his wife's birthday, writes out and hands to his wife the following: "I give this day to my wife, Sara, as a birthday present 500 shares of Sumatra Tobacco Company stock. [signed] Leopold Cohn." Cohn owns the stock, but it is in the name of his partnership and is in the firm's safe deposit box in New York. The partnership has been dissolved but the shares have not yet been reregistered in Cohn's name. Because it is impracticable to deliver the stock, the writing is a sufficient symbolic delivery and the gift is good. [*In re* **Cohn,** 187 A.D. 392 (1919)]

(a) Sealed instrument [§217]

Title to a chattel could be transferred at common law by a *deed*, as well as by delivery of the chattel, but the word "deed" referred only to a sealed instrument. At modern law, the distinction between sealed and unsealed instruments has been abolished, but it is probable that a sealed instrument may still be used for transferring a chattel without delivery of the chattel. [**Grymes v. Hone,** 49 N.Y. 17 (1872)]

(b) Unsealed instrument [§218]

Whether an unsealed instrument is effective today to make a gift without delivering the chattel is debatable. The cases are conflicting. A number of courts still follow the old rule that a gift by an unsealed writing is ineffectual without delivery of the chattel. But there are modern cases holding that a gift can be made by an ordinary writing.

Example: O, in a hospital about to undergo serious surgery, writes a note to her husband and puts it on a table by her bed: "In my bedroom closet you will find $75 and my savings bank book. I give these to you. Your kissing, loving wife." O's husband finds the note when he comes to the hospital. O dies in the operation. *Held:* 4 to 3, that no gift has been made. Although the informal writing establishes O's desire to make a gift, it does not satisfy the separate and distinct requirement of delivery because the donor was not by the writing deprived of her control over the property. [**Foster v. Reiss,** 112 A.2d 553 (N.J. 1955); *but see* the later New

Jersey case of **Scherer v. Hyland,** *supra,* §215—seemingly disapproves of *Foster*]

---

1) **Distinguish impracticability of manual delivery [§219]**

If manual delivery is *impracticable*, some courts may give effect to an informal writing as a symbolic delivery, although they would not permit a writing to suffice if manual delivery were practicable.

Example: O writes out and hands to A a memorandum reading: "I give my watch and my grand piano to A as a birthday present." O is wearing the watch, and the grand piano is in the room where O and A are. If the court permits symbolic delivery only where physical delivery is impracticable, O has made a gift of the piano but not of the watch, which she could easily hand over. If the court permits a gift by delivery of a writing whether or not manual delivery is impracticable, then O has made a gift of the piano and the watch.

---

2) **Exceptions—intangible interests [§220]**

A chose in action (*e.g.,* a debt) not evidenced by a written instrument can be transferred by a written assignment. A remainder interest, which has no physical existence, can also be transferred by a written assignment. [**Gruen v. Gruen,** 68 N.Y.2d 48 (1986)]

(3) **Delivery through third person [§221]**

A donor can deliver a chattel to a third party as agent to hold for the donee. If the third party is the *agent of the donor, no gift* takes place until the donor's agent delivers the chattel to the donee. *Rationale:* Because the donor can control her agent, she has not parted with dominion and control. On the other hand, if the third party is the *agent of the donee* or an *independent agent*, the gift is effective on delivery to the donee's agent.

EXAM TIP	**gilbert**

When a gift becomes effective may be important to an exam question. As indicated, the time of effectiveness of a gift through an agent can best be remembered by considering **who controls the agent**. A donor who has sent a gift via his own agent can theoretically recall the agent at the last minute; but a donor who delivers a gift to the **donee's agent** has no power to instruct the agent to return the gift. This rule is easy to state, but it is often difficult to determine whose agent the third party is. This usually depends on the intent of the donor, which may be unclear. You have to read the facts closely.

gilbert

	CIRCUMSTANCES	EXAMPLE
ACTUAL PHYSICAL DELIVERY	Donor **physically vests** donee **with possession** of the item such that donee has dominion and control over it	X hands a pearl necklace to Y
CONSTRUCTIVE DELIVERY	**Actual manual delivery is impracticable**; donor surrenders the **means** of obtaining possession and control	X, intending to give Y a two-ton safe and its contents, gives Y a slip of paper with the combination written on it
SYMBOLIC DELIVERY	**Actual manual delivery is impracticable**; donor hands over some object **symbolic of the thing given**	X executes a document stating that he is giving to Y a certain two-ton sculpture currently on loan to an art museum
DELIVERY THROUGH THIRD PERSON	Donor instructs **his agent to deliver** a gift to donee	X tells jewelry store (X's agent) to deliver a pearl necklace to Y
	Donor delivers gift **to agent of donee**	X personally delivers a pearl necklace for Y to Y's butler

Example: O sells Blackacre to A, taking back a promissory note by A to pay B $500. The note is secured by a mortgage on Blackacre. O sends the note and mortgage to his lawyer, telling the lawyer to record the mortgage and mail the note and mortgage to B, as a gift from O. The lawyer records the mortgage, but fails to mail the note and mortgage to B. O tells B that he has given her $500. A year later the lawyer returns the note and mortgage to O. If the lawyer is the donor's agent, there has been no delivery and no gift. [**Bickford v. Mattocks,** 50 A. 894 (Me. 1901)]

(a) Gift to be delivered on death [§222]

Often property will be handed to a third party with directions by the donor to deliver the property to the donee on the donor's death. This is a will substitute, and some courts formerly held it to be *testamentary* and *void*, because it was not in accordance with the requirements of the Statute of Wills (a written instrument signed in front of two witnesses, who also must sign, is required for a valid will in most jurisdictions). This is rather silly, because if the event were anything other than donor's death, the gift would be good—provided, of course, that the agent is the *agent of the donee*. Most modern cases uphold a gift where the property is delivered to a third party to be delivered to the donee on the donor's death. [**Innes v. Potter,** 153 N.W. 604 (Minn. 1915)]

1) Other contingencies [§223]

A direction to the third party to deliver to the donee *if the donee survives* the donor is usually held a valid delivery. The contingency can be any event, as long as it is one over which the donor has no control. If the donor can *control* the event, or if the donor can *get the property back* from the third party on demand (*i.e.,* revoke the gift), the attempted gift is not good. The donor has not surrendered dominion and control.

c. Revocable gifts [§224]

Although there are a few cases to the contrary, the general rule is that no gift is made when the donor retains the right to revoke the gift. It does not matter whether delivery has been made to the donee or to a third person for the donee. Retaining the power to revoke is said to be inconsistent with surrendering dominion and control (necessary for a gift) and also inconsistent with transferring a present interest.

Example: O deposits money in a bank account in the name of his two minor daughters, subject to his own order. O retains the passbook and makes deposits and withdrawals as he pleases in the names of his daughters.

O has no intention to vest control in his daughters until his death, and no gift has been made. [**Tygard v. McComb,** 54 Mo. App. 85 (1893)]

---

(1) Distinguish—revocable trust [§225]

A donor can transfer property to X in *trust* for a donee and retain the power to revoke the trust (*see infra,* §569). Revocable trusts are in wide use today. If a trust can be made revocable, why cannot a gift? Permitting the donor to retain *orally* the power to revoke a delivered gift would of course stir up much litigation if the donor changed her mind and wanted the object back. It would be conducive to fraud. But if the terms of the gift, including the power of revocation, are in a *written instrument* that accompanies delivery, it is not easy to say why a revocable gift should not be permitted—provided the object is still in the hands of the donee when the donor revokes the gift. There is no danger of fraud, and ritual and evidentiary purposes of delivery are satisfied. Perhaps the explanation is that the law of gifts still pays obeisance to the shibboleth that the donor must surrender dominion and control to make an effective transfer, whereas the law of trusts is more concerned with carrying out intent and less concerned with dogma.

d. Goods in possession of donee [§226]

If the goods are in the possession of the donee (usually as bailee), it is not necessary that they be redelivered to the donor and then delivered again from the donor to the donee. In this case, delivery is dispensed with; *proving the intent* of the donor *by clear and convincing evidence* is all that is necessary.

EXAM TIP	gilbert

Delivery is reliable and objective evidence of the donor's intent to make a gift. Because the delivery requirement is dispensed with when the donee already has possession, *donative intent must be very clear*.

e. Oral trusts [§227]

An oral trust of real property is forbidden by the Statute of Frauds, which requires a written instrument for the creation of an interest in land. The Statute of Frauds does not apply to personal property, and an oral trust of personal property can be created. There are two kinds of oral trusts—one where a third party is trustee and the other where the settlor is trustee.

(1) Transfer in trust [§228]

If O transfers property to X in trust for A, O must deliver the property to X. The ordinary rules of delivery (discussed above) apply.

(2) Declaration of trust [§229]

If O orally declares himself trustee of goods for the benefit of A, *no delivery is required*. It would be stupid to require O to deliver (hand over) goods to himself as trustee. This is a major loophole in the requirement of delivery. It is not necessary for O to use the words "declare myself trustee" if the evidence shows that O intended to hold the property as trustee.

---

e.g. Example: Thomas Smith buys some bearer bonds and puts them in his safe deposit box in an envelope reading: "13 P & A railroad bonds, $1,000 each, held for Tom Smith Kelly. [signed] Thomas Smith." Smith keeps an account book in which he credits the interest from the bonds to Tom, but does not give Tom any interest from the bonds before his death. The evidence is sufficient to hold that Smith declared himself trustee of the bonds for Tom. No delivery is required. The transfer in trust is valid. [*In re* **Smith's Estate,** 22 A. 916 (Pa. 1891)]

---

4. Acceptance [§230]

Acceptance by the donee is required for a gift. The donee can reject the gift if he wants. But the law *presumes acceptance* when the gift is beneficial to the donee. Sometimes this is stated this way: The gift takes effect immediately upon delivery, subject to the right of the donee to repudiate the gift.

C. Bona Fide Purchasers of Personal Property

1. Nature of Problem [§231]

With land, title records are kept in a county courthouse, and a purchaser can learn whether his seller has title to the land he wants to buy by searching the public records. With regard to personal property, generally there is no comparable system of recorded titles. (Imagine what kind of system would be required to document title to autos, television sets, watches, art, clothes, jewelry, books, cows, etc. It might, of course, be more feasible in these days of computer storage, but it still would have to contain a staggering amount of information all indexed so that the information about each item would be retrievable. Because personal property—unlike land—can be moved from state to state, or outside the country, it might have to include all personal property in the United States—or, for completeness, in the world!) Because the purchaser of personal property cannot easily ascertain that the seller has title, can the purchaser rely on the *possession* of the seller as transferring title to him? If the seller is in wrongful possession (*e.g.*, by theft or fraud), will the buyer prevail over the true owner? The rules discussed below apply to this situation.

2. General Rule [§232]

The general rule is that the seller can transfer *no better title than he has.* If the seller does not own the object or lawfully represent the owner, the buyer does not get title. [**Hessen v. Iowa Automobile Mutual Insurance Co.**, 190 N.W. 150 (Iowa 1922)] This is a harsh rule that has been mitigated to some extent by exceptions in favor of a *bona fide purchaser* ("BFP") in a *few situations*. First, consider the exceptions and then consider who is a BFP. The Uniform Commercial Code, enacted in all states, has changed the common law in some respects.

3. Exceptions

a. Seller has voidable title [§233]

If the seller has a "voidable" title, he can transfer a good title to a BFP. This exception is included in Uniform Commercial Code section 2-403(1) (enacted in all states): "A person with voidable title has power to transfer a good title to a good faith purchaser for value." A voidable title is one the *owner can void* (*e.g.*, where the title is acquired by fraud or by a check which bounces). [**Sheridan Suzuki, Inc. v. Caruso Auto Sales, Inc.**, 110 Misc. 2d 823 (1981)]

Example: Walter Gwynne falsely represents to O that he is Baldwin Gwynne, a man of financial responsibility. In reliance on this representation, O delivers a quantity of jewelry to Walter. Walter in turn sells it to A, a BFP. A wins over O. Why? O intended to transfer title to Walter, even though O was mistaken as to Walter's identity. O could have voided the title in Walter before Walter sold to A, a BFP, but, after A relies on Walter's possession, it would now be unfair for O to void the title. [**Phelps v. McQuade**, 220 N.Y. 232 (1917)]

---

(1) Reason for exception [§234]

There is a general equitable principle—which appears in various guises in the law—that where one of two innocent persons must suffer by the fraudulent act of a third person, the one who could have prevented the harm to the other should suffer the loss. Applied here, that principle means that O, rather than the BFP, should suffer the loss, because O could have prevented the loss to the BFP (by not delivering the goods to the imposter), whereas there is nothing the BFP could do to prevent loss to O.

(2) Distinguish—void title [§235]

A *voidable* title is one where the owner intends to pass title, but can void the transaction because of fraud, misrepresentation, or duress. A *void* title is one where the owner does not intend to pass title or has no capacity to do so. The best example is a title acquired by theft. A *BFP from a thief takes no title*. *Rationale:* If a purchaser from a thief were protected, owners would spend a larger amount of resources in securing their property from theft. Such "defense expenditures" are not socially productive. Also, persons whose property is stolen have done nothing to cause a third person (a BFP) to be harmed.

b. Estoppel [§236]

If the owner of goods by words or conduct *expressly or impliedly represents* that the possessor is the owner or is authorized to pass title, and this *induces reliance* by the purchaser, the owner is estopped to deny the truth of the representation. Estoppel is a general principle running through the law.

Example: O, a piano mover, delivers possession of a wagon to George Tracy, a new employee of O. To retain the business Tracy has built up for himself as a piano mover, O paints on the wagon the words, "George Tracy, Piano Mover." Tracy sells the wagon to B, a BFP. O is estopped to deny that Tracy is the owner. [**O'Connor v. Clark,** 32 A. 1029 (Pa. 1895)]

---

c. Entrusting goods to a merchant

(1) Common law rule [§237]

The common law principle of estoppel might apply to the situation where an owner entrusted goods to a merchant in the business of selling goods. But mere delivery of possession to the merchant was not enough to estop the owner. The owner must have done more, such as *stand by* while the merchant displays the goods with goods for sale, or clothe the merchant with *apparent authority* to dispose of the article (*e.g.*, giving the merchant a bill of sale or letting the merchant put his name on the item). [**Porter v. Wertz,** 68 A.D.2d 141 (1979)]

(2) Uniform Commercial Code [§238]

The Uniform Commercial Code ("U.C.C."), enacted in all states, provides for statutory estoppel as applied to entrusting goods to a merchant. This statutory estoppel does not replace but supplements the common law; if the facts come within *either* the requirements of common law estoppel *or* the requirements of the U.C.C., the owner is estopped. The U.C.C. provides that the *mere act of entrusting* is sufficient to protect the BFP; additional acts giving the merchant apparent authority to dispose of the article are not necessary. Section 2-403(2), (3) provides:

> (2) Any entrusting of possession of goods to a *merchant who deals in goods of that kind* gives him power to transfer all rights of the entruster to a *buyer in ordinary course of business.*

> (3) "Entrusting" includes any delivery and any acquiescence in retention of possession regardless of any condition expressed between the parties to the delivery or acquiescence and regardless of whether

the procurement of the entrusting or the possessor's disposition of the goods have been such as to be larcenous under the criminal law.

Example: O entrusts a painting to A, an art dealer, for examination. A gives the painting to a friend, B, a delicatessen employee. B, representing that he owns the painting, sells it to C, a BFP. If C had purchased the painting from A, a merchant, C would prevail over O. But because C bought the painting from B, O prevails over C for three distinct reasons: (i) B is not the merchant entrusted by O; (ii) B is not an art merchant; and (iii) the sale was not in "the ordinary course of B's business" because B did not deal in paintings. [*See* **Porter v. Wertz**, 53 N.Y.2d 696 (1981)]

---

4. Bona Fide Purchaser [§239]

A BFP is one who *does not know* of the seller's wrongful possession but has a *good faith belief* that the seller has title and, in addition, pays *valuable consideration*. A BFP is protected under the above exceptions to the general rule, but a buyer who is *not* a BFP is *never protected*.

Example: A obtains possession of O's watch by fraudulent representation, giving A a voidable title. A sells the watch to B, a BFP. B prevails over O. If A had *given* the watch to B, or if B had *known* of the fraud, B would not be a BFP and would not prevail over O.

---

a. Rationale

A BFP has a strong appeal to the conscience of a court, whereas a person who knows of the wrong or is not financially damaged has no such appeal to equity.

b. Inquiry notice [§240]

To be a BFP, a purchaser must have *no actual* notice of the seller's wrongful title *nor any inquiry notice*. "Inquiry notice" is notice the purchaser is deemed to have when the facts and circumstances should lead a reasonable person to make inquiries. From these inquiries, the purchaser would have learned of the defect in the seller's title.

Example: A, a poor man, acquires a very expensive oil painting from O on credit when he has no reasonable expectations of paying for it and no intention of paying for it. (This is fraud, and A has a voidable title.) A sells the painting to B. If the circumstances should make B suspicious (*e.g.*, A is dressed in rags, and B has earlier seen the painting hanging in O's shop), B must make inquiry of O to see if O has passed title to A. [*See* **Higgins v. Lodge**, 11 A. 846 (Md. 1888)]

Chapter Three: Possessory Estates

CONTENTS

Chapter Approach

Chapter Approach

This chapter and those following acquaint you with the historic "law of estates." The estate system originated in feudal times but still underlies our present property law. It is an entirely artificial way of thinking about ownership, known only to Anglo-American law, but something you must master. If it seems strange at first, be assured that it will become more familiar in time. The core ideas are essential tools of analysis for your Property exam and for everyday property problems.

This chapter covers three of the four possessory estates in land (there are also nonpossessory future interests, which will be discussed in chapter IV): (i) the *fee simple*; (ii) the *fee tail*; and (iii) the *life estate*. (The fourth, the *leasehold*, is discussed in chapter VI.) Estates are classified by *duration*. Remember that there are only four possessory estates, and any present possessory interest must be classified as one of these. To identify an estate:

1. Look for the **technical language** that creates the estate (*e.g.*, "and his heirs," "and the heirs of his body," etc.). Although this language may no longer be necessary to make a valid conveyance, lawyers use it, and it is often found on exams.

2. Consider how long the estate can **endure** (*e.g.*, forever, for someone's life, until the happening of some event, etc.).

And be sure to review the summary of possessory estates *infra*, §365.

A. Introduction

1. The Feudal Background [§241]

In 1066, William of Normandy crossed the English Channel, conquered England, and claimed it as his own. William parcelled out land to his supporters and imposed on England a highly organized feudal system. Out of the feudal system developed a system of estates in land, which is fundamental to modern property law.

a. Land tenure [§242]

A basic principle of the feudal system was that every landowner, save the king, had a lord above him. The king granted vast acreage to his tenants-in-chief, who in turn granted part of this large acreage to other tenants, who might subinfeudate further. Every tenant owed *services* to his lord, which might be fighting for the lord, laboring on the lord's land, furnishing foodstuffs for the lord's household, or payment of money rent. By this process of subinfeudation, a feudal ladder was developed, with the possessor of land at the bottom and the lords above him entitled to various services (comparable to modern rents).

(1) Feudal incidents [§243]

In addition to services, tenants were liable for *feudal incidents*, which generally came due on the tenant's death and were a form of inheritance tax. The principal incidents were *relief* (payment by the heir to relieve the land from the lord's grasp), *wardship* (the lord was entitled to possession of the land, including rents and profits, while the heir was a minor), *marriage* (the lord could sell the marriage of a minor heir), and *escheat* (the land reverted to the lord if the tenant died without heirs). The feudal incidents were very lucrative to the lords and, together with the services, provided the economic support for the feudal system. The feudal incidents were also important in the historical development of property law, for landowners tried to avoid them (much as people today try to avoid inheritance taxes). Courts laid down several rules that had the effect of preserving feudal incidents for the lords (*e.g.*, the destructibility of contingent remainders, *infra*, §464; the Rule in Shelley's Case, *infra*, §483; and the Doctrine of Worthier Title, *infra*, §507). And Henry VIII forced through Parliament the Statute of Uses (1536), which had the purpose of restoring the king's feudal incidents that clever lawyers had been able to bypass. The Statute of Uses (*infra*, §460) laid the foundation for modern conveyancing and the modern trust. The avoidance of taxation begot new property arrangements and continues to do so today.

2. The System of Estates

a. Historic development [§244]

Out of feudalism developed the system of estates in land, which remains central to our modern law, both in theory and in practice. Although a nonlawyer talks about owning "property" or "land," what he holds legally is an *estate* in land. An estate is an interest in land that *is or may become possessory*. More important at the moment, in understanding the development of the law, an estate is an interest *measured by some period of time*. In feudal days, a tenant was granted land by his lord for some period of time—*e.g.*, for life, for 10 years, for so long as he kept up the bridges. Gradually the law simplified and categorized these holdings by developing a system of estates. Dealing with standardized estates rather than with the hundreds of different tenurial arrangements as to duration made the law easier to administer. And so it came about that the judges recognized only three types of freehold estates and three types of leasehold estates. Lord and tenant had to fit their wishes into one of these six categories, although some variations within a category were permitted.

(1) **Distinguish—other meanings of estate [§245]**

The word "estate" is often used in other senses, such as referring to an area of land, *e.g.*, "Jones has an estate in the country," or to property in general, *e.g.*, "Jones died with an estate worth $100,000." Such usage does not occur in this chapter.

b. **Types of estates [§246]**

The common law developed the following estates, each indicating the period of time for which the land might be held.

(1) **Fee simple [§247]**

A fee simple is an estate that has the potential of *enduring forever.* It is created by O, the owner of Blackacre, granting the land "to A and his heirs." This estate resembles absolute ownership, and the holder of a fee simple is commonly called the owner of the land (*see infra*, §256).

(2) **Fee tail [§248]**

A fee tail is an estate that has the potential of enduring forever, but *will necessarily cease if and when the first fee tail tenant has no lineal descendants to succeed him in possession.* A fee tail is created by O granting the property "to A and the heirs of his body" (*see infra*, §300).

(3) **Life estate [§249]**

A life estate is an estate that will end necessarily *at the death of a person.* It is created by granting the property "to A for life" (*see infra*, §321).

(4) **Leasehold estate [§250]**

Leasehold estates include estates that endure: (i) *for any fixed calendar period* or any period of time computable by the calendar (called a "term of years" regardless of the length of the period); *or* (ii) from *period to period* until the landlord or tenant gives notice to terminate at the end of a period (called a "periodic tenancy"); *or* (iii) so long as *both the landlord and tenant desire* (called a "tenancy at will"). (Leasehold estates are dealt with in detail in chapter VI of this Summary.)

EXAM TIP   **gilbert**

Keep in mind that there are only these four present possessory estates. Any *present* estate in land has to be one of these four. There are no other options. To decide which estate it is, you need only to (i) look for the *special technical language* ("to A and his heirs"—fee simple; "to A and the heirs of his body"—fee tail, "to A for life"—life estate, and other language for leaseholds, *see infra*, §§258, 301, 322, 770, 775), and (ii) consider the *duration of the estate*. (See also *infra*, §255.)

c. Freehold and nonfreehold estates [§251]

The fee simple, fee tail, and life estate are "freehold" estates. Freehold was the highest form of holding under feudal tenure. The leasehold interests are not freehold because in the early feudal system they were not considered to be estates at all but merely personal contracts. The important difference between freehold and nonfreehold estates is that a freeholder in possession has *"seisin,"* whereas a leaseholder has only *possession*.

(1) Seisin [§252]

"Seisin" was an important concept in feudal times. A person seised of the land was responsible for the feudal services, and feudal incidents (taxes) were due on the death of a person holding seisin (a freehold tenant in possession). Hence, to keep wealth flowing to the top of the feudal ladder, some person always had to be responsible for these feudal charges. The rule was: There could never be an abeyance of seisin (*see infra*, §465).

d. Hierarchy of estates [§253]

At common law, estates were ranked according to their potential duration. A *fee simple* was longer in potential duration than a *fee tail*, which was longer than a *life estate*. All freehold estates were presumed to be longer in duration than a leasehold.

Example: O, owner of a fee simple, conveys a fee tail to A. (This leaves a reversion in O—the property will return to O when the fee tail expires.) A then conveys a life estate to B. (This leaves a reversion in A—the property will return to A at the death of B. If A's fee tail ends during B's life, the property will return to O.)

e. Estates in personal property [§254]

The law of estates developed at a time when land was the only property of substantial value, and it is sometimes called the law of estates in land. As personal property grew in amount and importance, the courts applied the system of estates to personal property. Because of the feudal origins of estates, there is technically a fee simple only in land ("fee" originally meant "fief"); the correlative estate in personal property is "absolute ownership." However, "fee simple" in land and "absolute ownership" of personal property are functional equivalents. "Absolute ownership," like the fee simple, can be divided into smaller possessory estates (such as a life estate), followed by future interests. Generally, the same types of possessory estates and future interests can be created in personal property as can be created in real property.

f. No new estates may be created [§255]

The fee simple, the fee tail, the life estate, and the leasehold estates are the only estates permissible. New types cannot be created. If an attempt is made to create a new type of estate, the language of the creating instrument will be construed to create an estate within *one of the existing* categories.

Example: Royal Whiton devises land "to my granddaughter Sarah *and her heirs on her father's side*." The highlighted words do not fit into any of the categories of estates. Royal is trying to create an estate that will descend only to Sarah's paternal kin. The law knows no such estate as this. The court will construe the highlighted words so that they fit within an accepted category of estate. The closest estate is a fee simple, created by a devise "to Sarah *and her heirs*." Hence Sarah has a fee simple, which she can dispose of by deed or will. If she does not transfer the fee simple, it will descend at her death to her heirs generally, maternal as well as paternal. [**Johnson v. Whiton**, 34 N.E. 542 (Mass. 1893)]

B. The Fee Simple

1. Fee Simple Absolute [§256]

A fee simple absolute is absolute ownership, so far as absolute ownership is known to Anglo-American law. It is of *potentially infinite duration* (therefore called a "fee"). There are *no limitations on its inheritability* (therefore called "simple"). It *cannot be divested*, nor will it end on the happening of *any* event (hence called "absolute").

EXAM TIP   **gilbert**

A fee simple absolute is what most lay people think of when they think of owning property. This estate gives the owner the *maximum rights* in the land.

---

a. Words of purchase and words of limitation [§257]

Estates are created by using appropriate words in a deed or will. *"Words of purchase"* identify the *person* in whom the estate is created. *"Words of limitation"* are words describing the *type of estate* created. Thus, where O conveys Blackacre "to A and her heirs," the words "to A" are words of purchase, identifying A as the taker. ("Purchase" here has nothing to do with the modern meaning of the word; rather it signifies only that the person takes by deed or will, and not by intestate succession.) The words "and her heirs" are words of limitation, indicating a fee simple.

b. Creation of a fee simple [§258]

At common law it was necessary to use words of inheritance ("and his heirs") to create a fee simple by deed. In early feudal times, the tenant held land only for his life; the lord had no obligation to accept his heir in his place (after all, the heir might be a weakling). Tenants quite naturally wanted the land to pass to their heirs at their death, and so the tenants bargained with the lords for inheritability. If the lord agreed to accept the tenant's heir in his place at his death, the lord granted the land "to the tenant and his heirs." Thus the lord assented to descent. In time, an inheritable estate known as a fee simple developed—and the words "and his heirs" were necessary to create it.

Example: O, owner in fee simple, conveys "to A in fee simple." *At common law*, A takes only a life estate. To create a fee simple, O should have conveyed "to A and his heirs."

(1) Heirs have no present interest [§259]

A grant "to A and his heirs" gives A's heirs no interest in the property. The words "and his heirs" are only words of limitation indicating that A takes a fee simple. A can sell or give away the fee simple, or devise it by will, thus depriving A's heirs of the land.

Example: O conveys land "to A and his heirs." A then gives the land to B. A's heir, H, has no interest in the land (only a hope of inheriting it) and cannot prevent the gift.

(2) Modern law [§260]

The ancient requirement of words of inheritance in a deed ("and his heirs") has been abolished in all states. Under modern law, a deed or will is *presumed to pass the largest estate the grantor or testator owned.* Thus, a conveyance of Blackacre "to A" conveys a fee simple if the grantor had a fee simple. But, in spite of the abolition of the necessity of using words of inheritance, lawyers, being creatures of centuries of habit, still use them in creating a fee simple.

EXAM TIP	gilbert

As indicated, under modern law, a transfer "to A" is sufficient to convey fee simple ownership. Words of inheritance (*i.e.,* "and his heirs") are **not** necessary. However, on your exam you are most likely going to find the *traditional technical language* ("to A and his heirs"), and so you should be familiar with it.

c. Transferability [§261]

The Statute Quia Emptores (1290) gave all freehold tenants the right to transfer their land without the lord's consent. Subsequently, in 1540, the Statute of Wills gave fee simple owners the right to devise their land. If the fee simple owner does not devise his land but dies without a will, the fee simple is inherited by the owner's heirs.

(1) Heirs defined [§262]

The word "heirs" means those persons who succeed to the *real property* of an intestate decedent (*i.e.,* one who died without a valid will) under a state's statute of intestate succession (sometimes called the *statute of descent*).

EXAM TIP — **gilbert**

For lawyers, remember that "heirs" is **not** a synonym for children, although it is sometimes used that way by nonlawyers. Thus, if O dies leaving a husband and a child, and under the intestate succession law the husband and child succeed to title to O's land, O's heirs are her husband and child.

(a) Spouse at common law [§263]

At English common law a spouse could not be an heir; he or she was given only curtesy or dower in real property (*see infra,* §§708-717). This disqualification of the spouse as an heir has been abolished in all states. In most states, dower and curtesy have been abolished, and the spouse is given a fractional share as heir of the decedent.

(b) Next of kin [§264]

The term "next of kin" refers to those persons who succeed to the *personal property* of an intestate decedent under the applicable statute of intestate succession (sometimes called the *statute of distribution*). At English law, the successors to real and personal property were not necessarily the same. Land passed under the rule of primogeniture to the eldest son ("the heir," as he was commonly referred to in England). Personal property was divided equally among all children. Primogeniture was abolished in this country shortly after the American Revolution, and today all children—male and female—share equally. In almost all states today the same persons succeed to a decedent's personal property as succeed to the decedent's land. Hence, in most states, "next of kin" and "heirs" are synonymous.

(2) Typical statute [§265]

It should be obvious from the above discussion of the meaning of "heirs" that the word "heirs" cannot be given content without looking at some statute of intestate succession. These statutes vary considerably from state to state, but the following represents the general pattern of the Uniform Probate Code, adopted in many states:

(a) Share of spouse [§266]

If the decedent leaves a spouse, the spouse takes one-half. The other one-half goes to the decedent's issue or, if no issue, to the decedent's parents or, if no parents, to the spouse.

(b) Share of issue

1) Issue defined [§267]

The word "issue" means children, grandchildren, great-grandchildren, and all further descendants. It is synonymous with "descendants," a term often used by nonlawyers for what lawyers call "issue."

2) Children's share [§268]

If the decedent leaves a spouse and children, the spouse takes half, and the children divide half. If the decedent leaves no spouse, the children take all in equal shares.

a) Representation [§269]

If a child *predeceases the decedent*, leaving issue, the issue *represent* the child and take the child's portion. This is called a *per stirpes* (by the roots) distribution. The principle of representation can get complicated when several issue predecease the decedent. (*See* Wills Summary.)

b) Grandchildren's share [§270]

Grandchildren do not take if their parent is alive. Generally speaking—and subject to much variation if the decedent leaves no children but only grandchildren and more remote issue—grandchildren share only under the principle of representation.

> **Example:** O dies intestate, leaving no spouse, a child A, and two sons of a child B who predeceased O. A and the two sons of B are O's heirs. A takes one-half; the two sons of B, representing B, divide the other half.

3) Adopted children [§271]

An adopted child is treated as a child of the adoptive parents and, in some states, as a child of the natural parents as well.

4) Nonmarital children [§272]

A child born out of wedlock inherits as a child of her mother and, if paternity is established, as a child of her father. (On inheritance from the father there is great variation from state to state.)

5) Stepchildren [§273]

Stepchildren do not take. Except for the spouse and adopted children, *only blood relatives* of the decedent take as heirs.

(c) Share of parents [§274]

If the decedent leaves issue, parents do not take. If the decedent leaves a spouse and no issue, parents take one-half and the spouse one-half. If the decedent leaves no spouse and no issue, parents take all.

(d) Collateral relatives [§275]

The term "collateral relatives" includes all blood kin except ancestors and descendants. Hence it includes brothers, sisters, nephews, nieces, uncles, aunts, and cousins. If the decedent leaves no spouse, issue, or parent, the collateral relatives take. The common law developed a complicated system for determining which collateral relatives took, and the rules for making this determination remain complicated today. (*See* Wills Summary.)

(e) Escheat [§276]

If a fee simple owner dies without a will and without heirs, the fee simple escheats to the state.

(3) Devisee and legatee defined [§277]

If a decedent leaves a will, the persons who are *devised* land are called *devisees*. The persons who are *bequeathed* personal property are called *legatees*.

EXAM TIP   **gilbert**

Keep the terms straight: The difference between heirs on the one hand and devisees and legatees on the other is that *heirs* take when decedent leaves *no will; devisees and legatees* take under a *will*.

---

2. Defeasible Fees [§278]

A fee simple can be created so that it is defeasible on the happening of some event, and the owner of the fee simple then loses, or may lose, the property. If the fee simple is defeasible, it is of course not absolute. The following are the three different kinds of defeasible fees simple. *Note:* All of these are called fees simple because they have the *potential* of infinite duration, although not the certainty. Defeasible fees are most commonly encountered in deeds *restricting the use* of land, but they may be used for other purposes as well.

a. Fee simple determinable

(1) Definition [§279]

A fee simple determinable is a fee simple estate so limited that it will *automatically end* when some specified event happens.

Example: O conveys Blackacre "to School Board so long as the premises are used for school purposes." The words "so long . . . purposes" are *words of limitation*, limiting the duration of the fee simple given. The School Board has a fee simple determinable that will automatically end when Blackacre ceases to be used for school purposes. When that event happens, the fee simple automatically reverts to O.

(a) Automatic termination [§280]

A fee simple determinable is a fee simple because it *may* endure forever. But, if the contingency occurs (Blackacre is used for other than school purposes, as above), the estate *automatically* ends. The estate terminates immediately on the occurrence of the event—nothing further is required—and the fee simple *automatically reverts* to the grantor. This is the distinguishing characteristic of the determinable fee.

(b) Other names for fee simple determinable [§281]

The fee simple determinable is sometimes called a "fee simple on a special limitation," "fee simple on a conditional limitation," or a "base fee," although these alternate names are now passing from usage. Whatever name is used, the same estate is meant.

(2) Creation [§282]

A determinable fee is created by language that connotes that the grantor is giving a fee simple only until a stated event happens. Traditional language to create this estate includes "to A *so long as* . . .," "to A *until* . . .," "to A *while* . . .," or language providing that on the happening of a stated event the land is to *revert* to the grantor. [**Mahrenholz v. County Board of School Trustees**, 417 N.E.2d 138 (Ill. 1981)]

(a) Motive or purpose [§283]

Words in an instrument that state the motive or purpose of the grantor do not create a determinable fee. For a determinable fee, it is necessary to use words *limiting the duration* of the estate.

Example: O conveys Blackacre "to Board of Education solely for the purpose of being used for the erection and maintenance of a public school." The Board erects a school. Thirty years later, the Board ceases to use Blackacre for a school. The Board has a fee simple absolute, not a fee simple determinable, and can do with Blackacre as it wishes. The words in the quotation marks merely state the grantor's motive. The grantor has retained no rights in Blackacre. [**Fitzgerald v. Modoc County**, 164 Cal. 493 (1913); **Roberts v. Rhodes**, 643 P.2d 116 (Kan. 1982); **Wood v. Board of County Commissioners**, 759 P.2d 1250 (Wyo. 1988); *but see* **Forsgren v. Sollie**, 659 P.2d 1068 (Utah 1983)—construing similar deed to create fee simple subject to condition subsequent (*see infra*, §286)]

(3) Transferability [§284]

A fee simple determinable may be transferred or inherited in the same manner as any other fee simple, as long as the stated event has not happened. But the *fee simple remains subject to the limitation* no matter who holds it.

(4) Correlative future interest [§285]

Because there is a possibility that the grantee's determinable fee may come to an end on the happening of the stated event, the *grantor* has a future interest called a *possibility of reverter*. A possibility of reverter may be retained expressly or may arise by operation of law. (The possibility of reverter is discussed more extensively *infra*, §§383 *et seq.*)

Example: O conveys Blackacre "to the Library Board so long as used for library purposes." By operation of law, O retains a possibility of reverter, which will automatically become possessory if and when the Library Board ceases to use Blackacre for library purposes.

b. Fee simple subject to condition subsequent

(1) Definition [§286]

A fee simple subject to condition subsequent is a fee simple that does not automatically terminate but may be *cut short* (divested) at the *grantor's election* when a stated condition happens.

Example: O conveys Blackacre "to A, but if liquor is ever sold on the premises, the grantor has a right to reenter the premises." The words "but if . . . premises" are *words of condition* setting forth the condition upon which the grantor can exercise her right of entry. They are not words limiting the fee simple granted A. A has a fee simple subject to condition subsequent. O has a right of entry. If O does not choose to exercise her right of entry when liquor is sold, the fee simple continues in A.

(a) Does not automatically end [§287]

A fee simple subject to condition subsequent is a fee simple because it may endure forever. If the contingency occurs, O merely has the *power* to reenter and to terminate the estate. The fee simple subject to condition subsequent *does not automatically end* on the happening of the condition. Rather, the estate continues in the grantee until the grantor *exercises* her power of reentry and terminates the estate. The grantor has the option of exercising the power or not.

EXAM TIP **gilbert**

Don't overlook this difference between a fee simple determinable and a fee simple subject to condition subsequent. The determinable fee *automatically* ends, regardless of whether the grantor does anything. With a fee simple subject to condition subsequent, the grantor *must act* to retake the property or the grantee's estate continues.

---

(2) Creation [§288]

A fee simple subject to condition subsequent is created by first giving the grantee an unconditional fee simple and then providing that the fee simple may be divested by the grantor or her heirs if a specified condition happens. Traditional language to create such an estate includes: "to A, *but if* X event happens . . .," or "to A, *upon condition* that if X event happens . . .," or "to A, *provided, however*, that if X event happens . . .," the grantor retains a right of entry.

(3) Transferability [§289]

This estate may be transferred or inherited in the same manner as any other fee simple until the transferor is entitled to *and does exercise* the right of entry.

(4) Correlative future interest [§290]

If the grantor creates a fee simple subject to condition subsequent, the grantor retains a *right of entry*. This interest is sometimes called a "right to reenter," a "power of termination," or a "right of reacquisition." But regardless of which name is applied, the law is the same. The law does not require that a right of entry be expressly retained by the grantor. If the words of the instrument are reasonably susceptible to the interpretation that this type of forfeitable estate was contemplated by the parties, the court will imply a right of entry. [*But see* **Storke v. Penn Mutual Life Insurance Co.**, 61 N.E.2d 552 (Ill. 1945)—court will not imply a right of entry where none is provided in a deed because equity will not aid a forfeiture] (The right of entry is discussed more extensively *infra*, §390.)

(5) Distinguished from fee simple determinable

(a) Construction of ambiguous language [§291]

These two estates are very similar and often the language in deeds can be classified either way. If the court has a choice, the *fee on condition subsequent is preferred* on the ground that the forfeiture is *optional* at the grantor's election and not automatic. The general policy of courts is to *avoid forfeiture* of estates ("equity abhors a forfeiture"). [**Storke v. Penn Mutual Life Insurance Co.**, *supra;* **Oldfield v. Stoeco Homes, Inc.**, 139 A.2d 291 (N.J. 1958)]

Example: O conveys "to A so long as intoxicating liquors are not sold on the premises, and if they are sold, O has a right to reenter." The words "so long as" point to a fee simple determinable. The retained right of entry points to a fee simple subject to condition subsequent. The court can classify the language to create either estate, but the fee simple subject to condition subsequent is preferred.

(b) Automatic vs. optional termination [§292]

The distinction between automatic and optional termination governs the consequences in several contexts. In cases of automatic termination, the fee simple goes back to the grantor by operation of law. Where termination is optional, the grantor must act affirmatively to terminate the fee simple estate.

1) Illustration—statute of limitations [§293]

In 1963, O conveys land "to School Board *so long as* used for a school, but if the Board ceases to use the land for a school, O retains *the right to reenter.*" In 1980, the Board ceases to use the land for a school but stays in possession. O does nothing. The statute of limitations is 20 years. If the Board has a fee simple determinable, the fee simple reverts to O in 1980, and the Board is thereafter in adverse possession. In the year 2000, the Board takes title by adverse possession. If the Board has a fee simple subject to condition subsequent, O's right of action is subject to the condition precedent that she elect to declare a forfeiture; hence, her right of action has not yet arisen and the statute of limitations has not run. However, some modern cases do not follow this theory, and hold that where O retains a right of entry, the statute of limitations begins to run from the time the condition is broken. [*See* **Johnson v. City of Wheat Ridge**, 532 P.2d 985 (Colo. 1975)]

(c) Restraints on marriage [§294]

Restraints on marriage are sometimes struck down as violations of public policy. If the purpose of the restraint is to *penalize* marriage, the restraint may be struck down. On the other hand, if the purpose is to give support until marriage, when the new spouse's obligation of support arises, the restraint is valid.

1) Limitation-condition distinction [§295]

Sometimes courts have resorted to a limitation-condition test to determine the validity of the restraint. A conveyance by O "to A and her heirs so long as she remains unmarried" (a fee simple determinable) is said not to be against public policy because O *intended* to give A *support* only until A's husband supported her. On the other hand, a conveyance by O "to A and her heirs, but if she marries, to B" is viewed as a penalty on marriage. Supposedly the distinction turns upon O's intent. Does O intend to provide A with support while single or to penalize A for marriage? The former is acceptable; the latter is not. But this technical distinction permits O to escape the dictates of public policy by carefully choosing the words. [**Lewis v. Searles,** 452 S.W.2d 153 (Mo. 1970)]

c. Fee simple subject to an executory limitation

(1) Definition [§296]

A fee simple subject to an executory limitation is a fee simple that, on the happening of a stated event, is automatically *divested* in favor of a *third person* (not the grantor).

Example: O conveys Blackacre "to School Board, but if within the next 20 years Blackacre is not used for school purposes, then to A." Observe that the forfeiture interest is in *another grantee*, A, and not in the grantor, O. A's future interest is called an *executory interest*. The School Board's possessory estate is called a *fee simple subject to an executory limitation*, or a *fee simple subject to an executory interest*.

Example: O conveys Blackacre "to School Board, so long as the property is used only for school purposes for the next 20 years, and if it is not, then to A." This example, in contrast to the preceding one, uses words of duration rather than condition. Words of duration, recall, are ones that create a fee simple determinable. (*See supra,* §282.) Accordingly, some lawyers say that here the School Board has a *fee simple determinable followed by an executory interest*. Others simply use the same label here as they do in the preceding example, where words of condition are used. In any event, A has an executory interest in each example.

(2) Comment

Do not worry too much about the fee simple subject to an executory limitation at this point. It will become much clearer in the next chapter (Future Interests), where the executory interest is explained in detail (§§434 *et seq.*). It must be mentioned here with the other types of defeasible fees for completeness, but the important thing to master at this point is the difference between the determinable fee, which *automatically expires*, and a fee on condition subsequent, which is *cut short*.

C. The Fee Tail

1. Historical Background [§297]

In feudal England, land was the basis of family power, status, and wealth. One of the chief objectives of landowners, particularly large landowners, was to keep land in the family. The fee tail was invented for just that purpose—to keep the land safe for succeeding generations.

a. The fee simple conditional [§298]

The first attempt of the landed lords to tie up land in the family was a *fee simple conditional*. This was created by a grant "to A and the heirs of his body." The judges held that A could convey a fee simple *if* a child were born to A. Thus, A's estate was thought of as a *fee simple conditional upon having issue.* If A had issue, A could convey a fee simple and transfer the land outside the family, cutting off the rights of A's issue and the reversioner.

b. Statute de Donis Conditionalibus (1285) [§299]

The landed lords were not happy with the judicial decisions that A could convey the land outside the family if A had a child. They sought relief in Parliament, which in those days was amenable to the wishes of the great lords. In 1285, Parliament enacted the Statute de Donis Conditionalibus. This statute abolished the fee simple conditional, and permitted the creation of a new estate in land, the fee tail.

2. Nature of Estate [§300]

A fee tail has two principal characteristics: (i) *it lasts as long as the grantee or any of his descendants survives*, and (ii) *it is inheritable only by the grantee's descendants.* (*See infra*, §304.)

3. Creation of Fee Tail [§301]

At common law, a fee tail was created by an instrument using words of inheritance and words confining succession to the issue of the grantee: "*to A and the heirs of his body.*" The term "heirs of the body" refers to the grantee's *issue* or *lineal descendants*. It includes not only children, but grandchildren and more remote descendants as well. The fee tail goes to each succeeding generation in turn.

4. **Characteristics [§302]**

The fee tail originally had two important characteristics:

a. **During tenant's life [§303]**

The tenant in fee tail for the time being (either the original grantee or his descendant) can do nothing to defeat the rights of the tenant's lineal descendants. In practical effect, he has *only a life estate*. On the death of the tenant in fee tail, the land automatically goes to his lineal descendants. *Caveat:* After 1472, the fee tail tenant could defeat the rights of his lineal descendants by disentailing (*see infra*, §313).

b. **On tenant's death [§304]**

The fee tail can be inherited only by the issue (lineal descendants) of the original grantee, and not by his collateral kin. If the blood descendants of the original grantee run out, the property is returned to the original grantor (or his heirs), or to any holder of the remainder named in the grant creating the fee tail. The fee tail cannot be devised by will.

5. **Types of Fees Tail [§305]**

Unless otherwise specified in the grant, a fee tail was inheritable by any issue of the fee tail tenant. However, the grantor could tailor the fee tail more specifically to his wishes. For example, a grantor could create a *fee tail male* that limited succession to male descendants of the grantee by granting "to A and the male heirs of his body." Likewise, a fee tail female could be created, but it was uncommon. Also, a grantor could create a *fee tail special*, which was inheritable only by the issue of a grantee and a specific spouse ("to A and the heirs of his body by his wife, B").

6. **Future Interests Following Fee Tail [§306]**

It was important to the landed aristocracy that when the fee tail expired, the land return to the family. Thus, a father might convey a tract of land to his second son, A, upon his marriage—"to A and the heirs of his body"—and desire the land to return to the father or to the father's eldest son (the heir and head of the family) if A and his issue expired. A might have a child who had a child who died without having a child, upon which event A's blood line would become extinct and the fee tail end. Fortunately for the father, the Statute de Donis Conditionalibus provided that the land would revert to him (the grantor) when the fee tail expired. It was also held that the father could direct that the land go to another upon the fee tail's expiration. Thus, the following future interests are possible to become possessory upon the expiration of the fee tail.

a. **Reversion [§307]**

O conveys Blackacre "to A and the heirs of his body." A has a fee tail; O has a reversion in fee simple to become possessory upon expiration of the fee tail. [**Long v. Long,** 343 N.E.2d 100 (Ohio 1976)]

b. Remainder [§308]

O conveys Whiteacre "to A and the heirs of his body, and if A dies without issue, to B and her heirs." A has a fee tail; B has a vested remainder in fee simple to become possessory on the expiration of the fee tail. B's interest is called a remainder, rather than a reversion, because a reversion can be created only in the grantor or testator's heirs. The analogous future interest in a grantee is called a remainder (*see infra*, §397).

c. Meaning of "dies without issue" [§309]

A remainder after a fee tail was usually introduced, as in the preceding example, by the words "if A dies without issue." What did this phrase "dies without issue" mean? As is easily seen here, when it follows a grant of a fee tail, it means "when A and all A's descendants are dead." In other words, it means the event terminating the fee tail. This construction of "dies without issue" was called *indefinite failure of issue* because the event awaited the indefinite future. Obviously it might happen hundreds of years from now.

(1) Preference for indefinite failure construction [§310]

The words "if A dies without issue" were first used in the context of a gift over following a fee tail and, as explained above, the indefinite failure of issue construction made perfect sense. English courts thought that once a phrase was defined by judges, it should have the same meaning in law thereafter regardless of whether the context was different. Hence, English courts laid down a rule that whenever "if A dies without issue" is used, it means *indefinite failure of issue* unless the grantor expressly states otherwise.

(a) A most peculiar rule of construction [§311]

Following this preference for the indefinite failure of issue construction, English courts applied it to this conveyance: "to A and his heirs, but if A dies without issue, to B and her heirs." The indefinite failure construction means when A and his descendants expire, B and her heirs get the land. That event is the same event that would terminate a fee tail in A, and so the judges, looking through form to substance, held that A had a fee tail, not a fee simple. Thus, there emerged a rule that if a remainder were limited to take effect on the death of the preceding (fee simple) tenant without issue, it converted the preceding fee simple into a fee tail. [**Caccamo v. Banning**, 75 A.2d 222 (Del. 1950)—applying rule of construction]

(2) American law [§312]

Almost all American states have abolished the preference for the indefinite failure construction. It makes no sense in contemporary American society where persons should not be presumed to intend gifts to take effect years in the future upon the expiration of a bloodline. If the grantor wants an indefinite failure construction, he must expressly say so in most states. Otherwise an instrument making a gift over to B "if A dies without issue" will be construed to mean a gift to B if, and only if, A leaves no issue alive at A's death.

7. Disentailing [§313]

The judges perceived many mischiefs in the fee tail, keeping land in the family generation after generation. No relief was to be expected from Parliament, controlled by the landed barons, so the judges set their ingenuity to work and invented a *fictitious lawsuit*, known as a **common recovery**, whereby a tenant in tail in possession could go into court and—after paying court and lawyer's fees—walk out with a *fee simple absolute*. The details of the common recovery are unimportant for purposes of this Summary; the important thing is that a tenant in tail by indulging in this fictitious lawsuit could turn his fee tail into a fee simple absolute, barring all the rights of issue, reversioners, and owners of the remainder. [**Taltarum's Case,** Y.B. 12 Edw. 4, 19 (1472)—approving the common recovery]

a. Disentailing by deed [§314]

In time simpler methods of disentailing evolved, until in the nineteenth century disentailing was permitted by a *deed* from the fee tail tenant to another.

> **Example:** O conveys Blackacre "to A and the heirs of his body, and if A dies without issue, to B and her heirs." By this conveyance A takes a fee tail, and B a vested remainder in fee simple. Thereafter A conveys by deed "to C and his heirs." The deed to C, purporting to convey a fee simple, gives C a fee simple absolute, cutting off all rights in A's issue and in B. C can now, if he wishes, convey a fee simple back to A. Hence any fee tail tenant can by deed convert his fee tail into a fee simple in another or in himself.

8. Status Under Modern Law

a. Fee tail still exists in a few states [§315]

The fee tail is permitted only in Delaware, Maine, Massachusetts, and Rhode Island. However, in these states, the fee tail tenant can at any time disentail and convey a fee simple absolute by deed, as explained above. Thus, a fee tail merely excludes collateral kindred of the grantee from inheriting the land. (A, the fee tail tenant, can even get around this limitation by conveying a fee simple to a "straw person," who then conveys the fee simple back to A. A's collateral kindred can now inherit the fee simple.)

b. Fee tail abolished in most states [§316]

The fee tail has been abolished in England and in all American jurisdictions except the four states mentioned above. [**Robins Island Preservation Fund, Inc. v. Southold Development Corp.,** 959 F.2d 409 (2d Cir. 1992)] The question then arises: What estates are created by a transfer "to A and the heirs of his body"? There are several statutory and judicial solutions.

(1) A has a life estate [§317]

A few states hold that A has a life estate or, what amounts to the same thing, an unbarrable fee tail for A's life, with a remainder in fee simple to A's issue.

(2) A has a fee simple [§318]

The large majority of states holds that A has a fee simple, but these states split on a subsidiary point. About half provide that A has a *fee simple absolute*; the justification for this view is that because A could disentail and convey a fee simple absolute, the law will treat A as having done so. The other half of states provide that A has a fee simple, but any remainder to become possessory on failure of issue is given effect if, and only if, *A leaves no descendants at his death*. The difference between the states can best be seen by an illustration.

Example: O conveys Blackacre "to A and the heirs of his body, and if A dies without issue, to B and her heirs." In half the states, A takes a fee simple absolute, and A's issue and B take nothing. In the other half, A takes a fee simple, and A's issue take nothing, but B takes a future interest that will become possessory if, and only if, at A's death no issue of A are alive. If A leaves issue at A's death, B's interest then disappears (or, using the technical word, "fails").

---

(3) A has a fee simple conditional [§319]

In South Carolina and Iowa, which do not recognize the Statute de Donis Conditionalibus (*see supra*, §299), a conveyance "to A and the heirs of his body" gives A a fee simple conditional. If a child is born to A, A can convey a fee simple. If a child is not born, A's estate ends at A's death. (*See supra*, §298.)

c. Drafting [§320]

No competent lawyer today uses the phrase "to A and the heirs of his body." Litigation may arise over its meaning. And the grantor's intent can be carried out far more specifically and clearly by creating a life estate in A followed by a remainder or remainders. Nonetheless, a transfer "to A and the heirs of his body" still occasionally crops up—usually in a homemade deed or will. Then the problems discussed above arise.

D. The Life Estate

1. Definition [§321]

A life estate is an estate that has the potential duration of one or more human lives. Life estates are very common today, particularly life estates in trust. When property is held by X in trust for A for life, A is entitled to all the rents and profits or other income from the property.

2. Types of Life Estates

a. For life of grantee [§322]

The usual life estate is measured by the grantee's life. Thus, where O conveys Blackacre "to A for life," the grantee, A, gets an estate in the land for so long as A lives. On A's death, the land reverts to O, the grantor.

b. Pur autre vie [§323]

Where the estate is measured *by the life of someone other than the owner of the life estate*, it is classified as a life estate pur autre vie (Law French term, meaning for the life of another). It comes to an end when the measuring life ends.

(1) Creation of life estate pur autre vie [§324]

A life estate pur autre vie can be created in one of two ways: (i) O conveys Blackacre to *B for the life of A*. B is a life tenant pur autre vie. A is the measuring life. The estate will end on A's death. If B dies before A, the life estate pur autre vie descends to B's heirs. Or (ii) A, a life tenant, *conveys her life estate* to B. B has a life estate pur autre vie. A remains the measuring life.

EXAM TIP　　　　　　　　　　　　　　　　　　　　　　**gilbert**

The first method of creating a life estate pur autre vie, in which the grant clearly states that it is for the duration of another person's life ("to A for the life of B"), is a fairly obvious example of a life estate pur autre vie, and you should be able to pick it out easily in an exam question. The second way, in which a *life tenant transfers her estate to another,* is much more subtle. To understand this second situation, you must understand two important points: (i) a life tenant can freely transfer her estate, but (ii) what the grantee gets is *not his own life estate*, but a life estate *for the life of the original life tenant* (pur autre vie). Thus, the grantee has the land to enjoy until the original life tenant dies, which in exam questions at least often is a very short period. So if, *e.g.,* the grantee is in the middle of a major construction project on the property when the original life tenant dies, the grantee's estate ends and he is out of luck, which is why this type of estate is not very desirable.

---

c. In a class [§325]

A life estate can be created in several persons, such as "to the children of A for their lives, remainder to B." Where a life estate is given to two or more persons, the principal question that arises is: What happens to the share of the first life tenant to die? Does this share go to the surviving life tenants or to those who hold the remainder? The usual construction is that it goes to the surviving life tenants and the remainder does not become possessory until *all* life tenants die.

d. Defeasible life estates [§326]

Like a fee simple, a life estate can be created so as to be determinable, subject to condition subsequent, or subject to an executory limitation.

Example: O conveys "to A for life so long as A remains unmarried." A has a life estate terminable upon marriage. (The restraint on marriage *might* violate the rule against restraints on alienation. *See supra*, §294, *and see infra*, §§344 *et seq.*)

Example: O conveys "to A for life, but if A does not use the land for agricultural purposes, O retains the right to reenter." A has a life estate subject to a condition subsequent.

Example: O conveys "to A for life, but if B marries during A's lifetime, to B." A has a life estate subject to an executory limitation.

e. Construction problems [§327]

Sometimes it is not clear what estate is created by the language used. Courts must then construe the instrument to determine whether the estate conveyed is a fee simple, life estate, or leasehold estate. Each case depends on its own facts and the *probable intent of the grantor*. The following are common examples of ambiguous language raising construction problems:

Example: "To my wife, W, so long as she remains unmarried." Does this create a fee simple determinable or a life estate determinable (on theory that the condition—marriage—could only happen during W's life)? *Majority view:* A *fee simple determinable* is created, even though the fee simple cannot be forfeited after W's death. [**Lewis v. Searles**, *supra*, §295]

Example: "To my wife, W, to be used as she shall see fit, for her maintenance and support." Does this give W a fee simple or a life estate with power to consume the principal? *Majority view:* A *fee simple* is created; the words "for her maintenance and support" merely state the reason for the gift. [**White v. Brown**, 559 S.W.2d 938 (Tenn. 1977)]

3. Alienability of Life Estate [§328]

A life tenant ordinarily is free to transfer, lease, encumber, or otherwise alienate her estate inter vivos. Of course, the transferee gets no more than the life tenant had—an estate that ends at the expiration of the measuring life.

4. Limited Utility of Legal Life Estate [§329]

A legal life estate is of limited utility because it is a very inflexible way of providing for successive ownership. Suppose that O dies, devising Blackacre to her husband, H, for life, and on his death, to their children. H may live a long time and various problems may arise that cannot be satisfactorily resolved except by going to court, and maybe not even then. Suppose that H wants to add a room on the house and needs to borrow money from a bank, giving the bank a mortgage. The bank will not lend money with only a life estate as security, for the bank's security ends at H's death. Or suppose that H wants to lease the land beyond his death, or wants to sell the land and move to a smaller place or more convenient location. It is possible for H to do what he desires if *all the owners of the remainder are adult, competent, and consent*. But if one of them is a minor, or dies leaving a minor heir, consent cannot be given without a lawsuit and the appointment of a guardian ad litem to represent the minor. Then too, even if all are competent, securing agreement from them may be difficult to achieve. Thus, H may be locked into a very inflexible position.

a. Equitable life estate [§330]

Far more satisfactory than a legal life estate is an *equitable life estate*. To create such, O can devise Blackacre *to X in trust* for H for life, remainder to O's children. X, the trustee, owns the legal fee simple and has the usual powers of a fee simple owner to sell, mortgage, or lease. H has the right to receive all income from Blackacre or to take possession of it. X, the trustee, must *manage* the property *prudently* and is held accountable for mismanagement. If desired, H can be named trustee by O. (For more on the trust, *see infra*, §§563 *et seq.*)

5. Waste

a. Definition [§331]

Waste is conduct by the life tenant that permanently impairs the value of the land or the interest of the person holding title or having some subsequent estate in the land. A common law form of action entitled "waste" lay against the life tenant for damages to the land. (Waste by a lessee is discussed in the landlord and tenant chapter, *infra*, §§965-970.)

(1) Rationale

There are two ideas underlying the doctrine of waste, and the court may choose to emphasize one or the other in a particular case. The first is that the *grantor intends* that the life tenant shall have the general use of the land *in a reasonable manner*, but that the land shall pass to the owner of the remainder as nearly as practicable *unimpaired in its nature, character, and improvements*. The second is that where two or more persons own interests in land, *fairness* requires that one shall not impose severe *economic damage* on the other.

b. Types of waste [§332]

Three different types of waste are recognized:

(1) Affirmative (voluntary) waste [§333]

Affirmative (or voluntary) waste occurs when the life tenant *actively causes* permanent injury by, *e.g.*, destroying buildings or ornamental trees on the land, or removing the natural resources (minerals, timber, etc.). However, cutting of trees in clearing woodland for conversion into more valuable cultivated farmland is not waste.

(2) Permissive (involuntary) waste [§334]

Permissive (or involuntary) waste occurs when the land is *allowed to fall into disrepair*, or the tenant fails to take reasonable measures to protect the land from the elements. [**Moore v. Phillips,** 627 P.2d 831 (Kan. 1981)] Failing to pay the *taxes* and allowing the property to be sold at a tax sale is treated as permissive waste.

(a) Insurance [§335]

The life tenant has no obligation to keep the property insured, and if a building burns down without the fault of the life tenant, this is not waste. [**Suydam v. Jackson,** 54 N.Y. 450 (1873)] Moreover, if the life tenant does insure, she is not required to rebuild the property for the remaindermen's benefit or hold the insurance proceeds in trust for the remaindermen. [**Ellerbusch v. Myers,** 683 N.E.2d 1352 (Ind. 1997)] In contrast, a trustee (*see supra*, §330) is required to insure the property and hold the proceeds in trust for the life tenant and remaindermen if the building burns down. Here is one obvious illustration of why a trust is preferable to a legal life estate.

(3) Ameliorating waste [§336]

Ameliorating waste occurs when the principal use of the land is substantially changed—usually by tearing down a building—*but the change increases the value of the land*. Ameliorating waste is actionable if the court finds that: (i) the grantor intended to pass the land with the specific buildings on it to the holder of the remainder; and (ii) the building can reasonably be used for the purposes built.

---

e.g. **Example:** In 1887, Isaac Brokaw erects a fine residence on Fifth Avenue and 79th Street in Manhattan. In 1913, Isaac dies, devising "my residence" to A for life, remainder to B. In 1929, A wants to take down the house (worth $300,000) and erect an apartment house (costing $900,000). This will increase A's income by $30,000 a year. A cannot take down the house because Isaac intended to pass "*my residence*" on to B, and the house is located in an area of fine houses and can reasonably be used as such. [**Brokaw v. Fairchild,** 135 Misc. 70 (1929)]

(a) Current use undesirable [§337]

If the house is located in an area that changes, perhaps by the location of factories and railroads nearby, so that it is no longer desirable as a residence, the life tenant can demolish the house, provided the value of the property is enhanced for business purposes. This result can be put on the ground that grantor's intent of passing the house on can no longer be carried out because changed conditions have made it impractical to do so. In that case, the house can be demolished if the parties will benefit economically. [**Melms v. Pabst Brewing Co.,** 79 N.W. 738 (Wis. 1899)]

c. Remedies for waste [§338]

The owners of the remainder may enjoin threatened waste by the life tenant or recover damages. If the ultimate future owner of the land is not now ascertained, damages may be impounded by the court pending determination of the ultimate takers.

COMPARISON OF TYPES OF WASTE		gilbert
TYPE OF WASTE	**CIRCUMSTANCES**	**EXAMPLE**
AFFIRMATIVE (VOLUNTARY) WASTE	Life tenant *actively causes* permanent injury to the land	Life tenant leases farmland for use as a toxic waste dump
PERMISSIVE (INVOLUNTARY) WASTE	Life tenant *allows land to fall into disrepair* or fails to take reasonable measures to protect the land from the elements	Life tenant fails to repair barn roof after a hail storm, leading to future water damage and decay
AMELIORATING WASTE	Life tenant substantially changes principal use of the land but the change *increases the value* of the land	Life tenant changes unproductive farmland into a lucrative shopping center

6. Sale of Property by a Court [§339]

If the life tenant and the owners of the remainder are all adults, competent, and agree, a fee simple in the land can be sold. If for some reason they cannot agree, can the life tenant get a court to sell the land, and order the proceeds reinvested in trust with the income paid to the life tenant?

a. Holders of the remainder are able to consent [§340]

If the holders of the remainder are all ascertained, adult, and competent, they can consent to the sale and the general rule is that a court will *not* give the life tenant relief in this case. The parties can bargain among themselves about sale and division of the proceeds.

(1) Equitable intervention [§341]

Equity may intervene and order sale of the property if the sale is necessary for the best interest of all the parties. This is a flexible remedy, which equity exercises sparingly, however, because of the underlying notion that the grantor wants *the land* itself (and not the economic value represented by the land) passed on to the holders of the remainder. [**Baker v. Weedon,** 262 So. 2d 641 (Miss. 1972)]

b. Holders of the remainder cannot consent [§342]

If the holders of the remainder cannot legally consent to the sale, because one or more is unascertained, underage, or incompetent, a court may order a sale if it finds that sale is in the best interests of the holders of the remainder.

c. Statutes [§343]

Statutes in many states authorize a court to sell a fee simple in land under specified conditions, upon petition of the life tenant. These statutes reflect a trend to loosen restrictions on a legal life estate, and to permit the life tenant to have the land sold and have the proceeds held in trust. Such statutes are more likely to appear in urbanized states than in farm states where the notion of "family farm" still holds sway. The breadth of the judicial doctrine of sale may also differ accordingly.

E. The Rule Against Restraints on Alienation

1. Introduction [§344]

The Statute Quia Emptores established, in the year 1290, a principle that land should be alienable. Working from that beginning, the courts laid down a number of rules designed to further the alienability of land. One of the most important is the rule *against direct restraints* on alienation. This rule invalidates certain types of restraints on certain types of estates.

2. Types of Restraints [§345]

There are three types of direct restraints:

a. Forfeiture restraint [§346]

A forfeiture restraint provides that if the grantee attempts to transfer his interest, it is forfeited to another person.

Example: O conveys Blackacre "to A and his heirs, but if A attempts to transfer the property by any means whatsoever, then to B and her heirs." This is a forfeiture restraint because the estate passes to another upon the attempted transfer.

---

b. Disabling restraint [§347]

A disabling restraint withholds from the grantee the power of transferring her interest.

> **Example:** O conveys Blackacre "to A and her heirs, but any transfer hereafter in any manner of an interest in Blackacre shall be null and void." This is a disabling restraint because the grantee cannot transfer her interest.

c. Promissory restraint [§348]

A promissory restraint provides that the grantee promises not to transfer his interest.

> **Example:** O conveys Blackacre "to A and his heirs, and A promises for himself, his heirs, and successors in interest that Blackacre will not be transferred by any means." This is a promissory restraint because the grantee made a promise that he will not transfer his interest.

3. Restraints on a Fee Simple

a. Total restraints [§349]

Any total restraint on a *fee simple*—either forfeiture, disabling, or promissory—is *void*. The grantee may therefore alienate the estate and suffer no penalty. In the preceding examples, A, the grantee, has a fee simple absolute, alienable at will.

(1) Rationale

Restraints on alienation take property out of the market, making it unusable for the best use dictated by the market. They tend to make property unmortgageable and therefore unimprovable, to concentrate wealth in the class already rich, and to prevent creditors from reaching the property to pay the owner's debts.

b. Partial restraints [§350]

A partial restraint is one that purports to restrict the power to transfer to specific persons, or by a specific method, or until a specific time. The older view is that partial restraints on alienation are to be treated like total restraints (*i.e.*, *void*). [**Hankins v. Mathews,** 425 S.W.2d 608 (Tenn. 1968)—forfeiture restraint for 10 years void] However, there are some established exceptions.

(1) Sale with consent of another [§351]

A deed may provide that the property may be sold only with the consent of another. Such a provision may be used in an attempt to control entry into a subdivision or neighborhood. Such provisions are usually held void. [**Riste v. Eastern Washington Bible Camp, Inc.,** 605 P.2d 1294 (Wash. 1980)]

> **Example:** Developer conveys lots in his subdivision by deeds containing the following provision: "And for the purpose of maintaining a high-class development, no owner of land hereby conveyed shall have the right to transfer the land without the written consent of the grantor." This covenant is void. The owners can sell to anyone without receiving the written consent of the grantor. [**Northwest Real Estate Co. v. Serio,** 144 A. 245 (Md. 1929)]

(2) Sale to a member of the club [§352]

A deed may provide that the property may be sold only to a member of a neighborhood association (*e.g.,* the Lake Watawga Association). Such a provision in effect gives the association power to veto a prospective buyer. If such a restriction on sale has no reasonable standards for admission to the association, giving the association members arbitrary power to deny membership, the provision in the deed is void. [**Lauderbaugh v. Williams,** 186 A.2d 39 (Pa. 1962)]

(3) Reasonable restraints doctrine [§353]

In more and more states, partial restraints on a fee simple are valid if reasonable. The restraint must have *a reasonable purpose* and be *limited in duration.* The reasonableness test is the modern trend. [**Horse Pond Fish & Game Club, Inc. v. Cormier,** 581 A.2d 478 (N.H. 1990)]

(a) Preemptive option [§354]

A preemptive option gives the optionee the right of first refusal if the owner decides to sell. A preemptive option is valid if the terms are reasonable regarding the price to be paid and the time allowed for exercise of the right. A preemptive option for fair market value is valid. [**Gale v. York Center Community Cooperative,** 171 N.E.2d 30 (Ill. 1961); **Procter v. Foxmeyer Drug Co.,** 884 S.W.2d 853 (Tex. 1994)]

(b) Sale of a cooperative apartment [§355]

A provision in a cooperative apartment agreement restraining sale of stock ownership without the consent of the building's board of directors is usually held valid. *Rationale:* Tenants of a cooperative are liable for the entire mortgage on the building—the entire building will be sold if one tenant defaults on mortgage payments and the other tenants do not make up the default. Because of the *financial interdependency* and living in close proximity to one another, cooperative apartment tenants need to assure themselves of the financial responsibility and desirability of the new lessees. A similar restriction on transferring a condominium unit may also be held valid for more or less the same reasons. [**Weisner v. 791 Park Avenue Corp.,** 6 N.Y.2d 426 (1959); **Penthouse Properties, Inc. v. 1158 Fifth Avenue, Inc.,** 256 A.D. 685 (1939)]

c.   Co-tenants [§356]

An agreement by tenants in common or joint tenants that they will not partition the property (*see infra*, §698) is valid if reasonable in purpose and limited in time.

Example: H and W own their home as tenants in common. After experiencing marital difficulties, H and W agree that neither shall transfer his or her interest to another, nor bring an action to partition the property. It is the intent of H and W to preserve the property as a home for the family. Because this restraint is limited to the life of H or W (whoever dies sooner), it is reasonably limited in time and is valid. [**Michalski v. Michalski,** 142 A.2d 645 (N.J. 1958)—holding agreement valid, but refusing to enforce it after nine years because of change in circumstances]

---

d.   Restraint on use [§357]

A restraint on the use of property makes the property less alienable by eliminating prospective purchasers who desire to make use of the property in a manner forbidden by the restraint. But restraints on the use of property have almost always been upheld. Even a restraint that the property can be used only by the grantee has been upheld. [**Mountain Brow Lodge No. 82 v. Toscano,** 257 Cal. App. 2d 22 (1967)]

e.   Racial restraints [§358]

Restraints prohibiting the transfer or use of the property to or by a person of a specified racial, religious, or ethnic group are not enforceable. Enforcement of a racially discriminatory restraint by the courts is *discriminatory state action* forbidden by the Equal Protection Clause of the Fourteenth Amendment of the United States Constitution.

(1)   Fourteenth Amendment [§359]

The Fourteenth Amendment to the United States Constitution provides that *no state* may deny persons equal protection of the laws—meaning, among other things, that no state can discriminate in granting or protecting property rights on the basis of race. *Judicial enforcement* of a racial covenant forbidding use of property by black persons is discriminatory *state action* forbidden by the Constitution. [**Shelley v. Kraemer,** 334 U.S. 1 (1948)]

Example: O conveys Blackacre "to A and his heirs, and A promises that Blackacre will never be used or occupied by nonwhite persons." Thereafter A sells to B, a black man, who moves onto Blackacre. O sues for an *injunction* prohibiting B from using Blackacre, and sues A for *damages* for having sold to B. Injunction and damages are judicial remedies ordinarily available for breach of a covenant. The court cannot grant O either an injunction or damages, because such judicial action would be *state action* interfering with B's right to enjoy property free of racial discrimination. [**Barrows v. Jackson,** 346 U.S. 249 (1953)]

(a) Condition subsequent [§360]

If O creates a racial restriction in the form of a condition subsequent, giving himself right of entry to enforce the condition, the right of entry cannot be enforced by a court. It falls under the ban of **Shelley v. Kraemer**, *supra*, on judicial state action that is discriminatory.

> **e.g.** **Example:** O conveys Whiteacre "to A and his heirs, but if Whiteacre is sold or leased to a black person, O may reenter and retake A's lot." A can sell or lease to a black person. O's right of entry cannot be enforced in court. [**Capitol Federal Savings & Loan Association v. Smith,** 316 P.2d 252 (Colo. 1957)]

(b) Determinable fee [§361]

Automatic termination of a fee simple determinable in land given a charity, terminable on *use* by nonwhite persons, has been held *not* to involve state action. No judicial action is required for the fee simple to revert. [**Evans v. Abney,** 396 U.S. 435 (1970); **Charlotte Park & Recreation Commission v. Barringer,** 88 S.E.2d 114 (N.C. 1955)] However, although such a determinable fee might not involve state action infringing on constitutional rights, it might well be in violation of civil rights statutes. (*See infra*, §§817 *et seq.*)

(2) Fair Housing Act [§362]

Racial restrictions may also violate the Fair Housing Act of 1968 (*see infra*, §821). Recording a deed with a racial restriction is prohibited by the Fair Housing Act. [42 U.S.C. §3604(c)]

RESTRAINTS ON ALIENATION OF FEE SIMPLE— EXAMPLES · gilbert

VOID RESTRAINTS	USUALLY VALID RESTRAINTS
• Total restraint	• Preemptive option (right of first refusal)
• Sale requiring consent of another	• Sale requiring consent of board of directors in cooperative apartment building (financial interdependency involved)
• Sale only to a member of a club with arbitrary power to deny membership	• Agreement by co-tenants not to partition (if reasonable in purpose and time)
• Racial restraint	• Restraint on use

4. Restraints on a Life Estate

a. Legal life estate [§363]

Because land owned for life is not marketable, as the life tenant may die at any time, a restraint on a life estate may add little practical inalienability—particularly where the holders of the remainder are unascertained and cannot join together with the life tenant in conveying a fee simple. Nonetheless, courts have struck down disabling restraints on a life estate, which have the effect of making the land legally inalienable. On the other hand, forfeiture and promissory restraints on a life estate (which can be released by the person holding the benefit of forfeiture or of the promise) have often been upheld.

b. Equitable life estate [§364]

A disabling restraint on an equitable life estate in trust is known as a *spendthrift trust*. It is valid in most states. (*See infra*, §574.)

---

e.g. **Example:** O conveys Blackacre and some IBM stock "to X in trust to pay the income to A for life, then on A's death to convey the trust property to B." A spendthrift clause is inserted in the conveyance providing that A cannot alienate her life estate or income interest, and that A's creditors cannot reach them. The clause is valid.

---

(1) Rationale

A restraint on an *equitable interest*, like the interest of A in the above example, does not prevent alienation of specific property. The trustee can sell the stock. But A cannot transfer to another her right to receive the income from the trust assets.

EXAM TIP   **gilbert**

This is an important point to remember: The rule against restraints on alienation applies *only to legal interests*. Restraints on the alienation of *equitable* interests (*e.g.*, spendthrift clauses in trust instruments) are valid.

F. Summary of Possessory Estates

1. Overview [§365]

This bare-bones digest of freehold possessory estates should serve as a review foundation for the law of future interests, which follows. After each of these estates, except the fee simple absolute, future interests will be created.

2. Fee Simple

PRESENT ESTATE	EXAMPLES	DURATION	CORRELATIVE FUTURE INTEREST IN GRANTOR	CORRELATIVE FUTURE INTEREST IN THIRD PARTY
FEE SIMPLE ABSOLUTE	"To A & his heirs"	Forever	None	None
FEE SIMPLE DETERMINABLE	"To A & his heirs so long as . . ." until . . ." while . . ."	As long as condition is met, then *automatically* to grantor	Possibility of Reverter	(*See* Fee Simple Subject to an Executory Interest, below)
FEE SIMPLE SUBJECT TO CONDITION SUBSEQUENT	"To A & his heirs, but if . . ." upon condition that . . ." provided that . . ." however . . ."	Until happening of named event *and* reentry by grantor	Right of Entry	(*See* Fee Simple Subject to an Executory Interest, below)
FEE SIMPLE SUBJECT TO AN EXECUTORY INTEREST	"To A & his heirs for so long as . . ., and if not . . ., to B"	As long as condition is met, then to third party	(*See* Fee Simple Determinable, above)	Executory Interest
	"To A & his heirs but if . . ., to B"	Until happening of event	(*See* Fee Simple Subject to Condition Subsequent, above)	Executory Interest
FEE TAIL	"To A & the heirs of his body"	Until A and his line die out	Reversion	None (but remainder is possible)
LIFE ESTATE (MAY BE DEFEASIBLE)	"To A for life," *or* "To A for the life of B"	Until the end of the measuring life	Reversion	None (*but see* below)
	"To A for life, then to B"	Until the end of the measuring life	None	Remainder
	"To A for life, but if . . ., to B"	Until the end of the measuring life *or* the happening of the named event	Reversion	Executory Interest

a. **Fee simple absolute**

"To A and his heirs." No future interest is possible after a fee simple absolute.

b. **Fee simple determinable**

"To A and his heirs *so long as* used for a library." The grantor has a possibility of reverter, which becomes possessory *automatically* on cessation of library use. If the conveyance provides that on cessation of library use the property will go to another grantee (B), rather than return to the grantor, the grantee (B) has a future interest called an executory interest.

c. **Fee simple subject to condition subsequent**

"To A and his heirs, *but if* the land is not used for a library, O has a right to reenter." The grantor has a right of entry, which he *may elect* to exercise or not.

d. **Fee simple subject to executory limitation**

"To A and his heirs, *but if* the land is not used for a library during the next 20 years, *to B*." B has an executory interest.

3. **Fee Tail**

"To A and the heirs of his body." The grantor has a reversion on expiration of the fee tail. If the conveyance creates a future interest in a grantee following a fee tail (*e.g.*, "and if A dies without issue, to B"), the future interest is a remainder.

4. **Life Estate**

"To A for life" or "to A for the life of B" (life estate pur autre vie). The future interest in the grantor following a life estate is a reversion. If the future interest is created in a grantee, it is ordinarily a remainder but can be an executory interest.

a. **Limited life estates**

A life estate may be made determinable, subject to condition subsequent, or subject to an executory limitation in the same manner as a fee simple may be so limited. For example, "to A for life or until remarriage" creates a life estate determinable.

Chapter Four:
Future Interests

CONTENTS

Chapter Approach

Chapter Approach

Now that you've mastered present possessory interests, you're ready to turn to future interests. The law of future interests has deep historical roots and an interdependent doctrinal structure that gives it a curious mathematical quality. More than any other field of law, it is law according to Euclid: It requires precision in analysis and rigor in doctrinal application. An approximate, rather than exact, understanding will not do. But don't despair, because the law of future interests is not difficult if approached correctly.

Your approach to future interests problems should follow two important rules:

(i) Pay careful attention to the *exact language* used in the grant; and

(ii) Read and analyze the interests in a grant *in sequence*.

Besides these two rules, you should keep in mind these other helpful hints:

1. **Classify the Present Estate**

    Classifying the present estate may help you figure out the future interests, because some future interests can follow only a particular type of present interest (*e.g.*, a possibility of reverter can follow only a determinable estate, and a right of entry can follow only an estate subject to a condition subsequent).

2. **Look at Who Has the Future Interest**

    If it is retained by the *grantor*, you've narrowed it down to a reversion, a possibility of reverter, or a right of entry. If it is given to someone *other* than the grantor, it must be a remainder or an executory interest.

3. **Think About How the Future Interest Will Become Possessory**

    For interests in a grantee, remember that a remainder waits patiently for the natural termination of the preceding estate, whereas an executory interest either divests the prior estate or springs out of the grantor's interest, in both cases cutting short the prior estate. For future interests remaining in the grantor, the reversion usually follows the natural termination of the prior estate (*e.g.*, after the life tenant dies). Similarly, the possibility of reverter does not cut short the preceding determinable estate, but succeeds it. On the other hand, the right of entry, like the executory interest, divests the preceding estate.

4. **Also Identify the Possessory Estate in Which the Future Interest Will Be Held**

    A future interest *will always be held in some possessory estate*. For example, if a grantor who owns in fee simple absolute conveys a fee simple determinable (*see supra*, §284), the grantor's future interest (which, you are about to see, is a possibility of reverter; *see infra*, §370) is most completely identified as a possibility of reverter *in fee simple absolute*. So as you study the future interests and examples below, take the time to identify the possessory estate in which the future interest will be held.

5. **Determine Whether the Interest Is Vested or Contingent**

A contingent interest either is given to an *unascertained person* or is subject to a *condition precedent*. Classify each interest in sequence by looking at the "words between the commas" setting off the interests. And distinguish between a condition precedent, which comes "between the commas," and a condition subsequent, which divests a vested interest. *Example—condition precedent:* "To A for life, then to B *if B survives A*, and if B does not survive A, to C." *Example—condition subsequent:* "To A for life, then to B, *but if B does not survive A*, to C."

6. **Apply the Following Rules to Contingent Interests**

    (i)   Destructibility of contingent remainders (applicable to contingent remainders only);

    (ii) The Rule in Shelley's Case;

    (iii) The Doctrine of Worthier Title; and

    (iv) The Rule Against Perpetuities.

Of these rules, the last is the most important and the most likely to be tested in an examination.

With these hints in mind (and memorization of the identifying factors of the estate; *see infra*, §578), you should be able to answer future interests questions.

A. Introduction

1. Future Interest Defined [§366]

A future interest is a nonpossessory interest capable of becoming possessory in the future. A future interest is a *present* interest in the sense that it is a presently *existing* interest. But it is *not* a presently *possessory* interest, and that is why it is called a future interest.

Example: O conveys Blackacre "to A for life, and on A's death to B." A has a possessory life estate. B has a future interest called a remainder. It will become possessory on A's death. Before A's death, the remainder exists as a property interest in Blackacre. As with other property interests, B can transfer the remainder to C, and B's creditors can reach the remainder. It is an existing property interest, which will become possessory in the future.

2. Categories Limited [§367]

Just as possessory estates are limited in number (fee simple, fee tail, life estate, leaseholds), so are future interests. There are only five categories of future interests: *reversion, possibility of reverter, right of entry, remainder,* and *executory interest.* (Remainders can be further divided into vested remainders and contingent remainders.) The language of each instrument creating a future interest must be construed so as to create one, and only one, of these future interests. Different rules apply to each future interest. This introduction contains a brief overview of the five future interests; then, each is discussed in detail later in the chapter.

3. Future Interests in the Grantor [§368]

Future interests are divided into two basic groups: (i) future interests *retained by the grantor*; and (ii) future interests *created in a grantee.* If the future interest is retained by the *grantor* (or, if retained by a will, by the testator's heirs), the future interest *must be* either a *reversion, possibility of reverter,* or *right of entry.*

a. Reversion [§369]

A reversion is a future interest left in the *grantor* after the grantor conveys a vested estate of a *lesser* quantum than he has.

> **Example:** O, owning Blackacre in fee simple, conveys Blackacre "to A for life." Because O did not convey a fee simple to anyone—but only a life estate, which is a lesser estate than a fee simple—O has a reversion. When A dies, Blackacre will revert to O. If O had conveyed a fee simple to A, O would not have a reversion.

b. Possibility of reverter [§370]

A possibility of reverter arises when a grantor carves out of her estate a *determinable* estate of the same quantum. In almost all cases it *follows a determinable fee.*

> **Example:** O conveys Blackacre "to the Board of Education so long as Blackacre is used for school purposes." The Board of Education has a determinable fee; O has a possibility of reverter. O's interest is not a reversion because O, owning a fee simple, has conveyed a fee simple determinable to the Board. All fees simple (absolute, determinable, subject to condition subsequent or executory limitation) are of the same quantum.

c. Right of entry [§371]

A right of entry is retained when the grantor creates an estate subject to condition subsequent and retains the power to cut short the estate.

> **Example:** O conveys Blackacre "to the Board of Education, but if the Board ceases to use Blackacre for school purposes, O retains a right to

reenter." The Board has a fee simple subject to condition subsequent; O has a right of entry.

---

d. Correlative estates [§372]

From the explanations above, it is easy to see that possessory estates have correlative future interests in the grantor:

(1) Life estate—reversion;

(2) Fee simple determinable—possibility of reverter;

(3) Fee simple on condition subsequent—right of entry.

4. Future Interests in Grantees [§373]

If a future interest is created in a grantee, it *must be* either a *remainder* or an *executory interest*.

a. Remainder [§374]

A remainder is a future interest in a grantee that: (i) has the *capacity of becoming possessory* at the expiration of the prior estates, and (ii) *cannot divest* the prior estates.

Example: O conveys Blackacre "to A for life, and on A's death, to B and her heirs." A has a possessory life estate; B has a remainder in fee simple. B's interest is a remainder because it can become possessory on A's death, and it will not divest A's life estate prior to A's death.

---

b. Executory interest [§375]

Generally speaking, an executory interest is a future interest in a grantee that, in order to become possessory, *must divest* or cut short the prior estate, or *spring out* of the grantor at a future date. The basic difference between a remainder and an executory interest is that a *remainder never divests* the prior estate, whereas an executory interest almost *always does*. Legal executory interests were not permitted prior to 1536; they were authorized by the Statute of Uses (1536).

Example—shifting executory interest: O conveys Blackacre "to A and his heirs, but if B graduates from law school, to B and her heirs." A has a fee simple subject to executory limitation; B has a shifting executory interest. B's interest can become possessory only by divesting A of the fee simple. A shifting interest is a useful device to shift title upon the happening of some uncertain event.

---

e.g. **Example—springing executory interest:** O conveys Blackacre "to my daughter A when she marries B." O retains the fee simple and creates an executory interest in A to spring out of O in the future when A marries B. A springing interest was, in early days, a useful device to give the groom assurances that the bride would come to the altar endowed with property.

SUMMARY OF TYPES OF FUTURE INTERESTS — gilbert

IN GRANTOR	IN A GRANTEE
• Reversion	• Remainder
• Possibility of Reverter	• Executory Interest
• Right of Entry	

EXAM TIP — gilbert

Note that there are only five future interests. To determine which type of future interest it is, first decide **who has the interest**—the grantor or the grantee. That narrows down the possibilities because if the **grantor** has the interest, it can only be one of three interests: reversion, possibility of reverter, or right of entry. If the **grantee** has the interest, it can only be a remainder or an executory interest. After that, **look at the present estate,** as that will often clue you in to what type of interest follows. Finally, for future interests in the grantee, determine whether the interest **cuts short a previous estate or naturally follows** it.

5. Legal or Equitable Interests [§376]

Future interests can be *legal* future interests or *equitable* future interests. Legal future interests are created without the imposition of a trust, such as where O conveys Blackacre "to A for life, remainder to B and his heirs." *Equitable* future interests are created in a trust. (The trust is explained in more detail *infra*, §§563 *et seq.*)

e.g. **Example:** O conveys property "to X *in trust* to pay the income to A for life, and on A's death to convey the trust assets to B." X is the trustee, owning a legal fee simple in the trust assets. A has an equitable life estate, and B has an equitable remainder. If X does not carry out his fiduciary duties, which include managing the property prudently and paying the income to A, A can sue X for misfeasance in office.

B. Reversion

1. **Definition [§377]**

   A reversion is a future interest left in the grantor after she conveys a vested estate *of a lesser quantum* than she has. A reversion may be expressly retained.

   Example: O conveys Blackacre "to A for life, then to revert to O." Where it is not expressly retained, a reversion will arise *by operation of law* where no other disposition is made of the property after expiration of the lesser estate.

   Example: O conveys Whiteacre "to A for life." O has a reversion in fee simple by operation of law.

   a. **Quantum of estates [§378]**

      As mentioned above, a reversion arises when the grantor transfers a vested estate of a *lesser quantum* than she has. The hierarchy of estates determines what is a lesser quantum: The fee simple is of longer duration than the fee tail; the fee tail is of longer duration than a life estate; the life estate is of longer duration than the leasehold estates.

      Example: O, owner of a fee simple, conveys a fee tail or a life estate to A. In either case, O has conveyed a lesser estate than O's fee simple. Therefore, O has a reversion.

      > **EXAM TIP**   gilbert
      >
      > Much of the time the reversion is *not expressly retained*; therefore, you must look for it. When you read the grant, check to see if O has conveyed all she had. If not—if she conveyed only a lesser estate—remember that there is a reversion in O.

   b. **Reversions are vested interests [§379]**

      All reversions are vested interests even though not all reversions will necessarily become possessory. Some reversions will certainly become possessory; *e.g.*, O conveys "to A for life, reversion to O." Other reversions may or may not become possessory (*see, e.g.*, example below).

      Example: O conveys Blackacre "to A for life, remainder to B if B survives A." O has a reversion because, if B dies before A, Blackacre will return to O at A's death. If A dies before B, Blackacre will go to B at A's death. Note that O does not have a contingent reversion. By common law dogma, *all reversions are vested*. So O has a vested reversion, which can be divested by B's interest becoming possessory at A's death.

      (1) **Significance [§380]**

          The significance of a reversion being vested is that it is *alienable, accelerates* into possession upon the termination of the preceding estate, and is *not subject to the Rule Against Perpetuities* (*see infra,* §§524 *et seq.*).

2. Alienability [§381]

A reversion has always been regarded as fully transferable both inter vivos and by way of testate or intestate succession. The transferee, of course, gets only what the transferor had—an interest that cannot become possessory until the preceding estate terminates.

EXAM TIP   **gilbert**

Keep in mind that any future interest that is transferable is also subject to involuntary transfer; *i.e.*, it is **reachable by creditors**.

---

3. Distinguish—Possibility of Reverter [§382]

Do not confuse a reversion with a possibility of reverter (*see infra*). Each is a distinct interest, with different characteristics. A possibility of reverter arises where the grantor carves out of his estate a *determinable estate of the same quantum.* Most often it arises where the grantor conveys a fee simple determinable. A reversion arises where the grantor conveys a *lesser estate* than he has and does not in the same conveyance create a vested remainder in fee simple. There is *no such interest as a "possibility of reversion."* Do not use the phrase as it is likely to confuse you.

C. Possibility of Reverter

1. Definition [§383]

A possibility of reverter arises when a grantor carves out of her estate a *determinable* estate of the *same quantum*. In almost all cases met in practice, a possibility of reverter follows a determinable *fee*, not some lesser determinable estate. Thus, for all practical purposes, a possibility of reverter is a future interest remaining *in the grantor* when a *fee simple determinable* is created. (For determinable fees, *see supra*, §§279 *et seq.*)

 Example: O conveys Blackacre "to A and his heirs so long as liquor is not sold on the premises." A has a determinable fee; O has a possibility of reverter.

EXAM TIP   **gilbert**

Note that as with the reversion, the possibility of reverter may **not be expressly retained** (*i.e.*, you won't see it in the grant). If you see a grant of a fee simple determinable, know that the grantor has a possibility of reverter unless the grant transfers the property to a **third party** upon the occurrence of the specified event.

---

a. Created only in grantor [§384]

A possibility of reverter *cannot be created in a grantee.* The analogous future interest created in a grantee is called an executory interest (*see infra*, §457).

2. Alienability [§385]

At common law, a possibility of reverter could not be transferred inter vivos. *Rationale:* A possibility of reverter was **not** viewed as an existing interest, but rather as a **mere possibility** of becoming an interest. Hence it was not a "thing" that could be transferred. However, on the death of the owner of a possibility of reverter, the possibility of reverter was treated as a thing; "it" descended to the owner's heirs.

a. Modern law [§386]

In most jurisdictions, a possibility of reverter is freely alienable, both during life and by will. *Rationale:* The possibility of reverter is now viewed as a **property interest**, and alienability is an inherent characteristic of any property interest. [**City of Carthage v. United Missouri Bank**, 873 S.W.2d 610 (Mo. 1994)]

b. Releasable [§387]

A possibility of reverter, although inalienable to a stranger at common law, was releasable to the owner of the determinable fee. A release made the land marketable.

3. Termination [§388]

Termination of a possibility of reverter is discussed below in connection with a right of entry. (*See infra*, §393.)

4. Valuation [§389]

When the government exercises eminent domain, taking title to land where a fee simple determinable is owned by A and a possibility of reverter is owned by B, it is necessary to value the separate interests. The majority rule is that the entire condemnation award belongs to A unless the fee simple determinable would expire (apart from the condemnation proceedings) within a reasonably short period. A minority sets the value of the determinable fee as the difference between full fair market value of a fee simple for all uses and the value of the land for the uses permitted. The difference between the value of the determinable fee and the full fair market value is the value of the possibility of reverter. [**Ink v. City of Canton**, 212 N.E.2d 574 (Ohio 1965); **Leeco Gas & Oil Co. v. County of Nueces**, 736 S.W.2d 629 (Tex. 1987)]

D. Right of Entry

1. Definition [§390]

When a grantor creates an estate subject to condition subsequent (*supra*, §286) and **retains the power to cut short** or terminate the estate, the grantor has a right of entry. Like a possibility of reverter, a right of entry cannot be created in a grantee. The right of entry is sometimes called "a power of termination."

Example: O conveys Blackacre "to A and his heirs, but if intoxicating liquor is ever sold on the premises, O has a right to reenter and retake Blackacre." A has a fee simple subject to condition subsequent; O has a right of entry for breach of the condition subsequent.

EXAM TIP	gilbert

You **will usually see** the right of entry (if there is one) expressed in the grant of an estate subject to a condition subsequent.

2. Alienability [§391]

At common law, a right of entry was inalienable inter vivos because it was treated as a chose in action, and choses were inalienable. It was not thought of as a property interest, but rather as a special right in the grantor to forfeit the grantee's estate if he wished. A right of entry could be released, however, to the owner of the fee simple, and it was inheritable by the heirs of the grantor.

a. Modern law [§392]

In some states, the right of entry is now alienable; in others, the common law is followed. Possibly in a few, a particularly harsh rule is followed: The mere attempt to transfer a right of entry destroys it.

Example: O conveys Blackacre "to Railroad Company, but if it fails to maintain an overpass, O has the right to reenter and retake Blackacre." Subsequently, O conveys the right of entry to his son. In the last group of states mentioned above, this attempt to convey the right destroys it, and the railroad has a fee simple absolute. [**Rice v. Boston & Worcester Railroad**, 94 Mass. 141 (1866); *compare* **Oak's Oil Service, Inc. v. Massachusetts Bay Transportation Authority**, 447 N.E.2d 27 (Mass. 1983)—holding right of entry alienable]

---

3. Termination [§393]

At common law, a right of entry or a possibility of reverter could endure indefinitely, and because it was inheritable, the grantor's heirs could exercise the right of entry or enforce the possibility of reverter hundreds of years after the grantor's death. These interests were not subject to the Rule Against Perpetuities, which generally prevented the creation of future interests to become possessory far in the future. (*See infra*, §§524 *et seq.*) This remains the law in the large majority of states. In some states, however, statutes have been enacted expressly limiting the period during which a possibility of reverter or right of entry can exist. The typical statute limits them to 30 years, after which the preceding fee simple becomes absolute. Some states have made the termination statute retroactive, applying it to existing possibilities of reverter and rights of entry. But state courts are divided on whether retroactive application is unconstitutional as a taking of property without compensation. [*See* **Texaco, Inc. v. Short**, 454 U.S. 516 (1982)—upholding an Indiana statute terminating existing unused mineral rights unless rights were rerecorded within two years]

FUTURE INTERESTS IN GRANTOR				**gilbert**
FUTURE INTEREST	CORRELATIVE PRESENT INTEREST	EXAMPLE	RIGHTS OF GRANTOR	ALIENABILITY
REVERSION	Life Estate	"To A for life."	Estate *automatically* reverts to grantor on life tenant's death	Transferable, descendible, and devisable
POSSIBILITY OF REVERTER	Fee Simple Determinable	"To A so long as alcohol is not used on the premises."	Estate *automatically* reverts to grantor upon the occurrence of the stated event	Transferable, descendible, and devisable
RIGHT OF ENTRY	Fee Simple Subject to Condition Subsequent	"To A on condition that if alcohol is used on the premises, O shall have the right to reenter and retake the premises."	Estate does *not* revert automatically; *grantor must exercise his right of entry*	Descendible and devisable, but some courts hold not transferable inter vivos

E. Remainder

1. Definition [§394]

A remainder is a future interest created in a *grantee* that is *capable of becoming a present possessory estate on the expiration of a prior possessory estate* created in the same conveyance in which the remainder is created. It is called a remainder because on the expiration of the preceding estate, the land "remains away" instead of reverting to the grantor. A remainder never divests or cuts short the preceding estate; instead it *always waits patiently* for the preceding estate to expire.

Example: O conveys Blackacre "to A for life, then to B if B is then living." B has a remainder because B's interest is capable of becoming possessory upon the termination of the life estate.

2. Essential Characteristics [§395]

The essential characteristics of every remainder are:

a. Must have preceding estate [§396]

A remainder can be created only by *express grant* in the *same instrument* in which the *preceding possessory estate* is created. Unlike a reversion, it *cannot* arise by operation of law. The old law said: "A remainder needs a preceding freehold to support it."

Example: O conveys "to A if A marries B." No preceding estate has been created by O in anyone; thus, A does not have a remainder. A has instead a springing executory interest (*see infra*, §455).

> **EXAM TIP** gilbert
>
> Remember that if *no preceding possessory estate* has been created in a transferee, the future interest is *not* a remainder.

b. Must follow a fee tail, life estate, or term of years [§397]

The estate preceding a remainder can be a fee tail, a life estate, or a term of years. A remainder can follow any of these estates. But a remainder cannot follow a fee simple (*see infra*, §399).

Example—fee tail: O conveys "to A and the heirs of his body, and if A dies without issue, to B and his heirs." If the fee tail has not been abolished (*see supra*, §315), A has a fee tail, and B has a remainder in fee simple.

Example—term of years: O conveys "to A for 10 years, then to B and his heirs." A has a term of years. B has a vested remainder in fee simple. At early common law, B's interest was not called a remainder. It was said that B had the fee simple subject to A's term of years. Lawyers put it this way because of the notion that a remainder needed a preceding freehold estate to support it. But today, lawyers call B's interest a remainder.

---

c. Must be capable of becoming possessory on natural termination of preceding estate [§398]

A remainder cannot divest a preceding estate prior to its normal expiration. A divesting interest in a transferee is an *executory interest*, not a remainder.

Example: O conveys "to A for life, then to B." B has a remainder because B takes when the preceding estate (A's life estate) expires.

Compare: O conveys "to A for life, but if B returns from Rome during the life of A, to B in fee simple." B does not have a remainder; rather,

B's taking divests A's estate and thus B has a shifting executory interest. (*See infra*, §456.)

---

(1) No remainder after a fee simple [§399]

A logical consequence of a rule that a remainder is an estate that becomes possessory on the natural termination of the preceding estate is that *there can never be a remainder divesting a fee simple*, which has an infinite duration. Any interest divesting or following a fee simple *must be an executory interest*, not a remainder. This rule applies to all types of fees simple, including a fee simple determinable (*see infra*, §457).

 Example: O conveys "to A and his heirs, but if A dies without issue surviving him, to B." B has an executory interest, not a remainder.

EXAM TIP	gilbert

To summarize, a remainder must **follow a preceding estate**—if there is no preceding estate, a future interest can't be a remainder. A remainder **can't follow a fee simple**—if you see a fee simple, a future interest can't be a remainder. And a remainder must be capable of becoming possessory **on the natural termination of the preceding estate**—if the future interest cuts off (divests) the previous estate, it can't be a remainder.

---

3. Estates in Remainder [§400]

An estate in remainder may be a fee simple, a life estate, a term of years, or, in those jurisdictions where such an estate is permitted, a fee tail.

Example: O conveys "to A for life, then to B for 10 years, then to C for life, then to D." B has a remainder for a term of years, C has a remainder for life, and D has a remainder in fee simple. (All of these remainders are vested; *see* below.)

---

4. Classification of Remainders [§401]

Remainders are classified either as "vested" or "contingent." A *vested* remainder is a remainder that is *both* created in an ascertained person *and* is not subject to any condition precedent. A *contingent* remainder is a remainder that is *either created in an unascertained person or subject to a condition precedent.*

a. How to classify [§402]

An appropriate—and easy—way to classify remainders is as follows: Take each interest *in sequence* as it appears in the instrument. Determine whether it is given to an ascertained person or is subject to a condition precedent. Classify it. Move on to the next interest and do the same thing. Classification of each interest *in sequence* is the key to correct classification.

To avoid confusion, *always* classify the interests *in order*.

Example: O conveys "to A for life, then to B and his heirs if B survives A, and if B does not survive A, to B's children and their heirs." Take each interest in sequence. First, "to A for life." This gives A a life estate. Second, "then to B and his heirs if B survives A." Stop at the comma, which ends B's interest, and classify it: B has a *remainder* because it is capable of becoming possessory on termination of the life estate and will not cut the life estate short. It is a remainder *in fee simple* ("B and his heirs"). It is a *contingent* remainder because it is subject to the express condition precedent, "if B survives A." Third, move on to the next interest, "and if B does not survive A, to B's children and their heirs." Classify it: The interest is a *remainder* because it is capable of becoming possessory on termination of the life estate and cannot cut the life estate short. It is a remainder to a class, B's children, *in fee simple*. It is a *contingent* remainder because it is subject to the express condition precedent, "and if B does not survive A." (*Note:* B and B's children have alternative contingent remainders; *see infra*, §428.) If the words of an instrument are classified *in sequence*, as in this example, the classification of remainders is not too difficult a task (at least with textbook examples, which are likely to be clearly framed to illustrate the rules).

---

(1) Why classify? [§403]

The common law drew—and still draws—a sharp distinction between vested and contingent remainders. Vested remainders were favored and contingent remainders disfavored. The judges thought contingent remainders were objectionable because they made land inalienable. Therefore, they laid down several rules designed to curtail contingent remainders: (i) the rule of destructibility of contingent remainders (*infra*, §464); (ii) the Rule in Shelley's Case (*infra*, §483); (iii) the Doctrine of Worthier Title (*infra*, §507); and (iv) the Rule Against Perpetuities (*infra*, §524). In addition, contingent remainders were not alienable, whereas vested remainders were alienable (*see infra*, §431). Thus, several legal consequences turn on whether a remainder is vested or contingent.

b. Vested remainders

(1) Definition [§404]

The most common definition of a vested remainder is the one given above: a remainder created *in an ascertained person* and *not subject to a condition precedent*. Gray defines it somewhat differently: "A remainder is vested in A, when throughout its continuance, A, or A and his heirs, *have the right to immediate possession, whenever and however the preceding freehold estates may determine.*" [John C. Gray, *The Rule Against Perpetuities* §101 (4th ed. 1942)] Gray's definition emphasizes that to be vested a remainder must be capable of going into possession whenever and however the preceding estates end—*i.e.*, right now.

> **Example:** O conveys "to A for life, then to B in fee simple." B (an ascertained person) has a remainder not subject to a condition precedent. The word "then" following a life estate is a word of art meaning "on the expiration of the life estate." Whenever and however the life estate terminates, B (or her representative) will be entitled to possession. B's remainder is vested.

(a) Condition precedent [§405]

A condition precedent is an *express condition* attached to the remainder, such as, "to B if B reaches age 30" or "to B if B survives A." *Note:* The expiration of the preceding estate (such as the death of the life tenant) is *not* a condition precedent.

(2) Subclassification of vested remainders [§406]

There are three different types of vested remainders: indefeasibly vested, vested subject to open, and vested subject to complete defeasance. These differences are explained *infra*. Generally speaking, however, the crucial distinction is between vested remainders on the one hand and contingent remainders on the other. For most purposes, all vested remainders have the same legal consequences (a principal exception is the treatment of remainders vested subject to open under the Rule Against Perpetuities, *infra*, §537). It is important to master these different types of vested remainders primarily because of the light they shed on how vested remainders are distinguished from contingent remainders.

(a) Indefeasibly vested remainder [§407]

When a remainder is indefeasibly vested, the holder of the remainder is *certain to acquire* a possessory estate at some time in the future, and is also certain to be entitled to *retain permanently* thereafter the possessory estate so acquired.

> **Example:** O conveys "to A for life, then to B and her heirs." B (or her representative) is certain to take possession on A's death. If B dies before A, B's heirs or devisees are entitled to possession. Thus, B's remainder is indefeasibly vested. (If B dies intestate and without heirs during A's life, B's remainder escheats to the state. At A's death, the state takes the property.)

(b) Vested remainder subject to open [§408]

When a remainder is vested subject to open, it is vested in a *class of persons*, at least one of whom is qualified to take possession, but the shares of the class members are not yet fixed because more persons can subsequently become members of the class.

Example: O conveys "to A for life, then to A's children." If A has no children, the remainder is contingent because no person qualifies as a child. If A has a child, B, the remainder is vested in B subject to "open up" and let in other children. B's remainder is sometimes called "vested subject to partial divestment." (Once the remainder has vested in B, the interests of the unborn children are called executory interests because they may partially divest B.)

EXAM TIP — gilbert

Generally, when an instrument creates a gift of a future interest in an open class (one in which more people could become members), existing class members have a *vested* remainder subject to open. But watch for a condition precedent, which will prevent the remainder from vesting. For example, "to A for life, remainder to those of B's children who survive A" creates a contingent remainder in B's children even if they are in existence—and even if B is dead—because the remainder is contingent on surviving A.

1) Class gifts [§409]

A class gift is a gift to a group of persons described as a class, *e.g.*, "children of A," "brothers and sisters of A," or "heirs of A." A class is either *open* or *closed.* It is open if it is possible for other persons to enter the class. *It is closed if it is not possible for others to enter the class.* In a gift to the "children of A," the class is closed if A is dead. It is not possible for other persons to come into the class. (A child of A in the womb is treated as in being from the time of conception if later born alive.)

EXAM TIP — gilbert

Remember that a class gift to "the children of A" remains open *until A's death.* It does not close simply because A has become too old or physically unable to have more children (see *infra*, §540).

(c) Vested remainder subject to divestment [§410]

When a remainder is vested subject to divestment, it is either vested subject to being divested by the operation of a *condition subsequent* or vested subject to divestment by an *inherent limitation* of the estate in remainder.

1) Illustration—condition subsequent [§411]

O conveys "to A for life, then to B, but if B does not survive A, to C." The vested remainder in B is subject to total divestment on the occurrence of a *condition subsequent* (B dying, leaving A surviving). C's executory interest will divest B if the condition subsequent happens.

2) Illustration—inherent limitation [§412]

O conveys "to A for life, then to B for life, then to C and his heirs." B has a vested remainder for life subject to total divestment if B fails to survive A. The divestment occurs because of the *inherent limitation* in a remainder for life: It fails if it does not become possessory within the life tenant's life. C has an indefeasibly vested remainder in fee simple.

3) Vested subject to open and to complete divestment [§413]

A remainder can be both vested subject to open and to complete divestment. For example, O conveys "to A for life, then to the children of A, but if no child survives A, to B." A, who is living, has a child, C. C has a vested remainder subject to open up and let in her brothers and sisters; it is also subject to complete divestment if A leaves no children surviving him (*i.e.*, if C and all other children of A die before A).

(3) Alienability [§414]

Vested remainders are alienable inter vivos and devisable by will. A vested remainder descends to heirs if not otherwise disposed of.

(a) Divested at death [§415]

A vested remainder can be so limited that it is not transmissible at death but is divested on death.

> **e.g. Example:** O conveys "to A for life, then to B, but if B does not survive A, to C." B's vested remainder is not transmissible. If B dies during A's life, B can pass nothing on B's death. In that case, C's executory interest would divest B at A's death and become a vested remainder.

c. Contingent remainders

(1) Definition [§416]

A remainder is contingent if it either is limited to an *unascertained person* or is subject to a *condition precedent*.

(2) Remainders in unascertained persons [§417]

A remainder in an "unascertained" person means the person is not yet born or cannot be determined until the happening of an event. Such a remainder is contingent.

(a) Illustration—unborn children [§418]

O conveys "to A for life, then to A's children." A has no children. The remainder is contingent because the takers are not ascertained at the time of the conveyance. If a child is born, the remainder vests in that child subject to open and let in other children born later.

(b) Illustration—heirs [§419]

O conveys "to A for life, then to B's heirs." B is alive. Because no one is an heir of the living (but only an heir apparent), the takers are not ascertained; therefore, the remainder is contingent. B's heirs will be ascertained only at his death. If B dies during A's life, the remainder will vest in B's heirs at B's death.

1) Meaning of "heirs" [§420]

"Heirs" means those persons who succeed to B's property *if B dies intestate* (*see supra*, §262). They are set forth in each state's statute of descent and distribution. Children and descendants are everywhere preferred over parents and more remote kin. To be an heir of B, a person must survive B. Dead persons do not inherit property. If, *e.g.*, B has a son, C, who dies before B, C is not an heir of B.

EXAM TIP   **gilbert**

Remember, a person *must be dead* to have an heir. Prior to death, one can only have an "heir apparent." Also, a dead person can never be an heir.

(c) Reversion [§421]

In each of the above examples, there is a reversion in O. *Note:* Whenever O creates a *contingent remainder* in fee simple, *there is a reversion in O.* Whenever O creates a *vested* remainder in fee simple, there is *never* a reversion in fee simple in O. The reason for this is as follows: In the case of a vested remainder in fee simple, the remainderman, by definition, stands ready to take whenever and however the previous estate ends. In the case of a contingent remainder, the remainderman will not be ready to take at the termination of the previous estate if the contingency has not yet been satisfied; hence, the interest must revert to O until the contingency occurs. So in the conveyance from O "to A for life, then to B's heirs," if B is alive when A dies, B's "heirs" are not determined and thus not ready to take. In the conveyance from O "to A for life, then to A's children," it is true that at A's death all of A's children, if any, are determined and thus ready to take. The catch is that, historically, a life estate could end by forfeiture before the death of the life tenant (*see infra,* §470). If this were to happen, A's life estate could terminate before A, still alive, had any children, so once again the interest must revert to O. Although this reason from history has faded away, the terminology persists. Hence, whenever O creates a contingent remainder in fee simple, it continues to be said that O has a reversion.

(3) Remainders subject to condition precedent [§422]

A remainder subject to a condition precedent is a contingent remainder. A condition precedent is an *express condition* set forth in the instrument (other than the termination of the preceding estate), which must occur before the remainder becomes possessory. This definition requires elaboration (*see* below).

(a) What is a condition precedent [§423]

A condition precedent is a condition expressly stated in the instrument. Suppose that O conveys "to A for life, then to B *if B marries C.*" B has a remainder subject to an express condition precedent. The condition precedent is marrying C. If B marries C during A's life, the remainder vests indefeasibly in B.

(b) What is not a condition precedent

1) Termination of preceding estate [§424]

The termination of the preceding estate is not a condition precedent. If it were, all remainders would be contingent, because no one is entitled to possession until the preceding estate has terminated.

2) Surplusage [§425]

Language that merely refers to the termination of the preceding estate is surplusage and does not create a condition precedent.

Example: O conveys "to A for life, and on A's death, to B." The words "on A's death" merely refer to the natural termination of the life estate and do not state a condition precedent. They are therefore surplusage and may be struck out. B's remainder is vested. [**Kost v. Foster,** 94 N.E.2d 302 (Ill. 1950)]

---

3) Survivorship [§426]

A remainder subject to a condition precedent *other than* survivorship is not also subject to an implied condition precedent of survivorship. *Remember:* The condition precedent must be expressly stated. Thus, if O conveys "to A for life, then to A's issue, and if A dies without issue, to B," B's remainder is contingent on A's dying without issue. It is **not** contingent on B's surviving A. Thus, if B dies before A, B's remainder passes to B's heirs or devisees, and if A subsequently dies without issue, B's heirs or devisees take the property.

REMAINDERS—CONTINGENT VS. VESTED	gilbert
CONTINGENT REMAINDERS	**VESTED REMAINDERS**
• Created in an **unascertainable** person (not yet born or cannot be determined)	• Created in an **ascertained** person
OR	*AND*
• Subject to a **condition precedent** expressed in the instrument	• **Not subject** to a **condition precedent**

(4) Distinguish—conditions subsequent [§427]

Sometimes it is difficult to distinguish between a vested remainder subject to divestment (*i.e.*, subject to a condition subsequent) and a remainder subject to a condition precedent. The test, according to Gray section 108 (*supra*, §404) is as follows: "Whether a remainder is vested or contingent depends upon the language employed. If the conditional element is incorporated into the description of, or into the gift to, the remainderman, then the remainder is contingent; but if, *after words giving a vested interest, a clause is added divesting it*, the remainder is vested."

EXAM TIP	gilbert
Whether a condition is precedent or subsequent depends on the words of the instrument. The words must be read *in sequence* and the interests classified *in sequence*.	

Example: O conveys "to A for life, then to B, but if B does not survive A, to C." B has a vested remainder subject to divestment by C's executory interest. The words "then to B" give B a vested remainder; the clause following is a divesting clause, giving the property to C if B dies before A.

Example: O conveys "to A for life, then to B if B survives A, but if B does not survive A, to C." B and C have alternative contingent remainders. A condition precedent has been expressly attached to B's remainder. O intended exactly the same thing as in the preceding example, but her intention was phrased differently. Here, O stated the condition of survivorship twice, once in connection with each remainder.

(a) Reversion in O with alternative contingent remainders [§428]

In the preceding example where alternative contingent remainders are created, there is a reversion in O. How is it possible for the property to revert to O? Inasmuch as B will take if B survives A, and if B does not survive A, C will take, it looks impossible for the property to revert to O. The answer? At common law *a life estate could terminate prior to the life tenant's death* by forfeiture or merger (*infra,* §§469-473). If this happened, neither B nor C would be ready to take on the termination of the life estate, and the property would revert to O. Or B and A can die simultaneously, so that neither survives the other and the conditions precedent on B's interest and C's interest can never be satisfied.

EXAM TIP **gilbert**

However unrealistic these possibilities may appear today, *in classifying future interests on an exam, you must assume that the life estate can terminate before the death of the life tenant* by forfeiture, merger, or simultaneous death of the grantees.

(b) Preference for vested remainders [§429]

If the instrument is ambiguous, the law favors a vested construction rather than a contingent one. [**Browning v. Sacrison,** 518 P.2d 656 (Or. 1974)]

Example: O conveys "to A for life, and at his death to A's children, the child or children of any deceased child to receive his or their deceased parent's share." Under the standard rule of construction, A's children take a vested remainder subject to condition subsequent at birth. Each child's interest is subject to being divested by his children if he dies before A. [**Kost v. Foster,** *supra,* §425]

---

1) Condition subsequent must be read carefully [§430]

In the above instrument, the condition subsequent is not operative to divest a child of A who dies before A *without children*. It is operative only to divest a child of A who dies before A *with children*. Thus, suppose A had two children, B and C, and C had a child, D. Then B and C died before A. B's share would go under his will as he devised, or to his heirs. C's share would be divested in favor of D. [*In re* **Estate of Houston,**

201 A.2d 592 (Pa. 1964); *In re* **Estate of Blough,** 378 A.2d 276 (Pa. 1977)]

EXAM TIP   **gilbert**

Where language is ambiguous, remember that the law favors early vesting. Thus, the preference is for *vested remainders subject to divestment* rather than contingent remainders or executory interests.

---

(5) Alienability [§431]

Vested remainders have always been alienable inter vivos and devisable by will. Contingent interests, including contingent remainders and executory interests, were not alienable inter vivos at common law, except in equity for a valuable consideration, by operation of the doctrine of estoppel, or where released to the owner of the possessory interest.

(a) Modern law [§432]

In a large majority of jurisdictions today, contingent interests are alienable inter vivos or, when survivorship is not a condition precedent, devisable by will. Of course, if the remainder is contingent because the limitation is to an unborn person, there is no one to make the conveyance, so the interest is inalienable.

(b) Creditor's rights [§433]

Generally, creditors can reach any alienable property interest the debtor has. The rule is: If the debtor can voluntarily transfer it, the creditor can reach it. Thus, creditors can reach vested remainders; they can also reach contingent remainders if they are alienable in the particular jurisdiction. [**Kost v. Foster,** *supra*]

F. Executory Interests

1. Historical Background of Uses

a. Origin of uses

(1) Development of equity [§434]

After the Norman Conquest (1066), the king imposed upon England a feudal system in which power was exercised by landowners. Royal judges were appointed to administer the system, but in time these law courts became formula-ridden, inflexible, and dominated by technical procedure. When persons failed to obtain a remedy at law, they turned to the king for relief. Their petitions were heard by the king's council, of which the chancellor was the most learned member. In time, the petitions came to be heard by the chancellor alone, and the chancellor gradually developed his own court—the court of chancery. In this court, which was independent of—and, indeed, was a rival of—the law courts, the chancellor administered a system of justice called equity. Chancery was a court of conscience, whereas the common law courts were courts of rules.

(a) Equitable remedies [§435]

The chancellor acted in personam (upon the person). His ultimate sanction was to imprison a person who disobeyed. He could not adjudicate title or award damages, as the law courts could. His remedy was an injunction ordering a person to do or not to do an act.

(b) Conflict with law courts [§436]

The chancellor's decrees often conflicted with decrees of the law courts, particularly when he ordered a person not to execute a judgment obtained in the law courts. Ultimately, James I decided that in a dispute between equity and law, equity would prevail.

(2) Development of the "use" [§437]

In feudal times, it was frequently found expedient to vest ownership of property in one person who would hold it for the use and benefit of another. One early example was where O, going off to fight a crusade, enfeoffed (*i.e.*, conveyed a freehold of land into the possession of) his brother, A, with the understanding that O's wife and children would have the *use* of the land. The common law courts refused to enforce uses, but the chancellor compelled the *feoffee to uses*, A, to hold the land in accordance with the understanding, on the ground that it was unconscionable to permit A to violate the confidence reposed in him.

(a) Note on terminology [§438]

In the above example, A is the *feoffee to uses*, and O's wife and children are the *cestuis que use*. In a similar arrangement in modern times, one would say A is the *trustee* and O's wife and children are the *beneficiaries*.

(b) Seisin [§439]

A, the feoffee to uses, was seised of the property by the feoffment from O. In enforcing the use in favor of O's wife and children, the chancellor did not move seisin from A. The chancellor merely directed A, holding seisin, to do certain things—or to go to jail.

(c) Rights of cestui que use [§440]

The feoffee to uses was required by the chancellor to *permit the cestui to take possession* or the profits of the land, to dispose of the land as the cestui instructed, and to protect the land.

b. Common law conveyancing before Statute of Uses and equitable bypasses [§441]

The common law courts had a number of restrictive rules related to conveyancing that could be circumvented in equity. In the text that follows, the restrictive rules of the law courts are discussed, and under each rule is a discussion of how a clever equity lawyer could arrange matters to avoid the rule.

(1) Livery of seisin required [§442]

At law, to pass title to land, the grantor must enfeoff the grantee in a ceremony called *livery of seisin*. The feoffment had to be performed on the land, by the parties going out onto the land and O handing over a clod or twig to A. This feoffment ceremony was useful evidence of a transfer of title in a society where few could read and write. But it was inconvenient to persons who might want to pass title in a London solicitor's office, rather than go onto the land, perhaps many miles from London.

(a) Bypass in equity [§443]

Equity offered a way to avoid the ceremony of livery. This was the *bargain and sale deed*. It worked this way: O executes a deed by which O *bargains and sells* Blackacre to A and his heirs *for a consideration* (say £100). At law, this was a nullity because seisin had not been manually conveyed on the land. But because A had paid money for the land, the chancellor thought it would be unconscionable for O to retain the land. Therefore, the chancellor required O to *stand seised for the use of A*.

(2) No springing interests [§444]

At law, a grantor could not create a freehold estate to *spring out* in the future, because O could not create a freehold estate without conveying seisin. Seisin had to be handed over—it could not spring from O in the future. An attempt to make seisin spring out from the grantor in the future (a springing interest) was a nullity at law.

Example: O conveys "to A and her heirs when she marries B." This attempt to make seisin spring out in the future was ineffective at law. Seisin remained in O.

(a) Bypass in equity [§445]

Under the highly commercial marriage arrangements of the times, the bride with a rich father had to come with dowry. But O would not want his daughter, A, to have the property that comprised the dowry until she married B. On the other hand, the bridegroom, B, would want assurances that A would have property upon marriage. Law would not permit seisin to spring out of O, the grantor, in the future. But the chancellor offered relief. If O would covenant (promise) to stand seised for the use of his daughter upon her marriage, the chancellor would enforce the promise. Upon marriage, O's daughter would be entitled to the use and profits from the land.

(3) No shifting interests [§446]

At law, a grantor could not create a future interest in a grantee that would cut short a freehold estate. This was known as a rule against shifting interests. The reasons for this rule were that O could not derogate from his grant to A, and O could not create a right of entry in a stranger, which a shifting interest resembled. (*Note:* A right of entry can be created only in the grantor; *see supra*, §390.)

Example: O has a son, B, who is studying for the priesthood in Rome, but he may return home. O conveys Blackacre "to A and his heirs, but if B returns from Rome, to B and his heirs." (There must have been a lot of going and coming from Rome in those days, because this is the standard example used in all the old texts.) By this conveyance, A takes a fee simple, and B has no interest recognized at law.

(a) Bypass in equity [§447]

The chancellor, unconcerned with the logic of the law courts, saw no harm in shifting interests that permitted O to plan for contingent events. Therefore, if O would "enfeoff X and his heirs to the use of A and his heirs, but if B returns from Rome, to B and his heirs," the chancellor would enforce the uses against X. X was said to stand seised to the use of A and, if the condition happened, B.

(4) Methods of creating a use [§448]

To get into the chancellor's court, the instrument had to *raise a use*, which gave the chancellor jurisdiction. To raise a use, one of the following three methods of transfer had to be employed.

(a) Feoffment to uses [§449]

If O "enfeoffed X and his heirs to the use of A and his heirs," O transferred seisin to X by the feoffment, and X held seisin to the use of A. Thus, a *feoffment to uses* raised a use.

(b) Bargain and sale [§450]

If O for a consideration executed a *bargain and sale deed* to A and his heirs, the deed raised a use in favor of A.

(c) Covenant to stand seised [§451]

If O *covenants under seal to stand seised* for the use of a *relative*, a use was raised, on the theory that natural love and affection sufficed as consideration for the use.

2. The Statute of Uses (1536)

a. Background of the Statute [§452]

By the sixteenth century, a large part of land in England was held in use. Feudal incidents (death duties; *see supra*, §243) were due only when seisin passed at death. Because the cestui que use did not have seisin, no death duties were payable at the cestui's death. To restore his feudal dues, Henry VIII determined to abolish the use. He forced through the Statute of Uses (1536). The purpose of the Statute was to abolish uses, turning them into legal estates that would be subject to all the usual feudal incidents on death of the legal owner. The Statute was very successful in reviving the crown's feudal incidents, which were not abolished until 1660, at the close of the Civil War.

b. What the Statute did [§453]

The Statute provided in substance that, "[i]f any person be seised of land to the use of another, the person having the use shall henceforth be deemed in lawful seisin and possession of the same lands in such like estate as he had in use." The Statute is said, therefore, to have "executed" or "converted" the use into a legal estate.

Example: After 1536, O enfeoffs "X and his heirs to the use of A and his heirs." The Statute "executes the use" and turns A's use into a legal fee simple in A. X gets nothing.

3. Springing and Shifting Interests Made Possible [§454]

By turning uses into legal estates, the Statute of Uses made possible *legal* shifting and springing future interests, recognized before 1536 in equity as uses. They became known as *executory interests*.

EXAM TIP   **gilbert**

How do you tell an executory interest from a remainder? If there is **no preceding estate**, the future interest must be an executory interest. If the future interest **follows a fee simple**, it must be an executory interest. And if the future interest does **not** follow the **natural termination of the preceding estate**, it must be an executory interest.

---

a. Springing interest [§455]

A springing executory interest is a future interest in a grantee that *springs out of the grantor* at a date subsequent to the granting of the interest, divesting the *grantor*. [**Abbott v. Holway,** 72 Me. 298 (1881)]

Example: O conveys "to A and her heirs if A quits smoking." A has a springing executory interest. It will divest the fee simple of O, the transferor, if it becomes possessory.

Example: O conveys "to A for 100 years if A so long live, then to A's heirs." The attempted contingent future freehold in A's heirs was void at law prior to the Statute of Uses because it was impossible to transfer seisin either to A (a termor) or to A's heirs (unascertained). After the Statute, the limitation to A's heirs was given effect as a springing executory interest. Seisin stays with O until the death of A, when it springs out to A's heirs.

b. Shifting interest [§456]

A shifting executory interest is a future interest in a grantee that divests a preceding estate in another grantee prior to its natural termination. The shifting interest, like the springing interest, divests a prior interest. The difference between them is that a *shifting* interest divests a *grantee*, whereas a *springing* interest divests the *grantor*.

Example: O conveys "to A and his heirs, but if B returns from Rome, to B and his heirs." A has a fee simple subject to an executory interest. B has a shifting executory interest. (B's interest *cannot* be a remainder, because it is a divesting interest, and remainders never divest.)

EXAM TIP   **gilbert**

It is not always necessary to know whether the executory interest is springing or shifting, as often it does not make any difference in your analysis. (And frankly, many professors are delighted if you even recognize it as an executory interest!) But if you need to identify the type of executory interest, think of the difference between the two this way: A *springing* executory interest *springs out of the grantor* (e.g., there is no preceding estate), and a *shifting* executory interest *shifts the estate from one grantee to another*.

Example: O conveys "to A for life, and on A's death, to B and his heirs, but if B does not survive A, to C and his heirs." C has a shifting executory interest—it vests, if at all, by cutting off B's vested remainder. Why is B's remainder vested? Remember to classify interests *in sequence*. B's interest comes first, and therefore must be classified first. Once it is classified as a vested remainder in fee, any further future interest in a grantee is necessarily a divesting executory interest. A remainder cannot follow a vested fee simple, either in possession or in remainder, and therefore C's interest cannot be a remainder if B's prior estate is a vested remainder in fee.

c. An oddity [§457]

An executory interest is always either a springing or a shifting interest—except in the case of a future interest in a grantee following a *fee simple determinable*. This executory interest is neither springing nor shifting because the fee simple determinable ends by its own special limitation. The executory interest does not divest it but rather *succeeds* it.

FUTURE INTERESTS IN GRANTEES

gilbert

FUTURE INTEREST	EXAMPLE	REVERSION IN GRANTOR FOLLOWING FUTURE INTEREST?	TRANSFERABLE?
INDEFEASIBLY VESTED REMAINDER	"To A for life, then to B."	No; remainder certain to become possessory	Yes; B's remainder transferable during life and at death
VESTED REMAINDER SUBJECT TO OPEN	"To A for life, then to A's children." A has a child, B. B has a vested remainder subject to open.	No; A's children are certain of possession	Yes; B's remainder transferable during life and at death
VESTED REMAINDER SUBJECT TO DIVESTMENT	"To A for life, then to B, but if B dies before A, to C." B has a vested remainder subject to divestment by C.	No; no possibility of property reverting to grantor	B's remainder transferable during life but not transferable at B's death if B predeceases A
CONTINGENT REMAINDER	(1) "To A for life, then to A's children." A has no children.	Yes	No; no child is alive
	(2) "To A for life, then to A's children who survive A." A has a child, B.	Yes	B's contingent remainder is transferable during life, but is not transferable at B's death if B predeceases A
	(3) "To A for life, then to B if B reaches 21." B is 17.	Yes	B's remainder is transferable during life, but remainder fails if B dies under 21
	(4) "To A for life, then to B's heirs." B is alive.	Yes	No; no one is heir of B until B dies
	(5) "To A for life, then to B if B survives A, and if B does not survive A, to C."	Yes	B's remainder is transferable during life, but fails if B predeceases A; C's remainder is transferable during life and at C's death if A is then alive
EXECUTORY INTEREST	(1) "To A, but if B returns from Rome, to B."	No	Yes
	(2) "To A for life, then to B, but if B does not survive A, to C."	No	C's executory interest is transferable during life and at C's death if A is then alive
	(3) "To A upon her marriage."	No reversion, but grantor has possessory fee until A's marriage	Yes

NOTE: In a few states, contingent remainders and executory interests are not transferable during life except in certain circumstances.

> **Example:** O conveys Blackacre "to Board of Education so long as used for school purposes, then to the Red Cross." The Red Cross has an executory interest. *Rationale:* There cannot be a remainder after any type of fee simple (*see supra,* §399). The only other permissible future interest in a grantee is an executory interest, so the interest in the Red Cross is called an executory interest.

d. Necessity of raising a use [§458]

For some years after the Statute of Uses, the grantor had to *raise a use* upon which the Statute would operate—if the grantor wished to create these new springing and shifting interests. If the grantor did not raise a use, to be converted by the Statute, he was caught within the old common law conveyancing rules. In time, courts held that a use on which the Statute could operate would be implied where necessary to carry out the intent of the parties. Today no special form of conveyance raising a use is necessary to the creation of executory interests. Springing and shifting interests can be created in any jurisdiction by an ordinary deed or by will.

4. Effect of Statute of Uses on Conveyancing [§459]

The Statute of Uses, for the first time, permitted legal title to be conveyed by a bargain and sale deed. Although feoffment was not abolished by the Statute, the convenience of transferring title by deed doomed the practice of livery of seisin of land, especially when the land was many miles removed from London. In 1677, the *Statute of Frauds* was enacted, requiring a *written instrument* to transfer title to land. The Statute of Frauds made livery of seisin obsolete unless accompanied by a written charter of feoffment.

5. Trust Arises After the Statute of Uses [§460]

The Statute of Uses revived the crown's feudal revenues considerably, but after feudal incidents were abolished in 1660, the crown had no pecuniary interest in the Statute of Uses, and the chancellors thereafter developed the modern trust—which made it possible again to separate the beneficial interest from the legal title.

a. Active duties imposed on trustee [§461]

The courts held that the Statute of Uses did not execute a use where the feoffee to uses had *active duties.* Before the Statute, the feoffee to uses occupied a passive position. The cestui que use was in possession, and the feoffee's primary duty was to convey the property as the cestui que use directed. The courts held that the Statute converted passive trusts only, and had no application where the feoffee was given active duties. Enforcing a use where there were active duties was, at bottom, purely an invention to circumvent the Statute of Uses.

b. The modern trust [§462]

Building on the idea that the Statute did not operate where the feoffee to uses was given active duties, the chancellors developed the modern trust. The trustee manages the property for the beneficiaries and has the active duties of management. In a trust, the trustee owns the legal title and the beneficiaries have rights against the trustee enforceable in equity. In addition, the beneficiaries have equitable rights in the property itself, *e.g.,* the right to the income from the trust property. Generally speaking, it is possible to divide these equitable rights (or "equitable title") into the same possessory estates and future interests as are permitted at law. (The trust is discussed in detail *infra, §§563 et seq.*)

Example: O conveys "to X and his heirs in trust for the benefit of A for life, then for B, and if B does not survive A, for C." X has the legal fee simple, A has an equitable life estate, B has an equitable vested remainder in fee, subject to being divested by C's equitable executory interest in fee.

G. Rules Restricting Contingent Remainders (Mostly Abolished)

1. Purpose of These Rules [§463]

Here we treat three of the ancient rules that had the purpose or effect of preventing the avoidance of death duties, which took the form of feudal incidents. The amazing thing is that these rules lasted centuries after the feudal incidents were abolished in 1660. But then a new reason arose to support them and give them an even broader reach. They made land alienable earlier.

2. Destructibility of Contingent Remainders [§464]

The rule of destructibility of contingent remainders was an important rule of the common law. This rule has been abolished in most states (*see infra, §481*), but because it may remain in effect in some, it is discussed here in the present tense.

a. Statement of rule [§465]

English judges laid down a rule that a legal contingent remainder in *land is destroyed if it does not vest at or before the termination of the preceding freehold estate.* If the preceding freehold terminates before the remainder vests, the remainder is struck down and can never take effect.

Example: O conveys Blackacre "to A for life, remainder to A's children who reach age 21." At A's death, his children are all under age 21. The remainder is destroyed. Blackacre reverts to the reversioner, O, who owns it in fee simple absolute.

---

(1) Rationale for rule

The common law abhorred an abeyance of seisin (*supra*, §252). Feudal incidents fell due upon the death of the person seised, and the location and continuity of seisin were important to the collection of feudal dues. Thus, the courts laid down this rule: If, upon termination of the preceding freehold, the holder of the remainder *is not able to take seisin* because his remainder is still contingent, the remainder is wiped out. In addition, the destructibility rule made land alienable earlier (at A's death in the preceding example).

b. Elements of the rule

(1) Preceding freehold [§466]

The preceding freehold estate in possession can be a fee tail or a life estate, both of which are estates having seisin. Because the fee tail is largely obsolete, this discussion will assume the freehold is a life estate. *The rule does not apply if the preceding estate is a leasehold*, because the termor does not have seisin.

Example: O conveys "to A for 100 years if A so long lives, then to A's children who reach age 21." Subsequently A dies, leaving an eldest child of 19. The destructibility rule has no application because A did not have a freehold.

---

(2) Termination of life estate [§467]

The life estate can terminate either on the death of the life tenant *or before the life tenant's death*. It is this later proposition that makes the rule more difficult than it appears.

(a) Natural termination of life estate [§468]

A contingent remainder that does not vest on the *natural* termination of the life estate (*i.e.*, at the life tenant's death) is destroyed.

Example: O conveys "to A for life, remainder to the heirs of B." B is alive. This conveyance creates a life estate in A, contingent remainder in the heirs of B, and a reversion in O. Subsequently A dies, survived by B. At A's death, B has no heirs, because no one can be an heir of the living. The contingent remainder in the heirs of B is destroyed, and O owns the land.

(b) Artificial termination of life estate [§469]

A contingent remainder that does not vest on the *artificial termination* of the life estate is destroyed. "Artificial termination" refers to the following methods of termination:

1) Forfeiture [§470]

At common law, a person forfeited his property by a tortious conveyance (*i.e.*, a conveyance by which a life tenant or a tenant in tail purported to convey a fee simple). Such a conveyance was treated as repudiating and destroying the old estate and claiming a new fee simple by disseisin, which was transferred. Any contingent remainders dependent on the grantor's old estate failed. Forfeiture for tortious conveyance is wholly obsolete in the United States.

2) Merger [§471]

If the life estate and a vested remainder or reversion in fee simple come into the hands of the *same person*, any intermediate contingent remainders are destroyed. The lesser estate (life estate) is merged into the larger (fee simple) and ceases to exist as a separate estate. A life tenant and reversioner can thus conspire to destroy contingent remainders.

---

e.g. **Example:** O conveys "to A for life, remainder to B if B survives A." While B is alive, A conveys her life estate to O. The life estate merges into the reversion, and B's contingent remainder is destroyed. O has a fee simple absolute.

---

a) Exception—fee tail [§472]

Life estates merge into a fee simple, but fees tail do not. Thus, suppose a conveyance "to A and the heirs of his body, and if A dies without issue, to B and her heirs if B is then living." A conveys his fee tail to O, the reversioner. B's remainder is not destroyed. (However, A can destroy B's remainder by disentailing; *supra*, §314.)

b) Exception—simultaneous creation [§473]

If a life estate and the next vested estate are created simultaneously, they do not merge *at that time* to destroy intervening contingent remainders. Thus, suppose that T devises Blackacre "to A for life, remainder to A's children who survive A." A is also T's heir and inherits the reversion. The life estate and reversion do not merge at that time; otherwise the intent of T in creating the remainder would be frustrated. But if *A subsequently conveys the life estate and reversion to B*, the estates then merge, destroying the contingent remainder.

c. Interests not affected by destructibility rule [§474]

The destructibility rule does not apply to the following interests in property.

(1) Vested remainders and executory interests [§475]

Vested remainders and executory interests cannot be destroyed by a gap in seisin. The destructibility rule *applies only to contingent remainders*.

e.g. **Example—vested remainder:** O conveys "to A for life, then to B for life, then to A's children who survive A." A conveys his life estate to O. The life estate cannot merge into the reversion because the vested remainder in B blocks it. O takes a life estate pur autre vie (for A's life).

e.g. **Example—executory interest:** O conveys "to A for 100 years if A so long lives, then to A's children who survive A." A has a term of years determinable. The children have an executory interest. It is not a remainder because there is no preceding freehold. There can be no contingent remainder after a term of years. A conveys his term to O. Seisin does not move from A to O because A, a termor, never had it (*see supra*, §251). Therefore, the children's executory interest is not affected. O now has a fee simple subject to A's children's executory interest but no longer subject to A's term of years.

e.g. **Example—executory interest:** O conveys "to A, but if A dies leaving children, to A's children who survive A, and if A dies without children, title shall return to O." A has a fee simple, subject to divestment by an executory interest in A's children who survive A, and subject also to a possibility of reverter in O. Later O conveys his interest to A, the fee simple owner. This cannot affect the executory interest in A's children. They take the land on A's death. [**Stoller v. Doyle,** 100 N.E. 959 (Ill. 1913)]

(2) Personal property [§476]

The destructibility rule has no application to personal property. There is no seisin in personal property, only in land.

(3) Interests in trust [§477]

Interests in trust (*i.e.*, equitable estates) are not subject to the destructibility rule. The trustee, owning the legal fee simple, has seisin. On expiration of the *equitable* life estate, seisin is not offered to the next estate—and therefore the destructibility rule, based on continuity of seisin, does not apply.

Example: O conveys Blackacre "to X and his heirs in trust to pay the income to A for life, then in trust to convey Blackacre to the children of A who reach age 21." Subsequently A dies, and his eldest child is 19. The remainder is not destroyed. The trustee, X, has seisin. Such children as reach age 21 will take the land.

---

d. Avoidance of rule [§478]

The destructibility rule can be easily avoided by a competent lawyer. The two most common ways of avoiding the rule are as follows.

(1) Term of years [§479]

If a drafter creates a term of years rather than a life estate, the destructibility rule can be avoided. (*See supra*, §475.)

(2) Trustees [§480]

The destructibility rule can also be avoided by creating *trustees to preserve contingent remainders*. The device works this way: O conveys "to A for life, then to X, Y, and Z as trustees for the life of A and to preserve contingent remainders, remainder to A's children who survive A." The trustees have a *vested* remainder following A's life estate. If the life estate terminates in any way, prior to A's death, the trustees step up and take seisin and hold it until A's death, paying the income to A. The purpose of this device was to *prevent artificial destruction* of contingent remainders by the termination of the life estate prior to the life tenant's death. If the life estate terminated before the death of A, the trustees took seisin, and blocked its passage on to the reversioner. Thus, A could not destroy the contingent remainders with the collusion of O.

e. Abolition [§481]

The destructibility rule has been abolished in the large majority of the states by judicial decision or statute. [**Abo Petroleum Corp. v. Amstutz,** 600 P.2d 278 (N.M. 1979)]

(1) Effect of abolition [§482]

Where destructibility is abolished, a contingent remainder takes effect if the contingency occurs *either before or after the termination of the life estate*. Thus, if O conveys "to A for life, remainder to A's children who reach age 21," and A dies leaving all children under 21, A's children take if and when they reach 21. Their interest takes effect in possession after A's death, and is called either an indestructible contingent remainder or an executory interest.

3. Rule in Shelley's Case [§483]

One of the great traps of common law conveyancing was the Rule in Shelley's Case. This rule has been abolished in most states (*see infra*, §505), but because it still exists in some, it is discussed here in the present tense. (*See* Restatement of Property section 312 for complete elaboration of the Rule.)

a. Statement of Rule [§484]

If (i) one instrument (ii) creates a freehold in land in A, and (iii) purports to create a remainder in A's heirs (or in the heirs of A's body), and (iv) the estates are both legal or both equitable, then the remainder becomes a remainder in fee simple (or fee tail) in A.

---

e.g. **Example—remainder to A's heirs:** O conveys "to A for life, then to A's heirs." The Rule in Shelley's Case converts the remainder limited to A's heirs into a remainder in fee simple in A. *Then* the doctrine of *merger* steps in, and A's life estate and vested remainder merge, giving A a fee simple in possession.

---

e.g. **Example—remainder to heirs of A's body:** O conveys "to A for life, then to the heirs of A's body." The Rule in Shelley's Case converts the remainder limited to "the heirs of A's body" into a remainder in fee tail in A. The fee tail is then changed into whatever estate is substituted for a fee tail under state law, probably a fee simple (*see supra*, §318). Then the remainder in A merges with A's life estate. [**Evans v. Giles,** 415 N.E.2d 354 (Ill. 1980)]

---

(1) Doctrine of merger [§485]

The doctrine of merger is an entirely separate doctrine from the Rule in Shelley's Case. The doctrine of merger is that a life estate in A and a remainder in A will merge unless (i) there is an intervening estate *or* (ii) the remainder in A is subject to a condition precedent to which his life estate is not subject. The doctrine of merger may or may not apply after the Rule in Shelley's Case has operated on the instrument.

b. Reasons for Rule

(1) Feudal tax evasion [§486]

The origin of the Rule in Shelley's Case is obscure, but it is probable that it arose to prevent feudal tax evasion. The feudal incidents (*supra*, §243) were due only if the new tenant acquired his interest by descent from the former tenant. The Rule in Shelley's Case makes the remainder into words of limitation, giving A the remainder, which may merge with A's life estate, giving A a descendible fee simple.

(2) Alienability [§487]

The Rule makes land alienable one generation earlier. In the preceding example, a fee simple can be conveyed by A immediately after the conveyance from O. The land is not tied up during A's lifetime. If the Rule in Shelley's Case has any modern justification, this is it.

(3) Does not apply to personal property [§488]

Because the original reasons for the Rule had no application to personal property, in which there were no feudal incidents, the Rule in Shelley's Case does not apply to personal property. [*But see* **Society National Bank v. Jacobson,** 560 N.E.2d 217 (Ohio 1990)—applying Rule to personal property]

---

e.g. Example: T devises her farm "to X as trustee, to be sold, with the proceeds to be held in trust to pay A the income for life, and on A's death to pay the principal to A's heirs." Under the doctrine of equitable conversion (*infra*, §1547), because the land must be sold on T's death and converted into personal property, equity treats the interests of A and A's heirs as being interests in personal property from the beginning. The Rule in Shelley's Case does not apply. However, if T had devised her farm "to X as trustee to pay A the income for life, and *on A's death either to sell the farm* and distribute the proceeds to A's heirs *or* to convey the farm to A's heirs," the case would be different. Because the sale is *optional*, equitable conversion would not apply to change the remainder to a remainder in personal property. The life estate and the remainder are both in land, and the Rule in Shelley's Case applies, giving A a fee simple. [**City Bank & Trust Co. v. Morrissey,** 454 N.E.2d 1195 (Ill. 1983)]

---

c. Operation of Rule [§489]

The Rule is more readily understood if each element of the Rule is separately analyzed.

(1) "If one instrument creates a freehold estate in A" [§490]

Although in England the freehold could be a fee tail or a life estate, all American cases applying the Rule in Shelley's Case have involved a *life estate*. Hence the discussion here assumes the freehold in A is a life estate. The life estate can be measured by A's life or it can be a life estate pur autre vie.

---

e.g. Example: O conveys "to A for the life of B, remainder to A's heirs." The Rule in Shelley's Case applies, and the Rule converts the remainder in A's heirs into a remainder in fee simple in A. A life estate in A (even measured by B's life) and a vested remainder in A comprise the totality of interests in the land; thus, A has a fee simple. *But compare:* If O had conveyed "to A for the life of B, remainder to B's heirs," the Rule in Shelley's Case would not apply. The life estate must be given to the ancestor of the heirs given the remainder.

(a) Life estate determinable [§491]

The life estate can be determinable or subject to condition subsequent.

Example: T devises a farm "to my wife W during her widowhood, and upon W's death or remarriage, remainder to W's heirs." The Rule in Shelley's Case applies, giving W the remainder. The remainder merges with W's life estate, giving W a fee simple.

(b) Life estate in remainder [§492]

The freehold can be a life estate in possession or a life estate in remainder. The Rule in Shelley's Case applies to a conveyance "to A for life, then to B for life, remainder to B's heirs." B has a remainder in fee simple.

1) Subject to condition precedent [§493]

If the life estate in A is subject to a condition precedent that is not also applicable to the remainder to A's heirs, the Rule in Shelley's Case does not apply. (The Rule might apply later, when the condition is met. *See infra,* §502.)

Example: O conveys "to A for life, then, if B marries C, to B for life, remainder to the heirs of B (whether or not B marries C)." The life estate is subject to a condition precedent that does not apply to the remainder. The Rule in Shelley's Case does not apply. (*But note:* If B marries C during A's life, the Rule in Shelley's Case *then* applies. *See infra,* §502.)

a) Remainder subject to same condition precedent [§494]

If the remainder is subject to the same condition precedent as the life estate, then the Rule in Shelley's Case applies. Thus if, in the preceding example, the language in parentheses had been omitted and the condition precedent of B marrying C were construed to be a condition precedent on the remainder as well as on B's life estate, the Rule in Shelley's Case would have applied. B would have taken a remainder in fee simple subject to the condition precedent of marrying C.

(2) "And purports to create a remainder" [§495]

The Rule applies to a remainder to the heirs of A, the life tenant, even though there is an intervening estate between the life estate and remainder. For example, the Rule applies to a conveyance "to A for life, then to B for life, then to A's heirs." A has a remainder in fee simple by the operation of the Rule. A's remainder does not, however, merge with his life estate; B's intervening remainder for life prevents merger.

(a) Contingent remainder [§496]

The remainder may be a remainder contingent on the happening of some condition precedent. Thus the Rule in Shelley's Case applies to a conveyance "to A for life, then to A's heirs if A survives B." A has a life estate and a contingent remainder, contingent on A's surviving B. The life estate and contingent remainder do not merge.

1) Note

It was noted above (*supra*, §493) that the rule did *not* apply if the life estate were subject to a condition precedent not also applicable to the remainder. But the Rule *does* apply in the converse situation, where there is a condition precedent on the remainder but not on the life estate. [Restatement (First) of Property ("Rest.") §312, comments o, p] This is simply an arbitrary distinction, without any reason.

(b) Executory interest [§497]

The Rule in Shelley's Case, as traditionally stated, applies only where a remainder, not an executory interest, has been created.

(3) "In A's heirs (or the heirs of A's body)" [§498]

The remainder must be given to A's heirs or heirs of the body in an indefinite line of succession rather than a specific class of takers.

(a) Indefinite line of succession [§499]

The distinction between "heirs" meaning those persons who take on A's death and "heirs" meaning an indefinite line of succession is hard to grasp. It is easier to understand in the English context of primogeniture, where the distinction originated. Under the doctrine of primogeniture, a person has only one heir, and therefore the word "heirs" can easily be taken to describe an indefinite succession of heirs. After primogeniture was abolished, the distinction became pretty ephemeral, and some courts have not grasped it—or have ignored it.

(b) Words meaning indefinite line of succession [§500]

The Rule in Shelley's Case does not apply to a remainder limited to "A's children" or "A's issue," because those words cannot be taken to mean heirs in an indefinite life of succession. The words "heirs" or "heirs of the body," however, are rather arbitrarily said to refer to heirs in an indefinite line of succession, unless the grantor shows he means something different.

Example: J.H. Sybert devises land "to Fred for life, and after his death to vest in fee simple in the heirs of his body." Fred dies childless, leaving his wife, Eunice, as his heir. Does the Rule in Shelley's Case apply so that Fred took a life estate and remainder in fee tail, which was converted by the fee tail statute into a remainder in fee simple, which merged with Fred's life estate, giving Fred a fee simple? If so, Fred's fee simple passes to his wife on Fred's death. If the Rule does not apply, the reversioner takes the land because Fred died without bodily heirs. The words "heirs of the body" are traditional words bringing the devise within Shelley's Case, and the Rule applies. [**Sybert v. Sybert**, 254 S.W.2d 999 (Tex. 1953)] If J.H. Sybert had said remainder "to Fred's issue," the Rule in Shelley's Case would not apply. Of course "heirs of the body" and "issue" describe exactly the same persons, but "issue" is said not to be a technical word signifying an indefinite line of takers. Rather it signifies persons who take at Fred's death. What this adds up to is that a remainder "to A's heirs" or "the heirs of A's body" are simply *magic words* triggering the Rule in Shelley's Case.

(4) "And the estates are both legal or both equitable" [§501]

The life estate and remainder must be either both legal or both equitable. If one is legal and the other is equitable, the Rule in Shelley's Case does not apply.

Example: O conveys Blackacre "to X in trust for the life of A to pay A the income and profits, remainder to the heirs of A." X has a legal life estate pur autre vie. A has an equitable life estate and A's heirs have a legal remainder in fee simple. Because A's life estate is equitable and the remainder to A's heirs is legal, the Rule in Shelley's Case does not apply. If X had been given a legal fee simple, the life estate and remainder would both be equitable, and the Rule in Shelley's Case would apply. [**City Bank & Trust Co. v. Morrissey**, *supra*, §488]

(5) Application of the Rule on a delayed basis [§502]

If the requirements for application of the Rule are not initially met at the time of the conveyance, *but are met subsequently*, the Rule in Shelley's Case will apply subsequently when the requirements are met.

---

e.g. **Example:** O conveys "to A for life, then, if B marries C, to B for life, remainder to the heirs of B (whether or not B marries C)." The Rule does not apply initially because the life estate in B is subject to a condition precedent not also applicable to the remainder to B's heirs (*see supra*, §493). But if B marries C during A's life, satisfying the condition, the Rule in Shelley's Case applies on B's marriage to C. (Thus, for a wedding gift B gets a remainder in fee simple.)

---

d. The Rule is a rule of law [§503]

The Rule in Shelley's Case is a rule of law (not a rule of construction) that applies regardless of O's intent. If the conveyance by O comes within its terms, the Rule in Shelley's Case applies regardless of what O wants.

EXAM TIP	gilbert

Remember the Rule in Shelley's Case *cannot* be avoided by expressions of intent, such as, "I intend that the Rule in Shelley's Case not apply." O's intent is irrelevant.

e. Avoidance of Rule [§504]

The Rule cannot be avoided by a direct expression of intent, but it can be avoided by failing to come within its requirements. A conveyance "to A for 100 years if A so long lives, then to A's heirs" is the standard device used by skilled drafters to avoid the Rule. The Rule does not apply because A has a *leasehold*, not a freehold.

f. Modern status [§505]

The Rule in Shelley's Case has been abolished by statute in the great majority of jurisdictions. The Rule apparently is still in effect in Arkansas, Delaware, Indiana, and possibly a few other states. In some states, the abolition of the Rule in Shelley's Case is fairly recent, so the old law, which remains applicable to conveyances made before abolition, will be of some concern for many years.

(1) Effect where abolished [§506]

If the Rule in Shelley's Case is abolished, a conveyance "to A for life, then to A's heirs" creates a life estate in A, and a contingent remainder in A's heirs.

4. Doctrine of Worthier Title [§507]

The Doctrine of Worthier Title is the third of the three rules restricting remainders dealt with here, the others being the destructibility rule and the Rule in Shelley's

Case. The Doctrine of Worthier Title has an inter vivos branch and (perhaps) a testamentary branch.

a. Common law Doctrine

(1) Inter vivos branch of Doctrine [§508]

When an inter vivos conveyance purports to create a *future interest* in the *heirs of the grantor*, the future interest is *void* and the grantor has a reversion. This rule is sometimes known as a rule against a remainder in the grantor's heirs.

 Example: O conveys "to A for life, then to O's heirs." The remainder to O's heirs is void, and O has a reversion.

(a) Original reason [§509]

The original reason for the Doctrine of Worthier Title is probably the same as for the Rule in Shelley's Case. Feudal incidents were due on *descent* of land. In the above example, feudal incidents would be due on O's death if he had a reversion passing to his heirs, but not if his heirs took by way of a remainder created during O's life. Hence the Doctrine prevented O from depriving his lord of feudal incidents by an inter vivos conveyance of this kind.

(2) Testamentary branch of Doctrine [§510]

If a person *devises* land to his *heirs*, the devise is void and the heirs take by *descent*. The simplest example of this is a devise by T "to A for life, then to T's heirs." The devise to T's heirs is void; T's heirs take the reversion after A's death by descent. The Restatement (First) of Property section 314(2) says the testamentary branch of the Doctrine of Worthier Title does not exist in this country. [*See In re* **Estate of Kern**, 274 N.W.2d 325 (Iowa 1979)—abolishing testamentary branch]

b. Modern rule [§511]

In view of the fact that the testamentary branch of the Doctrine is moribund or nonexistent, further references in this Summary to the Doctrine refer only to the inter vivos branch. The common law Doctrine of Worthier Title was a *rule of law* applicable to *land* only. The modern Doctrine of Worthier Title applies to *personal property* as well as to land. It is a *rule of construction*, not a rule of law. It raises a *presumption* that no remainder has been created, but this presumption can be rebutted by evidence of a contrary intent of the grantor.

EXAM TIP	gilbert

Note that the Doctrine of Worthier Title is different from the Rule in Shelley's Case: The Doctrine is a rule of **construction**, which may be rebutted by evidence of the grantor's intent; the Rule in Shelley's Case is a rule of *law* and the grantor's intent cannot change it.

---

(1) Justification [§512]

The Doctrine of Worthier Title can be justified as a rule designed to carry out the grantor's intent. It is assumed that grantors seldom intend to create a remainder in their heirs that they cannot change, and therefore, the Doctrine gives the grantor the right to change his mind by voiding the remainder and creating a reversion in the grantor. Another justification for the modern rule is that it makes property alienable earlier. In the above example, A and O can together convey a fee simple. If the Doctrine did not apply, a fee simple could not be conveyed until O's death, when O's heirs are ascertained.

c. Operation of Doctrine

(1) Limitation to heirs [§513]

For the Doctrine to apply, a future interest must be given to the grantor's "heirs" or "next of kin," or some equivalent term must be used. The Doctrine does *not* apply to a future interest limited to "O's children" or "O's issue," or to "O's heirs ascertained at the death of the life tenant A." [**Harris Trust & Savings Bank v. Beach,** 513 N.E.2d 833 (Ill. 1987); **Braswell v. Braswell,** 81 S.E.2d 560 (Va. 1954)] This requirement of the Doctrine is rather similar to the requirement of the Rule in Shelley's Case that the technical word "heirs" be used. (*See supra*, §500.)

(2) Kind of future interest immaterial [§514]

The Doctrine applies to a *remainder* or an *executory interest* limited to O's heirs. The future interest may be *legal* or *equitable*, or subject to a condition precedent other than the ascertainment of heirs.

(3) Preceding estate [§515]

The character of the estate preceding the future interest in O's heirs is immaterial. It may be a fee simple defeasible, fee tail, life estate, or term of years.

(4) Typical applications

(a) Revocation of trust [§516]

Suppose that O conveys property "to X in trust to pay the income to O for life, and on O's death to convey the trust assets to O's heirs." O retains no power to revoke. Subsequently, O wants to revoke the trust and get the property back. Under the law, a trust can be terminated if *all owners* of the equitable interests consent. Hence, if O's heirs do not have a remainder, but O has a reversion, O owns all the equitable interests in the trust and can terminate it. Under the Doctrine of Worthier Title, O is presumed to have a reversion and can terminate the trust. (Of course, contrary evidence can show that O intended to create a remainder in O's heirs and there has been considerable litigation over what contrary evidence is sufficient to rebut the presumption of a reversion.)

(b) Devise by O [§517]

Suppose that O conveys Blackacre "to A for life, then to A's issue, and if A should die without issue, then the land shall go to O's heirs." Subsequently O dies, devising all his property to B. O's heir is C. Under the Doctrine, O is presumed to have a reversion (and his heirs nothing). Therefore, O devises his reversion to B. Later A dies without leaving issue. B and not C owns Blackacre at A's death. [**Braswell v. Braswell,** *supra*]

(5) Effect of abolition of Rule in Shelley's Case [§518]

The abolition of the Rule in Shelley's Case has no effect on the Doctrine of Worthier Title. Suppose that O conveys Blackacre "to X in trust to pay the income to O for life, remainder to O's heirs." Under the Rule in Shelley's Case, the remainder limited to O's heirs becomes a reversion in O, which merges with O's life estate, giving O an equitable fee simple. If the Rule in Shelley's Case has been abolished, what happens? The Doctrine of Worthier Title presumes that the remainder is void and O has a reversion. Thus, the result is the same as under the Rule in Shelley's Case.

d. Abolition of Doctrine [§519]

The Doctrine of Worthier Title, unlike the Rule in Shelley's Case, apparently is still valid in many jurisdictions. It has been abolished in quite a few states, including California, Massachusetts, and New York. Where it has been abolished, the heirs of O take the future interest given to them under the instrument.

5. Recapitulation and Comparison [§520]

The destructibility rule, the Rule in Shelley's Case, and the Doctrine of Worthier Title should be compared. A comparison is helpful in remembering how the rules apply.

a. Destructibility rule [§521]

This rule applies only to *legal contingent remainders* in *land*. It does not apply to equitable interests, to interests in trust, nor to personal property. It is a *rule of law*, not a rule designed to carry out the grantor's intent.

b. Rule in Shelley's Case [§522]

This Rule applies to *legal and equitable remainders* in *land*. It does not apply to personal property. It is a *rule of law*, not a rule designed to carry out the grantor's intent.

c. Doctrine of Worthier Title [§523]

This Doctrine applies to *legal and equitable remainders* and *executory interests* in *real or personal property*. It is a *rule of construction* designed to carry out the grantor's intent, and can be overcome by contrary evidence of intent.

TECHNICAL RULES OF THE COMMON LAW

gilbert

	DESTRUCTION OF CONTINGENT REMAINDERS	RULE IN SHELLEY'S CASE	DOCTRINE OF WORTHIER TITLE
RULE	Contingent remainders are destroyed if not vested at time of termination of preceding estate.	If an instrument creates a freehold estate in A and a remainder in A's heirs, the remainder becomes a remainder in fee simple in A.	An inter vivos conveyance attempting to create a future interest in the grantor's heirs is ineffective, so grantor has a reversion.
EXAMPLE	"To A for life, remainder to A's children who reach 21."	"To A for life, then to A's heirs."	"To A for life, then to my heirs at law."
RESULT	If A has no children who are at least 21 at the time of her death, property reverts to grantor.	A has a fee simple.	A has a life estate; the grantor has a reversion.
MODERN STATUS	Abolished in most jurisdictions.	Abolished in most jurisdictions.	Generally treated as rule of construction (*i.e.,* raises a rebuttable presumption); does not apply in this country to testamentary grants.
MODERN RESULT	Property reverts to grantor; A's children have indestructible contingent remainder or an executory interest.	A has a life estate and A's heirs have a contingent remainder.	Grantor's heirs have a future interest given to them under the instrument.

H. The Rule Against Perpetuities

1. Historical Background [§524]

Beginning with the Statute Quia Emptores (1290), the idea of free alienation of property was an important force in the development of English property law. From feudal times to the nineteenth century, judges and the landed aristocracy engaged in a continuing series of running battles, the lords trying to find means of keeping land in the family, the judges trying to curb the dynastic devices invented by lawyers for the lords. The judges defeated the early dynastic device of the fee tail by permitting a fee tail tenant to engage in a fictitious lawsuit (known as a common recovery), which resulted in a fee simple (*see supra*, §313). Afterwards, lawyers for the landed aristocracy turned to the creation of life estates and remainders as dynastic devices, but the judges threw up new roadblocks or firmed up existing ones. The three main hindrances to the dynastic urge were the rule of destructibility of contingent remainders (*supra*, §464), the Rule in Shelley's Case (*supra*, §483), and the Doctrine of Worthier Title (*supra*, §507). But these rules applied only to remainders, and a century after the Statute of Uses (1536), it appeared that some new rule would be necessary to curb executory interests made possible by the Statute. No existing rule clearly prohibited the creation of an indefinite series of shifting executory interests. **Duke of Norfolk's Case,** 22 Eng. Rep. 931 (1682), laid the foundation for a new Rule Against Perpetuities. As finally agreed upon, the Rule applies to *all contingent future interests*, contingent remainders as well as executory interests. After the Rule developed fully, the older rules applicable to contingent remainders alone (destructibility and Shelley's Case) were abolished in most jurisdictions. Thus, the Rule Against Perpetuities stands today as the principal guardian against the control of the living by the dead hand. (For a detailed treatment of this Rule, *see* Future Interests Summary.)

2. Statement of Rule [§525]

The classic formulation of the Rule is by John Chipman Gray, one of the first great teachers of property law at Harvard: *No interest is good unless it must vest, if at all, not later than 21 years after some life in being at the creation of the interest.* Although Gray put the Rule in this one sentence, it took him more than 800 pages to explain it in the fourth edition of his treatise on the Rule. This subject will be covered in considerably fewer words here.

a. Reason for period [§526]

The judges selected lives in being plus 21 years as the permissible period for contingent interests to exist for this reason: A parent could realistically and perhaps wisely assess the capabilities of *living* members of the family, and so, with respect to them, the parent's judgment was given effect. Thus, the parent could protect the family from incompetent management during the lives of those he personally knew and until the first generation after them reached majority. The actual minority period, first tacked on to lives in being, was in time converted into a 21-year period in gross.

3. Interests Subject to Rule [§527]

The Rule applies to *contingent remainders* and *executory interests*. It does *not* apply to vested remainders or to future interests in the grantor (reversion, possibility of reverter, and right of entry), which are treated as vested upon creation.

> **Example:** O conveys "to A for life, then to A's children for their lives, then to B and his heirs." A has no children. The conveyance is entirely valid. The remainder for life given to A's children will vest, if at all, at A's death. The remainder in fee simple in B is a vested remainder when created.

EXAM TIP	gilbert

Although the Rule Against Perpetuities is one of the most feared and confusing rules of law you will ever encounter, there are some simple rules to help you apply it. One rule is that the Rule Against Perpetuities applies to *contingent remainders and executory interests*. When you see either of these on your exam, think about the Rule. On the other hand, you don't need to consider any of the *grantor's interests* (reversions, possibilities of reverter, rights of entry), as they are considered to be vested and thus safe from the Rule.

4. What-Might-Happen Is Test [§528]

The Rule is directed at the creation of *contingent* interests that *might vest* in the distant future (the distant future being defined as more than 21 years after the expiration of lives in being at the creation of the interest). If there is *any possibility* that a contingent interest will vest too remotely, the contingent interest is *void* from the outset. The thing to look for is the possibility of remote vesting. Courts do not wait to see what happens, but look at the interest at the time of creation and determine then if the interest will necessarily *vest or fail* within the perpetuities period set by the Rule. If it will not necessarily vest or fail within the period—if there is any possibility that it may vest beyond the period—it is void.

> **Example:** O conveys "to the first child of A who becomes a lawyer." A has a daughter D in law school. The gift is void. It is possible for the first child of A who becomes a lawyer to be a child not alive at the time of the conveyance. This is what *might happen*: D may die before becoming a lawyer. Then A, bereft at D's death and desiring a lawyer in the family, procreates another child—Hope—born two years later. The following year, A dies. Some 25 years later, Hope becomes a lawyer and claims the gift—but this is more than 21 years after the deaths of A and D (the only relevant lives). Thus, the gift is void.

a. Rule is a rule of proof [§529]

The preceding example illustrates that the Rule is a *rule of logical proof*. The person claiming that the gift is valid must prove without a shadow of a doubt that there is no possibility of it vesting too remotely. The person claiming that the gift is void must prove the opposite—*i.e.*, that there is a possibility of remote vesting. Whoever can prove the case wins.

(1) Possibility of vesting in time not sufficient [§530]

The Rule strikes down an interest if there is *any possibility* of remote vesting. It will not save the gift to prove that the gift *might* vest within the perpetuities period. To save it, it must *necessarily* vest or fail within the period. Hence, in the preceding example, D cannot save the gift by showing it might vest in her. She must prove that it cannot vest in any-one more than 21 years after A and D are dead, and that she cannot do.

(2) Vest or fail [§531]

The Rule says a contingent interest must *vest or fail* within a life in be-ing plus 21 years. The words "vest or fail" mean the contingency must be resolved, one way or the other, within that period.

EXAM TIP   **gilbert**

In analyzing Rule Against Perpetuities problems, keep in mind that the key is when the interest *could possibly vest*—not when it is likely to vest or even when it did. You must *examine the grant as of the time of its creation* and be sure that if the interest vests it will be within the period of the Rule (*i.e.*, life in being plus 21 years). If there is any possibility (no matter how absurd) that it could vest beyond the period, it is void.

---

5. Lives in Being [§532]

In solving perpetuities problems you are looking for a person in being when the future interest is created who enables you to prove the interest will vest or fail during that person's life, or at that person's death, or within 21 years after that person's death. If you find such a person, that person is the *validating* life (also known as the *measuring* life). If you do not find a validating life, the future inter-est is void unless it will necessarily vest or fail within 21 years.

a. Relevant lives [§533]

The only possible persons who can be used to prove validity are *persons who can affect vesting* of the interest. If you find a validating life, it will be a per-son who can affect vesting. All other persons can be ignored as irrelevant.

EXAM TIP   **gilbert**

Many people get themselves confused about lives in being and validating lives. Lives in being are merely people (not animals, plants, etc.) alive at the time the interest is created. Obviously, many people are alive at the time an interest is created, but the only ones you care about are those who can *affect vesting*—those are the lives who may enable you to prove the interest is valid. To find a life that proves the interest is valid, look first to the people *mentioned in the grant* and weed out the ones that do not affect vesting (*i.e.*, weed out the irrelevant lives). Then see if you can prove the interest will vest within the life of any one of the remaining relevant persons, or within 21 years after one of those persons' death. For example, if you have a grant "To A for life, then to B's children whenever born," consider whether you can prove the remainder will necessarily vest within the life of A or of B. It will vest within the life of B, because B's children will all be in being when B dies. So B is the validating life. Sometimes the validating life will *not be mentioned* in the instrument, but will be found in some person who

---

can affect vesting of the future interest. Usually this person or persons will be a parent or parents of the remaindermen. An example is: T bequeaths property to "such of my grandchildren as shall attain the age of 21." This is valid. The validating lives are T's children. You can prove the remainder will vest within 21 years after the death of T's children.

b. When lives in being determined [§534]

Generally speaking, the validating life must be a person *alive at the creation of the contingent interest*. Thus, if the interest is created by *will*, the validating life must be a person alive at the testator's death. If the interest is created by an *irrevocable inter vivos transfer*, the validating life must be a person alive at the date of the transfer. If the interest is created by a *revocable trust*, the validating life must be a person alive when the power of revocation ceases (usually at the settlor's death).

(1) Comment

Technically speaking, one should not say that the validating life must be a person *alive* at the creation of the contingent interest, but rather *alive or already deceased* at that time. For example, a testator who creates a contingent interest by will may qualify as a validating life, even though the testator is dead by the time the interest is created (a will is effective only at the testator's death).

(2) Child in womb [§535]

A child in the womb when the interest is created is treated as a life in being if the child is later born alive. Any actual periods of gestation are included within the permissible perpetuities period.

(3) Illustration—validating life

In a bequest "to A when A marries" or "to A's children," the validating life is A because the contingency (marriage or birth of children) must happen, if at all, within A's life plus a period of gestation thereafter. Thus the gift will vest, if at all, within A's life. If the bequest is "to A's children who reach 21," A is the validating life. Every child of A must necessarily reach 21 within 21 years of A's death plus a period of gestation. Thus the gift will vest, if at all, within 21 years after A's death.

(4) Illustration—no validating life (void gift)

T devises property "to A for life, then to A's children who reach 25." A has no children at T's death. The remainder is void because you cannot prove it will necessarily vest or fail within 21 years of A's death. Here is what *might happen*: Two years after T's death, C is born to A. The following year, A dies. Twenty-four years later, C reaches 25 and the remainder vests. Vesting has occurred more than 21 years after A's death. (No one other than A is useful in making the proof required, because A is the only life in being who can affect vesting. Try using Queen Elizabeth or Barbra Streisand, and you'll see you can't prove a thing by them.)

(5) Illustration—validating lives

Professor Jones gives $1,000 to be divided among all members of her property class who are admitted to the bar. This gift is good. The members of the property class are the validating *lives* (or, if you want to narrow it, the survivor of these persons is the validating *life*). The gift must vest or fail within the lives of the members of the property class. It will be known by the death of the survivor—and maybe sooner—which members of the class are admitted to the bar.

(a) Distinguish

How does this differ from the example in §528, "to the first child of A who becomes a lawyer," which is void? Here, the only possible takers are presently living members of the property class, and the condition precedent (admission to the bar) must happen, if at all, during their lives. In the earlier example, the taker—the first child of A to be a lawyer—might be a child of A not now alive.

6. Meaning of "Vest" [§536]

The four-letter word "vest" in the Rule has an uncommon ability to beget other four-letter words, for it is here that all the learning about vested and contingent remainders discussed earlier (*supra*, §§401 *et seq.*) becomes relevant—indeed, decisive. A vested interest is not subject to the Rule Against Perpetuities; a contingent interest is.

a. Exception—class gift [§537]

There is one major exception to applying the learning about vested and contingent remainders under the Rule Against Perpetuities. A *gift to a class* is not vested *in any member of the class until the interests of all members have vested*. Or to put it differently, a class gift is not vested under the Rule Against Perpetuities until *all class members are identified* and *all conditions precedent have been satisfied* for every member of the class. If the gift to one member of the class might vest too remotely, the whole class gift is void. This is known as the "all-or-nothing" rule.

Example: T devises "to A for life, then to A's children for their lives, then to A's grandchildren in fee simple." In 2006, T dies. The gift to A's children will vest, if at all, at A's death. It is valid. But the remainder to A's grandchildren is void. If A has a grandchild (B) alive at the time of T's death, the remainder is vested in B subject to open and let in other grandchildren (*see supra*, §408), *but it is not vested under the Rule Against Perpetuities*. The remainder is a class gift and will not vest until all takers are identified. They will not necessarily be identified at the death of A's children living in 2006; A can have an afterborn child who is A's last surviving child. Here is what might happen: In 2008, A has an afterborn child, Hope. In 2010, A and all of A's children and grandchildren alive in 2006 die in a common disaster. Only Hope, the afterborn child, survives. In the year 2036, Hope gives birth to a daughter, Faith. Hope dies in 2037. All of A's grandchildren can now be identified, and they will include Faith. But they have not all been identified within 21 years after the deaths of A and all of A's children and grandchildren alive in 2006. The entire class gift to A's grandchildren is void because this scenario might happen. [**Connecticut Bank & Trust Co. v. Brody,** 392 A.2d 445 (Conn. 1978)] Note, however, that if A had died before T, then the gift to the grandchildren would be valid because all of A's children would have been born by the time T's will became effective (*i.e.,* on T's death; *see supra,* §534). Hence, they could be used as validating lives.

(1) Rationale

A class gift is not vested under the Rule until all the class members are known and have vested interests *because* only at that point is the interest marketable. As a practical matter, property cannot be sold so long as some owners are unascertained. Hence, although a class gift may be vested in one member subject to open up and let in others, which may satisfy other rules restricting contingent remainders (*see supra,* §465), such a class gift does not satisfy the policy of the Rule Against Perpetuities against making property unmarketable too long.

b. Executory interest [§538]

An executory interest following a fee simple determinable or divesting a fee simple cannot vest in interest before it vests in possession. An executory interest following a determinable fee or divesting a fee simple *vests only when the condition happens and it becomes a possessory estate.*

7. Remote Possibilities [§539]

An interest is void under the Rule Against Perpetuities if by *any possibility*—however remote—the interest might vest beyond the perpetuities period. If a situation *can be imagined* in which the interest might not vest or fail within the relevant lives in being plus 21 years, the interest is void. The following cases illustrate the harsh and sometimes surprising consequences of a vivid judicial imagination and are what have brought the what-might-happen test into disrepute in recent years.

a. The fertile octogenarian [§540]

The law *conclusively presumes* that a person *can have children so long as the person is alive.* Evidence that a person is 80 years of age or has had a hysterectomy or vasectomy is irrelevant. After all, a person of any age can adopt a child. This principle is frequently overlooked by lawyers who naturally assume that 80-year-old persons will not have any more children, and proceed to draw instruments in violation of the Rule Against Perpetuities.

Example: T devises property "to Mary, and if Mary's line of descendants ever runs out, to the daughters then living of Elizabeth Jee (aged 80)." T is survived by Mary, Elizabeth, and four daughters of Elizabeth. The event upon which the Jee daughters' gift is conditioned—the death of Mary and all her descendants—is an event that may happen centuries hence. Is the gift to the Jee daughters valid? No. There is no relevant life by which they can prove the gift valid. Test them: The gift will not necessarily vest or fail at Mary's death, because the condition precedent ("expiration of Mary's issue") will not necessarily happen at Mary's death. Mary may leave an afterborn child who dies unmarried and without issue 50 years after Mary's death. Mary's bloodline would then expire. Nor will the condition precedent happen at Elizabeth's death. Why won't the gift vest, if at all, within the lifetimes of the Jee daughters living at T's death? The devise says to the Jee daughters "then living," which requires the takers to be alive when Mary's bloodline runs out, and, if they are not alive, the gift fails. The gift is void because it is to the Jee "daughters," including afterborn daughters. Elizabeth (aged 80) can have another daughter and this daughter may be alive when Mary's bloodline expires and may claim the gift. The gift thus may vest in the afterborn daughter more than 21 years after the death of Elizabeth, Mary, and the four living Jee daughters. [**Jee v. Audley**, 29 Eng. Rep. 1186 (1787)]

b. The unborn widow [§541]

The law assumes that a person's *surviving spouse* might turn out to be a person *not now alive*. For example, a man's present wife may die or be divorced, and the man may in the future marry a woman not now alive. This assumption leads to the unborn widow case.

Example: T devises property "to my son A for his life, then to my son's widow for her life, then to my son's issue who survive my son and his widow." The life estate in the son's widow is valid because it will necessarily vest or fail at the son's death. The remainder to the son's issue is void because it will not vest until the death of the son's widow, and she may be a person not now alive.

c. The slothful executor [§542]

It has been held that a bequest to vest "when my estate is settled" or "when my executor is appointed" violates the Rule because the named event may not happen within lives in being plus 21 years. The will may not be probated or the estate may be in litigation for decades. [**Ryan v. Beshk**, 170 N.E. 699 (Ill. 1930)]

EXAM TIP   gilbert

The fertile octogenarian, unborn widow, and slothful executor are the classic traps for the unwary. The first two are the more common. Whenever you see facts indicating that a life tenant is old, think about the fertile octogenarian problem. And whenever you see a grant to my "wife," "husband," or "spouse" **with no name given in the grant**, think about the unborn widow problem. Be careful not to allow your emotions to sway your answer when you encounter these situations on an exam. No matter how unjust the result, if there is **any** possibility that an interest might not vest or fail within the relevant lives in being plus 21 years, the interest is void.

8. Application to Defeasible Fees [§543]

The Rule Against Perpetuities does *not* apply to possibilities of reverter and rights of entry, which are regarded as vested interests, but it does apply to executory interests. This exemption of possibilities of reverter and rights of entry from the Rule has led to some strange results.

a. Fee simple determinable [§544]

A possibility of reverter is exempt from the Rule. An executory interest is subject to it. Any executory interest following a fee simple determinable that violates the Rule Against Perpetuities is struck out, as with a blue pencil, leaving the fee simple determinable standing. Whatever is left after striking out the void interest is given effect as written.

---

e.g. **Example:** O conveys Blackacre "to the School Board so long as used for school purposes, and if the land shall cease to be used for school purposes, to A and his heirs." A's executory interest, if valid, would be transmissible to A's heirs, and their heirs, and so on through time. It might not become possessory for centuries, and certainly it will not necessarily become possessory within A's life plus 21 years. A's executory interest is void. The language "and if the land shall cease to be used for school purposes, to A and his heirs," which is the language giving A an executory interest, is struck out. This leaves standing, "to the School Board so long as used for school purposes." This language gives the Board a fee simple determinable, which is not increased by striking out A's interest. Because the Board has only a fee simple determinable, which will automatically end when the land ceases to be used for school purposes, O has a *possibility of reverter*. [**First Universalist Society v. Boland,** 29 N.E. 524 (Mass. 1892); **City of Klamath Falls v. Bell,** 490 P.2d 515 (Or. 1971)]

---

(1) Criticism

The result in the example above is absurd in terms of policy. The land is tied up for exactly the same amount of time whether the future interest is an executory interest in a grantee or a possibility of reverter in the grantor. The result follows only because the possibility of reverter is exempt from the Rule, whereas the executory interest is subject to it.

(a) How O should do it [§545]

The lawyer for O can accomplish O's desires in the preceding example by using two deeds instead of one. The lawyer calls O, A, and a representative of the School Board into her office. The lawyer has prepared a deed reading, "O conveys Blackacre to A and his heirs." O hands this deed to A. A now owns Blackacre. The lawyer has also prepared a deed reading, "A conveys Blackacre to the School Board so long as used for school purposes." A hands this to the Board representative. This gives the Board a fee simple determinable, leaving a possibility of reverter in A exempt from the Rule Against Perpetuities. Thus, two pieces of paper rather than one will do the trick—and the lawyer may be liable for malpractice if she does not use them.

(2) Exception—gift over from one charity to another charity [§546]

If there is a gift to Charity A followed by a diverting gift to Charity B if a specified event happens, the executory interest in Charity B is *exempt from the Rule Against Perpetuities*. Thus, in the above example, if O had conveyed "to the School Board so long as used for school purposes, then to the Red Cross," the conveyance would be entirely valid. The reason for this exception is as follows. Charities are favorites of the law. A charitable trust can last forever. There is no objection to shifting enjoyment from charity to charity through time. *But note:* This exception applies *only* if *both* the possessory estate and the future interest are in charitable organizations.

EXAM TIP   **gilbert**

The charity-to-charity exception to the Rule comes up occasionally on exams. The important point to remember is that the exception applies only if the gift shifts *from one charity to another*. If the gift shifts from a private to a charitable use or from a charitable to a private use, the Rule Against Perpetuities applies and you must consider whether the interest is valid (and usually it is not).

---

b. Fee simple subject to an executory limitation [§547]

The example of the determinable fee above should be compared with a fee simple subject to an executory limitation. The difference in language is very slight but the difference in results is startling. Suppose that O conveys Blackacre "to the School Board, but if Blackacre shall cease to be used for school purposes, to A and his heirs." The executory interest in A is void under the Rule Against Perpetuities for the same reason A's executory interest in the preceding example is void. The language creating the executory interest—"but if Blackacre shall cease to be used for school purposes, to A and his heirs"—is struck out. This leaves a conveyance "to the School Board," which of course gives the Board a fee simple absolute. [**Proprietors of the Church in Brattle Square v. Grant,** 69 Mass. 142 (1855)]

EXAM TIP   **gilbert**

When a void interest is stricken, the interests are classified as if the void interest were never there. So *strike out the void interest* and see what you are left with. For example, if O conveys "to A for as long as no liquor is consumed on the premises, then to B," B's interest would be stricken, A would have a fee simple determinable, and O would have a possibility of reverter. In contrast, if O conveys "to A, but if liquor is ever consumed on the premises, then to B," B's interest and the condition are stricken, and A has a fee simple absolute.

---

c. Fee simple determinable created by will [§548]

A possibility of reverter is an interest retained by the grantor if the fee simple determinable is created by a deed; it is retained by the testator's heirs if the fee simple determinable is created by a will. A possibility of reverter cannot be created in a grantee—nor in a devisee. Hence, if the testator creates a fee simple determinable by will, followed by a void executory interest in a devisee, the testator's heirs have a possibility of reverter.

---

e.g. Example: T devises Blackacre "to the Baptist Church so long as used for church purposes, then to A. All the rest and remainder of my property I devise to B." A's executory interest violates the Rule Against Perpetuities and is struck out, leaving a determinable fee in the church. T's heirs—and *not B*—have a possibility of reverter. If B, the residuary devisee, were given the future interest after the determinable fee, B's interest as a residuary devisee would be an executory interest (just as A's interest as a specific devisee was an executory interest), and B's interest would be void. [*In re* **Pruner's Estate**, 162 A.2d 626 (Pa. 1960)]

---

(1) Massachusetts view [§549]

There is a Massachusetts case analyzing the above example in a different way: T created a fee simple determinable in the Church. A's executory interest is void under the Rule. This leaves a possibility of reverter in *testator*, which passes to B under the residuary clause. T's heirs take nothing. [**Brown v. Independent Baptist Church of Woburn**, 91 N.E.2d 922 (Mass. 1950)] This view is logically fallacious, and assumes T died twice. Observe that one crucial step in the reasoning is that "this leaves a possibility of reverter in testator." But this cannot be. Testator is dead! Property rights cannot be created in a dead person. The law substitutes testator's heirs for testator, and if the possibility of reverter is left in testator's heirs, it is their property and cannot be disposed of by the residuary clause. This Massachusetts view assumes that testator died once to create the determinable fee, leaving a possibility of reverter in the resurrected testator, who died a second time to pass the possibility of reverter to B. *Remember:* A possibility of reverter cannot be created in any transferee—neither a grantee in a deed nor a devisee in a will.

9. Application to Options [§550]

An option creates in the optionee a right to purchase the property on terms provided in the option. Because the option is specifically enforceable in equity by the optionee, it is regarded as creating in the optionee an equitable interest in property comparable to a contingent future interest. An option is void if it is possible to exercise the option more than 21 years after some life in being at its creation. [**Central Delaware County Authority v. Greyhound Corp.**, 588 A.2d 485 (Pa. 1991)] The policy reason for subjecting options to the Rule is that if someone has an option on the property, the owner will not improve it and no one else is likely to purchase it. Thus, options tend to make land unimprovable and inalienable.

Example: O conveys "to A and her heirs an option to purchase Blackacre for $10,000." This option is not limited to A's life, but can be exercised by A's heirs and their heirs long after A's death. The option is void.

a. Preemptive options [§551]

A preemptive option gives the optionee the right of first refusal if the owner desires to sell. If the preemptive option can be exercised beyond the perpetuities period, most courts hold the preemptive option—like an ordinary option—void. [**Ferrero Construction Co. v. Dennis Rourke Corp.**, 536 A.2d 1137 (Md. 1988); **Symphony Space, Inc. v. Pergola Properties, Inc.**, 88 N.Y.2d 466 (1996); *but see* **Shiver v. Benton**, 304 S.E.2d 903 (Ga. 1983)—*contra*] For treatment of preemptive options under the rule against unreasonable restraints on alienation, *see supra*, §354.

(1) Exception for condominium [§552]

A preemptive option in a condominium association giving the association the right to buy if the unit owner desires to sell, which permits the association to control who buys in, is not subject to the Rule Against Perpetuities. [**Cambridge Co. v. East Slope Investment Corp.**, 700 P.2d 537 (Colo. 1985)] For treatment of preemptive rights in condominiums or cooperatives under the rule against unreasonable restraints on alienation, *see supra*, §355.

b. Options in leases [§553]

An option in a tenant to renew the term or to purchase the property is not subject to the Rule Against Perpetuities. Such an option stimulates improvement of the property by the tenant and makes the property more, rather than less, marketable. [**Texaco Refining & Marketing, Inc. v. Samowitz**, 570 A.2d 170 (Conn. 1990)]

c. Uniform Statutory Rule Against Perpetuities [§554]

The Uniform Statutory Rule Against Perpetuities, adopted in about half the states, exempts options from the Rule Against Perpetuities. In these states apparently options may endure forever, unless they are subject to the rule against unreasonable restraints on alienation.

10. Wait-and-See Doctrine [§555]

Under the common law Rule Against Perpetuities, any possibility of remote vesting voids the interest. The what-might-happen test has come under fire in the last half-century for defeating reasonable dispositions on the assumption of possible events that, in fact, rarely occur. More than half the states have reformed the Rule by adopting the wait-and-see doctrine. Under the wait-and-see doctrine, the validity of interests is judged by *actual events* as they happen, and not by possible events that might happen. The validity of an interest is not determined at the time the interest is created. It is necessary to wait and see what actually happens.

a. Wait-and-see for the perpetuities period [§556]

Some of the states adopting the wait-and-see doctrine wait out the common law perpetuities period before declaring the contingent interest void. The common law perpetuities period is measured by the lives that can affect vesting plus 21 years. [**Hansen v. Stroecker,** 699 P.2d 871 (Alaska 1985); *In re* **Estate of Anderson,** 541 So. 2d 423 (Miss. 1989); **Merchants National Bank v. Curtis,** 97 A.2d 207 (N.H. 1953); *In re* **Estate of Pearson,** 275 A.2d 336 (Pa. 1971); **Fleet National Bank v. Colt,** 529 A.2d 122 (R.I. 1987)]

b. Wait-and-see for ninety years [§557]

The Uniform Statutory Rule Against Perpetuities (*supra,* §554) rejects waiting for the common law perpetuities period and calls for waiting for 90 years. If a contingent interest satisfies the what-might-happen test of the common law, or actually vests within 90 years, it is valid under the Uniform Rule.

c. Criticism [§558]

The wait-and-see doctrine has been criticized primarily on two grounds: (i) not knowing whether an interest is valid or void may prove inconvenient; and (ii) the doctrine results in the extension of the dead hand and of more wealth being tied up in trust.

d. Drafting [§559]

The wait-and-see doctrine and cy pres doctrine (below) are saving devices for the lawyer who drafts an instrument that violates the common law Rule Against Perpetuities. But no instrument is competently drafted if you must wait and see if it is valid or if it must be reformed by a court. Even in states adopting wait-and-see or cy pres, a careful lawyer drafts an instrument that is valid under the common law Rule.

11. Cy Pres Doctrine [§560]

The second reform of the Rule Against Perpetuities, adopted in a handful of states, is the cy pres doctrine (law French for "as near as possible"). Under the cy pres doctrine, an invalid interest is reformed, within the limits of the Rule, to approximate most closely the intention of the creator of the interest. Exercising the reformation power, a court can reduce age contingencies to 21 years or make some other appropriate change to reform the invalid interest. [*In re* **Estate of Chun Quan Yee Hop,** 469 P.2d 183 (Haw. 1970); *In re* **Estate of Anderson,** *supra,* §556]

(e.g.) **Example:** O conveys "to A for life, remainder to A's children who reach age 25." The remainder to A's children is void, as explained *supra,* §537. Exercising the reformation power, a court may reduce the age contingency to 21 years, thus saving the gift.

EXAMPLE	VALIDITY	EXPLANATION
"To A for life, then to A's children for life, then to B."	Valid	B's remainder is vested on creation.
"To A for life, then to A's children for life, then to A's grandchildren."	Invalid	A may have a child after the interest is created and so may have **grandchildren beyond the perpetuities period**.
"To School Board so long as it is used for a school, then to the Red Cross."	Valid	This falls within the charity-to-charity exception.
"To School Board so long as it is used for a school, then to A."	Invalid	The interest may vest in A's heirs or **devisees hundreds of years from now**. (A's interest is stricken.)
"To B for life, remainder to those of B's siblings who reach age 21."	Valid	B's parents can be used as measuring lives.
"To B for life, then to such of B's children who become lawyers."	Invalid	B may have a child **born after the disposition** who becomes a lawyer **more than 21 years** after B's death.
"To A for life, then to his wife, W, for life, then to A's surviving children."	Valid	No unborn widow problems because the gift is to W, a life in being.
"To A for life, then to his widow for life, then to A's surviving descendants."	Invalid	**Unborn widow problem**.
"To X for life, then to Y, but if at her death Y is not survived by children, then to Z."	Valid	Y is the measuring life.
"To M for life, then to M's children for their lives, then to M's grandchildren." M is 80 years old and has had a hysterectomy.	Invalid	**Fertile octogenarian problem**.
"Trust income to Polo Club. At the death of A, B, C, D, and E (all born today at Obie Hospital), the corpus to Z and his heirs."	Valid	A, B, C, D, and E are measuring lives.
"The residue of my estate to my descendants who are living when my estate is distributed."	Invalid	Administrative contingency—the **slothful executor problem**.

a. Cy pres coupled with wait-and-see [§561]

The large majority of states adopting wait-and-see also provide for judicial reformation of any disposition that does not in fact vest within the wait-and-see period. Hence, reformation is postponed until the end of the wait-and-see period.

12. Abolition of Rule [§562]

A number of states, pushed by bankers for the rich, have abolished the application of the Rule Against Perpetuities to future interests in a trust. As of 2006, these states are Alaska, Arizona, Colorado, D.C., Delaware, Florida, Idaho, Illinois, Maine, Maryland, Missouri, Nebraska, Nevada, New Hampshire, New Jersey, Ohio, Rhode Island, South Dakota, Utah, Virginia, Washington, Wisconsin, and Wyoming. Most of these states permit perpetual trusts, although a few fix a time limit, ranging from 150 to 1,000 years. Perpetual trusts can have certain tax advantages, such as being free from federal estate and generation-skipping transfer taxes. For example, federal tax law permits a donor to transfer up to $2 million (scheduled to increase to $3.5 million in 2009) into a trust for the donor's descendants, paying income to descendants in successive generations, with no federal estate or generation-skipping transfer taxes payable on the deaths of the settlor's descendants. This tax-exempt *dynasty trust* can last as long as local perpetuities law permits. If local law permits perpetual trusts, a tax-exempt dynasty trust can go on forever. Because of the tax advantages of dynasty trusts, lawyers for the rich in other states may push to exempt trusts from the Rule Against Perpetuities. A new struggle against dynastic wealth, which originally brought on the Rule Against Perpetuities (*see supra*, §524), may ensue, bringing new rules to curb the dead hand.

I. The Trust

1. Trust Defined [§563]

A trust is a fiduciary relationship with respect to property in which one person, the *trustee*, holds the legal title to property subject to equitable rights in *beneficiaries*. It is basically a device whereby one person manages property for the benefit of others. The person who creates a trust is called the *settlor* (who, as our grandfathers would have said, makes a settlement in trust).

2. Creation of a Trust [§564]

To create an express trust, the settlor must manifest an intent to do so. To create a trust of land, a written instrument (deed or will) is required by the Statute of Frauds. But an oral trust of personal property is permitted. Ordinarily, a trust is created by a written instrument naming the trustee, specifying the rights of the life beneficiaries and the remaindermen, and setting forth the powers of the trustee. To create a trust, it is also necessary to deliver property to the trustee to manage.

a. Trustee [§565]

Any person with legal capacity can be trustee. The settlor can serve as trustee, a beneficiary can serve as trustee, or an independent third party can serve as trustee.

(1) Fees [§566]

The trustee is entitled to a fee for managing the trust property. The fee can be waived, *e.g.*, where a child manages property as trustee for a parent (or vice versa).

b. Testamentary trust [§567]

A testamentary trust is a trust created by will. It arises at the death of the settlor.

c. Inter vivos trust [§568]

An inter vivos trust is created by the settlor during life.

(1) Revocable trust [§569]

An inter vivos trust can be made either revocable or irrevocable by the settlor. If the trust instrument provides that the trust is revocable and the settlor subsequently revokes the trust, the trust property is returned to the settlor. It is important to note that a donor probably cannot make a revocable gift without creating a trust (*see supra*, §224; *infra*, §1606). Hence, whenever a person wants to make a revocable transfer, a revocable trust is the appropriate route. A revocable trust is a substitute for a will, because it can be revoked until death, and revocable trusts are widely used to avoid probate (*see infra*, §1607). [**Farkas v. Williams**, 125 N.E.2d 600 (Ill. 1955)]

3. Powers of a Trustee [§570]

The trustee ordinarily has very broad powers of management, either by the terms of the trust instrument or by statute or common law. The trustee can sell the trust assets and invest the proceeds in other assets. The trustee can give leases and mortgages on real property. Generally, the trustee has power to manage the property in the same manner as an intelligent person would manage her own property.

4. Duties of a Trustee [§571]

A trustee is held to the highest standards of conduct in administering the trust. If the trustee breaches a fiduciary duty, the trustee is *personally liable*.

a. Prudent investor rule [§572]

The trustee has the duty of making the trust property productive, which includes the duty to invest the trust property in a prudent fashion and receive a reasonable return of income. In investing the trust assets, the trustee must exercise that degree of care, skill, and prudence as would be exercised by a *reasonably prudent person* in managing her own property. In most states, the trustee must *diversify* the trust investments. It is deemed imprudent to "keep all the eggs in one basket." [**Blankenship v. Boyle**, 329 F. Supp. 1089 (D.D.C. 1971)]

b. Undivided loyalty [§573]

The trustee owes the beneficiaries of the trust undivided loyalty. He must reap no personal advantage from his position and must not put himself in a position where a conflict of interest is possible. The trustee cannot borrow trust funds or buy any of the trust assets. Self-dealing in any form is *absolutely prohibited*. [**Blankenship v. Boyle**, *supra*]

EXAM TIP   **gilbert**

Keep in mind that this prohibition against self-dealing also applies to sales or loans to the trustee's *relatives and business associates*, and to corporations of which the trustee is a director, officer, or principal shareholder. The trustee's good faith or actual benefit to the trust is irrelevant.

---

5. Spendthrift Trusts [§574]

A spendthrift trust is one in which the settlor imposes a valid restraint on alienation, providing that the beneficiary *cannot transfer* his interest *voluntarily* and that his *creditors cannot reach it* for the satisfaction of their claims. Despite the general invalidity of restraints on alienation (*see supra*, §363), the validity of spendthrift restrictions on *equitable* interests in trust has been recognized in most American states. [**Broadway National Bank v. Adams**, 133 Mass. 170 (1882)]

---

e.g. Example: S transfers a fund in trust to pay the income to A for life, remainder to B. The trust instrument provides: "Each beneficiary, A and B, is hereby forbidden to alienate his or her interest, nor shall the interest of any beneficiary be subject to claims of his or her creditors." A cannot transfer her life estate, and her creditors cannot reach it. Thus, A has a stream of income from the trust for A's life, which A's creditors cannot reach. In some states an exception is made for A's spouse and children, who can, by court order, require the trustee to pay income to them for support. [**Howard v. Spragins**, 350 So. 2d 318 (Ala. 1977)]

---

a. Rationale

The legal title to the trust assets is in the trustee, and the specific trust assets are alienable by the trustee. The trustee can change investments if desirable. Therefore, the *trust assets* are not made inalienable by a restraint on the equitable interests. All the restraint on the equitable life estate does is to make the stream of income inalienable. The policy issue then is whether it is wise to permit trust beneficiaries—beneficiaries of inherited wealth—to enjoy a stream of income unreachable by creditors, when workers' wages are subject to garnishment by creditors. Views on this matter have been sharply divided.

b. Self-settled trust [§575]

A person cannot create a spendthrift trust for her own benefit, but only for the benefit of others. Thus, a person who makes $5 million cannot protect herself from her creditors, but she can give the $5 million to a daughter as beneficiary of a spendthrift trust, thus protecting the daughter from the daughter's creditors.

6. Constructive Trusts [§576]

In property cases, a court may sometimes impose a *constructive trust* on a party. When this is done the "constructive trustee" must hold the property to which he has legal title for the benefit of another person. This is a judicial remedy to prevent fraud or unjust enrichment of a party.

 Example: Son murders mother. A court may impose a constructive trust on son, requiring son to hold his inheritance for the benefit of other heirs.

---

a. Distinguish—express trust [§577]

A constructive trust is an equitable remedy—treating a person as a trustee when he is in fact not one. Except for the language of trust used, it has little in common with the express trust used to manage property.

J. Summary of Future Interests

1. Introduction [§578]

In reviewing future interests, you may find the following table useful. It sets forth all types of future interests following the various possessory estates. If you can classify the future interests correctly, you should have no problem in classifying future interests on an examination.

2. Future Interests in the Grantor (or in Testator's Heirs If Created by Will)

These arise by *operation of law* when the grantor does not transfer his entire estate, or they can be *expressly created*.

a. Reversion

A reversion is an interest remaining in a grantor who transfers a *vested estate of a lesser quantum* than he has. A reversion can follow any kind of possessory estate except a fee simple. If O, owner of a fee simple, makes a conveyance of a fee tail, a life estate, or a term of years and does not create a vested remainder in fee simple, O has a reversion.

(1) Fee tail

O conveys "to A and the heirs of his body." O has a reversion because a fee tail is an estate of a shorter duration than a fee simple.

(2) Life estate

— O conveys "to A for life." O has a reversion. If A subsequently conveys "to B for B's life" or "to C for 90 years," A (as well as O)

gilbert

FUTURE INTEREST		EXAMPLE	CORRELATIVE PRESENT INTEREST(S)	SUBJECT TO RULE AGAINST PERPETUITIES?
IN GRANTOR	**REVERSION**	"To A for life."	Fee Tail, Life Estate, Term of Years	No
	POSSIBILITY OF REVERTER	"To A so long as liquor is not sold on the premises."	Fee Simple Determinable	No
	RIGHT OF ENTRY	"To A, but if liquor is sold on the premises, O has a right to reenter."	Fee Simple Subject to Condition Subsequent	No
IN GRANTEE	**INDEFEASIBLY VESTED REMAINDER**	"To A for life, then to B."	Fee Tail, Life Estate, Term of Years	No
	VESTED REMAINDER SUBJECT TO OPEN	"To A for life, then to A's children." A has a child, X.*	Fee Tail, Life Estate, Term of Years	Yes—As long as the class remains open
	VESTED REMAINDER SUBJECT TO DIVESTMENT	"To A for life, then to **B**, but if B predeceases A, to C." (**B** has a vested remainder subject to divestment)	Fee Tail, Life Estate, Term of Years	No
	CONTINGENT REMAINDER	"To A for life, then to A's surviving children."	Fee Tail, Life Estate, Term of Years	Yes
	SPRINGING EXECUTORY INTEREST	"To A when she passes the bar exam."	Fee Simple, Fee Tail, Life Estate, Term of Years	Yes
	SHIFTING EXECUTORY INTEREST	"To A for life, then to B, but if B predeceases A, to **C**." (**C** has a shifting executory interest)	Fee Simple, Fee Tail, Life Estate, Term of Years	Yes

*Remember that if A has no children, the remainder is contingent because no person qualifies as a taker.

has a reversion. By the hierarchy of estates, a life estate pur autre vie and a term of years are estates of shorter duration than a life estate.

— O conveys "to A for life, remainder to B if B survives A." O has a reversion.

— O conveys "to A for life, remainder to B if B survives A, but if B does not survive A, to O." O has a reversion because O has not transferred a vested remainder in fee.

— O conveys "to A for life, remainder to B." O does *not* have a reversion.

(3) Terms of years

— O conveys "to A for 99 years." O has a reversion.

— O conveys "to A for 99 years, and then to A's heirs." O has a reversion.

b. Possibility of reverter
A possibility of reverter is a future interest remaining in the grantor when the grantor creates a determinable estate of the *same quantum* as the grantor had. Almost always a possibility of reverter follows a fee simple determinable. A possibility of reverter becomes possessory *automatically*.

— "To A and her heirs so long as intoxicating liquors are not sold on the premises." The grantor has a possibility of reverter, which arises by operation of law, because only a determinable fee was granted.

c. Right of entry
A right of entry is a future interest retained by the grantor giving the grantor *power to terminate*, at his election, the estate granted. Usually it is retained when granting a fee simple subject to condition subsequent.

— "To A and her heirs, but if intoxicating liquors are sold on the premises, O has a right to reenter." O has a right of entry, which he can exercise or not when the condition is breached.

3. Future Interests in Grantees (or Devisees in a Will)
These cannot arise by operation of law, but *must be expressly created.*

a. Remainder
A remainder is a future interest in a grantee that is capable of becoming possessory *on the expiration of the preceding estate*. A remainder never divests

the preceding estate. A remainder cannot follow a fee simple, but can follow any other kind of possessory estate. Remainders are vested or contingent. A *vested* remainder is created in an ascertained person and is not subject to a condition precedent. A **contingent** remainder either is created in an unascertained person or is subject to a condition precedent. (In every example below where a contingent remainder is created, O has a reversion.)

(1) Fee tail

— O conveys "to A and the heirs of her body, and if A dies without issue, to B." B has a vested remainder. The words "if A dies without issue" are surplusage, merely referring to the expiration of the fee tail, and do not state a condition precedent.

— O conveys "to A and the heirs of her body, and if A dies without issue, to B if B is then alive." B has a contingent remainder, subject to the condition precedent of B surviving the expiration of the fee tail.

(2) Life estate

— O conveys "to A for life, then to B." B has a vested remainder.

— O conveys "to A for life, then to B's heirs." B is alive. B's heirs have a contingent remainder because the takers are unascertained.

— O conveys "to A for life, then to B if B reaches age 25." B is age 15. B has a contingent remainder because it is subject to a condition precedent.

— O conveys "to A for life, then to B if B survives A, and if B does not survive A, to C." B and C have alternative contingent remainders; each is subject to a condition precedent.

— O conveys "to A for life, then to B, and if B does not survive A, to C." B has a vested remainder subject to divestment.

— O conveys "to A for life, then to A's children." If A has no child, the remainder is contingent because the taker is unascertained. If A has a child, B, the remainder is vested in B subject to open up and let in other children born to A. B's remainder is sometimes called a vested remainder subject to partial divestment.

(3) Term of years

O conveys "to A for 10 years, then to B." B has a vested remainder.

b. Executory interest

An executory interest is a future interest in a grantee that *may divest another grantee* (a shifting executory interest) or may **spring out of the grantor** at a future date (a springing executory interest). An executory interest can divest any type of possessory estate or future interest.

(1) Fee simple

— O conveys "to A, but if B returns from Rome, to B." B has a shifting executory interest, which will divest a fee simple if the condition happens.

— O conveys "to B if B marries A." B has a springing executory interest, which will divest O's fee simple if B marries A.

— *Exception to rule:* O conveys "to A so long as used for a library during the next 20 years, and if not so used, to B." B has an executory interest even though it will not divest the preceding fee simple determinable. It is an executory interest because of the rule that a remainder cannot follow a fee simple.

(2) Fee tail

O conveys a cottage "to A and the heirs of his body, but if A inherits the family manor, to B." B has a shifting executory interest.

(3) Life estate

— O conveys "to A for life, but if B returns from Rome during A's life, to B." B has a shifting executory interest which may divest A's life estate.

— O conveys "to A for life, then to B, but if B does not survive A, to C." C has a shifting executory interest which may divest B's vested remainder.

— O conveys "to A for life, then one day after A's death, to B." B has a springing executory interest which will divest O's fee simple one day after A's death.

(4) Term of years

— O conveys "to A for 10 years, but if A does not keep up the fence, to B for the balance of the term." B has a shifting executory interest which may divest the term of years.

— *Exception to rule:* O conveys "to A for 100 years if A so long lives, then to A's heirs." A's heirs have an executory interest even though it will not divest the preceding term of years determinable. It is an executory interest because before the Statute of Uses one could not have a contingent remainder following a term of years. In modern times, the interest in A's heirs is sometimes called a contingent remainder.

Chapter Five:
Concurrent Ownership and Marital Rights

CONTENTS

Chapter Approach

Chapter Approach

The preceding chapters dealt with *successive* ownership (*e.g.*, a life estate in A, followed by a remainder in B). Property can also be owned by two or more persons *concurrently*. For example, A and B can be *concurrent* owners of a possessory fee simple, a life estate, or even a remainder.

Exam questions on concurrent ownership generally require you to determine from the facts what type of concurrent interest is involved. The common law recognized three forms of concurrent ownership: (i) the tenancy in common; (ii) the joint tenancy; and (iii) the tenancy by the entirety. The chief distinguishing features of each are:

1. *Tenancy in common*—two or more persons own the property with *no* right of survivorship between them; when one tenant in common dies, her interest passes to her heirs or devisees.

2. *Joint tenancy*—two or more persons own the property *with a right of survivorship;* when one joint tenant dies, the survivor(s) takes all. Remember that the common law required the four unities (time, title, interest, and possession) for a joint tenancy.

3. *Tenancy by entirety*—exists only between *husband and wife,* with a *right of survivorship* that *cannot be severed* without consent of both spouses.

Questions regarding concurrent ownership may also involve the rights and duties of the co-tenants. Recall that, with the exception of survivorship rights and certain rights under a tenancy by the entirety, the rights and duties of co-tenants are basically the same regardless of the type of co-tenancy.

In addition to concurrent ownership, this chapter also discusses the somewhat related issue of marital property rights. Marital property law is in the process of change in the United States. The common law and modern property rights of spouses, including rights in community property, will be discussed. Because these topics are but a small part of most Property courses, the discussion here is brief, but it will provide you with the common law background necessary to understand many of today's laws.

A. Tenancy in Common

1. Nature of the Tenancy [§579]

A tenancy in common is a form of concurrent ownership wherein each co-tenant is the owner of a separate and distinct share of the property, which has not been divided among the co-tenants. Each owner has a separate *undivided interest* in the whole. Tenancies in common can arise by an express conveyance or devise to persons as tenants in common or when persons inherit property from a decedent.

a. Right to possession [§580]

Each tenant in common has the right to possess and enjoy the *entire property,* subject to the same right in each co-tenant. One co-tenant can go into possession of the whole unless another co-tenant objects. The co-tenants can come to any agreement about possession they desire. If they are in conflict over possession, a court may order partition of the property or give some other remedy, discussed below.

> **Example:** O dies, leaving Son and Daughter as her heirs. Daughter has the right to, and does, move into the house. Unless Son objects, there is no problem with respect to the right to possession.

b. No right of survivorship [§581]

When a tenant in common dies, her interest passes to her devisees or heirs. It does *not* go to the surviving tenant in common. There is no right of survivorship among tenants in common.

EXAM TIP   **gilbert**

The chief difference between a tenancy in common and a joint tenancy is this: A tenant in common has *no right of survivorship*, whereas a joint tenant has a right of survivorship.

> **Example:** A and B are tenants in common. Subsequently A dies intestate, leaving H as her heir. H takes A's share, and B and H now are tenants in common.

c. Equal shares not necessary [§582]

Equal shares are not necessary for a tenancy in common. A and B can be tenants in common, with A holding a three-fourths interest and B holding a one-fourth interest. It is *presumed* that the shares of tenants in common are equal, but this presumption can be overcome by evidence that unequal shares were intended. If A and B, who are not related to each other, purchase property as tenants in common, and A puts up three-quarters of the purchase price and B one-quarter, it will likely be held that A did not intend to make a gift to B, and that the parties have undivided interests proportionate to the consideration each paid. If B is a natural object of A's bounty, a gift from A to B does not seem so unlikely. In this case, the unequal consideration paid by A and B may be insufficient by itself to overcome the presumption of equal shares.

d. Same estates not necessary [§583]

Tenants in common can have different types of estates. Suppose that A and B are tenants in common, and that A dies, devising her half interest to C for life, remainder to D. C now owns a life estate and D a remainder in a one-half interest held in a tenancy in common with B.

2. Alienability [§584]

A tenant in common can sell, give, devise, or otherwise dispose of her undivided share in the same manner as if she were the sole owner of the property. For example, in the preceding illustration, A died devising her one-half interest to C for life, remainder to D. Thus, each share of a tenancy in common can be divided into a life estate and future interests, or among a new group of concurrent owners.

Example: A and B are tenants in common. Subsequently A conveys her one-half interest to C, D, and E as tenants in common. Thereafter, B, C, D, and E are tenants in common, B owning a one-half undivided interest and C, D, and E each owning a one-sixth undivided interest.

---

3. Presumption of Tenancy in Common [§585]

Under modern law, whenever a conveyance is made to two or more persons who are not husband and wife, they are presumed to take as tenants in common and not as joint tenants. (As to conveyances to husband and wife, *see infra*, §§602, 639.) This presumption can be overcome by evidence that a joint tenancy is intended.

EXAM TIP	gilbert

If in an exam question you see a conveyance "to A and B," and A and B are not a married couple, A and B have a *tenancy in common*. For A and B to get a *joint tenancy* (*see infra*), the grant must *expressly indicate* that a joint tenancy is intended, usually done by an express mention of the right of survivorship. (If A and B are a married couple, a conveyance "to A and B" usually will create a *tenancy by the entirety* if the jurisdiction recognizes that estate, unless evidence shows that the grantor intended some other estate; *see infra*, §639.)

B. Joint Tenancy

1. Nature of the Tenancy [§586]

A joint tenancy is a form of concurrent ownership wherein each co-tenant owns an undivided share of property (as in tenancy in common), and the surviving co-tenant has the right to the whole estate. The *right of survivorship* is the distinctive feature of the joint tenancy. There is no limit on the number of persons who can hold together as joint tenants. On the death of each joint tenant, the property belongs to the surviving joint tenants, until only one is left. The tenant who lives longest takes the property by herself.

a. Conveyance or devise required [§587]

A joint tenancy can be created by deed or by will, or by a joint adverse possession. Joint tenancy does ***not*** arise where persons inherit property by intestate succession. Heirs always take as tenants in common.

b. Real or personal property [§588]

A joint tenancy can be created in either real or personal property.

2. Four Unities Requirement

a. Fiction of one entity [§589]

By a common law fiction, joint tenants are regarded as composing ***one entity***. Each joint tenant is seised *per my et per tout* (by the share or moiety and by the whole). In theory, then, each ***owns*** the undivided ***whole*** of the property; this being so, when one joint tenant dies, ***nothing passes*** to the surviving joint tenant or tenants. Rather, the estate simply continues in survivors freed from the participation of the decedent, whose interest is extinguished. Thus, the surviving joint tenant is entitled to the whole by the right of survivorship, but no interest has passed to the surviving joint tenant. The interest of the dying joint tenant simply vanishes. This is a rather odd theory, but it can have important consequences.

Example: State Blue imposes an inheritance tax on all property passing from a decedent by devise, bequest, or intestate succession. A and B are joint tenants. A dies. No inheritance tax is imposed on B by a statute taxing the ***passing*** of property at death.

---

(1) No right to devise [§590]

Because the dying joint tenant's interest ***vanishes at her death***, she cannot devise it by will. There is no property in her estate for her will to dispose of. Similarly, the creditors of a joint tenant cannot attach the tenant's share after the tenant's death because the share disappeared at death.

b. The four unities [§591]

Because joint tenants are seised of the undivided property as one fictitious entity, the common law requires that their interests be ***equal*** in all respects. They must take their interests (i) at the ***same time,*** (ii) by the ***same instrument,*** (iii) with ***identical interests,*** and (iv) with an ***equal right to possess*** the whole property. If these four unities of time, title, interest, and possession were not present, a joint tenancy could not be created at common law. When a grantor failed to create a joint tenancy because one of the four entities was not present, a tenancy in common was created. This still remains the law in most states, though some states say a joint tenancy can be created "if the grantor intends it"—a position that may lessen the importance of the four unities requirement.

(1) Unity of time [§592]

The interest of each joint tenant must vest at the same time. For example, suppose that O conveys Blackacre "to A for life, then to the heirs of A and the heirs of B as joint tenants." The heirs of A are ascertained at A's death, and the heirs of B are ascertained at B's death. Because the holders of the remainder are ascertained at different times, the heirs of A cannot take as joint tenants with the heirs of B. They take as tenants in common.

(2) Unity of title [§593]

All joint tenants must acquire title by the same deed or will, or by a joint adverse possession.

EXAM TIP   **gilbert**

The unity of title requirement has been most frequently litigated in a situation involving a conveyance by a sole owner to himself and another as joint tenants. This most often occurs in a conveyance by a husband to himself and his wife as joint tenants. Watch for this fact pattern on exams, and remember that if the grantees don't acquire title *by the same instrument* (or by adverse possession) *and at the same time*, they are not joint tenants, but tenants in common under the common law rule.

(a) Conveyance by H to H and W [§594]

A conveyance by H "to H and W as joint tenants" violates the *unities of time* and *title*. Because of the common law rule that one person cannot convey to himself, the conveyance by H "to H and W as joint tenants" is viewed as in reality only a conveyance of a one-half interest by H to W. Because the unities of time and title are lacking, at common law H and W held as tenants in common.

1) Use of a strawperson [§595]

Where H wants to convey "to H and W as joint tenants," he can accomplish his wishes by conveying the property to a "strawperson." (A strawperson is a person not intended to have any beneficial interest in the property, who must convey as directed by the beneficially interested parties. A strawperson is usually a lawyer or the lawyer's secretary.) After H conveys to the strawperson, the strawperson conveys "to H and W as joint tenants." The second deed complies with the four unities rule.

(b) Modern law [§596]

The common law rule that a conveyance by a sole owner to himself and another as joint tenants created only a tenancy in common has been abolished by statute in many states, although a few of these statutes permit only a direct conveyance from *one spouse* to both spouses as joint tenants. Courts have sometimes avoided the common law rule by saying that H is conveying to a different entity (H and W) of which H is only a part. Hence, in most states a conveyance by H "to H and W as joint tenants" will create a joint tenancy. [**Miller v. Riegler,** 419 S.W.2d 599 (Ark. 1967)]

EXAM TIP gilbert

Whenever you see a fact situation on an exam where the grantor is trying to create a joint tenancy in himself and another person, *discuss the unity of title and of time problems* unless the facts state that the common law rule has been changed in the particular jurisdiction. Even though many states no longer require a strawperson to convey title at the same time and by the same instrument, most professors want a discussion of the four unities.

---

(3) Unity of interest [§597]

Because in theory joint tenants hold but one estate as a single entity, the interest of each joint tenant must be *equal in an estate of one duration.* It is not possible, *e.g.,* for O to create a joint tenancy by conveying "one-half to A and his heirs, and one-half to B for life, A and B to hold as joint tenants." A and B would hold as tenants in common, which does not require unity of interest (*see supra,* §583).

(a) Equal shares [§598]

To create a joint tenancy, the shares of each joint tenant must be equal. One joint tenant cannot be given a one-third share and the other a two-thirds share, for example. However, after the joint tenancy is created, any joint tenant can petition a court to terminate the joint tenancy by a partition sale. Upon sale of the property in equity, the court—acting to achieve fairness—may divide the sale proceeds in accordance with the proportionate consideration paid. In other words, the creating instrument must give the joint tenants equal shares, but an equity court may choose to ignore this to do equity on partition sale (*see infra,* §697). (Similarly, in a joint bank account, the parties, during life, usually are held to own interests in proportion to the net contributions of each. *See infra,* §631.)

(b) Another interest in same property [§599]

Property can be divided into fractional shares, one of which is owned by persons as joint tenants and the other owned by persons as tenants in common. This is best seen by an illustration.

---

e.g. Example: O conveys Blackacre as follows: "a one-half undivided interest to H and W as joint tenants, and a one-half interest to A." As between themselves, H and W are joint tenants, and if H dies first, W will own the entire one-half interest relieved of H's participation. As between H and W on the one hand and A on the other, the parties are tenants in common. There are no survivorship rights between A and the joint tenants H and W.

(4) Unity of possession [§600]

Unity of possession requires that each joint tenant have the right to possession of the whole. After a joint tenancy is created, the joint tenants can agree that one joint tenant has the exclusive right to possession. Such an agreement *does not break the unity of possession;* the joint tenant out of possession is merely waiving his right to possession. Obviously any other rule would be very inconvenient. The law likes joint tenants to settle problems over possession by agreement between themselves, out of court, and such agreements would not likely take place if they caused the severance of the right of survivorship.

THE JOINT TENANCY FOUR UNITIES REQUIREMENT	**gilbert**
UNITY OF TIME	Interest of each joint tenant must **vest at same time**
UNITY OF TITLE	All joint tenants must **acquire title by same deed or will**, or by joint adverse possession
UNITY OF INTEREST	Interest of each joint tenant must be **equal** in an estate of one duration (identical interests)
UNITY OF POSSESSION	Each joint tenant must have **right to possession of the whole**

3. Creation of Joint Tenancy

a. Presumption

(1) Common law [§601]

At common law, it was *presumed* that any *conveyance* or *devise* to two or more persons (other than husband and wife) created a joint tenancy, unless a contrary intent was clearly set forth. This presumption favored sole ownership over multiple ownership, and the reasons for it lie in the feudal system. Being able to look to one rather than to several owners for feudal services and incidents was more convenient for the lord. Shared responsibility was more difficult to enforce. Joint tenancy was preferred by the tenant class too because it reduced the burdens due the lord. Although each tenant in common owed the services separately, in a joint tenancy, with its fiction of one entity, any number of joint tenants comprised only one tenant owing services.

(a) Husband and wife [§602]

Husband and wife were presumed at common law to take as tenants by the *entirety*. (*See infra*, §§604, 638.)

(2) American law [§603]

In all American jurisdictions, the common law *presumption of a joint tenancy has been abolished*, either by statute or judicial decision. The presumption today is that a conveyance to two or more persons creates a *tenancy in common*. [**Gagnon v. Pronovost**, 71 A.2d 747 (N.H. 1949); *In re* **Michael's Estate**, 218 A.2d 338 (Pa. 1966)] In a few states, the joint tenancy itself has been abolished.

(a) Husband and wife [§604]

Statutes abolishing the common law presumption sometimes do not apply to husband and wife, who were presumed at common law to take as tenants by the entirety. In some states, husband and wife are still presumed to take as tenants by the entirety. In a few states, husband and wife are presumed to take as joint tenants. (*See infra*, §639.)

(b) Distinguish—executors and trustees [§605]

The presumption of tenancy in common does *not apply to executors and trustees*, who are presumed to hold as joint tenants. Upon the death of one fiduciary, the surviving fiduciary continues to manage the estate or the trust property. It would be very inconvenient—and not what the testator or settlor intended—to have the heirs of the dead fiduciary come in and claim to be co-executors or co-trustees. Joint tenancy among executors and trustees remains even in states that have otherwise abolished joint tenancies.

b. Overcoming presumption of tenancy in common [§606]

A joint tenancy can be created only by *express words* in an instrument indicating an intent to create a joint tenancy. The clearest way to create a joint tenancy is to convey "to A and B *as joint tenants with the right of survivorship, and not as tenants in common*." These words will create a joint tenancy, but anything less might not. [*But see* **Jones v. Green**, 337 N.W.2d 85 (Mich. 1983)—holding such words create a joint life estate with remainder in fee simple in the survivor by erroneously equating this language with that discussed *infra, §609*] Courts have been rather harsh in demanding clear expressions of intent. Compare the following conveyances, which may not create a joint tenancy.

(1) "To A and B as joint tenants" [§607]

In some states, a joint tenancy can be created *only if survivorship is expressly provided for.* Hence a conveyance "to A and B as joint tenants" is insufficient to create a joint tenancy.

(2) "To A and B jointly" [§608]

The decisions are divided over whether a conveyance "to A and B jointly" will create a joint tenancy. Some courts view the word "jointly" as equivocal because it is often used, by nonlawyers, to describe a tenancy in common as well as a joint tenancy.

(3) "To A and B as joint tenants, and to the survivor and his heirs" [§609]

This phraseology looks very similar to the phraseology given above for creating a joint tenancy, but there is one important difference. There is an express gift here "to the survivor and his heirs" (it does not say "to A and B with the right of survivorship"). Does this express gift mean that A and B take a co-tenancy for their joint lives with a contingent remainder to the survivor rather than a joint tenancy? The cases are divided. Some hold this language creates a tenancy in common in A and B for life, with remainder to the survivor. [**Albro v. Allen,** 454 N.W.2d 85 (Mich. 1990)—holding "to A and B as joint tenants with full rights of survivorship" created life estate in A and B with remainder to survivor] Others hold this language creates a joint tenancy. [**Palmer v. Flint,** 161 A.2d 837 (Me. 1960)]

(a) Difference in effect [§610]

If A and B hold a joint tenancy, either A or B can convey her interest to C, severing the unities of time and title and thus terminating the joint tenancy. B and C would then hold as tenants in common. Hence, either joint tenant can destroy the right of survivorship. If A and B hold a co-tenancy for their joint lives, with remainder to the survivor, neither A nor B acting alone can destroy the contingent remainder in the survivor. If A conveys to C, C takes A's life estate and A's interest in the contingent remainder, but B's rights are not affected.

(b) Where joint tenancy abolished [§611]

A few states, in an excess of zeal to clear away the remnants of feudalism, abolished the joint tenancy in the last century. In such states, a deed "to A and B as joint tenants with right of survivorship" is construed to create a tenancy in common in A and B for their joint lives, with remainder in fee in the survivor. As stated above, the chief difference between this construction and a joint tenancy is that the survivor's remainder in the whole cannot be destroyed without consent, whereas the joint tenant's right of survivorship can be. [**Holbrook v. Holbrook,** 403 P.2d 12 (Or. 1965)]

EXAM TIP   **gilbert**

The presumption of tenancy in common is strong. Therefore, only when you see *express language* in an instrument indicating an intent to create a joint tenancy can you be certain that you have a joint tenancy. If you see "to A and B *as joint tenants with the right of survivorship*," you can safely assume a joint tenancy was intended. A grant "to A and B *as joint tenants and not as tenants in common*" may be enough, but a few states require that the right of survivorship be mentioned. *But note:* The specific language above is important only when you are interpreting an instrument to determine what the grantor intended. If an exam question tells you that A and B hold the property "in joint tenancy," don't fight the facts—accept that A and B are joint tenants. The right of survivorship language is important only when you are *interpreting* a deed, will, or other instrument.

(4) Extrinsic evidence [§612]

Where the client directs a lawyer to create a joint tenancy and the lawyer fails to create a joint tenancy by omitting required words of survivorship, a recent case has held that the deed may be reformed by clear and convincing evidence that a joint tenancy was intended. [*In re* **Estate of Vadney**, 83 N.Y.2d 885 (1994)] Reformation of lawyers' errors is a recent development, which avoids legal malpractice suits.

4. Severance of Joint Tenancy [§613]

Any joint tenant can at any time destroy the right of survivorship by severing the joint tenancy. Upon severance, the joint tenancy becomes a tenancy in common, and the right of survivorship is destroyed. At common law, severance occurred automatically when one or more of the four unities were severed. Modern law generally follows the proposition that severance of one of the four unities severs the joint tenancy. But inasmuch as one of the unities can be unknowingly severed, without intent to destroy the right of survivorship, in situations where a joint tenant conveys less than her entire share, some courts look to the intent of the parties in determining whether there is a severance.

a. Conveyance by joint tenant [§614]

Each joint tenant has the right to convey her interest. A conveyance of the tenant's entire interest or share severs the joint tenancy with respect to that share. Either a conveyance to a third person or to another joint tenant severs the share conveyed from the joint tenancy. A deed to a third person severs the joint tenancy even though the other joint tenant does not know about the deed. [**Crowther v. Mower**, 876 P.2d 876 (Utah 1994)]

Example: A, B, and C are joint tenants. A conveys his share to D, thus destroying the unities of time and title between B and C and their new co-tenant, D. B and C remain joint tenants between themselves, but D holds her share as a tenant in common with them. If B subsequently dies, C owns a two-thirds interest and D a one-third interest as tenants in common. [**Giles v. Sheridan**, 137 N.W.2d 828 (Neb. 1965)] If A had conveyed his share to B, a co-tenant, rather than to a third party, D, the result would be similar. B would hold one-third as a tenant in common, and B and C would hold two-thirds as joint tenants. If B subsequently died intestate, C would own a two-thirds interest and B's heirs a one-third interest as tenants in common. [**Jackson v. O'Connell,** 177 N.E.2d 194 (Ill. 1961)]

---

(1) Contract to convey [§615]

A contract by one joint tenant to convey her interest in the property, which is specifically enforceable in equity, may sever the joint tenancy. Under the doctrine of "equitable conversion" (*infra,* §§1547 *et seq.*), the execution of a contract gives the buyer equitable ownership and converts the seller's legal ownership into a contract right to receive the selling price. Thus, the unity of interest is severed in equity.

(a) Contract by all tenants [§616]

On the other hand, a contract to convey land signed by *all* of the joint tenants has been held not to sever the joint tenancy for two reasons. First, the parties did not intend to sever. Second, even applying equitable conversion, the parties have a unity of interest in equity. [**Estate of Phillips v. Nyhus,** 874 P.2d 154 (Wash. 1994)]

(2) Conveyance to self [§617]

Under old law a joint tenant who wished to convert the tenancy to a tenancy in common had to convey to a strawperson, who conveyed back to the joint tenant. The common law required that, in order to have a legal transfer, one person must convey to *another* person, and not to herself; hence the joint tenant could not convey directly to herself. Some recent cases have permitted a joint tenant to unilaterally sever the tenancy by conveying her interest to herself without using an intermediary. [**Riddle v. Harmon,** 102 Cal. App. 3d 524 (1980)]

b. Mortgage by joint tenant [§618]

When one joint tenant gives a mortgage on the joint tenancy property, does this sever the joint tenancy because the unity of interest is destroyed? Jurisdictions are not in agreement on this question. Generally, courts divide between jurisdictions following the title theory of mortgages and those following the lien theory.

(1) Title theory states [§619]

At common law, a mortgage had the effect of conveying the *legal title* to the mortgagee (money lender); the mortgagor (borrower) kept an *equity of redemption* entitling the mortgagor to get legal title back on payment of the mortgage ("redeem the mortgage"). Because a mortgage by a joint tenant conveys the legal title of the joint tenant, the mortgage destroys the unity of interest and severs the joint tenancy. It cannot be revived by the mortgagor's paying off the mortgage. The title theory of mortgages is still followed in a number of states, but in some of them the consequences have been whittled away by the equitable idea that the mortgagee holds title only for security purposes, and the courts reach the same results as in lien theory states.

Example: A and B are joint tenants of Blackacre. A borrows $5,000 from Security Bank and gives Security Bank a mortgage on A's interest in Blackacre. Under the title theory of mortgages, the joint tenancy is severed. A and B hold as tenants in common. Subsequently A pays off the debt and discharges the mortgage. Then A dies intestate. A's interest passes to his heirs. B has no right of survivorship.

(a) Criticism

Severance by one joint tenant giving a mortgage may not carry out the intent of the mortgagor, who may intend her interest to pass to the surviving joint tenant subject to the mortgage. She probably has no knowledge of the four unities requirement and the severance doctrine. Automatic application of the doctrine may lead to inadvertent severance.

(2) Lien theory states [§620]

Most states hold that the mortgagee does not have legal title, but rather a security interest called a lien. Legal title remains in the mortgagor. In lien theory states, a mortgage does not sever the joint tenancy but the states differ on whether the *surviving joint tenant takes one-half subject to the mortgage if the debt is not paid off before the debtor joint tenant dies.* This difference is best seen by an illustration.

Example: Suppose that A and B are joint tenants of Blackacre, located in a lien theory state. A gives a mortgage on her interest in Blackacre. This does not sever the joint tenancy. B still has a right of survivorship. Now suppose that A dies. Does B take A's interest subject to the mortgage or does B own the entire interest in Blackacre free of the mortgage? Jurisdictions split on this question. Some hold that B takes A's interest subject to the mortgage. This view seems fair to the mortgagee, who would otherwise lose his security. It also protects B's survivorship rights. Other courts hold that B has the right to A's half unencumbered by the mortgage. [**Harms v. Sprague,** 473 N.E.2d 930 (Ill. 1984); **Brant v. Hargrove,** 632 P.2d 978 (Ariz. 1981); **People v. Nogarr,** 164 Cal. App. 2d 591 (1958)] This latter position has this consequence: A lender who knows of the rule will not give credit to one joint tenant; a lender who does not know of it loses his security if the debtor dies, and the survivor gets a windfall.

	TITLE THEORY STATE	LIEN THEORY STATE
INTEREST HELD BY MORTGAGEE (LENDER)	Legal title	Security interest (lien)
INTEREST HELD BY MORTGAGOR (JOINT TENANT)	Equity of redemption	Legal title
EFFECT	Unity of interest destroyed; joint tenancy severed	Joint tenancy survives

EFFECT OF MORTGAGE ON JOINT TENANCY — **gilbert**

c. **Lease by joint tenant [§621]**

One joint tenant has the right to lease her interest in the property, even over the objection of the other joint tenant. [**Swartzbaugh v. Sampson,** 11 Cal. App. 2d 451 (1936)] Does the conveyance of a leasehold sever the joint tenancy? This question basically involves the same issues as severance by giving a mortgage, and not surprisingly the courts divide in the same ways.

(1) **Common law—lease severs [§622]**

The classical common law was that the conveyance of a leasehold destroyed the unity of interest because the lessor joint tenant had only a reversion in the property whereas the other joint tenant had a fee simple. Their interests after the lease were different. This view makes logical sense and parallels the title theory of mortgages, but is subject to the same criticism that it results in unintentional severance.

(2) **Modern view—lease does not sever [§623]**

The modern view is that there is no severance by one joint tenant giving a leasehold, and the surviving joint tenant takes the whole. But the cases split over *whether the surviving joint tenant takes one-half subject to the lease.* The split is similar to that over whether the surviving joint tenant takes subject to a mortgage given by the dead tenant. One view holds that the surviving joint tenant takes subject to the leasehold on a one-half interest. Another view is that the survivor holds the entire property not subject to the lease. Under this view, a lessee can protect himself against the risk of the lessor dying only by having all joint tenants sign the lease or by requiring the lessor to sever the joint tenancy beforehand. [**Tenhet v. Boswell,** 18 Cal. 3d 150 (1976)]

d. **Agreement among joint tenants [§624]**

Joint tenants can agree among themselves that one tenant has the right to exclusive possession (*supra,* §600). Such an agreement does not sever the joint tenancy. Joint tenants can make an agreement to hold as tenants in common. Such an agreement severs the joint tenancy even though none of the four unities is broken. In this situation ***intention,*** rather than the four unities, ***controls.***

(1) Divorce [§625]

Divorce does not terminate a joint tenancy between husband and wife, but in most states a property settlement agreement can sever a joint tenancy if the parties so intend. [**Porter v. Porter,** 472 So. 2d 630 (Ala. 1985)] Courts sometimes infer such an agreement from the divorce proceedings.

Example: H and W own a family home as joint tenants. On divorce, H and W sign a property settlement agreement providing that W shall remain in the family home with the children, but that on W's remarriage or on the youngest child reaching 21 years of age, the home shall be sold and the proceeds divided equally between H and W (now ex-H and ex-W). W dies soon thereafter and H claims the family home is still in joint tenancy. If it is held in tenancy in common, W's half interest will descend to her children and not go to H by right of survivorship. From these facts an agreement to hold as tenants in common may be inferred. [**Mann v. Bradley,** 535 P.2d 213 (Colo. 1975)]

---

e. Murder of one joint tenant by another [§626]

If one joint tenant murders the other, most courts hold that this effects a severance, converting the joint tenancy into a tenancy in common. The murderer thus cannot take the victim's share by right of survivorship. [**Duncan v. Vassaur,** 550 P.2d 929 (Okla. 1976); **Estate of Grund v. Grund,** 648 N.E.2d 1182 (Ind. 1995)—applying same rule to tenancy by the entirety] This view is adopted by Uniform Probate Code section 2-803.

f. Simultaneous death [§627]

Suppose A and B, joint tenants, die simultaneously in a plane crash. Who takes the property? Half goes to A's estate and half goes to B's. The Uniform Simultaneous Death Act, enacted in almost all states, provides: "Where there is no sufficient evidence that two joint tenants or tenants by the entirety have died otherwise than simultaneously the property so held shall be distributed one-half as if one had survived and one-half as if the other had survived. If there are more than two joint tenants and all of them have so died the property thus distributed shall be in the proportion that one bears to the whole number of joint tenants." [Uniform Simultaneous Death Act §3 (1940)]

5. Avoidance of Probate [§628]

The joint tenancy is a useful estate, particularly between husband and wife, because it ***avoids probate.*** When a person dies either intestate or testate, probate proceedings have to be opened in a local court in order to, among other things, change the title from the decedent to the new owner. Probate is time consuming and costly—executor's commissions, lawyer's fees, and court costs must be paid. With joint tenancy there is no need to change the title at a joint tenant's death, because the surviving joint tenant owns the whole by virtue of the right of survivorship. Hence joint tenancy avoids probate. It is very common for husband and wife to hold the family home in joint tenancy (or tenancy by the entirety).

6. Joint Bank Accounts [§629]

In a *joint and survivor bank account*, either party on the account can withdraw the amount deposited and the *survivor takes whatever sum is remaining* in the account when the other joint tenant dies. If a depositor, O, is aging or sick and needs another person, A, to pay bills, the depositor may open a joint bank account intending it to be a "*convenience account*." If a convenience account is the depositor's intent, A can lawfully write checks during the depositor's life to pay bills but A has *no rights of survivorship*. Because joint bank accounts can be used as a "true" joint and survivor account or as a convenience account, much litigation results as to which type of account was intended by the depositor.

a. Presumption [§630]

The *presumption* is that by signing a joint tenancy card at the bank, which provides survivorship rights, O, the depositor, intends to open a true joint and survivor account with A, the other party, having full rights of survivorship. In most states, however, this presumption can be overcome by clear and convincing evidence that a convenience account was intended. In a few states, to avoid litigation as to the depositor's intent, signing a joint and survivor account form is conclusive, and no evidence of a contrary intent is admissible. [**Wright v. Bloom,** 635 N.E.2d 31 (Ohio 1994)]

b. Lifetime rights [§631]

The majority of states holds that the joint account belongs during the lifetime of the parties to the parties in proportion to the net contributions of each to the sums on deposit. Thus, if O contributes all the money, O during her lifetime owns all the money, and A can withdraw it only with the express or implied consent of O. This has implications for creditors. The creditors of A can only reach the amount on deposit proportionate to A's contribution. (Compare a joint tenancy in real property, where O and A are deemed to own equal shares. *See supra,* §598.)

c. Will substitute [§632]

A joint bank account can also be used purely as a will substitute. In such case, the depositor, O, does not intend A to have any right to withdraw money in the account until O dies. If extrinsic evidence shows this is the depositor's intent, many courts in the past held the joint bank account invalid because no gift is made during life; the account is a testamentary act not executed with the formalities required for a will (two witnesses, declaration that instrument is a will, etc.). The older cases held that the designated beneficiary under a joint account intended solely as a payable-on-death account takes nothing at death. Here again, the presumption is that the depositor intended to create a true joint and survivor account, but this can be overcome by clear and convincing evidence to the contrary. [**Malone v. Walsh,** 53 N.E.2d 126 (Mass. 1944)]

(1) Totten trust [§633]

A *savings* account opened by O, as *trustee* for A, with the right in O to withdraw all sums deposited, was upheld in *In re* **Totten,** 179 N.Y. 112 (1904). Even though this arrangement is almost purely testamentary, and A has virtually no rights until O dies, the court saw no room for fraud in this banking arrangement and validated the "Totten trust" as a "poor man's will." The theory is that, because the account is in trust form, the law of trusts applies. A trust can be revocable and used as a will substitute (*see supra,* §569).

(2) Uniform Probate Code [§634]

Uniform Probate Code section 6-101, enacted in many states, provides that a payable-on-death account is valid. If payable-on-death bank accounts are permitted, then the depositor can pick whichever account serves his purpose. It is not necessary to use a joint account as a payable-on-death account in disguise. Less litigation as to the depositor's true intention will result.

C. Tenancy by the Entirety

1. Nature of the Tenancy [§635]

A tenancy by the entirety is a form of concurrent ownership that can be created *only between a husband and wife,* holding as *one person.* The tenancy by the entirety is like the joint tenancy in that the four unities (plus a fifth—the unity of marriage) are required for its creation, and the surviving spouse has the right of survivorship.

EXAM TIP	gilbert

Remember a tenancy by the entirety can be created *only* between a husband and a wife. Do not use it for any other type of co-tenants.

a. Fiction of one person [§636]

It is of the essence of tenancy by the entirety that a husband and wife are considered in law to be one person. As one person, they do not take the estate by the moieties or shares; rather both—holding as one—are seised *per tout et non per my.* The fiction that a husband and wife are one person reflected the realities of English common law. A married woman was not a legal person; her husband represented her interests. Although today a married woman is a legal person and her husband's control of her property has been completely abrogated in all states, the peculiar legal fiction of unity of a husband and wife still underlies the tenancy by the entirety and causes trouble.

b. Severance by one tenant impossible [§637]

Although the tenancy by the entirety resembles the joint tenancy in that the same four unities are required for its creation, it is unlike the joint tenancy in that severance of the tenancy by one tenant is not possible. Neither tenant acting alone can sever the four unities and destroy the right of survivorship.

EXAM TIP   **gilbert**

This is the chief difference between a tenancy by the entirety and a joint tenancy, and an important point to remember. Neither tenant by the entirety *acting alone* can do anything to destroy the right of survivorship.

---

2. Creation of Tenancy by the Entirety

a. English common law [§638]

At English common law, a husband and wife were legally one, and therefore it was impossible for a husband and wife to hold with each other as tenants in common or as joint tenants. They were not considered separate entities and thus could not hold separate moieties (shares). Therefore, a conveyance to H and W "as joint tenants" or "as tenants in common" created a tenancy by the entirety in H and W. This old rule has been *abolished* in all states. Modern law permits a husband and wife to take as tenants in common or as joint tenants.

b. Modern presumption [§639]

Where the conveyance is unclear, most states that retain the tenancy by the entirety *presume* that a conveyance to a husband and wife creates a tenancy by the entirety. This presumption can be rebutted by evidence that some other estate was intended. To this extent, the old common law preference for a tenancy by the entirety is retained. [**Adamson v. Adamson,** 541 P.2d 460 (Or. 1975)] In a few states that have the tenancy by the entirety, a husband and wife, like others, are presumed to take as tenants in common. And in a few others, a husband and wife are presumed to take as joint tenants (a middle position between the common law presumption and the presumption applicable to nonmarried persons).

c. Conveyance to unmarried persons [§640]

If a conveyance is made to two unmarried persons to hold as tenants by the entirety, it does not create a tenancy by the entirety. Some courts hold such a conveyance creates a joint tenancy, on the theory that a joint tenancy is closer to the grantor's intent than a tenancy in common. Others apply the ordinary presumption of a tenancy in common.

3. Rights of Tenants During Marriage

a. English common law [§641]

Because of the fiction that a husband and wife were one, and the husband was that one, the tenancy by the entirety was heavily loaded in favor of the husband at common law.

(1) Husband's rights [§642]

The husband had the following rights:

(a) Right to possession [§643]

The husband had the right to exclusive possession and all the rents and profits while the tenancy endured. The husband could convey this right to a third party, giving the third party the right to possession—completely excluding the wife from possession. Inasmuch as creditors can reach what a person can voluntarily transfer, the husband's creditors could reach this right and sell it to pay the husband's debts.

(b) Right of survivorship [§644]

The husband had the right to the entire property if he survived the wife. The husband could transfer this right to a third person, and the husband's creditors could reach it.

Example: H's creditor seizes and sells H's interest in Blackacre, owned by H and W as tenants by the entirety. The purchaser at the creditor's sale is entitled to possession and rents and profits. If W dies before H, the purchaser owns the entire interest in Blackacre at W's death, when her right of survivorship is extinguished. If H dies before W, W's right of survivorship gives her the entire interest in Blackacre at H's death.

(2) Wife's right of survivorship [§645]

The wife had the right to the entire property if she survived the husband. This was the only right the wife had in a tenancy by the entirety. The right of survivorship could not be destroyed without the wife's consent, and it remained in the wife *even after the husband conveyed his entire interest* in the property. The wife's right of survivorship was not alienable by the wife without her husband's consent (recall that she was not a person sui juris). Therefore, her creditors could not reach it.

(3) No right to partition [§646]

Neither spouse had the right to a judicial partition of the property. Neither spouse acting alone could have had the property sold because the other spouse's right of survivorship could not be extinguished without his or her consent.

(4) Not unconstitutional [§647]

Although the husband's rights in a common law tenancy by the entirety were much greater than those of the wife, this was held not to be a violation of the Equal Protection Clause of the Constitution. The tenancy by the entirety is an optional type of tenancy deliberately chosen by the grantor or by the husband and wife. [**D'Ercole v. D'Ercole,** 407 F. Supp. 1377 (D. Mass. 1976)] Fortunately this question cannot arise with respect to any *new* tenancies by the entirety because the rights of husband and wife now have been made equal by legislation in all states.

b. Modern law

(1) Married Women's Property Act [§648]

In the nineteenth century, each American state enacted a Married Women's Property Act. These acts were passed to remove the common law disability of married women to control and dispose of their property. They provided, generally, that a married woman was able to receive, hold, manage, and dispose of real and personal property as if she were a single woman. (A single woman was under no disability at common law and could do with her property anything a man could.) The Married Women's Property Act did not specifically mention the wife's interest in a tenancy by the entirety, and hence it fell to the courts to apply the principle of the acts to entirety property. The position taken on the effect of the Married Women's Property Act on the tenancy by the entirety has important consequences for creditors, because a creditor can reach only such property as the debtor can voluntarily assign. The states can now generally be classified as taking one of two positions.

(a) Act forbids either spouse to convey separately [§649]

The courts in the majority of states recognizing the tenancy by the entirety hold that the equality intended by the Married Women's Property Act can be achieved in this way: (i) give both husband and wife equal rights to possession during the marriage (thus, with respect to possession, putting the wife in the same position the husband had at common law), and (ii) forbid both husband and wife, acting alone, to convey his or her interest (thus, with respect to voluntary transfer and creditors, putting the husband in the same position the wife had at common law). Under this view, creditors of one spouse cannot reach the property because neither the husband nor the wife acting alone can transfer his or her interest. [**Sawada v. Endo,** 561 P.2d 1291 (Haw. 1977); **Robinson v. Trousdale County,** 516 S.W.2d 626 (Tenn. 1974)] Doubtless this exemption from creditors is one of the main reasons for the survival of the tenancy by the entirety. It serves to protect the family home from assignment by one spouse and from creditors of one spouse.

(b) Act gives wife same rights husband had [§650]

Some courts hold that the Married Women's Property Act had the purpose of giving the wife the same rights as the husband had at common law. Thus, with respect to a tenancy by the entirety, the wife acquires the right to possession of one-half and the right to convey her interest in the same manner as the husband could at common law. Neither spouse can destroy the right of survivorship of the other. (This view is taken in New York and New Jersey, among other states.)

1) Creditors' rights [§651]

Because each spouse can voluntarily convey his or her interest, a creditor of the husband can seize and sell his interest and a creditor of the wife can seize and sell her interest. [**Coraccio v. Lowell Five Cents Savings Bank,** 612 N.E.2d 650 (Mass. 1993); **King v. Greene,** 153 A.2d 49 (N.J. 1959)]

Example: H and W own Blackacre as tenants by the entirety. W's judgment creditor, A, levies execution on W's interest, which is sold to B on execution sale. B is entitled equally to possession with H until H or W dies. If H dies first, B alone owns Blackacre. If W dies first, H alone owns Blackacre.

---

a) Criticism

The interest of one spouse, sold subject to survivorship rights in the other spouse, may not bring on a creditors' sale a price commensurate with its economic value. An execution sale of an interest defeasible if the nondebtor spouse survives may result in a sacrificial sale of the interest.

b) Partition after sale [§652]

A purchaser from H or W, including a purchaser at an execution sale, is a tenant in common with the other spouse during the lives of the spouses, but if the property is a family home, partition is not available to the purchaser. Equity refuses to grant partition in an attempt to protect the nondebtor spouse in the family home, but the nondebtor spouse must pay one-half the reasonable rental value to the purchaser. [**Newman v. Chase,** 359 A.2d 474 (N.J. 1976)]

(2) Forfeiture under drug laws [§653]

Federal drug laws provide for the forfeiture to the government of any property used in the sale of illegal drugs. Any interest in the property of an innocent owner is exempt from forfeiture. Suppose, then, that H sells illegal drugs from property owned by H and W as tenants by the entirety.

What part of the tenancy by the entirety is forfeited? Courts have held that the government is in the same position as a creditor of the drug-dealing spouse and can reach whatever interest of H a creditor can reach. Thus, W's protection against federal forfeiture of a tenancy by the entirety may differ from state to state. [**United States v. 1500 Lincoln Avenue,** 949 F.2d 73 (3d Cir. 1991); **United States v. 2525 Leroy Lane,** 910 F.2d 343 (6th Cir. 1990)]

(a) Innocent owner defense [§654]

Note that the property used in dealing drugs is forfeited except to the extent the owner did not know of or consent to the illegal activity (called "the innocent owner defense"). Thus, property owned solely by W used by her husband for dealing drugs can be forfeited unless she did not know of or consent to his activity. W's claim that she consented under a generalized fear of her husband is not a defense. To take advantage of the innocent owner defense, W must show that she consented under duress—a threat of immediate harm that she could not reasonably escape. [**United States v. Sixty Acres in Etowah County,** 930 F.2d 857 (11th Cir. 1991)]

(b) State forfeiture laws [§655]

Although federal drug laws provide that an innocent owner's share of property will not be forfeited, some state laws provide for forfeiture of property used in committing various offenses with no exemption of an innocent owner's interest. It has been held that forfeiture statutes are constitutional ("not unfair") even though an innocent owner's interest is included in the forfeiture. By taking title as a co-owner, the innocent owner takes the risk of forfeiture by the other co-owner. [**Bennis v. Michigan,** 516 U.S. 442 (1996)—car owned by H and W forfeited when H arrested using car for sexual activity with prostitute]

4. Divorce of Spouses [§656]

In most states, a divorce terminates the unity of husband and wife and therefore the tenancy by the entirety. In some states, the tenancy by the entirety is converted into a joint tenancy, but in most it is converted into a tenancy in common on the theory that the spouses do not want survivorship rights after divorce.

5. Tenancy by the Entirety in Personal Property

a. Common law rule [§657]

Because at common law the husband was the owner of his wife's personal property, a tenancy by the entirety in personal property was a logical impossibility. Michigan, New Jersey, and New York are the chief states still prohibiting a tenancy by the entirety in personal property, although the reason for the prohibition has completely disappeared. In these states, an attempt to create a tenancy by the entirety in personal property will create either a joint tenancy (as the closest equivalent) or a tenancy in common.

TYPE OF TENANCY	DEFINITION	CREATION	TERMINATION
TENANCY IN COMMON	Each tenant has a distinct, proportionate, undivided interest in the property. There is *no right of survivorship*.	"To A and B." Only unity required is possession.	May be terminated by partition.
JOINT TENANCY	Each tenant has an undivided interest in the whole estate, and the surviving co-tenant has a right to the whole estate (*right of survivorship*).	"To A and B as joint tenants *with the right of survivorship*." (Without survivorship language, it may be construed as a tenancy in common.) Joint tenants must take: • *Identical interests*; • From the *same instrument*; • At the *same time*; • With an *equal right to possess* (The four unities).	The right of survivorship may be severed, and the estate converted to a tenancy in common by: a conveyance by one joint tenant, agreement of joint tenants, murder of one joint tenant by another, or simultaneous death of joint tenants. A joint tenancy can be terminated by partition (voluntary or involuntary).
TENANCY BY THE ENTIRETY	*Husband and wife* each has an undivided interest in the whole estate and a *right of survivorship*.	"To H and W." Most states presume a tenancy by the entirety in any joint conveyance to husband and wife where the four unities (above) are present.	The right of survivorship may be severed by divorce, mutual agreement, or execution by a joint creditor. Tenancy by the entirety cannot be terminated by involuntary partition.

(1) Conversion of real to personal property [§658]

When, in these states, real property held by the entirety is converted into personal property, either by a voluntary act (*e.g.*, by sale) or by an involuntary act (*e.g.*, where a building burns and is replaced by insurance proceeds, or land is condemned), the proceeds cannot be held in tenancy by the entirety. [**Hawthorne v. Hawthorne**, 13 N.Y.2d 82 (1963)]

b. Majority rule [§659]

Most states recognizing the tenancy by the entirety permit it to be created in personal property (except possibly in a joint bank account; there, because either spouse can withdraw all funds, an inseverable right of survivorship is not possible). These states reason that the basis for the common law prohibition was destroyed by the Married Women's Property Act, which abolished the husband's ownership of the wife's personal property. [**Carlisle v. Parker**, 188 A. 67 (Del. 1936)]

6. Modern Status [§660]

The tenancy by the entirety is not recognized in about half the states. Some states have refused to recognize it because the common law unity of husband and wife, on which the estate is based, is repugnant to modern ideas of the marital relationship. Courts in other states have held that the tenancy by the entirety was abrogated by the Married Women's Property Act. In the eight community property states, the tenancy is not recognized because it is thought to be inconsistent with the equality principle underlying the community property system.

D. Rights and Duties of Co-Tenants

1. Introduction [§661]

The rights and duties of co-tenants are more or less the same regardless of the type of co-tenancy. Of course, a joint tenant or a tenant by the entirety has a right of survivorship, and a tenant in common does not. And a tenant by the entirety may be legally unable to convey his or her interest without the consent of the spouse. And the common law unity of husband and wife may give tenants by the entirety different rights than other co-tenants. But these matters aside, the rights and duties of co-tenants are similar. Unless otherwise noted, the following discussion applies to all co-tenants.

2. Possession by One Co-Tenant [§662]

Each co-tenant is equally entitled to the possession and enjoyment of the entire co-tenancy property. No co-tenant may exclude another co-tenant from any part of the property. Obviously these general rules are not very helpful when one co-tenant goes into exclusive possession. What rights has the co-tenant out of possession?

a. **Agreement by parties [§663]**

Co-tenants can agree among themselves that one co-tenant has the right to exclusive possession. The law encourages parties in conflict to resolve the conflict by private agreement rather than by a lawsuit. A private agreement regarding possession does not sever the unity of possession nor does it sever a joint tenancy (*see supra,* §§600, 624).

b. **Accounting for reasonable rental value by co-tenant in possession [§664]**

Must a co-tenant in possession pay a reasonable rental value to the co-tenant out of possession? Suppose that A and B are co-tenants. A goes into exclusive possession. B voluntarily remains out of possession. Must A pay B one-half the fair rental value of the property?

(1) **Majority rule [§665]**

If B is not excluded (ousted) by A, A is entitled to use and occupy every part of the property without paying any amount to B. B cannot recover a share of the rental value of the land unless B has been *ousted* by A, or A agreed to pay B, or A stands in a fiduciary relationship to B. [**Pico v. Columbet,** 12 Cal. 414 (1859); **Spiller v. Mackereth,** 334 So. 2d 859 (Ala. 1976); **Barrow v. Barrow,** 527 So. 2d 1373 (Fla. 1988); **Cummings v. Anderson,** 614 P.2d 1283 (Wash. 1980)]

(a) **Rationale**

This rule promotes the productive use of property. It rewards the co-tenant who goes into possession and uses the property. It also follows logically from the premise that each co-tenant has the right to possession of all, and not merely a proportionate share, of the property.

(b) **Carrying charges [§666]**

Because A, in possession, does not have to pay rent to B, it is deemed fair that A must bear the ordinary expenses of upkeep (*e.g.*, taxes, mortgage interest, repairs). If taxes and mortgage interest exceed the fair rental value of the property, A has a right of contribution from the other co-tenants. Similarly, A will be credited for payment of more than A's proportionate share in an accounting or partition action.

(c) **Ouster [§667]**

In a jurisdiction following the majority rule, if one co-tenant ousts another co-tenant, she must pay the ousted co-tenant his share of the reasonable rental value of the property.

1) **Definition [§668]**

Ouster is an act by one co-tenant that *deprives another co-tenant of the right to possession.* There is an ouster when an occupying co-tenant refuses to admit another co-tenant into possession. Ouster also occurs if the occupying co-tenant denies the title of another co-tenant. It may occur if the occupying co-tenant refuses to pay an appropriate rental value demanded by a co-tenant out of possession. It may even occur where the occupying co-tenant does not reply to a letter making such a demand. It is a flexible definition by which a court tempers the majority rule, and makes it fairer to the tenant out of possession. [**Olivas v. Olivas,** 780 P.2d 640 (N.M. 1989)—holding H not ousted when he moved out of house as a result of marital discord]

2) Remedies [§669]

An ousted co-tenant can bring a suit to collect his share of the reasonable rental value or a suit to partition the property. The former action is sometimes called a suit for mesne profits. Mesne profits are the reasonable value of the *use* of land, not the profits actually made.

(2) Minority rule [§670]

In a minority of states, A must account to B for B's share of the *reasonable rental value* of the premises. [**Lerman v. Levine,** 541 A.2d 523 (Conn. 1988); **McKnight v. Basilides,** 143 P.2d 307 (Wash. 1943); *but see* **Fulton v. Fulton,** 357 P.2d 169 (Wash. 1960)—dismissing McKnight rule as dictum and shifting Washington back to majority rule]

(a) Rationale

This rule places the burden on the occupying co-tenant to show an agreement by the co-tenants that she was not to pay. By putting the burden on the person who will reap economic gain (the occupying co-tenant), and penalizing her if the parties act ambiguously, this rule induces co-tenants to come to an agreement as to the payment of rent. An agreement is desirable because it lessens litigation over the parties' rights.

(b) Carrying charges [§671]

The occupying co-tenant is accountable for her share of the *net reasonable rental value,* after deducting expenses of upkeep.

3. Accounting for Rents Received from a Third Party [§672]

Any rents or other income collected by a co-tenant from a third party must be shared equally with the other co-tenants if the income exceeds the collecting co-tenant's proportionate share. The collecting co-tenant must account to the others for their proportionate shares. This rule was established by the Statute of Anne (1704). The collecting co-tenant must account for the net amount actually received, not for the reasonable rental value of the land. [**Carr v. Deking,** 765 P.2d 40 (Wash. 1988)]

Example: A and B are co-tenants. A leases the land to C for $1,000 a year. A must pay B $500 out of each $1,000 payment A receives.

---

a. Time of accounting [§673]

When a co-tenant has a right to an accounting during the existence of the co-tenancy, she can bring a suit for an accounting. Or she can wait and demand an accounting in a partition action, which separates the co-tenants and adjusts their rights in a final settlement. In a final accounting in a partition action, the court can require a tenant to account from the beginning of the tenancy. The statute of limitations does not begin to run until the termination of the co-tenancy, because a co-tenant is viewed as a fiduciary. (A statute of limitations does not run on a trustee from the time of breach, but rather only from the time the fiduciary relationship terminates.) [**Goergen v. Maar,** 2 A.D.2d 276 (1956)]

4. Exploiting Natural Resources [§674]

A co-tenant is accountable for profits derived from a use of land that permanently reduces its value.

a. Minerals [§675]

If a co-tenant operates mines or oil wells, she is not entitled to take her fair share of the minerals in place, because of the difficulty in estimating the amount and value of the minerals. Instead, the co-tenant must pay a proportionate part of the net amount received for the extracted minerals to her co-tenants.

(1) Amount payable [§676]

The general rule is that the co-tenant must account for the net amount received for the minerals as they are extracted. But if the co-tenant is in the business of processing and selling minerals, it has been held that the extracting co-tenant is accountable for the net profits realized from her processing business. [**White v. Smyth,** 214 S.W.2d 967 (Tex. 1948)] The case is supportable on the rationale that requiring the extracting co-tenant to account for profits from her processing business induces her to come to an agreement with her co-tenants before extracting minerals. The same rationale supports the minority rule regarding payment of rent to a co-tenant out of possession. It places the burden of reaching agreement on the active party, and hence is economically efficient.

(2) Distinguish—farming [§677]

A co-tenant who excludes her co-tenants and farms the land is accountable for the fair rental value of the land, not the net profits received from her farming operation.

b. Timber [§678]

Unlike products underground, timber can be seen and a fractional share apportioned easily. For this reason, some courts hold that one co-tenant can cut her proportionate share of the timber without being liable to her co-tenants for its value. If she cuts more than her share, she must account. Other courts hold that, to prevent overcutting, no co-tenant can cut a share of the timber without the consent of the co-tenants.

5. Actions by Co-Tenant to Protect Property [§679]

The general principle is that a co-tenant who pays money to keep up the property, which benefits all co-tenants, is entitled to reimbursement for more than her proportionate share of costs. But this is subject to exceptions and qualifications. The courts try to do what is just and equitable under the circumstances. The discussion below states the usual rule, but there are variations in particular jurisdictions.

a. Taxes [§680]

Each co-tenant has the *duty to pay her share of taxes*, in order to protect the property from a tax foreclosure sale. If one co-tenant pays more than her share of taxes, she can compel the other co-tenant to reimburse her immediately, or she can wait and present her claim in a suit for partition.

(1) Exception—co-tenant in possession [§681]

If the paying co-tenant is in sole possession, she has the duty to pay the taxes and mortgage interest up to the amount of the reasonable rental value of the property. She can compel contribution only if taxes and other carrying charges exceed the reasonable rental value.

(2) Rent received from third person [§682]

If the paying co-tenant receives rent from a third person, she must account to her co-tenant for the net rents received after deducting taxes and other carrying charges.

b. Interest on mortgage [§683]

Interest on a mortgage is treated the same way as taxes. These are "compulsory" carrying charges. A co-tenant who pays interest on the mortgage can compel contribution from nonpaying co-tenants who are personally liable on the mortgage. If the nonpaying co-tenant is not personally liable on the mortgage, the paying co-tenant can foreclose a lien on the other's interest.

(1) Payment on principal [§684]

If a co-tenant pays off the *principal* of the mortgage, she is subrogated to the mortgagee and has whatever rights the mortgagee has. Paying off a mortgage gives the paying co-tenant a lien on the property, which the mortgagee had. If the other co-tenant does not pay his share of the principal when it falls due, the paying co-tenant can foreclose the lien by having the property sold to pay the lien. In addition, if the mortgage is a joint obligation of the co-tenants, the paying co-tenant can get a *personal judgment* against the other co-tenant in the amount of his proportionate share. [**Giles v. Sheridan,** *supra*, §614]

c. Repairs [§685]

At common law, repairs were (and in many jurisdictions still are) treated differently from taxes and interest on mortgages. Repairs are voluntary; no person has a duty to make them. Hence the common law rule is that a co-tenant who makes repairs *cannot compel contribution* from her co-tenants. She must wait until an accounting action or partition action. In an accounting for rents received from a third person or for reasonable rental value, she can *set off the amount (over and above her share) spent on repairs*. In a partition sale, she may be reimbursed for repair expenses over and above her share before the sale proceeds are distributed. *But note:* This common law approach has been changed in some jurisdictions. Some jurisdictions now permit an action for contribution if the repairs were *necessary* and if (in some jurisdictions) she gave *notice* to the other co-tenants.

d. Improvements [§686]

Just as co-tenants generally do not have a duty to repair, no co-tenant has a duty to improve. Thus, an improving co-tenant cannot compel contribution from her co-tenant. But in other respects, improvements are not treated like necessary repairs. There may be no reimbursement for them at all. The general principle applicable to improvements is that the improver should get the *value added* by the improvements, and if the improvements add no value, the improver is not reimbursed. The improver bears the risk. Thus, in accounting for rents received or for fair rental value, the improver is credited only with the amount of increased rent or rental value attributable to the improvements. Similarly, in a partition action, where the property is physically partitioned, the court will give the improver the portion of the property containing the improvements if feasible. If a partition sale is ordered, the improving co-tenant receives the *value added* to the property by (not the cost of) the improvements. If the improvements add no value, the improver receives nothing for them.

> **e.g. Example:** A and B are co-tenants of land that costs $20,000. A erects a building thereon at a cost of $10,000. On partition sale the property is sold for $55,000, the land being worth $30,000 and the building worth $25,000. From the proceeds A should receive one-half the value of the land ($15,000) and the whole value of the building ($25,000), for a total of $40,000. B should receive $15,000.

EXAM TIP   **gilbert**

Don't confuse the standard for reimbursement for repairs with that for improvements. A co-tenant who makes repairs to the property generally cannot compel contribution from her co-tenant but may be reimbursed for **the amount of the repairs** in the event of an accounting or partition. A co-tenant who makes an improvement to the property may only be reimbursed for the **value added** to the property by the improvements.

---

6. Co-Tenants as Fiduciaries [§687]

A co-tenant is not, strictly speaking, a fiduciary. She does not hold her interest for the benefit of another. On the other hand, a co-tenancy is not a relationship between strangers where the parties can be expected to be guarding their respective interests. In view of this, courts sometimes treat one co-tenant as the fiduciary of another.

a. When deemed fiduciaries

(1) Confidential relationship [§688]

If a confidential relationship exists among the co-tenants, any co-tenant who acquires an outstanding title or lien on the property is deemed to have acquired it on behalf of all the co-tenants. A confidential relationship may arise when two persons buy property together as co-tenants, each relying on the good faith of the other.

(2) Inherited title [§689]

Co-tenants who acquire their interests by will or intestate succession are usually regarded as fiduciaries with respect to each other. Ordinarily such co-tenants are siblings or have some other family tie, and their expectations are that the other co-tenants will act in good faith toward them.

b. Acquisition of outstanding title [§690]

The event that most commonly triggers fiduciary liability is the acquisition of an outstanding superior title. The most frequently litigated cases involve purchase by a co-tenant at a tax sale or on foreclosure of a mortgage. There is a great divergence of opinion in these cases. The following are the general rules, but the equities in a particular case may be controlling.

(1) Tax sale [§691]

Each co-tenant has a duty to pay taxes on the property. If a co-tenant in a fiduciary relationship buys the property at a tax sale, or buys it from the purchaser within the period of redemption, she holds it for the benefit of all the co-tenants. The other co-tenants have the right to preserve their interests in the property by contributing their share of the sum expended to the purchasing co-tenant. [**Massey v. Prothero**, 664 P.2d 1176 (Utah 1983)]

(2) Foreclosure of mortgage [§692]

If all the co-tenants are liable on the debt securing the mortgage, and one co-tenant buys the property at the mortgage foreclosure sale, she is entitled to reimbursement from her co-tenants to the extent she paid their shares of the indebtedness. Conversely, the other co-tenants have the right to contribute to the purchase price within a reasonable time and reclaim their shares. [**Laura v. Christian**, 537 P.2d 1389 (N.M. 1975)]

7. Adverse Possession [§693]

A co-tenant can adversely possess against another co-tenant, and if the adverse possession continues for the statutory period, it will ripen into title in the adverse possessor. However, merely going into exclusive possession or collecting rents is insufficient to establish adverse possession. Similarly, refusing to admit a co-tenant into possession is not enough. To establish herself as an adverse possessor, a co-tenant must give the other co-tenants clear and unequivocal *notice of repudiation of the common title.* Any co-tenant has the right to be in possession of co-tenancy property. Hence, if the acts of the possessor are susceptible of explanation consistent with the existence of the common title, such acts do not give notice. [**Mercer v. Wayman,** 137 N.E.2d 815 (Ill. 1956); **Shives v. Niewoehner,** 191 N.W.2d 633 (Iowa 1971)]

8. Partition [§694]

Any tenant in common or joint tenant has the right to bring a suit in partition. This is an equitable proceeding in which the court either physically divides or sells the common property, adjusts all claims of the parties, and separates them. When co-tenants are squabbling and cannot come to any agreement, the judicial remedy of partition terminates the co-tenancy and divides the common property. Partition is not available to tenants by the entirety because neither spouse can destroy the right of survivorship of the other spouse.

a. Partition in kind [§695]

The court may order physical partition of the property into separate tracts if that is feasible. Once the land is physically partitioned, each party owns her tract alone in fee simple. If the separate tracts are not equal in value, the court will require one tenant to make a cash payment, called *owelty,* to the other tenant to equalize values. [**Delfino v. Vealencis,** 436 A.2d 27 (Conn. 1980)]

---

e.g. **Example:** A court partitions land into two tracts: tract 1 worth $20,000, and tract 2 worth $18,000. The co-tenant who is assigned tract 1 will have to pay the other tenant $1,000 in cash, so that each ends up with property worth $19,000.

---

b. Partition sale [§696]

If physical partition is not feasible or in the best interests of the parties, the court will order the property sold and the sale proceeds divided equally among the co-tenants. Houses, apartment buildings, urban lots, and commercial property do not usually lend themselves to physical partition. Instead, sale is ordinarily ordered by the court. Rural land is the type most often physically partitioned, but even there the court will order the land sold if the total value of the land will be materially less if partitioned into separate tracts. [**Johnson v. Hendrickson,** 24 N.W.2d 914 (S.D. 1946)]

(1) Division of proceeds [§697]

The presumption is that on partition of the property, each co-tenant is entitled to an equal share in the proceeds, subject to adjustments for payment of taxes, interest, repairs, and improvements (*supra,* §§680-686). This presumption is rebuttable by evidence that the co-tenants intended unequal shares. This most often occurs when there are unequal contributions to the purchase price. If no gift was intended by a co-tenant making a larger contribution, she is entitled to a proportionately larger share of the proceeds.

c. Agreement not to partition [§698]

Co-tenants may agree not to partition the land. If the agreement is for a reasonable purpose and for a reasonable length of time, such as the life of a co-tenant, it is not invalid as a restraint on alienation (*supra*, §356). But because partition is an equitable proceeding, if the court finds the agreement harsh or oppressive it will refuse to enforce the agreement and will grant partition. [**Michalski v. Michalski**, *supra*, §356]

E. Marital Rights on Divorce

1. Common Law [§699]

At common law, on divorce the husband's property belonged to the husband and the wife's to the wife. However, the husband had the obligation of supporting his wife for her lifetime. This obligation ordinarily continued after divorce. A court, on divorce, would award the wife support (called *alimony*), unless the wife had been unfaithful or had otherwise forfeited her right to support.

2. Modern Law [§700]

Statutes in all states have modernized divorce law in attempts to bring equality to husbands and wives. The central idea is that the poorer spouse (usually the wife) should be given a share in the property owned by the richer spouse to compensate her for her efforts in making the marriage a material success. Whether modern divorce law has resulted in equality for wives is widely debated.

a. Alimony [§701]

Alimony (now usually called *support*) is no longer owed by the husband to the wife for her life. The husband has the obligation of supporting the wife for a limited period of time until she can reenter the job market and support herself. This is sometimes called *rehabilitative alimony*. But for a woman who has been out of the job market and laboring in the home for many years, rehabilitative alimony is highly unlikely to put her in an equal position with her husband.

b. Property division [§702]

At common law, the wife had no claim to the husband's property. In all common law property states today, a wife is entitled to *equitable distribution* of a fractional share of the husband's property (and vice versa if the wife is the rich one). The equitable distribution statutes vary. Some authorize the divorce court to divide *all property* of the spouses, regardless of the time or manner of acquisition. Others authorize division of *all property acquired during marriage* by any means. Still others imitate the community property system and authorize division only of property acquired during marriage *from earnings*. Equitable distribution requires a court to consider a broad range of factors, including the length of the marriage, the earning capacity of the spouse, and the childcare responsibilities of one spouse. [*In re* **Marriage of King,** 700 P.2d 591 (Mont. 1985); **Painter v. Painter,** 320 A.2d 484 (N.J. 1974)]

(1) Professional degrees [§703]

During marriage one spouse may have acquired a professional degree while the other spouse has supported him. On divorce, should the supporting spouse receive any benefit from the degree? It seems unfair for one spouse to come out of marriage with increased earning power acquired at the expense of the other without some compensation being given to the supporting spouse. The courts have divided three ways:

(a) Not divisible property [§704]

Some courts have held that increased earning power from a professional degree is not "property," and therefore it is not divisible on divorce. "Putting hubby through" is just tough luck. [*In re* **Marriage of Graham,** 574 P.2d 75 (Colo. 1978)]

(b) Reimbursement alimony given [§705]

Some courts have held that the appropriate remedy is to give the supporting spouse reimbursement alimony. This is a restitution remedy, which returns to the supporting spouse the cost of her investment in the other spouse's degree. When the cost of her investment is returned to her, she can make a new investment, perhaps in a degree for herself. [*In re* **Marriage of Francis,** 442 N.W.2d 59 (Iowa 1989)]

(c) Divisible property [§706]

New York has held that earning power increased during the marriage by acquiring a professional degree or celebrity status is property subject to equitable division. Thus, the supporting spouse is awarded a share in the value of her investment in human capital. [**O'Brien v. O'Brien,** 66 N.Y.2d 576 (1985); **Elkus v. Elkus,** 169 A.D.2d 134 (1991)]

(2) Goodwill [§707]

Most courts hold that goodwill acquired in the practice of law or medicine is property to be taken into account on equitable division. Thus, if the wife is a lawyer, the husband is entitled to a share of the value of the wife's practice, including accounts receivable and goodwill that will produce future business. [**Prahinski v. Prahinski,** 582 A.2d 784 (Md. 1990)]

F. Marital Rights on Death

1. Common Law

a. Dower [§708]

At common law, a wife has dower in all *freehold land* (i) of which her husband is *seised during marriage* and (ii) which is *inheritable by issue* born of the marriage. Dower is a life estate in one-third of each parcel of qualifying land.

Example: H dies, owning Blackacre in fee simple. W is entitled to a life estate in one-third of Blackacre. H's heirs and devisees take Blackacre subject to W's dower.

---

(1) In land seised during marriage [§709]

Dower attaches only to land of which the husband is seised during marriage. The husband has to be in possession of a freehold estate. Thus, dower does *not* attach to any *leasehold* interest of the husband, nor to any *remainder* interest the husband has following a life estate in another. Nor does dower attach to the *personal property* of the husband, in which there is no seisin, nor to any *equitable interest* of the husband, where the trustee holds seisin. [**Chaplin v. Chaplin**, 24 Eng. Rep. 1040 (1733)]

(2) In land inheritable by issue [§710]

For dower to attach, it must be *possible for issue* born of the marriage *to inherit* the land from the husband. Actual birth of issue is immaterial. Thus, dower does not attach to land in which the husband has only a *life estate*. Nor does it attach to land the husband owns with another person as *joint tenants* with the right of survivorship.

(3) Rights during husband's life [§711]

Dower attaches to the land the moment the husband is seised during marriage. Until the husband dies, dower is *inchoate*—a word indicating that the wife has an interest that is not yet, but may become, possessory. Once inchoate dower attaches, the wife prevails over any subsequent purchasers of the property and over any attaching creditors of the husband. They take the property *subject to her dower*.

Example: H, married to W, purchases Blackacre, taking title in his own name. On purchase, W has inchoate dower in Blackacre. No subsequent person can cut out her dower if she survives H. Later H sells to a bona fide purchaser who has no notice of W's dower interest. H

---

dies. W is entitled to a life estate in one-third of Blackacre. The purchaser takes the land subject to W's dower.

(a) Release of dower [§712]

Because dower rights prevail over subsequent purchasers, a purchaser from a married man must have his wife release dower in order to take free of it. This means the wife must sign the deed, releasing her dower. If the purchaser does not know if the seller is married, the purchaser takes the risk.

(b) Divorce [§713]

An absolute divorce puts an end to the marriage and to inchoate dower. A legal separation does not bar dower.

EXAM TIP   **gilbert**

The rule of dower is simple: Once inchoate dower has attached, a wife *cannot lose dower unless* she *consents* or the couple is *divorced*.

---

(4) Rights on husband's death [§714]

On the husband's death, leaving his wife surviving, dower gives his wife the right to possession *for her life* of *one-third* of *each parcel* of land subject to dower. Unless the surviving wife and the heir or devisee agree otherwise, dower in each parcel is assigned to the wife by a court.

(5) Statutory abolition [§715]

Dower has been abolished in all jurisdictions except Arkansas, Iowa, Kentucky, Michigan, and Ohio. In these states the surviving spouse can elect dower or a forced share (*see infra,* §718). Because the latter is almost always greater, the primary function of dower is to require both spouses to sign deeds to land.

b. Curtesy [§716]

At common law, on the wife's death, a surviving husband had curtesy, which was roughly comparable to dower but somewhat different. First, the husband had curtesy only if issue were born of the marriage (giving the husband an incentive to produce issue). Second, the husband received a life estate in *all* of his wife's lands, and not merely a third of them, as in dower. This reflected the notion that males should control the land whereas females needed only support.

(1) Statutory abolition [§717]

By modern statutes, curtesy has been abolished wherever dower has been abolished. Where dower has been retained, dower has been extended to the husband and the different estate of curtesy abolished. Thus, the treatment of spouses is the same in all states except Michigan, where dower is given to wives but not to husbands and curtesy has been abolished.

2. Modern Statutory Elective Share [§718]

Almost all common law property states give the surviving spouse an elective share in the *decedent's property owned at death*. The share is usually one-half or one-third or some other fraction determined by the length of the marriage. The elective share is in both real and personal property.

a. Election required [§719]

The surviving spouse has the option ("election") of taking a forced share *or* taking what the decedent spouse left her by will. If she elects her forced share, what she was left by will is credited against the forced share.

b. Inter vivos transfers [§720]

Most states provide that an inter vivos revocable trust created by the decedent spouse is subject to the elective share of the surviving spouse. If this were not done, then one spouse could completely defeat the surviving spouse by creating a revocable trust, which remains under the complete control of the settlor spouse. In some states courts say a revocable trust is reachable by the surviving spouse if made with the intent to deprive her of her marital rights, but in most states intent is irrelevant. The revocable trust is reachable because the decedent spouse could revoke it. [**Sullivan v. Burkin**, 460 N.E.2d 572 (Mass. 1984); **Newman v. Dore**, 275 N.Y. 371 (1937)] In a few states, however, the elective share is limited to the decedent's probate estate and does not extend to an inter vivos revocable trust.

c. Antenuptial transfers [§721]

Secret transfers made before marriage, when marriage is contemplated, may be deemed fraudulent as to the surviving spouse. If deemed fraudulent, such transfers are subject to the surviving spouse's elective share. Fraudulent intent is ordinarily presumed when the gift is made without the knowledge of the prospective spouse. [**Strong v. Wood**, 306 N.W.2d 737 (Iowa 1981)]

d. Extended elective share [§722]

Although the original elective share legislation gave the surviving spouse a share of the decedent's *probate estate only*, many states in recent years have extended the elective share to also include property not passing through the decedent's probate estate (*e.g.*, life insurance, joint tenancies, retirement plans, inter vivos trusts where the decedent retained a life estate). [*See, e.g.*, Uniform Probate Code §2-202—extending elective share to an "augmented estate," meaning probate estate augmented with other property. The details of augmented estate statutes are quite complex and can happily be left to a course on Wills]

G. Community Property

1. Introduction [§723]

Eight states (Arizona, California, Idaho, Louisiana, Nevada, New Mexico, Texas, and Washington) have community property between married couples. In Alaska, married couples may elect to hold their property as community property. The system of community property is traceable to French or Spanish influence in the South and West. The summary below can only sketch the general idea of community property. Many variations exist in each of these states. (For a detailed discussion, *see* Community Property Summary.)

a. Basic theory of community property [§724]

Community property rests on a notion that husband and wife are a marital partnership (a "community"), that both contribute to the material success of the marriage, and that both should share equally in material acquisitions. Community property is owned in equal undivided shares by the spouses. Community property in one form or another exists throughout the continent of Europe, but it never crossed the English channel. Under the pressure of a militaristic feudalism, the English judges suppressed any tendencies toward community property. And by the time the feudal period had ended, the legal subjugation of the wife to the husband had become entrenched. Hence, while husband and wife shared earnings equally on the continent, in England all earnings belonged to the wage earner who was, in the vast majority of cases, the husband. Community property recognizes and rewards the work of a spouse who stays at home and does housework. Common law property does not.

2. What Is Community Property? [§725]

Community property consists of *earnings* of either spouse *during marriage* and property acquired through earnings. Property owned by either spouse *before marriage* or acquired after marriage by *gift, descent, or devise* is *separate property*. This division of property follows from the basic theory that husband and wife should share equally material acquisitions resulting from the labor of either during marriage.

a. Income from community property [§726]

Once property is characterized as community property, all income and proceeds of sale of the property are community property. If new assets are purchased with community funds, the new assets are community property. One spouse cannot, without the other's consent, change community property into separate property. Remember, community property belongs to both husband and wife.

Example: H earns $1,000 from his job at General Dynamics. H uses the $1,000 to buy 10 shares of Beta stock in his own name. The Beta stock is community property, even though held in H's own name. H cannot change community property (earnings) into his separate property without W's consent.

> **EXAM TIP**   **gilbert**
>
> How *title* is held is *not* controlling in defining community property; whether the asset is traceable to *earnings during marriage* is controlling.

b. Income from separate property [§727]

In Idaho, Louisiana, and Texas, the income from separate property is community property; in other states, the income from separate property retains its separate character. Where the characterization of the property is doubtful, there is *a strong presumption in favor of community property*.

3. Commingling of Community and Separate Property [§728]

If community and separate property have been commingled in such a manner that it is impossible to ascertain and identify each source, the commingled whole will be presumed to be community property.

Example: H and W maintain a bank account depositing therein both earnings and income received from separate property. If no records are kept as to which deposits are separate property and which are community, the commingled whole will be treated as community. The same result occurs when H and W buy a parcel of land using both separate and community funds to pay the purchase price and keep no records.

4. Community Labor Used to Enhance Separate Property [§729]

Where one spouse devotes time and effort in managing his or her separate property, thus increasing its value, the enhanced value is partly attributable to the spouse's separate investment and partly due to the spouse's skill and industry. The enhancement due to the spouse's skill and industry belongs to the community. How is this calculated? The rules are best seen by an illustration:

Example: At the time of marriage, H owns a business valued at $100,000. After marriage, H continues to manage the business. Profits of $80,000 have accumulated. What portion of the profits is community and what portion is separate property? First, the court must decide if the *chief* contributing factor in realizing profits is the capital investment of H or the personal efforts of H. If the court finds that the *greater factor was H's efforts* (a community asset), the court will allocate a fair return (say 7% per annum) on the $100,000 investment to H as his separate property and allocate any excess to community property. On the other hand, if the court finds that H's personal services were not the greater factor in creating profits, the court will allocate the reasonable value of H's services to community property (say a salary of $10,000 a year), and allocate the balance to separate property. [**Beam v. Bank of America,** 6 Cal. 3d 12 (1971)]

5. Conveyance of Share [§730]

Neither spouse acting alone can convey *his or her share* of community property, except to the other spouse. However, by *agreement of the parties*, community property may be converted into the separate property of either spouse, or conversely, separate property may be converted into community property.

6. Management of Community Property [§731]

Either husband or wife, acting alone, can manage community property; either can sell it, lease it, invest it, etc. Thus, technically, H has the right to manage W's earnings as well as his own, and W has the right to manage H's earnings as well as her own. Each is a fiduciary in exercising management powers. Each must use good faith in exercising authority and for breach of the fiduciary duty each is liable to the other spouse.

Example: H and W own 100 shares of GM stock as community property. W decides the stock should be sold, and she sells the stock for its market price. She reinvests the proceeds in GE stock. Sale and reinvestment is within W's power.

a. Real property [§732]

Usually land held as community property cannot be sold except with the consent of both husband and wife.

b. Business interest [§733]

A spouse who is managing a business that is community property has the sole management and control of the business.

Example: W, a lawyer, operates a law practice. W maintains a bank account in her own name in connection with her law practice. W has sole management powers over the bank account and all of the personal property used in her practice. H cannot sell the desks in W's office, nor draw on the business bank account.

c. Gifts [§734]

The community property states follow different rules respecting gifts of community property by one spouse. In some states, a spouse may make reasonable gifts and, in others, gifts not in "fraud" of the other spouse. In still other states, the nondonor spouse may set aside the gift entirely.

7. Rights at Dissolution of Marriage [§735]

When the marriage is dissolved by divorce, community property is usually divided equally. When the marriage is terminated by the death of one spouse, the decedent spouse has the right to transfer his or her one-half of the community property by will to anyone.

8. Uniform Marital Property Act [§736]

The Uniform Marital Property Act, promulgated in 1983, adopts the principles of community property although it avoids that term. The Act provides that all property acquired *during marriage other than by gift or inheritance is marital property*. This is the definition of community property in community property states. All other property is *individual* property. Husband and wife have equal interests in marital property, and their rights in it during marriage and on divorce or death are more or less the same as the rights of spouses in community property. In 1984, Wisconsin became the first and only state to adopt the Uniform Marital Property Act.

9. **Migrating Couples [§737]**

Property rights in earnings are determined by the state of domicile when the property is earned. If the couple is domiciled in a separate property state, the earnings of each are the separate property of each. If domiciled in a community property state, the earnings of both are community property. Once the property rights are determined, they do not change if a couple changes domicile. Community property acquired in a community property state remains community property when the couple moves to a common law property state. Similarly, separate property from earnings acquired while the couple was domiciled in a common law property state remains separate property when they move to a community property state.

a. **Elective share [§738]**

Community property states do not have elective share statutes. They protect the surviving spouse by giving her during life half the property earned by the other spouse. Thus, when an older couple moves to a community property state from a separate property state, where the husband has worked and acquired substantial property, the wife loses her protection in the form of the elective share of the former domicile. To remedy this situation, California and a few other community property states (but not Texas) have enacted "quasi-community property" statutes. These statutes treat as community property—for purposes of distribution on death or divorce—all property earned in a separate property state that would have been treated as community property if the couple had been domiciled in a community property state. Thus, if a couple moves to California from Illinois, where the husband worked and accumulated $500,000, California gives the wife one-half of this on divorce or death of the husband.

b. **Choice of law [§739]**

When a couple is involved in a transaction, part of which occurs in a common law property state and part of which occurs in a community property state, the question may arise as to which state law should be applied. Generally state courts apply the law of the state having the *most significant relationship* with the parties and the transaction. It is easier to state this rule than apply it, however, because evaluating the competing state policies involved often results in disagreement among the judges. [**Pacific Gamble Robinson Co. v. Lapp,** 622 P.2d 850 (Wash. 1980)]

H. Rights of Unmarried Partners

1. Common Law Marriage [§740]

Where common law marriage is recognized, an unmarried man and woman who agree to be married, hold themselves out to the public as married, and conduct their affairs as a married couple are lawfully married. That is known as common law marriage. The couple has all the rights of persons married with benefit of clergy. Common law marriage used to be widely recognized in the United States, but it has been abolished in most states.

2. Contracts Between Unmarried Partners [§741]

Courts have taken different views about the rights of unmarried cohabitants on dissolution of their relationship.

a. Express contract [§742]

An express contract between the partners providing how the couple's property will be divided on separation or death is enforceable in most states. In some states the contract can be oral. [**Cook v. Cook,** 691 P.2d 664 (Ariz. 1984); **Morone v. Morone,** 50 N.Y.2d 481 (1980)] *But note:* A contract between the parties cannot give them the status rights conferred by the state on married persons (*e.g.,* elective share, inheritance rights, split-income tax return, marital deduction, spousal benefits under Social Security).

(1) Contract not enforceable [§743]

Illinois has taken the view that an express or implied contract by unmarried partners is unenforceable because to enforce the contract would be to reinstitute common law marriage abolished by the legislature. In addition, the court thought that enforcing such contracts would weaken the institution of marriage and family. [**Hewitt v. Hewitt,** 394 N.E.2d 1204 (Ill. 1979)]

b. Implied contract [§744]

In some states a contract to share property or to support one partner can be implied from the conduct of the parties. If an implied contract is found by a court, it is enforceable. In addition to enforcing the contract, the aggrieved party may be entitled to have a constructive trust imposed by an equity court on the other party's assets to prevent unjust enrichment. [**Marvin v. Marvin,** 18 Cal. 3d 660 (1976); **Watts v. Watts,** 405 N.W.2d 303 (Wis. 1987)]

c. Partnership theory [§745]

The Mississippi court has held that where the parties create a relationship akin to a partnership, in which the parties embark on a joint venture and rely on each other, the property acquired through their joint efforts will be equitably divided when they break up. [**Pickens v. Pickens,** 490 So. 2d 872 (Miss. 1986)]

d. Quantum meruit [§746]

A party who is not entitled to recover under any of the above theories may be entitled to recover on a quantum meruit basis, to prevent unjust enrichment. Quantum meruit gives the aggrieved party restitution for the value of services rendered.

3. Same-Sex Partners [§747]

Same-sex partners may, like opposite-sex cohabitants, make contracts governing their property rights. However, with one exception to date, same-sex couples are not permitted to enter into marriage and acquire rights granted married persons as a matter of status. The exception is Massachusetts. That state's supreme court has held that the state constitution precludes the state from denying the incidents of marriage to same-sex couples *who are residents of the state.* [**Goodridge v. Department of Public Health,** 798 N.E.2d 941 (Mass. 2003)] As to other states, a handful, while not permitting same-sex marriage, do extend some recognition to same-sex couples. California provides for domestic partnerships with rights and responsibilities that are essentially the same as those of legally married parties. New Jersey provides for more limited domestic partnerships whereby the partners are eligible to receive certain health and retirement benefits but not marital property rights. Hawaii permits same-sex couples to register as "reciprocal beneficiaries," a status that confers inheritance rights. Vermont goes considerably further, providing for "civil unions" conferring the same benefits, protections, and responsibilities as are granted to married spouses under state law.

a. Rent-controlled apartment [§748]

In New York City, rent-controlled apartments on the tenant's death can be passed to a member of the deceased tenant's "family." It has been held that in this context the word "family" includes a same-sex partner living in the apartment. [**Braschi v. Stahl Associates,** 74 N.Y.2d 201 (1989)]

b. Discrimination statutes [§749]

A number of states have passed statutes forbidding discrimination in housing or employment because of sexual orientation. Some cities have passed ordinances giving to same-sex partners certain limited rights.

Chapter Six:
Landlord and Tenant

CONTENTS

Chapter Approach

This chapter covers the major topics on landlord-tenant law. Of all the various areas of property, landlord-tenant law has undergone the most change during the last 50 years. On the whole, it has been revised to give tenants more rights and landlords less. Revisions have not been accepted in all states however nor, where accepted, have they had uniform content. These recent changes are discussed in this chapter.

As another general comment to this area of law, remember that landlord-tenant law is a blend of property law and contract law. Thus, even though a lease is a contract, it is also a transfer of a property interest; hence, depending on the particular facts, sometimes property law will prevail over contract law, and at other times, the opposite will be true.

More specific considerations for study are:

1. **Types of Tenancies**
   Be sure you can identify the four types of tenancies:

   - *Tenancy for years*—fixed period with beginning and ending dates; may be less than a year;

   - *Periodic tenancy*—period to period (*e.g.,* month to month) until notice of termination given;

   - *Tenancy at will*—no stated duration, continues until landlord or tenant desires an end; and

   - *Holdover tenancy* or *tenancy at sufferance*—tenant remains after the end of tenancy.

2. **Landlord's Duties**
   In most jurisdictions, the landlord has a duty:

   - *To deliver possession* at the beginning of the lease;

   - *Not to interfere with the tenant's quiet enjoyment* (watch for issues of actual or constructive eviction); and

   - *To provide habitable premises* (at common law, the landlord generally had no duty, but courts today, at least as to residential tenancies, often find a duty imposed by an express warranty, implied covenant, or a statutory duty).

A landlord is generally **not liable** for torts unless the tort is related to a concealed dangerous condition, common areas, public use, or if the landlord has a statutory or contractual duty to repair. But landlords' tort liability may be increasing.

3. Tenant's Duties

The tenant *must pay rent*! Also, a tenant has a duty:

- *Not to damage the premises* beyond fair wear and tear; and

- *Not to disturb other tenants*.

Remember that the *tenant's duties may be independent* of duties of the landlord. Thus, the tenant may have a duty to pay rent even though the landlord has breached one of the landlord's duties.

4. Landlord's Remedies

The landlord may use the common law right of distress (abolished or statutorily altered in many states), statutory liens, security deposits, or rent acceleration clauses. Of course, the landlord's most common remedy is *eviction*.

5. Assignment and Sublease

Be sure you determine from the facts of your question whether there has been an *assignment* (a transfer of the entire interest under the lease) or a *sublease* (transferor retains an interest in the leasehold). Check to see whether the lease allows such a transaction. And also determine who is liable for rent and other obligations.

6. Other Topics

Recall that the landlord's right to select tenants may be limited by legislation (*e.g.*, Fair Housing Act, state law, etc.).

Finally, note that landlord-tenant questions on your Property exam will involve issues touching on at least some of the above topics. Other topics may be reserved for other courses (*e.g.*, "housing"). Obviously, which topics you'll see on your exam will depend on your professor.

A. Introduction

1. Background [§750]

Landlord-tenant law developed during feudal agrarian times to regulate the relationship between a landlord and his tenant farmer, an able-bodied man. Possession of the land itself was the important thing. Any buildings thereon were crude and could be fixed by the tenant. Because the law developed for the agricultural tenant, it imposed very few duties on the landlord. At early common law, the only duty the landlord had was not to evict the tenant so long as the rent was paid. In the second half of the twentieth century, this law has seemed in various respects unsatisfactory for the urban dweller, and it is now in the process of modernization and adaptation to the needs of the urban tenant.

a. Chattel real [§751]

Although there is some dispute, the tenancy for years probably arose as a moneylender's device to avoid the church's strict prohibition against collecting interest on a loan. O, a landowner in need of money, would borrow a sum from a moneylender and in return transfer to the moneylender a portion of O's land for a period of time. The rents and profits from the land took the place of interest on the loan. Because of its beginning as a moneylender's device, a leasehold—like a mortgage today—was categorized as personal, not real, property. It was called a "chattel real." This peculiar categorization still lingers, and wherever it is necessary to classify a property interest as realty or personalty, a leasehold—a "chattel real"—is classified as personalty.

2. Property Law and Contract Law Both Applicable [§752]

Landlord-tenant law is a blend of property law and contract law. This results from a lease being both a *conveyance of an estate in land* and a *contract containing promises* between landlord and tenant. Originally the lessee's rights were purely contractual, but from the sixteenth century onward the courts treated the lease as creating a possessory interest in land. For 400 years, property theory has dominated landlord-tenant law, but since World War II contract theory has been in the ascendant. It is important to see the difference between these two ways of analyzing the landlord-tenant relationship.

a. Lease is a conveyance of leasehold estate [§753]

Landlord-tenant law traditionally rests on a conception that the lease is a conveyance of property and that the tenant has purchased a leasehold estate in land. The parties to the conveyance can agree that the purchase price (known as rent) is payable at the beginning of the term, at the end, or in equal installments over the period. The tenant is entitled to possession of the estate, which the tenant has the duty of maintaining. If a building on the land burns down, the tenant must continue to pay rent for the leasehold. The landlord has only the right to reenter and repossess the land on breach of a covenant by the tenant (usually the covenant to pay rent). To put all this in a nutshell, the traditional property rule is that the tenant has bought an estate in land and assumes the risks of caring for the estate.

b. Lease is a contract [§754]

A lease is a contract containing promises (usually called covenants) of the parties. Most modern leases contain numerous covenants—promises to pay rent, taxes, or insurance; to repair; or to use the property for certain purposes. The lease is a document governing the relationship of landlord and tenant over the term of the lease. What happens when one party does not perform his promise? Can the other party withhold performance? Under contract law, covenants are deemed to be *mutually dependent*. If L does not do what L promises to do, T can refuse to do what T promises to do. The performance of one party's promise is dependent on the performance of the other party's promise.

(1) Independent covenant rule in leases [§755]

Until the last 50 years, promises in leases were assumed to be *independent of the other party's performance*. The conception of a lease as creating a property interest was preferred to the conception of a lease as creating promises. For example, suppose that L rents T a house for four years; L promises in the lease to paint the house, and T promises to pay rent. After T moves in, L fails to paint the house. T is stuck for the rent. The performance of T's promise to pay rent is not dependent on the performance of L's promise to paint. The fundamental—and controlling—idea is that T purchased a four-year term in the land, and T must pay the agreed consideration for the specific thing for which T bargained. L's promise to paint is viewed as merely an incidental promise, enforceable in a lawsuit by T against L for damages. The disadvantage of the independent covenant rule is that T cannot break the lease on L's failure to perform, but has to sue for damages. However, modern law is coming more and more to apply contract law where a landlord breaches a covenant.

c. *Interesse termini* [§756]

Under the common law, until the tenant enters, he has no estate in land, only an *interesse termini*, a contract right to enter. The notion is that the tenant's *property* rights begin when he takes possession; before that he has only *contract* rights. The idea of *interesse termini* is fading from the law, but it might support a holding that if the tenant breaks the lease before taking possession, the landlord can sue for contract damages but not for rent. It is not likely to make a difference, because in most cases contract damages will be equal to rent.

3. Lease Distinguished from Other Relationships [§757]

To have a landlord-tenant relationship, the landlord must transfer to the tenant the *right to possession* of the premises. A leasehold is the only interest apart from freehold estates that gives the holder the right to possession. Other interests, such as an easement, license, or profit, entitle the holder to *use* another's land, but do not give possession. (These nonpossessory interests are discussed in chapter VII.)

EXAM TIP   **gilbert**

Recall that there are *only four present possessory estates* in land. The first three (discussed in chapter III) are the fee simple, fee tail, and life estate. The fourth estate is the leasehold. Thus, a present estate that provides the holder *with possession* must fit into one of these four categories.

---

a. Transfer of possession is the key [§758]

An instrument creating a landlord-tenant relationship contemplates that the lessee will control the leased property and exclude others from it. It is the *right to possession* that distinguishes the lessee's interest from an easement, license, or profit. Possession is, of course, a word of many meanings, and often refers both to facts and to the legal conclusion that a party should be protected by calling him a possessor. Whether a particular transaction results in a transfer of possession, and is a lease, depends primarily on the intention of the parties. [**Friend v. Gem International, Inc.,** 476 S.W.2d 134 (Mo. 1971)] What the parties call the transaction is important, but *not conclusive*. Other guides to intention are:

(1) Defined area [§759]

Because possession implies possession of a defined area and not a right to wander at large, the more specific the description of boundaries, the more likely it is that a lease has been created.

(2) Rent reserved [§760]

A lease usually calls for periodic payment of rent, whereas an easement is usually purchased with a lump sum payment. The reservation of a periodic rent indicates a lease.

(3) Duration [§761]

A lease is usually limited in time, whereas an easement is not. A grant of a property right for a specific duration, not unlimited in time, indicates a lease.

(4) Uses permitted [§762]

Because possession of a space implies that the space can be used for a wide variety of uses, the more the use of the space is limited, the more likely it is that a lease has *not* been created.

b. Oil and gas "lease" [§763]

A landowner ordinarily transfers oil and gas rights to a well operator by an instrument denominated a "lease." A typical instrument conveys "the right to drill for oil and gas for five years and so long thereafter as oil or gas is produced." This "lease" does not create a landlord-tenant relationship between landowner and operator. Jurisdictions split over the nature of the lessee's interest. Some states hold that an oil and gas lease is a conveyance of a *fee simple determinable* in the minerals in place (determinable on cessation of oil and gas exploration or production). Other states hold the lessee has a *profit a prendre* (the right to take away something that is affixed to or part of the land). Landlord-tenant law, developed in the contexts of farm leases, commercial leases, and residential leases, is inappropriate for regulation of the rights of the landowner and oil operator. A special body of law has developed for oil and gas interests.

c. Billboard "lease" [§764]

An instrument giving the lessee the right to erect signs or billboards, although denominated a "lease," does not ordinarily create a landlord-tenant relationship.

It is usually deemed to give the sign company an *easement* to come on the land and erect and maintain a sign. Easement law is more appropriate to the context than landlord-tenant law. [**Baseball Publishing Co. v. Bruton**, 18 N.E.2d 362 (Mass. 1938)]

d. Lodging agreements [§765]

Agreements to furnish lodging may differ in a great many respects, particularly the following: the length of time of occupancy, the control exercised by the occupant, and the nature and extent of services furnished by the owner of the property. The test in each case is to determine whether the *control of the occupant over the premises* is so great as to make the occupant a tenant or is so small as to make the occupant a licensee. Whether the parties intend the consequences of a landlord-tenant relationship is an important factor in this determination. [**Cook v. University Plaza,** 427 N.E.2d 405 (Ill. 1981)]

(1) Hotel guest [§766]

A guest in a hotel room is usually treated as a *licensee*. The brief duration of the guest's stay, the large control usually retained by the hotel, and the services furnished indicate that the hotel did not intend to give the transient guest exclusive possession of the room. Nor does the hotel or the guest contemplate that the guest will have the remedy of ejecting the prior occupant who does not vacate.

(2) Apartment hotel [§767]

Renting a unit in an apartment hotel at a weekly or monthly rental, particularly where the renter supplies furniture for the rooms, may create a *landlord-tenant* relationship, even though maid service is furnished.

(3) Rooming house [§768]

A lodger in a rooming house is usually treated as a *licensee*, not as a tenant. Courts emphasize that where the owner retains keys and furnishes housekeeping service, the owner has retained general control, and thus the lodger is not a tenant. However, if the rented room is unfurnished or if housekeeping service is not provided, a lease is probably created.

e. Legal differences between leases, licenses, and easements [§769]

The legal consequences of characterizing an instrument as creating a lease rather than a license or easement are chiefly: (i) a lease can be oral, but an easement is subject to the Statute of Frauds and requires a written instrument; and (ii) of these relationships, *only a tenant has a possessory interest in land* and can bring a possessory action such as ejectment, trespass, or nuisance. A holder of an easement or license must bring a different kind of lawsuit for interference with her rights.

B. Types of Tenancies and Their Creation

1. Tenancy for Years

a. Definition [§770]

A tenancy for years is an estate that lasts for some maximum *fixed period of time* or for a period of time computable by a formula that results in fixing *calendar dates* for beginning and ending, once the term is created or becomes possessory. The period may be a certain number of *days, weeks, months, or years,* but regardless of the period, the tenancy is called a tenancy for years or a term of years. Examples of terms of years: "Ten years from the date of this lease," "one year from next Christmas," "from the date of this lease until next Christmas." In all of these examples, the beginning and ending calendar dates can be fixed. Unless there is a statute to the contrary, a term of years may be created for any number of years, even 1,000.

EXAM TIP	gilbert

A tenancy for years is what you get when you rent an apartment under a one-year lease. The *beginning and ending dates are set* in the lease, and the lease *automatically ends at the end of the period*. But don't be fooled by the term "tenancy for *years*." Keep in mind that this estate can last *any fixed period of time*—even a certain number of days. Thus, a lease for the period of "March 17 through March 21 of this year" is a tenancy for years.

(1) Tenancy of no fixed period terminable on some event [§771]

Although the definition of a tenancy for years requires that a calendar date be fixed or computable for its ending, in a few cases where the lease is terminable on some event but of no fixed period, courts have held that a tenancy for years has been created. The primary example of this is where O leases to A "for the duration of the war." This type of lease does not fit easily within any of the permissible categories, but the tenancy for years is the closest approximation of the parties' intention. Why? Because a tenancy for years cannot be terminated unilaterally by either party prior to the event fixing termination, it gives the parties the benefit of their bargain. (A periodic tenancy or a tenancy at will can be terminated prior to the event.) But there are some cases that hew strictly to the requirement that a term of years have a calendar date fixed for ending, and deem a lease terminable on some uncertain event to create a periodic tenancy or a tenancy at will or, if the event is in the control of the tenant, a life estate determinable. [**Womack v. Hyche**, 503 So. 2d 832 (Ala. 1987)]

(2) Term of years determinable [§772]

A term of years (and a periodic tenancy as well) may be made terminable on some event, or subject to condition subsequent, in the same manner as a freehold may be made terminable on an event. Thus, if L rents to T for 10 years "so long as used for a sawmill," a 10-year *term of years determinable* is created. Notice that the maximum term is fixed, although the tenancy may end earlier.

(3) Day of beginning and ending [§773]

Unless the parties specify otherwise, a lease begins on the earliest moment of the beginning day and ends immediately before midnight on the date set for termination. Thus, a lease of one year "from July 1 next" is usually held to begin at 12:01 a.m. on July 1 and end at midnight the next June 30.

b. Termination of tenancy for years [§774]

Because the parties know precisely when a term of years will end, a term of years expires at the end of the stated period *without either party giving notice.* This is the chief difference between a term of years and a periodic tenancy, which requires notice for termination.

2. Periodic Tenancy

a. Definition [§775]

A periodic tenancy is a tenancy for a period of some fixed duration that *continues for succeeding periods* until either the landlord or tenant *gives notice* of termination. *Examples:* "To T from month to month," or "to T from year to year." If notice of termination is not given, the tenancy is *automatically extended* for another period. In this way the periodic tenancy differs from a term of years, which automatically ends on the day set.

EXAM TIP   **gilbert**

An example of a periodic tenancy is when you rent from month to month, but it can be from year to year or any other period. So how do you tell a tenancy for years from a year-to-year tenancy? The periodic tenancy has **no set ending date**; it continues until one party gives the other proper notice, while the tenancy for years will automatically end at the end of the period with no notice required.

---

(1) Extensions are part of same tenancy [§776]

Although the tenancy carries over from one period to the next, it is basically the same tenancy and not a new tenancy each term. Consequently, all of the conditions and terms of the tenancy are carried over and are applicable in each subsequent period, unless there are express provisions to the contrary.

b. **Creation of periodic tenancies [§777]**

A tenancy from period to period may be created by agreement of the parties or by operation of law.

(1) Creation by express agreement of the parties [§778]

The landlord and the tenant may expressly create an estate that is to extend from period to period. For example, "L to T for one year, and at the end of such term, the lease shall continue in effect from month to month, unless one of the parties shall end this lease by notice in writing delivered at least one month prior to the end of the term in which such notice is given." At the outset, T has an estate for one year (a term of years), which at the expiration of the first year becomes an estate from period to period (month to month), which will continue as such until the requisite notice is given.

(2) Creation by agreement only as to rent period [§779]

More frequently, a tenancy from period to period arises by implication where land is leased with no set date for termination, but provision is made for payment of rent monthly, quarterly, annually, etc. The tenant has a periodic tenancy measured by the rental periods. Thus, if T rents an apartment beginning June 1 and pays monthly rent, T is a tenant from month to month.

(a) Annual rent payable monthly [§780]

Where the lease provides for an *annual* rent *payable monthly* (*e.g.*, "$6,000 per annum, payable $500 on the first day of every month commencing January 1"), is the estate from year to year or month to month? At common law (and in most jurisdictions today), if an annual rent is specified, the estate is from year to year, even though the rent is required to be paid in monthly installments. It is said that the monthly payments are merely for the convenience of the parties. This view is sometimes applied only to leases of *agricultural land*, and not to leases of dwellings, on the theory that farmland is almost always rented on a yearly basis.

1) Minority view [§781]

A contrary view holds that the payment of rent on a monthly basis presumptively makes the tenancy one from month to month—even where it is a one-twelfth installment of a specified yearly rent. But this view, where followed, is usually applied only to leases of *dwellings*, and not to leases of agricultural land.

2) Why it matters [§782]

If the lease is from year to year, six months' notice is required for termination according to the common law rule (which is often modified by statute or by a provision in the lease). If the tenant does not give six months' notice, the landlord can hold the tenant for another year's rent. If the tenancy is month to month, either the landlord or the tenant can terminate the tenancy on one month's notice (below).

(3) Creation by operation of law [§783]
A tenancy from period to period may arise in certain cases even in complete absence of any agreement of the parties.

(a) Where tenant holds over after expiration of the term [§784]
Where a tenant holds over (remains in possession) after the end of the term, the landlord may elect to consent to the tenant's staying over and hold the tenant liable for further rent as a periodic tenant for an additional term. (*See infra*, §809.)

EXAM TIP — **gilbert**

Pay attention to this rule. In most jurisdictions, when a tenant for years holds over after the tenancy has expired, the lease is **not renewed for another term**. Rather, a **periodic tenancy** for another term is created. This means that the landlord and tenant are obliged to follow the old lease's provisions for rent, etc., but now either party can get out of the deal by giving the other proper notice. (*See infra*, §§809-813.)

(b) Where tenant takes possession under an invalid lease [§785]
If L leases Blackacre to T for 10 years at $500 per month, but for some reason the lease is unenforceable or void—*e.g.*, due to lack of formalities required by the Statute of Frauds—but T nevertheless goes into possession under the invalid lease, what result? The mere entry into possession by T creates a *tenancy at will*. However, the *payment of rent* periodically *converts* the tenancy at will into a tenancy from *period to period* arising by operation of law. (*See infra*, §806.)

c. Requirement of notice of termination [§786]
Probably the most distinctive feature of a periodic tenancy is that it *continues until proper notice* of termination is given. Except where required by statute or the lease, the notice can be either oral or written.

(1) Common law rules

(a) How much notice need be given [§787]
To terminate an estate from period to period, notice must be *equal to the length of the period* itself (*e.g.*, month, week, etc.) with the *exception* that if the tenancy is from year to year, only *six months'* notice is required. By agreement, however, the parties to a periodic

tenancy may shorten the amount of notice required, or eliminate the requirement of notice altogether. (*See also infra,* §791.)

(b)   Notice must specify last day of period [§788]

The notice must fix *the last day of the period* as the date for termination and not some intervening date. Thus, in the case of a month-to-month tenancy commencing on the first day of each month, if notice is given on January 20, terminating the tenancy on February 20, the notice is insufficient to terminate on February 20. (Under one view (below), the notice will not terminate the lease on the last day of February either, because it does not specify that date.)

(c)   When notice must be given [§789]

The notice must be given so that the tenant or landlord will receive the required amount of notice prior to the expiration of the current term. For example, in a year-to-year tenancy, commencing on January 1, the notice must be given sometime prior to July 1 in order to terminate the estate on the following December 31. If the notice is given on July 2, the year-to-year tenancy will not end on the next December 31. Some courts go even further and hold that an ineffective notice does not terminate the periodic tenancy at the end of the following period. Thus, a notice given July 2, 2006, terminating the tenancy on December 31, 2006, has *no effect at all.* It does not terminate the lease on the earliest date a termination is possible, December 31, 2006, because it does not specify that day. The tenant is stuck with the rent until proper notice is given. [**Moudry v. Parkos,** 349 N.W.2d 387 (Neb. 1984); **Arbenz v. Exley, Watkins & Co.,** 50 S.E. 813 (W. Va. 1905)]

EXAM TIP	gilbert

A common exam question on periodic tenancies concerns notice of termination—how much notice is required and at what time it must be given. Remember that the notice must be: *equal to the period* (*i.e.,* a week's notice for a week-to-week tenancy, a month's notice for a month-to-month tenancy, *but* only six months' notice for a year-to-year tenancy); must end the tenancy *on the last day of the period*; and must be given so that the other party has the *full notice period*.

1)   Restatement position [§790]

The Restatement (Second) of Property declines to follow the common law rule and provides that "if the date stated in the notice for termination is not the end of a period or is too short a time before the end of a period, the notice will be effective to terminate the lease at the earliest possible date after the date stated." This rule seems more likely to carry out the terminating party's intention than the common law rule discussed above. [Restatement (Second) of Property ("Rest. 2d"), Landlord & Tenant §1.5, comment f]

(2) Statutory modifications [§791]

Statutes in many states reduce the six months' notice required to terminate a tenancy from year to year to one month's notice. It is thought that six months' notice is unreasonably long. Statutes in a few states go further and provide that a month-to-month tenancy can be terminated on any day, and not only on the last day of the period, provided one month's notice before the day specified is given. [*See* Cal. Civ. Code §1946] This is a debatable change, because a landlord or a tenant may find it hard to rent an apartment in the middle of the month.

3. Tenancy at Will

a. Definition [§792]

A tenancy at will is a tenancy of *no stated duration* that endures only so long as *both* landlord and tenant desire. Either can *terminate it at any time.* Consequently, its potential duration is not very great. A tenancy at will can arise expressly or, more often, by operation of law when the intended tenancy fails for some reason.

EXAM TIP | **gilbert**

The key identifiers for a tenancy at will are that there is *no stated duration* to the tenancy and *either party can terminate* it at any time. However, it is not very common because of those factors (what tenant wants a tenancy where she can be thrown out at any time?). As indicated, if you do see a tenancy at will, it is most likely to have arisen by operation of law, *e.g.,* when the tenant takes under an invalid lease. But even in that case, remember that the payment of *rent converts* it from a tenancy at will *to a periodic tenancy*. (*See supra, §785, and infra, §806.*)

---

(1) Tenant's possessory rights [§793]

A tenant at will is not merely a licensee. She has an estate in land; she has *possession.* The tenant can maintain an action of trespass against third persons who intrude on the premises, or even against the landlord if he enters without having first terminated the tenancy.

(2) Tenancy terminable by only one party [§794]

A leasehold that is terminable at the will of *only one* of the parties is not a tenancy at will. By definition, a tenancy at will must be terminable by the landlord or by the tenant and not by one of them alone. The first step in determining what estate is created if only one party can terminate the tenancy is to ascertain whether or not the power to terminate is affixed to a term of years or periodic tenancy.

(a) **Lease for certain duration terminable by one party [§795]**

If a provision for termination by one party is grafted onto a term of years or a periodic tenancy, the lease creates a *determinable tenancy*, not a tenancy at will. (*See supra,* §772.)

Example: L leases a house "to T for one year, with a proviso that L can terminate at any time." This creates a determinable term of years, terminable at the will of L.

Example: L leases land "to T from year to year for use as storage space. T has the right to terminate the lease at any time." L can terminate the lease only in accordance with the law respecting periodic tenancies. T can terminate at any time.

(b) **Lease for no certain duration [§796]**

If a leasehold has no certain duration (*i.e.,* is not an estate for years or a periodic tenancy by its terms), but is terminable at will by one party, the courts are split:

1) **Tenancy at will [§797]**

Some courts imply a power of termination *in the other party* because there is no certain duration. Thus, a tenancy at will is created.

Example—termination by landlord only: L leases land to T "for and during the pleasure of the landlord." This creates a tenancy at will, and L or T can terminate at any time.

Example—termination by tenant only: L leases land to T "for as many years as T desires" at a yearly rent of $300. This creates a tenancy at will, and L also can terminate at any time. [**Nitschke v. Doggett,** 489 S.W.2d 335 (Tex. 1972)]

2) **Determinable life estate [§798]**

Other courts hold that if the agreement does not create a term of years or periodic tenancy, but the tenancy is to continue so long as the tenant wills, the tenant has a life estate determinable.

Example: L leases land to T "so long as T should wish." This creates a life estate in T, determinable on his death or prior relinquishment of possession. [**Garner v. Gerrish,** 63 N.Y.2d 575 (1984)]

b. Termination [§799]

At common law, neither landlord nor tenant had to give any notice for a period of time as a prerequisite to terminating a tenancy at will. The tenancy at will terminated on the day notice of termination was received by the other party. However, most states today have statutes that require some sort of notice to terminate a tenancy at will. Usually 30 days' notice is required, but often this requirement is imposed on the landlord and not the tenant. [*See, e.g.,* N.Y. Real Prop. Law §228]

(1) Termination by assignment [§800]

A tenancy at will cannot be assigned, and it terminates if either the landlord or the tenant attempts to assign it.

4. Statute of Frauds [§801]

A term of years, periodic tenancy, or tenancy at will may be created by an express provision in a written lease. But where there is no written instrument, problems arise concerning the application of the Statute of Frauds and the type of tenancy that can be created by an oral agreement.

a. Short-term lease exception [§802]

The English Statute of Frauds (1677) provided that all leases must be in writing except a lease for three years or less. This is known as the "short-term lease exception," and was put in the statute to permit oral leases of short duration, which are not uncommon. Most American states by statute have reduced the short-term lease exception to *one year*. An oral lease for more than one year (or whatever period that measures the short-term lease exception) creates only a tenancy at will.

(1) No short-term lease exception [§803]

In a few states, the Statute of Frauds does not contain any exception for short-term leases. An oral lease of any duration (*e.g.,* for two months) creates only a tenancy at will. However, each of these states requires a 30-day notice to evict a tenant at will. Hence, as a practical matter, an oral lease creates a tenancy for at least a 30-day period.

b. Oral lease to commence in the future [§804]

Suppose on July 15 a landlord orally leases to a tenant "for one year commencing next January 1." Is this lease valid? Under the lease provision of the Statute of Frauds referred to above, it is valid because it is for only one year. But the English Statute of Frauds had a section on contracts in addition to a section on leases. The section dealing with contracts required all agreements not to be performed within one year *from the making of the contract* to be in writing. As discussed above, a lease is a contract, and this contracts section could apply to leases. Under this section, the above lease would be void because it cannot be entirely performed within one year from July 15. The majority of courts hold that the contracts section of the Statute of Frauds is not applicable to leases because leases are expressly dealt with in the section on leases. Thus, an oral lease to commence in the future is valid if the term does not exceed one year. The Restatement adopts this view. [Rest. 2d, Landlord & Tenant §2.1, comment f]

c. Option to renew oral lease [§805]

Where there is an oral lease that is renewable at the option of the lessee, the lease is usually treated as extending to the end of the option period. Thus, if the oral lease is for a one-year term, with an option to renew for another year, the lease is treated as a two-year lease and is void if the short-term exception in the Statute of Frauds is one year.

(1) Minority view

A minority holds that the original period and the option period are separable, and only the option that extends the duration beyond the short-term exception is void. This minority view is adopted by the Restatement. [Rest. 2d, Landlord & Tenant §2.1, comment c]

d. Entry and paying rent under an invalid lease [§806]

Although an oral lease not complying with the Statute of Frauds is void, entry by a tenant under an oral lease creates a *tenancy at will*. As soon as the tenant pays rent, *a periodic tenancy* is created. However, there is some difference of opinion as to what is the period of the periodic tenancy.

(1) Year-to-year tenancy [§807]

The majority view is that a year-to-year tenancy is created, regardless of how the rent is calculated in the void lease and of how rent is paid. *Rationale:* Because the invalid lease was necessarily for a term exceeding one year, a year-to-year tenancy comes closest to approximating the parties' intention. (*But note:* Because it is a year-to-year tenancy, notice must be given to terminate it. The notice requirements might surprise the parties, who think the (invalid) term will end automatically without notice.)

(2) How rent is calculated [§808]

Another approach is to determine the length of the period by how the rent is calculated in the invalid lease. If the rent is calculated on an annual basis, even though payable monthly, a year-to-year periodic tenancy will be created.

> **Example:** T enters under a written 10-year lease, not signed by L or T, and therefore invalid. The lease is to end January 31, 2016. T makes rent payments specified in the lease, which are calculated on an annual basis, even though payable monthly. T is a year-to-year tenant, and at common law, six months' notice is required to terminate the tenancy. (*Note:* No notice would have been required to terminate the 10-year

term, but notice is required to terminate the periodic tenancy. Hence if L notifies T in November 2015 to vacate on January 31, 2016, when the 10-year period expires, L has not given sufficient notice to terminate the periodic tenancy, and T is entitled to stay until January 31, 2017.) [**Darling Shops Delaware Corp. v. Baltimore Center Corp.**, 60 A.2d 669 (Md. 1948)]

5. Holdover Tenant [§809]

When a tenant who was rightfully in possession wrongfully remains in possession (holds over) after termination of the tenancy, he is called a *tenant at sufferance*. The tenant at sufferance is not really a tenant at all because he is not holding with the permission of the landlord. On the other hand, he is not a trespasser either, because his original possession was not wrongful. He is in a peculiar situation, called a tenancy at sufferance, which lasts only until the landlord *evicts* the tenant *or elects to hold the tenant to another term*. The prior tenancy of the holdover tenant may be a tenancy for years, a periodic tenancy, or even a tenancy at will. Thus, if T has a one-year lease expiring October 1, and T stays on until October 2, L can elect to hold T to another term. Or if T is a periodic tenant, and L serves T with notice to quit and T does not leave when required, L can hold T to another period.

a. Rationale

The holdover doctrine, permitting the landlord to hold the holdover tenant to another term, is justified as a deterrent to holding over, which is thought not to be in the best interest of tenants as a class who should be able to move in promptly upon expiration of an old tenancy. However, the holdover doctrine has been criticized as imposing a penalty disproportionate to fault.

b. Excuses [§810]

The common law admitted *no excuses* for holding over. The tenant holding over was liable for another term regardless of extenuating circumstances.

> **Example:** T's one-year lease expires October 1. T begins moving on September 26, but becomes ill. T's clerks continue moving but do not finish until October 11. In the meantime, on October 6, T dies. L elects to hold T's estate to another term of a year. T's illness is no excuse, and T's estate is liable for another year's rent. [**Mason v. Wierengo's Estate**, 71 N.W. 489 (Mich. 1897)]

(1) Modern law [§811]

Most modern cases give a tenant relief where the tenant does not intend to hold over but is forced to do so by circumstances beyond the tenant's control. The relief is that the landlord cannot elect to hold the tenant to another term if the tenant vacates as soon as possible in light of the circumstances. This view, which relieves the tenant only when moving is a near impossibility and beyond the tenant's control, is endorsed by the

Restatement. [Rest. 2d, Landlord & Tenant §14.4, comment i] At least one court has gone further and has relieved the holdover tenant even without extenuating circumstances where a dilatory tenant held over for a few hours, on the ground that the damage to the landlord was de minimis. [**Commonwealth Building Corp. v. Hirschfield**, 30 N.E.2d 790 (Ill. 1940)] The difficulty with this last view, of course, is where to draw the line in deciding what is de minimis. If the landlord has no new tenant in prospect, is she damaged much if the old tenant holds over 15 days or 30? If this last view is accepted, why not push it to its logical end and give the landlord only actual damages suffered from the holdover plus reasonable rental value for the period held over? The calculation of actual damages might be hard to measure. An arbitrary penalty might be cheaper to administer. (*Compare* the penalty imposed by the Uniform Residential Landlord and Tenant Act, *infra*, §814—three months' rent or actual damages.)

c. **Length of new term [§812]**

In most jurisdictions, holding over gives rise (at the landlord's election) to a periodic tenancy; in the rest, it results in a term of years. As to the basis for the length of the period or term, some courts hold it is the way *rent is reserved* in the original lease, and other courts hold it is the *length of the original term* or period—but the maximum length in each case is limited to one year. According to the Restatement, holding over results in a periodic tenancy measured by the way rent is computed, up to a maximum period of one year. [Rest. 2d, Landlord & Tenant §14.4, comment f]

Example: L leases to T for five years, ending on November 4, reserving a yearly rent of $7,000. T holds over, surrendering possession on November 27, after the lease has expired. Under any of the above views, L is entitled to elect to hold T over as tenant for another year. (If T does not abandon the property but stays on and L accepts rent, T is a periodic tenant from year to year. A periodic tenancy with periods determined by how the rent is calculated in the lease usually results.) [**A.H. Fetting Manufacturing Jewelry Co. v. Waltz**, 152 A. 434 (Md. 1930); *but see* **Crechale & Polles, Inc. v. Smith**, 295 So. 2d 275 (Miss. 1974)]

---

d. **Provisions of new term [§813]**

Except with respect to length, the new tenancy is governed by the provisions in the old lease, including provisions for payment of rent and any covenants made by the parties. If the landlord notifies the tenant that the tenant must pay a higher rent if he holds over, the holdover tenant may be liable for the higher rent unless he notifies the landlord that he refuses to pay. Silence by

TYPE OF LEASEHOLD	DEFINITION	CREATION	TERMINATION
TENANCY FOR YEARS	Tenancy that lasts for some *fixed period of time*.	"To A for 10 years."	Ends at the end of the stated period without either party's giving notice.
PERIODIC TENANCY	Tenancy for some fixed period that *continues for succeeding periods* until either party *gives notice* of termination.	"To A from month to month." *or* "To A, with rent payable on the first day of every month." *or* Landlord elects to bind holdover tenant for an additional term.	Ends by notice from one party at least equal to the length of the time period (*e.g.,* one full month, for a month-to-month tenancy). *Exception:* Only six months' notice is required to terminate a year-to-year tenancy.
TENANCY AT WILL	Tenancy of *no stated duration* that lasts as long as both parties desire.	"To T for and during the pleasure of L." (Even though the language gives only L the right to terminate, L or T may terminate at any time.) *or* "To T for as many years as T desires." (Even though the language gives only T the right to terminate, L or T may terminate at any time.)	Usually ends after one party displays an intention that the tenancy should come to an end. May also end by operation of law (*e.g.,* death of a party, attempt to transfer interest).
TENANCY AT SUFFERANCE	Tenant *wrongfully holds over* after the termination of the tenancy.	B's lease expires, but B continues to occupy the premises.	Terminated when landlord evicts the tenant or elects to hold the tenant to another term.

the tenant is usually deemed implied consent. [**David Properties, Inc. v. Selk,** 151 So. 2d 334 (Fla. 1963)]

e. Statutory modifications of landlord's remedies [§814]

Statutory modifications of the landlord's remedies against the holdover tenant are not uncommon. These modifications usually weaken the landlord's remedies in the belief that the penalties are disproportionate to the act. Section 4.301(c) of the Uniform Residential Landlord and Tenant Act ("URLTA"), which is a comprehensive residential landlord-tenant code enacted or copied in more than a dozen jurisdictions, provides:

> If the tenant remains in possession without the landlord's consent after expiration of the term of the rental agreement or its termination, the landlord may bring an action for possession and if the tenant's holdover is willful and not in good faith the landlord may also recover an amount not more than [three] month's periodic rent or [threefold] the actual damages sustained by him, whichever is greater, and reasonable attorney's fees. If the landlord consents to the tenant's continued occupancy [the tenancy is week to week in case of a roomer who pays weekly rent, and in all other cases month to month].

(1) Holding over willfully [§815]

URLTA section 4.301(c) penalizes only a tenant who willfully holds over. Some statutes imposing a double rent on a holdover tenant are not expressly limited to willful holdovers, but courts have construed these penalty statutes strictly and declined to apply them unless the holdover is willful. [**Jones v. Taylor,** 123 S.W. 326 (Ky. 1909)] *See also supra,* §811, discussing a refusal of courts to apply the common law doctrine where the holdover is excusable. The majority of courts believe an excusable holdover should not be penalized by statute or judicial doctrine, but willful holdovers should be.

C. Selection of Tenants

1. Introduction [§816]

Historically, a seller or a landlord was free to sell or rent to whomever he pleased. But federal and state statutes now prohibit discrimination in the sale or rental of property on various grounds—including race, religion, or national origin. These statutes differ in many details, as outlined below. These statutes ordinarily apply to both *sale and rental* of property. Because it is convenient to treat them in one place in this Summary, they are treated here in connection with landlords and tenants because leasing is discussed first in this Summary, before sale.

2. Civil Rights Act of 1866 [§817]

The 1866 Civil Rights Act, enacted by Congress after the Civil War, provides: "All citizens of the United States shall have the same right, in every State and Territory, as is enjoyed by white citizens thereof to inherit, purchase, lease, sell, hold, and convey real and personal property." [42 U.S.C. §1982] This Act is commonly referred to as "section 1982" of the United States Code. Although this Act was long thought to bar only racial discrimination by states, the Supreme Court in **Jones v. Alfred H. Mayer Co.,** 392 U.S. 409 (1968), held that the Act barred "all racial discrimination, private as well as public, in the sale or rental of property."

a. Bars racial or ethnic discrimination only [§818]

Section 1982 forbids discrimination against African-Americans, as well as against any "identifiable classes of persons who are subjected to intentional discrimination solely because of their ancestry or ethnic characteristics," as opposed to their place of origin or religion. [**St. Francis College v. Al-Khazraji,** 481 U.S. 604 (1987)]

EXAM TIP   **gilbert**

Remember that section 1982 applies *only to racial or ethnic discrimination*. Thus, a person refused a lease because she is a follower of Hare Krishna cannot sue under section 1982. She could sue, however, under the Fair Housing Act, *infra*.

---

b. Applies to all property transfers [§819]

Section 1982 applies to sale or rental of *all property*, not just to housing. Thus, if a landlord refuses to rent a commercial building to a prospective tenant because he is black, the prospective tenant can sue under section 1982. (But he could not sue under the Fair Housing Act, below, which deals only with housing.)

c. Remedies [§820]

Although section 1982 was couched in declaratory terms and did not provide any explicit method of enforcement, courts have fashioned effective remedies. The remedies for a person discriminated against under this Act are an injunction against the landlord or seller, or damages.

3. Fair Housing Act of 1968 [§821]

In 1968, Congress enacted the Fair Housing Act as Title VIII of the Civil Rights Act of 1968. The Fair Housing Act makes it unlawful to refuse to sell or rent a *dwelling* to any person because of race, color, religion, or national origin. [42 U.S.C. §3604] In 1974, the Act was amended to prohibit discrimination on the basis of sex. In 1988, the Act was further amended in two ways: (i) it prohibits discrimination against persons with children except in senior citizen housing; and (ii) it prohibits discrimination against handicapped persons.

a. Advertising [§822]

In addition to prohibiting discrimination in renting or selling, the Act prohibits advertising or making *any public statement* that indicates any discriminatory preference. [42 U.S.C. §3604(c)] A statement to a tenant or prospective tenant that the landlord will not rent to persons protected by the Act violates the Act. [**Jancik v. Department of Housing & Urban Development**, 44 F.3d 553 (7th Cir. 1995)—holding advertisement "mature person preferred" indicates a preference based on familial status (no children)]

b. Exemptions [§823]

The Fair Housing Act provides that private clubs, dwellings for religious organizations, and certain specified persons are exempt from the Act. The purpose of these exemptions is to protect some types of close personal relationships from what is thought to be an invasion of privacy.

(1) Single-family dwelling [§824]

A person leasing or selling a dwelling she owns is exempt if she: (i) does not own more than three such dwellings, (ii) does not use a broker, and (iii) does not advertise in a manner that indicates her intent to discriminate. [42 U.S.C. §3603(b)(1)]

(2) Small owner-occupied multiple unit [§825]

A person is exempt if she is offering to lease a room or an apartment in her building of four units or less, one unit of which she occupies, and she does not advertise in a discriminatory manner. This is known as the "Mrs. Murphy exception," an allusion to "Mrs. Murphy's boarding house." [42 U.S.C. §3603(b)(2)]

(3) Distinguish—no exemption under section 1982 [§826]

The Civil Rights Act of 1866 [now 42 U.S.C. §1982] does not have any exemptions for a single-family dwelling or for "Mrs. Murphy." Section 1982 applies to sales or rentals by an owner of a single-family dwelling or by Mrs. Murphy. A person denied admittance to Mrs. Murphy's apartments must sue under section 1982 rather than the Fair Housing Act of 1968.

Example: O inserts an advertisement in a newspaper offering to rent a room in her house to a white person. O is in violation of the Fair Housing Act prohibition against discriminatory advertising. If O does not advertise, she is not in violation of the Fair Housing Act if she refuses to rent to blacks. However, if O refuses to rent to blacks, O is in violation of section 1982, which contains no exemption for owner-occupied dwellings.

c. Enforcement [§827]

An aggrieved person may sue the seller or landlord in federal court, without regard to the usual jurisdictional requirements as to diversity of citizenship and dollar amount in controversy, and with the right to a court-appointed attorney if he cannot afford one. The court may give the plaintiff an injunction, actual damages, and punitive damages. [42 U.S.C. §3612]

4. Proving Discrimination [§828]

To prove a violation of the Fair Housing Act or section 1982, the plaintiff must *first* establish a *prima facie case*. To make a prima facie case, the plaintiff must show that (i) she is a member of a statutorily protected class, (ii) she applied for and was qualified to rent the designated dwelling, (iii) she was denied the opportunity to inspect or rent the dwelling, and (iv) the housing opportunity remained available for others. *Second*, if the plaintiff makes a prima facie case, *the burden shifts* to the defendant to produce evidence that the refusal to rent was motivated by *legitimate considerations* having *nothing* to do with the plaintiff's race, religion, ethnic origin, sex, disability, or family status. If race (or other protected status) is even one of several motivating factors, the statute is violated. *Third*, once the defendant introduces evidence of his alleged legitimate reasons, the burden shifts back to the plaintiff to show that the alleged legitimate reasons are *pretextual* and not the real reasons. [**Soules v. United States Department of Housing & Urban Development,** 967 F.2d 817 (2d Cir. 1992); **Asbury v. Brougham,** 866 F.2d 1276 (10th Cir. 1989); **Hobson v. George Humphreys, Inc.,** 563 F. Supp. 344 (W.D. Tenn. 1982)]

5. Kinds of Discrimination

a. Disproportionate effect on one race [§829]

Unlawful practices under the Fair Housing Act include not only those motivated by a *racially discriminatory purpose*, but also those that *disproportionately affect racial minorities* and lessen housing opportunities for them. Thus, a policy of racial ceiling quotas on rentals to prevent white flight and maintain an integrated apartment complex violates the Act. [**United States v. Starrett City Associates,** 840 F.2d 1096 (2d Cir. 1988)]

b. Sex discrimination [§830]

The Fair Housing Act prohibits sex discrimination in the rental or sale of housing. "Sex discrimination" includes harassing tenants for sexual favors. [**Grieger v. Sheets,** 689 F. Supp. 835 (N.D. Ill. 1988)]

c. Familial status [§831]

The Fair Housing Act prohibits discrimination on the basis of "familial status" (existence of children under age 18 in the family unit). Whether restrictions limiting the number of occupants per bedroom discriminate against families with children is currently the subject of much litigation. The theory is that occupancy restrictions have a disparate impact on families with children. [*See* **United States v. Badgett,** 976 F.2d 1176 (8th Cir. 1992)]

(1) Exemption [§832]

The Fair Housing Act exempts from the familial status provisions (i) housing occupied solely by people 62 years of age or older and (ii) housing units at least 80% occupied by at least one person 55 or over. The "55 and over" exemption is further qualified in that the units must have significant facilities and services specifically designed to meet the physical or social needs of older persons. [**Park Place Home Brokers v. P-K Mobile Home Park,** 773 F. Supp. 46 (N.D. Ohio 1991)—holding ordinary mobile home park does not meet the last requirement above]

d. Disabilities [§833]

The 1988 amendment to the Fair Housing Act prohibited discrimination against handicapped persons. "Handicap" is broadly defined as "a physical or mental impairment which substantially limits one or more of such person's major life activities." [42 U.S.C. §3602(h)] A statutory exception excludes drug addicts as handicapped, but recovering drug addicts and alcoholics are handicapped persons within the meaning of the Act. Persons with AIDS are handicapped. [**Poff v. Caro,** 549 A.2d 900 (N.J. 1987)]

(1) Reasonable accommodation [§834]

The Fair Housing Act sections protecting handicapped persons provide that it is discrimination for a landlord to refuse to *make reasonable accommodations* in rules or services when such accommodations may be necessary to afford a handicapped tenant equal opportunity to use and enjoy a dwelling. Thus a landlord with a "no pets" policy might have to accommodate a deaf person by permitting a "hearing dog" to bark at the doorbell or telephone. [**Bronk v. Ineichen,** 54 F.3d 425 (7th Cir. 1995)]

6. State Statutes [§835]

A number of states have statutes prohibiting discrimination in selling or renting, generally protecting the same classes as specified in the federal Fair Housing Act. Some statutes go further than the federal act and protect tenants from discrimination because of marital status, sexual orientation, or age.

COMPARISON OF CIVIL RIGHTS ACT AND FAIR HOUSING ACT		gilbert
	CIVIL RIGHTS ACT §1982	**FAIR HOUSING ACT**
PROTECTION	Bars *racial or ethnic* discrimination only	Bars *racial and ethnic* discrimination, *and* discrimination based on *religion, national origin, sex, disability,* and *against persons with children*
TYPE OF PROPERTY	Sale or rental of *all property*	Sale or rental of *dwelling only*; also includes advertising for sale or rental of dwelling
EXEMPTIONS	None	Private clubs, religious organizations, qualifying owner of 1 to 3 single-family dwellings, qualifying owner-resident of building with 4 or fewer units, qualifying senior citizen housing

a. Marital status [§836]

Several state statutes prohibit discrimination on the basis of "marital status." Does this term include unmarried cohabiting couples? Some courts have held "no," on the theory that it was not the legislature's purpose to protect fornication and erode the institution of marriage. [**State by Cooper v. French,** 460 N.W.2d 2 (Minn. 1990)] But California has held that the term "marital status" protects cohabiting unmarried persons from discrimination, even if the landlord refuses to rent to them because of her religious beliefs. [**Smith v. Fair Employment & Housing Commission,** 12 Cal. 4th 1143 (1996)]

7. Admission to Public Housing [§837]

Each public housing authority is empowered to adopt "desirability standards" to determine eligibility for admission. But inasmuch as the housing authority is a governmental body, these standards must offer the prospective tenants due process of law. Courts have held that a standard cannot exclude applicants as a class but can be weighed only in the individual's case. For example, persons with criminal records cannot be excluded as a class, but a person's particular record can be taken into account in weighing desirability. Courts have also required public housing authorities to institute "objective scoring systems" to establish preferences.

a. Eviction [§838]

A federal drug forfeiture statute provides for forfeiture of any property used in selling illegal drugs (*see supra,* §653). Thus, if a tenant in a public housing project sells drugs, the tenant may forfeit the apartment. However, the apartment is not forfeited if the drug seller is one of several occupants in the apartment and the owner of the leasehold does not know of the drug activity. Only the drug dealer can be evicted. [**United States v. Leasehold Interest in 121 Nostrand Avenue,** 760 F. Supp. 1015 (E.D.N.Y. 1991)]

D. Landlord's Duty to Deliver Possession

1. Legal Right to Possession [§839]

The landlord has the duty to transfer to the tenant at the beginning of the tenancy the *legal right to possession.* The landlord warrants that she has the legal right to possession and is transferring this to the tenant. If another person has *paramount title* and is legally entitled to possession, the landlord is in default.

a. Paramount title [§840]

"Paramount title" refers to any title or interest in the leased land, held by a third party at the time the lease is made, that is paramount to the interest of the landlord. For example, before leasing, L gives M a mortgage on the property, which M records; M has paramount title. Or L has given a prior recorded lease to another tenant. Or L does not own the property at all.

b. Tenant's remedies prior to entry [§841]

If on the commencement of the term a paramount title exists that could prevent the tenant from enjoying the use contemplated by the parties, and of which the tenant is *unaware* when he signs the lease, the tenant *prior to entry* may *terminate the lease*. The tenant does not have to begin his tenure if after signing the lease he discovers a possibility that he will be evicted by a paramount claimant. If the tenant *knows of the paramount title at the time he signs the lease*, however, the tenant is presumed to *waive* the possibility of eviction by the paramount claimant. In other words, the landlord must make full disclosure of the risks to the tenant before the lease is signed.

c. After tenant enters into possession [§842]

After entry by the tenant, the mere existence of a paramount title does not breach the landlord's duties. The tenant has *no remedy unless he is actually evicted* by paramount title. Once the tenant takes actual possession, he is assumed to have accepted the landlord's title as adequate for his use of the property. The traditional way of putting this is to say that, after entry by the tenant, the landlord's covenant of quiet enjoyment is not breached by the mere existence of a paramount claim.

EXAM TIP   **gilbert**

Note that timing is everything here. The tenant's right depends on whether he is in possession. *Before the tenant takes possession*, the *mere threat posed by a paramount title* will allow the tenant to avoid the lease. However, once the *tenant has taken possession* of the property, the existence of paramount title is not a breach of the landlord's duty, and the tenant has no rights unless there is *actual interference* with the tenant's enjoyment.

---

2. Actual Possession

a. "English rule" (majority view) [§843]

In most jurisdictions, the landlord has the duty to deliver to the tenant *actual possession*, as well as the *right to possession*, at the beginning of the term. If the previous tenant has not moved out when the new tenant's lease begins, and the landlord does not remove the person within a reasonable period of time, the landlord is in default. This is known as the "English rule," and is adopted by the Restatement. [Rest. 2d, Landlord & Tenant §6.2; **Adrian v. Rabinowitz**, 186 A. 29 (N.J. 1936)]

(1) Rationale

This carries out the intention of the parties because the tenant bargains for *use* of property, not a lawsuit against the prior tenant. Furthermore, the landlord is more likely to know if the previous tenant will move out and is in a better position to pressure him to do so. Finally, the landlord is usually much more familiar with eviction procedures than the tenant, and can evict the holdover tenant at less cost. The last two reasons suggest it is more efficient to put the duty on the landlord than on the tenant.

(2) Tenant's remedies [§844]

For the landlord's failure to provide actual possession, the tenant has several remedies. The tenant can terminate the lease and recover damages sustained by having to obtain quarters elsewhere. Or the tenant can affirm the lease, refuse to pay rent for the portion of the term during which he was kept out of possession, and recover damages. Damages include costs of renting other premises in excess of the rent specified in the lease, costs of ousting the holdover tenant, and loss of anticipated business profits (proven to a reasonable degree of certainty) that the landlord could have foreseen. [Rest. 2d, Landlord & Tenant §10.2; *but see* **Adrian v. Rabinowitz**, *supra*—lost profits of a newly established business were too speculative for recovery but, in the alternative, if recoverable, they had not been proven]

b. "American rule" (minority view) [§845]

In some jurisdictions, the landlord has *no duty* to deliver actual possession at the commencement of the term, and hence is not in default under the lease when the previous tenant continues wrongfully to occupy the premises. This is known as the "American rule"—although it is actually a *minority* view. [**Teitelbaum v. Direct Realty Co.**, 172 Misc. 48 (1939); **Hannan v. Dusch**, 153 S.E. 824 (Va. 1930)]

(1) Rationale

Several reasons are advanced for the American rule. First, the lease conveys a leasehold to the tenant. It is up to the tenant to take possession of his property if he wants it. Second, the tenant has the right to evict the holdover by summary proceedings and needs no additional remedy against the landlord. Third, the landlord should not be held liable for the tortious act of the holdover. Fourth, because the landlord is not required to evict a trespasser after the tenant takes possession, the landlord should not be required to evict a trespasser before the tenant takes possession. These reasons are either technical or question-begging and do not address the fundamental issues of fairness and efficiency.

(2) Remedies against the holdover tenant [§846]

Because the incoming tenant cannot sue the landlord when actual possession is not available, what remedies has the incoming tenant against the tenant holding over? The incoming tenant generally has the same rights against the holdover as a landlord would have. The incoming tenant can sue to evict the holdover and recover damages. Or the incoming tenant can treat the holdover tenant as tenant for another term, with rent payable to the incoming tenant (*see supra,* §§809 *et seq.*). Because the purpose of the holdover doctrine and penalty is to give the person with the right to possession more clout to recover possession, it should extend to the incoming tenant with the right to possession.

E. Landlord's Duty Not to Interfere with Tenant's Quiet Enjoyment

1. Covenant of Quiet Enjoyment [§847]

A tenant has a right of quiet enjoyment of the premises, without interference by the landlord. This right arises from the landlord's *covenant of quiet enjoyment,* which may be expressly provided in the lease. If not expressly provided, such a covenant is *always implied in every lease.*

a. Dependent covenant [§848]

As noted *supra* (§755), covenants in leases were, at common law, independent. But there was this exception: The tenant's covenant to *pay rent was always dependent* on the landlord's performance of the covenant of quiet enjoyment. Thus, if the landlord breached this covenant by evicting the tenant, the tenant's obligation to pay rent ceased.

b. Breach [§849]

The covenant of quiet enjoyment can be breached by either actual or constructive eviction.

2. Actual Eviction [§850]

If a tenant is physically evicted from the *entire* leased premises—either by the landlord or by someone with paramount title—the tenant's *rental obligation ceases.* Having been deprived of possession of the entire premises, the tenant may treat the lease as terminated, and his liability for further rent under the lease as discharged. He may also collect damages from the landlord for breach of covenant.

a. Partial eviction by landlord [§851]

If the tenant is evicted from *any portion of* the leased premises by the landlord, his rent obligation *abates entirely* until possession thereof is restored to him. The tenant may stay in possession and refuse to pay rent. [**Smith v. McEnany,** 48 N.E. 781 (Mass. 1897)]

e.g. **Example:** L leases T a farm of 40 acres. Subsequently L takes possession of an unused barn on the 40 acres and stores corn in it. T may stay in possession and refuse to pay any rent until L gives up the barn.

(1) Rationale

It is said that the obligation to pay rent rests on the tenant's possession of the entire leasehold, and that the landlord cannot apportion her own wrong. But this is merely to state a conclusion. The result—and perhaps the reason—is to impose a penalty on the landlord who interferes with the tenant's use of any part of the premises. This rule may be an efficient way to protect a tenant. Other remedies available to the tenant may be costly or unsatisfactory. If the law gives the tenant only damages, this requires a lawsuit. If the law gives the tenant only the right to terminate the lease and leave, the tenant may not be able to find other equivalent quarters.

(2) Restatement view [§852]

The Restatement rejects the rule of complete rent abatement for partial actual eviction on the grounds that this is unjust to the landlord. It adopts a rule of *partial rent abatement* and in addition gives the tenant the other usual remedies of termination or damages for breach of the covenant. [Rest. 2d, Landlord & Tenant §6.1]

b. Partial eviction by paramount title [§853]

Where the tenant is evicted from a part of the premises *by a third party* with paramount title, which interferes with the tenant's use contemplated by the parties, the tenant may terminate the lease, recover damages, *or* receive a *proportionate rent abatement*. If the tenant continues in possession, he remains liable for the reasonable rental value of the portion he possesses. [Rest. 2d, Landlord & Tenant §4.3]

---

e.g. **Example:** L leases a lot and building to T, including an easement to cross an adjacent lot to reach a side entrance. In good faith, L assumes this easement exists, but after the lease is executed, litigation establishes that there is no such easement. The owner of the adjacent lot then prevents T from crossing it. This is an eviction by paramount title. T may stay on the premises and receive an abatement of the rent by the amount by which the agreed rent of the property exceeds its reasonable rental value without the easement.

---

(1) Distinguish—partial eviction by landlord [§854]

If the landlord partially evicts the tenant, the tenant may stay in possession and pay no rent (*see supra*, §851). But if a third party partially evicts the tenant, the tenant does not have the option of staying in possession and paying no rent. The reason for this distinction is this: Under the recording acts, a third party may have a paramount claim in the leased land only if the tenant has actual or constructive notice of the claim. If the tenant has notice, the tenant takes the leasehold with the knowledge that he may be ousted by a third party. It is unfair to penalize the landlord for a third party exercising paramount rights of which the tenant is aware or, as in the example above, which the landlord does not believe to exist.

3. Constructive Eviction [§855]

Where, through the fault of the landlord, there occurs a *substantial interference with the tenant's use and enjoyment* of the leased premises, so that the tenant can no longer enjoy the premises as the parties contemplated, the tenant may terminate the lease, vacate the premises, and be excused from further rent liability. This is known as the doctrine of constructive eviction.

a. Dependent promises doctrine expanded [§856]

The doctrine of constructive eviction applies where the tenant is left in possession but the tenant's use and enjoyment is disturbed. Using this doctrine, the courts expanded the application of the contract doctrine of dependent promises from cases of actual eviction to situations where the landlord prevented the tenant from getting the enjoyment bargained for. The doctrine serves to make the tenant's obligation to pay rent dependent on the landlord's performance of her covenant of quiet enjoyment. It gives the tenant the remedy of termination of the tenancy. Without that remedy, the tenant could only sue for damages—a costly and inefficient remedy in many situations.

b. Distinguish—actual eviction [§857]

Actual eviction requires physical expulsion or exclusion from *possession*. If the landlord changes the locks or bars entry, the eviction is actual. If the landlord interferes with *enjoyment*, but does not bar entry, the eviction is constructive.

EXAM TIP   **gilbert**

It is important to distinguish between actual and constructive eviction because the tenant's remedy varies with each. In the case of *actual, partial eviction,* the tenant can remain in possession of the rest of the premises and refuse to pay rent. This option is *not* available in the case of constructive eviction. If the tenant wants to stop paying rent in a constructive eviction scenario, he must *abandon* the premises and *terminate the tenancy*.

Example: T, a lawyer, rents office space in a glass-enclosed, air-conditioned building. The windows are sealed. L promises comfortable use of the premises for 24 hours a day. L turns off the air-conditioning at 6 p.m. T wants to work late, but finds the office too hot and stuffy to work in after 6 p.m. T refuses to pay rent on the ground that this is an actual, partial eviction that results in the abatement of all rent (*see supra,* §851). However, L's actions constitute a constructive, not an actual, eviction. Because this is not an actual partial eviction, T cannot stay in the office and refuse to pay rent. T may claim constructive eviction, which releases him from the rent obligation, but to do so, T must abandon the premises. [**Barash v. Pennsylvania Terminal Real Estate Corp.**, 26 N.Y.2d 77 (1970); *but compare* **Minjak Co. v. Randolph,** 140 A.D.2d 245 (1988)—granting rent abatement]

---

c. **Elements of constructive eviction**

(1) **Substantial interference [§858]**

To have a constructive eviction, the tenant's use and enjoyment (as distinguished from possession) must be *substantially interfered with*. "Substantial interference" is measured objectively; it is what a reasonable person would regard as fundamentally incompatible with the use and enjoyment for which the parties bargained. Courts usually take into consideration the *purposes* for which the premises were leased, the *foreseeability* of this type of interference, the *potential duration* of the interference, the *nature and degree of harm caused*, and the availability of *means to abate* the interference. Courts can and do differ over what is substantial interference. [**Reste Realty Corp. v. Cooper**, 251 A.2d 268 (N.J. 1969)—water flooding basement office substantial interference; **Jacobs v. Morand,** 59 Misc. 200 (1908)—bedbugs, cockroaches, and ants not substantial interference and must be abated by the tenant]

(a) **Disclosure prior to lease [§859]**

If the landlord knows of defects in the premises (such as a leaky roof or the existence of cockroaches), she may be under a duty to disclose these to the tenant. Under tort law, the landlord is under a duty to disclose concealed dangers (*see infra*, §876). It is arguable that the landlord should be under a similar duty for contract purposes, even in the absence of physical injury. This argument usually states that it is fraudulent for the landlord not to tell the tenant of concealed and known substantial defects. [**Leech v. Husbands,** 152 A. 729 (Del. 1930)]

(b) **Tenant's knowledge [§860]**

If the tenant knows of the interference before taking possession, and then takes possession, the tenant has *waived* the interference.

(c) **Notice to landlord [§861]**

Prior to claiming constructive eviction, the tenant must give notice to the landlord of the objectionable conduct and the landlord must fail to remedy the situation within a reasonable time.

(2) **Tenant must vacate premises [§862]**

A tenant cannot claim a constructive eviction unless and until he vacates the premises. He *cannot remain in possession* and either refuse to pay rent or receive damages under this doctrine. If the tenant stays on, there is no eviction and the rent obligation continues. (Courts in some jurisdictions permit the tenant to remain in possession and bring suit for damages. *See infra,* §865.) Also, the tenant takes a chance when he determines that the circumstances amount to a constructive eviction, and vacates the premises within a reasonable time, possibly at some expense, because the court may not find a constructive eviction. [**Thompson v. Shoemaker,** 173 S.E.2d 627 (N.C. 1970)]

(a) Declaratory judgment [§863]

A tenant may be able to stay in possession and bring an equitable action for a declaratory judgment that the landlord's actions constitute a constructive eviction. Such declaratory relief permits the tenant to know, before vacating the premises, whether he is justified in vacating. [**Charles E. Burt, Inc. v. Seven Grand Corp.,** 163 N.E.2d 4 (Mass. 1959)]

(b) Damages after vacation [§864]

If the tenant vacates the premises on constructive eviction, this action terminates the lease. The tenant has no further rent liability. However, the tenant can recover from the landlord for damages suffered because of constructive eviction, including the difference between rent paid and reasonable rent value, expenses in obtaining substitute premises, loss of profits caused by landlord's actions, etc.

(c) Restatement view [§865]

The Restatement rejects the requirement that the tenant must abandon the property before claiming constructive eviction. The Restatement gives the tenant the right to: (i) terminate, or (ii) stay on and receive damages or a rent abatement or employ certain self-help remedies. *Rationale:* The tenant should receive what he bargained for. If the tenant's only remedy is to vacate, the doctrine of constructive eviction has limited usefulness in giving the tenant what he bargained for, particularly the poor tenant who lacks the funds to find decent housing elsewhere. [Rest. 2d, Landlord & Tenant §6.1]

(3) Fault of landlord [§866]

The interference with the tenant's quiet enjoyment must result from some act or failure to act by the landlord. Generally, a tenant cannot claim a constructive eviction growing out of the wrongful acts of a third party (*e.g.,* another tenant) unless that party's acts were induced by, or committed with the express or implied consent of, the landlord.

(a) Acts of landlord [§867]

Any act of the landlord (*e.g.,* playing a stereo very loudly at 2 a.m.) or any failure to act (*e.g.,* not providing heat) that substantially interferes with the tenant's use and enjoyment is sufficient for constructive eviction. Where the tenant claims constructive eviction for the landlord's nonfeasance (failure to act), the landlord must have some legal duty to act, the breach of which deprives the tenant of use and enjoyment, and thus breaches the covenant of quiet enjoyment.

EXAM TIP   **gilbert**

The most significant modern cases concerning acts of the landlord involve *failure of the landlord* to furnish heat or services or to repair in violation of an express or implied covenant to do so. Look for these fact patterns on your exam, as these facts will probably raise issues of constructive eviction.

Example: L leases a commercial building to T. The use of the basement is necessary for the conduct of T's business, which L knows. After every rainstorm, the basement floor is covered by two inches of water. Finally, one rainstorm brings five inches of water. T moves out within a week. Even in the absence of an express covenant to keep the basement waterproof, most courts will imply such a duty as necessary to the tenant's enjoyment of the premises, which the parties contemplated. T has been constructively evicted. [**Reste Realty Corp. v. Cooper,** *supra,* §858—agreement to pay rent and agreement to waterproof cellar were independent covenants]

(b) Acts of other tenants [§868]

Whether the acts of other tenants will suffice for constructive eviction depends on whether the landlord can control the behavior of other tenants and can be regarded as at fault in not controlling it. As a general rule, the landlord is *not responsible* for one tenant causing annoyance to another tenant, even though the annoying conduct would be constructive eviction if done by the landlord herself, and even though the landlord can legally control the other tenant's conduct. [**Sciascia v. Riverpark Apartments,** 444 N.E.2d 40 (Ohio 1981)]

1) Exceptions [§869]

There are two recognized exceptions to the general rule. First, the landlord has a duty not to permit a *nuisance* on the premises. Thus, if the landlord rents to prostitutes whose conduct is lewd or immoral, the landlord is in breach of her duty, and the conduct of others is attributable to her. [**Dyett v. Pendleton,** 8 Cow. 727 (N.Y. 1826); **Milheim v. Baxter,** 103 P. 376 (Colo. 1909)] Second, the landlord has a duty to control *common areas* under her control (*see infra,* §877). If the objectionable conduct takes place in common areas, the conduct is attributable to the landlord. [**Phyfe v. Dale,** 72 Misc. 383 (1911)]

2) **Modern trend [§870]**

A modern trend appears to be developing that holds the landlord responsible for other tenants' acts if the landlord has the legal ability to correct the conditions and fails to do so. The reason is that the landlord is in a better position to stop the objectionable conduct than is the tenant. [Rest. 2d, Landlord & Tenant §6.1, comment d]

---

e.g. **Example:** L leases an apartment to T, and also rents a cocktail lounge next door to X. The lease to X provides that L can terminate the lease if the noise disturbs the neighboring tenants. T complains to L of the loud noise of X. L does nothing. Because L can control the noise of X by terminating the lease, the noise is a constructive eviction. [**Blackett v. Olanoff,** 358 N.E.2d 817 (Mass. 1977)]

ACTUAL VS. CONSTRUCTIVE EVICTION — gilbert

TYPE	DEFINITION	REMEDIES IF EVICTION BY LANDLORD	REMEDIES IF EVICTION BY OTHERS
ACTUAL EVICTION			
- TOTAL	*Physical expulsion or exclusion* from possession of *entire* premises	Tenant may *terminate* lease, *pay no more rent*, and *collect damages*	If by person with paramount title—same (may *terminate* lease and *pay no more rent* and *collect damages*)
- PARTIAL	*Physical expulsion or exclusion* from possession of *part* of premises	Tenant may stay *in possession* and pay *no rent until possession is restored*	If by person with paramount title—tenant may *terminate* lease and seek damages, *or* stay *in possession* and pay *proportionate amount of rent*
CONSTRUCTIVE EVICTION	*Substantial interference* with *use and enjoyment* of premises	Tenant *must vacate* in order *to stop paying rent* or *receive damages*	*No remedy* (*i.e.,* no constructive eviction by third party) *unless* landlord has duty not to permit nuisance or to control common areas

d. Covenant not to compete [§871]

A covenant by the landlord that he will not compete with or rent to a competitor of the tenant is usually deemed to be so important to the tenant's enjoyment of the property that breach of the covenant by the landlord is treated as a constructive eviction. [**University Club v. Deakin,** 106 N.E. 790 (Ill. 1914)]

(1) Dependent covenant analysis [§872]

The extension of the constructive eviction doctrine to breach of non-competition covenants means in effect that the payment of rent depends on the performance of the noncompetition covenant. But why should a noncompetition covenant be singled out for such treatment? A noncompetition covenant is, after all, not favored by the law because it protects a monopoly. And why should commercial tenants be given rights denied to residential tenants? It has been suggested that the noncompetition cases rest on a principle that all promises of the landlord that are *a significant inducement to the making of a lease* are dependent. It has been then argued that this principle logically extends to all types of promises, and not just to noncompetition promises. The Restatement adopts this view, and provides that all *significant promises, express and implied*, are dependent. Breach by the landlord relieves the tenant of performance. [Rest. 2d, Landlord & Tenant §7.1] If this view is adopted by courts, then contract law will finally triumph over property law in the area of landlord and tenant. [*See* **Teodori v. Werner,** 415 A.2d 31 (Pa. 1980)—adopting Restatement view]

F. Landlord's Duty to Provide Habitable Premises

1. Landlord's Duty at Inception of the Lease

a. Common law [§873]

Under the common law, there is no implied covenant by the landlord that the premises are in tenantable condition or are fit for the purposes intended. The rule is *caveat lessee* (*i.e.,* "let the lessee beware"). Before he purchases his estate in land, the tenant is able to *inspect the premises* and thus protect himself. Unless the landlord gives an express warranty, the landlord has no duty to the tenant with respect to the condition of the premises. The tenant takes them "as is." [**Franklin v. Brown,** 118 N.Y. 110 (1889); **Anderson Drive-In Theatre, Inc. v. Kirkpatrick,** 110 N.E.2d 506 (Ind. 1953)]

(1) Exceptions [§874]

Four exceptions to the rule of caveat lessee are recognized.

(a) Furnished house for short term [§875]

Where there is a *short-term* lease of a *furnished house* (such as a summer cottage), a covenant is implied that the premises are tenantable. *Rationale:* The tenant in such a situation has no time to inspect or put the premises in tenantable condition. [**Ingalls v. Hobbs,** 31 N.E. 286 (Mass. 1892)]

(b) Hidden (latent) defects [§876]

When defects or dangerous conditions are *known* to the landlord and *not easily discoverable* by an ordinary inspection, the landlord has a duty to disclose the defects. *Rationale:* The tenant cannot discover the defects in an ordinary inspection, and nondisclosure borders on fraud. (If the landlord fraudulently represents the condition of the premises, she is liable to the tenant.)

(c) Common areas [§877]

The landlord has a duty to maintain safe and sanitary *common areas.* *Rationale:* The tenant will not have an incentive to maintain areas, such as stairways, used by all tenants, may not have access to some common facilities, and cannot be expected to make capital outlays to repair them.

(d) Building under construction [§878]

When a building is being constructed for a particular use, and the lease is executed *before the building is finished*, a covenant is implied that the building will be fit for the purposes intended. *Rationale:* The tenant has no opportunity to inspect the premises when the lease is executed.

(2) Independent covenants rule [§879]

Even if there is an express warranty of suitability or habitability, or if the tenant comes within one of the exceptions, the tenant must *overcome the independent covenants rule* if the tenant wants to terminate the lease or be excused from rent. Under the independent covenants rule, the tenant is *not excused* from performance (paying rent) by the landlord's breach, and the tenant's remedy is to sue the landlord for damages. This remedy is time-consuming and the legal expenses may be costly. If the tenant desires to terminate the lease, he must—under the common law—prove constructive eviction, discussed above, and move out. Thus, if the roof leaks in a summer cottage, the tenant can (i) sue for damages, or (ii) move out if he proves a constructive eviction by a substantial interference with his use and enjoyment.

b. Implied covenant of habitability [§880]

In recent years, a growing number of courts have held (or statutes have provided) that there is an implied covenant of initial habitability and fitness in leases of urban dwellings, including apartments. They have further held that the *dependent covenant doctrine* applies, and that a tenant *is relieved of his obligations* when the landlord breaches the implied covenant of habitability. [**Pines v. Perssion**, 111 N.W.2d 409 (Wis. 1961); **Lemle v. Breeden**, 462 P.2d 470 (Haw. 1969)] (Compare this implied covenant of habitability at the *inception* of the lease with a *continuing* covenant of habitability discussed *infra*, §893. In most respects they are the same, but in some they differ.)

(1) Various rationales [§881]

The implied covenant of habitability has been justified on several grounds: (i) A modern urban residential tenant does not have time to inspect the premises and put them in tenantable condition. (ii) The landlord knows more about the defects and is in a better position to remedy them. (iii) Housing codes, imposing duties on the landlord, have not been effectively enforced. More effective housing code enforcement will result from giving tenants the right to sue when premises are untenantable. Constructive eviction, requiring vacation of the dwelling, is not a viable remedy in times of housing shortage. (iv) Because of the housing shortage, tenants have much less bargaining power than landlords. (v) Uniform Commercial Code sections 2-314 and 2-315 imply a warranty of fitness for the purpose intended in a sale by a merchant or where the buyer relies on the seller's skill. By analogy, similar warranties should be applied to the sale of a leasehold. (Analogy to the U.C.C. supports implying a warranty at the inception of the lease, but does not support implying a *continuing duty* on the landlord to maintain the premises.)

(a) Criticism

The implied warranty of habitability has been criticized on economic grounds. It is claimed that placing this duty on the landlord will lead to increased rents to cover the upgraded housing, or to abandonment by the landlord, or to less investment in new housing. The end result of imposing obligations on the landlord, it is argued, is that the poor will lose more housing facilities. [**Chicago Board of Realtors, Inc. v. City of Chicago**, 819 F.2d 732 (7th Cir. 1987)] But this claim has been much disputed. Some argue that if imposing a duty on the landlord reduces the stock of low-income housing, perhaps this will result in the government's providing more housing for low-income persons. Under this view, the implied warranty of habitability is a strategic political move to put pressure on Congress to subsidize more low-income housing.

(b) Commercial leases [§882]

Some of the reasons given above for the implied warranty in residential leases are equally applicable to commercial leases, particularly the small commercial or office tenant. Courts are now beginning to hold that the covenant of initial suitability should be implied in commercial leases as well as in residential dwellings. [**Davidow v. Inwood North Professional Group,** 747 S.W.2d 373 (Tex. 1988)]

(2) Scope of warranty [§883]

The scope of the initial warranty of habitability has not received as much attention as has the scope of the continuing duty of habitability (*infra*, §§895-897). The cases have applied one of two standards.

(a) Latent defects only [§884]

Some courts have held that the landlord is responsible for latent defects only. In one of the early cases implying the covenant, it was said: "[I]t is a covenant that at the inception of the lease, there are no *latent* defects in facilities vital to the use of the premises for residential purposes because of faulty original construction or deterioration from age or normal usage." [**Marini v. Ireland,** 265 A.2d 526 (N.J. 1970)] This statement, limiting the warranty to latent defects, does not extend the warranty far beyond the second exception to the common law rule (*see supra*, §876). The statement has been repeated by several courts, but it does not seem to mean much in view of the imposition by these same courts of a continuing duty on the landlord to maintain the premises in tenantable condition, remedying patent defects as well as latent ones. If the landlord does not have to remedy patent defects initially, he has to remedy them thereafter. The latent-patent distinction might be important on the issue of waiver, however. If the defect is patent and seen by the tenant, the landlord may claim that the tenant waived it when he discovered it before signing the lease. (On waiver of the implied warranty, *see infra*, §887.)

(b) Housing code [§885]

Some courts hold that the local housing code sets the standard of the landlord's duty. A substantial violation of the housing code is a violation of the implied covenant of habitability. The Restatement provides that leased property "is unsuitable for residential purposes if it would be unsafe or unhealthy for the tenant to enter on the leased property and use it as a residence." [Rest. 2d, Landlord & Tenant §5.1, comment e] It goes on to say that a "significant violation" of the housing code "which has a substantial impact upon safety or health" is conclusive that the premises are untenantable, but that other modes of proving untenantability are acceptable.

(3) Remedies for breach [§886]

The remedies for breach of a covenant of habitability include the usual contract remedies of damages, restitution, and rescission. In addition, they may include using the rent for repair and rent withholding. The remedies are the same for the initial covenant of habitability as are provided for the continuing covenant of habitability and are discussed below in connection with the continuing covenant. The basic choice of the tenant in most cases is to move out and recover any prepaid rent *or* to stay in possession and recover damages (rent reduction). (How damages are calculated is discussed *infra*, §§901-904.)

---

e.g. **Example:** T leases a house from L. T moves in and finds that the house is filled with rats, the roof leaks, and the toilet does not work. T can rescind the lease, move out, and sue for her rent deposit; *or* she can stay in possession and sue for damages; or, in some states, she can use a reasonable amount of the rent money to remedy the defects.

---

(4) Waiver by tenant [§887]

Suppose that a tenant is willing to take the premises "as is." May the tenant waive the implied warranty of habitability? The tenant can waive minor defects, but it may be *against public policy* to permit the tenant to waive defects that make the premises unsafe or unsanitary. Because one of the reasons for implying a covenant of habitability is to encourage enforcement of the housing code by tenants, tenants may not be able to waive code requirements. The cases so far decided do *not permit waiver of a substantial breach.* [**Javins v. First National Realty Corp.,** 428 F.2d 1071 (D.C. Cir. 1970)] In those jurisdictions that do not permit waiver, patent as well as latent defects should be covered by the implied warranty (*compare supra,* §884).

(a) Analogy to contract law [§888]

The duties imposed on the landlord under the implied warranty of habitability go beyond the bounds of ordinary contract law. Contract law permits the sale of property "as is." In refusing to permit tenants to waive the landlord's duty, courts are trying to put pressure on landlords to rehabilitate dwellings. The moving force is not contract law, but to find a way to upgrade the housing stock.

c. Statutory duties [§889]

In many states, statutes have been enacted that impose on the landlord an affirmative duty to put residential premises in a tenantable condition prior to leasing them. [*See, e.g.,* URLTA §2.104, discussed *infra,* §914—specifically lists what defects will render leased premises untenantable]

d. Illegal lease [§890]

A lease of premises the *landlord knows* are in substantial violation of the municipal housing code is an illegal agreement *if the code prohibits rental* of premises in violation of the code. If the lease is an illegal agreement, the landlord cannot enforce any *covenant* to pay rent. The landlord can sue only for the reasonable rental value of the premises as they exist. [**Brown v. Southall Realty Co.,** 237 A.2d 834 (D.C. 1968)]

2. Landlord's Duty to Repair After Entry by Tenant

a. Common law [§891]

At common law, the landlord has **no duty to maintain and repair** the premises. At early common law, when the rule was formulated, most leases were agricultural leases, and the tenants were able-bodied men who could, and were expected to, make repairs on simple farm dwellings. The essential thing the tenant bargained for was possession of the land; the buildings were incidental.

(1) Landlord's covenant to repair [§892]

The parties can **by agreement** put the duty to repair on the landlord. But even where there is such an agreement, the landlord's covenant to repair might be deemed **independent** of the tenant's covenant to pay rent. On that view, if the landlord fails to repair, this breach does **not excuse** the tenant from rent payments. The tenant's only remedy is to sue the landlord for damages or specific performance, unless the landlord's breach results in substantial interference that justifies the tenant's vacating the premises and claiming constructive eviction. (*See supra*, §855.)

b. Implied covenant of habitability [§893]

A large majority of courts have, since the 1960s, implied on the part of the landlord a **continuing covenant of habitability** in leases of urban dwellings. They have also held that the dependent covenant doctrine of contract law applies, and thus a violation of the covenant by the landlord is a defense to an action by the landlord for payment of rent. For the landlord to sue on the tenant's covenant, the landlord must have performed her own. The continuing covenant of habitability is similar to the covenant implied at the inception of the lease, which most states now imply. Thus, under modern law in most states, a landlord has a duty of delivering habitable premises and of maintaining them in habitable shape. [**Javins v. First National Realty Corp.**, *supra*, §887; **Pugh v. Holmes**, 405 A.2d 897 (Pa. 1979); **Hilder v. St. Peter**, 478 A.2d 202 (Vt. 1984)]

(1) Rationale

Almost all the reasons given for implying a covenant of habitability at the inception of the lease (*supra*, §881) support the imposition of a continuing duty of maintenance on the landlord. In addition, the tenant bargains for, and expects to get, continuing services, including maintenance, from the landlord.

(a) Commercial leases [§894]

Covenants of habitability have in a few cases been implied in commercial leases when it appears that the commercial tenant has bargained for continuing maintenance by the landlord. This will more likely be the case where the landlord rents an office in a building than where the landlord rents the entire building. [**Davidow v. Inwood North Professional Group,** *supra*, §882]

(2) Scope of warranty [§895]
Courts differ on what standards are used to measure the landlord's duty. Generally they fall into one of two groups:

(a) Housing code [§896]
Some courts hold that the standards are those of the housing code. If there is a substantial violation of the housing code, the landlord's warranty is breached. Minor violations not affecting habitability do not constitute a breach. [**Javins v. First National Realty Corp.,** *supra*; Rest. 2d, Landlord & Tenant §5.5]

(b) Fit for human habitation [§897]
Some courts require that the premises be "fit for human habitation" or use similar language in respect to the standard. A violation of the housing code is compelling evidence of breach, but not conclusive. The standard as applied may be higher or lower than the housing code requirements. In these jurisdictions, continued loud noise could be a breach of warranty even though it is not a violation of the housing code. [**Boston Housing Authority v. Hemingway,** 293 N.E.2d 831 (Mass. 1973)]

(3) Notice to landlord [§898]
If the landlord is unaware of the condition, must the tenant give the landlord notice of the condition and a reasonable time to repair? Several courts, assuming that the implied warranty incorporates a *fault standard*, have stated that the landlord has a reasonable time to repair after notice is given. The Restatement agrees that the landlord is not in breach until a reasonable time has passed after the tenant has given the landlord notice. [Rest. 2d, Landlord & Tenant §§5.1, comment d, 5.4, comment g]

(4) Remedies for breach [§899]
The tenant's covenant to pay rent is dependent on the landlord's performance of her duties under the implied warranty of habitability. On breach by the landlord, the tenant has the following remedies:

(a) Terminate lease [§900]
The tenant may terminate the lease, vacate the premises, and recover damages. Damages may include relocation costs and the fair market value of the lease (the difference between the agreed rent and the fair market rent).

 Example: L leases an apartment to T for two years at a rental of $300 per month. After six months, L breaches the warranty by failing to furnish heat. T terminates the lease. The reasonable rental value of the apartment is now $350 a month. T can recover $900 from L. This figure represents $50 a month for 18 months, which is the advantage of the lease T is losing by terminating.

(b) Continue lease and recover damages [§901]

The tenant may continue the lease and recover damages. Damages ordinarily will be a rent reduction, but it is not yet entirely clear how the courts will calculate the damages.

1) Pay-for-premises-as-is rule [§902]

One method of measuring damages has the purpose of making the tenant pay only for the value of what he is receiving (the premises as is). Damages are measured by the difference between the agreed rent and the fair market rental value of the premises *as they are* during occupancy by the tenant in the unsafe or unsanitary condition. This method results in no damages *if the agreed rental is the fair market rental for the premises as is*, and thus it does not serve to goad landlords into rehabilitation. For this reason, it will probably be rejected by courts.

Example: T rents a slum apartment for $100 a month, which is the fair market rent for the apartment *as is*. If up to code (and as impliedly warranted), the apartment would rent for $200 a month. T should pay only for what he is receiving, which is worth $100 a month. Therefore, T can claim no damages.

2) Loss-of-bargain rule [§903]

A second method is to attempt to give the tenant what he bargained for. This is achieved by measuring damages by the difference between the fair market rental value of the premises *if they had been as warranted* and the fair market value of the premises *as is*. The agreed rent is assumed to be the fair rental value *as warranted* (not *as is*). This measure of damages appears to be winning judicial approval. [**Hilder v. St. Peter,** *supra*, §893; **Teodori v. Werner,** *supra*, §872]

Example: T rents an apartment at $100 a month. The condition of the apartment deteriorates over several years. T sues for damages. The court finds the market rental for the apartment as warranted is $160 a month, and the market rental for the apartment as is is $80 a month. Therefore, the tenant is losing the difference between $160 (as warranted) and $80 (as is), which is $80 a month. The tenant receives a rent abatement of $80, cutting his rent to $20 a month. If the difference between the rental value as warranted and the rental value as is had exceeded $100 a month, T could live in the apartment rent free! (Theoretically, if damages were $110 a month, L should pay T $10 a month to live in the apartment, but probably no court would give damages in excess of the agreed rent.)

3) Damages for discomfort and annoyance [§904]

A few cases have given damages for emotional distress unaccompanied by physical injury (tort damages). [**Hilder v. St. Peter**, *supra*; **Simon v. Solomon**, 431 N.E.2d 556 (Mass. 1982); **Haddad v. Gonzalez**, 576 N.E.2d 658 (Mass. 1991)]

(c) Continue lease and use rent to repair [§905]

In some jurisdictions, if the landlord fails to repair after notice, the tenant may use a *reasonable amount* of rent to repair the defective conditions. [**Marini v. Ireland**, *supra*, §884] This remedy is also provided for in the Restatement if the tenant first gives notice to the landlord and makes only reasonable expenditures. [Rest. 2d, Landlord & Tenant §11.2] A statutory repair and deduct remedy may be more specific than the judicial remedy of "reasonableness" and therefore more useful to tenants. For example, California Civil Code section 1942 permits the tenant to use up to one month's rent for repairs (remedy available no more than twice in a one-year period).

(d) Continue lease and withhold rent [§906]

Section 11.3 of the Restatement provides that the tenant may, after notice to the landlord, place his rent in escrow until the default is eliminated. Apparently no case has specifically granted this as a judicial remedy, but, with Restatement approval, this remedy may develop.

1) Distinguish—retaliatory eviction [§907]

If the tenant: (i) claims the lease is illegal because of violations of the housing code, (ii) reports the violations to the authorities, and (iii) withholds rent, the landlord cannot evict the tenant if the landlord's motive is to retaliate for reporting housing code violations. (*See infra*, §921.)

(e) Defense to landlord's rent action [§908]

Set forth above are affirmative actions that a tenant may take on the landlord's breach of the implied covenant of habitability. The tenant may also defend, in an action by the landlord for rent, that the agreed rent is not due because of the landlord's breach. This defense rests on the dependent-covenants rule—that the duty to pay rent is dependent on the landlord's performance.

1) **Distinguish—non-rent action [§909]**

If the landlord brings an eviction action that is not based on failure to pay rent, but rather is based on her right to possession at the expiration of the tenancy, the landlord's breach is not a defense available to the tenant. In a month-to-month tenancy, *e.g.*, the landlord can terminate it at any time, for any reason, on 30-day notice to quit. Breach of implied warranty is not a defense to a possessory action based on a notice to quit. Because the landlord is not suing for a breach of covenant by the tenant, which is dependent on the landlord's performance, the landlord's breach is irrelevant. The only defense to an action to evict because the tenancy has terminated is that the landlord is retaliating against the tenant's acts. (*See infra*, §921.)

TENANT'S REMEDIES FOR BREACH OF IMPLIED WARRANTY OF HABITABILITY	**gilbert**
REMEDY	**RESULT**
TERMINATE LEASE AND RECOVER DAMAGES	Tenant *vacates the premises* and recovers *damages* (e.g., relocation costs and the difference between the lease rent and cost of substitute premises)
CONTINUE LEASE AND RECOVER DAMAGES	Tenant *remains in possession* and recovers *damages* (rent reduction): (i) the difference between the agreed rent and the fair market value of the premises as they are, or (ii) the difference between the fair market value of the premises if they had been as warranted and the fair market value of the premises as is
CONTINUE LEASE AND USE RENT TO REPAIR	Tenant remains in possession and may *use a reasonable amount of rent to repair* the defective conditions
CONTINUE LEASE AND WITHHOLD RENT	Tenant remains in possession and, after notice to the landlord, places his *rent in escrow* until the default is eliminated
USE AS DEFENSE AGAINST LANDLORD'S ACTION FOR RENT	Tenant may use the landlord's breach *as a defense* in an action by the landlord for rent

(5) **Waiver by tenant [§910]**

According to the cases so far decided, a waiver of the landlord's obligations under the implied covenant of habitability is not permitted. The primary purpose of implying the obligation is to give tenants power to enforce the housing code, and it would be against public policy to permit tenants to waive that power (*see supra*, §887).

(a) URLTA view [§911]

Section 2.104(d) of the URLTA (*see supra,* §814) provides that the lease can shift the duty of repair to the tenant if: (i) the agreement is not for the purpose of evading the obligations of the landlord and is set forth in a *separate writing* and supported by *adequate consideration*, and (ii) the work is not necessary to cure noncompliance with the housing code. Hence, the parties can agree separately in consideration of a reduced rent that the tenant shall maintain the premises, provided the agreement does not shift to the tenant the burden of complying with the housing code. The tenant can be given the duty of painting and minor repairs, but not the duty of curing housing code violations.

(b) Restatement view [§912]

The Restatement provides that the parties may agree to decrease the landlord's obligations unless the agreement is "*unconscionable* or significantly *against public policy.*" [Rest. 2d, Landlord & Tenant §5.6] An agreement is unconscionable when it would shock the conscience if enforced. This—as well as "against public policy"—is a vague and imprecise phrase, but the Restatement spells out seven factors to weigh in determining unconscionability or public policy. These include the extent to which the waiver interferes with the enforcement of the housing code; the type of property leased; whether the waiver serves a reasonable business purpose and is a result of conscious negotiations; whether the waiver is part of a boilerplate lease document (an adhesion contract); whether the waiver imposes unreasonable burdens on a tenant who is poor and has unequal bargaining power; and whether the parties were represented by counsel.

c. Statutory duties of landlord [§913]

Many states have enacted legislation imposing a duty on the landlord to maintain residential premises in habitable condition. The statutes usually spell out the standard of habitability, whether the duty can be waived, and the tenant's remedy for breach. In addition to the remedies mentioned above, developed by the courts, statutes often give the tenant additional remedies going beyond what the courts have so far approved.

(1) URLTA [§914]

The URLTA imposes duties on the landlord equivalent to those imposed by the judicially implied covenant of habitability. Section 2.104 of the Act imposes on the landlord the duty of keeping the premises "in a fit and habitable condition." No distinction is made between latent and patent defects. If the landlord violates her statutory duties, the tenant may send written notice to the landlord telling her to fix the problems or consider the lease terminated. If the landlord refuses, the tenant may, after written notice, sue for damages, sue for an injunction, or take advantage of the following self-help remedies. [URLTA §4.101]

(a) Repair and deduct [§915]

If the defect can be cured by application of one-half the periodic rent, the tenant may correct the condition at the landlord's expense. [URLTA §4.103]

(b) Essential services [§916]

If the landlord fails to supply heat, water, hot water, or other essential service, the tenant may procure the service and deduct the cost from the rent. In addition, the tenant may find substitute housing while the service fails and be excused from paying rent while the service failure continues. [URLTA §4.104]

(2) New York statutes [§917]

New York statutes enacted to deal with substandard housing provide the following remedies:

(a) Abatement of rent after six months' violation [§918]

New York Multiple Dwelling Law section 302-a provides that if a serious housing code violation is not cured within six months after official notice by the building inspector, no rent shall be recovered if the tenant pays the rent due into court. None of the rent accruing after the end of the six-month period goes to the landlord, even if she ultimately corrects the violation. She forfeits the rent as a penalty. This remedy depends on the enforcement agency issuing a citation. Tenants cannot proceed without this.

(b) Rent withholding [§919]

New York Real Property Actions and Proceedings Law section 755 provides for a stay of an action for nonpayment of rent or to evict a tenant for nonpayment when the premises have housing code violations serious enough to amount to a constructive eviction, provided the tenant deposits with the clerk of the court all rent due when the stay is issued. In other words, if there is a constructive eviction, the tenant does not have to move out, but may pay rent into court. The court then may release the rent to pay for repairs. If the code violations are cured, the deposited rent is paid to the landlord. There is no machinery for getting repairs made. All depends on an individual tenant's initiative to repair his apartment. Also, rent is not suspended as under Multiple Dwelling Law section 302-a.

(c) Receivership [§920]

New York Real Property Actions and Proceedings Law section 770 was enacted to cure the defects in sections 302-a and 755, above. It provides that on application of one-third of the tenants of a building in dangerous condition, the court may order all rents from all tenants in the building paid to an administrator appointed by the court. The administrator is a rent receiver and uses the deposited rents to remedy the conditions found to exist in the building.

d. Retaliatory eviction [§921]

If a tenant reports the landlord for violation of the housing code, the landlord might try to evict the tenant or might refuse to renew the lease at the end of the leasehold term. For example, in a month-to-month tenancy, the landlord might try to evict the tenant after a 30-day notice. Some cases hold that a landlord, acting under retaliatory motivation, cannot evict a tenant. Retaliatory action is a defense against eviction, even in summary eviction proceedings. [**Haddad v. Gonzalez,** *supra,* §904; **Edwards v. Habib,** 397 F.2d 687 (D.C. Cir. 1968)] This defense is also adopted by the Restatement. [Rest. 2d, Landlord & Tenant §§14.8, 14.9]

(1) Interference with statutory right [§922]

Most of the retaliatory eviction cases involve a tenant complaining about violation of a *housing code*. In granting the tenant a defense against retaliatory eviction, the courts have emphasized that the retaliatory action frustrates the legislative policy underlying the housing codes. Enforcement of the codes depends in part on tenants reporting violations. If landlords could inhibit enforcement by evicting tenants who report violations, the effectiveness of the housing codes—and the legislative intent—would be frustrated. The basic rationale underlying the doctrine of retaliatory eviction is that it is essential to the effectiveness of the housing codes. [**Dickhut v. Norton,** 173 N.W.2d 297 (Wis. 1970)]

(2) Interference with judicially created right [§923]

Cases to date have mostly involved retaliation by the landlord for reporting statutory violations or for involvement in a tenants' union. [**Hillview Associates v. Bloomquist,** 440 N.W.2d 867 (Iowa 1989); **Imperial Colliery Co. v. Fout,** 373 S.E.2d 489 (W. Va. 1988)] But it seems likely that courts will extend the retaliatory eviction defense to cases where the tenant complains to the landlord of violations of the implied warranty of habitability. URLTA section 5.101 extends the retaliatory eviction defense to complaints to the landlord of a violation of the landlord's obligations.

EXAM TIP   gilbert

If on an exam you are presented with a novel basis for a retaliatory eviction defense, **consider the public policy** behind the defense in making your argument.

---

(3) Proof of motive [§924]

Whether a landlord's primary motivation is retaliation is a question of fact. The burden of proving a retaliatory motive is on the tenant. If the tenant can show that the landlord's action: (i) was discriminatory against the defendant tenant and (ii) followed the tenant's reporting of violations at the first opportunity, the burden shifts to the landlord to prove her primary motivation is not retaliatory. The Restatement provides that each case turns on its own facts. [Rest. 2d, Landlord & Tenant §14.8, comment f]

(a) Retaliation by rent increase [§925]

The retaliatory eviction defense can be used in a suit where the landlord is not retaliating directly but retaliating indirectly. For example, if T reports housing code violations, and then L increases T's rent and moves to evict T for nonpayment of the increased rent, T can plead retaliatory eviction if T can show that the rent increase is retaliatory. [**Schweiger v. Superior Court,** 3 Cal. 3d 507 (1970)]

(4) Tenant in default [§926]

A tenant in default in payment of rent cannot assert a retaliatory eviction defense. However, a tenant is *not in default* if the tenant is acting legally in withholding rent. The tenant is acting legally if under a statutory right he is using the rent money to make repairs or is withholding rent. If the lease is illegal, because renting the premises is in violation of the housing code, the tenant is not in default if he refuses to pay rent.

(5) When landlord can evict [§927]

The landlord cannot evict if she has a retaliatory motive. When a court holds that the landlord's primary motivation is not retaliatory, she may evict. In the meantime, the tenant can remain in possession and withhold or abate rent. The tenant may have to pay the landlord the reasonable rental value of the premises as is, which the landlord must sue for. A suit for rental value is not a summary proceeding and may take years.

Example: T refuses to pay rent because L is unwilling to make repairs on a dwelling that contains numerous housing code violations. L sues to evict T for nonpayment of rent. T defends that the lease is invalid under **Brown v. Southall Realty Co.** (*supra*, §890), and T does not owe any rent. T wins. Thereafter, L serves T with a 30-day notice to quit and subsequently sues T in unlawful detainer. T defends that the eviction is in retaliation for assertion of a *Southall Realty* defense. L alleges she is unwilling to make repairs and intends to take the dwelling off the market. *Held:* The retaliatory eviction defense is available to T. If L is removing the unit from the market for retaliatory motives, she cannot evict T, as that would inhibit private enforcement of the housing codes. L can evict T only if she makes the necessary repairs or takes housing off the market for *sound business reasons*. [**Robinson v. Diamond Housing Corp.,** 463 F.2d 853 (D.C. Cir. 1972)]

(a) Landlord stops utilities [§928]

If the landlord cannot evict the tenant, can the landlord stop paying the utility bills? Statutes in a number of states prohibit the landlord from attempting to evict a tenant by refusing to pay for utilities. The landlord must evict the tenant by using the judicial process. Self-help measures are forbidden (*see infra,* §1024). These statutes sometimes impose severe penalties on a landlord who tries to evict a tenant by cutting off utilities.

(6) State statutes [§929]

In many states, statutes prohibit retaliatory acts. The statutes vary, particularly on presumptions of retaliatory motive and the kinds of tenant acts protected against retaliatory eviction. Some of these statutes extend the retaliatory eviction defense to commercial tenancies. [*See* Rest. 2d, Landlord & Tenant §14.8, statutory note]

G. Landlord's Tort Liability

1. Introduction [§930]

The ordinary scope of duty in negligence cases is this: Where a person can foresee that if she does not use ordinary care and skill in a situation she will cause danger of injury to another person, a duty arises to use ordinary care and skill to avoid such danger. Negligence involves recognizing danger of injury and doing nothing about it. At common law, with a few recognized exceptions, the landlord had no duty to make the premises safe. The tenant took the premises as is. *Caveat lessee* (*i.e.,* "let the lessee beware") was the rule. After the tenant took possession, the tenant—the possessor—was responsible for tort injuries.

a. Contract and tort liability compared [§931]

The preceding section of this chapter discussed the landlord's duty to provide habitable premises. As we saw, modern courts have implied a warranty of habitability. The question now arises whether it is sound to continue to allow the landlord to escape liability for personal injury when the landlord is liable for damages for not maintaining the dwelling. There is this important difference in the two duties: A judgment for damages for breach of the duty of habitability probably cannot exceed the agreed rent. A judgment for personal injury can be as large as the injury suffered, perhaps thousands of dollars. Extending the landlord's tort liability would theoretically subject the landlord to the possibility of large costs, which she would pass along to the tenants in the form of higher rents. But this may be more theoretical than real, because landlords can and do insure against personal injury. The cost passed on to the tenant may be only the cost of the insurance premium. An impecunious tenant may not take out insurance, and if society wants personal injury insured against, the only practical solution may be to impose the burden on the landlord, who may pass it on to the tenant. Thus, at bottom, the issue seems to be: Who should pay the cost of an accident? The party injured or the tenant class by way of an insurance premium built into the rent? Much of the old law was laid down without spreading of the risk through insurance in mind.

2. Dangerous Condition Existing at Time of Lease [§932]

As stated above, the common law general rule is *caveat lessee*. The tenant is buying a term and takes it in the condition it is in. Therefore, the landlord is *not liable for injuries* to the tenant due to a dangerous condition of the premises. Nor is the landlord liable to the tenant's guests, because the tenant has assumed the risk of warning guests (*see infra*, §934). (Tenant's "guests" include members of the tenant's family, invitees, licensees, and others lawfully on the premises.) There are several important exceptions to the general rule, narrowing its strict application.

a. Concealed dangerous condition (latent defect) [§933]

If the landlord *knows or should know of a dangerous condition*, and also has reason to believe that the *tenant will not discover* this condition and realize the risk, the landlord has a duty to disclose the dangerous condition. If the landlord does not disclose, she is liable for injuries caused thereby to the tenant or the tenant's guests. *Rationale:* It is said that it is either negligent or fraudulent to fail to give a warning of a hidden danger, but this exception also has an economic basis. If the landlord discloses the defect to the tenant, the tenant can minimize the risk by remedying the defect or avoiding it. Both on grounds of fairness and efficiency, the tenant should not be held to assume the risk unless he can reasonably discover the defect on inspection. [**Johnson v. O'Brien,** 105 N.W.2d 244 (Minn. 1960)]

Example: L owns two apartments, numbered 1 and 2, which are joined by a connecting door. L papers over the door, and it cannot be discovered from an inspection of apartment 1. T leases apartment 1 and L does not tell T of the door. Subsequently a person enters apartment 1 through the papered-over door, beats up T, and carries off T's stereo set. L is liable for both T's personal injuries and loss of property. [**Myron W. McIntyre, Ltd. v. Chanler Holding Corp.,** 172 Misc. 917 (1939)]

---

(1) No liability after disclosure to tenant [§934]

If the tenant is made aware of the defect and accepts the premises "as is," the tenant assumes the risk. Moreover, after disclosure to the tenant, the landlord is not liable to *guests* of the tenant. The tenant has not only assumed the risk for himself; he has assumed the duty to warn others. *Rationale:* It is said that the landlord cannot stand guard and warn visitors for the tenant in possession. It is also said that the tenant's failure to remedy the defect is a superseding cause of the ultimate injury. [Restatement (Second) of Torts ("Rest. 2d, Torts") §356] But these are not very satisfactory reasons. Nonliability to the tenant's guests is not consistent with negligence law generally, which does not exonerate a negligent person simply because the dangerous condition she creates is no longer under her control.

b. Public use [§935]

Where the lease contemplates that the premises will be used as a *place of public admission* (*e.g.,* store, restaurant, theatre, etc.), the landlord is liable for injury to members of the public *if* the landlord: (i) *knows or should know of the dangerous condition*, (ii) has reason to expect that the *tenant will probably not correct* the condition before admitting the public, and (iii) *fails to exercise reasonable care to remedy* the condition. The reason for imposing liability on the landlord is that it will facilitate commerce and keep costs of doing business low if the public can go about its business in reasonably safe premises. Hence the landlord may not permit the land to be used in a manner that involves a *public, rather than a private*, danger. [Rest. 2d, Landlord & Tenant §17.2]

(1) What is public use [§936]

A few courts have limited the public use exception to situations where the lease contemplates use by a large number of persons at one time (*e.g.,* a store or lecture hall). But the majority do not so limit it, and impose liability on the landlord when only two or three members of the public will be on the premises at any one time (*e.g.,* a doctor's office). It is the *nature of the use*, and the *expectations* of the public, and not the number of admissions, that creates the landlord's duty.

(2) Liability limited to persons entering for public purposes [§937]

Because the landlord's liability is based on her knowledge that the tenant plans to use the premises for purposes involving entry by the public before the defective condition is corrected, the landlord's liability extends *only* to persons who enter the premises *for the purposes for which the public is invited*.

> **Example:** T leases a lecture hall from L for a free public lecture. L knows that one of the steps at the entrance is defective and dangerous. L points this out to T (thereby complying with L's duty under the first exception) and advises T to repair it. T replies that he does not think the step is dangerous and sees no need to repair it. A, coming to a lecture, slips on the step and is injured. L is liable to A. B, coming to paint the lecture hall when no lecture is being held, slips on the step and is injured. L is not liable to B.

(3) Defect must exist at beginning of lease [§938]

If the defect does not exist at the beginning of the lease, and *arises after* the tenant takes possession, the landlord has no liability under the public use exception.

(4) Tenant's promise to repair [§939]

If the tenant promises to repair the defect, the landlord may remain liable if she has reason to expect that the tenant will admit the public before repairing. The landlord's duty is not relieved unless she has no reason to expect that the public might be admitted to unsafe premises.

3. Defects Arising After Tenant Takes Possession [§940]

The general rule is that the landlord has *no liability* for personal injury from dangerous conditions that arise *after* the tenant takes possession. The duty of care to keep the premises safe rests on the person in possession, the tenant.

Example: L leases a house to T situated on a hill above the street. The house has a depressed passageway along the side, giving access to the rear of the house. The passageway is protected from the sloping bank of the hill by a retaining wall. At the time of the lease the retaining wall is in a safe condition. Subsequently, a crack appears in the retaining wall, and two years later the wall falls on a young nephew of the tenant, injuring him. L is not under a statutory duty to repair. L has no liability for the injury. [**Bowles v. Mahoney**, 202 F.2d 320 (D.C. Cir. 1952)]

---

a. Repairs undertaken [§941]

If the landlord *voluntarily undertakes* to make repairs, although not legally obligated to do so, she owes a duty *to exercise reasonable care* in the undertaking. If she makes repairs in a negligent manner, the landlord is liable to those who do not know of her negligence and are injured by her careless or unskillful workmanship.

EXAM TIP | **gilbert**

A landlord's duty regarding repairs is a fairly common topic in landlord-tenant questions. Keep in mind that although the landlord generally has **no duty to make repairs**, and faces **no liability** for personal injury from dangerous conditions, **if she decides to make repairs**, she must act reasonably. Thus, if she does the work herself but is negligent, or if she hires someone else whom she knows (or should know) is not doing a careful job, she will be liable for damages.

---

(1) Knowledge of tenant [§942]

The landlord is not liable when she undertakes repairs if the tenant knows or should know that the repairs have been negligently made. Liability is imposed under this exception to the general rule because of the *reliance of the tenant* on the landlord's acts, and where there is no reliance there is no liability. Oddly enough, knowledge by the tenant of the landlord's negligence also bars a suit by the tenant's guest, even though the guest relies on the deceptive appearance of safety. In such a case, the landlord can assume that the tenant will warn his guests.

> **Example:** In October, T leases a house from L. The roof leaks, and in repairing the roof, L removes the gutter. L knows that without a gutter rain will drain onto the front porch steps and freeze, resulting in icy steps. L intends to reinstall the gutter. T complains about the absence of the gutter. In January, before L reinstalls the gutter, rain falls and freezes, and a guest of T slips on the icy steps and is injured. L is not liable because T had knowledge of the danger and should have warned his guest. [**Borders v. Roseberry,** 532 P.2d 1366 (Kan. 1975)]

4. Common Areas Controlled by Landlord [§943]

If the landlord leases part of the property and retains *control of common areas* (such as halls, walks, elevators, etc.), the landlord is liable for physical injury if the landlord could have reasonably discovered the condition and made it safe. This *duty of reasonable care* over common areas is the same as any owner-occupier has toward guests.

> **Example:** T slips and falls on the icy sidewalk leading to L's apartment house. L is liable if L knew or should have known of the ice and did not take reasonable steps to remedy it (*e.g.*, by putting sand on it or otherwise).

a. Criminal intrusion [§944]

If the landlord can reasonably foresee the risk of criminals coming into the building by way of common areas under the control of the landlord, the landlord may be liable for physical harm caused by criminal intrusion if necessary precautions are not made.

> **Example:** T is assaulted in the lobby of his apartment house, which is located in an area where such assaults are common, increasing, and foreseeable. L has neither a doorman on duty nor an adequate security system. Some recent cases hold that L is liable to T. The liability may be based on the landlord's control of common areas. Or, if the landlord has reduced security, the liability may be based on an implied contractual duty not to reduce security (tenant's expectations). [**Walls v. Oxford Management Co.,** 633 A.2d 103 (N.H. 1993); **Feld v. Merriam,** 485 A.2d 742 (Pa. 1984)—L liable only if L has assumed a duty of protecting tenants and has negligently performed that duty]

5. Landlord Contracts to Repair [§945]

If the landlord expressly promises to repair and maintain the premises, the older cases hold this promise does *not carry with it tort liability*. The injured tenant can sue only in contract, and damages may be limited to the cost of the repair or to the agreed rent. The reason is that the parties did not contemplate tort liability (which can be large) but only contractual liability. Carrying the contract analysis one step further, older cases also hold that guests of the tenant, who are not a party to the contract, cannot sue because of lack of privity of contract. (Even if the contract is construed to be a third-party beneficiary contract, the tenant's guests may still be limited to contract damages and cannot recover damages for personal injuries.)

a. Modern law [§946]

Although the old law is still followed in some jurisdictions, a majority of states now find the landlord who *contracts to repair* liable in tort to the *tenant and to his guests*. By holding the landlord liable in tort to the tenant's guests, the privity of contract issue is circumvented. *Rationale:* Because of the landlord's promise, the tenant will rely on it and forgo efforts to remedy the condition. Hence the tenant will not minimize the risk. Society wants the risk minimized. [**Faber v. Creswick**, 156 A.2d 252 (N.J. 1959); Rest. 2d, Landlord & Tenant §17.5]

6. Landlord Under Legal Duty to Repair [§947]

The landlord may have a statutory duty to repair the premises, or the jurisdiction may imply a covenant of habitability. This will probably be the case in most jurisdictions with respect to residential leaseholds. What effect does the legal duty to repair have on the landlord's tort liability?

a. Statutory duty to repair [§948]

If the landlord has a statutory duty to repair (such as imposed by a housing code), the landlord may be liable to the tenant and the tenant's guests who are injured as a result of the failure to repair. [**Whetzel v. Jess Fisher Management Co.**, 282 F.2d 943 (D.C. Cir. 1960); **Kanelos v. Kettler**, 406 F.2d 951 (D.C. Cir. 1968)]

b. Implied covenant of habitability [§949]

Should the landlord be liable in tort if personal injury results from a breach of the implied warranty of habitability? Cases now impose liability only for the landlord's *negligence*. The plaintiff must show that the landlord knew or should have known of the violation and failed to correct the situation within a reasonable time. [**Peterson v. Superior Court**, 10 Cal. 4th 1185 (1995), *overruling* **Becker v. IRM Corp.**, 38 Cal. 3d 454 (1985)—imposed strict liability]

7. Modern Trend—Landlord Liability [§950]

It seems clear that the landlord's tort liability is undergoing a change. Tort liability has already been imposed where the landlord has a statutory duty to repair or breaches the implied covenant of habitability. But the landlord's liability is likely to be extended to situations beyond these. Landlords will probably be treated like all persons who must exercise reasonable care not to subject others to an unreasonable risk of harm. The basic tort issues, such as foreseeability and unreasonableness of the particular risk or harm, will control. The old general rule of limited landlord tort liability, with its elaborate exceptions, has already been abandoned in some jurisdictions. [**Sargent v. Ross,** 308 A.2d 528 (N.H. 1973); **Williams v. Melby,** 699 P.2d 723 (Utah 1985)]

Example: T rents from L an apartment with a balcony. The balcony has a faulty railing, about which the landlord knows and warns T. Several months later, T invites a woman to a dinner party in his apartment. She steps out on the balcony and leans against the railing. It gives way, and she falls to the ground and is injured. L is liable to the woman under ordinary tort principles. [**Young v. Garwacki,** 402 N.E.2d 1045 (Mass. 1980)]

---

8. **Exculpatory Clauses [§951]**

An "exculpatory clause" is a lease provision that purports to exonerate the landlord from some or all responsibility and liability. The exculpatory clause may purport to relieve the landlord from all liability for personal injury resulting from the landlord's negligence. Courts are split on the validity of such provisions.

a. **Traditional view [§952]**

The traditional view is that an exculpatory clause relieving the landlord of liability for personal injury is *valid* because of freedom of contract. Thus, by inserting an exculpatory clause in the lease, the landlord can be effectively insulated from any liability to repair or maintain the premises. *Rationale:* Public policy is not offended by the parties bargaining to limit their rights and duties regarding each other at the time they enter into the leasehold. The tenant may contract to assume the risk for himself and his guests. [**O'Callaghan v. Waller & Beckwith Realty Co.,** 155 N.E.2d 545 (Ill. 1959), *reaffirmed in* **Sweney Gasoline & Oil Co. v. Toledo, Peoria & Western Railroad,** 247 N.E.2d 603 (Ill. 1969); *but see* 765 ILCS 705/1—reverses cases and provides exculpatory clauses relieving landlord of liability for personal injury unenforceable]

b. **Modern trend [§953]**

Because of the disparity of bargaining power between landlord and tenant in modern times with a housing shortage, and where the tenant has no practical choice but to accept the lease as offered, several modern courts have held that exculpatory clauses in residential leases are *against public policy* and void. The courts have objected to the fact that relieving the landlord of tort liability subjects others to an unreasonable risk of harm. [**McCutcheon v. United Homes Corp.,** 486 P.2d 1093 (Wash. 1971)]

c. **Statutes [§954]**

Statutes in many states provide that exculpatory clauses relieving the landlord from liability in tort are void. Often these statutes apply to residential leases only, but some apply to all leases. [*See* Rest. 2d, Landlord & Tenant §17.3, statutory note—listing statutes in California, Illinois, Massachusetts, New York, and Ohio, among other states] URLTA section 1.403 provides that no residential rental agreement may relieve the landlord of tort liability.

H. Tenant's Duties

1. Duty to Pay Rent [§955]

The tenant has a duty to pay any rent reserved in the lease. Traditionally, the duty to pay rent is an *independent obligation*—not dependent on the landlord's performance of her obligations. Thus, if the landlord fails to repair, rent is still payable. In many jurisdictions the duty to pay rent is now dependent on performance of the landlord's obligations if the premises are residential. If the landlord does not perform, the tenant can terminate the lease and move out, withhold rent, or receive a rent abatement (*see supra*, §§899 *et seq.*).

a. Implied agreement [§956]

If rent is not reserved, the tenant has a duty to pay the *reasonable rental value* of the use of the property (quantum meruit). [**Gunn v. Scovil**, 4 Day 228 (Conn. 1810)] The reasonable rental value is not rent, however, and the landlord's remedies on default are not the same as her remedies on default of rent. (*See infra*, §§988 *et seq.*)

b. Illegal agreement [§957]

If the rental agreement is illegal because the housing code forbids renting property in substandard condition, the tenant has no duty to pay rent. [**Brown v. Southall Realty Co.**, *supra*, §927] But the tenant must pay the reasonable rental value of the premises.

c. Rent passes with reversion [§958]

The right to rent is attached to the landlord's reversion. If the landlord sells the property to another, the transferee is entitled to future rents. However, the right to rent is not inseparable from the reversion. The landlord can expressly reserve the right to rent when she transfers the reversion, or she can assign the rents without assigning the reversion.

d. Nonapportionment of rent [§959]

In the absence of an agreement to the contrary, rent falls due only on the last day of the lease term. Rent does not accrue from day to day, but accrues and falls due simultaneously at the end of the term.

Example: On April 1, L leases Blackacre to T, with rent of $200 payable monthly. On June 18, L dies, and the will devises L's reversion in Blackacre to A, and leaves the residue of the estate to B. A, owner of the reversion on June 30, is entitled to the entire $200 due on June 30.

e. Rent control [§960]

Many cities have enacted rent control ordinances. Rent control is a form of price regulation. Regulating rents has been held constitutional on the theory that it bears a rational relation to a legitimate public purpose: the welfare of housing consumers. [**Pennell v. City of San Jose,** 485 U.S. 1 (1988)]

(1) Reasonable return [§961]

Although constitutional in general, rent control ordinances must provide a landlord with a just and reasonable return on her property. If the rent control law does not provide for procedural mechanisms that will give the landlord a fair return under changing economic conditions, it is confiscatory and a taking of the landlord's property without compensation (in violation of the Takings Clause of the United States Constitution—*see infra,* §§1463, 1471).

(2) Eviction of tenant [§962]

Under rent control ordinances, the landlord cannot evict a tenant at the end of a term and rent to a new tenant at the market rate. If the landlord could, rent control would be undermined. It would provide security of tenure at the existing rent only during existing terms. So rent control provisions have always been accompanied by provisions requiring renewal of a lease unless there is *good cause* for eviction (*e.g.,* default in rent payments). [**Fresh Pond Shopping Center, Inc. v. Callahan,** 464 U.S. 875 (1983)]

2. Duty to Occupy Premises [§963]

The tenant has bought an estate in land, and the tenant can occupy the property or not as the tenant elects. Unless failure to occupy results in permissive waste (*see supra,* §334, *and infra,* §965), the tenant has no liability for failure to occupy.

a. Percentage leases [§964]

A court may make an exception in this rule in a commercial lease if the rent is for a percentage of sales on the premises (known as a "percentage lease"). Most percentage leases require a fixed monthly rent plus a percentage of sales. In such a case a court may imply a duty of the tenant to occupy *and conduct the business* if the circumstances indicate the parties so intended. Most cases refuse to imply a duty where the fixed minimum rent is substantial. [**College Block v. Atlantic Richfield Co.,** 206 Cal. App. 3d 1376 (1988); **Piggly Wiggly Southern, Inc. v. Heard,** 405 S.E.2d 478 (Ga. 1991); **Mercury Investment Co. v. F.W. Woolworth Co.,** 706 P.2d 523 (Okla. 1985)]

3. Duty to Repair [§965]

In the absence of a duty on the part of the landlord to repair (imposed by statute, implied covenant of habitability, or express covenant), the tenant has a duty to make *ordinary repairs* to keep the property in the same condition as at the commencement of the term, *ordinary wear and tear excepted.* The tenant does not have to make substantial repairs, but he must protect the premises from damage, usually by the elements. He must treat the premises in such a way that no substantial injury is done to them during his tenancy. Sometimes the tenant's duty to repair is referred to as "liability for permissive or involuntary waste." [**Suydam v. Jackson**, *supra*, §335]

a. Death and decomposition of tenant [§966]

It has been argued that the tenant's estate is liable for damages if the tenant dies and his body decomposes in the apartment before it is discovered. The argument rests on the common law duty to redeliver the premises in the same general condition as they were at the time of letting. This argument has been rejected on the ground that the damages occurred as a result of unavoidable circumstances over which the tenant had no control. [**Kennedy v. Kidd**, 557 P.2d 467 (Okla. 1976)]

b. Tort liability [§967]

To the extent that the tenant has a duty of repair, the tenant is liable to persons injured as a result of his failure to repair. [**King v. Cooney-Eckstein Co.**, 63 So. 659 (Fla. 1913)]

c. Covenant by tenant to repair [§968]

The tenant may expressly covenant to repair and maintain the premises. In the past, courts have usually enforced this covenant, whatever the cause of the damage. The tenant's duties in this respect extended even to ordinary wear and tear, unless expressly excluded by the covenant. But there is no duty to repair structural failures or damage resulting from fire or other casualty unless such duty is expressly included in the covenant. However, if the repairs are ordered by governmental authority (such as removing asbestos or earthquake hazards), recent cases treat the question as one of interpreting the lease and analyzing several factors in determining the parties' intent as to liability for the particular repair. [**Hadian v. Schwartz**, 8 Cal. 4th 836 (1994)]

4. Duty Not to Damage Premises [§969]

If the tenant *substantially damages* the premises by an affirmative act, the tenant is liable to the landlord. This is sometimes known as voluntary or affirmative waste. The damage must be substantial, with effects extending well beyond the tenant's term. Attaching a wooden closet to a wall or putting a decorative frame around a window is not waste.

a. Changes in the premises [§970]

Under the old common law rule, the tenant was liable for substantial changes in the premises, even if the changes increased the value of the property. The landlord was entitled to get the premises back in the same condition as they were leased. A change that increased the value of the premises was known as *ameliorating waste*. In modern times, courts have held that a long-term tenant may change a structure if the economic value is not diminished. For example, the replacement of old built-in cabinets with new ones is not actionable by the landlord. [**Sigsbee Holding Corp. v. Canavan**, 39 Misc. 2d 465 (1963); *compare* **Melms v. Pabst Brewing Co.**, *supra*, §337]

5. Duty Not to Disturb Other Tenants [§971]

Absent a covenant in a lease, there is *no common law duty* of a tenant not to make noise or otherwise disturb other tenants. The only duty of the tenant in this respect is *not to commit a nuisance*. All possessors of land have a duty not to commit a nuisance (*see infra*, §§1311 *et seq.*). It is common, however, for residential apartment leases to provide a covenant by the tenant that he will not substantially interfere with the enjoyment by other tenants of their apartments. Breach of such a covenant permits the landlord to evict the tenant. Covenants of this type tend to be judicially construed by a rule of reason. The amount of noise and disturbances permitted depends upon the particular context. Even if the covenant does not have a rule of reason written in it, but is a covenant to make "no noise or disturbance," a court will likely interpret it to mean "no unreasonable noise or disturbance." This construction in effect makes the court and not the landlord the arbiter of the defendant's conduct. [**Louisiana Leasing Co. v. Sokolow**, 48 Misc. 2d 1014 (1966)]

6. Acts of Third Party Relieving Tenant of Duty [§972]

The tenant may be relieved of his duty to pay rent by acts of a third party that make it impossible or difficult to continue the lease. One must start from the proposition, however, that the tenant has purchased a term and assumed the risk. This was the old law. [**Paradine v. Jane**, 82 Eng. Rep. 897 (1647)—holding tenant assumed risk of war] Modern doctrines have carved exceptions in that proposition, but it still has considerable vitality.

a. Use becomes illegal [§973]

Where a use of property becomes illegal after the lease is made, a court may—in some circumstances—hold that the tenant may terminate the lease and stop paying further rent.

(1) Where restricted to one use [§974]

Where the parties intend that the premises be used for *one particular use only*, which becomes illegal, the tenant is excused from further liability for the rent. In effect the courts imply a condition that the lease is made on an implied condition that the one use intended remain legal. It is considered oppressive and unfair to hold the tenant when he can make *no use* of the property. [**Brunswick-Balke-Collender Co. v. Seattle Brewing & Malting Co.**, 167 P. 58 (Wash. 1917); Rest. 2d, Landlord & Tenant §9.2]

(2) Where several uses permitted [§975]

Where the parties intend that the premises be used for one use, but the tenant is free to make other uses, and the intended use becomes illegal, the tenant cannot terminate the lease. It is not considered oppressive to hold the tenant when he *can make other uses* of the property than those intended. In this situation, the tenant takes the risk that the use will become illegal. The Restatement generally adopts this position, but adds that a tenant may terminate "if it would be unreasonable to place on the tenant the burdens of the lease after converting to the other use." [Rest. 2d, Landlord & Tenant §9.2(2)]

(3) Permit required for use [§976]

When the lease restricts the tenant to one particular use that is legal *only if a permit or zoning variance is obtained* from a governmental agency, the tenant *cannot terminate* the lease if the permit is not granted. The tenant assumes the risk of obtaining the permit. [**Warshawsky v. American Automotive Products Co.,** 138 N.E.2d 816 (Ill. 1956)]

(a) Minority views

A minority of jurisdictions put the risk on the landlord and excuse the tenant from liability for rent if the permit is not granted. They reason that the burden on the tenant is too oppressive because he cannot make any further use of the land. The Restatement excuses the tenant if he makes a good faith effort to obtain the permit. [Rest. 2d, Landlord & Tenant §9.2, comment a]

b. Frustration of purpose [§977]

The tenant may terminate the lease in case of *extreme hardship* if the purpose of the lease is frustrated. The most frequent form of frustration is governmental action that makes the intended use of the premises extremely difficult. This doctrine originated as part of contract law and has been applied to *commercial* leases.

(1) Requirements [§978]

Courts have been more hesitant to relieve tenants of their bargains than promisors generally. They have imposed strict requirements on the frustration doctrine. For the tenant to be relieved of liability: (i) the use that has been frustrated must have been *contemplated by both* landlord and tenant as the use for which the premises were let; (ii) the frustration must be *total or near total*, imposing extreme hardship on the tenant; and (iii) the frustrating event must *not have been foreseen or foreseeable* by the parties. If it was foreseeable, the risk is ordinarily placed on the tenant.

Example: In August 1941, L leases a building to T for the sole purpose of selling new cars. The lease is for five years. In January 1942, after the outbreak of the war, the federal government restricts the sale of new cars to persons with preferential priorities, and orders Detroit to cut back on car production. L offers to waive the restriction on use, says he will accept an assignee if T can find one, and offers to reduce the rent if T cannot operate profitably. T refuses to stay on. On March 15, 1942, T vacates the premises, claiming frustration of purpose. The frustration doctrine does not apply to T, and T continues to be liable for rent. Why? First, the frustration has not been total, and the hardship is not extreme. Some new car sales are still possible. T has merely lost part of his expected profits. Second, the risk was reasonably foreseeable because in June 1940, Congress authorized the President to mobilize the automobile industry for national defense. The public anticipated that production would soon be restricted. T assumed the risk unless T can show that the circumstances were wholly outside the contemplation of the parties. [**Lloyd v. Murphy,** 25 Cal. 2d 48 (1944)]

(2) Impossibility of performance [§979]

The frustration doctrine is similar to, but not identical with, the contract doctrine of impossibility of performance. Both require the showing of extreme hardship. In the case of impossibility, *performance* must be literally impossible or extremely difficult or illegal. In the case of frustration, the *purposes* are frustrated, while performance is still possible. The doctrines are related, sometimes confused, and not always separable.

EXAM TIP **gilbert**

Try to keep these terms straight. With the *frustration* doctrine, the *purpose of the lease is frustrated*. For example, if in a contract to lease land for its timber a forest fire burns down almost all of the trees before the lease begins, the purpose of the lease is frustrated because the tenant will not be able to use the land for its timber. But the tenant may still be held to the lease if forest fires are foreseeable. In contrast, with the doctrine of *impossibility* of performance, *performance is literally impossible* or extremely difficult or illegal. For example, if in a contract to lease an apartment, the apartment building burns down before the lease begins, it is impossible for the tenant to take possession of the apartment unit because it no longer exists.

---

c. Destruction of the premises [§980]

At common law, destruction of the building on the leased property did not terminate the lease or relieve the tenant of his obligation to pay rent. *Rationale:* The leasehold (estate in land) survived the destruction, and the land was the important part of the bargain. The common law rule is unsuited to most urban leases where the lease is primarily of the building, not the land. Statutes in a large majority of states have been enacted providing that, if the lease does not provide to the contrary, the tenant may terminate the lease and cease paying rent if the premises are destroyed by fire, the elements, or any cause other than the tenant's own negligence. [*See* Rest. 2d, Landlord & Tenant ch. 5, statutory note, item 2; URLTA §4.106] Some courts also have so held. [*See, e.g.,* **Albert M. Greenfield & Co. v. Kolea,** 380 A.2d 758 (Pa. 1977)]

d. Eminent domain [§981]

A permanent taking of all the leased property by condemnation proceedings *extinguishes* the leasehold. The lessee is entitled to compensation for the taking of the leasehold (*see* below). However, if the government takes the property for a limited period of time shorter than the duration of the lease (*e.g.*, to store munitions during an emergency), the lease is *not terminated.* The tenant's duty to pay rent continues unabated. The tenant is entitled to recover from the government the value of the occupancy taken. [**Leonard v. Autocar Sales & Service Co.,** 64 N.E.2d 477 (Ill. 1945)]

7. Rights and Duties Relating to Fixtures [§982]

When the tenant attaches a chattel to the premises, he may want to remove it on termination of the lease. The common law made it difficult to do so. Two rules were applied: (i) fixtures belong to the landlord; and (ii) attached chattels that are not fixtures are forfeited to the landlord if they are not removed before the end of the lease.

a. Fixtures belong to landlord [§983]

The common law rule is that fixtures cannot be removed from the premises by the tenant. Fixtures become part of the realty and therefore the property of the landlord. Thus the key question arises: What is a fixture?

(1) Fixture defined [§984]

The word "fixture" has proven difficult to define. The English view is that a chattel that has been *permanently attached* to land is a fixture. Thus the focus is on what is "permanent" and what is "attached." American courts have generally rejected the English view as unworkable and have held that whether a chattel is a fixture depends on the *intention of the tenant.* The intention is determined by objective criteria, such as the nature of the article, the manner in which it is attached, and the amount of damage that would be caused by its removal. [**Sigrol Realty Corp. v. Valcich,** 12 A.D.2d 430 (1961)]

EXAM TIP   **gilbert**

Remember, the fact question as to whether something is a fixture is one of *intent*, either expressly stated or otherwise implied from the facts. Did the tenant intend to make the item a permanent part of the premises?

---

(2) Exception—trade fixtures [§985]

An exception to the rule is recognized to allow a tenant to remove trade fixtures—*i.e.*, those installed for the purpose of carrying on a trade or business.

(a) Rationale

This encourages economic investment for trade. The tenant is liable to the landlord, however, for *material damages caused by removing* trade fixtures. [**Cameron v. Oakland County Gas & Oil Co.,** 269 N.W. 227 (Mich. 1936); **Handler v. Horns,** 65 A.2d 523 (N.J. 1949)]

To encourage investment, "trade fixture" has been broadly defined (*e.g.*, "trade fixtures" has been held to include improvements of property for agricultural purposes as well as for commercial trading or manufacturing purposes [**Old Line Life Insurance Co. v. Hawn,** 275 N.W. 542 (Wis. 1937)]).

(3) Modern trend [§986]

The modern trend is to be very liberal in permitting the tenant to remove any chattel he installs on the leased premises, whether or not used in trade or business, as long as substantial damage is not caused. The Restatement provides that the tenant may remove his annexations "if the leased property can be and is restored to its former condition after the removal." [Rest. 2d, Landlord & Tenant §12.2(4)] The annexations may involve a considerable investment by the tenant, and there is no reason to require a gift of this investment to the landlord.

b. Removal before end of term or forfeit [§987]

If the annexations do not belong to the landlord (*i.e.*, they are *not "fixtures"*), the tenant *must remove them before the end of his term* or they become the property of the landlord. The rule has been criticized on the ground that because the tenant does not lose title to his unattached chattels remaining behind, he should not lose title to attached chattels he is entitled to remove. On the other hand, if the tenant can foresee the need for removal, the landlord will be inconvenienced if the tenant does not remove his annexations before the end of the lease.

I. Landlord's Remedies

1. Means of Assuring Performance [§988]

The landlord has a number of means to assure performance of the tenant's duties. The principal concern of the landlord, of course, is the continuing payment of rent. The means available to the landlord to secure the rent may be provided by common law rule, by statute, or by a clause in the lease.

a. Distress (seizure of tenant's chattels)

(1) Common law [§989]

At common law, if a tenant was in arrears in rent, the landlord could, *without notice* to the tenant, enter upon the premises and *seize whatever chattels she could find* and hold them as security until the rent was paid. This was known as the right of distress or the right of distraint. Because of the possibilities of injustice, some states have abolished the common law right of distress and have not substituted a similar statutory right. [*See* Rest. 2d, Landlord & Tenant §12.1, statutory note, item 5c]

(2) Statutory distress [§990]

Statutes in many states have abolished the common law right of distress and have substituted therefor a statutory right similar to distress. These statutes usually *eliminate the self-help feature* (seizure by the landlord) or require peaceable entry. [*See* Rest. 2d, Landlord & Tenant §12.1, statutory note, item 5a]

(a) Constitutionality [§991]

The Constitution provides that no state shall deprive any person of his property without due process of law. Statutory or common law creditor remedies may be action by the state (*see* discussion of "state action" *supra*, §359). If so, these remedies must provide the debtor with due process. Principally, due process means that the debtor must have prior notice and a judicial hearing before property is taken. In the early 1970s, statutes providing a remedy of distress were held to be state action and unconstitutional if the tenant had *no prior notice and hearing* by a public official before the property was taken. [**Hall v. Garson,** 468 F.2d 845 (5th Cir. 1972)]

b. Statutory liens [§992]

Many states have statutes that create *liens* of one sort or another *on the tenant's personal property* located on the rented premises. [*See* Rest. 2d, Landlord & Tenant §12.1, statutory note, item 5] Some states create a general landlord's lien on all the tenant's personal property, which gives the landlord priority over other creditors; but no right to possession is conferred, and the landlord must institute judicial proceedings to foreclose her lien if the rent is in arrears. [**Jordan v. Talbot,** 55 Cal. 2d 597 (1961)]

c. Security deposits [§993]

Lease provisions commonly require the tenant to make a security deposit at the time the lease is executed to assure the tenant's performance. The landlord promises to return this money to the tenant at the end of the term if the tenant has not breached any covenant.

(1) Landlord is debtor [§994]

A security deposit creates a debtor-creditor relationship: The landlord owes the money to the tenant at the end of the lease. But the tenant, as a general creditor, has no priority over other creditors of the landlord. Statutes have been enacted in some states giving the tenant priority over any creditor with respect to the amount of the security deposit. Often the statutes state that the money is held by the landlord in trust or in escrow. [**Mallory Associates, Inc. v. Barving Realty Co.,** 300 N.Y. 297 (1949); Mich. Comp. Laws §554.604]

(2) On termination of lease [§995]

On the termination of the lease, the landlord must return to the tenant the amount of the security deposit that *exceeds the landlord's actual damages* (*e.g.,* cost of repossession and any unpaid rent). The tenant is due an accounting of the sum. [**Garcia v. Thong,** 895 P.2d 226 (N.M. 1995)]

(a) Interest [§996]

Statutes in some states require the landlord to pay the tenant interest on the sum held as a security deposit. [*See, e.g.,* N.Y. Gen. Oblig. Law §§7-103, 7-105] But there is no general common law rule that the landlord must pay interest.

(b) Liquidated damages [§997]

The lease may provide that the landlord may keep the sum deposited as liquidated damages. Such a provision is a penalty, however, and is enforceable *only if* actual damages are not readily ascertainable and the deposit is reasonably related to the probable damages.

(c) Penalty for not accounting [§998]

Statutes in some states penalize landlords for failing to give tenants an itemized list of deductions from the security deposit. For example, the URLTA provides that the tenant may recover the sum due him together with damages in an amount equal to twice the amount wrongfully withheld, plus reasonable attorneys' fees. [URLTA §2.101] These statutes sometimes apply to "prepaid rent" as well as to security deposits, if the purpose of the prepaid rent is to secure the tenant's performance.

(3) Distinguish—"bonus" [§999]

If a payment is made to the lessor as a bonus for executing the lease, with no provision for any rebate to the tenant at the end of the lease, the landlord may retain the entire sum. The tenant has no right to the return of any portion thereof.

(4) Distinguish—"prepaid rent" [§1000]

If the rent is prepaid for some future period (*e.g.,* prepayment of $500 for the last month's rent), the prepaid rent may be retained by the landlord if the tenant terminates the lease prematurely. *Rationale:* The parties may make the rent payable at any time, and under the rule of nonapportionment of rent (*supra,* §959), the advance payment belongs to the landlord on premature termination by the tenant. Because forfeiting prepaid rent looks like a penalty, courts may construe agreements, when possible, as security deposits (requiring repayment to the tenant) rather than prepaid rent.

d. Rent acceleration clause [§1001]

A standard lease usually contains a clause providing that the rent for the balance of the term shall become *payable in full on the tenant's default* in payment of rent or some other obligation. This is known as a rent acceleration clause. Most courts uphold a rent acceleration clause. [**Fifty States Management Corp. v. Pioneer Auto Parks, Inc.**, 46 N.Y.2d 573 (1979)] *Rationale:* Because the parties may contract for payment in advance of rent for the entire term, they have the right to contract that the entire rent shall become payable on the happening of a contingency. The Restatement adopts this position. [Rest. 2d, Landlord & Tenant §12.1, comment k]

(1) Landlord cannot terminate lease *and* accelerate rent [§1002]

If a landlord elects to accelerate rent, the landlord cannot terminate the lease and demand possession also. Nor can she retake possession on abandonment by the tenant and accelerate the rent. The landlord must choose to treat the tenant as a purchaser of the term for which she is demanding payment now by accelerating the rent, or choose to terminate the lease, thereby cancelling her claim for future rent. To allow the landlord to demand rent and at the same time take possession (equivalent in value to rent) would allow double recovery and be unconscionable.

---

e.g. **Example:** L leases a store to T for five years at $1,000 a year with a rent acceleration clause. After two years, T defaults. L can elect to terminate the lease or to hold T to the lease and accelerate the rent (with $3,000 being due on T's default). If L collects $3,000 from T and thereafter relets the store for T's benefit (*see infra*, §1034), L must account to T for the rent received from the new tenant.

---

e. Waiver of service and confession of judgment [§1003]

Standard form leases often provide that, on default in rent, the tenant waives the right of service of process and authorizes anyone to confess judgment on his behalf. If this clause is effective, the landlord can get a judgment against the tenant for the total rent due for the remainder of the lease plus the costs and attorneys' fees for the action *without the tenant receiving notice*. In most states, confession of judgment clauses are invalid. [*See, e.g.*, URLTA §1.403; Cal. Civ. Code §1953(a)]

2. Eviction of Tenant [§1004]

The landlord may wish to (i) evict the tenant *during the term of the lease* for nonpayment of rent or for other cause or (ii) evict the tenant who holds over *after the term expires*. The landlord's remedies may differ according to whether she is evicting during the term of the lease or after the lease expires. Her remedies are usually more limited during the term of the lease.

a. Termination for breach of covenant [§1005]

At old common law, the landlord had no power to terminate a lease if the tenant did not pay rent. The landlord's remedy was to sue for the rent due. [**Brown's Administrators v. Bragg**, 22 Ind. 122 (1864)] Statutes in most states now give the landlord *power to terminate a lease for nonpayment* of rent when due. As for other covenants, such as a covenant to repair, the independent covenants rule still applies, and the breach of a covenant by the tenant does *not give the landlord power* to terminate the lease and evict the tenant.

(1) Lease provisions [§1006]

In view of the independent covenants rule, almost all leases contain express provisions authorizing the landlord to terminate the lease on breach of *any covenant* by the tenant. The covenant might relate to payment of rent, repair, keeping dogs, making noise—whatever the tenant promises to do or not do. These provisions for termination are known as "forfeiture clauses." Forfeiture clauses are ordinarily construed as creating in the landlord an optional right of entry for breach of condition.

(a) Notice of default and time to cure [§1007]

Where nonpayment of rent is the basis of forfeiture, the landlord must *notify* the tenant of default and demand rent, and then give the tenant *a reasonable time to pay*. If the tenant does not pay within a reasonable time, the landlord then can notify the tenant that she has elected to terminate the lease. "Equity abhors a forfeiture," and requires the landlord, *before exercising her right of entry*, to alert the tenant to the consequences of his failure to pay. If the dependent covenants doctrine applies to other covenants (*e.g.*, a covenant to repair), it is likely that the courts will similarly require the landlord to request the tenant to perform and give him a reasonable time to do so before declaring a forfeiture. Restatement (Second) of Property, Landlord and Tenant section 13.1, comments h and k, so provide.

EXAM TIP   gilbert

For an exam question in which the landlord is trying to evict her tenant for breach of a covenant, check first to see if there is a lease, and if so, what the pertinent terms are. The lease may give the landlord the right to terminate the lease for many reasons. But if there is no relevant lease provision, remember that a tenant can be evicted **only for nonpayment of rent** (and not the breach of other covenants), and then **only if proper notice** procedures are followed.

(b) Trivial default [§1008]

Regardless of the language of the lease, the breach must be material or substantial to cause forfeiture. A trivial breach will not cause forfeiture. [**Foundation Development Corp. v. Loehmann's, Inc.**, 788 P.2d 1189 (Ariz. 1990)]

(2) Waiver [§1009]

The landlord may expressly or impliedly waive her right to terminate upon breach. The landlord's acceptance of rent from the tenant *with knowledge* of the breach is generally held to constitute such a waiver.

Example: T assigns the lease to X in breach of a covenant against assignment. Thereafter L accepts rent from X. L has waived the breach.

(a) Reliance on practice of waiver [§1010]

The landlord can waive the right to prompt payment by accepting delayed payment of rent. If the landlord does this several times, then she must warn the tenant that she will insist on prompt payment in the future before she can terminate the lease because of delayed payment.

b. Eviction through judicial process [§1011]

If the landlord is entitled to evict the tenant for breach of a covenant or for holding over at the end of a lease, the landlord may resort to the following judicial remedies.

(1) Suit in ejectment [§1012]

The landlord may bring an action in ejectment to recover possession of the premises. However, such an action does not take precedence over other civil litigation and may not come to trial for some time. As a result, a suit in ejectment is *rarely brought* by a landlord.

(2) Summary proceedings [§1013]

Every state has a *summary proceeding* whereby the landlord can recover possession quickly and at low cost. Often this proceeding is called an action for "forcible entry and detainer" or "unlawful detainer." It is called forcible entry because the tenant is viewed as having tortiously, or wrongfully, acquired possession by holding over. [*See* Rest. 2d, Landlord & Tenant §14.1, statutory note]

(a) Notice to quit [§1014]

Statutes usually require that before bringing a summary action, the landlord must give the tenant notice to quit, but the required notice may be very short (*e.g.*, three days) because it is assumed that the tenant knows that he is holding over unlawfully. If the landlord is terminating the lease under a forfeiture clause because of nonpayment of rent, the landlord usually must give the tenant notice that rent must be paid or the lease will be terminated after three days.

(b) Issues that can be raised [§1015]

Because the proceeding is summary, the issues that can be raised are very limited. The landlord must prove that the lease has terminated, or that she has lawfully exercised her right to forfeit for nonpayment of rent. It is sometimes said that the sole issue is whether the landlord or the tenant has the right to possession. [**People** *ex rel.* **Tuttle v. Walton,** 2 Thompson & Cook 533 (N.Y. 1874)]

1) Defenses [§1016]

The tenant can assert only those defenses which, if proven, would either preserve his possession as a tenant or preclude the landlord from recovering possession. The tenant cannot defend on the ground that the landlord had no title or that the lease was fraudulent, because, even if successful, the tenant would not be entitled to remain in possession. The landlord, as prior possessor, would have the superior right to possession. The tenant *can* defend on the ground that a landlord-tenant relationship does not exist because the lease is illegal, and therefore no rent is due, or that the landlord refused to accept a timely payment of rent.

2) Modern trend [§1017]

In recent cases, where the landlord has been in breach of a statutory duty to repair or an implied covenant of habitability, courts have permitted the tenant to defend on the ground that no rent is due. The theory is that the duty to pay rent is dependent upon the performance of the landlord's duty to maintain the property in habitable condition. [**Jack Spring, Inc. v. Little,** 280 N.E.2d 208 (Ill. 1972)] *Rationale:* Refusing summary eviction where the landlord is in breach of a duty of maintenance will give poor tenants a better bargaining position to enforce the landlord's repair obligations.

3) Constitutionality [§1018]

A state law that denies the tenant the right to defend on the ground that the landlord has breached her duty to repair is constitutional. Housing is not a fundamental right, and therefore no compelling state interest need be shown to justify the statute. [**Lindsey v. Normet,** 405 U.S. 56 (1972)]

(c) Not allowed for purpose of retaliation [§1019]

Eviction for the purpose of retaliating against the tenant's assertion of his rights regarding maintenance of the premises may be forbidden. (*See supra,* §§921 *et seq.*)

c. Self-help [§1020]

The states take various positions on whether self-help by the landlord is permissible. If it is not, the landlord is liable for damages to the tenant and his chattels if she resorts to self-help.

(1) Common law [§1021]

If the tenant had no right to continue in possession, the old common law permitted the use of such force as was necessary to expel the tenant. Because of too many breaches of the peace, the statute of 5 Richard II, ch. 8 (1381) made forcible entry by the landlord a crime. The criminal statute of Richard II has been accepted or reenacted in almost all American states. However, in civil suits, the courts did not change the rule that the landlord was not liable for using reasonable force.

(2) Reasonable force permitted [§1022]

In this country, a few states apparently still follow the common law rule that the landlord may use *reasonable force* to expel the tenant, without court process of any kind.

(3) Peaceable entry permitted [§1023]

Some jurisdictions hold that the landlord can enter only by *peaceable* means. But what is peaceable? Definitions vary considerably. Changing the locks and locking out the tenant has been held forcible, not peaceable. This effectively guts the self-help rule, as it is difficult to imagine circumstances that might be found peaceable if changing the locks is forcible.

(4) Self-help not permitted [§1024]

A growing number of states prohibit self-help in recovering possession and require the landlord to resort to a statutory remedy. If she does not, she is liable in damages. [**Berg v. Wiley,** 264 N.W.2d 145 (Minn. 1978); **Vasquez v. Glassboro Service Association,** 415 A.2d 1156 (N.J. 1980)]

(5) Lease provision authorizing self-help [§1025]

A lease may provide that the landlord is authorized to use self-help in retaking possession on the tenant's default. Most courts hold such a provision valid. A minority hold the provision void, as violating public policy against self-help. [**Jordan v. Talbot,** *supra*, §992]

3. Abandonment by Tenant [§1026]

If the tenant has no right to vacate the property but abandons it, the landlord may have several options: (i) *terminate* the lease; (ii) *let the premises lie idle and sue the tenant for rent* as it comes due; or (iii) *retake possession* and attempt to relet the premises. There is a great deal of conflict in the cases regarding the remedies available to the landlord.

a. Landlord terminates lease [§1027]

The landlord may terminate the lease on the tenant's abandonment; this effects a *surrender.* The tenant is liable only for rent accrued and for damages caused by the abandonment. The landlord's remedy of distress and the landlord's lien (*supra,* §§989-992) cease on termination of the lease. If the landlord keeps the lease alive under other options (below), these remedies do not cease.

(1) Common law rule—no damages for anticipatory repudiation [§1028]

The common law rule, applicable to leases but not to other contracts, is that the landlord cannot terminate the lease (rescind) and receive damages for anticipatory breach of contract. The theory is that a covenant to pay rent does not create an enforceable obligation until the rent is due. If the landlord terminates the lease prior to the due date, she is not entitled to the rent. Hence, if the landlord wants damages, the landlord must keep the lease alive, wait until rent is due, and then sue. This rule is still followed in some states.

(2) Anticipatory repudiation allowed [§1029]

In some states, anticipatory repudiation of the contract by the landlord is allowed when the tenant makes it clear he will pay no further rent. If allowed, the landlord's damages are determined by the difference between the rent agreed upon in the lease and the fair rental value over the balance of the term. [**Sagamore Corp. v. Willcutt,** 180 A. 464 (Conn. 1935)]

Example: T leases a building from L for five years at $1,000 a year. After two years, T abandons the building. L accepts the surrender and relets to another for $800 a year. Under the common law rule, T is not liable for the difference of $200 a year for three years (*i.e.,* $600), which is L's damage. If damages for anticipatory breach are allowed, L can recover $600 from T, discounted to its present value.

b. Landlord stands by and does nothing [§1030]

Under another option, the landlord may leave the premises vacant and sue the tenant for rent as it comes due under the lease.

(1) No duty to mitigate damages [§1031]

Under the older view the landlord does *not have any duty to mitigate* damages by finding another tenant. *Rationale:* The tenant has bought a term in the landlord's land. If the tenant chooses not to use it, it is not the landlord's fault. The tenant still owes the rent as it comes due. [**Gruman v. Investors Diversified Services, Inc.,** 78 N.W.2d 377 (Minn. 1956); **Holy Properties, Ltd. v. Kenneth Cole Productions, Inc.,** 87 N.Y.2d 130 (1995)]

Example: T leases a building from L for five years at $1,000 a year. After two years, T abandons the building. L does not reenter. L can sue T for the annual rent as it comes due.

(a) Criticism

This rule views the lease as a conveyance of property and is inconsistent with modern cases, which more and more view the lease as a contract. Moreover, it is wasteful of resources to permit the landlord to do nothing. Modern contract law imposes on promisees a duty to mitigate damages, reducing costs.

(2) Recent trend [§1032]

In a growing number of states, probably a majority, the landlord *has a duty to mitigate* damages. A lease is treated as any other kind of contract and is not viewed, on this issue, through property glasses. If the landlord must mitigate damages, the landlord cannot leave the premises vacant and sue for rent as it comes due. [**Sommer v. Kridel,** 378 A.2d 767 (N.J. 1977); **Lefrak v. Lambert,** 89 Misc. 2d 197 (1976); **United States National Bank v. Homeland, Inc.,** 631 P.2d 761 (Or. 1981); *and see* URLTA §4.203—landlord must mitigate damages]

(3) Rent acceleration clause [§1033]

To avoid the rule that the landlord must wait to sue for rent as it falls due, a rent acceleration clause is often inserted in the lease. It provides that the rent for the balance of the term shall become payable in full on the tenant's default of payment of rent or some other obligation. Most courts hold these clauses valid. (*See supra,* §1001.)

c. Landlord repossesses and relets [§1034]

Instead of standing by, the landlord may *reenter and repossess* the property for the purpose of renting it out to another tenant. Indeed, if the landlord must mitigate damages (*see supra,* §1032), the landlord must repossess. On the other hand, if the landlord has no duty to mitigate damages and the landlord reenters, the cases go two ways. In some jurisdictions, repossession deprives the tenant of possession and effects a surrender (*see supra,* §1027). If it does, the tenant is excused from further rent liability, but not necessarily from liability for damages. [**Lennon v. United States Theatre Corp.,** 920 F.2d 996 (D.C. Cir. 1990)] In other jurisdictions this effects a surrender only if the landlord intends to terminate the lease; otherwise the landlord is acting as agent for the tenant in reletting.

J. Assignment and Subletting

1. Assignment [§1035]

Unless the lease prohibits it, a tenant or landlord may freely transfer his interest in the premises. At common law, if the tenant transfers the *entire remaining term* of his leasehold, he has made an assignment, and the assignee comes into *privity of estate* with the landlord. Privity of estate makes the landlord and the assignee *liable to each other on the covenants* in the original lease that run with the land. Similarly, if the landlord assigns the reversion, the assignee and the tenant are in privity of estate.

Example: L leases to T. T promises to pay $200 a month rent. T assigns the leasehold to T2. L can sue T2 on the promise to pay $200 a month rent. They are in privity of estate with each other.

a. Privity of estate [§1036]

Privity of estate is an ancient concept developed to give the landlord the right to sue the assignee of the tenant on the covenants in the lease, and to give the assignee the right to sue the landlord on her covenants. In the example above,

T promises to pay $200 a month rent. After assignment, L cannot sue T2 on a theory of privity of *contract* because T2 did not make the promise to L. To circumvent the lack of privity of contract, the courts invented the concept of *privity of estate*. An assignee of the tenant is said to be in privity of estate and is liable on the covenants in the lease. Similarly, the landlord is liable to the assignee on the landlord's covenants (*e.g.*, the covenant to repair). If, in the above example, L assigns her reversion to L2, *L2 is in privity of estate with T2*, and each is liable to the other on the covenants in the lease. Hence, parties who are in privity of estate have a landlord and tenant relationship.

(1) Privity of contract [§1037]

If there is privity of contract (*i.e.*, the plaintiff and defendant have agreed with each other to do or not do certain things), their obligations bind them regardless of whether they are in privity of estate. Thus, in the above example, after the assignment, L can sue T on his promise to pay rent, because T made the promise to L. L and T are in privity of contract. [**Samuels v. Ottinger,** 169 Cal. 209 (1915)] L can *also sue* T2 on the promise because L and T2 are in privity of estate. Being able to sue two persons is, of course, an advantage to L, because one of them, T or T2, might be judgment proof or difficult to get into court.

EXAM TIP   **gilbert**

Many students find the terms "privity of contract" and "privity of estate" confusing, but the terms are not that difficult to understand. The basic things you need to know are:

Privity of contract is simply the term used to describe why the original landlord and tenant are liable to each other—as *parties to the contract*.

$$L \xleftrightarrow{\text{contract}} T$$

Privity of estate is the term used to describe why an assignee and an original party to the contract are liable to each other—the *assignee takes the estate his assignor had*. In effect there is a *new landlord-tenant relationship* between the assignee and the other party to the original contract.

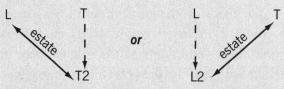

If *a tenant's assignee breaches* a covenant in the lease (*e.g.,* fails to pay rent), the landlord can sue the assignee because of privity of estate and can *also sue the original tenant* because of privity of contract. (Likewise, if the landlord's assignee breaches, the tenant can sue the assignee and the original landlord.)

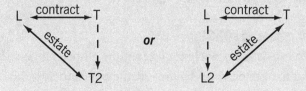

---

2. Sublease Distinguished from Assignment [§1038]

The common law rule is that if a tenant transfers *less than the entire remaining term* of his leasehold, he has made a sublease, and he becomes the landlord of the sublessee. The sublessee *is not in privity of estate* with the landlord and cannot sue or be sued by the landlord. [**Neal v. Craig Brown, Inc.**, 356 S.E.2d 912 (N.C. 1987)] Because the sublessee has made *no contract with the landlord*, he cannot sue or be sued on a contract either. The crucial question, then, is: When is a transfer an assignment and when is it a sublease?

COMPARISON OF ASSIGNMENTS AND SUBLEASES			gilbert
	ASSIGNMENT BY LANDLORD	**ASSIGNMENT BY TENANT**	**SUBLEASE BY TENANT**
CONSENT	Tenant's consent not required.	Landlord's consent may be required by lease.	Landlord's consent may be required by lease.
PRIVITY OF ESTATE	Assignee and tenant are in privity of estate.	Assignee and landlord are in privity of estate.	Sublessee and landlord are *not in privity of estate*. Original tenant remains in privity of estate with landlord.
PRIVITY OF CONTRACT	Assignee and tenant are *not in privity of contract*. Original landlord and tenant remain in privity of contract.	Assignee and landlord are *not in privity of contract*. Original tenant and landlord remain in privity of contract.	Sublessee and landlord are *not in privity of contract*. Original tenant remains in privity of contract with landlord.
LIABILITY FOR COVENANTS IN LEASE	Assignee liable to tenant on all covenants that run with the land because of privity of estate.	Assignee liable to landlord on all covenants that run with the land because of privity of estate.	Sublessee is *not personally liable* on any covenants in the original lease and *cannot enforce* the landlord's covenants.
	Original landlord remains liable to original tenant on *all* covenants in the lease because of privity of contract.	Original tenant remains liable for rent and *all* other covenants in the lease because of privity of contract.	Original tenant remains liable for rent and *all* other covenants in the lease and can enforce the landlord's covenants.

a. Reversion retained [§1039]

At common law, a transfer by a tenant is a sublease if the tenant *retains a reversion* in the property after the transfer. If the tenant does not retain a reversion, the transfer is an assignment. A reversion is a period of time within the term of the leasehold when the tenant will again be entitled to possession; *i.e.,* the tenant has not transferred the entire remaining term of the leasehold. The common law position is still adhered to in many states. [**Krasner v. Transcontinental Equities, Inc.,** 70 A.D.2d 312 (1979)]

---

e.g. **Example:** L leases to T for 10 years. One month later, T transfers a nine-year term to T2. This is a sublease, because T retains a reversion (T will be entitled to possession after T2's nine years are up). T is T2's landlord. L is not in privity of estate with T2. L cannot sue T2 on covenants in the original lease, and T2 cannot sue L.

---

b.   Right of entry retained [§1040]

Suppose that the tenant transfers the leasehold to another tenant and does not retain a reversion, but retains a *right of entry* if a covenant is breached. The typical case is where the tenant transfers the entire remainder of his term to another, at a higher rent than he is paying, with a right to reenter if the rent is not paid.

(1)   Application

L leases to T for 10 years with rent of $200 a month. Five years later, T transfers the remainder of the term to T2 for a rent of $250 a month. T retains the right to reenter and retake possession if T2 does not pay the rent promised. (This right is reserved in a forfeiture clause, discussed *supra,* §1006.) Is the transfer to T2 an assignment or a sublease?

(a)   Common law view [§1041]

The common law view is that such a transfer is an *assignment*, not a sublease, because T retained no reversion. The right of entry reserved by T is viewed as merely a means of enforcing T2's contractual obligations. Because it is an assignment, there is privity of estate between L and T2, so that L can hold T2 personally liable for the rent reserved in the L to T lease ($200 per month).

(b)   Modern view—right of entry makes it a sublease [§1042]

A substantial number of modern cases hold that such a transfer is a *sublease*, and not an assignment. The reservation of the right to reenter for nonpayment of rent is deemed a "contingent reversionary interest," so that the transfer is a sublease even though no actual reversion is retained by T. Because it is a sublease, there is no privity of estate between L and T2. Thus, if T2 fails to pay the rent, L cannot sue him directly. [**Davis v. Vidal,** 151 S.W. 290 (Tex. 1912)] This is the position of the Restatement. [Rest. 2d, Landlord & Tenant §15.1, comment i]

1)   Landlord's remedies [§1043]

This does not mean that L is without a remedy. L can *sue T for rent* based on privity of contract. L can *evict T2* for breach of the promise to pay rent made in the L to T lease as readily as he could evict T. The distinction is that because this is only a sublease, there is no privity of estate, and hence L cannot hold T2 *personally* liable for rent.

c. Minority view—intention controls [§1044]

A few recent cases have rejected both the common law rule that retention of a reversion is necessary for a sublease and the rule that retention of a right of entry is sufficient to create a sublease. These cases hold that the *intent* of the parties determines whether a transfer is an assignment or a sublease, and that reservation of an additional rent by itself is an indication that the parties intended a sublease. On the other hand, the transfer of the lease for a lump sum, even if payment is to be made in deferred installments, indicates an assignment. [**Jaber v. Miller,** 239 S.W.2d 760 (Ark. 1951); **Ernst v. Conditt,** 390 S.W.2d 703 (Tenn. 1964)]

3. Duty to Pay Rent [§1045]

A promise to pay rent is a covenant running with the land, which means the promisee can sue any person on the covenant with whom she is in privity of estate. Covenants running with the land are discussed more fully below, but the promise to pay rent is such an important covenant that it is singled out here for special attention. The general rule is that a landlord can sue for rent any person who is either in *privity of contract* with the landlord as to the rent obligation, *or* who has come into *privity of estate* with the landlord so as to be bound by the rental covenants in the lease.

a. Assignment [§1046]

As already indicated, an assignment establishes privity of estate between the landlord and the assignee; thus, the *assignee is personally liable* for the rent even though no mention is made of it in the assignment.

(1) Liability of original tenant [§1047]

Although the assignee is liable for the rent, the *original tenant also remains liable* for the rent, in the event the assignee fails to pay, because the original tenant *contracted* with the landlord. The assignment terminates his interest in the leasehold, but does not affect his contractual liability to the landlord. [**Samuels v. Ottinger,** *supra*, §1037]

---

e.g. **Example:** L leases to T. T promises to pay rent. T assigns his leasehold to T2. T2 is liable for the rent provided in the L to T lease. L can also sue T for rent because T remains liable on his promise to pay rent.

(a) T is surety [§1048]

When the assignee, T2, becomes liable for the rent, he is *primarily* liable because he has the benefit of possession. The original tenant's,

T's, liability, based on privity of contract, is *secondary*. This means that, although L can sue either T or T2, if T has to pay, he can seek recovery from T2. T is said to be a surety. According to the rules of suretyship, if T2 and L materially change the terms of the lease, so as to prejudice T, T is released as a surety. [**Gerber v. Pecht,** 104 A.2d 41 (N.J. 1954)]

(b) Release by landlord [§1049]

The only way T can escape his duty to pay rent is by an express or implied *release* from his promise to L. The mere fact that L consents to the assignment and accepts rent from T2 is not an implied release of T. These acts give L additional rights against T2, but from them, one *cannot* infer an intent to give up her rights against T.

(c) Novation [§1050]

If L consents to the assignment to T2 and *releases* T and, in exchange for the release, T2 undertakes the promises in the lease, there is a *novation*. A novation is a new contract between L and T2, and the previous contract between L and T is extinguished. T is now out of the picture, and there is now privity of contract *and* privity of estate between L and T2.

(2) Liability of assignee [§1051]

The assignee, T2, is liable only for the rent accruing during the time he holds the leasehold. He is not liable for rent accruing prior to the assignment, nor for rent accruing after he reassigns—because the effect of any reassignment is to terminate the privity of estate with L. [**Reid v. Weissner & Sons Brewing Co.,** 40 A. 877 (Md. 1898); **A.D. Juilliard & Co. v. American Woolen Co.,** 32 A.2d 800 (R.I. 1943)]

(a) Application

L leases land to T for $200 a month. T becomes one month in arrears. T then assigns the leasehold to T2, who becomes four months in arrears. T2 assigns to T3, reserving a rent of $250 a month.

1) L recovers from T3 [§1052]

L can recover $200 a month from T3 for the time T3 is assignee. During this time, L and T3 are in privity of estate. (L cannot recover the extra $50 reserved in the assignment to T3.)

2) L recovers from T2 [§1053]

L can recover $800 from T2 because during the four months of default L and T2 were in privity of estate. [**First American National Bank v. Chicken System of America, Inc.,** 616 S.W.2d 156 (Tenn. 1980)]

3) L recovers from T [§1054]

L can recover $1,000 (five months' rent in default) from T because the parties are in privity of contract. In turn, T is *subrogated* to L's claim against T2 for the rental in arrears during the time that T2 held the leasehold, so that T could recover $800 from T2 if T pays L the rent due for these four months.

b. Sublease [§1055]

If the tenant subleases, the sublessee is *not personally liable* to the landlord for rent.

(1) Rationale

There is neither privity of contract nor privity of estate between the landlord and the sublessee. The tenant-sublessor, of course, remains obligated to pay rent. If he does not pay, the landlord can terminate the lease and oust the sublessee. To prevent such ouster and forfeiture of the master lease, the sublessee may pay the landlord the rent due her from the tenant-sublessor (and offset this against any rental provided in the sublease).

c. Third-party beneficiary suits [§1056]

If an assignee or sublessee expressly *assumes the covenants of the master lease*, the assignee or sublessee is directly liable to the landlord, who is a third-party beneficiary of the contract between the tenant and his assignee or sublessee. The liability of the assignee or sublessee for performance of his promise continues, even though there is a further assignment of the leasehold. [**First American National Bank v. Chicken System of America, Inc.,** *supra*]

Example: L leases to T. T sublets to T2, who promises to perform all obligations of T under the lease from L. T2 later assigns his interest to T3, who fails to pay the rent. L can sue T2 for the rent owed by T3. Having expressly assumed the lease obligations, T2 is bound to perform his contract notwithstanding the assignment of his entire interest to another.

---

4. Covenants Against Assignment or Sublease [§1057]

Unless there is a covenant to the contrary, a leasehold is *freely transferable* by the tenant. It may be assigned or sublet without the landlord's consent.

a. Express covenants [§1058]

Many landlords insist that the lease contain a covenant against transfers by the tenant. Such a covenant is valid, but, being a restraint on the transfer of land, it is *strictly construed.* Thus, a covenant "not to assign" does not prevent the tenant from subleasing, and a covenant "not to sublease" does not prevent an assignment. A transfer by will or by operation of law without a will is not a breach of the covenant; nor is an involuntary transfer (*e.g.*, by execution or bankruptcy). [**Krasner v. Transcontinental Equities, Inc.**, *supra*, §1039]

b. Arbitrary denial of consent [§1059]

If the lease contains a covenant against transfer without the landlord's consent, the older view is that the landlord *may arbitrarily refuse to accept* a new tenant. She has no duty to mitigate damages, as an ordinary contracting party does under ordinary contract principles. The property conception of a lease as a conveyance of a term prevails. [**Gruman v. Investors Diversified Services, Inc.**, *supra* §1031; **21 Merchants Row Corp. v. Merchants Row, Inc.**, 587 N.E.2d 788 (Mass. 1992)—commercial leases; **Slavin v. Rent Control Board of Brookline**, 548 N.E.2d 1226 (Mass. 1990)—residential lease; **Dress Shirt Sales, Inc. v. Hotel Martinique Associates**, 12 N.Y.2d 339 (1963)]

Example: L leases a building to T for $2,000 a month for 10 years. T cannot make a profit in his business after two years. T produces X, a highly satisfactory and suitable person, and proposes that L agree that T can sublet to X for $1,750 a month. (This will cut T's losses to $250 a month.) L can refuse to accept X for any reason except an illegal reason such as violation of the civil rights laws.

---

(1) Minority view [§1060]

In a growing number of jurisdictions, the landlord's denial of consent must be *reasonable*. [**Kendall v. Ernest Pestana, Inc.**, 40 Cal. 3d 488 (1985)] This is the position taken by the Restatement. [Rest. 2d, Landlord & Tenant §15.2]

(2) What is reasonable? [§1061]

Where a lease provides that the landlord may not unreasonably withhold her consent or a court reads that into a lease, what factors determine what is reasonable? Courts have applied an objective test to determine whether the landlord is acting *as a reasonably prudent person* in withholding consent. The landlord may look at factors such as the financial responsibility of the proposed new tenant and his suitability for the building, but the landlord cannot consider her general economic advantage (*i.e.*, she cannot refuse consent as a stratagem to get T to terminate the lease). [**Kendall v. Ernest Pestana, Inc.**, *supra*; **Palmer v. 309 East 87th Street Co.**, 112 Misc. 2d 667 (1982)]

c. Waiver of covenant [§1062]

The landlord may expressly or, by her acts, impliedly waive the covenant against assignment of sublease. Implied waiver usually occurs when the landlord accepts rent from the assignees with the knowledge of the assignment.

(1) Rule in Dumpor's Case [§1063]

Where the landlord expressly consents to one assignment, the Rule in **Dumpor's Case** [76 Eng. Rep. 1110 (K.B. 1578)] states that the covenant thereafter becomes unenforceable. The rationale is that the covenant is single, and *once waived, the covenant is destroyed.*

(a) Criticism

The Rule makes no sense, as the obvious purpose of such a covenant is to assure the landlord that a responsible tenant is in possession throughout the term of the lease. Nonetheless, the Rule has been retained by many courts in this country, although it is now abolished by statute in England. The Restatement rejects the Rule. [Rest. 2d, Landlord & Tenant §16.1, comment g]

(b) Exceptions [§1064]

There are numerous exceptions to the Rule in Dumpor's Case, developed in attempts to avoid a questionable rule, of which the following are the most prominent:

1) Covenant binding lessee and assigns [§1065]

If the covenant not to assign without the landlord's consent is expressed as binding on the lessee *and his assigns*, an assignment by the lessee with consent of the landlord does not free the assignee from the binding force of the covenant. [**Childs v. Warner Bros. Southern Theatres, Inc.**, 156 S.E. 923 (N.C. 1931)]

2) Landlord's limited consent [§1066]

If the landlord, when consenting, expressly states that her consent is to this assignment only and not to future assignments as well, the Rule in Dumpor's Case does not apply.

5. Covenants Running to Assignees

a. Introduction [§1067]

For the landlord to be able to enforce a covenant in the lease against the tenant's assignee, or for the tenant to be able to enforce a covenant in the lease against the landlord's assignee, the following requirements must be met. [*See* Rest. 2d, Landlord & Tenant §§16.1, 16.2]

(1) Intention [§1068]

The parties to the lease must intend that the covenant run to assigns.

(2) Privity of estate [§1069]

The assignee must be in either privity of estate or privity of contract with the person who is suing or being sued. Privity of estate means, generally speaking, that the person succeeded to the estate of a party to the

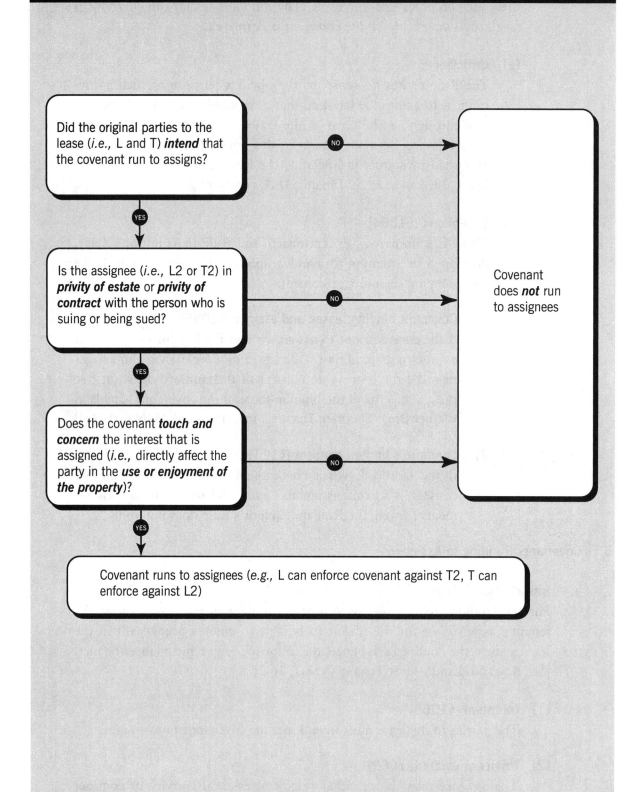

Did the original parties to the lease (*i.e.,* L and T) ***intend*** that the covenant run to assigns?

NO

Is the assignee (*i.e.,* L2 or T2) in ***privity of estate*** or ***privity of contract*** with the person who is suing or being sued?

NO

Does the covenant ***touch and concern*** the interest that is assigned (*i.e.,* directly affect the party in the ***use or enjoyment of the property***)?

NO

YES

YES

YES

Covenant does ***not*** run to assignees

Covenant runs to assignees (*e.g.,* L can enforce covenant against T2, T can enforce against L2) contract. (*See* discussion *supra*, §1036.) If the assignee has *promised* to perform the covenant (*see supra*, §1056), the assignee's liability rests on privity of contract as well as on privity of estate.

(3) Touch and concern [§1070]

The covenant must touch and concern the interest that is assigned, be it the leasehold or the reversion. "Touch and concern" means, basically, that the covenant directly affects the party *in the use or enjoyment of the property*.

(a) Two ends to covenant—burden and benefit [§1071]

There are two "ends" to a covenant, the burden end and the benefit end. Whoever makes the promise has the burden end. Whoever has the benefit of the promise has the benefit end. For the burden or benefit end to run to assignees, the promise must touch and concern the interest of the assignee.

Example: L leases to T. T promises to repair. T assigns his leasehold to T2. If L sues T2 on the covenant to repair, L must show that the *burden* touches and concerns the leasehold. If L assigned the reversion to L2, who sued T2, L2 would have to show also that the *benefit* touches and concerns the reversion.

(b) Generally both burden and benefit touch and concern leased land [§1072]

In the great majority of covenants in leases, if *either end* touches and concerns, *the other will* too, because the covenant will have some direct relationship to the use or enjoyment of the leased property in which both parties have an interest. The covenant to pay rent, *e.g.*, touches and concerns the leasehold because it is the price paid for possession. It touches and concerns the reversion because it directly affects the value of (enjoyment of) the reversion.

(c) Personal covenant [§1073]

If a covenant does *not touch and concern* the promisor's interest, it is personal to the promisor. The promisor continues to be liable on the personal promise after assignment if the parties so intend.

b. Covenant to do or not to do a physical act on the leased premises [§1074]

Covenants to do or not to do a physical act include covenants to repair, to conduct business in a certain manner, not to remove fixtures, to furnish heat, and to deliver up premises in good condition.

(1) Runs with leasehold [§1075]

A covenant by the *tenant or by the landlord* to do or refrain from doing a physical act *on the leased premises* touches and concerns the *leasehold* and runs with it.

> **e.g** **Example:** L leases property to T for one year. T covenants to repair. T assigns to T2. L can enforce the covenant to repair against T2. If L rather than T had covenanted to repair, T2 could have enforced the covenant against L. The covenant runs with the leasehold.

(2) Runs with reversion [§1076]

If the landlord or tenant makes a covenant to do or not do a physical act *on the leased land*, such as to furnish heat or to repair, the covenant runs to assigns of the reversion.

c. Covenant to pay money [§1077]

A covenant to pay money touches and concerns if it is paid for an improvement on the property or to protect the property to make it more valuable. Similarly, a covenant to pay taxes or insurance, which protects both landlord and tenant, runs both with the leasehold and reversion. [Rest. 2d, Landlord & Tenant §16.1, comment b, illus. 8]

d. Tenant's covenant to insure for benefit of landlord

(1) Insurance proceeds used for rebuilding [§1078]

A covenant by the tenant to insure the property touches and concerns *if* the lease requires the landlord to use the insurance proceeds for rebuilding. In that case, the insurance proceeds are substituted for the building leased.

(2) Insurance proceeds not used for rebuilding [§1079]

If the insurance proceeds can be pocketed by the landlord, who does not have to rebuild, the covenant is personal and does not touch and concern. [**Masury v. Southworth,** 9 Ohio St. 340 (1859); **Burton v. Chesapeake Box & Lumber Corp.,** 57 S.E.2d 904 (Va. 1950)]

(a) Restatement position [§1080]

The Restatement takes the position that a promise to insure touches and concerns even though the landlord does not have to use the proceeds to rebuild. The Restatement says the promise touches and concerns the tenant's leasehold because it affects his use and enjoyment (it is affected by the disaster insured against). It touches and concerns the landlord's reversionary interest because it enhances its value. [Rest. 2d, Landlord & Tenant §16.1, comment b, illus. 8]

e. Promise to arbitrate disputes [§1081]

A promise to arbitrate disputes arising under a lease touches and concerns the land. [**Abbott v. Bob's U-Drive,** 352 P.2d 598 (Or. 1960)]

f. Implied covenants [§1082]

An implied covenant, such as the covenant of quiet enjoyment or an implied warranty of habitability, can be enforced against whoever is the landlord at the time the covenant is breached. If L transfers the reversion to L2, L is not liable for a breach of the covenant occurring after the transfer.

Chapter Seven: Easements and Covenants

CONTENTS

Chapter Approach

Landowners often want to make agreements with their neighbors respecting the use of one or both of the parcels of land. These agreements can be divided into two broad categories: (i) rights arising from a *grant* of a right by one landowner to another (known as *easements* or *profits*), and (ii) rights arising from a *promise* respecting the use of land by one landowner to another (known as a *real covenant* or an *equitable servitude*). These rights are frequently found in subdivision developments and in condominiums, as well as between neighboring landowners.

1. **Easements**

   The most important questions about easements relate to their *creation* and *termination*. An easement can be created by an express agreement, by estoppel, by implication from an existing use when land is divided, by necessity when land is divided, and by prescription. Pay particular attention to the requirements that must be met to have an easement of the designated type.

2. **Real Covenants**

   The most important issue about real covenants is whether they will *run to assignees*. Privity of estate is required for the covenant to run. Privity is a difficult concept. Concentrate on it and get it straight. Remember also that the remedy for breach of a real covenant is *damages*.

3. **Equitable Servitudes**

   The most important issues about equitable servitudes relate to creation, enforcement by assignees or third parties, and termination. Note that unlike real covenants, equitable servitudes can be *implied* from a *general plan*. The rules for the running of equitable servitudes to assignees are technical and you should master them. Privity of estate is *not* required, but the covenant must touch and concern and, generally, the benefit must be to neighboring land. Also, look carefully at whether the assignee has notice of the covenant when she buys, for if she does not, she is not bound by the covenant. The remedy for breach of an equitable servitude is an *injunction* or enforcement of a *lien*.

The law in this chapter is technical, but if you concentrate on how these servitudes may be created, when they bind assignees, and when they may be terminated, you will be well prepared for any such question on your exam.

A. Easements

1. Introduction

a. Definition [§1083]

An easement is a grant of an interest in land that entitles a person to *use* land possessed by another.

b. Types of easements [§1084]

Easements are either affirmative or negative.

(1) Affirmative easement [§1085]

The owner of an affirmative easement (sometimes called a positive easement) has the right to *go onto* the land of another (the "servient land") and do some act on the land. Most easements are affirmative. For example, when O, the owner of Blackacre, grants to A a right of way across Blackacre, an affirmative easement has been created.

(2) Negative easement [§1086]

The owner of a negative easement can *prevent* the owner of the servient land from doing some act on the servient land. Negative easements are rare and are dealt with *infra*, §§1184 *et seq.*

c. Easements appurtenant or in gross [§1087]

All easements are either appurtenant to other land or in gross.

(1) Easement appurtenant [§1088]

If an easement *benefits* its owner *in the use of another tract of land*, it is appurtenant to that land. The land benefited is called the *dominant tenement*; the land burdened is the *servient tenement*. The servient tenement usually is, but does not have to be, adjacent to the dominant tenement.

---

e.g. **Example:** Whiteacre is located between Blackacre and a public road. O, owner of Whiteacre, conveys to A, owner of Blackacre, a right to cross Whiteacre to reach the public road. The easement over Whiteacre is appurtenant to Blackacre (the dominant tenement).

(a) Passes with dominant tenement [§1089]

An easement appurtenant is attached to the dominant tenement and ordinarily passes with the tenement to any subsequent owner of the tenement. In the above example, the benefit of the easement across Whiteacre will pass to any subsequent owner of Blackacre.

1) Exception—personal easement [§1090]

If the grant of an easement creates appropriate limiting terms, however, it will not pass to subsequent owners of the dominant tenement.

(e.g.) Example: O, owner of Whiteacre, grants a right of way over his land to his neighbor, A, owner of Blackacre. The conveyance provides that the right of way shall exist "only so long as A lives on Blackacre." This easement is appurtenant but also *personal*. If A sells Blackacre to B, the easement terminates and B has no right of way. Nor does A, because A no longer lives on Blackacre.

---

(2) Easement in gross [§1091]

If an easement does not benefit its owner in the use and enjoyment of his land, but merely *gives him the right to use the servient land*, the easement is in gross. "In gross" is the term used to signify that the benefit of the easement is not appurtenant to other land. An appurtenant easement cannot be separated from its dominant tenement and turned into an easement in gross, unless the owners of the dominant and servient tenements make a new agreement permitting that. An easement in gross usually can be assigned if the parties so intend. (*See infra*, §1169.)

(e.g.) Example: O, owner of Greenacre, grants to Heylook Billboard Co. the right to erect a sign on Greenacre. Heylook owns no land. The easement is in gross and can be assigned by Heylook if the parties so intend. If O sells Greenacre to A, the burden of the easement passes with the ownership to A. [**Baseball Publishing Co. v. Bruton,** *supra*, §764]

EXAM TIP	**gilbert**

The term "in gross" means only that the easement is *not appurtenant*. It does not mean that the easement is personal to the holder and cannot be assigned.

---

(3) Easement appurtenant favored [§1092]

If an instrument creating an easement is ambiguous, courts generally construe it as creating an easement appurtenant to land rather than an easement in gross. [**Martin v. Music,** 254 S.W.2d 701 (Ky. 1953); **Burcky v. Knowles,** 413 A.2d 585 (N.H. 1980); **Maranatha Settlement Association v. Evans,** 122 A.2d 679 (Pa. 1956); **Mitchell v. Castellaw,** 246 S.W.2d 163 (Tex. 1952); **Green v. Lupo,** 647 P.2d 51 (Wash. 1982)]

(a) Rationale

An appurtenant easement is favored for several reasons. *First, intent.* The parties usually have in mind that the easement will benefit a *tract* of land. In addition, if the benefit of the easement will be more useful to a successor owner of that tract than to the original owner of the easement after he sells the tract, this indicates the parties intended an appurtenant easement. *Second, land value is increased.* An easement appurtenant increases the value of the dominant land, presumably by more than it decreases the value of the servient land. To purchase an easement, the buyer will have to pay something more than the damage to the servient tenement in order to strike a bargain with the seller. Thus, an easement appurtenant increases the total value of land. An easement in gross does not increase the value of any land, and it in fact decreases the total value of land by the amount of damage to the servient tenement.

 Example: A, owner of Blackacre, wants to purchase an easement of way across Whiteacre, owned by O. Such an easement will increase the value of Blackacre by $100; it will damage Whiteacre by $60. At a price somewhere between $60 and $100, O and A will strike a bargain that will make them both better off. If O sells the easement for $75, the total value of land has increased by $40. O has made a gain of $15 (the amount O receives in excess of his damage), and A has made a gain of $25 (the amount the easement is worth to A less what A pays). If A owns no land, so that the easement is in gross, the total value of land would be decreased by the amount of damage to Whiteacre ($60).

---

d. Interest in land [§1093]

An easement is an interest in land. This means, among other things, that the burden passes to subsequent owners of the servient land. The owner of an easement does not have merely contract rights against the original grantor of the easement, but also has rights against all successors to the grantor.

e. Distinguish—profit [§1094]

A profit (or profit a prendre) is the right to *take something off* another person's land that is part of the land or a product of the land. Profits include crops, timber, minerals, wild game, and fish. When a profit is granted, an easement to go on the land and remove the subject matter is implied. The rules applicable to easements generally apply to profits.

f. Distinguish—license [§1095]

A license is *permission* to go on land belonging to the licensor. Licenses are very common: The plumber repairing a stopped-up drain, UPS delivering packages, and guests at a party all have licenses. A license can be oral or in writing. A license generally is *revocable* at the will of the licensor.

Example: O tells A that A can park on O's land. O's oral license gives A permission to park. O can revoke the license at any time.

---

(1) Construction [§1096]

Cases sometimes arise where the issue is whether a person has a license or an easement in gross. For example, an apartment house owner may give A the sole and exclusive right to install and maintain laundry machines in the owner's apartment house. If this is a license, it is not binding on a new owner of the apartment house; but if it is an easement, it is binding on a new owner who has notice of it. Reflecting a hostility to easements in gross, which clog title, courts usually construe agreements such as these, which do not give A exclusive possession of any definite space, as licenses. [**Todd v. Krolick,** 96 A.D.2d 695 (1983)]

(2) Irrevocable licenses [§1097]

A license may become irrevocable in certain limited situations.

(a) License coupled with an interest [§1098]

A license coupled with an interest cannot be revoked. A license coupled with an interest is one that gives the licensee the right to remove a chattel of the licensee, which is on the licensor's land. Thus, if O sells A a car located on O's land, A has an irrevocable license to enter and remove the car.

(b) Estoppel [§1099]

A license may become irrevocable under the rules of estoppel. If the licensee has constructed substantial improvements on either the licensor's land or the licensee's land, relying on the license, in many states the licensor is estopped from revoking the license. The theory is that it would be unfair to the licensee to permit revocation after he spends money in reliance. [**Camp v. Milam,** 277 So. 2d 95 (Ala. 1973); **Stoner v. Zucker,** 148 Cal. 516 (1906); **Holbrook v. Taylor,** 532 S.W.2d 763 (Ky. 1976); *but compare* **Rase v. Castle Mountain Ranch, Inc.,** 631 P.2d 680 (Mont. 1981)]

---

e.g. **Example:** O gives an adjoining property owner, A, oral permission to go on O's land and erect a tile drain thereon to protect A's property from natural water drainage. A does so at substantial expense and with O's knowledge. O is estopped now to revoke permission. [**Ricenbaw v. Kraus,** 61 N.W.2d 350 (Neb. 1953)]

---

1) Criticism

When a court estops O in the preceding example, it is giving the entitlement to A at no cost, and permitting A to damage O to the extent of O's actual loss in value. O, being a good neighbor and casually saying yes, may not have realized the amount of damage he would suffer. Perhaps a fairer remedy would be to permit A to continue the license on payment of damages to O. This remedy would mean that the good neighbor who gave permission not anticipating any great harm by the license would not suffer any actual loss.

2) How long irrevocable [§1100]

The First Restatement of Property says that irrevocability exists only for whatever time is required to enable the licensee to reap the fruits of his expenditures. [Rest. §519] Some courts have held that irrevocability is limited to the life of the pertinent structure or improvement. A few courts hold that an irrevocable license is like an easement and is capable of lasting forever. [**Cooke v. Ramponi,** 38 Cal. 2d 282 (1952)]

3) Minority view—estoppel rejected [§1101]

Some courts hold that the licensor will not be estopped to revoke the license. *Rationale:* An oral irrevocable license, like an oral easement, falls within the Statute of Frauds. Refusing to enforce the oral agreement induces the parties to reduce their agreement to writing, avoiding lawsuits over oral statements and ambiguous expectations. Moreover, in fairness, a writing should be required so that the good neighbor who gives casual permission, without thinking of the permanent damage to his land, will not be bound. [**Croasdale v. Lanigan,** 129 N.Y. 604 (1892)]

(3) Theatre tickets [§1102]

A theatre ticket is something of an anomaly. A theatre ticket is a contract between the theatre owner and the buyer entitling the buyer to see a performance in a designated seat. The ticket, which is a memorandum that might satisfy the Statute of Frauds, could be held to create an easement, but this would give the ticket holder the right to use self-help to enter and to eject someone sitting in her seat. Courts have held that a ticket creates a revocable license, but this is not an interest in land so as to permit self-help. The ticket holder can be denied admission or ejected by the theatre owner. Her remedy is to sue the theatre owner for breach of contract. *Rationale:* The theatre owner does not want to incur ill will, is likely to be fair in settling disputes between patrons, and is the most efficient "order keeper" in the situation. [**Marrone v. Washington Jockey Club,** 227 U.S. 633 (1913)]

(4) Assignability [§1103]

A license is usually presumed to be personal and nonassignable, but if the parties so intend, it can be made transferable. A theatre ticket, for instance, is assignable.

2. Creation of Easements [§1104]

Easements may be created by *express grant or reservation*, by *implication*, or by *prescription*.

a. Creation by express grant [§1105]

An easement over the grantor's land may be granted to another. This is known as an easement created by grant.

(1) Statute of Frauds [§1106]

An easement, being an interest in land, must satisfy the Statute of Frauds. Unless one of the exceptions to the Statute applies, creation of an easement requires a *written instrument signed by the grantor*. If the grantor does not sign a written instrument but instead orally gives the grantee permission to enter land, the grantee has a *license* to use the land (*see supra*, §1095). The exceptions to the Statute of Frauds include the usual ones of fraud, part performance, and estoppel; easements by implication and prescription; and easements lasting less than one year. [**Berg v. Ting,** 886 P.2d 564 (Wash. 1995)]

EXAM TIP　　　　　　　　　　　　　　　　　　**gilbert**

Don't forget that a failed attempt to create an easement may still result in a license. Thus, if a grantor attempts to *orally grant an easement* (and there are no applicable Statute of Frauds exceptions), the grantee does *not* have a valid easement but does have a *license*.

---

(2) Duration of easement [§1107]

An easement can be created to endure for a person's life, for a period of years, or forever. If it endures forever, it is called an easement in fee simple.

(3) Construction of ambiguous instrument [§1108]

In some deeds it is difficult to tell whether the grantor intended to grant an easement or to grant a fee simple. Generally, a grant of a *limited use*, or for a *limited purpose*, or of an identified space *without clearly marked boundaries* creates an easement. Similarly, a sale of an interest for less than the fair market value of a fee simple indicates an easement. If the owner of the servient land pays taxes, and the used space is not separately assessed, this also indicates an easement.

Example: O grants A a 40-foot strip "for a road." The limited purpose indicates that an easement is created. [**Preseault v. United States,** 100 F.3d 1525 (Fed. Cir. 1996)]

(a) Presumption of a fee simple [§1109]

Courts sometimes presume that the grantor conveys the largest interest he can convey, unless expressly limited. This presumption favors a fee simple construction. So too does use of a warranty deed, which guarantees "title." [**Urbaitis v. Commonwealth Edison,** 575 N.E.2d 548 (Ill. 1991)]

b. Creation by reservation [§1110]

An easement may be reserved by the grantor over the land granted. If the grantor conveys land, reserving an easement, the land conveyed is the servient tenement.

(1) Reservation in favor of grantor [§1111]

An easement could not be reserved at early common law because only rights "issuing out of the land" (such as rents or feudal services) could be reserved. English courts eventually found a way around this restriction by inventing the *regrant theory*. Under the regrant theory, a deed from O to A purporting to reserve an easement in O was treated as conveying a fee simple absolute to A, who by the same instrument *regranted an easement* to O. Hence, A was treated as the grantor of a reserved easement. The fact that A, the grantee, had not signed the deed regranting an easement to O was initially bothersome, but courts ultimately held that the grantee had, by accepting the deed, bound himself to it. Although the conditions that gave rise to the regrant theory no longer exist, the regrant theory still plagues us.

(a) Exception of an easement [§1112]

At common law, a reservation differed from an exception. A reservation is the regrant of a *new easement*, not previously existing. An exception is a provision in a deed that excludes from the grant some *preexisting right*.

---

e.g. **Example:** O, owner of Blackacre, conveys an easement over Blackacre to A. Subsequently O conveys Blackacre to B "except for an easement previously granted to A." The *preexisting* easement in A is excepted. It could not be reserved because it has previously been granted to A.

---

1) Note

The distinction between an exception and a reservation has all but disappeared in American law, when a new easement has been retained, and the words exception and reservation are often treated as synonymous. Thus, today, if O "excepts" an easement in himself, it will be treated as a reservation.

(2) Reservation in favor of a third party

(a) Common law [§1113]

At common law, an easement could not be reserved in favor of a third party. The reasons for this prohibition lay in feudal notions of conveyancing and in the theory that the grantee *regranted to the grantor* the easement. This common law prohibition is still followed in a majority of states. [**Estate of Thomson v. Wade,** 69 N.Y.2d 570 (1987)]

1) Solution—two pieces of paper [§1114]

This rule serves only as a malpractice trap and ought to be eliminated. It can easily be circumvented by putting the third party in the position of the grantor. This can be done by using two pieces of paper. Suppose that O wants to convey Blackacre to A and reserve an easement for parking in favor of her church across the street. First, O conveys Blackacre to the church. Second, the church conveys Blackacre to A reserving an easement in itself. It is likely that a lawyer will be liable for malpractice if she does not use two pieces of paper to accomplish her client's wishes.

EXAM TIP — **gilbert**

Watch for fact patterns in which a grantor reserves an easement for someone else. Under the majority view, an easement can be reserved only for the *grantor*. An attempt to reserve an easement for anyone else will likely be held *void*.

---

2) Distinguish—covenants [§1115]

A covenant, unlike an easement, can be created to benefit a third party. (*See infra*, §§1188 *et seq.*)

(b) Minority view [§1116]

Some modern cases hold that an easement may be reserved in favor of a third person. There is no reason to prohibit this in modern law. Moreover, if the easement is invalidated, the grantee is unjustly enriched by getting more than she bargained for (*i.e.*, she pays the value of land with an easement and gets land without an easement). [**Willard v. First Church of Christ, Scientist,** 7 Cal. 3d 473 (1972)] Section 2.6 of the Restatement (Third) of Property, Servitudes (2000), referred to hereinafter as the Restatement of Servitudes, provides that an easement may be created in favor of a third party.

c. Creation by implication [§1117]

An easement by implication is created by *operation of law*, not by a written instrument. It is an exception to the Statute of Frauds. However, an easement can be implied only in very narrowly defined circumstances indicating that the parties intended an easement or that an easement is a necessity. Implied easements thus are limited to two kinds: (i) an intended easement based on an *apparent use existing* at the time the servient tenement is separated from the dominant tenement, and (ii) an easement by *necessity*.

(1) Easement implied from existing use [§1118]

If, prior to the time a tract of land is divided into two lots, a use exists on the "servient part" that is reasonably necessary for the enjoyment of the "dominant part" and which the court finds the parties intended to continue after the tract is divided, an easement may be implied. The requirements for implication are discussed below.

gilbert

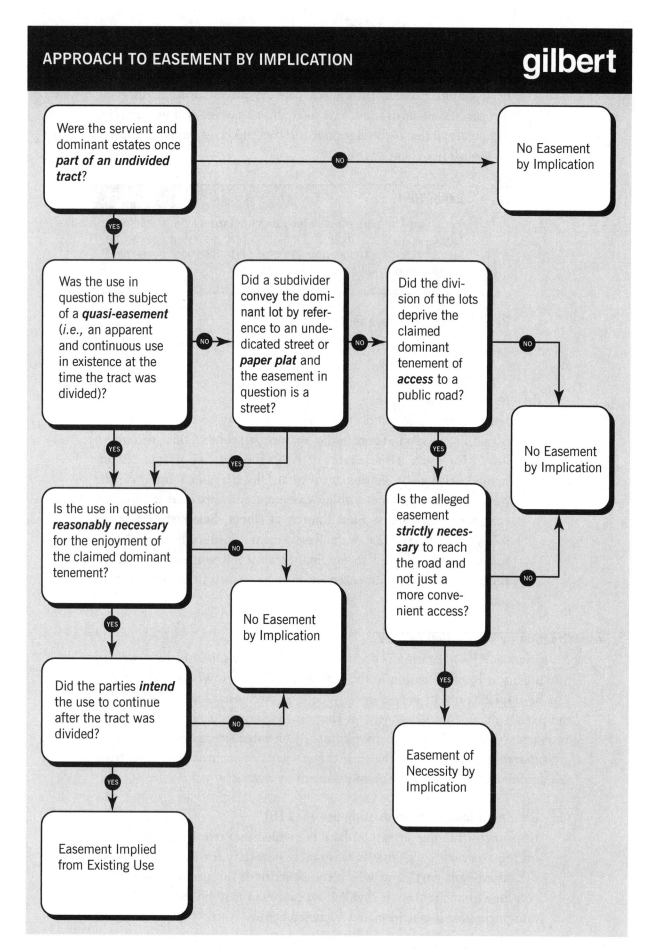

Were the servient and dominant estates once *part of an undivided tract*?

→ NO → No Easement by Implication

YES ↓

Was the use in question the subject of a *quasi-easement* (*i.e.*, an apparent and continuous use in existence at the time the tract was divided)?

→ NO → Did a subdivider convey the dominant lot by reference to an undedicated street or *paper plat* and the easement in question is a street?

→ NO → Did the division of the lots deprive the claimed dominant tenement of *access* to a public road?

→ NO → No Easement by Implication

YES ↓ (quasi-easement)   YES ↓ (paper plat)

Is the use in question *reasonably necessary* for the enjoyment of the claimed dominant tenement?

→ NO → No Easement by Implication

YES ↓

Did the parties *intend* the use to continue after the tract was divided?

→ NO → No Easement by Implication

YES ↓

Easement Implied from Existing Use

YES ↓ (access)

Is the alleged easement *strictly necessary* to reach the road and not just a more convenient access?

→ NO → No Easement by Implication

YES ↓

Easement of Necessity by Implication

(a) Implied only over land granted or reserved when tract divided [§1119]

An easement can be implied only over land granted or reserved when a tract is divided into two or more parcels. If an easement is implied in favor of the *grantee*, the easement is created by *implied grant* to the grantee. If an easement is implied in favor of the *grantor*, the easement is created by *implied reservation* to the grantor.

Example: O owns Blackacre, a large tract of land. A house is built on the back of the tract, serviced by a driveway leading to the street. O divides Blackacre into two lots, and sells the back lot with the house on it (lot 1) to A. O retains the front lot with the driveway on it (lot 2). Provided the other requirements of implied easements are met, a court will imply a *grant* to A of an easement of way over lot 2. If O had retained lot 1, and sold lot 2 to A, a court would imply a *reservation* of an easement over lot 2.

---

1) Implied only in favor of dominant tenement [§1120]

An easement in gross will not be implied. An easement by implication must benefit a dominant tenement created by dividing a tract into two or more lots.

(b) Existing use at time of tract division [§1121]

At the time a tract is divided into two or more lots, a use of one part of the tract must exist from which it can be inferred that an easement permitting its continuation was intended. This existing use is often called a *quasi-easement*. It is not a legal easement, because O cannot have an easement in his own land. It can arise as an easement only when O divides the land into two lots. However, a quasi-easement is a use of the land that would resemble an easement if the tract were divided into two lots. In the example above, the driveway on Blackacre, before division by O, is a quasi-easement.

1) Apparent [§1122]

To have a quasi-easement, the previous use must be *apparent*. It is apparent if a grantee could, by a reasonable inspection of the premises, discover the existence of the use (*e.g.*, a "beaten path"). "Apparent" does not mean the same thing as "visible"; a nonvisible use may be apparent. Thus, *e.g.*, underground drains may be apparent even though not visible, if the surface connections would put a reasonable person on notice of their presence.

Example: O builds two houses on his property, Blackacre. O installs a sewer line to service these houses; the sewer line runs from the street to house 1 and then to house 2. O sells house 1 to A. Although the sewer running under house 1 is not visible, A could discover that it serviced house 2 as well as house 1 by calling a plumber in for an inspection. It has been held that an implied sewer easement has been reserved to house 2 because the sewer is apparent. [**Van Sandt v. Royster**, 83 P.2d 698 (Kan. 1938); **Otero v. Pacheco**, 612 P.2d 1335 (N.M. 1980); *but see* **Campbell v. Great Miami Aerie No. 2309**, 472 N.E.2d 711 (Ohio 1984)]

---

2) Continuous [§1123]

The previous use must be *continuous*, not sporadic. The requirement of continuity is based on the idea that the activities should be such that there is a great probability that the use was known to the parties at the time of the grant, from which an intent can be inferred that the parties wanted the use to continue. Thus, courts interpret "continuous" to include a permanent physical change in the land for a particular use. Thus, the improvement of a roadway by paving is a permanent change of the land, and hence a continuous use, although the roadway is not used every day.

3) Conveyance by paper plat [§1124]

If, before building a street, a subdivider conveys a lot by reference to an undedicated street or a paper plat, the requirement of a quasi-easement is *waived*. The purchaser receives an easement by implication at least in such streets as abut the purchaser's lot, and perhaps in all of the streets delineated on the plat, even though not yet in existence. *Rationale:* The purchaser buys in reliance on the street being opened, and pays a price commensurate with a lot with easements. [**Highland Construction, Inc. v. Paquette**, 697 So. 2d 235 (Fla. 1997); **Putnam v. Dickinson**, 142 N.W.2d 111 (N.D. 1966)]

(c) Reasonable necessity [§1125]

The easement must be necessary for the enjoyment of the claimed dominant tenement. Necessity is an important circumstance in implying an easement on the basis of an existing use, because it probably affects the intention of the parties as to whether the existing use is to continue. In most jurisdictions *reasonable necessity*, and not strict necessity, is required. This is a flexible requirement. Relevant factors in determining reasonable necessity include cost and difficulty of establishing a new road or other alternate use, and whether the price paid reflects the expected continued use of the servient portion of the original tract. [**Granite Properties Limited Partnership v. Manns**, 512 N.E.2d 1230 (Ill. 1987)]

1) Necessity where easement reserved [§1126]

In older cases, courts were reluctant to imply an easement reserved by the grantor. An implied reservation was thought to be in derogation of the deed of the fee simple, and gave the grantee less than the deed called for. An implied grant of an easement, on the other hand, was not in derogation of the deed but rather gave the grantee some additional rights. In modern times, some courts still refuse to imply an easement by reservation except in cases of strict necessity. [**Mitchell v. Castellaw**, *supra*, §1092] In many states, a stronger showing of necessity is required for an implied reservation than for an implied grant. [**Adams v. Cullen**, 268 P.2d 451 (Wash. 1954)] In perhaps the majority of states, the amount of necessity required is the same for both an implied reservation and an implied grant of an easement.

(2) Easement by necessity [§1127]

An easement by necessity is implied if the owner of a tract of land divides the tract into two lots and by this division deprives one lot of access to a public road or utility line. An easement of way over the lot with access to the public road or utility line is implied. Usually an implied easement of way by necessity must be strictly necessary and not just a more convenient access. The doctrine of easements by necessity rests either on the ground that *public policy* requires a way of access to each separate parcel of land or on the ground that, because access is essential to use, the parties *intended* to create an easement but overlooked putting it in the deed. [**Hurlocker v. Medina**, 878 P.2d 348 (N.M. 1994)]

Example: O owns Blackacre, the southern border of which fronts on a public road. O conveys the northern half of Blackacre to A. By this division, the northern half of Blackacre is deprived of access to a public road. An easement by necessity is implied over the southern half of Blackacre in favor of the northern half of Blackacre. [**Reese v. Borghi**, 216 Cal. App. 2d 324 (1963); **Roy v. Euro-Holland Vastgoed, B.V.**, 404 So. 2d 410 (Fla. 1981); **Finn v. Williams**, 33 N.E.2d 226 (Ill. 1941); **Berkeley Development Corp. v. Hutzler**, 229 S.E.2d 732 (W. Va. 1976)]

(a) Implied only over landlocking parcel [§1128]

An easement by necessity is implied only when land is divided. The necessity must exist when the tract is severed. The easement is implied only over that portion of the divided tract that blocks access to a public road from the landlocked parcel. An easement by necessity cannot be implied over land that was never owned by the common grantor of the dominant and servient tenements. [**Othen v. Rosier**, 226 S.W.2d 622 (Tex. 1950)]

(b) No existing use required [§1129]

An easement by necessity, unlike an easement implied on the basis of existing use, does not require an existing use at the time a tract is divided into two lots. Even if the land is virgin timber land, and there are no roads on it, an easement by necessity is implied when it is divided so as to landlock a part.

(c) Location of easement [§1130]

The owner of the servient parcel has the right to locate the easement by necessity, provided the location is reasonably convenient. The servient owner is best capable of locating the easement so as to do the least damage to the servient land, thereby reducing costs. [**Palmer v. Palmer,** 150 N.Y. 139 (1896)]

(d) Easements other than ways [§1131]

An easement by necessity might be implied in situations where an easement for something other than road access is claimed. For example, an easement for a sewer or for light and air might be implied when the severed parcel is deprived of access to a sewer or light and air. However, to date, courts have refused to imply such easements on the ground that sewage can be removed by truck and buildings can be equipped with artificial light and air. Moreover, it is far less likely that the parties intended, but forgot, to create an easement for sewage or light and air than that they intended to provide access to a landlocked lot, which is essential to its use. Inasmuch as the parties probably did not think sewage or light and air access was part of their bargain, the parties are left where they are. Thus, easements by necessity have so far been limited to easements of way. [**Maioriello v. Arlotta,** 73 A.2d 374 (Pa. 1950)]

(e) Termination of necessity [§1132]

An easement by necessity lasts only so long as it is necessary. It terminates when the necessity ceases. [**Palmer v. Palmer,** *supra*]

1) Distinguish—quasi-easement

An easement implied on the basis of a *quasi-easement* may continue forever, even after any element of necessity disappears.

d. Creation by prescription

(1) Historical development [§1133]

Statutes of limitations applicable to actions to recover possession of land did not apply to easements because an easement is a nonpossessory interest. Yet the same policies that underlie the law of adverse possession apply to long use of an easement. Thus, the courts developed the doctrine that an easement could be acquired by prescription, *i.e.*, by an *adverse use* for a requisite period.

(a) English law [§1134]

Searching for a way to establish the doctrine of prescription, the English courts developed the *fiction of the lost grant*. If a person had been using another's land for the requisite period, the court presumed that she was doing so under a grant from some former owner, which grant was now lost. The presumption of grant was conclusive once the requisite period had passed, and was applied even though it was later admitted that no grant had ever been made.

(b) American law [§1135]

The fiction of the lost grant has been rejected in most American jurisdictions. In this country, the doctrine of prescription has been developed as a matter of public policy by analogy to the law of *adverse possession*. If the statute of limitations for adverse possession is 20 years, the prescriptive period for acquiring an easement is likewise 20 years. Generally, the same requirements for adverse possession are applied to an easement by prescription. Hence, the same period and same issues are generally involved in acquiring an easement by prescription as are involved in acquiring a fee simple by adverse possession.

(2) Elements of prescription [§1136]

For prescription, the usual elements required for adverse possession must be shown: *open and notorious use; adverse and under a claim of right; continuous and uninterrupted* throughout the requisite period. [**Brocco v. Mileo,** 170 A.D.2d 732 (1991); **Community Feed Store, Inc. v. Northeastern Culvert Corp.,** 559 A.2d 1068 (Vt. 1989)]

(a) Open and notorious use [§1137]

The use must be made without any attempt at concealment. This requirement is most often litigated in cases involving underground sewers and drains. If the sewer could be reasonably discovered on inspection (*e.g.*, surface connections are visible), this requirement is satisfied.

(b) Under a claim of right [§1138]

A claim of a prescriptive easement must be under a claim of right, and not with permission of the owner of the land. But, as with adverse possession, a court may apply an objective or a subjective test to a "claim of right." Under the objective test, it is sufficient that the acts of the user appear to the community to be under a claim of right (*see supra*, §98). Under the subjective test, the user must in good faith believe that he has a right to use the servient land (*see supra*, §99).

---

e.g. **Example:** A and B own adjoining lots. Pursuant to an oral agreement, A and B construct a cement driveway, half on A's lot and half on B's lot. Each pays half the cost. Some 25 years later, A conveys her lot to C, and B conveys his lot to D. C and D squabble, and D forbids C to use the driveway. C claims a prescriptive easement. Under the objective test, C and D have reciprocal prescriptive easements over the other's lot. [**Fischer v. Grinsbergs,** 252 N.W.2d 619 (Neb. 1977)] If A and B believed they had a right to use the driveway because each contributed to construction, even under the subjective test C and D can have prescriptive easements. [**Shanks v. Floom,** 124 N.E.2d 416 (Ohio 1955)—prescriptive easement due to expense of constructing driveway (similar to estoppel to revoke license)] The courts are split in these common driveway situations, however; much depends on the particular facts as to whether the user thought she had a right to use the common driveway or was using it permissively.

---

1) **Permissive use changes to adverse [§1139]**

Prescriptive rights cannot be acquired where the use is permissive. [**Finley v. Botto,** 161 Cal. App. 2d 614 (1958)] However, if a person uses the land of another with permission and subsequently begins to do acts that reasonably should put the owner on notice that the user is *claiming a right* to use the land, the use becomes adverse. For example, if O gives A permission to use a driveway, and A subsequently tears down a gate across the driveway or widens and paves the driveway, these subsequent acts begin adverse use. [**Hester v. Sawyers,** 71 P.2d 646 (N.M. 1937)] But if A merely repairs the driveway, this is insufficient to put O on notice that A is claiming use as of right. [**Lunt v. Kitchens,** 260 P.2d 535 (Utah 1953)]

2) **Color of title and payment of taxes not required [§1140]**

In some states, statutes require color of title and payment of taxes for adverse possession. Neither is required for a prescriptive easement. These particular statutory requirements for adverse possession have been ignored by the courts in developing the analogous law of prescription.

(c) **Continuous use [§1141]**

The adverse use must be continuous, but this does not mean constant. Indeed, the use of an easement ordinarily involves only periodic use. Continuity requires a continuous claim of right and periodic acts which, given the nature of the type of easement claimed, give notice to the owner that an easement is being claimed.

Thus, driving or walking across another's land, whenever headed in that direction, is sufficient to establish a prescriptive easement, even though this is not done every day.

1) Seasonal use [§1142]

Grazing cattle on another's land during the grazing season every year establishes sufficient continuity, even though the season is only a few months long. Similarly, hunting or fishing rights can be acquired by prescription despite long intervals between use. The difficult thing in hunting and grazing cases is to distinguish between seasonal use with a claim of right to continue it season after season and, on the other hand, sporadic or occasional trespasses. Sporadic and occasional trespasses do not give rise to a prescriptive easement. [**Romans v. Nadler,** 14 N.W.2d 482 (Minn. 1944)]

a) Easement in gross [§1143]

It is possible to acquire a prescriptive easement in gross. For example, if a hunting club hunts on the land of another every hunting season, the club members may acquire a prescriptive easement.

2) Tacking [§1144]

Tacking is allowed in prescription, just as it is allowed in adverse possession. One prescriptive user can tack on to his period of use the prescriptive use of a predecessor in interest. Transfer of the dominant tenement establishes the necessary privity if the grantor intends to transfer with it the use which is ripening into an easement.

(d) Uninterrupted use [§1145]

If the adverse use is interrupted by the owner of the land being used, the prescriptive period ends. If the adverse use begins again after interruption, a new prescriptive period begins. The central question is: What constitutes an interruption? In adverse possession the owner can interrupt the adverse possession only by entry upon the land or by bringing a lawsuit. But in prescription, there is some authority in jurisdictions following the fiction of the lost grant (*see supra*, §1134) that the owner can interrupt adverse use by merely protesting the use (*e.g.*, mailing a letter to the user). This authority assumes that the fiction of the lost grant is rebutted when the owner says, "I do not grant you an easement; stop using my property." [**Dartnell v. Bidwell,** 98 A. 743 (Me. 1916)] In jurisdictions rejecting the fiction of the lost grant, the owner must effectively interrupt the adverse use. A sign or oral protest will not suffice.

EASEMENT BY PRESCRIPTION—SUMMARY OF ELEMENTS   **gilbert**

FOR AN EASEMENT BY PRESCRIPTION, THE USE MUST BE:

☑ *Open and notorious* (*i.e.,* without any attempt at concealment)

☑ Under a *claim of right* and not with permission of the landowner

☑ *Continuous* (not necessarily constant; just normal use, such as grazing during grazing season)

☑ *Uninterrupted* by owner's entry upon the land, bringing suit, or—in some states—protesting use

(3) Public easements [§1146]

In most jurisdictions, the public at large can acquire a public easement in private land by prescription if members of the public use the private land in a manner meeting the requirements for prescription. If the public uses land for a roadway, the presumption is that the use is adverse (under a claim of right), just as it is for an individual claim of easement. On the other hand, if the public uses vacant, undeveloped land, the presumption is that the use is permissive. It is deemed not to give notice to the owner of a claim of right. Therefore, except for a public road, it is difficult to acquire a public easement by prescription.

(a) Minority view [§1147]

In some states, the general public *cannot* acquire prescriptive rights in private property. *Rationale:* The owner's cause of action runs against the specific trespassing individuals and not against the public at large. Therefore, the statute of limitations only bars the owner from suing the individuals who trespassed. [**State ex *rel.* Haman v. Fox,** 594 P.2d 1093 (Idaho 1979)]

(b) Customary rights [§1148]

In Florida, Hawaii, and Oregon, courts have revived the medieval doctrine of customary rights in beaches. If the public has used the beach (the dry sand area in private ownership) for so long that "the memory of many runneth not to the contrary," the public has a customary right to use the beach. [**State ex *rel.* Thornton v. Hay,** 462 P.2d 671 (Or. 1969)] In New Jersey, the public may use the privately owned dry sand area to the extent needed in the exercise of the public's right under the public trust doctrine to use the wet sand area and the water. [**Matthews v. Bay Head Improvement Association,** 471 A.2d 355 (N.J. 1984)]

3. Scope of Easements [§1149]

After an easement is created, questions may arise about what use the easement owner can make of the easement or about what interference by the servient owner is permissible. These questions are treated as questions of the scope of the easement.

a. General rule [§1150]

The scope of an easement depends on the intention of the parties. In ascertaining this intent, a court may examine whether the easement was created expressly or by prescription, what changes in use might reasonably be foreseeable by the parties, and what changes in use are required to achieve the purpose of the easement under modern conditions and preserve the usefulness of the easement to the dominant tenement. The court will also look at whether the increase in the burden is unreasonable.

b. How easement was created

(1) Express easement [§1151]

If the easement was *expressly* created, the court will look at the language of the instrument, together with the surrounding circumstances, in order to determine the parties' intent.

(a) Easement of way [§1152]

An easement of way is a favorite of the law because surface access is essential to the use and productivity of land. An easement of way is given a scope that permits it to meet the needs of the dominant tenement as it normally develops. It may be used in ways reasonably foreseeable by the parties or, if not foreseeable, by ordinary means of transportation as those means normally evolve. There is a strong public policy that land have access necessary to make it useful under contemporary conditions. [**Sides v. Cleland**, 648 A.2d 793 (Pa. 1994)]

---

e.g. **Example:** In 1876, O grants A a right of way over Blackacre to reach Whiteacre, which is used for a slaughterhouse. Animals are brought in by cart, slaughtered, and animal products removed by cart. After 35 years, the slaughterhouse burns, and Whiteacre is used for farming. Farm machinery is moved in and out over the easement. Whiteacre is then sold for commercial use. Modern vehicles can use the easement to reach Whiteacre. The easement is not limited to the modes of transportation (horse and cart) in use in 1876. Nor is the easement limited to vehicles reaching land used only for a slaughterhouse or for a farm. If the use of the dominant tenement changes to commercial use, trucks may use the easement. The purpose of the easement is to gain access to the dominant tenement, however it is used. [**Cameron v. Barton**, 272 S.W.2d 40 (Ky. 1954)]

---

(2) Implied easements

(a) Existing use [§1153]

If an easement is implied on the basis of a use existing at the time of severance of a tract into two parcels that the parties intended to continue, the scope is generally the same as an express easement. Changes that reasonably might have been expected or that are necessary to preserve the utility of the easement are permitted.

(b) Easement by necessity [§1154]

In case of an easement by necessity, the extent of necessity determines the scope.

(3) Easements by prescription [§1155]

It is more difficult to increase the burden of an easement by prescription than any other kind of easement. The uses that give rise to the easement can continue, but there is no basis for assuming the parties intended the easement to accommodate future needs. After all, the owner of the servient land (O) might not have objected to A crossing O's land to pick apples on A's land, which use gave rise to the prescriptive easement, but the owner would have objected to a whole stream of traffic generated by a subdivision on A's land. Thus, if a prescriptive easement is acquired by use to reach a house, and the use of the dominant tenement is changed from residential to commercial, the added burden of traffic probably will not be permitted on the prescriptive easement. [**S.S. Kresge Co. v. Winkelman Realty Co.,** 50 N.W.2d 920 (Wis. 1952); *but compare* **Farmer v. Kentucky Utilities Co.,** 642 S.W.2d 579 (Ky. 1982)—prescriptive easement for utility wires includes right to clear trees under the wires; **Glenn v. Poole,** 423 N.E.2d 1030 (Mass. 1981)—prescriptive easement acquired to haul wood and gravel and to reach land for truck storage could continue to be used when dominant land was used for garage and repair shop and increase in burden was moderate]

EXAM TIP   **gilbert**

Questions on easements often ask whether the easement holder can increase the scope of the easement. Remember, the courts will look to the *intent of the parties*, based on any written instruments and the circumstances at the time the easement was created. Courts will also consider whether the increase will *unreasonably burden* the servient tenement. Generally, an express or implied easement of way (the most common exam fodder) can be increased in scope to meet the needs of the dominant tenement as they normally develop. However, courts are slow to increase the scope of an easement of way obtained through *prescription* because while the servient owner might not have objected to some slight use of her land (e.g., the creation of a footpath to pick apples), she might have strongly objected to heavier use (e.g., driving a truck onto her land to pick apples).

---

c. **Subdivision of dominant tenement [§1156]**

As a general rule, if the dominant estate is subdivided, each subdivided lot has a right to use easements appurtenant to the dominant estate. An easement is appurtenant to every part of the dominant tenement. However, there is an important limitation on use of an easement by subdivided lots: The servient estate is not to be burdened to a greater extent than was contemplated at the time the easement was created and is necessary to accommodate normal development of the dominant estate. Obviously it is a question of judgment, weighing all the circumstances, as to when the increase in burden becomes unreasonable. Use by four subdivided lots may be permitted, but use by 40 lots may be viewed as excessive. [**Bang v. Forman,** 222 N.W. 96 (Mich. 1928)—subdividing three lots into 26 lots creates unreasonable burden; **Cushman Virginia Corp. v. Barnes,** 129 S.E.2d 633 (Va. 1963)—subdividing 126-acre tract not unreasonable burden; **Cox v. Glenbrook Co.,** 371 P.2d 647 (Nev. 1962)—subdividing into 40 to 60 lots may constitute unreasonable burden, but court refuses to declare in advance]

d. **Use for benefit of nondominant land [§1157]**

An easement granted for the benefit of lot 1 cannot be used for the benefit of lot 2, even though the same person owns lots 1 and 2. The dominant owner cannot increase the scope of the easement by using it to benefit a nondominant tenement. [**S.S. Kresge Co. v. Winkelman Realty Co.,** *supra,* §1155]

Example: O, owner of Whiteacre, grants to A an easement of way over Whiteacre for the benefit of Blackacre, which A owns. Subsequently A buys Greenacre, adjacent to Blackacre, and erects a building on Greenacre and Blackacre. Access to this building is across the easement on Whiteacre. O can enjoin A, preventing the use of the easement to provide access to the portion of the building on Greenacre. [**Penn Bowling Recreation Center, Inc. v. Hot Shoppes, Inc.,** 179 F.2d 64 (D.C. Cir. 1949); *but compare* **Brown v. Voss,** 715 P.2d 514 (Wash. 1986)—holding O might be given damages against A rather than an injunction if, all things considered, an injunction would be inequitable] If it is impossible for an injunction to be effective in preventing the use of the easement for access to Greenacre, the easement will be extinguished entirely. A will pay the penalty of forfeiture if A extends the easement to other land in such a way that use for the dominant tenement only cannot be effectively policed. [**Crimmins v. Gould,** 149 Cal. App. 2d 383 (1957); *but compare* **Frenning v. Dow,** 544 A.2d 145 (R.I. 1988)—holding A should be given opportunity before easement was entirely extinguished by excessive use to propose a plan that would subject the use to monitoring by the servient owners and ultimate enforcement by the court]

---

e. **Change in location of easement [§1158]**

If an easement has been granted in a specific location, or has been located by mutual agreement of the parties, the location cannot thereafter be changed by one party acting unilaterally. The location can be changed only by mutual consent.

Example: O, owner of Whiteacre, grants A an easement of way in a specific location on Whiteacre. Subsequently O wants to erect a building in this location and move the easement to another location on Whiteacre, which would be just as convenient to A. O cannot move the location of the easement without A's consent. [**Sakansky v. Wein,** 169 A. 1 (N.H. 1933)]

(1) Widening of easement [§1159]

If the width of an easement is specified in the grant, or if it existed at the time of the grant so that it can be inferred that the parties intended it to remain the same width, the easement cannot be widened without the consent of the servient owner.

(2) Restatement view [§1160]

Restatement of Servitudes section 4.8 permits the servient owner to relocate the easement or make reasonable changes in its dimension when necessary to permit normal development of the servient estate, provided the changes do not unreasonably interfere with the easement holder's use. This view is also taken in **Umphres v. J.R. Mayer Enterprises,** 889 S.W.2d 86 (Mo. 1994).

f. Use by servient owner [§1161]

The servient owner has the right to use the servient land in ways that do not unreasonably interfere with the easement. The servient owner may erect a structure over an easement of way, provided enough headroom is provided for the passage of vehicles below. Similarly, the owner of the servient land may use the easement itself, provided it is not an exclusive easement and the use does not unreasonably interfere with the rights of the owner of the easement.

Example: O grants to a water company an easement to lay water pipes across O's land. O can grant similar rights to others for the same purpose, provided these subsequent rights do not interfere with the rights of the water company. [**City of Pasadena v. California-Michigan Land & Water Co.,** 17 Cal. 2d 576 (1941)]

g. Division of easements in gross [§1162]

Can an easement or profit in gross be "divided" or "apportioned," *i.e.,* transferred to two or more persons and used by them independently of each other? This turns primarily on whether the easement is "exclusive" or "nonexclusive."

(1) Nonexclusive easement [§1163]

A nonexclusive easement is one that is enjoyed both by the easement holder and the servient owner (*e.g.,* both have the right to hunt on the land). Absent authority in the grant, the easement holder cannot divide the right among others who use it independently. To do so would constitute excess competition with the servient owner for the use or sale of the rights. [Rest. Servitudes §5.9]

(2) Exclusive easement [§1164]

An easement in gross is exclusive if the holder has the exclusive right to enjoy it (*e.g.*, the only person who can hunt). The owner of an exclusive easement can divide it and transfer it to others who can use it independently, unless the original grant prohibits this. [**Henley v. Continental Cablevision**, 692 S.W.2d 825 (Mo. 1985)—holding telephone company with exclusive easement for lines could permit cable television company to string cables from its poles]

(a) Overuse of profit in gross [§1165]

Even though a profit (*supra,* §1094), like an easement, can be divided among several persons, overuse of the profit by these persons—each seeking to maximize his wealth—can lead to the depletion of natural resources. To regulate use of profits in gross, courts invented the *"one-stock" rule*. The one-stock rule is: When two or more persons own a profit in gross they must use the profit as one stock. Neither can operate independently of the other. One owner can veto use by the other because consent of all is required. The one-stock rule has been applied to easements in contexts where overuse of the easement may result in destroying the resource. [**Miller v. Lutheran Conference & Camp Association**, 200 A. 646 (Pa. 1938)]

(b) The "one stock" rule [§1166]

Almost all profits are held in gross; they are not appurtenant to land. A usual profit is the right to take timber, minerals, or sand on O's land. Suppose that A has the exclusive right to take sand from Blackacre. If A desires, A can extract all the sand now, but A will not do so because what A extracts and sells today A cannot extract and sell tomorrow. If A were to sell the sand today, A would bear the loss if prices rose tomorrow. A will set an optimum rate of extraction based on the present price of sand relative to its expected future price. If A assigns the right to dig sand to B and C, B and C must act as "one stock" in extracting sand and not as independent owners. B and C both must agree on the rate of extraction. Why? Without this rule, B and C would have an economic incentive to take as much sand as fast as possible, before the other took it. If B took all the sand today, the cost of having no sand tomorrow would be borne by B and C and not by B alone. If B and C must act as a single owner, agreeing on the rate of extraction, they will set a rate of extraction that takes into consideration future demand and prices. The "one stock" rule thus inhibits consuming natural resources without regard to future needs.

(c) Restatement of Servitudes [§1167]

Restatement of Servitudes section 5.9 rejects the one-stock rule as a way of controlling overuse. It provides for a "reasonable" test to govern how much the competing owners can use the easement, analogizing to the reasonableness use doctrine used to govern riparian rights (*see supra*, §35).

4. Transfer of Easements

a. Easement appurtenant [§1168]

When the dominant tenement is transferred, any easements appurtenant are transferred with it, unless the appurtenant easement is also personal in its terms (*see supra*, §1090). Similarly, the burden of an easement appurtenant passes with the servient land when transferred. An easement appurtenant is thought of as "attached" to the dominant land, and it benefits the possessor of that land, including an adverse possessor. Of course, the owners of the servient and dominant tenements may make a contrary agreement if they wish. By mutual consent, they can "detach" the easement and either "attach" it to other dominant land or convert it into an easement in gross, but neither party acting alone can do this.

EXAM TIP   **gilbert**

It is important to remember that the easement appurtenant *passes with the benefited land*. Don't be fooled by questions that make you think it must be specifically mentioned in the deed.

---

b. Easements in gross [§1169]

Easements in gross may present special problems regarding transferability. If the benefit of an easement in gross is inherited by or assigned to a large number of persons, it may be difficult to locate these persons (or their heirs upon their deaths), making it difficult to secure a release of the easement or to clear up title. (Compare an easement in gross to an easement appurtenant, where the dominant owner is always known and available to bargain with.) With this danger in mind, courts have sometimes restricted the transfer of the benefit of an easement in gross.

(1) Commercial easements in gross assignable [§1170]

In some old cases, courts held that the benefits of easements in gross were not assignable. But the general rule today is that the benefit of a commercial easement in gross is assignable, and a noncommercial easement in gross is assignable if the parties so intend. [**Miller v. Lutheran**

Conference & Camp Association, *supra,* §1165] Commercial easements in gross are those that have primarily *economic benefit* rather than personal satisfaction. The large majority of easements in gross are of this kind: railroad rights-of-way, gas pipe lines, and utility easements. *Rationale:* It would be unacceptable public policy for a transportation or utility company to lose its easements when it merged with another company. Moreover, the problem of locating multiple unknown owners does not arise with most commercial easements in gross, which are held by utility companies or railroads. Finally, if commercial easements in gross are not assignable, utility companies will buy a fee simple for their lines, rather than an easement; this is undesirable because a fee simple, unlike an easement, cannot be terminated by abandonment or by acts of the owner. [**Geffine v. Thompson,** 62 N.E.2d 590 (Ohio 1945)]

(2) Restatement view [§1171]

The First Restatement of Property provided that only commercial easements in gross were assignable. Restatement of Servitudes section 4.6 provides that all easements in gross are transferable unless contrary to the intent of the parties.

c. Profits in gross [§1172]

Profits in gross (*e.g.,* the right to take timber or minerals) have always been assignable. Inasmuch as profits in gross could give rise to the same problem of multiple and unknown owners, it is odd that courts put more restrictive rules on easements. Perhaps the fact that assignability of profits has resulted in no serious problems is an argument for holding all easements in gross assignable.

5. Termination of Easements [§1173]

An easement may be terminated in accord with its express terms (*see supra,* §§1090, 1107) or in any of the ways discussed below.

a. By unity of title [§1174]

An easement is a right in the land of *another.* If the title to the easement and title to the servient tenement come into the hands of one person, the easement is extinguished. This usually happens when one person buys the dominant tenement and the servient tenement. Once the easement is extinguished, it is *not revived* by subsequent separation of the tenements into two ownerships. [*Compare* **Castle Associates v. Schwartz,** 63 A.D.2d 481 (1978)—easement not extinguished by merger of title of dominant tenement with *one of two* servient tenements when the other servient tenement was necessary for enjoyment of easement]

b. By act of dominant owner

(1) Release [§1175]

The owner of an easement may release the easement to the servient owner by a *written* instrument. An oral release is ineffective because of the Statute of Frauds. However, if the owner of an easement orally releases it to the servient owner, and the servient owner *expends money in reliance* on the oral release (such as erecting a building on the easement), the easement owner is estopped to plead the Statute of Frauds. The easement is extinguished by the oral release and action in reliance.

(2) Nonuse [§1176]

Mere nonuse of an easement, like nonuse of a fee simple, does *not* extinguish the easement. A power company, *e.g.*, which has an easement for electric lines across Blackacre, does not lose the easement merely because the lines are not built. The easement is not extinguished no matter how long the nonuse continues. [**Lindsey v. Clark,** 69 S.E.2d 342 (Va. 1952)]

(3) Abandonment [§1177]

Although neither oral release nor nonuse alone is sufficient to terminate an easement, if the owner of an easement *acts* in such a way as to indicate an *unequivocal intent* to abandon the easement, the easement is abandoned. Such acts can include an oral release or nonuse coupled with failure to maintain the easement, or permitting the easement to be blocked by others, or establishing a substitute easement elsewhere. [**Preseault v. United States,** *supra*, §1108; **Flanagan v. San Marcos Silk Co.,** 106 Cal. App. 2d 458 (1951)]

Example: A, owner of Blackacre, has an easement to use a common driveway located half on adjacent Whiteacre. A builds a barn on the part of the driveway located on Blackacre, which makes further use of the driveway impossible. The easement is abandoned. [**Hickerson v. Bender,** 500 N.W.2d 169 (Minn. 1993)]

EXAM TIP   **gilbert**

Don't confuse mere nonuse with abandonment. Nonuse alone does not extinguish the easement. On the other hand, if the owner of the easement acts in a way that indicates an *unequivocal intent to abandon* the easement, such as allowing the easement to be blocked or an oral release coupled with failure to maintain, the easement is abandoned.

---

(4) Alteration of dominant tenement [§1178]

If an easement is granted for a particular purpose, and an alteration of the dominant tenement makes it impossible to achieve the purpose any longer, the easement is extinguished.

Example: O, owner of Blackacre, grants to A, owner of the adjacent lot, an easement of view from the windows of A's present house across Blackacre to Main Street (on the other side of Blackacre). A subsequently moves her house to the rear of her lot, where it has no view of Main Street from any of its windows. The easement is extinguished. [**Hopkins the Florist, Inc. v. Fleming,** 26 A.2d 96 (Vt. 1942)]

(a) Particular purpose [§1179]

Whether an easement is limited to a particular purpose may, in any individual case, be debatable. However, courts are reluctant to construe an easement to be limited for a particular purpose when this is not clearly and unequivocally stated. An easement for light and air "for the windows of A's dwelling," *e.g.*, is usually construed to be for the benefit of A's **building**. "Dwelling" describes A's present use, but does not limit the purpose of the easement, and the easement is not extinguished if A uses the building for something other than a dwelling. [**First National Trust & Savings Bank v. Raphael,** 113 S.E.2d 683 (Va. 1960)]

(5) Easement by necessity [§1180]

An easement by necessity terminates when the necessity ends. If the dominant owner acquires other access by conveyance or prescription, the easement by necessity is extinguished. (*See supra*, §1132.)

c. By act of servient owner

(1) Destruction of servient tenement [§1181]

An easement in a structure (*e.g.*, a right to use a stairway) is terminated if the building is destroyed without fault of the owner of the servient estate (*e.g.*, by fire or act of God). If the building is destroyed by the *intentional* act of the servient owner, the easement is not extinguished. The servient owner is liable in damages to the owner of the easement, and a court may require the servient owner to create in any new building a stairway for the use of the dominant owner. [**Rothschild v. Wolf,** 20 Cal. 2d 17 (1942)]

(a) Minority view

One state holds an easement can be destroyed by the intentional destruction of the building by the servient owner. [**Union National Bank of Lowell v. Nesmith,** 130 N.E. 251 (Mass. 1921)]

(2) Prescription [§1182]

If the servient owner interferes with an easement in an adverse manner (*e.g.*, by erecting a fence across a roadway), the servient owner can extinguish the easement by prescription. The requisite elements of adversity are the same as for the creation of an easement by prescription. However, where an easement has been created but no occasion has arisen for its use and the servient owner fences his land, the servient owner is not deemed to act adversely until the dominant owner demands that the easement be opened and the servient owner refuses to do so. [**Castle Associates v. Schwartz,** *supra,* §1174]

d. By change of conditions [§1183]

The doctrine of change of conditions in the neighborhood, which may prevent the enforcement of a real covenant or equitable servitude (*see infra,* §1277), is *not* applicable to easements. [**Waldrop v. Town of Brevard,** 62 S.E.2d 512 (N.C. 1950)]

EXAM TIP gilbert

When confronted with an exam question involving overuse or misuse of an easement, remember that such use ***does not terminate*** the easement. The appropriate remedy for the servient owner is an injunction against the misuse. Reasonable use of the easement may continue.

---

6. Negative Easements [§1184]

A negative easement gives the easement holder the right to prevent the servient owner from using her land in some way.

a. Types limited [§1185]

Negative easements are rare and are generally not permitted unless one of four types recognized by early English law: easements for *light*, for *air*, for *subjacent or lateral support*, or for the *flow of an artificial stream*. These four negative easements permit two neighbors to agree that neighbor A will not block neighbor B's windows, will not dig so as to undermine B's house, or will not interfere with an aqueduct bringing water to B's farm. However, the list of negative easements is not necessarily closed, and new decisions may expand the list. Solar easements, scenic easements, and conservation easements are new types of negative easements recognized in recent years.

Example: Blackacre, a hillside lot, has a view over Whiteacre to the sea. O, owner of Whiteacre, grants to A, owner of Blackacre, an easement of view beginning 20 feet above the ground level of Whiteacre. This will enable A to see the sea and prevent B from building above 20 feet and blocking the view. At common law this would not have been permitted as a negative easement because it is not one of the four permitted types. However, in this country in modern times an easement of view or scenic easement has been permitted as a negative easement. Although the easement is not for light and air, it resembles the same. [**Petersen v. Friedman,** 162 Cal. App. 2d 245 (1958)]

---

(1) Why types are limited [§1186]

Almost all types of purported negative easements can be treated as a *promise* by the servient owner not to use his land in a certain way. In the above example, O could have *promised* A not to build any structure over 20 feet high, in which case A would not have an easement but a covenant. (*Remember:* An easement is a *grant* of an interest in land; a covenant is a *promise* respecting use of land.) Courts have not found it necessary to expand the categories of permissible negative easements because they can classify the right to prevent a neighbor from doing something on his land as an equitable servitude (a "promise").

b. Cannot arise by prescription [§1187]

In the United States, negative easements (for light and air, support, drainage) *cannot* arise by prescription. The reason is that prescription bars a *cause of action*, and where the owner has no cause of action, prescription does not apply.

Example: In 1980, A builds a house four inches from A's property line adjoining B's land. A's windows overlook B's land. In 2006, B proposes to erect a building on B's side of the property line, six inches away from A's windows. Although B's building will block A's light and air, A does not have a prescriptive negative easement for light and air over B's land and cannot stop B from building. *Rationale:* Because between 1980 and 2006 B did not have a cause of action against A (to force A to close up her windows), B had no cause of action on which the statute of limitations has run. It would be unfair to give A a prescriptive right that B could not prevent from arising. [**Parker & Edgarton v. Foote,** 19 Wend. 309 (N.Y. 1838)]

B. Real Covenants

1. Introduction

a. What running covenants are about [§1188]

A covenant is a *promise* to do or not to do a certain thing. The covenants considered in this chapter are promises relating to the *use* of land. Typically they are promises to do something on land (*e.g.*, a promise to maintain a fence) or a promise not to do something on land (*e.g.*, a promise not to erect a commercial building). The promise to do something is an *affirmative promise*. The promise not to do something is a *negative promise*. If the promisee sues the promisor for breach, the law of contracts is applicable. If, however, a person who buys *the promisee's land* is suing or a person who buys *the promisor's land* is being sued, the law of property, as set forth in the rest of this chapter, is applicable. These property rules determine when a successor owner can sue or be sued on an agreement to which he was not a party.

b. Remedies for breach [§1189]

If the promise is breached, the promisee or his successor may want one of two things: (i) money damages, or (ii) an injunction or decree requiring specific performance of the promise. If the promisee wants money damages, he must sue *in law*. If the promisee wants an injunction or specific performance, he must sue *in equity*. In England (and still in a few states in this country), law and equity are separate courts. In most American jurisdictions, law and equity have been merged into one court. Nonetheless, even with one court, the plaintiff must ask for legal relief (money damages) or equitable relief (injunction or specific performance). If the plaintiff asks for money damages, the rules developed by the old law courts are applicable. If the plaintiff asks for equitable relief, the rules developed by the equity courts are applicable.

c. Real covenant defined [§1190]

A real covenant is a covenant that runs with the land *at law*. It is enforceable at law by a successor owner of the promisee's land and, concomitantly, is enforceable against a successor to the promisor's land. If the plaintiff wants money damages, the plaintiff must show that the covenant qualifies as a real covenant. The plaintiff must satisfy the requirements for the covenant to run at law.

(1) Personal liability only [§1191]

A real covenant gives rise to personal liability only. It is enforceable only by an award of money damages, which is collectible out of the general assets of the defendant.

Example: O conveys Blackacre to A, and A promises for herself, her heirs, and assigns not to erect a slaughterhouse on Blackacre. The covenant is for the benefit of adjacent Whiteacre, owned by O. The deed is recorded, giving notice to subsequent purchasers. A sells Blackacre to B. B erects a slaughterhouse. O decides to enforce the promise as a real covenant. O is entitled to money damages from B in the amount that Whiteacre is devalued by having a slaughterhouse next door. (This promise can also be enforced as an equitable servitude in equity. Equity will enjoin B, prohibiting erection of the slaughterhouse, if O sues for an injunction before the slaughterhouse is erected.)

---

(2) Distinguish—equitable servitude [§1192]

An equitable servitude is a covenant enforceable *in equity* by or against successors to the land of the original parties to the contract. Hence, if the plaintiff wants equitable relief (injunction or specific performance), the plaintiff must show that the covenant qualifies as an equitable servitude. Different rules may be applicable to the enforcement of covenants in equity than are applicable in law. (Equitable servitudes are discussed *infra*, §§1218 *et seq.*)

(3) Distinguish—condition [§1193]

Land use may be controlled by a condition as well as by a covenant. A condition provides for *forfeiture* upon breach of the condition, whereas a covenant is enforceable only by an award of money damages (real covenant) or an injunction (equitable servitude). A condition is imposed when the grantor conveys a *fee simple determinable* or a *fee simple subject to condition subsequent* (*see supra*, §§279, 286).

2. Creation

a. Writing required [§1194]

At common law a real covenant had to be in writing and under seal. The requirement of a seal has been abrogated, but a writing is still required. Note that a real covenant will not be implied, nor can it arise by prescription.

b. Grantee bound without signing [§1195]

Most deeds are signed only by the grantor. Such a deed is known as a deed poll. By accepting a deed poll, the grantee is bound by any covenants in the deed to be performed by the grantee.

3. Enforcement By or Against Assignees [§1196]

The major issue involving real covenants is whether the *burden* of the covenant will run to successor owners of the promisor's land. It is also sometimes an issue whether the *benefit* will run to successor owners of the promisee's land. The burdened tract is analogous to the servient tenement under the law of easements. The benefited tract is analogous to the dominant tenement. Easements run to successive owners of the tracts involved because easements are interests in land (part of the title). Covenants, on the other hand, did not start out as interests in land, but rather only as promises concerning the use of land, and so courts laid out different rules for when these promises run to successors.

a. Requirements for burden of covenant to run at law [§1197]

The requirements for the burden to run are: (i) the contracting parties must *intend* that successors to the promisor be bound by the covenant (*see infra*, §1199); (ii) there must be (at least in some states) *privity of estate* between the original promisor and promisee as well as privity of estate between the promisor and his assignee (*see infra*, §§1202, 1210); (iii) the covenant must *touch and concern* the land (*see infra*, §1215); and (iv) a subsequent purchaser of the promisor's land must have *notice* of the covenant (*see infra*, §1216). Each of these requirements will be examined in detail below.

b. Requirements for benefit of covenant to run at law [§1198]

The requirements for the benefit to run are: (i) the parties must so *intend*; (ii) some form of *privity of estate* may be required (*see infra*, §1212); and (iii) the benefit must *touch and concern* land owned by the promisee. As we shall see, traditionally the requirements for running of the benefit were somewhat more lenient than for the running of the burden.

c. Intention of the parties [§1199]

The intention of the parties that the burden and benefit run is usually found in the language of a deed or contract. The instrument may read "these covenants shall run with the land," or "the grantee promises for herself, her heirs, and assigns." If the instrument is unclear, the court will look at the purpose of the covenant and all the circumstances to ascertain the parties' probable intent. [**Charping v. J.P. Scurry & Co.,** 372 S.E.2d 120 (S.C. 1988)]

(1) Necessity of word "assigns" [§1200]

In **Spencer's Case,** 77 Eng. Rep. 72 (1583), the court laid down three requirements for the burden of a covenant to run at law. The first pertained to the intention to bind assigns: If the covenant concerns a *thing that is not in being* at the time the covenant is made but is to be built or created thereafter, the burden of the covenant will not bind assigns unless they are *expressly mentioned*. For example, if A promises B that A will build a wall, A's assignee is not bound unless A promises on behalf of herself *and her assigns*. This technical rule has been abolished in the large majority of states, which hold that intention is to be gathered from the whole instrument and not from the presence or absence of the word "assigns."

d. Privity of estate [§1201]

Inasmuch as the requirement of privity of estate is the most baffling requirement for most students, it is set forth here in detail. In the analysis of privity of estate, it is necessary to keep separate two kinds of privity of estate: (i) a specified relationship existing between the original promisor and promisee (known as *horizontal privity*), and (ii) a specified relationship between an original party to the contract and an assignee (known as *vertical privity*).

(1) Horizontal privity—relationship between the contracting parties

(a) Running of the burden [§1202]

For the *burden* of a covenant to run to assignees, the traditional rule is that the original parties to the covenant must be in privity of estate. This requirement was laid down in **Spencer's Case,** *supra.* Privity of estate was not defined in that case, and later courts had to decide what the phrase meant. In **Spencer's Case,** the original parties were landlord and tenant, the covenant by the tenant to build a wall was in the lease, and the landlord was trying to enforce the covenant against the assignee tenant. The court found on these facts that there was privity of estate. But which was the important fact that put the parties in privity of estate? It could be (i) that they were landlord and tenant, (ii) that they both had interests in the land, or (iii) that the promise was in a conveyance of a term of years.

1) English view [§1203]

In England it was ultimately decided that the parties to a promise are in privity of estate only if they are in a landlord and tenant relationship. [**Keppell v. Bailey,** 39 Eng. Rep. 1042 (1834)] The judges wanted to curtail restrictions on a fee simple, largely because England at the time had no recording system and covenants could not be discovered by a prospective purchaser from an inspection of the land. Hence, in England, the burden of a covenant runs at law only if it is contained in a lease; the burden of a covenant given by a fee owner does not run at law to assignees. A covenant by a fee owner is enforceable against assignees only in equity as an equitable servitude.

2) Mutual interest [§1204]

Massachusetts and a few other states took the position that what put the parties in privity of estate in **Spencer's Case** was the fact that the landlord and the tenant *both have an interest in the property*. Hence, applying this view of privity to a covenant by a fee owner, the burden will run if one party has an interest (apart from the covenant) in the land of the other. For example, if O divides Blackacre into two lots, and sells one lot to A, reserving an easement for the benefit of the other lot, a promise by A to maintain a fence along the lot line will be enforceable against A's successors. O and A both have interests in A's land: A owns the fee simple and O owns an easement. If O had not reserved the easement, the promise would not be enforceable against A's successors. In effect, then, for the burden of a covenant to run at law in Massachusetts, the covenant must be coupled with an easement. [**Morse v. Aldrich,** 36 Mass. 449 (1837)]

3) Successive relationship [§1205]

A third view of privity—said to be the majority—is that the important fact in **Spencer's Case** was that the covenant was contained in a *conveyance* of an interest in land. Applying this view to a covenant by a fee owner, privity of estate is present where the promise is contained in a conveyance of the fee simple, *i.e.*, where one of the original parties to the promise succeeds to an estate previously owned by the other party. [**Wheeler v. Schad,** 7 Nev. 204 (1871); **Runyon v. Paley,** 416 S.E.2d 177 (N.C. 1992)]

Example: O, a developer, conveys lot 1 to A. A promises not to use lot 1 for commercial purposes. A sells lot 1 to B. The burden of the covenant runs to B because the promise was in the deed from O to A. If A had made a promise to O in a separate instrument a week after the conveyance from O to A, the burden of the covenant would not run to B because O and A were not in privity of estate (a grantor-grantee relationship) when the promise was made.

4) Restatement view [§1206]

First Restatement of Property section 534, synthesizing the jurisdictions, says privity of estate is satisfied by either a mutual relationship or a successive relationship. [**Moseley v. Bishop,** 470 N.E.2d 773 (Ind. 1984)]

a) Restatement policy

The First Restatement of Property objected to the *burden* of covenants running *at law*, and put as many technical roadblocks in the way as arguably could be supported by the cases. The Restatement had no policy objection to the benefit running at law or to burden and benefit running in equity. Why? The Restatement theory was that a judgment for damages—which could result in unlimited personal liability—was much more objectionable than an injunction or foreclosing a lien—which limited the defendant's liability to the value of the land. This theory is, of course, of dubious soundness because in most cases a judgment for damages will result in a smaller loss to the defendant than would an injunction (*see infra*, §1224). Because an injunction is usually worth more to the plaintiff, it is the remedy usually sought.

5) Minority view—not required [§1207]

A minority view holds that horizontal privity is not required for running of the burden. [**Gallagher v. Bell,** 516 A.2d 1028 (Md. 1986)] For example, Restatement of Servitudes section 5.2 repudiates the First Restatement and provides that horizontal privity is not necessary for the burden to run.

EXAM TIP   **gilbert**

Horizontal privity concerns only the *original* parties. Even if successors in interest are trying to enforce the covenant, you must look only to the original covenanting parties to determine horizontal privity.

(b) Running of the benefit [§1208]

At common law, the *benefit* of a covenant could run without the covenanting parties being in privity of estate. [**Pakenham's Case**, Y.B. Hil. 42 Edw. 3, pl. 14 (1368)] What primarily motivated the courts was the desire to keep land free of burdens undiscoverable by a purchaser on inspection of the land. A benefit did not adversely affect marketability. First Restatement section 548 restates the common law view that horizontal privity is not required for running of the benefit, and this is the position taken by modern cases.

EXAM TIP   **gilbert**

When answering exam questions on covenants, remember that in many states the *burden* of the covenant will run to successors only if there is horizontal privity—a successive relationship between the parties such as grantor-grantee or, in some states, a mutual relationship such as lessor-lessee. Horizontal privity is *not* required, however, for the *benefit* of the covenant to run to a successor.

---

(2) Vertical privity—the interest transferred to assignee [§1209]

Vertical privity means the party suing or being sued succeeded to the estate of the original promisee or promisor. [**Runyon v. Paley**, *supra*, §1205]

(a) Running of the burden [§1210]

For the burden to run to a successor owner of the land, the successor must be in vertical privity of estate with the original promisor. Under First Restatement section 535, vertical privity of estate was defined to mean succession to an estate of the same duration as owned by the original promisor. If, *e.g.*, the original promisor owned a fee simple, the covenant will run only to a person succeeding to a fee simple—and not to some lesser interest, such as a life estate.

Example: Suppose that O owns Whiteacre and Blackacre. A buys Blackacre from O. A promises O, his heirs, and assigns that A, his heirs, and assigns will not erect a pizza parlor on Blackacre, which would be objectionable to Whiteacre. Subsequently A devises Blackacre to his wife, W, for life. W erects a pizza parlor. W is not liable for damages. She did not succeed to the whole fee simple A had.

---

1) Runs with estate in land [§1211]

From the above discussion, you should see that although we talk about "covenants running with the land," in fact the covenant runs with the *estate in land*. It annexes itself to that estate and goes to successive owners of that particular estate.

(b) Running of the benefit [§1212]

When the issue is whether the benefit (rather than the burden) runs, First Restatement section 542 says the benefit will run to assigns of *any interest* in the land, not just to assigns of an estate of the same duration as held by the original promisee. Thus, in the example above, if O devised Whiteacre to his wife for life, O's wife could sue A on the promise or she could sue any successors to A's whole fee simple. But O's wife could not sue A's wife because A's wife did not succeed to the whole fee simple. The reason for this different treatment of burden and benefit was the Restatement's dislike of burdens running (*see supra*, §1206).

(c) Restatement of Servitudes view [§1213]

Restatement of Servitudes section 5.2 discards the requirement of vertical privity for running of both the burden and the benefit. Instead, the Restatement draws a distinction between *affirmative* and *negative* covenants. Negative covenants are treated like easements, which run to successors because they are interests in land. Affirmative covenants, requiring the burdened owner to perform an act, are treated differently because they are viewed as more onerous than negative covenants. The burdens and benefits of affirmative covenants run to persons who succeed to an *estate of the same duration* as owned by the original parties, including in most cases an adverse possessor. But affirmative covenants do not run to persons who hold lesser estates than those held by the original parties to the covenant. Special rules are set forth for when affirmative burdens run to lessees and life tenants, who must perform them, and when they can enforce the benefit. [Rest. Servitudes §§5.3, 5.4]

(d) Exception—homeowners' association [§1214]

A homeowners' association may sue to enforce the benefit of a covenant even though the association succeeds to no land owned by the original promisee. The homeowners' association is regarded as the agent of the real parties in interest who own the land. [**Neponsit Property Owners' Association v. Emigrant Industrial Savings Bank**, 278 N.Y. 248 (1938)]

EXAM TIP   **gilbert**

Although many students cringe when they hear the terms "horizontal privity" and "vertical privity," recall the discussion of privity of contract and privity of estate with regard to assignments and subleases (*supra*, §§1036-1037).

Horizontal privity is simply the term used to describe the relationship between the original promisor and promisee—the *parties to the covenant*.

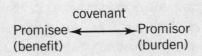

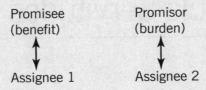

Vertical privity is the term used to describe the relationship between an original party to the covenant and an assignee.

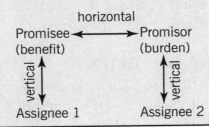

In many states, the **burden** of the covenant will run at law (*i.e.*, the covenant may be enforced against Assignee 2) only if there is **both horizontal and vertical privity**. The running of the **benefit** (*i.e.*, allowing Assignee 1 to enforce the covenant) generally requires **only vertical privity**.

e. Touch and concern [§1215]

For the burden to run with the burdened land, the covenant must touch and concern the burdened land. Likewise, for the benefit to run with the benefited land, the covenant must touch and concern the benefited land. Inasmuch as this is a requirement in equity as well as in law, and as most of the cases involve equitable servitudes, this requirement is discussed in connection with equitable servitudes, *infra*, §§1245 *et seq.*

f. Notice [§1216]

A bona fide purchaser of the burdened land is not bound at law if he has no notice of the covenant. The same notice requirement is applicable to equitable servitudes, discussed *infra*, §§1260 *et seq.*

EXAM TIP   **gilbert**

Remember that the notice requirement will protect **only bona fide purchasers for value**. Someone who does not give value may be bound by a covenant at law (not equity) even if he has no actual or constructive notice of the covenant.

---

g. Liability of original promisor after assignment [§1217]

After the promisor assigns the land, does the promisor remain personally liable on the contract? If the covenant is a promise to do or not to do some act on the burdened land, the covenantor has **no liability** after assignment. The covenantor has no control over the land after assignment, so it would be unfair to hold him liable for performance of the covenant by the assignee or subsequent assignees. With this type of covenant, the courts imply that the parties intended that the covenantor's liability cease with assignment. [**Gallagher v. Bell**, *supra*, §1207; Rest. Servitudes §4.4]

C. Equitable Servitudes

1. Introduction

a. Definition [§1218]

An equitable servitude is a covenant—whether or not running with the land at law—that *equity* will enforce against *assignees* of the burdened land who have *notice* of the covenant. The usual equitable remedy granted is an *injunction* against violation of the covenant.

b. Historical development [§1219]

As noted above (*supra*, §1203), the law courts in England refused to permit a covenant by a fee simple owner to run with the land to an assignee, primarily because England had no recording system that would permit subsequent purchasers to discover covenants and it was deemed unfair to subject purchasers to such risks. On the other hand, the industrial revolution had demonstrated the need for enforceable running covenants. One tract of land might need to have power supplied by the owner of a neighboring tract and his successors. The owner of one tract might want to prevent economic loss by a factory or incompatible use locating next door. As urban land use intensified, it was seen that benefits could be gained from running covenants. In the middle of the nineteenth century, equity stepped in to resolve these conflicting considerations by holding that a covenant would be enforced in equity against a subsequent purchaser *with notice* of the covenant (thus obviating the main objection of the law courts).

(1) Tulk v. Moxhay [§1220]

The famous case of **Tulk v. Moxhay**, 41 Eng. Rep. 1143 (1848), originated equitable servitudes. In this case, Tulk sold Leicester Square in London to Elms, who promised for himself, his heirs, and assigns not to build on the Square. Elms conveyed the Square to Moxhay, who had notice of the covenant. Moxhay proposed to build on the Square, and Tulk sued for an injunction. The chancellor granted the injunction. The chancellor deemed it inequitable that a covenant should be unenforceable against a subsequent purchaser where the purchaser acquired the land with knowledge of the restriction. The purchaser, Moxhay, probably supposed himself bound by the covenant and probably paid less for the land than he would have had to pay for unburdened land. To hold the covenant unenforceable would give Moxhay an advantage he did not bargain for and would unjustly enrich him. From this acorn grew a new servitude known as an equitable servitude.

(2) Theory of enforcement [§1221]

The theory underlying an equitable servitude was at one time disputed. Some early courts and scholars said that equity was merely granting specific performance of a contract against an assignee with notice. Ultimately, however, most courts shifted away from this theory. The right to specific performance of the contract (like equitable conversion, *infra*, §1547) was deemed to give the promisee an interest in the land. When the promise was negative (not to do something), the right was thought of as an equitable interest analogous to a negative easement. The Restatement and practically all the recent cases now take the view that an equitable servitude is an interest in land.

c. Equitable servitude compared with real covenant [§1222]

The principal differences between an equitable servitude (enforceable in equity) and a real covenant (enforceable in law) are as follows:

(1) Remedy [§1223]

Different remedies are available for breach of an equitable servitude than are available for breach of a real covenant. If a promisee seeks *damages* from an assignee, the promisee must go into law and attempt to enforce the promise as a real covenant. If the promisee seeks an *injunction*, or enforcement of a consensual lien securing a promise to pay money, the promisee must go into equity and ask for enforcement of an equitable servitude.

(a) Remedies compared [§1224]

In the usual case, the plaintiff wants an injunction, not damages. An injunction is worth more to the plaintiff than damages. For example, assume a subdivision is restricted to residential use. A wants to put a commercial building on her lot. If A's lot is available for commercial use, the value of A's lot will increase from $25 to $100. A will make a gain of $75. On the other hand, commercial use of A's lot will damage B's house next door, causing a $30 loss in value. If B sues for and is awarded damages, B gets $30. If B sues for and gets an injunction, B has a right that B can sell to A for more than $30. Because A will make a gain of $75 if she can build commercially, and B will be damaged only $30 by A's commercial building, B should "sell his injunction" to A for a price somewhere between $30 and $75; then both A and B are better off. The difference between the damage to B and the value to A ($45) is an economic gain available to the parties by trading. If A buys B off for $55, B has a profit of $25 and A has a profit of $20. As a general rule, then, an injunction permits B to reap some of the gain from trading with A, whereas a judgment for damages gives all the gains from trade ($45) to A. A naturally would prefer to have a judgment for damages, rather than an injunction, awarded to B.

EXAM TIP   **gilbert**

When answering exam questions, be sure to remember that the crucial difference between real covenants and equitable servitudes is the *remedy sought*. If money *damages* are sought, you must use the real covenant analysis. If a party seeks an *injunction*, you must consider whether the requirements for enforcement as an equitable servitude have been met. A single promise can create both a real covenant and an equitable servitude.

---

(2) Creation [§1225]

A real covenant must be in writing. In many states an equitable servitude will be *implied* (*see infra*, §1229).

(3) Privity of estate [§1226]

Horizontal privity of estate is not required in equity. Nor is vertical privity required for the burden to run. The court, in enforcing an equitable servitude, is enforcing an interest in land analogous to an easement, which is enforceable against any person who interferes with it. On the other hand, when a person other than the original promisee is enforcing the *benefit*, in some states such person must show that he acquired title to his land from the promisee, either before or after the original covenant was made. (*See infra*, §1242.)

EXAM TIP   **gilbert**

In contrast to real covenants, which require vertical and horizontal privity of estate for burdens to run, and vertical privity for benefits to run, in most states *no privity of estate is required* for an equitable servitude to be enforceable by and against assignees.

---

(4) Touch and concern and notice [§1227]

Both real covenants and equitable servitudes require that the covenant touch and concern land. Neither is enforceable against a subsequent bona fide purchaser without notice of the covenant.

(5) Restatement of Servitudes position [§1228]

The Restatement of Servitudes applies the same rules to real covenants and equitable servitudes, thus abolishing any distinction between them. Generally these rules are those now applied to equitable servitudes, but the Restatement goes further and abolishes a number of technical rules restricting equitable servitudes discussed later in this chapter.

DISTINGUISHING CHARACTERISTICS OF REAL COVENANTS AND EQUITABLE SERVITUDES **gilbert**		
	REAL COVENANTS	**EQUITABLE SERVITUDES**
CREATION	Writing is *always* required	Writing is *usually* required but may arise by *implication* from common scheme of development of a residential subdivision
RUNNING OF BURDEN	Requires: • Horizontal privity (shared interest in land, apart from the covenant, by *original* covenanting parties; or covenant put in a deed from grantor to grantee), *and* • Vertical privity (successor holds entire interest held by covenanting party)	No privity required
RUNNING OF BENEFIT	Vertical privity required	No privity required in most states
REMEDY	Damages	Injunction

2. Creation [§1229]

Inasmuch as an equitable servitude is an interest in land, most courts hold that the Statute of Frauds requires a writing signed by the promisor. As with real covenants, acceptance of a deed signed only by the grantor binds the grantee as promisor (*see supra*, §1195). However, there is one important exception to the requirement of a writing: Negative equitable servitudes may be implied from a general plan for development of a residential subdivision. This exception, followed in a majority of states, is discussed below.

a. Negative servitude implied from a general plan [§1230]

In the case of a restricted residential subdivision, many courts will imply a negative servitude on a lot even though there is no writing creating the servitude on that lot. This is usually done on the theory of equitable estoppel: Where a purchaser, buying a lot restricted to residential use, relies on the promise of the subdivider to restrict the other lots and makes a substantial investment, the subdivider and any assignee of the other lots are estopped to plead the Statute of Frauds.

(1) The circumstances [§1231]

Suppose that a developer is marketing a tract of 50 lots. The developer sells off 30 lots by deeds containing covenants by the respective grantees that each will use his lot for residential purposes only. The developer orally assures all 30 grantees that this will be an exclusively residential development and that similar restrictions will be inserted in subsequent deeds. Then the developer sells off two corner lots to gasoline companies by deeds containing no covenants. The gasoline companies want to erect service stations. If (i) the developer had a *general plan* of an exclusively residential subdivision, *and* (ii) the gasoline companies had *notice* of the covenants in the 30 prior deeds, the court will imply a covenant in the deeds to the gasoline companies restricting their lots to residential purposes only. [**Turner v. Brocato,** 111 A.2d 855 (Md. 1955); **Sanborn v. McLean,** 206 N.W. 496 (Mich. 1925); **Buffalo Academy of the Sacred Heart v. Boehm Bros.,** 267 N.Y. 242 (1935); **Mid-State Equipment Co. v. Bell,** 225 S.E.2d 877 (Va. 1976); Rest. Servitudes §2.14]

(a) General plan required [§1232]

A court will imply a reciprocal negative servitude only if the evidence shows that the developer had a reasonably uniform general plan for development of all lots of the same character. [**Evans v. Pollock,** 796 S.W.2d 465 (Tex. 1990)] On the basis of this general plan, it is inferred that the purchasers bought in reliance on the general plan and in the expectation of being able to enforce subsequently created equitable servitudes similar or identical to the restrictions imposed on their lots.

(b) Evidence of general plan [§1233]

The general plan must exist at the time the developer sells the first burdened lot within the general plan. If the plan arises later, it cannot impose burdens on lots previously sold without the burdens. [**Davis v. Huey,** 620 S.W.2d 561 (Tex. 1981)] Evidence of a general plan includes a recorded plat with restrictions, the developer exhibiting to buyers a map or plat of the entire tract on which restrictions appear, oral representations of the developer with respect to restrictions to be imposed on the remaining land, and statements made in sales brochures or advertising. Or, a general plan can be shown by the fact that the developer inserted similar covenants in a substantial number of the deeds in the subdivision *prior* to the deed to defendant. Restrictions inserted in other deeds *after* the deed to defendant do not show a general plan at the necessary time. [**Graham v. Beermunder,** 93 A.D.2d 254 (1983)]

Example: Subdivider CG (common grantor) sells off lot 1 to A. No restrictions appear on any plat or map. Subsequently, CG sells off the remaining lots in the subdivision, restricting them to residential use. Lot 1 is not bound by the restrictions. If a number of lots in the subdivision are sold off before the plan arises, the court may find "no general plan" because of the apparent inequity of enforcing burdens against some, but not all, owners in the subdivision.

EXAM TIP   **gilbert**

Questions involving negative servitudes implied from a general plan are fairly common on law school exams and fairly easy to spot. They almost always will involve a general plan for an exclusively residential subdivision and a purchaser who wants to intrude with a commercial use. You should enforce the negative servitude (*i.e.*, prohibit the commercial use) if there is evidence that (i) the developer had a plan calling for *development of all the lots in the same character* and (ii) the *plan existed* no later than the time the parcel in question was sold.

---

(2) Kind of servitude implied [§1234]

A servitude similar to a *reciprocal negative easement* is implied. This label is quite descriptive. The servitude must be *reciprocal*; *i.e.*, a similar covenant must bind other lots in the subdivision. It must be a *negative* or *restrictive* covenant, forbidding some use of land; the court will not imply affirmative covenants, requiring the purchasers to do something. And the servitude is in the nature of an *easement*; *i.e.*, it is an interest in land.

(3) Covenants not implied [§1235]

Some courts refuse to imply reciprocal negative servitudes in a residential subdivision. In California, an equitable servitude must be created by a written instrument identifying the burdened lot. It will not be implied from the existence of restrictions on other lots in a subdivision. [**Riley v. Bear Creek Planning Committee,** 17 Cal. 3d 500 (1976)] If a recorded subdivision map contains restrictions on the property, which are said to be covenants running with the land, such written restrictions are enforceable by and against subsequent purchasers in the subdivision. [**Citizens for Covenant Compliance v. Anderson,** 12 Cal. 4th 345 (1995)] Massachusetts also will not imply negative servitudes. [**Sprague v. Kimball,** 100 N.E. 622 (Mass. 1913)]

b. Using general plan to show who has the benefit [§1236]

Even in jurisdictions that do not imply restrictions from a general plan, a general plan can be used to show who the developer intended to have the benefit of written restrictions on other lots. If there is a general plan, then prior and subsequent purchasers of lots within a subdivision can enforce a written restriction on a restricted lot. It is inferred from the plan that the developer intended to confer a benefit on all lot owners. [**Snow v. Van Dam,** 197 N.E. 224 (Mass. 1935)] A general plan can be used to determine who can enforce restrictions in jurisdictions that imply restrictions from a general plan as well as in jurisdictions that do not imply restrictions.

---

e.g.   **Example:** Developer, owner of 50 lots in a subdivision, sells these lots with restrictions limiting use to residential purposes only. The deeds do not indicate who has the power to enforce the restrictions. If the developer has a general plan of substantial uniformity, all purchasers in the subdivision—whether they buy their lots before or after the owner they are suing—can enforce the restrictions.

(1) Developer's right to modify [§1237]

If the developer retains the right to modify the restrictions imposed on lots to be sold in the future, some cases have held that this is evidence of intent to benefit the developer personally and not the neighbors in the subdivision. The retention of the right to modify may negate the existence of enforcement rights in the lot owners. [**Suttle v. Bailey,** 361 P.2d 325 (N.M. 1961)] On the other hand, several cases and Restatement of Servitudes section 2.14, comment h, take the position that the developer's right to modify does not destroy the power of the lot owners to enforce the general plan as it finally takes form. [**Berger v. Van Sweringen Co.,** 216 N.E.2d 54 (Ohio 1966)]

c. Real covenants [§1238]

Real covenants, unlike equitable servitudes, have not been implied by courts. The reason may be that courts deem it unfair to impose personal liability on a person without an express agreement. An implied servitude, enforceable only by injunction or lien, limits liability to the value of the land. Or the reason may be that equity has traditionally been willing to brush aside formalities in carrying out the parties' intent.

3. Enforcement By or Against Assignees [§1239]

For an equitable servitude to be enforced by a successor to the promisee or against a successor to the promisor, certain requirements must be met.

a. Intent [§1240]

The contracting parties must intend that the servitude be enforceable by and against assignees. No technical words such as "assigns" (possibly required for a covenant to run at law) are required. (*See supra,* §1200.) The court ascertains intent from the purpose of the covenant and the surrounding circumstances.

b. Privity of estate [§1241]

Privity of estate is relevant in equity only when the person trying to enforce the benefit does not own land that was once owned by the original promisee. In some states, such a person cannot enforce the benefit.

(1) The ghost of privity [§1242]

Privity of estate, somewhat redefined, survives in a few states as a requirement for enforcing an equitable servitude. The person seeking to enforce the covenant *must trace his title to the original promisee.* In describing this requirement, courts say the plaintiff must be in "privity of estate" with the original promisee, but this meaning of vertical privity differs from what has been discussed earlier. Under this requirement, all purchasers in a subdivision can enforce a restriction imposed by the developer, because they trace title from the developer. But a third party who did not buy any land from the person imposing the restriction cannot enforce the restriction. Similarly, a third party that owns no land, such as the Sierra Club, cannot enforce a restriction because the party cannot trace title to land from the developer. [**Malley v. Hanna,** 65 N.Y.2d 289 (1985); **Neponsit Property Owners' Association v. Emigrant Industrial Savings Bank,** *supra,* §1214]

(2) Third-party beneficiary theory [§1243]

In a large majority of states, any third-party beneficiary can enforce a covenant in law or in equity if the contracting parties so intend. This follows modern contract law, which puts no restrictions on the kinds of third-party beneficiaries who can enforce contracts. In these jurisdictions, privity of estate is irrelevant in enforcing equitable servitudes.

(3) Distinguish—easements [§1244]

At common law, and in a majority of states, an easement cannot be reserved in favor of a third person (*see supra,* §1113). On the other hand, an equitable servitude analogous to a negative easement can be enforced by third parties. Such a result seems irrational, but it is the law of, *e.g.,* New York. Restatement of Servitudes section 2.6 makes all servitudes (easements and covenants) enforceable by third parties if the parties to the transaction so intend.

c. Touch and concern requirement

(1) General rule [§1245]

For the burden to run with the burdened land in equity as well as in law, the covenant must touch and concern the burdened land. And likewise, for the benefit to run with the benefited land, the covenant must touch and concern the benefited land. Equity generally applies the same touch and concern test as is applied at law. It is difficult to give any but the most generalized statement of the meaning of "touch and concern." Early cases asked whether the covenant burdens or benefits a party in the *physical use or enjoyment* of particular land, but this proved too narrow a test. Some covenants, particularly negative covenants, merely *enhance the value* of the benefited land, but they have been held to touch and concern the benefited land as well as the burdened land.

(a) Function of requirement [§1246]

The function of the touch and concern requirement is to permit courts to stop covenants from running when the social utility of the covenant is outweighed by the fettering of the burdened property. A market economist would say that if there are no harmful third-party effects, the court, in deciding whether a covenant touches and concerns, should try to approximate the decision the present land-owners would reach in a negotiation free of transaction costs. If the value of the benefit exceeds the burden, the present landowners would reimpose the covenant because it would be to the advantage of both. Because the benefited party values the right more, the benefited party would pay the burdened party for the right. Under this theory, the relative values of the benefit and burden are very important in deciding whether a covenant touches and concerns. The First Restatement appears to have some such theory in mind when it states, "the burden will not run if the burden imposed is obviously greater than the benefit given. There must be such a relation between benefit and burden that the performance of the promise has, in the particular case, some reasonable prospect of promoting land utilization as a whole." [Rest. §537, comment h]

(2) Specific applications

(a) Negative covenants [§1247]

Covenants not to do a physical act (*e.g.*, not to erect commercial buildings) touch and concern. These covenants affect the burdened owner in the physical use of his land. Restrictive covenants also *enhance the value* of the benefited land, even though they may not affect the benefited owner in the physical use of his land. Covenants containing building restrictions, enhancing the value of the benefited land, have always been held to touch and concern. [**Runyon v. Paley,** *supra*, §1205]

1) Covenants not to compete

a) Burden side [§1248]

A covenant not to compete restricts the promisor in the *physical use* he may make of his land. Hence, it touches and concerns the *burdened* land as much as a covenant restricting the property to residential use. Most courts have so held, provided the covenant is reasonable in its duration and in the area it encompasses. [**Dick v. Sears-Roebuck & Co.,** 160 A. 432 (Conn. 1932); **Dunafon v. Delaware McDonald's Corp.,** 691 F. Supp. 1232 (W.D. Mo. 1988)]

b) Benefit side [§1249]

The benefit of a covenant not to compete clearly enhances the value of the covenantee's land, but it is debatable whether it affects him in the physical use of his land. Nevertheless, a majority of courts hold that *enhancement of commercial value* is enough to satisfy the requirement of touch and concern. Massachusetts formerly held that the benefit of a covenant not to compete does not touch and concern land. [**Shell Oil Co. v. Henry Ouellette & Sons Co.,** 227 N.E.2d 509 (Mass. 1967)] This holding, coupled with the rule that the burden will not run if the benefit is in gross (*see infra*, §1255), meant that the burden of a covenant not to compete would not run. However, the old Massachusetts cases have now been overruled; reasonable covenants not to compete now run in Massachusetts when they facilitate orderly and harmonious commercial development. [**Whitinsville Plaza, Inc. v. Kotseas,** 390 N.E.2d 243 (Mass. 1979)]

(b) Affirmative covenants [§1250]

In England, only negative covenants are enforceable as equitable servitudes. This refusal to enforce affirmative covenants rests either on the idea that an equitable servitude is in substance a negative easement or on the perceived difficulty of supervising performance by a mandatory injunction. In some early cases in this country, particularly in New York and New Jersey, this English restriction on equitable servitudes was influential. Today, however, this position has been largely abandoned. Most courts permit affirmative covenants to run both in law and equity; they usually are held to touch and concern the land. [**Lake Arrowhead Community Club, Inc. v. Looney,** 770 P.2d 1046 (Wash. 1989)—holding affirmative covenant runs to purchaser at tax sale] Nonetheless, if an affirmative covenant imposes a substantial burden on property which receives no benefit from it and fetters land in perpetuity, a court may find it does not touch and concern. [**Eagle Enterprises, Inc. v. Gross,** 39 N.Y.2d 505 (1976)]

1) Performance off land [§1251]

If the act is to be performed off the burdened land, without benefiting the burdened land, the covenant does not touch and concern the burdened land.

Example: O conveys Blackacre to A, who promises to keep a house on Whiteacre in repair. The benefit touches and concerns Whiteacre, but the burden does not touch and concern Blackacre.

Compare: On the other hand, if the act to be performed off the burdened land benefits the burdened land, the covenant does touch and concern. A typical covenant of the latter type is a promise to perform (or not perform) an act regarding maintenance of common areas in a condominium.

(c) Covenants to pay money [§1252]

Covenants to pay money for some improvement that benefits the promisor by enhancing the value of his property touch and concern even though the improvements are on other land. Typically these covenants provide that the landowner or condominium owner will pay a certain sum each year to maintain common spaces. If the formula for calculating the sum is reasonably clear, a covenant to pay an annual fee is enforceable against assigns. [**Streams Sports Club, Ltd. v. Richmond,** 440 N.E.2d 1264 (Ill. 1982); **Regency Homes Association v. Egermayer,** 498 N.W.2d 783 (Neb. 1993); **Neponsit Property Owners' Association v. Emigrant Industrial Savings Bank,** *supra,* §1242]

1) Lien [§1253]

A covenant to pay money is normally enforced by an action at law for breach of contract. To give the promisee an additional remedy, a deed often will retain a lien on the land to enforce the promise. If the burden of the covenant does not run at law, so that no personal judgment can be obtained against the assignee of the promisor, the *land* can be reached by equitable process to satisfy the consensual lien.

(d) Restatement of Servitudes view [§1254]

Restatement of Servitudes section 3.2 "supersedes" the touch and concern requirement with more specific tests for unenforceability, including reasonableness. The Restatement provides separate grounds for refusing to enforce a servitude at its inception and for refusing to enforce a servitude which, although reasonable in the beginning, subsequently becomes unreasonable. So too in **Davidson Bros. v. D. Katz & Sons, Inc.,** 579 A.2d 288 (N.J. 1990), the court held that rigid adherence to the touch and concern requirement was no longer warranted, and that enforceability of a covenant would depend on its reasonableness.

(3) Covenant with benefit in gross [§1255]

When the benefit of a covenant does not touch and concern land (*i.e.,* is in gross), the majority rule is that the burden will not run. In other words, the burden will not run unless the benefit is tied to land. What is the reason for this rule? A brief historical explanation will show its origin and its misapplication in the United States.

(a) English rule [§1256]

English courts refused to recognize an easement in gross. Easements must be tied to land. When the equitable servitude developed, they viewed it as an "interest analogous to a negative easement." Therefore, quite logically, the English courts held that the burden of an equitable servitude (analogous to a legal easement) will not run if the benefit is in gross. For a servitude to run, there must be both a servient and a dominant tenement. [**London County Council v. Allen,** [1914] 3 K.B. 642]

---

e.g. **Example:** The Urban Housing Commission sells land to A, extracting a promise from A that A will use the land only for residential purposes. A sells the land to B. If the Urban Housing Commission owns no land benefited by the promise, the covenant is not enforceable against B.

(b) American law—equitable servitudes [§1257]

In this country, easements in gross are recognized, and the burden of the easement runs with the land. Therefore, if an equitable servitude is an "interest analogous to an [American] easement," the burden should run even if the benefit is in gross. Most courts, however, followed the English view, paying no mind to its basic assumption that equitable servitudes were analogous to easements. [**Snow v. Van Dam,** *supra*, §1236; **Neponsit Property Owners' Association v. Emigrant Industrial Savings Bank,** *supra*, §1252]

1) Rationale

The rule possibly can be justified on the following grounds: (i) Where a burden devalues land, public policy requires an accompanying benefit to other land, resulting in a net increase in land value. (ii) Where the benefit is in gross, finding the owner or owners to buy them out is more difficult than when the benefit is in the owner of neighboring land.

2) Minority view [§1258]

Some courts hold that the burden of a covenant will run even though the benefit is in gross. They see no reason to distinguish between covenants and easements. [**Merrionette Manor Homes Improvement Association v. Heda,** 136 N.E.2d 556 (Ill. 1956); **Pratte v. Balatsos,** 113 A.2d 492 (N.H. 1955)] Section 2.6, comment d, of the Restatement of Servitudes provides that the burden will run, both in law and equity, where the benefit is in gross.

(c) American law—real covenants [§1259]

Although the analogy to legal easements is not made with respect to real covenants, it has been held that the policies underlying the rule in equity (*see supra*, §1257) are applicable to covenants at law. Thus, if a covenant will not run in equity because the benefit is in gross, neither will a covenant run at law. [**Caullett v. Stanley Stilwell & Sons, Inc.,** 170 A.2d 52 (N.J. 1961)]

d. Notice [§1260]

If the assignee is a subsequent purchaser for valuable consideration without notice of the servitude, he does not take subject to it. If the assignee has notice, he is bound if the servitude is otherwise enforceable. Notice can be actual, record, or inquiry.

(1) Actual notice [§1261]

If the assignee has actual knowledge of the covenant in a prior deed, he clearly has notice.

(2) Record notice [§1262]

If the covenant is in a deed to the assignee's lot, he has record notice. If the covenant is in a deed or deeds to other lots in a subdivision conveyed by the developer to prior grantees, the assignee has record notice if the deeds to neighboring lots are in the assignee's *chain of title* (*i.e.*, he must read them because by operation of law he has notice of their contents). However, there is a split of authority as to whether covenants contained in prior deeds out to other grantees in the same tract from a common grantor, which purport to restrict use of all lots in the tract, are in a subsequent grantee's chain of title (*see infra*, §1776). Some courts hold that prior deeds out from a common grantor to other purchasers in a subdivision are in the chain of title of a subsequent purchaser from the developer. [**Guillette v. Daly Dry Wall, Inc.**, 325 N.E.2d 572 (Mass. 1975)] Other courts hold they are not in the chain of title, and the subsequent grantee does not have record notice of their contents. [**Buffalo Academy of the Sacred Heart v. Boehm Bros.**, *supra*, §1231]

Example: Developer CG sells off 40 lots by deeds containing identical residential restrictions. CG sells off lot 41 to A without restrictions. A has no actual notice of the contents of prior deeds. If the prior deeds are in A's chain of title, A may be subject to an implied restriction if there is a general plan, or A will be subject to an express restriction if the prior deeds expressly bind the common grantor's retained land. If the prior deeds are not in A's chain of title, A is not subject to an implied covenant nor to an express covenant contained in those deeds.

(3) Inquiry notice [§1263]

At least one court has held that a purchaser buying into a built-up residential area where the houses appear to have been built in accordance with a plan should look at the other deeds out from the developer to see if any basis for an implied covenant exists. Regardless of whether such prior deeds are in the purchaser's chain of title, the lay of the land puts him on inquiry notice to look at the deeds of the neighboring lots from the developer. [**Sanborn v. McLean**, *supra*, §1231]

REQUIREMENTS FOR THE RUNNING OF BENEFITS AND BURDENS	COVENANTS		EQUITABLE SERVITUDES	
	BENEFIT	BURDEN	BENEFIT	BURDEN
INTENT	✓	✓	✓	✓
NOTICE		✓		✓
TOUCH & CONCERN	✓	✓	✓	✓
HORIZONTAL PRIVITY		✓		
VERTICAL PRIVITY	✓	✓		

4. Construction of Covenants [§1264]

A covenant will be construed so as to carry out the intention of the parties in light of the purpose of the covenant. Some of the more frequently recurring construction problems involve the following matters.

a. Single-family dwelling [§1265]

Covenants in residential subdivisions usually prohibit use of the property except for a single-family dwelling. But what is a "single-family dwelling"? Much litigation has ensued over this question.

(1) Group homes [§1266]

Does a group home constitute a single-family dwelling or does "single-family" imply that the occupants must be related by blood, marriage, or adoption? The cases are not all in agreement, but the most recent cases take a functional approach and ask if the particular group home functions with a traditional family housekeeping structure and atmosphere. Public policy also favors including in residential settings group homes for individuals with physical or mental disabilities. Group homes for the disabled are almost always classified as single-family dwellings, whereas a fraternity house would not be. [**McMillan v. Iserman**, 327 N.W.2d 559 (Mich. 1982)—residential mental health facility; **Blevins v. Barry-Lawrence County Association for Retarded Citizens,** 707 S.W.2d 407 (Mo. 1986)—developmentally disabled persons; **Hill v. Community of Damien of Molokai,** 911 P.2d 861 (N.M. 1996)—AIDS; **Rhodes v. Palmetto Pathway Homes, Inc.,** 400 S.E.2d 484 (S.C. 1991)—mentally disabled persons]

(a) Fair Housing Act [§1267]

The federal Fair Housing Act prohibits discrimination against handicapped persons in the sale or rental of a dwelling (*see supra*, §833). Discrimination also includes a refusal to make reasonable accommodations when necessary to afford handicapped persons equal opportunity to use a dwelling. Enforcement of a residential covenant against a group home for the disabled—even if the term "single-family" is construed to exclude group homes—is a violation of the Fair Housing Act. [**Hill v. Community of Damien of Molokai,** *supra*]

(2) Commercial use [§1268]

Persons often use their houses for home occupations. If a covenant restricts the use of property to "residential use" only, what home occupations come within or outside that term? Baking cakes for sale, repairing cars, practicing medicine, child day care? The cases tend to be resolved on their own facts, emphasizing any increased traffic or change in the character of the neighborhood. [**Metzner v. Wojdyla,** 886 P.2d 154 (Wash. 1994)]

b. Whether residential use only implied [§1269]

A covenant that does *not specifically* limit use of land to residential may do so inferentially by providing, "no dwelling house shall be built closer than 20 feet from the street or cost less than $25,000," or something similar. Some courts, hostile to covenants, construe them literally and refuse to imply a general prohibition against nonresidential use from specific restrictions on dwelling size, cost, or location. [**Groninger v. Aumiller,** 644 A.2d 1266 (Pa. 1994)] But other cases construe the restrictions in a manner to achieve their purpose of protecting the character of the neighborhood. These cases imply a general restriction for residential use from specific restrictions on dwellings. [**Joslin v. Pine River Development Corp.,** 367 A.2d 599 (N.H. 1976)]

c. Architectural controls [§1270]

Many modern subdivisions contain covenants that every building to be erected shall be approved by an architectural control committee. The standards governing approval may be very general or vague. Courts have held that specific standards are not necessary, but the architectural control committee must act reasonably and in good faith. [**Rhue v. Cheyenne Homes, Inc.,** 449 P.2d 361 (Colo. 1969); **Jones v. Northwest Real Estate Co.,** 131 A. 446 (Md. 1925)] This good faith rule has been criticized for failing to protect against arbitrary action in fact, because the burden of establishing bad faith is too costly for most landowners to undertake.

d. Exclusion of churches [§1271]

Churches and religious schools can be excluded from residential areas by restrictive covenants. The majority of courts hold that it is not state action for a court to enjoin religious use of residentially restricted land. [**Ginsberg v. Yeshiva of Far Rockaway,** 45 A.D.2d 334 (1974), *aff'd*, 36 N.Y.2d 706 (1975)]

e. Racial restriction [§1272]

A covenant prohibiting use of the property by a person of a particular race cannot be enforced by the courts. Judicial enforcement of racial covenants is *state action* (action by the state) which deprives a person of equal protection of the laws. Racially discriminatory action by the executive, legislative, or judicial branches of the state is forbidden by the Constitution. Thus, although the covenant is not void, it cannot be enforced. [**Shelley v. Kraemer,** *supra*, §360]

5. Termination of Covenants and Servitudes

a. Merger [§1273]

If the title to the land benefited and the title to the land burdened come into the hands of one person, real covenants and equitable servitudes, like easements, merge into the fee simple and cease to exist. *Rationale:* The owner of the benefited land cannot sue himself for damages or an injunction; therefore, there is no enforceable covenant. If one parcel is subsequently sold, new covenants will have to be imposed if the owner wants a covenant.

b. Equitable defenses to enforcement [§1274]

Any of the following may be asserted as defenses to enforcement where an equitable servitude is claimed.

(1) Estoppel [§1275]

If a benefited party acts in such a way as to lead a reasonable person to believe that the covenant was abandoned, and the burdened party acts in reliance thereon, the benefited party may be estopped to enforce the covenant. [**Fink v. Miller,** 896 P.2d 649 (Utah 1995)]

(2) Relative hardship [§1276]

As a general rule, a court of equity may deny an injunction when the hardship to the defendant is great and the benefit to the plaintiff is small. But where the right to the benefit of a servitude is clear, the defense of disproportionate harm and benefit is usually not persuasive. [**Mohawk Containers, Inc. v. Hancock,** 43 Misc. 2d 716 (1964); **Rick v. West,** 34 Misc. 2d 1002 (1962); **Loeb v. Watkins,** 240 A.2d 513 (Pa. 1968)]

(3) Change of conditions in neighborhood [§1277]

The most frequently asserted defense to equitable enforcement of a servitude is that the character of the neighborhood has so changed that it is impossible any longer to secure in substantial degree the benefits of the restrictive covenants. If this is shown, equity will refuse to enforce the covenant. [**El Di, Inc. v. Town of Bethany Beach,** 477 A.2d 1066 (Del. 1984); **Trustees of Columbia College v. Thacher,** 87 N.Y. 311 (1881)] However, for the defense of change of conditions to succeed, most courts require either that (i) the change *outside* the subdivision must be so pervasive as to make *all lots* in the subdivision unsuitable for the permitted uses, or (ii) substantial change must have occurred *within the subdivision* itself. Change outside the subdivision that affects only the border lots in a subdivision is not sufficient to prevent enforcement of the covenant against the border lots. [**Camelback Del Este Homeowners Association v. Warner,** 749 P.2d 930 (Ariz. 1987); **Bolotin v. Rindge,** 230 Cal. App. 2d 741 (1964); **Pettey v. First National Bank,** 588 N.E.2d 412 (Ill. 1992); **Western Land Co. v. Truskolaski,** 495 P.2d 624 (Nev.1972); **Montoya v. Barreras,** 473 P.2d 363 (N.M. 1970)]

Example: Developer restricts a subdivision to residential use. Subsequently, commercial development and traffic increase on the borders of the subdivision. The owner of a border lot within the restricted tract wants to develop commercially. The courts refuse to permit the border lot owner to develop commercially unless the purposes of the restrictions can no longer be achieved for any owner because of changed conditions. *Rationale:* If the purchaser of a border lot has paid a lower price because it is a buffer lot, to permit the border owner to develop would give him a benefit he did not bargain for and deprive the owners of inner lots of a benefit paid for.

---

(4) Effect on right to damages [§1278]

Theoretically, the above defenses are equitable defenses, and if successful the plaintiff still may have a right to damages. But in fact the damage remedy is rarely used. It has been suggested that efficiency and fairness would be better served by giving the owners of benefited lots damages rather than an injunction in many cases of changed conditions. [*See* Mass. Gen. Laws ch. 184, §30—denying injunctive relief and giving damage remedy only if any of several enumerated conditions are found to exist; *and see* **Blakeley v. Gorin,** 313 N.E.2d 903 (Mass. 1974)—statute held constitutional]

c. Abandonment [§1279]

An easement burdening other land may be abandoned by the holder of the easement (*see supra,* §1177). But an affirmative covenant, such as an obligation to pay money, cannot be abandoned. One cannot walk away from an obligation and terminate liability. But this means that affirmative covenants may be onerous, because all of the landowner's assets may be reached to pay the obligation. Restatement of Servitudes section 7.12 provides for modification or termination of affirmative covenants when the obligation is in perpetuity or becomes excessive. But these rules do not apply to obligations to a community association or reciprocal obligations imposed in a common plan. [**Pocono Springs Civic Association v. MacKenzie,** 667 A.2d 233 (Pa. 1995)]

gilbert

	EASEMENT	PROFIT	LICENSE	REAL COVENANT/ EQUITABLE SERVITUDE
DEFINITION	A grant of an interest in land that allows someone to use another's land	Right to take part of the land or a product of the land of another	Permission to go onto another's land	Promise to do or not to do something on the land or related to the land
EXAMPLE	Owner of parcel A grants owner of parcel B the right to drive across parcel A	O allows A to come onto O's land to cut and remove timber	O allows the electrician to come onto his land to fix an outlet	O conveys an adjoining parcel to A. A promises not to build a swimming pool on the property
WRITING	Generally required. *Exceptions:* • Implication • Necessity • Prescription	Required	Not required. *Note:* An invalid oral easement is a license	Required. *Exception:* Equitable servitude may be implied from general plan of development of residential subdivision
TERMINATION	• Express terms • Unity of title (merger) • Release • Abandonment • Alteration of dominant tenement • End of necessity • Destruction of servient tenement • Prescription • Change of conditions	Same as Easement	Usually revocable at will. May be irrevocable if coupled with an interest or if licensor estopped by licensee's expenditures	• Merger • Estoppel • Hardship • Change of conditions • Abandonment • Eminent domain

d. Eminent domain [§1280]

When the government by eminent domain takes title to the burdened land and condemns the covenant as well, the majority rule is that the government must pay damages to the owner of the benefited land. The measure of damages usually is the difference in value of the benefited lot with and without the benefit of the covenant. The underlying theory is that a real covenant or equitable servitude is a property interest analogous to an easement, and it must be paid for when removed by the government. [**Southern California Edison Co. v. Bourgerie**, 9 Cal. 3d 169 (1973)]

D. Common Interest Communities

1. Introduction [§1281]

In the last 50 years, common interest communities have mushroomed in the United States. These communities include condominiums, cooperatives, and subdivisions with homeowners' associations enforcing covenants. What ties all these housing communities together is the fact that they are run by private governments (boards) that enforce and make rules, assess charges, and make repairs and improvements.

2. Condominiums [§1282]

The condominium form of ownership—which has been widely used in other parts of the world—was virtually unknown in this country until the early 1960s. Since that time, it has captured the popular imagination and is increasing rapidly in use. In this country, condominium ownership has taken the form of individual ownership of individual units organized with common areas, and mutual rights and obligations in the common areas. Statutes have been enacted in all states authorizing condominiums. All condominium developments must conform to the state statute. A condominium usually consists of apartments, but it can consist of commercial units, separate houses, or townhouses.

a. Essential features [§1283]

Each condominium development consists of individual units, common areas, and perhaps "limited common areas."

(1) Unit ownership [§1284]

Each individual unit (apartment, office, store) is owned separately in *fee simple*. The boundaries of a unit are sometimes defined as the interior surfaces of the perimeter walls, floors, and ceilings. The unit may include a space restricted to use by the unit owner, even if the space is not within the boundaries of the individual unit, *e.g.*, a parking space, storage room, balcony, or patio.

(2) Common areas [§1285]

The entire condominium except the individual units is called the common area. This includes walls, staircases, elevators, swimming pools, etc. The common area is owned by all owners of the units as *tenants in common*.

(a) No right to partition [§1286]

Unlike the ordinary tenant in common, the condominium owner has no right to partition the common areas so long as the structure remains intact.

(b) Easement for entrance and support [§1287]

A nonexclusive easement for entrance and exit and for support, through the common areas, is appurtenant to each unit.

(3) Financing [§1288]

Each unit owner may finance the purchase of her unit independently of all other owners in the project. The unit owner gives the mortgage lender, who finances the purchase, a *separate mortgage* on her unit, for which she alone is responsible. The failure of one unit owner to make payments permits the mortgagee to foreclose on that unit. The other unit owners are not affected. Thus, so far as the mortgage is concerned, there is no financial interdependency with other owners. But there may be financial interdependency by virtue of monthly charges to keep up the common areas.

b. Creation of a condominium

(1) Declaration of condominium or master deed [§1289]

A condominium is ordinarily created by a declaration or master deed stating that the owner is creating a condominium to be governed by the provisions of the state condominium act. Most states require that the declaration be recorded in the county recorder's office. The declaration may contain many details of the organization of the condominium or, alternatively, these may be set forth in separate bylaws signed by each unit owner at the time of purchase of the individual unit. The declaration and bylaws attempt to solve in advance problems that may arise from condominium ownership. Among the matters dealt with are the following:

(a) Owners' association [§1290]

All owners of units are members of the condominium association. An elected board of directors runs the association. Until all of the units are sold, the developer may keep control of the association and management. [**Barclay v. DeVeau**, 429 N.E.2d 323 (Mass. 1981)]

(b) Management [§1291]

The board can manage the condominium or, more commonly, a professional manager is employed.

(c) Owner's fraction [§1292]

Each owner's fractional share of the whole project is set forth. This usually fixes permanently the unit owner's proportionate interest in the common areas, including her share of the common expense and her interest in the whole project upon its destruction. Because each unit is taxed separately, the assessor may value the project as a whole and then use this fraction to compute the property tax on a unit.

(2) Rules of conduct [§1293]

The originating document (declaration of condominium or master deed) may provide for certain rules of conduct. Or the promulgation of rules may be left to subsequent action by the membership association or board. Generally, the test of validity of these rules is "reasonableness," but courts are moving toward applying different standards of judicial review to different types of rules.

(a) Restrictions in originating documents [§1294]

Restrictions appearing in the originating document have a very strong presumption of validity. The trend is to strike down these original covenants only if they are arbitrary or violative of public policy or a constitutional right. The reason for this distinction is that buyers voluntarily agree to be governed by these terms when they buy in and are entitled to rely on the enforceability of restrictions in an originating document. [**Nahrstedt v. Lakeside Village Condominium Association,** 8 Cal. 4th 361 (1994); *and see* **Noble v. Murphy,** 612 N.E.2d 266 (Mass. 1993)—upholding no-pet restriction; **Hidden Harbour Estates, Inc. v. Basso,** 393 So. 2d 637 (Fla. 1981)—upholding prohibition of any exterior alteration without board approval; *but see* **Portola Hills Community Association v. James,** 4 Cal. App. 4th 289 (1992)—refusing to enforce ban on satellite dishes because plaintiff's dish not visible by neighbors; **Bernardo Villas Management Corp. v. Black,** 190 Cal. App. 3d 153 (1987)—refusing to enforce ban on trucks in carports because plaintiff's pickup was new and clean] Note that *Nahrstedt* disapproved of both *Portola Hills* and *Bernardo Villas* on grounds that the courts were not deferential enough to the strong presumption of validity of restrictions in condominium declarations and, further, that reasonableness must be determined by reference to common interest development as a whole and not by an individualized analysis of one homeowner's situation.

(b) Restrictions subsequently adopted [§1295]

Restrictions not in the originating documents but adopted by a board subsequently must be reasonable. A court may give a less deferential review to a subsequent bylaw change than it gives to a covenant in the originating documents. The reliance interest of the buyers is not so strong with respect to subsequent changes. Here courts may balance the importance of the new rule's objective with the importance of the individual interest infringed upon. [**O'Buck v. Cottonwood Village Condominium Association,** 750 P.2d 813 (Alaska 1988)—upholding ban on television antennae and requiring payment of fee for cable; **Hidden Harbour Estates, Inc. v. Norman,** 309 So. 2d 180 (Fla. 1975)—upholding ban on alcoholic beverages in clubhouse; **Winston Towers 200 Association v. Saverio,** 360 So. 2d 470 (Fla. 1978)—striking bylaw amendment which prohibited replacement of pet because retroactive]

c. Administration of common areas

(1) Expenses of maintenance [§1296]
The statute or condominium declaration should, and ordinarily does, provide that unit owners are liable for their shares of common expenses. The provisions for financial contributions are covenants, and to be enforceable against subsequent purchasers must comply with the requirements for covenants running with the land in law or equity (*see supra*, §§1188 *et seq.*).

(a) Enforcing payment [§1297]
Most declarations and some statutes provide for the imposition of a lien to enforce collection of assessments for common expenses. This lien may be foreclosed by the management in the same manner as a mortgage on real property.

(2) Tort liability [§1298]
Individual unit owners are, of course, subject to tort liability for injuries occurring inside their respective units. In addition, all of the unit owners are jointly liable for injuries occurring in the common areas that they own as tenants in common. The owners' association may also be liable for such injuries (on the ground that it has assumed management and control of the common areas), but this has no effect on the owners' personal liability. As a practical matter, each purchaser of a condominium unit will have to make sure the owners' association maintains adequate liability insurance to cover her personal liability for such injuries. Tortious conduct for which owners are liable includes failure to maintain common areas such as halls, elevators, and boilers; failure to supervise pools or playgrounds where children congregate; violation of housing codes, etc. [**Dutcher v. Owens,** 647 S.W.2d 948 (Tex. 1983)—unit owners' liability for torts in common area limited to pro rata share of ownership]

d. Restrictions on transfer [§1299]
Restrictions are often imposed on the transfer of a condominium unit. A typical

restriction usually prohibits transfer of the condominium unit without the consent of the association. These restrictions run into the following problems.

(1) Restraint on alienation [§1300]

In a condominium, the unit owner owns a fee simple. As previously discussed (*supra*, §§349 *et seq.*), direct restraints on transferring a fee simple have usually been held void, and the question arises whether a restraint on a condominium unit will be governed by the same rule as is usually applied to a fee simple. The courts have been more tolerant of restraints on a condominium unit, because of the interdependent ownership, and the rule appears to be that a restraint is valid if it is a reasonable means of accomplishing valid objectives. [**City of Oceanside v. McKenna,** 215 Cal. App. 3d 1420 (1989); **Aquarian Foundation, Inc. v. Sholom House, Inc.,** 448 So. 2d 1166 (Fla. 1984); *but see* **Laguna Royale Owners Association v. Darger,** 119 Cal. App. 3d 670 (1981)]

(2) Illegal racial discrimination [§1301]

The Fair Housing Act (*supra*, §821) prohibits discrimination in sale or rental of housing on grounds of race, ethnic origin, religion, sex, family status, or handicap. The Civil Rights Act of 1866 (*supra*, §817) bars all racial discrimination in the sale or rental of property. If it can be shown that the condominium association (or cooperative or homeowners' association) is using restrictions on transfer and screening procedures with the intent or effect of illegally discriminating, the association can be enjoined from doing so, and may be liable in damages. [**Wolinsky v. Kadison,** 449 N.E.2d 151 (Ill. 1983)]

3. Cooperatives [§1302]

A cooperative apartment house usually takes the following form: A corporation holds legal title to an apartment building. Shares of stock are sold to the persons who will occupy the apartments; the amount of stock required to live in the building depends on the value of the apartment (size, location, etc.). In addition to owning stock in the corporation, the occupants receive leases from the corporation. The leases may be for long terms (99 years) or for short, renewable terms. Thus, the residents in a cooperative are *both tenants* (under their leases with the cooperative corporation) *and owners* of the cooperative corporation (by virtue of stock interests).

a. Basic characteristics [§1303]

The tenant-shareholders elect a board of directors, which operates the building. Rent may be increased or decreased by the board of directors, depending on the operational costs.

(1) Liability for mortgage payments [§1304]

The entire project (land and buildings) is normally subject to a blanket mortgage. This mortgage has priority over the occupancy leases, which means that, in the event of foreclosure, the lender (mortgagee) will wipe out each tenant's interest. The risk of foreclosure of the blanket mortgage means that each tenant is in effect obligated to come up with any deficiency if other tenants fail to pay the rent. Because of the financial interdependency of the tenants, there is substantial risk to cooperative members if there are many rent defaults.

(2) Liability for taxes, maintenance, and repairs [§1305]

Repairs within each apartment are the responsibility of each tenant (the lease normally so provides). Taxes and repairs to the building exterior and common areas are normally the responsibility of the cooperative corporation. If the rent payments are insufficient, the corporation raises the rent accordingly so that each tenant ends up paying her proportionate share.

b. Restrictions on transfers [§1306]

Normally both the lease and stock interest of each tenant are subject to restrictions on transfer. The purpose of these restrictions is to assure the remaining tenants that the new tenant will be compatible and financially responsible. Problems that arise are similar to those discussed in connection with condominiums (*see supra*, §1299). There may be more justification for a restraint in a cooperative than in a condominium, however, because the cooperative members are in a joint financial venture, whereas the condominium owners are not. The cooperative has more need to be assured of the financial responsibility of the purchaser.

(1) Restraint on alienation [§1307]

The cooperative owners own leaseholds, not fees simple. Most cases hold that inasmuch as a restraint on a *leasehold* is valid, as is a restraint on sale of stock, a restraint on sale of a cooperative apartment is valid. [**Penthouse Properties, Inc. v. 1158 Fifth Avenue, Inc.**, *supra*, §355] However, the courts are split over whether the cooperative corporation can arbitrarily withhold its consent to transfer. New York holds that it may. [**Weisner v. 791 Park Avenue Corp.**, *supra*, §355] Most courts apply a reasonableness test to restrictions on transfer of a cooperative apartment. The restriction must be reasonably tailored to the purposes of assuring financial responsibility and social compatibility. The application of the restriction to particular buyers is reviewable by a court. [**Mowatt v. 1540 Lake Shore Drive Corp.**, 385 F.2d 135 (7th Cir. 1967)]

(2) Preemptive option [§1308]

Rather than retaining the right to veto the transfer, the cooperative corporation may retain the *right of first refusal* (a preemptive option) if any member wishes to sell her stock and lease. Preemptive options restrain alienation, and to be valid must be *reasonable* in purpose *and* duration.

Again, courts have been very liberal in upholding preemptive options in cooperative ventures. [**Gale v. York Center Community Cooperative,** *supra,* §354] Preemptive options in cooperatives and condominiums have been held not subject to the Rule Against Perpetuities.

c. Termination of lease [§1309]

The corporation may terminate the lease if the tenant fails to pay her assessed share of common expenses or violates rules of conduct established by the corporation. [**Green v. Greenbelt Homes, Inc.,** 194 A.2d 273 (Md. 1963)]

(1) Limitation [§1310]

The rules of conduct promulgated by the board of directors are unenforceable if they are arbitrary or unreasonable. [**Justice Court Mutual Housing Cooperative, Inc. v. Sandow,** 50 Misc. 2d 541 (1966)—regulation prohibiting the playing of musical instruments after 8 p.m. and by any one person more than 1½ hours per day held unreasonable and unenforceable; hence, termination of lease of pianist not allowed]

Chapter Eight:
Rights Against Neighbors

CONTENTS

Chapter Approach

Chapter Approach

The law has long given the possessor of land various rights against neighbors. These rights include the right to be free of a *nuisance* nearby, the right to *support* so that the land does not fall in, and rights in *airspace*. (These rights may also include rights in streams and in underground water, but water rights have been covered earlier at §§22 *et seq.,* in connection with the rule of capture.)

For questions concerning these rights, consider the following:

1. For *nuisance,* be sure to distinguish between a nuisance (interference with the use and enjoyment of land) and a *trespass* (invasion of the possessor's interest in exclusive possession). Also consider the *remedies* available (injunction and damages) and whether one is more appropriate than another in a particular case.

2. Regarding the *right to support,* remember that the right extends to both lateral support (support from adjacent land) and subjacent support (support from ground below).

3. *Airspace* issues may arise in questions about navigable airspace and flight paths (remember that the government sets the standards), or those about solar enjoyment (where the type of use—solar power source vs. garden requirements—may determine whether the right will be enforced).

In all of these areas, *economic analysis* may well influence the courts' decisions, and thus should probably be considered in your answer.

A. Nuisance

1. In General [§1311]

A "nuisance" is an unprivileged interference with a person's *use and enjoyment of her land.* Relief from nuisance was awarded at common law under the basic maxim that one must use her property so as not to injure that of another. A nuisance is termed a *"private nuisance"* when it involves interference with the private use and enjoyment of one or a number of nearby properties. It is a *"public nuisance"* when the interference is with a right common to the general public.

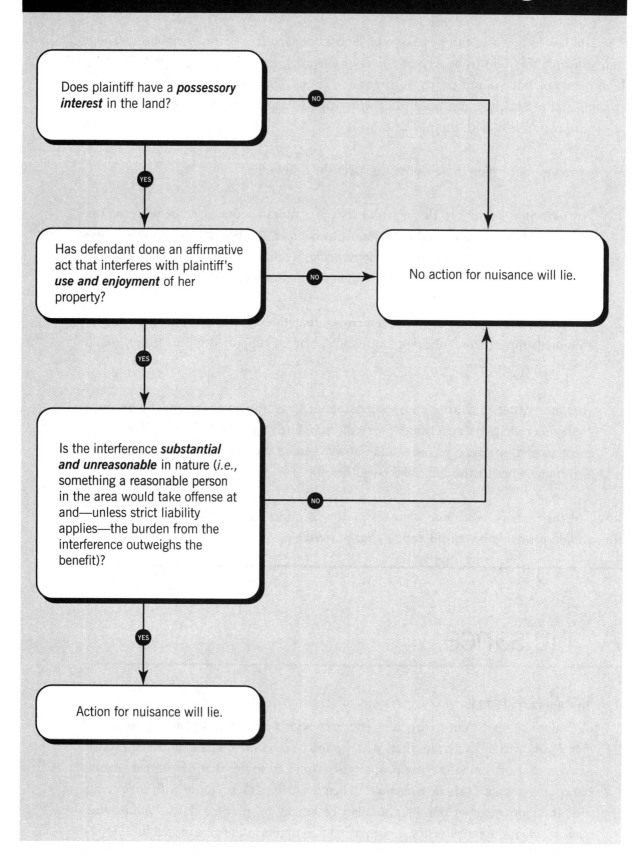

Does plaintiff have a *possessory interest* in the land?

NO

Has defendant done an affirmative act that interferes with plaintiff's *use and enjoyment* of her property?

YES

NO

No action for nuisance will lie.

Is the interference *substantial and unreasonable* in nature (*i.e.,* something a reasonable person in the area would take offense at and—unless strict liability applies—the burden from the interference outweighs the benefit)?

YES

NO

Action for nuisance will lie.

YES

2. Private Nuisance

a. Definition [§1312]

A private nuisance is conduct that causes a *substantial interference* with the private use of land and is either (i) *intentional and unreasonable*, or (ii) *unintentional but negligent*, reckless, or resulting from an abnormally dangerous activity (for which there is strict liability). [**Waschak v. Moffat**, 109 A.2d 310 (Pa. 1954); Rest. 2d, Torts §822] A person cannot sue claiming a private nuisance unless she has a *property interest* that is affected or alleges bodily harm as the result of the activities complained of.

(1) Intentional nuisance [§1313]

The usual type of nuisance is an intentional and unreasonable act that continues over time and is known to interfere with another's enjoyment of land. The primary factor in determining an intentional nuisance is the *unreasonableness of the interference* with the neighbor's use and enjoyment. Under the Restatement (Second) of Torts, any intentional invasion of an interest in the private use and enjoyment of land is unreasonable, and therefore a nuisance, if the *gravity of the harm outweighs the utility of the actor's conduct*. [Rest. 2d, Torts §826(a)] Balancing the gravity of the harm against the utility of the conduct requires an examination of particular factors in each case. [**County of Westchester v. Town of Greenwich**, 745 F. Supp. 951 (S.D.N.Y. 1990); **Page County Appliance Center, Inc. v. Honeywell, Inc.**, 347 N.W.2d 171 (Iowa 1984); **Escobar v. Continental Baking Co.**, 596 N.E.2d 394 (Mass. 1992)] Even if the utility of the conduct outweighs the gravity of the harm, an activity can still be a nuisance if the harm is *serious* and the defendant can *afford to pay* those damaged. [**Hendricks v. Stalnaker**, 380 S.E.2d 198 (W. Va. 1989); **Crest Chevrolet-Oldsmobile-Cadillac, Inc. v. Willemsen**, 384 N.W.2d 692 (Wis. 1986); Rest. 2d, Torts §826(b)]

(a) Gravity of harm [§1314]

The Restatement lists the following factors to be considered in determining the gravity of the harm: (i) the *extent* of the harm; (ii) the *character* of the harm; (iii) the *social value* of the use or enjoyment invaded; (iv) the *suitability* of the use invaded to the locality; and (v) the *burden* on the person harmed of avoiding the harm. [Rest. 2d, Torts §827]

(b) Utility of conduct [§1315]

The Restatement lists the following factors to be considered in determining the utility of the conduct of the invader: (i) the *social value* of the primary purpose of the conduct; (ii) the *suitability* of the conduct to the character of the locality; and (iii) the *impracticability* of preventing or avoiding the invasion. [Rest. 2d, Torts §828]

(c) Fault [§1316]

The fault of the defendant is not controlling, but the failure of the defendant to use due care in avoiding the harm may be a ground for imposing liability. In some cases, courts have imposed liability on the defendant even though she has taken all reasonable precautions and is in no way at fault. They have concluded that the gravity of the harm outweighed the utility of the conduct. [**Pendoley v. Ferreira**, 187 N.E.2d 142 (Mass. 1963)—existing well-operated piggery enjoined as nuisance when new homes built in area]

1) Comment

There may be an *economic* justification for this result in that total value to society will be increased by the cessation of the defendant's activity, but the question of whether it is *fair* to put the cost of abating the conflict on the defendant is another matter.

(d) "Nuisance per se" vs. "nuisance in fact" [§1317]

Courts sometimes distinguish between a "nuisance per se" (an activity that is a nuisance no matter how reasonable the defendant's conduct) and a "nuisance in fact" (an activity that is unreasonable under the particular facts). However, the distinction is of dubious value, because it conflicts with the basic concept that a nuisance is determined by whether the activity causes an *unreasonable interference* with the use of another's land—not whether the activity is unreasonable regardless of the use of the other land. The tendency of courts that have found nuisances per se is to limit them to unduly hazardous activities (*e.g.*, storage of explosives), unlawful activities, or highly objectionable uses in the particular district.

(2) Unintentional act [§1318]

An unintentional act may give rise to a nuisance when the conduct in question is reckless or negligent or involves abnormally dangerous activities. Nuisances of this type are uncommon, but an example is the storage of dangerous explosives.

b. Types of unreasonable interference [§1319]

The practical meaning of the term "nuisance" can best be grasped by looking at the particulars of various cases in which the interference has been held to be a nuisance.

(1) Character of the harm

(a) Depreciation of property value [§1320]

Use of property in a manner that depreciates the value of surrounding property is *not enough by itself* to constitute a nuisance. Even so, it is an important factor in proving that there is substantial injury to the plaintiff. In the case of "psychological" nuisances (cemeteries, funeral homes, etc.), depreciation of neighboring property values may be the underlying or controlling factor.

(b) Discomfort [§1321]

Serious discomfort and inconvenience in the use of land is another important factor in determining a nuisance. Objectionable noise, odors, or smoke are frequently the interference complained of. The standard of unreasonable interference is measured by the sensibilities of the average person. [**Rose v. Chaikin,** 453 A.2d 1378 (N.J. 1982); **Morgan v. High Penn Oil Co.,** 77 S.E.2d 682 (N.C. 1953)]

1) Sunlight [§1322]

Older cases held that cutting off a neighbor's sunlight by building next to the property line was not a nuisance. [**Fontainebleau Hotel Corp. v. Forty-Five Twenty-Five, Inc.,** 114 So. 2d 357 (Fla. 1959)] But this view may change as a result of the development of solar collectors, which provide cheap energy. It has been held that blocking a neighbor's roof solar collector can be enjoined as a nuisance. [**Prah v. Maretti,** 321 N.W.2d 182 (Wis. 1982)]

2) Spite fences [§1323]

A spite fence, erected solely to harm the neighbor and of no economic benefit to the erecting party, can be enjoined as a nuisance. Such conduct has no social utility.

(c) Fear of harm [§1324]

If the use is a dangerous one that puts the adjoining neighbor in fear of harm, this is a significant factor in declaring a nuisance (*e.g.,* storage of high explosives, mental hospital, leprosarium). The reasonableness of the fear is tested by general community beliefs and extrinsic evidence based on experience. And, of course, even though people fear a use, it may be permitted to exist because it has high social value.

e.g. **Example:** The owner of Blackacre wants to put a "halfway house" on Blackacre to provide temporary residence for selected parolees from state prison. It has been held that a halfway house, which has a high social value, is not a nuisance in a residential area because the fear of bringing criminal activity to the neighborhood is speculative. Until established and tried, the halfway house is an "unknown quantity." [**Nicholson v. Connecticut Half-Way House, Inc.,** 218 A.2d 383 (Conn. 1966); *but see* **Arkansas Release Guidance Foundation v. Needler,** 477 S.W.2d 821 (Ark. 1972)]

(2) Character of the neighborhood [§1325]

The character of the neighborhood is of great importance in determining a nuisance. Residential areas are often given a preferred status and are protected against incompatible uses.

(a) Use authorized by zoning ordinance [§1326]

A zoning ordinance is admissible in court to show community policy with respect to desirable land use within a neighborhood. However, the fact that the defendant's use of her land is consistent with local zoning is *not controlling* in an action for private nuisance. Even though the ordinance may permit the use generally, the specific activity may be carried out in such a manner as to constitute an unreasonable interference with the particular adjoining properties. [**Boomer v. Atlantic Cement Co.**, 26 N.Y.2d 219 (1970)—cement plant located in industrial district declared a nuisance]

(3) Social value of the conflicting uses [§1327]

One of the primary objects of nuisance law is to avoid the more serious harm. Society does not want to resolve conflicts in such a way as to make it poorer. If one party's conduct has great social value (*e.g.*, a factory employing many people), a court will be reluctant to enjoin it as a nuisance. On the other hand, if the harm is serious and the payment of damages will not shut down the plant, the court may order the payment of damages for nuisance and refuse to enjoin the activity.

Example: Atlantic Cement Co. has invested $45 million in its plant, which employs 300 people. Dirt and smoke emanating from the plant cause $185,000 in permanent damage to A's property. It has been held that A cannot enjoin Atlantic for this nuisance, but can collect $185,000 in damages. [**Boomer v. Atlantic Cement Co.**, *supra*]

---

(4) Priority in time [§1328]

Another important factor is which of the conflicting uses was first located in the vicinity. If the defendant's use was first, the plaintiff has *"come to the nuisance"* and has a less appealing case because she could have avoided the harm. Economic analysis supports the "coming to the nuisance" defense in many cases (*see infra*, §1343).

EXAM TIP — gilbert

Coming to the nuisance is a popular exam ploy. Watch out for a fact pattern with a sympathetic defendant—such as a farmer whose family has been raising pigs on the same plot of land for generations without complaint from neighboring farmers, but who has been receiving complaints over the past five years from rich urban lawyers who have moved into country estates built by developers who bought out all of the farmer's neighbors. If the lawyers file a nuisance action, although some courts will take into account the plaintiffs' coming to the nuisance, *in no court will that fact be determinative*—all other relevant factors will also be considered, such as the suitability of the farmer's use to the neighborhood, the value of the properties in question, the costs of eliminating the condition complained of, and the social benefits of allowing the use to continue.

---

c. Distinguish—trespass [§1329]

A *physical invasion* of another's land can be either a trespass or a nuisance.

A trespass is an actionable invasion of a possessor's interest in exclusive *possession* of land. A nuisance is an actionable invasion of a possessor's interest in the *use and enjoyment* of land. Both unintentional and intentional trespass can give rise to liability. Unintentional trespass is treated much the same as unintentional nuisance (*see supra,* §1318); in essence, the plaintiff must show that the invasion is unprivileged and the result of reckless or negligent conduct. *Intentional trespass*, however, is treated differently from intentional nuisance. Intentional trespass is actionable *even if no substantial injury results*. *Intentional nuisance*, on the other hand, requires more. The plaintiff must show (i) unreasonable interference (*see supra,* §1313); and (ii) substantial injury. In terms of remedies, in trespass the plaintiff is entitled, usually as a matter of right, to damages for past conduct and an injunction against future trespass. In nuisance, the court may, in its discretion, give damages for past conduct or *permanent damages for future conduct* or an injunction. The remedies for nuisance are more flexible than for trespass.

(1) Air pollution [§1330]

Air pollution can be classified as a trespass on the theory that unseen but measurable particles are entering the plaintiff's land. Or it can be classified as a nuisance, an interference with plaintiff's enjoyment of clean air. Restatement (Second) of Torts section 826(b) (*supra,* §1313) permits a court to treat air pollution as a nuisance—even if the utility of the conduct outweighs the gravity of the harm—if the harm is serious and the defendant can afford to pay those damaged. One of the purposes of section 826(b) is to give courts, in cases where they would be very reluctant to close down a plant having great utility to the public, the option of treating a suit for air pollution as a suit in nuisance, and giving permanent damages.

COMPARISON OF TRESPASS AND NUISANCE — gilbert

	TRESPASS	NUISANCE
DEFINITION	Actionable invasion of a possessor's interest in exclusive *possession* of land	Actionable invasion of a possessor's interest in the *use and enjoyment* of land
STANDARD FOR RELIEF	An *intentional* or negligent, unprivileged physical intrusion	Intentional, reckless, negligent, or abnormally dangerous conduct; unreasonable interference; *and* substantial injury
REMEDY	Damages for past conduct *and* an injunction against future trespass (as a matter of right)	Damages for past conduct *or* permanent damages for future conduct *or* an injunction (in court's discretion)

d. Economic analysis [§1331]

Economic analysis is increasingly used by modern courts in solving problems of nuisance, including what remedy to give. Indeed, the law of nuisance is hardly ever taught anymore without an economic analysis; therefore, a brief exposition is appropriate. Suppose that landowner A has a factory on her land belching smoke into the air, which flows across to landowner B, who has an amusement park on his land. The smoke interferes with the patrons' enjoyment of the park. This simple hypothetical case is useful to focus the economic issues.

(1) Who is at fault? [§1332]

Neither A nor B is solely the cause of the harm. Both are responsible, because of the conflicting uses A and B make of their respective parcels. If B's land were most valuable when devoted to some use where smoke is unobjectionable, there would be no conflict and no harm. Now, given B's use as an amusement park, should the court allow B to harm A (by enjoining A's smoke emission as a nuisance) or allow A to harm B (by refusing to enjoin A)? The economic problem is to avoid the more serious harm, although other factors, particularly fairness, may be important in a judicial determination of the appropriate solution.

(a) Neither party alone causes conflict [§1333]

Under economic theory, the party emitting the smoke is no more the cause of the conflict than the party sensitive to the smoke. The conflict requires the presence of both parties. Courts have sometimes talked about "higher uses," usually in protecting a residential area from noise or smoke or such, giving the "higher use" an advantage, but this does not make economic sense. If the factory has a greater market value than the homes, then society values the factory higher; it is worth more to society.

(b) Externalities [§1334]

An externality is a cost (or benefit) of any given action that is not taken into consideration by the actor in determining the level of that activity that is optimal from the actor's point of view. Economic theory suggests that resources will generally be allocated more efficiently if the costs (and benefits) of different actions are "internalized," *i.e.*, taken into account by economic actors in determining the optimal level of their activities. It is economically inefficient for a business to impose a cost of doing business on others and not internalize it. In the above example, an external cost of the factory, which A imposed on B, is that B's land is made unsuitable for uses sensitive to smoke. An external cost of B's use of land as an amusement park is that A's land is made unsuitable for activities that conflict with an amusement park.

(2) Coase theorem [§1335]

The economic problem in all cases of harmful effects is how to maximize the social value of production by putting land to its most valuable use while internalizing costs. Suppose the cost to A of installing smoke abatement equipment is $100, and the damage to B's land is $50. If the right to belch smoke is given A, A will continue to do so because B will give A only $50 to stop, and it is worth $100 to A to continue. If the right to stop the smoke is given B, B will sell the right to smoke to A at somewhere between $50 and $100, because the right is worth only $50 to B and is worth $100 to A. A sale will make them both better off. Thus, regardless of whether A or B is given the right, it will end up in A's hands by operation of the market, at least in most cases where costs of conducting transactions are low. If the figures are reversed, so that installing smoke abatement equipment would cost A $50 and the smoke damage to B's land is $100, A would install the smoke equipment no matter where the right is initially assigned. If assigned to A, B will pay A something between $50 and $100 to install the equipment. If assigned to B, A would install the equipment for $50 rather than buy out B's right for $100. Thus the *market* determines whether the activity (smoke emission) will continue, not the initial allocation of rights by the courts. The initial allocation only makes one party richer and will not stop pollution. This argument was first made by Nobelist Ronald Coase and is known as the Coase theorem. [Ronald H. Coase, The Problem of Social Cost, 3 J.L. & Econ. 1 (1960)]

(3) Transaction costs [§1336]

The Coase theorem, which provides that the market will move the right to the highest valued use, depends on the assumption that transaction costs are zero or low. It assumes that A and B can easily transfer rights to each other at little or no cost. This may be an unrealistic assumption. Transaction costs include costs of obtaining *information* about persons with whom one must deal, conducting *negotiations, coming to terms* with the other party or parties, and *enforcing* any bargains made. The more parties involved, the higher the transaction costs.

(a) The holdout problem [§1337]

Suppose that A's factory belches smoke over a large residential area so that 50 neighbors (and not just B) suffer damage. Assume the total damage to the neighbors is $50 ($1 each) and the cost of smoke abatement equipment is $100. If each neighbor is given the right to enjoin A, A has to buy all the neighbors out. It would be to the economic benefit of everyone if this occurred, but A is not likely to be able to buy *all* 50 neighbors out at a price under $100. Each neighbor would have an incentive to *hold out* for an exorbitant price, more than the $1.99 A would be willing to pay each neighbor.

If A were to buy up the right from 49 neighbors for $97.51, it would be worthless unless A also were to buy out the final neighbor. Knowing that A will lose $97.51 if he (the final neighbor) will not sell, the last neighbor holding out will price his right higher than $1.99, which means the total cost to A would exceed $100. Therefore, A will not buy out the neighbors and the right to enjoin A will stay with the neighbors, where it was initially allocated. The market does not work to modify the initial allocation.

1) Caveat

A can avoid the holdout if she does not make a firm commitment to buy any rights until she is sure that all sellers will agree to sell at a total price of less than $100. But negotiating with 50 neighbors is time-consuming and costly. The deal may not be made because the information cost of finding out at what price each of the 50 neighbors will sell and A will buy exceeds the possible gain of $50 from the trade.

(b) The free rider problem [§1338]

Suppose that in the above example the damage to the 50 neighbors was $100 and the cost of smoke abatement equipment was $50. Suppose also that A's activity was not deemed a nuisance by the court, thus allocating the right to A. To achieve the least economic harm, the 50 neighbors should get together, pay A something between $50 and $100, and get A's agreement to install smoke abatement equipment. A and the 50 neighbors will all be better off if this is done. However, there is a tendency for each neighbor to desire a *free ride* and not to cough up his share: "Let the others do it." Thus, it is difficult to bring about the transfer, transaction costs are too high, and the right stays where allocated. A continues to belch smoke.

(c) The strategic behavior problem [§1339]

If A or B behaves in a "strategic" way in an effort to get as much of the gains from trade as possible, bargaining may be difficult to achieve. Suppose that A's smoke damages B's land in the amount of $50, that the cost to A of installing smoke abatement equipment is $100, and that B is entitled to an injunction. Both A and B are better off if a trade takes place with A paying B a sum more than $50 and less than $100. The difference between the value of the right to B and the value to A is called "gains from trade." The question is who will get how much of the gains from trade by bargaining. If B holds out for $90, and A offers "a top" of $80, no trade will take place, and haggling can go on and on—with transaction costs mounting. Parties may behave in a strategic way, particularly where they can trade only with each other (*i.e.*, A is the only person who will pay B more than $50, and B is the only person who can prevent the $100 loss to A; this situation is called a bilateral monopoly).

(d) Query—are transaction costs ever low? [§1340]

The holdout and free rider problems mean that when there are many parties, the costs of transacting are high. When there are few parties, transaction costs may be made high by strategic behavior.

(4) Initial allocation [§1341]

The initial allocation of the right is called the "entitlement." How should the initial allocation of the right be made? Should A be given the entitlement? Or should B be given the entitlement? Below are some suggested solutions. Economic arguments are given in (a) and (b), moral arguments in (c) and (d).

(a) Give to highest valued user [§1342]

If the market says that the right is going to end up with the party who most values it, allocate it there initially and avoid transaction costs. By eliminating transaction costs, the *total wealth* of society is increased. Economic analysis favors reduction of costs. Another way of phrasing this argument is to say: Allocate the liability (not the right) to the cheapest cost avoider, the person who can eliminate the conflict at the least monetary cost. This will reduce *total costs to society*.

(b) First in time prevails [§1343]

If one of the conflicting uses is established before the other, the first user may have an irretrievable or "sunk" cost of investment, which the second user may not now have. The first user should prevail at least to the extent that the second user should be forced to buy out the first user. This will require the second user to internalize the cost imposed on the first user and to choose among competing location sites, knowing it must bear this cost. [**Spur Industries, Inc. v. Del E. Webb Development Co.**, 494 P.2d 700 (Ariz. 1972)] Thus, the second user chooses a location on the basis of the cheapest cost, which is to society's benefit. Also, by permitting established uses to continue unharmed, the court avoids "demoralization costs," which might arise if a court enjoins a long-established use because of incompatibility with some use newly arrived on the scene.

1) Criticism

Awarding the entitlement to the first in time might be efficient and fair where (i) the defendant established her use at a time when she could not reasonably foresee the conflict, and (ii) the activity was not a nuisance at the time it was established.

But if there were external costs at the time the activity was begun, it seems both inefficient and unfair not to require the defendant to take these into account by giving damages to the damaged parties.

(c) Wealth redistribution [§1344]

Assume the cost to A of installing smoke abatement equipment is $100, and the smoke damage to B is $50. If the right is given to A to continue to belch smoke, A is $100 richer and B is $50 poorer. The market will not reallocate the right. If the right is given to B to enjoin A, B is richer by $50 or, if the market subsequently reallocates the right, by some amount between $50 and $100 (whatever price A and B come to for transferring that right) and A is poorer by the same amount. Thus, the initial allocation affects the wealth position of A and B. A court might decide to allocate the right to A if B is very rich and A poor, or to allocate the right to B if the situation were reversed. The theory would be that society prefers to equalize wealth. This is not an economic argument but a public policy argument based on *fairness*.

1) Fairness in other contexts [§1345]

Fairness may also be argued in other contexts. If A can pass the cost of abating the harm on to the consumers, so that the cost is spread, this may be deemed fair. If B bought the land at a market price for smoky land and did not pay the price for unsmoky land, it may be deemed unfair to give the right to stop the smoke to B on the ground that B will reap a benefit B did not bargain for. (The economic loser is the person who initially suffered the decrease in land value because of A's smoke, though of course in determining net loss, it is necessary to determine if the "harmed" land rose in value because A's use as a factory brought more people into the area and increased the value of land.)

(d) Healthy environment [§1346]

Another noneconomic argument for allocation of the property right (or entitlement) is that it is morally right for society to guarantee a minimally healthy environment. A person should not be subject to certain health risks, no matter how economically inefficient such a policy might be. Thus, if A's smoke is deemed "unhealthy," allocate the entitlement to B. This argument usually has a strong appeal when phrased in words such as "healthy environment," "air quality," and the like, but the costs of achieving these goals cannot be disregarded. A variation on this argument is to set up an order of preferred activities, as is done in cumulative zoning, which prefers housing over commercial uses. This, in effect, makes the allocation in accordance with how "harm" is intuitively perceived by the court or legislature.

e. Remedies

(1) Judicial remedies [§1347]

In determining what remedy to give in cases of land use conflict, a court has the four choices below. The basic choice of remedy is between injunctive and damage relief. When an injunction is granted, the plaintiff receives the entitlement or property right; the plaintiff can refuse to sell this right if the defendant does not offer enough. When damages are given, the invader is in effect given power to destroy the entitlement of plaintiff on payment of its value, objectively determined by a jury. Thus, the remedy has an important impact on the wealth position of the parties (if not on whether the activity will cease). To illustrate, assume A is a factory owner and B is the owner of an amusement park.

(a) Enjoin A [§1348]

The court may grant B an injunction forbidding A to emit smoke. B then has the right. A and B can then bargain and, according to the Coase theorem, transfer the right to A. B is made richer by the entitlement and is also in a strong position to get most of the gains from trade. [**Estancias Dallas Corp. v. Schultz**, 500 S.W.2d 217 (Tex. 1973)]

1) High transaction costs [§1349]

If transaction costs are very high (if, *e.g.*, the plaintiffs were 50 neighbors), the right as initially allocated would probably not be transferred, even though it would be to society's economic advantage (*see supra*, §1337). For this reason, some have suggested that the second or third remedy, which leaves the right with the highest valued use while giving damages to the other party, is appropriate in such a situation.

(b) Give B damages [§1350]

The court may refuse an injunction but grant B damages. This has the effect of giving the right to B, but forcing a sale of it to A (damages). Because the forced sale is at the price of B's damage, B gets his damages but A gets all the possible gains from trade. [**Boomer v. Atlantic Cement Co.**, *supra*, §1327]

1) Taking for private use [§1351]

It is arguable that this remedy results in A "taking" B's property. Because the Constitution prohibits taking of private property for private use, this remedy is arguably unconstitutional. However, if it is assumed that neither party alone is at fault in conflicting land use (*see supra*, §§1332-1334), this argument begs the question of whose property is being taken. A might claim that an injunction against her would be the taking of her property. In recent cases, this argument has been rejected on the ground that the question is what *remedy* a court of equity should fashion, not whether A is taking B's property.

(c) Enjoin A and give A damages [§1352]

The court may grant B an injunction against A *and* require B to pay A damages. This has the effect of giving the right to B, but forcing B to pay A for it. This solution tends to bring about efficient resource allocation because B, who claims the right is worth more to B than to A but is unwilling to or cannot bargain with A for transfer of the right, is forced to back up his claim for a judicially enforced transfer with cash. However, this solution may not be feasible when there are many potential Bs, and high transaction costs. [**Spur Industries, Inc. v. Del E. Webb Development Co.**, *supra*, §1343]

(d) Refuse B any remedy [§1353]

The court may refuse to grant B any remedy—either an injunction or damages.

3. Public Nuisance

a. Definition [§1354]

A public nuisance affects the *general public*, whereas a private nuisance affects only particular individuals. A public nuisance is widespread in its range or indiscriminate in its effects. Uses classified as public nuisances include gambling, prostitution, nude sunbathing, air pollution, and rock festivals. The underlying test of a public nuisance is the same as for private nuisance: *substantial* harm caused by *intentional and unreasonable* conduct or by conduct that is *negligent or abnormally dangerous*. Unreasonableness turns primarily on the gravity of the harm balanced against the utility of the activity. A suit to stop a public nuisance is usually brought by the attorney general.

b. Enforcement by private persons [§1355]

A private individual may act against a public nuisance *only* if she can show that the nuisance is *specially injurious* to her. The person does not have to own any affected land (as in private nuisance), but she must show that the damage to her is of a *different kind* than the damage to the public at large. It is not enough to show that she suffers the same kind of harm as the general public but to a greater extent.

Example: A pollutes a navigable stream so that it is no longer fit for drinking and swimming. This is a public nuisance. A fish hatchery downstream whose business is ruined thereby is entitled to bring suit.

(1) Standing to sue [§1356]

The reason for the requirement of "special injury" is to avoid an excessive number of lawsuits seeking to enforce public rights. The suit should be brought by a public official. However, in recent years, under pressure from environmentalists, standing to sue for public nuisance has been liberalized by statutes and decisions. In some states, a private person can sue as a *representative* of the general public or in a class action.

EXAM TIP   **gilbert**

Be careful not to confuse the requirements to bring a *private nuisance action* with those for a private individual to bring a *public nuisance action*. To claim a private nuisance, a person must have a property interest that is affected or must allege bodily harm. For a private individual to have standing to sue against a public nuisance, that person need not own any affected land, but must show a special injury different from the public at large.

---

c. Use authorized by statute [§1357]

If a use is authorized by statute or ordinance, it is not a public nuisance and cannot be enjoined. Even so, what would be a public nuisance (in the absence of a statute authorizing it) may be treated as a private nuisance if special injury is shown. Zoning ordinances are not defenses to a private nuisance suit (*see supra*, §1326).

B. Right to Support

1. In General [§1358]

The right to support of one's land from the lands adjoining is one of the incidents of ownership. It is sometimes called a "natural right." There are two kinds of support involved. "Lateral support" is support that land receives from the adjacent land. "Subjacent support" is support that land receives from underlying strata.

2. Right to Lateral Support

a. Right to support of land [§1359]

A landowner is *strictly liable* if she changes her land use so as to withdraw lateral support from her neighbor and cause her neighbor's land to slip or fall in. It is no defense that the excavator acted with the utmost care and not negligently. The absolute right to support of land is based on the idea that fairness requires that adjacent landowners not disturb the natural conditions so as to deprive the other's land of lateral support.

(1) Retaining walls [§1360]

If an excavator builds a retaining wall to support the adjoining parcel, she and her successors in interest have the duty thereafter to *maintain the wall.* Although a landowner is not liable for failure of support because of an act of God (erosion, storm, flood, etc.), decay or deterioration of a retaining wall is not an act of God so as to relieve the excavator from liability. Once a landowner changes the natural conditions and erects an artificial support, she and all subsequent owners of the changed property have a duty to maintain such support. [**Gorton v. Schofield,** 41 N.E.2d 12 (Mass. 1942); **Noone v. Price,** 298 S.E.2d 218 (W. Va. 1982)]

b. Right to support of buildings on land

(1) Majority view [§1361]

Strict liability for withdrawal of lateral support to a neighbor's property does not extend to buildings on the neighbor's land. There is no obligation to support the added weight of buildings. Where an adjacent landowner excavates and provides sufficient support to sustain the weight of the neighboring land in its natural state, *but the neighboring land slips because of the weight of the buildings on it*, the excavator is not liable *in the absence of negligence*. On the other hand, if land would have slipped even in its natural state (*i.e.*, without the buildings) because of the excavation, the neighbor who withdraws support to the land, resulting in damage to the building, is *strictly liable* for damage to the land and the building. The crucial fact is whether the weight of the building placed so much pressure on the land that the building caused the subsidence when the neighbor withdrew support. If it did, the neighbor is liable only for negligence. [**Noone v. Price,** *supra*]

(a) Note—noncontiguous lands

A negligence standard, rather than strict liability, governs lateral support from noncontiguous land. [**Puckett v. Sullivan,** 190 Cal. App. 2d 489 (1961)]

(2) Minority view [§1362]

In a minority of states, an adjacent landowner has the same strict liability for failing to support neighboring buildings as she has with respect to land. Statutes and city ordinances adopt this position in many states. It is likely that this view is the law in all the large cities in this country. It is also the view of the Restatement (Second) of Torts section 817.

(a) Policy issues

Protecting through strict liability the person who builds first encourages development. In protecting the first developer, strict liability for lateral support of buildings is efficient because it imposes the costs on the second developer, who can more easily avoid them (*see supra,* §1343). It may appear unfair, however, because it allows the first developer to increase the support burdens on neighbors and perhaps devalue their land. The same conflict in policy appears in nuisance law over whether priority in time controls what is a nuisance (*see supra*, §1343).

EXAM TIP   **gilbert**

Keep in mind that at common law, strict liability for withdrawal of lateral support did not apply where the damaged land was improved with buildings; instead, if the weight of the building caused slippage of the land, the excavating landowner was liable *only for negligence*. However, the common law rule has been replaced in some states, most large cities, and the Restatement (Second) of Torts. If you get an exam question involving a building that collapsed because of a neighbor's excavation, be sure to mention both views. Also note that the minority (Restatement Second) position protects the first builder and so encourages development, but also discourages development somewhat because it imposes (slightly) increased costs on subsequent builders.

---

c. **Subsidence from withdrawal of water [§1363]**

As discussed *supra* (§23), a landowner usually has absolute ownership of all the percolating ground water under the land. She can sink wells, drying up neighboring wells, with impunity. If the landowner sinks wells and causes subsidence of neighboring land, is she liable? Some courts have applied the rule of absolute ownership of percolating water and have held that the landowner is not liable unless she carries off some soil in the process or reduces the lateral support of the land. This seems unfair and inefficient because it does not require the owner of the well to take adequate precautions. More modern cases hold that an owner of a well is liable for negligence in withdrawing water that causes adjacent land to subside. [**Friendswood Development Co. v. Smith-Southwest Industries, Inc.**, *supra*, §23]

3. **Right to Subjacent Support [§1364]**

Whenever mineral estates are severed from the surface, the surface occupant has a right of subjacent support against the mineral owner. This right differs from the right to lateral support in two respects: (i) the mineral owner must support the land with the buildings existing on it when the mineral estate is severed (*i.e.*, the mineral owner is strictly liable for subsidence of the land and any existing buildings); and (ii) the mineral owner is liable for negligently damaging springs and wells, but under the usual rule that an adjacent owner has absolute ownership of the percolating water under her land (*see supra*, §23), the adjacent owner is not liable for interfering with percolating ground water of her neighbors.

C. Rights in Airspace

1. **Navigable Airspace [§1365]**

The surface owner may be protected against intrusions in the overlying airspace that impair her present or potential use of the surface. She may be able to recover in trespass or, where there are repeated intrusions, in nuisance.

a. Navigational servitude [§1366]

An ancient maxim says that the surface owner has a right to exclusive possession to the heavens. However, the modern world pays little heed to this maxim. Aircraft have a navigational servitude (right to cross airspace) above the surface land. The distance above surface land at which the servitude begins may be set by proper government authority. The real test of a surface owner's rights is whether use of airspace *harms the surface owner*. If it does not harm the surface owner, intrusions in airspace by aircraft are not actionable.

b. Noisy flights as inverse condemnation [§1367]

If the noise of airplanes flying over land constitutes a direct and continuing interference with the enjoyment and use of the surface, a governmental body may have taken property for which compensation must be paid under the Constitution.

---

e.g. **Example:** Low-flying military aircraft from a nearby field fly directly over a chicken farm and frighten the chickens, causing production to fall off. The chicken farm is forced to go out of business. The federal government has taken, by inverse condemnation, an easement for noisy flights over the farmer's land and must pay damages. [**United States v. Causby,** 328 U.S. 256 (1946)]

---

(1) Inverse condemnation [§1368]

Inverse condemnation is an action brought by an owner against a governmental body having the power of eminent domain. The purpose of the action is to recover the value of property that in effect has been taken by the government, although no formal exercise of the power of eminent domain has occurred. (*See infra*, §1483.)

(a) Public body must be sued [§1369]

This theory can be applied only to governmental units with the power of eminent domain. The *government* or *airport commission* must be sued—*not* the airlines.

(2) Rights of neighboring landowners [§1370]

A landowner whose land is near, but not directly under, the flight path may suffer nearly as much noise and air pollution as those owners directly under the flight path. However, because an aircraft has not entered the landowner's airspace, it may be difficult for the landowner to claim a taking of an easement for noisy flight. On the other hand, a few state courts *have permitted* a recovery on the theory that the *noise* constitutes a physical invasion interfering with the neighboring owner's enjoyment of the surface. [**Martin v. Port of Seattle,** 391 P.2d 540 (Wash. 1964); *but see* **Ferguson v. City of Keene,** 238 A.2d 1 (N.H. 1968)—cause of action in nuisance, but not inverse condemnation, would lie]

c. Noisy flights as a nuisance [§1371]

If noise pollution from airplanes is classified as a nuisance, the landowner can collect damages. [**Ferguson v. City of Keene,** *supra*]

(1) Injunction not available [§1372]

Note, however, that a court cannot issue an injunction, as this would interfere with the regulation of air traffic by the appropriate governmental agencies. In addition, an injunction would be an economically inefficient way to allocate airspace, because it would require the airline to buy out the landowners, each of whom might hold out for an unreasonable price. The award of damages means that the landowners are forced to sell a navigational servitude for noisy flights at a price set by a jury.

(2) Neighboring landowners may recover [§1373]

Because a nuisance does not necessarily involve a physical invasion of the landowner's space, this theory permits recovery of damages by landowners whose airspace is not entered by the airplanes, but whose enjoyment and use is substantially harmed.

(3) Nongovernmental defendant [§1374]

Under this theory, a nongovernmental defendant (such as an airline) can be sued by the landowner. Because of governmental immunity from tort in some states, this theory might not be available against a governmental defendant (which would have to be sued under the inverse condemnation theory).

EXAM TIP   **gilbert**

Noisy overflight fact patterns are a favorite with some law professors. On an exam, if you see overflights interfering with activities on the ground, be sure to note the following:

- Overflights can constitute a *taking* of an easement, and the landowner can bring an action for *inverse condemnation*.

- Because an action for inverse condemnation alleges a taking without just compensation as required by the Fifth Amendment, the *action can be brought only against a government agency* (e.g., the military if they are making the overflights, the airport authority, or perhaps the Federal Aviation Administration if they approved the flights); private parties are *not* subject to the proscriptions of the Fifth Amendment.

- Private parties may be liable in *nuisance* for noisy overflights, but check the facts carefully. Remember, nuisance will lie only for a *substantial interference that is unreasonable as measured by the sensibilities of an average person*. If the overflights interfere with an uncommon or ultrasensitive use of land (e.g., mink farming), they might not be actionable.

---

2. **Solar Enjoyment [§1375]**

Whether a landowner has a cause of action in nuisance for her neighbor's blocking of sunlight is a question on which there is, to date, a split of judicial opinion. It has been held that such a cause of action does not lie. [**Fontainebleau Hotel Corp. v. Forty-Five Twenty-Five, Inc.,** *supra*, §1322—neighboring hotel blocking sun on swimming pool] It has also been held that a cause of action in nuisance does lie for blocking sunlight. [**Prah v. Maretti,** *supra*, §1322—blocking neighbor's solar collector] If such a cause of action does lie, it is probable that the court, in balancing the utility of the conduct against the harm, will give more protection to solar collectors than to sunlight for gardens or swimming pools.

a. **Economic issue [§1376]**

The economic issue, discussed earlier in other contexts, is whether it is more efficient to have a fixed definition of solar rights, which can be easily transferred to the higher valued use if there are low transaction costs, or a reasonableness test. If only two neighbors are involved, under the Coase theorem (*supra*, §1335), the right will end up with the party who values it more, regardless of whether the court says solar blockage is or is not a nuisance. If so, judicial costs can be saved by having a fixed rule. However, when many parties are affected, the reasonableness test of nuisance, which lets the court determine who has the right, has greater economic justification because of the high transaction costs involved (*see supra*, §1336).

Chapter Nine: Public Land Use Controls

CONTENTS

Chapter Approach

The use of land is often controlled by local governments. The primary tool used by government is the *zoning* ordinance. But governments may also use *subdivision regulation* and *eminent domain*.

For purposes of study:

1. Remember that the authority for zoning comes from the state, and so a zoning ordinance must conform to the state's enabling act or it is *ultra vires* (void because it is beyond the authority of the local body).

2. Also consider the constitutional limitations on these land use controls:

    —   *Zoning power* may be limited by various constitutional provisions. Current "hot" topics, raising difficult and unsettled constitutional issues, include regulatory takings and aesthetic regulations. Be sure to look for constitutional problems when you see *exclusionary zoning*—zoning that excludes a particular group.

    —   Although the *power of eminent domain* is usually upheld, recall that when the government takes land it must be for a *public use* (defined broadly by the Supreme Court) and there must be *just compensation* paid (generally fair market value).

A. Zoning

1. Theory of Zoning [§1377]

By dividing up a city into use zones from which harmful uses are excluded, zoning purports to prevent one landowner from harming his neighbor by bringing in an incompatible use. In a sense, zoning is nuisance law made predictable by declaring in advance what uses are harmful and prohibited in the various zones. Indeed, this is the theory used in the classic case upholding zoning from constitutional attack, **Village of Euclid v. Ambler Realty Co.,** 272 U.S. 365 (1926). But zoning has purposes beyond preventing harm. Modern zoning often regulates uses to achieve public benefits or to maximize property values (the tax base) in the city. Zoning also has a darker side: It has been used, *e.g.*, to exclude low-income groups who cannot afford the housing permitted in the city.

a. Separation of uses [§1378]

The most fundamental means by which zoning accomplishes its purposes is the separation of conflicting uses, which are classified on a scale from "highest" use to "lowest" use. The highest use is deemed the least harmful to others, the lowest the most harmful. Separation of uses into different districts is sometimes called "Euclidean zoning," after the *Euclid* case holding it valid.

(1) Highest use—housing [§1379]

Zoning laws embody the assumption that wholesome housing (the central objective) must be protected from harmful neighbors. Thus, commerce and industry are excluded from residential zones because they are deemed harmful to housing. Even within residential zones there is a hierarchy of desirable uses. A single-family house, the "highest" use, is protected from the harmful effects of less desirable housing by being in an exclusive single-family house zone. Excluded are two-family houses and apartments. Similarly, in a two-family house district, lower residential uses such as apartments are excluded.

(2) Commercial and industrial districts [§1380]

Commercial use is "lower" than residential. Zoning codes typically divide commercial districts into several different kinds. C-1, *e.g.*, might provide for convenience shopping (grocery, drugstore, etc.), C-2 for a regional shopping center, and C-3 for a downtown commercial district. Industrial uses, which are "lower" than commercial, are similarly divided. The purpose of such divisions is to separate light from heavy industry and commerce.

(3) Principle of cumulative uses [§1381]

The principle of cumulative uses underlies zoning law. It states that *higher* but not lower uses are permitted in any district. Accordingly, in an apartment district, single-family and two-family houses can be erected, but no commercial or industrial uses are permitted. In certain situations, however, the ordinance may not be cumulative and may exclude higher uses. For example, it is rather common today for a zoning ordinance to forbid residential or commercial use in an industrial park district. The purposes of such noncumulative ordinances are to prevent discord between houses and industry and to keep land available for industry in the industrial park.

b. Density controls [§1382]

Density controls are rules that indirectly control the number of people using an area of land. They may include height limitations, setback requirements, and minimum lot and house sizes.

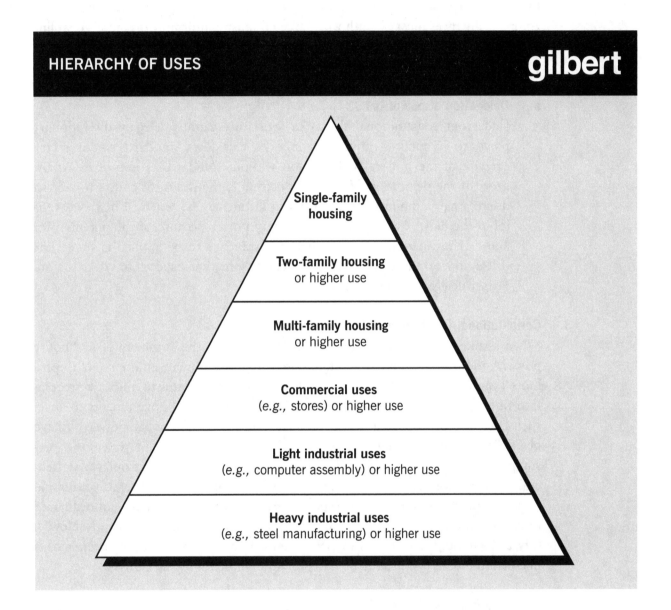

2. Source of Zoning Power [§1383]

Zoning ordinances are usually enacted by a city or a county to apply to land within its local jurisdiction. But under our governmental scheme, the state legislature is the sovereign power, and a city or county has no power to zone unless given such power by the state legislature. The act giving power to zone is called the *enabling act*. All zoning ordinances must be authorized by and must conform to the state's enabling act. Any zoning ordinance that does not conform to the enabling act is *ultra vires* (*i.e.*, beyond the authority of the local body) and is therefore void.

a. Delegation of power [§1384]

Under our constitutional theory, a legislature cannot delegate discretionary power to an administrative body unless it lays down standards to govern the exercise of the power. A delegation without standards is improper. At the heart of the delegation of powers doctrine is the desire of courts to restrict discretionary administrative powers so far as may be practical in view of the job to be done. Courts fear discretionary power because of the potential for abuse. Thus in zoning cases, where the standard to be applied is vague, the delegation of authority can be attacked (sometimes successfully) as an improper delegation of power.

3. Constitutional Limitations [§1385]

When a state enacts an enabling act, it does so under the authority of its "police power," the legislative power a state has to regulate human affairs so as to promote health, safety, welfare, and morals. The power of states to authorize regulation of property use by zoning laws and the power of local governments to enact such laws have been specifically upheld as valid uses of the police power. [**Village of Euclid v. Ambler Realty Co.**, *supra*, §1377] Although zoning laws enjoy a presumption of validity, like any other legislation, zoning laws must not violate federal (and, if more restrictive, state) constitutional provisions. The constitutional requirements must be met with respect to *each individual lot*. Thus, an ordinance might be valid in general, but be *invalid as applied* to a particular lot. [**Nectow v. City of Cambridge**, 277 U.S. 183 (1928)] Any argument that a zoning ordinance is unconstitutional must usually be based on one of the following clauses.

a. Due Process Clause [§1386]

The Due Process Clause of the Fourteenth Amendment provides: "No State shall . . . deprive any person of life, liberty, or property, without due process of law. . . ." A rough conceptualization of the effect of this clause divides it into *procedural* and *substantive* due process. Zoning actions may violate either form of due process.

(1) Procedural due process [§1387]

A landowner may argue that a zoning action has deprived him of procedural due process if it has been enacted without notice to him and without his having had an opportunity to be heard. However, courts have drawn a distinction between *legislative* actions (such as enacting a zoning ordinance for the entire city) and *administrative* actions. For legislative actions, notice does not have to be given to each landowner affected, whereas for administrative actions, it does have to be given. Administrative actions include variances and special exceptions, which are granted by the zoning board of adjustment (*infra*, §§1416-1422). In some states, zoning ordinance amendments by the city council affecting a few lots are treated as administrative decisions, on the theory that it is fair and reasonable to require notice to affected parties (including neighbors) where the action affects only a few. [**Fasano v. Board of County Commissioners,** 507 P.2d 23 (Or. 1973)]

(2) Substantive due process [§1388]

Substantive due process refers to fundamental rights and liberties, as found by the federal or state supreme courts, but not enumerated in the Bill of Rights. Prior to the mid-1930s, the United States Supreme Court struck down economic and social legislation deemed unwise on the ground that it violated (substantive) due process of law. The court was severely criticized for requiring legislatures to conform with its notions of proper economic and social policy, which it read into the Due Process Clause. In the 1930s, the court beat a retreat, and with rare exceptions since then it has not struck down economic and social legislation on grounds of violation of due process. The current test for whether federal substantive due process has been violated is: Does the ordinance bear a *rational relationship to a permissible state objective*? If so, the ordinance is valid under the Due Process Clause. The ordinance must be *a* rational way of achieving the objective, not necessarily the best way. [**Village of Belle Terre v. Boraas,** 416 U.S. 1 (1974)] Legitimate state objectives have been held to include public health, safety, and general welfare. Inasmuch as almost all zoning ordinances involve a means of achieving these objectives that is not wholly irrational, few zoning ordinances are struck down under the rational relationship test. [**Pierro v. Baxendale,** 118 A.2d 401 (N.J. 1955)]

(a) Strict scrutiny standard [§1389]

If the zoning ordinance infringes on a *fundamental right* (*e.g.*, the right to vote, the right to free speech, the right to interstate travel, etc.), the burden is on the state to justify the legislation by showing that it has a *compelling state interest* in the legislation's objective. This standard is called strict scrutiny, because it requires that a statute be examined very closely. However, strict scrutiny is rarely applied under the Due Process Clause to zoning ordinances, because housing has been held *not* to be a "fundamental" right. [**Lindsey v. Normet,** *supra*, §1018; *but see* **Moore v. City of East Cleveland,** 431 U.S. 494 (1977)—constitutional protection given to the right of traditional family to live together (*see infra*, §1448)] Even though exclusionary zoning ordinances may infringe on the right to travel and settle in the community, it is difficult to raise that issue in federal courts (*see infra*, §1456).

(3) State due process requirements [§1390]

Like the federal Constitution, state constitutions also require that legislation not deprive a person of due process of law. As to a state constitution, the state supreme court is the final arbiter of its meaning. Although the United States Supreme Court has interpreted the Due Process Clause in the federal Constitution in such a way as to limit severely its application to laws regulating the use of property, state supreme courts have continued to recognize that the *state* due process clause has *considerable substantive*, as well as procedural, content. Under this clause, state courts strike down legislation they deem "arbitrary" or "unreasonable," even though it may be *a* rational way of achieving the objective. Despite the fact that state courts, interpreting state constitutions, give a broader reach to the state due process clause than does the United States Supreme Court interpreting the federal Constitution, zoning ordinances remain presumptively valid. [*See* **Guimont v. Clarke**, 854 P.2d 1 (Wash. 1993)]

b. Equal Protection Clause [§1391]

The Equal Protection Clause of the Fourteenth Amendment provides: "No State shall . . . deny to any person within its jurisdiction the equal protection of the laws." As applied to zoning, this clause requires that landowners who are similarly situated be similarly treated, except where treating them differently can be justified. The difference between the Due Process Clause and the Equal Protection Clause is generally this: Under the Due Process Clause, the question is whether the government can take away the right. Under the Equal Protection Clause, the question is whether the government can take away the right from these persons and not from others. To establish a violation of the Equal Protection Clause, the plaintiff must prove a *discriminatory purpose or intent*. Discriminatory effect is not enough. [**Village of Arlington Heights v. Metropolitan Housing Development Corp.,** 429 U.S. 252 (1977)]

(1) Rational relationship standard [§1392]

The validity of most zoning regulations under the Equal Protection Clause is measured by the rational relationship test that is also applicable under the Due Process Clause. The legislation only has to bear a *rational relation* to a *permissible state objective*. [**Village of Belle Terre v. Boraas,** *supra*, §1388]

(2) Strict scrutiny standard [§1393]

If the zoning ordinance operates by reference to a *suspect classification* (*i.e.*, race, national origin, religion, or possibly age or sex), the burden is on the state to justify the legislation by showing it has a *compelling state interest* in the legislation's objective. The ordinance is strictly scrutinized. Thus, a zoning ordinance that restricts blacks to one district and whites to another would violate the Equal Protection Clause. However, strict scrutiny is rarely applied under the Equal Protection Clause to zoning ordinances because they rarely operate by reference to a suspect classification. (*See also infra*, §1454.)

c. Takings Clause [§1394]

The Fifth Amendment to the Constitution provides: ". . . nor shall private property be taken for public use without just compensation." (State constitutions have similar provisions.) Although this amendment is expressly applicable only to the federal government, it has also been held applicable to the states under the Fourteenth Amendment, which requires the states to provide citizens with due process of law. Because of this, courts sometimes do not clearly indicate whether they regard the issue as one of taking or as one of due process. They mix the two. But this is confusing because due process is basically a question of rational relationship between means and ends (or substantive due process), whereas taking involves rather different matters, such as whether the ordinance prevents harm or secures a benefit (discussed *infra*, §§1472 *et seq.*). So, too, the remedy for a violation of due process and the remedy for a taking may be different. If an ordinance violates due process, it is void. If an ordinance is a taking, the landowner's remedy is an injunction against its enforcement or, possibly, interim or permanent damages. (*See* the discussion of remedies under regulatory takings, *infra*, §1483.) For clarity, it is wise to keep the due process issue and the taking issue separate.

d. Summary [§1395]

To sum up, the arguments made against zoning actions are principally these:

(1) Ultra vires [§1396]

The action is not authorized by, or violates an express provision of, the enabling act.

(2) Improper delegation [§1397]

The action is unconstitutional because the delegation of discretionary authority to the local decisionmaker is without any governing standards.

(3) Procedural due process [§1398]

The action—an administrative decision—was taken without notice and hearing to the affected parties.

(4) Substantive due process [§1399]

The action deprives persons of due process of law because (i) it lacks a rational relationship to a permissible state objective, or (ii) it infringes on a fundamental right and cannot be justified by a compelling state interest. Or, under a state due process clause, the action is arbitrary or unreasonable.

POSSIBLE CHALLENGES TO ZONING ORDINANCE | gilbert

ULTRA VIRES	An argument that the zoning ordinance is beyond the authority of the zoning body and therefore void. Must *look to enabling act* adopted by state; states may delegate this aspect of their police power.
FEDERAL DUE PROCESS (PROCEDURAL)	An argument that the zoning ordinance was improperly adopted. If the zoning action was legislative (general in effect), individual notice is not required. If the zoning action was administrative (affecting only one, or in some states a few parcels of land), the landowner must be *notified* and given an *opportunity to be heard*.
FEDERAL DUE PROCESS (SUBSTANTIVE)	An argument that the ordinance is not reasonable and so is invalid. Unless a fundamental right is involved (and it seldom is), the zoning action need only bear a *rational relationship to a permissible state objective*, such as health, safety, and welfare concerns. Almost every zoning action will pass this standard.
STATE DUE PROCESS (SUBSTANTIVE)	Similar to federal due process, but many states require *more* than is required under federal law and might find a rational ordinance unreasonable.
FEDERAL EQUAL PROTECTION	An argument that the zoning action has the purpose or intent *to discriminate*. Most zoning actions will be tested under the rational relationship test and will be upheld.
FEDERAL TAKINGS CLAUSE	An argument that the zoning action has taken property *without just compensation*. Most zoning actions will not constitute a taking.

(5) Equal protection [§1400]

The action deprives persons of equal protection of the laws because (i) it has no rational relationship to a permissible state objective, or (ii) it operates by reference to a suspect classification and cannot be justified by a compelling state interest.

(6) Taking [§1401]

The action takes the plaintiff's property without compensation.

4. Nonconforming Uses [§1402]

A nonconforming use is a *use in existence when the zoning ordinance is passed* that is not permitted in the district under the new zoning ordinance. Nonconforming uses are allowed to remain because requiring immediate termination would be either a violation of substantive due process or an unconstitutional taking of property rights. (*See infra*, §1472.) Nonetheless, nonconforming uses may be limited or terminated under certain conditions (below).

a. Limits on changing use [§1403]

A zoning ordinance may *prohibit expanding* a nonconforming use beyond the precise space it occupied when the ordinance was enacted. Or an ordinance may stipulate that a nonconforming building, if destroyed by fire, *cannot be rebuilt* without complying with the ordinance. Or an ordinance may prohibit *change to another nonconforming* use. [**Town of Belleville v. Parrillo's, Inc.**, 416 A.2d 388 (N.J. 1980)]

b. Amortization [§1404]

A zoning ordinance may provide that the nonconforming use must terminate after a specified period of time. The ordinance may provide for different amortization periods, depending on the amount of investment in the use and building. These ordinances have been challenged as being unconstitutional, sometimes successfully.

(1) Majority view—amortization valid [§1405]

The majority of courts has held such ordinances constitutional as a reasonable exercise of the police power—not in violation of due process and not a taking. Nonetheless, the ordinance must be reasonable *as applied* to each nonconforming use terminated. If not reasonable as applied to each particular landowner, it is unconstitutional as to that landowner. [**City of Los Angeles v. Gage**, 127 Cal. App. 2d 442 (1954)—five years for removal of plumbing business reasonable; **Village of Valatie v. Smith**, 83 N.Y.2d 396 (1994)—termination of nonconforming mobile home use on transfer of ownership valid as a form of amortization (*but compare infra*, §1419)]

(2) Minority view—amortization unconstitutional [§1406]

A minority of courts have held amortization ordinances unconstitutional as a taking of property without compensation. [**Ailes v. Decatur County Area Planning Commission,** 448 N.E.2d 1057 (Ind. 1983); **Hoffmann v. Kinealy,** 389 S.W.2d 745 (Mo. 1965); **City of Akron v. Chapman,** 116 N.E.2d 697 (Ohio 1953); **PA Northwestern Distributors, Inc. v. Zoning Hearing Board,** 584 A.2d 1372 (Pa. 1991)]

c. Vested rights [§1407]

If a person has acquired a "vested right," the zoning cannot be changed so as to deny the person a right to proceed. A vested right generally arises when the person spends a substantial sum in reliance on a building permit. [**Stone v. City of Wilton,** 331 N.W.2d 398 (Iowa 1983)] A minority view creates vested rights any time a building permit is legally granted.

5. Administration of Zoning Ordinance

a. Comprehensive plan [§1408]

Section 3 of the Standard Zoning Enabling Act requires that local zoning ordinances "be made in accordance with a comprehensive plan." To prepare the plan, the enabling act requires that a planning commission composed of citizens be appointed by the mayor or other executive officer. The commission employs a staff of expert professional planners to prepare plans and give it advice. The commission also recommends to the local legislative body a zoning ordinance to implement the comprehensive plan.

(1) Legal effect of plan [§1409]

A master or comprehensive plan is a guide for development within the city; it states policies and guiding principles. Its adoption by the commission or by the local legislative body does not have the legal consequence of restricting the use of property. To restrict the use of property, the plan must be implemented by the local legislature enacting a zoning ordinance or subdivision regulations, which have legal effect. A comprehensive plan places an important constraint on exercise of discretionary powers.

(2) Existence of comprehensive plan [§1410]

Many cities have not prepared written comprehensive plans, but have enacted zoning ordinances. Zoning ordinances not based on plans are generally held valid on the theory that a separate, comprehensive plan is not required; the zoning ordinance itself is the plan. Indeed, even if a separate plan is required, it has been held that the plan can consist of policies of the planning commission, as evidenced by documents or testimony of the commission members. It does not necessarily have to consist of a formal document. Under this interpretation, a comprehensive plan means comprehensive *planning*.

b. Amendment of zoning ordinance [§1411]

The enabling act provides that the zoning ordinance can be amended by the local legislative body rezoning a particular parcel of land. The local legislative body is advised by the planning commission on amendments, but it does not have to follow the commission's advice.

(1) Spot zoning [§1412]

An amendment not in accordance with the comprehensive plan is "spot zoning." Spot zoning is unlawful. Although spot zoning usually involves rezoning one lot in violation of the plan, the zoning of one lot differently from its neighbors could, in a particular context, be in accordance with a comprehensive plan. In determining what is spot zoning, size or number of lots rezoned—while important—is not controlling; deviation from the plan is controlling. [**Miss Porter's School, Inc. v. Town Plan & Zoning Commission,** 198 A.2d 707 (Conn. 1964); **Save Our Rural Environment v. Snohomish County,** 662 P.2d 816 (Wash. 1983); **Anderson v. Island County,** 501 P.2d 594 (Wash. 1972)]

(2) Amendments generally presumed valid [§1413]

The traditional view is that zoning amendments, like zoning ordinances, are presumptively valid, and the burden is on persons objecting to the amendment to prove that it is not in accordance with a comprehensive plan. However, abuses in the zoning amendment process have caused some courts in recent years to tighten up the standards applicable to zoning amendments. These standards are generally designed to make it harder for a proponent to procure a zoning amendment. They are not yet widely followed.

(a) "Change or mistake rule" [§1414]

One way to tighten up on amendments is to shift the burden of proof. Accordingly, it has been held by some courts that there is no presumption of validity of piecemeal amendments. The original zoning is presumptively valid and *correct*. To sustain a piecemeal change therein, the proponent must show strong evidence of *mistake* in the original ordinance or of a *substantial change in conditions*. [**MacDonald v. Board of County Commissioners,** 210 A.2d 325 (Md. 1965)]

(b) Must show public need [§1415]

Another way of tightening up is to narrow the applicable standards for amendments. Accordingly, it has been held that in proving that the proposed amendment is in accordance with the comprehensive plan, the proponent must show that there is a *public need* for a change of the kind proposed, and that such need will be best served by changing the zoning of the proponent's parcel *as compared with other available parcels*. Findings of fact and written reasons by the zoning commission supporting the amendment may also be required. [**Fasano v. Board of County Commissioners,** *supra*, §1387; **Snyder v. Board of County Commissioners,** 595 So. 2d 65 (Fla. 1991)]

c. Variances [§1416]

Because of the difficulty in drawing a general zoning ordinance that takes into account all the various existing shapes, sizes, topographical features, and peculiar conditions of every lot in the city, zoning enabling acts provide for a *board of adjustment* (sometimes called the board of zoning appeals) to grant relief by way of variance where the restrictions contained in the ordinance cause the owner *"practical difficulty"* or *"unnecessary hardship."* The board of adjustment is composed of citizens appointed by the mayor or other chief executive and is a body different from the planning commission.

(1) Standards for variances [§1417]

The standards for a variance are *practical difficulty* or *unnecessary hardship*, for which the evidence should be strong because the variance is a departure from the uniform plan. The hardship must be due to unique circumstances, *i.e.*, peculiar to the particular lot. If the hardship conditions generally exist in the neighborhood, an amendment to the zoning ordinance, not a variance, is proper. The hardship must *not* be *self-created*. The variance must not result in substantial detriment to the public health, safety, or welfare, and it must not be a substantial departure from the comprehensive plan. [**Puritan-Greenfield Improvement Association v. Leo**, 153 N.W.2d 162 (Mich. 1967); **Clark v. Board of Zoning Appeals**, 301 N.Y. 86 (1950)]

Example: The zoning ordinance requires a 20-foot building setback from the street. Because of the shallowness of the lot, which was created before the zoning ordinance was enacted, it is not practicable to set back a new building 20 feet. This is a proper case for a variance. If the shallow lot were created *after* the enactment of the zoning ordinance, the difficulty would be self-created, and a variance would be improper. [**Commons v. Westwood Zoning Board of Adjustment**, 410 A.2d 1138 (N.J. 1980)]

(a) Distinguish—use vs. bulk variance [§1418]

In the above example, a *bulk* variance is illustrated. A *use* variance, permitting a use prohibited in the district, is much more destructive of the master plan and in effect is an amendment. In some states, use variances cannot be granted by the board of adjustment or are held to a higher standard of proof of no reasonable return. [**Village Board v. Jarrold**, 53 N.Y.2d 254 (1981)]

EXAM TIP   **gilbert**

Variance issues appear on exams with some frequency. Remember to mention the basics: If because of a *unique circumstance* (e.g., the atypically small size of a landowner's lot) compliance with the zoning ordinance (e.g., a setback requirement) would cause *practical difficulty or unnecessary hardship*, a variance may be granted.

(2) Runs with the land [§1419]

A variance, when granted, runs with the land to successive owners. It cannot be granted to expire when the owner transfers the property or dies. Zoning thus relates to the property without regard to the person who owns it. [**St. Onge v. Donovan**, 71 N.Y.2d 507 (1988)]

(3) Conditions attached [§1420]

A variance may be granted on the applicant's meeting certain specified conditions. The conditions must be reasonable and must relate to the proposed use of the property and be aimed at minimizing adverse impact on the surrounding area. [**St. Onge v. Donovan**, *supra*]

d. Special exception [§1421]

A special exception to a zoning ordinance is one allowable where certain conditions specified in the ordinance are met. It has frequently been confused with a variance, but a theory other than individual hardship underlies the special exception. The theory is that certain uses can peacefully coexist with their neighbors when specified conditions occur. The board of adjustment is empowered to determine whether the conditions specified in the ordinance are met. Sometimes the special exception is called a "special use" or "conditional use." [**Kotrich v. County of DuPage**, 166 N.E.2d 601 (Ill. 1960)]

Example: A zoning ordinance specifies that a nursery school is permitted in a residential district if adequate off-street parking is provided, no more than 30 students are enrolled, and play space is fenced and screened by a hedge. This is a special exception.

(1) Standards for special exception [§1422]

Legislative power cannot be delegated to an administrative agency unless the standards are sufficiently clear to prevent gross arbitrariness. Delegation of power without standards is improper. Sometimes the standards set forth in the ordinance for granting a special exception are especially vague. For example, a nursery school might be permitted in a residential district "when compatible with the neighborhood" or "with permission of the board of adjustment." Despite the lack of procedural safeguards and standards, the majority of courts have usually upheld provisions for special exceptions without clear standards. They have held that the general purposes in view ("health, safety, and general welfare of the community") are a sufficient safeguard to control the board's discretion, provided the board gives reasons for its action. [**Cope v. Inhabitants of the Town of Brunswick**, 464 A.2d 223 (Me. 1983); **Zylka v. City of Crystal**, 167 N.W.2d 45 (Minn. 1969)]

EXAM TIP **gilbert**

Watch for special exception situations on your exam. Schools, hospitals, and funeral homes often must (or wish to) be located in residential areas. This is permissible *if* the zoning ordinance so provides and any conditions specified in the ordinance (*e.g.*, provision of off-street parking) are met. The rationale is that these uses can peacefully coexist with neighbors if the conditions are met.

---

e. Discretionary or non-Euclidean zoning [§1423]

Under the zoning ordinance upheld in the *Euclid* case, the only means of flexibility provided were variances and special exceptions. These proved to be insufficient. More flexibility was required than the early planners thought. As a result, cities have experimented with various types of non-Euclidean or discretionary zoning, which have generally been upheld after some initial judicial objection. The gist of the judicial objection is that these techniques give planners great discretion, and open the door to favoritism, unfairness, and unpredictability. However, the trend is to uphold these discretionary devices as necessary to effective public land planning.

(1) Contract zoning [§1424]

Where a city agrees to zone or rezone a particular tract of land on condition that the owner execute a contract or covenant restricting the use of the tract in specified ways, this is called "contract zoning" or "conditional zoning." It is a method whereby, on application by the owner, the city can tailor planning considerations to the particular tract, permitting the owner to develop the land in ways that do not harm the neighborhood. Planners consider it useful in bringing flexibility to zoning. [**Collard v. Incorporated Village of Flower Hill,** 52 N.Y.2d 594 (1981)]

---

e.g **Example:** A landowner wishes to put a light manufacturing plant on a lot zoned residential. If the owner will agree by covenant to provide a buffer strip park to protect nearby houses, the city will agree to rezone the land for light industrial use. The owner executes the covenant in favor of the city; the city rezones the land.

---

(2) Density zoning [§1425]

After World War II, developers often desired to develop large tracts of land and use their spaces in a way different from that permitted by the zoning ordinance. Typically, the developer wanted to build houses on smaller lots (clustering them) and use the space saved for some recreational use for the homeowners—a park, riding trails, tennis courts. The overall density would remain the same, as under traditional development, but the homeowners would have some common amenity that made the subdivision more desirable. To permit this, cluster zoning or density zoning laws were enacted. Thus, density zoning provides developers with an option to use spaces in various ways, provided a specified overall density of population is maintained.

(3) Floating zones [§1426]

Another method of introducing flexibility is the floating zone. A floating zone is a zone provided in the ordinance to which no land is assigned on the zoning map until a landowner makes such a request and is granted that zoning classification. Such reclassification is made by amendment to the zoning map. Such a zone is said to "float" over the city; no one knows where it will land. The planners argue that this allows them to postpone making a specific site selection until a specific proposal is made; it prevents over-zoning for uses before they are needed. And it offers the extra dollars that might come from the floating zone to the first landowners to come up with an acceptable proposal.

Example: The city council decides it needs a limited industrial district somewhere in the city. The zoning ordinance is amended to create a limited industrial district (F-1), which sets forth the requirements (25 acres minimum), conditions (sufficient off-street screened parking; 200-foot setback from street, with grassy front lawn), and uses permitted (non-noisy light industry). No land in the city is placed in an F-1 district. The zone "floats" over the city. Subsequently landowner A, whose tract is in a residential district, applies for rezoning to F-1. A's tract meets the criteria set forth in the ordinance. The city council rezones the tract F-1.

(a) Criticism

It has been asserted that floating zones are in violation of the requirement of a comprehensive plan, which gives predictability as to future use. Thus, it is argued, floating zones are not permitted by the enabling act. It is also claimed that floating zones deny equal protection of the laws, because when and where the zone will "come to rest" lies in the arbitrary discretion of the planning commission. Some courts agreed in the early days of floating zones and struck them down. But now courts uphold floating zones by analogizing them to the variance and special exception procedures, where a comparable amount of discretion is permitted. [**Rodgers v. Village of Tarrytown**, 302 N.Y. 115 (1951)]

(4) Planned unit development [§1427]

In a planned unit development ("PUD") district, the developer with a large tract of land can mix uses—*e.g.*, some single-family houses, some apartments, some neighborhood shopping, even an unobjectionable industry. The developer can ignore specific lot and density requirements if the overall density of the development does not exceed that of standard lot-by-lot development. The requirements for a PUD classification may be set forth in the ordinance and ordinarily require a large amount of land. The test, as with an amendment, is whether the rezoning is in accordance with a comprehensive plan. [**Cheney v. Village 2 at New Hope, Inc.**, 241 A.2d 81 (Pa. 1968)]

(a) Criticism

It has been argued that the PUD district violates the enabling act on the theory that by mixing uses and ignoring lot lines it violates the essence of zoning, which is lot-by-lot development. And, like the floating zone, it does not give predictability to what is permitted in the neighborhood (a virtue of Euclidean zoning). It is unlikely that such arguments would succeed today where the market demand for planned unit developments, thought to represent advanced ideas for flexible planning, is strong. Planned unit development, however, gives largely discretionary powers to the planning authorities, which is to some extent the antithesis of the zoning upheld in the *Euclid* case (*see supra*, §1377).

f. Zoning by referendum [§1428]

Because of public hostility to certain types of uses, mainly certain types of multiple dwellings, zoning ordinances in some cities in recent years have been amended to provide that a zone change *amendment* can be made only by a public referendum. Although the requirement of a referendum may have the effect of excluding low-income housing and may have a disproportionate effect on one race, mandatory referendums have been upheld as constitutional. It has been held that a referendum is a legislative act that cannot, by itself, violate the Due Process Clause. To violate that clause the *result* of the referendum must not be a rational method of achieving a permissible public objective. Nor is a referendum an unconstitutional delegation of legislative power to a limited group uncontrolled by any standard; it is direct legislation by the voters. [**City of Eastlake v. Forest City Enterprises, Inc.,** 426 U.S. 668 (1976)] The reasoning of the Supreme Court in *Eastlake* is not necessarily applicable to *administrative* decisions (such as variances and special exceptions). A referendum for administrative decisions may be an improper delegation of power without standards. [**Arnel Development Co. v. City of Costa Mesa,** 28 Cal. 3d 511 (1980)]

NON-EUCLIDEAN ZONING—EXAMPLES	**gilbert**
CONTRACT ZONING	City agrees to zone or rezone a particular tract if owner contracts to restrict the use in a certain way (*e.g.,* city will rezone for light industrial if owner erects a buffer zone).
DENSITY ZONING	Ordinance focuses on overall density of an area rather than having lot size restrictions (*e.g.,* small lots are permitted, but more land is set aside for parks).
FLOATING ZONES	Zoning ordinance establishes a zone (*e.g.,* light industrial) but does not assign it to a particular location until a landowner requests reclassification to the zone.
PLANNED UNIT DEVELOPMENT	Owner of a large tract of land is allowed to mix uses as long as overall density limits are not exceeded.
BY REFERENDUM	Rezoning (usually for multi-family dwellings) is allowed only if approved by public referendum.

6. **Purposes of Zoning [§1429]**

Although zoning legislation with the purpose of protecting the public health or safety is clearly within the police power, three other purposes have been much litigated in recent years: zoning for aesthetic objectives; zoning against adult bookstores and cinemas; and zoning for preservation of historic buildings and open space.

a. **Zoning for aesthetic objectives**

(1) **Old doctrine [§1430]**

In the late nineteenth century, the courts laid down the rule that the police power cannot be used to accomplish objectives that are primarily aesthetic. There is no statutory or constitutional basis for this doctrine; it is simply a restriction that the courts, cognizant of the subjectivity of what is beautiful, imposed on the legislatures, usually municipal legislatures. The doctrine may owe something to the fact that zoning was originally conceived as a scheme to deal with nuisance. Older nuisance cases drew a distinction between offenses to the sight, which are not actionable because they are considered to be neither substantial nor tangible, and offenses to the other senses, which are actionable.

(2) **New doctrine [§1431]**

In recent years, many state courts, discarding the old doctrine, have held that cities may enact regulations primarily for aesthetic objectives. Some of these courts, attempting to put some limitation on what can be legislated in the name of beauty and to read some standard into the delegation of power, have said that the standard to be applied to aesthetic ordinances is whether the prohibited use offends the sensibilities of the *average person* and tends to *depress property values*. Inasmuch as the sensibilities of the average person will be reflected in property values, this standard boils down to whether the prohibited uses deemed ugly will lessen property values. This tends, it is alleged, to make aesthetic judgments more objective.

(a) **Architectural review boards [§1432]**

Most courts now uphold the power of city architectural review boards to deny building permits for proposed buildings that the board disapproves. Because the standards these boards apply are often vague and difficult to apply, they raise problems of improper delegation of power and equal protection of the laws. A favorite standard is that the building must "conform to the existing character of the neighborhood and not cause a substantial depreciation in neighboring property values." Such a standard has been upheld, even when the "existing character" of the neighborhood is not entirely uniform. [**State *ex rel.* Stoyanoff v. Berkeley,** 458 S.W.2d 305 (Mo. 1970); *but see* **Anderson v. City of Issaquah,** 851 P.2d

744 (Wash. 1993)—holding a substantially similar statute to be unconstitutionally vague]

(b) Advertising signs [§1433]

It has long been held that commercial advertisements may be prohibited in residential areas, on the theory that they are harmful to the quiet and tranquility sought in residential areas. If the commercial use itself can be excluded, the advertisement of it can also be excluded. But problems arise when *political* advertisements are banned or when *commercial billboards* are banned from *commercial areas*. Here the zoning ordinance may conflict with the First Amendment right of freedom of speech.

1) Political advertisements [§1434]

Political speech occupies a preferred position and is given greater protection than most other kinds of speech. Political speech includes comment on any matter of public interest. For example, ordinances prohibiting political signs entirely in front yards of residential areas have usually been held void, because adequate alternative means of communication are not available to the owners. [**City of Ladue v. Gilleo,** 512 U.S. 43 (1994)]

2) Commercial advertisements [§1435]

First Amendment protection of commercial speech is an emerging area of the law. Although not protected at all until 1975, in that year, the United States Supreme Court held that commercial speech enjoys a substantial amount of First Amendment protection, but the Court has yet to carve out exactly what that amount is. The most recent pronouncement on the regulation of billboards from the Supreme Court is **Metromedia, Inc. v. City of San Diego,** 453 U.S. 490 (1981), and that case settled little. San Diego had enacted an ordinance banning outdoor advertising signs throughout the city, with a few exceptions. Signs advertising goods sold on the premises ("on-site" advertising) were allowed, as were signs falling into 12 specific categories (one of which was "temporary political campaign signs"). Seven justices explicitly concluded that the city's interest in avoiding visual clutter was sufficient to justify a prohibition of billboards, but a majority of justices voted to invalidate the specific ordinance as in violation of the First Amendment. The reasoning of the justices differed considerably. Four justices in a plurality opinion concluded that the ordinance was void because it was not content-neutral. The ordinance contained an exception for on-site commercial advertising but lacked a similar exception for noncommercial messages. Thus, it restricted too little speech because of the exceptions based on the signs' messages. Other justices thought the ordinance eliminated the billboard as an effective medium of communication for noncommercial messages, and thus prohibited too much protected speech.

b. Zoning against adult entertainment [§1436]

Cities have adopted various measures to deal with adult bookstores, cinemas, and other places of entertainment. A zoning ordinance that permits adult entertainments, but disperses or limits them to certain zones, is constitutional. The chief constitutional difficulty with such ordinances is equal protection because adult theatres are discriminated against whereas other theatres are not. That appears to be discrimination on the basis of content of speech (impermissible), but nonetheless such classification has been held constitutional as serving a substantial government interest while allowing reasonable alternative places for adult entertainment. [**City of Renton v. Playtime Theatres, Inc.**, 475 U.S. 41 (1986)] The Supreme Court has since increased a city's power to regulate adult entertainment. A city's ban on nude dancing, which once was held to involve freedom of expression protected by the First Amendment [**Schad v. Borough of Mount Ephraim**, 452 U.S. 61 (1981)], was upheld by the Court. [**Barnes v. Glen Theatre, Inc.**, 501 U.S. 560 (1991), *and see* **City of Erie v. Pap's A.M.**, 529 U.S. 277 (2000)]

EXAM TIP   **gilbert**

Early on, the Supreme Court seemed squeamish when it came to zoning ordinances that restricted facilities that allowed nude dancing. The Justices agreed that nude dancing conveys a message, is entitled to some First Amendment protection, and deserves its "place in the sun" (or "moon") somewhere within a city, even if limited to city outskirts. However, the Court seems to have retreated—even a *total ban* on establishments that allow nude dancing *can be upheld* because of the government's substantial interests in combating crime and the secondary effects caused by the presence of such facilities. Thus, if an exam question deals with a flat-out total ban on nude dancing, don't hesitate to find the ban valid.

---

c. Zoning and religious establishments [§1437]

The Religious Land Use and Institutionalized Persons Act of 2000 ("RLUIPA") [42 U.S.C. §§2000cc - 2000cc-5] prohibits: (i) land use regulations that impose substantial burdens on religious exercise unless the government demonstrates that the regulation is in furtherance of a compelling state interest and is the least restrictive means of furthering that interest; (ii) regulations that treat religious institutions unequally relative to nonreligious institutions or otherwise discriminates against them; and (iii) total exclusion of religious institutions from a jurisdiction. There have been a number of constitutional challenges to the legislation, based on the First Amendment's Free Exercise Clause, but no decisive determination of the issue to date.

e.g. Example: Due to inadequate classroom space, Westchester Day School, a religious school, applies for a special use permit to construct a new school building and to renovate other existing buildings on its campus. The permit is denied. Under the RLUIPA, the zoning board's denial of the permit application places a substantial burden on religious exercise because, by precluding the construction of needed facilities, the board significantly interfered with the school's ability to provide its students with an adequate and effective education. Moreover, denial of the permit may not be the least restrictive means of addressing the government's interests, because any potential increase in traffic caused by the project could be mitigated by, *e.g.*, retiming traffic lights, widening streets, an improved busing program, or an enrollment cap, and any adverse environmental impact due to the size of the proposed building could be mitigated through imposition of conditions (*see supra*, §1420). [**Westchester Day School v. Village of Mamaroneck**, 417 F. Supp. 2d 477 (S.D.N.Y. 2006)]

d. Zoning for preservation [§1438]

In recent years, there has been increasing public demand to preserve open spaces, wildlife areas, and historic structures. These ordinances have been challenged on the ground that they "take" property without compensation. Whether property is "taken" depends on analysis of the economic loss to the landowner weighed against the reasonable need for the legislation to accomplish a substantial public purpose. (*See infra*, §1472 *et seq.*)

(1) Historic preservation

(a) Historic districts [§1439]

Ordinances directed toward preservation of historic districts are generally valid. The standard usually applied in judging a new building's conformity with the "character of the district" is much clearer in a historic district than in the ordinary city residential district because the existing architecture is normally of a uniform character (*e.g.*, Georgian or French Quarter, etc.). This standard minimizes the likelihood that an architectural board will violate equal protection in its decisions. Furthermore, control of historic preservation districts is not a taking of property. The preservation of a historic district often results in *gain*, not loss, to the landowners, so there is a reciprocity of benefit from the regulation. (*See infra*, §1479.)

(b) Individual landmarks [§1440]

Preservation of individual buildings that are deemed historically important but are not in a historic district raises serious equal protection and "taking" problems not raised by general district-wide regulations. Because there is no historic district with many owners affected, the designation of a single historic building can impose a large cost on one individual who reaps no reciprocity of benefit. The landmark case is now **Penn Central Transportation Co. v. City of New York,** 438 U.S. 104 (1978). The Supreme Court, sustaining New York City's landmark law, which prohibited building an office tower above Grand Central Terminal, held that the owners could not establish a "taking" merely by showing that they had been denied the right to exploit the airspace, a valuable property interest. The court held the taking issue in this context must be resolved by focusing on the uses *permitted,* not on the uses prohibited (*i.e.,* on what has been left the owner, not on what the owner has lost). The uses permitted included *continuing use* as a terminal containing office space, which the Court regarded as Penn Central's *primary expectation concerning use.* In addition, subject to certain limitations, Penn Central could sell its development rights in its airspace to other developers in the neighborhood. Altogether, the income from the terminal and the possible sale of development rights provided Penn Central with a *reasonable return* on its investment.

(2) Preservation of open space

(a) Agricultural zoning [§1441]
A city may establish policies regarding conversion of agricultural land on the edge of the city to urban development. It may hold land in an agricultural zone until such time as the land is needed for urban purposes. [**Philippi v. City of Sublimity,** 662 P.2d 325 (Or. 1983)]

(b) Wetlands zoning [§1442]
Ordinances have been enacted regulating and sometimes prohibiting fill of wetlands, usually defined as swamp, marsh, beach, or land subject to tidal action or storm flooding. The public purpose is preservation of ecological systems and the natural environment, as well as aesthetic enjoyment. Most state courts now uphold wetlands preservation legislation. The theory used to sustain wetlands preservation legislation is that it is not a "taking" to prohibit future activities that would be *harmful* to the public. It does not matter that the existing uses of wetlands—wildlife observation, hunting, haying, shellfish harvesting, and aesthetic enjoyment—may be of little economic value, if the purpose of the ordinance is to prevent public harm. [**Just v. Marinette County,** 201 N.W.2d 761 (Wis. 1972)] (*See* discussion of harm theory of taking, *infra,* §1476.)

7. Exclusionary Zoning [§1443]
Zoning can be used to purposefully exclude various groups from the community or from certain districts. Excluded persons may be unmarried or unrelated persons

who live together as a family, low-income persons, or racial minorities. Even where there is no intention to exclude these persons, the zoning ordinance may in fact result in exclusion. Bear in mind the difference between intentional and de facto exclusion, which may be an important distinction in some cases.

a. Nontraditional families [§1444]

At the heart of the zoning system is the protection of the single-family home. But what is a single family? How is it defined? Legislatures have defined it in various ways, usually in terms of persons being related by blood, marriage, or adoption. If the definition bears a *rational relationship* to the objective of preserving "family values" and quiet seclusion, the definition passes muster under the United States Constitution. [**Village of Belle Terre v. Boraas,** *supra,* §1392] Several state courts, however, have held that occupancy restrictions based on biological or legal relationships violate the state constitution because the definitions do not bear a rational relationship to the city's goal of controlling density. [**Charter Township of Delta v. Dinolfo,** 351 N.W.2d 831 (Mich. 1984); **State v. Baker,** 405 A.2d 368 (N.J. 1979); *and see* **Borough of Glassboro v. Vallorosi,** 568 A.2d 888 (N.J. 1990)—holding ordinance defining family as "a stable and permanent living unit, being a traditional family or the functional equivalent thereof" encompassed a house shared by 10 students]

(1) Excluding group homes [§1445]

If the ordinance excludes group homes for persons with handicaps, it may come in conflict with the Fair Housing Act, which prohibits discrimination in housing against persons with handicaps (*see supra,* §821). Discrimination includes the refusal to make reasonable accommodations in rules necessary to afford handicapped persons equal opportunities to housing.

(a) Occupant caps [§1446]

The Fair Housing Act exempts any "reasonable" zoning regulation restricting the maximum number of persons permitted to occupy a dwelling. The Supreme Court has held that family composition rules that *cap the total number of occupants* are exempt, but rules designed to preserve the family character of the neighborhood by focusing on the *composition of households* are not exempt. A family composition rule (*e.g.,* a maximum of five unrelated occupants or an unlimited number of related occupants) is not a maximum occupancy restriction. Thus, under a family composition rule, the city must take reasonable steps to accommodate group homes of the handicapped. [**City of Edmonds v. Oxford House, Inc.,** 514 U.S. 725 (1995); *and see* **Doe v. City of Butler,** 892 F.2d 315 (3d Cir. 1989)—holding six-person limit on transitional dwelling might violate FHA if it made group home for abused mothers with children not economically feasible]

(b) Reasonable accommodation [§1447]

In accommodating group homes, a city may not require a permit for group homes that is not also required for other multiple-residence dwellings. A special permit requirement reflects prejudice against handicapped persons and does not bear a rational relationship to a legitimate state objective. [**City of Cleburne v. Cleburne Living Center, Inc.,** 473 U.S. 432 (1985); **Association for Advancement of the Mentally Handicapped, Inc. v. City of Elizabeth,** 876 F. Supp. 614 (D.N.J. 1994); *but compare* **Familystyle of St. Paul, Inc. v. City of St. Paul,** 923 F.2d 91 (8th Cir. 1991)—upholding ordinance dispersing group homes for mentally ill persons]

(2) Excluding traditional family [§1448]

If the definition of family excludes the traditional family, including the extended family, the ordinance requires a *higher standard* of justification than rational relationship (but less than strict scrutiny). The Supreme Court has struck down, as violating substantive due process, an ordinance defining a family so that a grandmother could not live with her son and her two grandchildren where the grandchildren were not both children of the son. The court held the ordinance intruded into the traditional family and had only a marginal relationship to the permissible zoning objectives of preventing overcrowding and congestion. The Court thus has given constitutional protection to the tradition of uncles, aunts, cousins, and grandparents sharing a household—a protection it has not extended to students or unmarried persons living together. [**Moore v. City of East Cleveland,** *supra,* §1389]

EXAM TIP	gilbert

NIMBYs (**N**ot **I**n **M**y **B**ack **Y**ard) appear frequently in law school exams. It seems no one wants a landfill, nuclear waste facility, or group home in his neighborhood. If you see an exam question where a zoning board caters to the fears of NIMBYs and adopts an ordinance prohibiting a group home, remember the following points:

- The federal Constitution generally will not prohibit a ban on *unrelated* persons living together (think "frat house"), but the Fair Housing Act might if the ban discriminates against persons with handicaps.

- The Fair Housing Act has an exception for ordinances that cap the total *number* of persons who live within a home, but not ordinances that attempt to limit occupants by composition (*e.g.,* no more than five *unrelated* persons).

- An attempt to limit the number of traditional *family members* (including extended family) probably will be found unconstitutional.

---

b. Low-income persons [§1449]

Various types of land use controls may be enacted that have the purpose or effect of limiting housing to the affluent in a particular district, or excluding low-income persons entirely from the community. Ordinances may stipulate a minimum house size, minimum lot size, or minimum front footage—all of which may have the effect of limiting development to more expensive homes and excluding cheaper types of housing from the community. Excessive subdivision requirements for off-site and on-site improvements can also drive up the cost of housing. Zoning ordinances may prohibit entirely certain cheaper types of housing units—usually apartments and mobile homes. [**Vickers v. Township Committee,** 181 A.2d 129 (N.J. 1962)—upholding exclusion of mobile homes] A conflict thus arises between preserving the character of the community and making housing available to all persons.

(1) Validity of density controls

(a) Rational relationship test [§1450]

The older cases tended to uphold density controls under the rational relationship test. Inasmuch as such controls tended to prevent overcrowding and bore a rational relationship to density, they were valid, even though they operated to exclude low-income groups from entry into the community or portions thereof. Since the 1960s, particularly in New Jersey and Pennsylvania, courts have begun to scrutinize the rationality of density controls more carefully when they have an exclusionary effect. For example, it has been held a violation of substantive due process to exclude all apartments from a developing city. [**Fernley v. Board of Supervisors,** 502 A.2d 585 (Pa. 1985)]

(b) Enabling act violation [§1451]

Another theory for invalidating some exclusionary devices is that the enabling act, authorizing the division of the city into zoning districts, requires the city to provide space somewhere for each type of housing. Thus, under the enabling act a newly developing city must provide for all types of housing within its borders. [**Britton v. Town of Chester,** 595 A.2d 492 (N.H. 1991)]

(c) Fair share test [§1452]

The *Mount Laurel* decision of the New Jersey Supreme Court has become famous for laying down a requirement that each community must provide its fair share of housing needs in the region. *Mount Laurel I* [**Southern Burlington County NAACP v. Township of Mount Laurel,** 336 A.2d 713 (N.J. 1975)] held that a city's zoning regulations, which did not provide opportunity for a fair share of the region's need for low-income and moderate-income housing, were in violation of the *state* constitutional requirements of *substantive due process* and *equal protection* because the regulations were not concerned with the general welfare of all persons. The intent of the town legislature is not controlling; the effect of excluding low-income persons is. Eight years later, after the township did very little to comply with the constitutional mandate of providing housing opportunities for low-income persons, the court in **Mount Laurel II** [**Southern Burlington County NAACP v. Township of Mount Laurel,** 456 A.2d 390 (N.J. 1983)] reaffirmed the requirement of opportunities for constructing a fair share of low-income housing. [*See also* **Hills Development Co. v. Township of Bernards,** 510 A.2d 621 (N.J. 1986)—upholding state Fair Housing Act, intended to implement *Mount Laurel* decision; *and see* **Surrick v. Zoning Hearing Board,** 382 A.2d 105 (Pa. 1977)—following fair share test]

(2) Growth controls [§1453]

Ordinances with the purpose of slowing growth of housing, so that construction of necessary public facilities such as schools and sewers can keep pace, have an obvious exclusionary impact on outsiders trying to settle in the city. These ordinances have been attacked primarily (i) as being in violation of due process because they lack a rational relation to the public welfare, and (ii) as being a taking of property inasmuch as some landowners may not be able to develop for 10 or more years. However, growth control ordinances have been *upheld* if the purpose is not exclusionary, and the ordinance is a rational method of timing development according to a comprehensive plan. The purpose is not exclusionary if the ordinance is not aimed at excluding low-income housing and growth is not permanently halted, but rather is put on a timetable. And as for rationality, the courts find it rational to time development of housing so that it does not outrun the building of schools, sewers, and other public facilities. [**Construction Industry Association v. City of Petaluma,** 522 F.2d 897 (9th Cir. 1975)] Slow-growth ordinances, if reasonable from a regional perspective, have also been held not to unlawfully interfere with the constitutional right to travel and settle. [**Associated Home Builders v. City of Livermore,** 18 Cal. 3d 582 (1976)] At the heart of these cases is a conflict between protecting the natural environment and opening suburbia to low-income housing.

c. Racial exclusion [§1454]

A zoning ordinance that has an exclusionary effect is not *unconstitutional* solely because it has a racially discriminatory impact. A racially discriminatory *intent or purpose* must be shown to prove a constitutional denial of equal protection of the laws. Intent can be shown by such facts as disproportionate impact; a clear pattern of discrimination, unexplainable on grounds other than race; the historical background of the challenged ordinance; departures from normal procedures; and the statements of the local legislators. If such intent is shown, the ordinance violates the Equal Protection Clause. [**Village of Arlington Heights v. Metropolitan Housing Development Corp.,** *supra,*

§1391; *and see* **Bean v. Southwestern Waste Management Corp.**, 482 F. Supp. 673 (S.D. Tex. 1979)—holding intent not proven to site hazardous waste facilities in minority areas]

(1) Fair Housing Act [§1455]

A discriminatory intent is required to make out a constitutional violation under the Equal Protection Clause, but under the Fair Housing Act (*supra*, §821), plaintiffs need only show that there is a *discriminatory effect* in the municipality's refusal to rezone to allow low-income housing. A discriminatory effect makes out a prima facie case that the Act is violated, which the city must rebut with persuasive, legitimate reasons. Thus, it is easier to prove a violation of the Act than of the Constitution. [**Huntington Branch, NAACP v. Town of Huntington**, 844 F.2d 926 (2d Cir. 1988)—holding exclusion of apartments from all-white neighborhoods made out a prima facie case of discrimination, which was not rebutted by city's alleged concerns]

EXAM TIP   **gilbert**

When presented with a fact pattern on an exam where zoning results in racial exclusion, keep in mind that it is easier to prove a violation of the Fair Housing Act than a violation of the Equal Protection Clause of the Constitution. To prove a violation of equal protection, it is not enough merely to show a discriminatory effect; it must also be shown that the government action was undertaken **with the intent** or purpose to discriminate. Under the Fair Housing Act, on the other hand, to prove a violation, a plaintiff need only show that a refusal to rezone has a discriminatory effect.

---

d. Federal courts [§1456]

It is difficult to litigate exclusionary ordinances in federal courts. To have *standing* to litigate a municipal ordinance in federal court, a plaintiff must show a *"case or controversy"* between himself and the defendant. The controversy cannot be hypothetical. To challenge a zoning ordinance as exclusionary, the plaintiff must allege "specific, concrete facts demonstrating that the challenged practices harm *him*," *i.e.*, that he suffers some injury in fact. Harms that are suffered by others or by the public at large, or that are speculative, are not sufficient. Thus, *nonresidents* of a city, housing developers, and nonprofit groups interested in promoting low-income housing cannot sue the city in federal court, alleging that exclusionary zoning denies them the opportunity of finding housing in the city, unless they can show a substantial probability that the injury complained of would be redressed if the zoning were struck down. For standing, a plaintiff must (i) have a current involvement, contractual or otherwise, with a *specific housing proposal on a specific lot*, which is prevented by the ordinance, and (ii) be within the *zone of interest* protected by the particular constitutional provision involved. The constitutional right to travel or migrate, *e.g.*, *cannot* be asserted by a *builder's association* or by *residents within the city* because their right to travel is not being interfered with. Thus, they cannot challenge the exclusionary zoning in federal court on that ground. Only a resident outside the city who wants to move into the city and has contracted to buy (or has bought) a specific lot in the city can raise the right to travel issue. [**Construction Industry Association v. City of Petaluma**, *supra*, §1453—building association could attack ordinance on due process grounds, not on right to travel grounds]

(1) Fair Housing Act [§1457]

Standing to litigate a *federal* statute, such as the Fair Housing Act, is governed by a different rule than the rule on standing to litigate state legislation in federal courts. Standing requirements are much more liberal. Courts have permitted third parties to sue to vindicate rights of minorities under the Fair Housing Act, on the theory that Congress intended to define standing broadly.

B. Subdivision Control and Maps

1. Subdivision Regulations [§1458]

Pursuant to an enabling act, cities may enact subdivision regulations to govern the development of new tracts of land. Subdivision regulations apply when land is to be divided for development. Subdivision regulations differ from zoning ordinances: Zoning ordinances regulate land *use*, while subdivision regulations lay down *conditions for approval of a subdivision plan*. Ordinances usually provide that a building permit will not be granted unless there is compliance with subdivision regulations. Subdivision regulations may lawfully give the planning authority considerable discretion in determining whether the layout of a proposed subdivision satisfies the needs of public health and safety. [**Durant v. Town of Dunbarton**, 430 A.2d 140 (N.H. 1981)]

a. On-site beneficial improvements [§1459]

Subdivision regulations generally require the subdivider to put in paved streets with curbs and gutters in an approved layout, and to install street lights, water mains, and sewers. If these requirements, which benefit the subdivision buyers in the physical use of their homes, are reasonable, they are valid.

b. Off-site improvements [§1460]

Cities may require the developer to dedicate a certain amount of land for a public park, school site, or street widening, or, in lieu thereof, to contribute a sum to a public fund to purchase land for such purposes. These requirements have been upheld if the need for such facilities is attributable to the developer's activity. [**Jenad, Inc. v. Village of Scarsdale**, 18 N.Y.2d 78 (1966)] But if the city's demands on the subdivider are not logically connected with, or not roughly proportionate to, the burdens created by the subdivider, they may be held to be an unconstitutional taking of the subdivider's property (*see infra*, §§1481-1482).

2. Official Maps

a. Street maps [§1461]

The enabling act may provide that if a city adopts a street plan, locating future streets on maps, no one will be permitted to build in the location of a mapped street. The purpose of an official map locating unbuilt streets is to save costs in the future, when the city exercises eminent domain and condemns the land. (If the land is not built upon, the city will not have to pay for improvements.) The question arises whether mapping future streets is a "taking" of the private property that is mapped for future use as a street. It has been held that the mere mapping of future streets is not a "taking" because it does not divest the owner of title and does not interfere with any present use of the property. However, *when the owner applies for and is denied a building permit* in the mapped street, denial is a "taking" unless there is a special hardship procedure in the act whereby an owner is permitted to build in a mapped street if the owner is substantially damaged by denial of a permit to build. Thus, most map acts require the municipality to allow the owner, upon application, to build something that will give a reasonable return. [**State *ex rel.* Miller v. Manders,** 86 N.W.2d 469 (Wis. 1957)]

b. Park maps [§1462]

The enabling act may provide that a city can map land to be acquired in the future for a public park or playground, and freeze development of the land for a set period, usually one year. This gives the city a right to prevent development for one year of lands it wants to acquire for a park. If the city elects to map land for acquisition in this way, it may have to pay the landowner the price of an "option" to purchase land for one year, for this is what, in effect, the city has taken from the landowner. [**Lomarch Corp. v. Mayor & Common Council,** 237 A.2d 881 (N.J. 1968)—requiring compensation for the "option" taken]

C. Eminent Domain

1. In General [§1463]

The federal, state, and local governments have the power of eminent domain, *i.e.,* the power to take title to property against the owner's will. The Fifth Amendment to the Constitution provides ". . . nor shall private property be taken for public use, without just compensation." Although the Fifth Amendment is expressly applicable only to the federal government, it has been held applicable to the states as well under the Due Process Clause of the Fourteenth Amendment. Under the Takings Clause there are three major questions: (i) What is a "public use"? (ii) What is a "taking"? (iii) What is "just compensation"?

2. What Is Public Use? [§1464]

Observe that the Fifth Amendment limits the power of eminent domain to taking property "for public use." What then is "public use"?

a. Public use or purpose? [§1465]

The Fifth Amendment speaks of public use, and in earlier times some courts, construing similar provisions in state constitutions, held that to exercise eminent domain, the public must have the *right to use* the condemned property. This might be called the "narrow reading" of the public use requirement. In modern times, most courts, including the United States Supreme Court, have held that the term "public use" means the condemnation must *benefit the public*. Under the broader construction, most condemnations are permissible.

Example: The state enacts a law permitting a private person to erect a dam on a stream, which will collect water and flood riparian upstream land. The dam builder must compensate the upstream owners. In effect, the lower riparian is given a right to flood an upper riparian for the purpose of erecting a dam to provide power. Under the narrow construction—the right to use by the public—the law is void. Under the public purpose construction, the law is valid: The public purpose is the generation of hydroelectric power.

---

b. Public purpose very broad [§1466]

The Supreme Court has held that as a matter of federal constitutional law a public purpose may be found even in cases where the government action transfers ownership from one private party to another. Examples include cases involving urban renewal, where the government takes blighted land and resells it to a developer under a redevelopment program. [**Berman v. Parker**, 348 U.S. 26 (1954)] Later cases have gone further, finding that the public use requirement is met even if the land taken is not blighted, such as where the government takes land concentrated in a few owners and transfers it to former tenants in fee simple [**Hawaii Housing Authority v. Midkiff**, 467 U.S. 229 (1984)], or takes the land of homeowners and transfers it to private developers as part of a plan to promote economic development in depressed areas [**Kelo v. City of New London**, 125 S. Ct. 2655 (2005)]. The Supreme Court uses a rational basis approach—upholding the exercise of the eminent domain power as long as it is *rationally related* to a conceivable public purpose—and grants the government great deference. But states can, and some do, take a much stricter stance, either by examining the government program with strict scrutiny [*see, e.g.,* **Southwestern Illinois Development Authority v. National City Environmental, L.L.C.**, 768 N.E.2d 1 (Ill. 2002)], or by applying strict "per se" (or "categorical") standards [*see, e.g.,* **County of Wayne v. Hathcock**, 684 N.W.2d 765 (Mich. 2004)].

3. What Is a "Taking"? [§1467]

Federal and state government (and by delegation, local governments), under the

gilbert

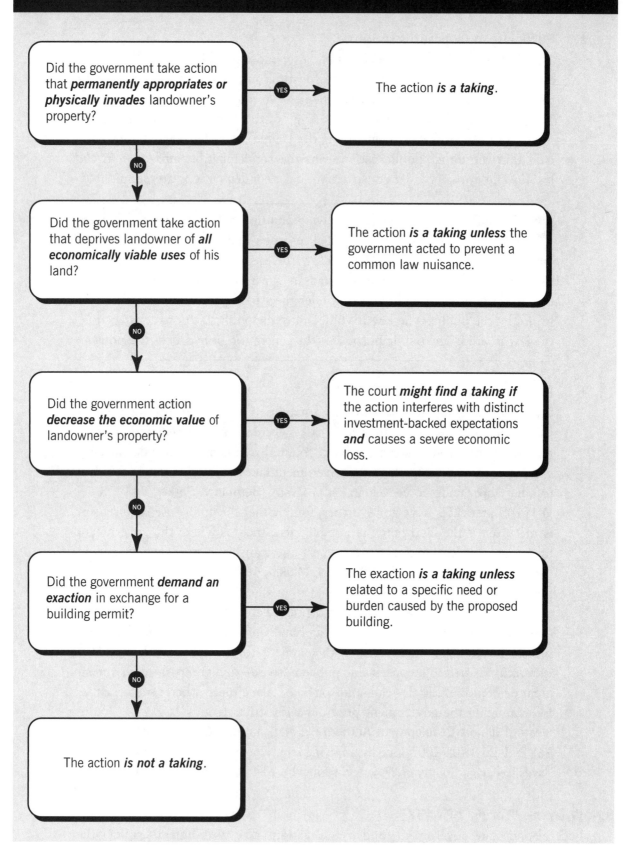

Did the government take action that **permanently appropriates or physically invades** landowner's property?

YES → The action **is a taking**.

NO ↓

Did the government take action that deprives landowner of **all economically viable uses** of his land?

YES → The action **is a taking unless** the government acted to prevent a common law nuisance.

NO ↓

Did the government action **decrease the economic value** of landowner's property?

YES → The court **might find a taking if** the action interferes with distinct investment-backed expectations **and** causes a severe economic loss.

NO ↓

Did the government **demand an exaction** in exchange for a building permit?

YES → The exaction **is a taking unless** related to a specific need or burden caused by the proposed building.

NO ↓

The action **is not a taking**.

power of eminent domain, can "take" property in various ways. The first way is straightforward: an action brought by the government to condemn property. The second way—permanent physical occupation authorized by the government—always results in a taking. The third way, the category of so-called regulatory takings, is more complicated.

a. Condemnation action to take title to property [§1468]

If the government formally exercises its power of eminent domain by bringing a condemnation proceeding and taking title to the land, the government has of course taken the property and must pay for it.

b. Physical occupation or invasion [§1469]

Any *permanent physical occupation or invasion by the government* is a taking. This is the first *per se* or *categorical rule*: No argument, the government must pay. Physical occupation is the functional equivalent of depriving the owner of title, because the owner's power to exclude others is the essence of property (*see supra*, §175), and physical invasion by the government compromises that power. Thus, the government must pay compensation, no matter how trivial the invasion. Physical invasion includes undue noise that interferes with the use and enjoyment of the surface of the owner's land. [**United States v. Causby**, *supra*, §1367] If the occupation or invasion is *not permanent*, a more complex balancing test is used by the courts (*see infra*, §§1477-1480). [**Kaiser Aetna v. United States**, 444 U.S. 164 (1979)]

(1) By third parties [§1470]

If the government does not invade property itself but *authorizes* third parties to permanently occupy private property, the same categorical rule applies. For example, the Supreme Court held that a statute authorizing private cable TV companies to install cables in apartment buildings, over the landlord's objection, is a physical invasion of the landlord's property and a taking. [**Loretto v. Teleprompter Manhattan CATV Corp.**, 458 U.S. 419 (1982)] Once again, however, if the occupation is not permanent, the balancing test applies (*see infra*, §§1477-1480).

(2) By tenants [§1471]

If a rent control program *requires* landlords to lease units at controlled rents for an indefinite period, and does not allow withdrawal from the rental market entirely, the regulation is a taking of the landlord's property without compensation. [**Seawall Associates v. City of New York**, 74 N.Y.2d 92 (1989)] But if the program is *voluntary* in the sense that landlords may opt out of the rental market rather than lease units at controlled rents, then there is no taking. [**Yee v. City of Escondido**, 503 U.S. 519 (1992)]

c. Regulatory takings not involving physical occupation or invasion [§1472]

Regulatory takings can arise from government action that involves physical occupation or invasion (*see supra*, §1469). More commonly, however, they arise from regulations that do not involve occupation or invasion but rather affect the *use and value of the land*. The authority to regulate property for the purpose of protecting public health, safety, welfare, and morals arises out of the federal government's enumerated powers, and the state government's police power. But regulatory activity might, for a variety of reasons, work a taking, depending on the application of various tests. By and large, the relevant tests have been developed by the United States Supreme Court and include the following:

(1) Destruction of *all* economic value [§1473]

In **Lucas v. South Carolina Coastal Council**, 505 U.S. 1003 (1992), the Supreme Court announced a new categorical rule: If the regulation deprives land of *all economically beneficial uses*, it is a taking *unless* the government can justify its actions as *preventing a common law nuisance* (*see infra*, §1476). Common law nuisances include those acts defined as nuisances by judicial common law (*see supra*, §§1311 *et seq.*) and not by the legislature.

EXAM TIP   **gilbert**

Keep in mind that this rule applies only if the regulation deprives the land of *all* economic value, which is bound to be exceedingly rare. Regulatory control of uses deemed harmful (but not amounting to common law nuisances) that *diminish* but do not wipe out all value will be subject to the balancing test discussed *infra*, §§1477-1480.

(a) By regulation enacted before purchase [§1474]

In **Palazzolo v. Rhode Island**, 533 U.S. 606 (2001), the Court held that purchase of land *after* enactment of a regulation reducing or destroying the land's value does not foreclose takings claims. A regulation that would otherwise be an unconstitutional taking is not transformed into a valid measure simply because the affected land was purchased after the regulation.

(b) For a limited time [§1475]

A regulation that destroys all economic value of a parcel of land, but for a *limited time*—as in the case of a development moratorium—is not necessarily a categorical taking under *Lucas*. Rather, all of the relevant circumstances must be considered under the balancing test (*see infra*, §§1477-1480) to determine whether there has been a taking. [**Tahoe-Sierra Preservation Council, Inc. v. Tahoe Regional Planning Agency**, 535 U.S. 302 (2002)]

(c) Exception—control of common law nuisances [§1476]

A third categorical rule is that no taking results if the government regulates to control common law nuisances or nuisance-like activity; the government should not have to pay to regulate activities that are harmful to the public. [*See, e.g.,* **Hadacheck v. Sebastian,** 239 U.S. 394 (1915)—upholding a zoning ordinance prohibiting continuation of a brickyard in a residential area] The rationale here is that when a regulation has the purpose or effect of protecting against a *harm*, it is an exercise of the police power and noncompensable; but when the regulation aims to extract a *benefit*, it is a taking and the owner must be compensated. The difficulty is that the distinction between harms and benefits can be arbitrary, absent some well-defined norm against which to judge the conduct in question.

Example: Regulation A prohibits continued operation of a brickyard that has been annoying residential neighbors. Regulation B forbids the owner of a wooded parcel from razing the trees and developing the land, which would deprive the public of the benefits of wildlife conservation. Because regulation A protects against a *harm*, no taking results. On the other hand, regulation B promotes a public *benefit* and results in a compensable taking.

Compare: Regulation C prohibits the filling of wetlands. The regulation could be construed to control a public harm (*e.g.,* prevent pollution by the manmade fill) *or* create a public benefit (*e.g.,* wildlife conservation). [*See* **Just v. Marinette County,** 201 N.W.2d 761 (Wis. 1972)]

---

(2) Diminution in value [§1477]

Perhaps the first regulatory takings case was **Pennsylvania Coal Co. v. Mahon,** 260 U.S. 393 (1922). The Supreme Court, in a decision by Justice Oliver Wendell Holmes, struck down a Pennsylvania statute forbidding coal mining that caused the subsidence of any house in the area. Before the statute was enacted, the coal company had sold the surface rights to the land to Mahon, but had reserved the right to remove the coal thereunder and to undermine the surface. Because the statute made it commercially impracticable to mine the coal, and thus had nearly the same effect as the complete destruction of the mineral rights, the Court held the statute invalid as a taking without compensation. Said Justice Holmes: "The general rule at least is that while property may be regulated to a certain extent, *if regulation goes too far it will be recognized as a taking.*" Hence, a very large reduction in the value of regulated property may be a taking, but smaller reductions are not. Where the line is to be drawn is hardly clear, and in this sense the rule is very different from the three categorical rules considered above. This test is in essence a *balancing test*: If a government regulation of a use that is not a common law nuisance imposes too great a burden on property owners, the government must provide compensation.

(a) What "property" is considered in the test? [§1478]

In *Pennsylvania Coal*, the Court looked only at the rights to the coal, which had been severed from the surface rights. Because the coal rights could not be exercised without buying out the homeowners, the coal that had to be left in place lost all of its value. But, as Justice Brandeis asked in dissent, what about the coal that could be mined? As an example of this problem, consider a parcel of land which is half wetlands and half not. The government then forbids development of the wetlands. Is a court to determine that the relevant "property" is the wetlands subject to regulation? If so, it has lost all of its value and a taking would likely result. Or is the court to determine that the relevant "property" is the whole parcel, which has lost only half (at most) of its value? This is known as the question of *conceptual severance*, also referred to as the *denominator problem*. Although the issue has not been subject to principled resolution, in practice the courts tend to look at the whole parcel of which the regulated part is a portion. Thus, takings are seldom found to occur based on the diminution-in-value test, unless the *whole parcel loses all* or virtually all of its value. For example, a case subsequent to *Pennsylvania Coal*, involving virtually identical facts, considered only the loss in value caused by having to leave support pillars of coal in place, and thus found no taking. [*See* **Keystone Bituminous Coal Association v. DeBenedictis**, 480 U.S. 470 (1987)]

(b) Other factors to consider

1) Reciprocal advantages and disadvantages [§1479]

Holmes suggested another consideration in the *Pennsylvania Coal* decision, having to do with what he called "an average reciprocity of advantage." Zoning regulations provide a good example. If a parcel of land is zoned for single-family housing only, no doubt there is a loss of value compared to the situation where the property could be used for any purpose whatsoever. On the other hand, because neighboring parcels in the single-family zone are equally limited, there is an offsetting advantage to each and every landowner in the zone, realized by the fact that neighboring property in the zone cannot be used for purposes that would lower the value of the lots limited to single-family housing (*e.g.*, commercial use). This consideration is sometimes referred to as *implicit compensation in kind*.

2) Investment-backed expectations [§1480]

The basic approach of *Pennsylvania Coal* was given a fuller exposition in **Penn Central Transportation Co. v. City of New York,** *supra*, §1440. The Court there held that in determining the taking issue, one must consider not only the economic impact of the regulation on the landowner, but, more particularly, the degree to which the regulation interferes "with distinct investment-backed expectations." But, alas, the Court has never bothered to define just what this means. Some state courts have interpreted the phrase in such a way as to find distinct investment-backed expectations only in instances where regulations interfere with investments *already made*, as opposed to regulations limiting possible future investments. This implies that if someone purchases land after a regulation limiting its use has already been enacted, the landowner has no distinct investment-backed expectation. The Court, however, has held that this does not necessarily follow. [*See* **Palazzolo v. Rhode Island,** *supra*, §1474]

(3) Exactions [§1481]

When a property owner applies for a building permit, the city may impose a condition on the development that does not benefit the owner but benefits the city. These conditions are commonly called "exactions." For example, in **Nollan v. California Coastal Commission,** 483 U.S. 825 (1987), the exaction was a public path across the owner's property for beach access. *Nollan* held that the condition must be *logically related* to the *specific* public need or burden that the owner's building creates or to which it contributes; *i.e.*, there must be an "essential nexus" between the legitimate government interest and the condition exacted by the city. The condition must be a credible way of securing the government interest, which dispels any suspicion that the exaction is a subterfuge designed to secure a benefit for the public without payment. Subsequently, in **Dolan v. City of Tigard,** 512 U.S. 374 (1994), the Court went further and held that in addition to satisfying the essential nexus test, conditions imposed on owners must bear a *"rough proportionality" to the negative impact* of the development on the public. In other words, the owner can be required to pick up a cost roughly proportionate to the injury inflicted on the city.

Example: The Nollans applied for a permit to demolish the bungalow on their beachfront property and replace it with a three-bedroom house. The permit was conditioned on the Nollans' allowing the public to use a path across their property for beach access. The Court held that an outright ban on construction of the house did not logically relate to the public's interest in beach access; *i.e.*, there was no essential nexus. On the other hand, if the condition would have protected the public's ability to see the beach notwithstanding construction of the house (*e.g.*, a height restriction), then the essential nexus test may have been met. Thus, the Nollans were entitled to compensation for the taking. [**Nollan v. California Coastal Commission,** *supra*]

e.g. **Example:** Dolan owned a store in the downtown business district. Her property was partially located in a flood plain. Dolan applied for a permit to expand her store and add a parking lot. The permit was conditioned on Dolan's dedicating 10% of her property for improvement of a storm drainage system and for a bicycle path. Other regulations required that 15% of the property be kept as open space. The Court first determined that an essential nexus existed between the condition imposed and the state's legitimate interest in preventing flooding and reducing traffic congestion. Next, the Court held that the cost imposed on Dolan was not roughly proportionate to the injury inflicted on the city—there was no reason given why the flood control area had to be public, when the 15% required open space could be used as a private flood control area. Thus, Dolan was entitled to compensation for the taking. [**Dolan v. City of Tigard,** *supra*]

(a) Distinguish—impact fees [§1482]

Impact fees are *monetary*, rather than physical, *exactions*. The courts are split on whether *Nollan* and *Dolan* apply to impact fees.

e.g **Example:** Ehrlich applied for a permit to demolish the health club on his property and erect a 30-unit condominium complex. He demolished the facility before the permit allowing him to construct the condominium was approved. The city, which had considered purchasing the health club prior to its demolition in order to preserve its recreational nature, granted the permit on the condition that Ehrlich pay $280,000 "to be used for additional public recreational facilities." The court first determined that the monetary exaction would substantially advance the city's legitimate interest in alleviating the shortage of public recreational resources (essential nexus). However, as in *Dolan*, the court did not find that the cost imposed on Ehrlich was roughly proportionate to the injury inflicted on the city—the public would receive $280,000 worth of recreational facilities for free when the money could have been raised by the public itself or through a private party (*e.g.*, health club membership fees). Thus, Ehrlich was entitled to compensation for the taking. [**Ehrlich v. City of Culver City,** 911 P.2d 429 (Cal. 1996)—noting that the city may be able to justify a monetary exaction of some lesser amount]

(b) Note

The *Nollan* and *Dolan* rules apply only to exactions, not to takings

GOVERNMENT ACTION THAT RESULTS IN PER SE TAKING	GOVERNMENT ACTION THAT DOES *NOT* RESULT IN PER SE TAKING (APPLY BALANCING TEST)
• Government **condemns** land	
• Government **permanently** occupies land (*e.g.*, government-built dam causes permanent flooding of private property)	• Government **temporarily** occupies land (*e.g.*, government-built dam causes temporary flooding of private property)
• Government **authorizes** third parties to occupy land (*e.g.*, cable TV company installs cables in apartments over landlord's objection)	
• Law **requires** landlord to lease units at controlled rents	• Rent control ordinances allow landlord to **voluntarily** lease units at controlled rents
• Law (whether enacted before or after purchase) **destroys all economically viable use** of land	• Law **temporarily** deprives land of all economically valuable use (*e.g.*, development moratorium)
	• Law prohibits continued operation of a **common law nuisance**
	• Law **reduces the value** of land or an interest in land (*e.g.*, mineral interest)
	• Government imposes exaction that **logically relates to a legitimate government interest** (essential nexus) **and bears a rough proportionality** to the negative impact on the public

generally. Thus, government-imposed *conditions* on land use are constrained by proportionality requirements, while governmental *regulations* on land use are not.

EXAM TIP   **gilbert**

If you see a fact situation where the government condemns land, you know it's a taking and the government has to pay. But because that situation is so easy, it isn't likely to be a question on your exam. So remember to watch for other types of takings such as *permanent* physical occupations or invasions by the government (or a third party authorized by the government), and regulations that destroy *all* economic value. Both of these are per se takings and require the government to pay. An even more involved question may present a regulation that causes *only a diminution in the value* of the property. In that case, you must apply a balancing test to determine whether the government has to pay the landowner. Finally, if the government grants a *permit on condition* that the developer give up some of his land (or in some states pay a fee) for public purposes, look at whether (i) there is an *essential nexus* between the legitimate government interest and the condition imposed, and (ii) the condition bears a *rough proportionality to the negative impact* of the development on the public.

---

d. Remedies for regulatory takings [§1483]

Logic suggests that the remedy for regulatory takings should be *compensation*, and so it is. The suit for compensation usually proceeds by way of an action in *inverse condemnation*, so-called because the landowner is suing for compensation instead of the government instituting formal condemnation proceedings. If there is a taking under one of the applicable tests for regulatory takings reviewed above, the government is liable for *interim damages* for the period beginning when the regulation first takes the owner's land and ending when the government decides to rescind or amend the regulation; if it chooses to do neither, then *permanent damages* are awarded. [**First English Evangelical Lutheran Church v. County of Los Angeles**, 482 U.S. 304 (1987)] If the regulation in question is unconstitutional because, *e.g.*, it is not for a legitimate public purpose, then of course the measure will be invalidated. Damages might also be available, however, for deprivation of constitutional rights under color of law. [42 U.S.C. §1983]

e. State constitutional law [§1484]

In applying the taking tests enunciated by the United States Supreme Court, state courts have often been less analytical than the highest Court. State courts sometimes say that in testing the validity of the police power action they must balance private loss against public gain. If the gain outweighs the loss, the landowner is not compensated. Courts often do not give specific content to the balancing test. If the test means that when the totality of society's welfare gains is greater than the individual's loss no compensation is due, the test can be used only rarely to strike down legislation because the legislature is better equipped than courts to determine economic efficiency, *i.e.*, that aggregate social values will be increased by the legislative action.

However, as applied, the test indicates the court is not balancing exclusively economic gains and losses, but also is adding to the scales its notions of fairness. The more doubtful the efficiency of the legislation, and the more unfair it seems, the more compelling must be its justification. The taking test may resemble substantive due process (*supra*, §1388). [**Karches v. City of Cincinnati,** 526 N.E.2d 1350 (Ohio 1988)]

4. What Is Just Compensation?

a. Market value [§1485]

Generally speaking, the requirement of just compensation means that the owner must be paid fair market value for the property taken. Fair market value is the price in cash for which the property would change hands in a transaction between a willing buyer and a willing seller (*i.e.*, neither acting under any compulsion to buy or sell). Fair market value does not mean the value to the owner, who might place a higher value on the property than other persons do. Property may have subjective value to the owner that is not compensated in the market. Thus, the owner whose property is condemned may be penalized.

(1) Justification for market value test [§1486]

The market value test is justified on efficiency grounds. It is the easiest, least costly test to apply. If just compensation required that the owner be given the value the owner placed on the property, it would be difficult to ascertain the value and there would be potential for fraud.

(a) Criticism

The fair market value test does not award objectively verifiable costs to the owner (*e.g.*, moving expenses). It also imposes on the owner who does not agree with the government's offer the cost of hiring a lawyer to fight out fair market value in court. Apart from depriving the owner of the unique value the property has for the owner, the fair market value test leaves the owner at a substantial disadvantage. This has been called, however, "part of the burden of common citizenship." [**United States v. 564.54 Acres of Land,** 441 U.S. 506 (1979)]

(b) Exception—special purpose property [§1487]

Where there is no relevant market for the property, *any just and equitable method* of valuation may be employed. A special purpose property (*e.g.*, school, church, park) for which no realistic market exists may be valued by replacement cost, depreciated original cost, capitalization of income, or some other just and equitable method.

(2) Loss of business [§1488]

When there is a business on the condemned land, the business itself is not condemned and thus it must move. It may be, for various reasons, that the business cannot be moved successfully to another location. The owner is *not* entitled to be paid for the taking of the business, which, if destroyed, is merely an unintended incident of the taking of land.

(3) Expectations about possible future uses [§1489]

The market value test takes into account the possibility of future uses as well as existing uses. A buyer, believing there is some possibility of different and more valuable use in the future, may be willing to pay something extra for this speculation. In ***instructing the jury***, the judge must tell the jury to consider any evidence that a willing buyer would have considered the possibility of rezoning and would have paid more based on the possibility of future use. The jury must determine for itself whether it thinks the zoning change is reasonably probable. If not reasonably probable, that element of value should be disregarded. [**State *ex rel.* Commissioner of Transportation v. Caoili,** 621 A.2d 546 (N.J. 1993)]

(a) Expectations about leasehold renewal [§1490]

When the government condemns a leasehold interest with improvements, it must pay the lessee the value of the leasehold with improvements. The expected useful life of the improvements and expectations that the landlord will renew the lease must be considered as part of market value. [**Almota Farmers Elevator & Warehouse Co. v. United States,** 409 U.S. 470 (1973)]

(b) Expectations about rights revocable by government [§1491]

Some Supreme Court cases seem to establish that the government does not have to pay the owner for a value the government has created, or that the government can take away by regulation. [**United States v. Fuller,** 409 U.S. 488 (1973)—government condemned land adjacent to federal land on which condemnee possessed revocable government grazing permits; government did not have to pay for element of value based on use of condemnee's lands in combination with federal permit lands] The theory excluding this element of value (because the government could destroy it) could logically be applied to condemnation of property subject to zoning regulations. If that were done, whatever value that could be removed by regulation would not be compensable on a taking by eminent domain.

---

e.g. **Example:** O owns farmland zoned for residential purposes (and for those purposes worth $100 an acre). The state could lawfully rezone O's land to agricultural purposes (and for those purposes worth $40 an acre). The state condemns O's land. Under present law, the state must pay O $100 an acre. Under the above theory, the state would pay O $40 an acre, assuming any regulation more restrictive than an agriculture-only zone would be going too far.

b. Partial taking [§1492]

If only part of the property is taken, the owner is entitled to recover for resulting damages to the part not taken. These are called "severance damages." There are two basic methods (with variations thereof in the several states) of determining the owner's compensation where there is a partial taking.

(1) Before and after rule [§1493]

The owner is entitled to the difference between the value of the *entire tract* before taking and the value of the *remainder* left in him after taking. This rule is the easiest to apply and is more consistent with realistic market appraisal techniques.

e.g. Example: O owns a tract of land in the country, on which his house is situated. The tract is worth $400,000. The state takes a portion of the tract for an expressway, which will depreciate the value of the house because of the noise from the expressway. The value of the land taken is $75,000. The remainder, after taking, is worth $150,000. Thus, there is consequential damage (damage resulting from the state's use of the portion taken as a freeway) of $175,000. Under the before and after taking rule, O is entitled to $250,000—*i.e.*, $400,000 (original value) less $150,000 (value of remainder). [**Dennison v. State**, 22 N.Y.2d 409 (1968)]

(2) Value plus damage rule [§1494]

The second method of determining what the owner gets on partial taking is to give him the sum of the value of the part taken and any net damages to the remainder after offsetting benefits. Unlike the before and after rule, this method evaluates separately the value of the tract taken and the damages to the remainder. [**Merrill Trust Co. v. State**, 417 A.2d 435 (Me. 1980)] The two methods reach the same result in the preceding example— *i.e.*, $175,000 (consequential damage) plus $75,000 (value of land taken) equals $250,000. They lead to different results where net special benefits are realized by the remainder. Under the value plus damage method, any special benefits to the remainder are set off against the remainder only; under the before and after test, special benefits are set off against the value of the entire property.

e.g. Example: O's land is worth $400,000. The state takes a portion of O's land in order to create a park. The land taken was worth $75,000. The remainder after the taking is worth $350,000, because proximity to the park has increased the value of the land. Therefore, under the value plus damage method, O is entitled to $75,000 (value of land taken). The special benefit of $25,000 to the remainder can be offset only against damage to the remainder, not against the value of the land taken.

Chapter Ten:
The Sale of Land

CONTENTS

Chapter Approach

Chapter Approach

The sale of land is ordinarily a two-step process: First, a *contract of sale* is signed by the buyer and seller. Then, after a couple of months or more, the *closing* takes place. At the closing, the seller *delivers a deed* to the buyer, and the buyer hands the seller a *check for the purchase price*. This two-step process is necessary because the buyer—after signing the contract but before paying the purchase price—needs time to check out the seller's title (discussed *infra*, §§1517 *et seq.*), to arrange financing, and to take steps to move onto the premises.

Problems regarding the sale of land (both on exams and in "real life") generally arise, if at all, during the period between the signing of the contract and the closing date. The buyer may learn of title defects or the premises may burn down. For these and other reasons, the buyer (or seller) may wish to rescind the contract while the other party wants to enforce it. Remember that *specific performance* (as well as *rescission* and *damages*) is a remedy for the breach of a land sale contract. Also keep in mind that the *doctrine of equitable conversion* may determine who bears the loss if the property has been destroyed.

At the closing, another party may be represented—the *mortgagee*. To pay for the property, the buyer may have secured a purchase money mortgage, or the seller may have previously mortgaged the property. In any case, remember that a mortgagee has a major interest in the land; any time a question mentions a mortgage, don't overlook this interest in your answer.

After closing, questions may arise as to the seller's liabilities if title proves defective or if the building proves defective. Review the *seller's warranties* (contained in the deed) at the end of this chapter.

Favorite topics for examination include attempted rescission by the buyer before closing, delivery of the deed, and the seller's warranties after closing.

A. The Contract for Sale of Land

1. Broker's Role [§1495]

Almost all houses and a large percentage of other real property are sold through a broker. The seller signs a contract with the broker, giving the broker the right to list and show the property to prospective buyers and, if the property sells, to collect a commission out of the purchase price. The broker's commission may run from 5 to 8% of the selling price. Two major legal issues involving brokers are:

THE SALE OF LAND—A TIMELINE

This chart represents the chronological progression from contract through recording.

PARTIES ENTER INTO LAND SALE CONTRACT →	TIME BETWEEN CONTRACT AND CLOSING →	CLOSING →	RECORDATION
1. Contract must be in writing (Statute of Frauds).	1. Buyer investigates Seller's title. If defective, Buyer must notify Seller and give him an opportunity to cure.	1. Title passes if deed is validly executed and delivered. Valid execution requires a writing signed by the grantor containing an adequate description of the parcel. Valid delivery requires intent by the grantor to immediately part with legal control.	Buyer records deed to protect her title against a subsequent bona fide purchaser.
2. Presumption that time is not of the essence unless so stated.	2. During this time, the risk of loss is on Buyer.	2. When title passes, the land sale contract usually is extinguished by merger into the deed (along with the implied warranty of marketability).	
3. Implied warranty of marketability arises.		3. The only basis for a suit by Buyer after title passes is an express covenant, if any, in the deed. There are six possible covenants: Seisin Right to Convey Against Encumbrances Quiet Enjoyment Warranty Further Assurances	

(1) Price [§1503]

If the price has been agreed upon, it must be set forth. Failure to put it in the memorandum makes the contract unenforceable. However, if no price has been agreed upon, the court may imply an agreement to pay a reasonable price if such an agreement is inferable from all the circumstances. [*Compare* **Wiley v. Tom Howell & Associates,** 267 S.E.2d 816 (Ga. 1980)—holding contract to sell at "appraised" value unenforceable]

(2) Conditions

(a) Financing [§1504]

Many contracts to purchase contain a clause providing that the offer to purchase is contingent on the purchaser obtaining the necessary amount of financing. This "subject to financing" clause may be held void for vagueness unless the surrounding circumstances indicate what amount and terms the parties had in mind. [**Gerruth Realty Co. v. Pire,** 115 N.W.2d 557 (Wis. 1962)] If the clause is interpreted to mean that the loan must be in such amount and on such terms as the buyer considers necessary, the buyer must act in good faith and use reasonable diligence in procuring a loan. [**Bushmiller v. Schiller,** 368 A.2d 1044 (Md. 1977); **Lynch v. Andrew,** 481 N.E.2d 1383 (Mass. 1985)]

(b) Building permit [§1505]

A contract may be conditioned on the buyer obtaining from the public authorities all the necessary permits for erecting or altering a building or obtaining a zoning change. As with a condition about obtaining financing, the buyer must use reasonable efforts to obtain the permits or zone change. If the buyer does not submit any plans to the public authority or apply for a zone change, the buyer is in default. [**Sechrest v. Safiol,** 419 N.E.2d 1384 (Mass. 1981)]

c. Oral contract

(1) Part performance [§1506]

Part performance is an equitable doctrine that allows a court of *equity*, under certain circumstances, to specifically enforce an *oral* contract for the sale of an interest in land. If a buyer or seller sues *at law* for damages, the doctrine of part performance is not applicable in most states; the doctrine is applicable only in a suit in equity for specific performance.

(a) Acts of "unequivocal reference to a contract" [§1507]

What acts constitute part performance, taking the contract out of the Statute of Frauds and making it enforceable, vary considerably from state to state. But most courts require acts of unequivocal reference to a contract, *i.e.,* acts done by the parties that make sense only as having been done pursuant to a contract. Thus, if the buyer (i) *pays* all or part of the purchase price, *and* (ii) enters into *possession, and* (iii) *makes improvements*, the contract is enforceable, because the court assumes the buyer would not do these acts without a contract. Such acts supply sufficient evidence of the contract. Inasmuch as the purpose of requiring acts of "unequivocal reference to a contract" is to give reliable evidence of the contract, the requirement is not insisted on if the seller admits to making the contract or the contract is clearly proved. [**Gardner v. Gardner,** 454 N.W.2d 361 (Iowa 1990); **Shaughnessy v. Eidsmo,** 23 N.W.2d 362 (Minn. 1946)]

1) Variations on part performance [§1508]

In some states, the contract is enforceable if the buyer merely takes *possession* under circumstances referable to a contract. This is known as the English rule. Other states require that the buyer also *make payments or improvements*. Still other states require the buyer to go further and show, in addition to these acts of part performance, *irreparable injury if the contract is not enforced*. Usually this is shown by the buyer's making valuable improvements that cannot be compensated in money.

2) Injurious reliance theory [§1509]

Another theory of part performance is that it is intended to prevent injurious reliance on the oral contract. Restatement (Second) of Contracts section 129 adopts this theory. It provides that a contract may be specifically enforced if the party seeking enforcement proves the contract and, *in reasonable reliance on the contract*, "has so changed his position that injustice can be avoided only by specific enforcement." This position is in line with the modern trend to relax the Statute of Frauds. [**Roundy v. Waner,** 570 P.2d 862 (Idaho 1977); **Hickey v. Green,** 442 N.E.2d 37 (Mass. 1982)] But the requirement of unequivocal acts probably survives in most states.

EXAM TIP   **gilbert**

On your exam, if the parties have entered into an *oral* contract for the purchase of land, there has been part performance, and one of the parties is trying to back out of the deal, your answer should first point out that generally oral contracts for the sale of land are unenforceable under the Statute of Frauds. You should then note that there is an exception for *part performance that unequivocally references* a contract. The buyer's making payments, moving onto the property, and making valuable improvements is powerful evidence that a contract exists. If the buyer in your question has done less, the decision can go either way, depending on state law.

(b) Suit by seller [§1510]

Most suits for specific performance alleging part performance are brought by the buyer against the seller. Suppose that the buyer performs some acts of part performance, enough to justify specific performance by the buyer, and then the buyer wants to back out of the deal. Can the seller sue the buyer for specific performance of an oral contract? Some older cases refused to grant the seller specific performance based on the buyer's acts that caused economic loss to the buyer. The seller, seeking to circumvent the Statute of Frauds, could not take advantage of the buyer's acts. However, most courts now hold that if the property has been changed by the buyer so as to lessen its value or to prevent the seller from being restored to his original position, specific performance will be granted. Other courts go further and hold the seller can sue under the principle of "mutuality" of remedies: If the buyer can sue for specific performance, the seller can also. [**Pearson v. Gardner,** 168 N.W. 485 (Mich. 1918)]

(c) Contracts to devise [§1511]

The doctrine of part performance may be applied to oral contracts to devise land at death in exchange for services. However, courts are more reluctant to enforce oral contracts to devise than to enforce oral contracts to sell, because in the former case one party is dead and cannot testify. When oral contracts to devise are enforced, courts emphasize that the proof of the promise is clear and convincing, the promisee changed to a detrimental position in reliance on the promise, and failure to enforce would be unconscionable (*i.e.,* is grossly harsh or would work a fraud).

Example: A alleges that T, an old man, promised to devise A his house if A moved in and looked after T for the rest of his life. A moved in and looked after T, who subsequently died, leaving a will devising the house to B. If a court finds that A's acts are not unequivocally referable to a contract (but that A acted merely in the expectation of reward), A is not entitled to enforce the alleged contract. If A is denied specific performance, A has an action in law for quantum meruit (the monetary value of services rendered). [**Burns v. McCormick,** 233 N.Y. 230 (1922)]

---

1) Uniform Probate Code [§1512]

In an effort to reduce litigation, Uniform Probate Code section 2-514, adopted in many states, takes a hard line against enforcing oral contracts to devise. The Code provides that: (i) the will must set forth the material provisions of the contract, (ii) the will must expressly refer to the contract and to extrinsic evidence proving its terms, or (iii) a separate writing signed by the decedent must evidence the contract.

(2) Estoppel [§1513]

In a few states, part performance is not recognized. In these states, estoppel is the theory used to enforce an oral contract to sell land. Estoppel applies where unconscionable injury would result from denying specific performance after one party has been induced by the other seriously to change his position in reliance on the contract. [**Baliles v. Cities Service Co.,** 578 S.W.2d 621 (Tenn. 1979)]

(3) Revocation [§1514]

A written contract for the sale of land can be *revoked* by *oral* agreement of both parties in a majority of states. *Rationale:* The Statute of Frauds applies to the *making* of a contract, not to the *revocation* thereof. [**Niernberg v. Feld,** 283 P.2d 640 (Colo. 1955)] However, in some states, the revocation must be in writing; the theory is that the contract creates equitable title in the buyer (*see* "equitable conversion," *infra*, §1547), and revocation of the contract is in reality a *transfer* of this equitable title back to the seller.

4. Time of Performance [§1515]

Even though the contract sets a specific date for performance ("the closing date"), the contract is enforceable in equity *after* that date if performance is offered within a reasonable period thereafter. The time for performance is treated as a formal rather than an essential term of the contract. [**Kasten Construction Co. v. Maple Ridge Construction Co.,** 226 A.2d 341 (Md. 1967)]

a. Effect of "time of essence" provision [§1516]

Because the rule in equity can leave the liabilities of the parties uncertain for a substantial period of time, well-drafted contracts always provide that *"time is of the essence."* If this clause is in the contract and one party does not tender performance by the specified date, the other party is thereby *excused* from performance.

Example: In one case where payment was to be made before 2:30 p.m. on December 19, and time was stated to be of the essence, and the buyer produced the payment at 3:00 p.m. on December 19, it was held that the buyer could not enforce the contract. [**Doctorman v. Schroeder,** 114 A. 810 (N.J. 1921)]

5. Marketable Title

a. Implied in contract [§1517]

Unless there is a provision in the contract of sale to the contrary, it is implied that the seller must furnish the buyer with good and marketable title at closing. This implication will be made even though the contract calls for a conveyance by quitclaim deed (which makes no warranties of title). The reason is that the contract calls for a conveyance of land, and the seller cannot convey land unless he has title to it. [**Wallach v. Riverside Bank,** 206 N.Y. 434 (1912)]

EXAM TIP   **gilbert**

Watch out for questions where the seller agrees only to give a quitclaim deed (*see infra,* §1635). Most deeds include a warranty that valid title was passed at the time of closing; a quitclaim deed makes no such warranty. Nevertheless, the seller is ***not relieved*** from the duty ***to provide marketable title*** at closing. Thus, if the buyer discovers a defect in title before closing, she can seek to rescind the contract. However, if she discovers defects ***after*** closing, she will not be able to rescind or get damages from the seller because the implied duty to provide marketable title ***ends at closing***; after that the seller is liable only for warranties made in the deed, and a quitclaim deed does not warrant title.

---

(1) Contract provisions [§1518]

If the contract requires the seller to provide the buyer with an *insurable* title, only a title insured by a title insurance company and not a marketable title is required. If the contract calls for a "good *record* title," the seller must offer a marketable title based on recorded documents alone, not upon adverse possession. [**Tri-State Hotel Co. v. Sphinx Investment Co.,** 510 P.2d 1223 (Kan. 1973)]

b. Marketable title defined [§1519]

A marketable title is a title reasonably free from doubt, one which a prudent purchaser would accept. Although a perfect title is *not* required, the title must be such that there is no reasonable probability that the buyer will be subjected to a lawsuit. [*In re* **Estate of Oppelt,** 203 N.W.2d 213 (Iowa 1972)]

(1) Good record title [§1520]

A seller can show marketable title by producing a good *record title* or, in many states, by showing title by *adverse possession.* Good record title means, generally speaking, that there was a conveyance (usually many years ago) by a sovereign state then holding ownership, and thereafter there are, on record, transfers of title from the original grantee to the seller. In addition, good record title means that there are no recorded encumbrances, such as mortgages and easements, on the property. A person who has a good record title has an unencumbered fee simple, provable from the public records.

(a) Record search [§1521]

Because of the burden of searching title back to its original source, local practice may limit backward search to some definite period, such as 60 years. Title searchers assume that the statute of limitations will bar any earlier defect, although this is not necessarily the case. The risk of limiting a search to a 60-year period is deemed acceptable, in view of the high cost of further search back to the inception of private title. The risk may be covered by the seller's warranties of title (*see infra*, §§1631 *et seq.*) or by title insurance (*see infra*, §§1807 *et seq.*). In determining whether the seller has good record title, courts usually consider local practices regarding the period of record search.

(2) Adverse possession [§1522]

Unless marketable title "of record" is called for, many states hold that marketable title can be based on adverse possession. Adverse possession must be ***clearly proven***. The seller must offer the buyer ***written evidence or other proof*** admissible in court that the buyer can use to defend any lawsuit challenging title. [**Conklin v. Davi,** 388 A.2d 598 (N.J. 1978)] In a few states, marketable title cannot be shown by adverse possession unless a quiet title action has eliminated the record owner's rights.

c. Defects in title

(1) Defects in record chain [§1523]

Title may be unmarketable because of a defect in some prior instrument constituting part of the chain of title. For example, a deed might not be acknowledged before a notary (required for recordation), or the land descriptions in the chain may not match, or an old mortgage is not discharged on the records.

(2) Private encumbrances [§1524]

As a general rule, marketable title means an unencumbered fee simple. Mortgages, liens, covenants, and easements make title unmarketable unless the buyer waives them. However, a mortgage is not an encumbrance if the seller pays it off before closing or at closing with the proceeds from the sale.

(a) Easements [§1525]

An easement that lessens the value of the property (such as an easement by a neighbor for a right of way) makes title unmarketable. An easement that benefits the property (*e.g.*, a utility easement to service the property) does not necessarily make title unmarketable. Although a ***majority holds that such easements are encumbrances***, a ***minority*** holds that an open and visible easement for the benefit of the property known to the buyer before he makes the contract is not an encumbrance. Under the minority view, much depends on the expectations of the buyer, including what future use he plans to make of the property.

(b) Covenants [§1526]

Restriction on the use of property, imposed by private covenant, makes title unmarketable. It is assumed that the buyer wants to use the property for any purpose permitted by zoning regulations, and not merely continue its present use. On the other hand, if the contract expressly states that the property has been purchased for a particular use, and such use is permitted by the private covenants, title may be held marketable.

(c) Express waiver [§1527]

The contract of sale may enumerate the encumbrances and the buyer may waive them. Or the contract may provide that the seller shall furnish the buyer with a list of encumbrances prior to closing, and failure of the buyer to disapprove within a few days after receipt will be deemed a waiver. However, a waiver of an encumbrance in the contract of sale is not a waiver of a *violation* of the encumbrance when the buyer does not know of the violation. Thus, if in the contract the buyer waives building restrictions, and it is then found that the building on the property violates the restrictions, the buyer can rescind. [**Lohmeyer v. Bower,** 227 P.2d 102 (Kan. 1951); **Laba v. Carey,** 29 N.Y.2d 302 (1971)]

EXAM TIP   **gilbert**

Remember that a seller has the right to satisfy a mortgage or lien at closing **with the proceeds** of the sale. Thus, the buyer cannot claim title is unmarketable because it is subject to a mortgage prior to closing, if the closing will result in marketable title.

---

(3) Zoning restrictions [§1528]

Zoning laws and subdivision restrictions generally do **not** make title unmarketable. They are not considered encumbrances. However, even though zoning regulations do not generally affect marketability of title, if zoning restrictions are imposed *after* the buyer signed the contract, and these restrictions would materially interfere with or frustrate the buyer's contemplated use of the property, many courts will refuse to enforce the contract against the buyer. Some courts proceed on the theory of frustration of purpose. Others proceed on the ground that it would be unfair to grant specific performance in such event. [**Clay v. Landreth,** 45 S.E.2d 875 (Va. 1948)]

(a) Violations of zoning regulations [§1529]

If the property is in violation of a zoning ordinance or subdivision law, and correction of the violation can be demanded by the government, the title is usually held unmarketable. *Rationale:* To force the purchaser to take the property may force a lawsuit on the purchaser.

The purchaser may be sued by the government to correct the violation. [**Lohmeyer v. Bower**, *supra*; **Bethurem v. Hammett**, 736 P.2d 1128 (Wyo. 1987)]

---

e.g **Example:** P contracts to buy land and a building thereon from V. The land is in a single-family residence zone. After the zoning ordinance was passed, V cut up the house into two apartments in violation of the ordinance. P can rescind on the ground that title is unmarketable. (If the land were in an apartment zone, the title would be marketable.)

---

6. Defects in the Premises

a. Caveat emptor [§1530]

The old rule was that the seller did not have to disclose any defects in the condition of the premises unless a defect was fraudulently concealed. The buyer had the opportunity to inspect, and caveat emptor (let the buyer beware) applied.

(1) Exceptions [§1531]

Even in those states still professing to apply caveat emptor, exceptions are blossoming. For example, where a seller publicized her house locally as inhabited by poltergeists, it has been held that an out-of-town buyer who did not know of the reputation for poltergeists can rescind the contract of sale. The seller created the situation, and a physical inspection by the buyer was highly unlikely to reveal the poltergeists. [**Stambovsky v. Ackley**, 169 A.D.2d 254 (1991)]

b. Duty to disclose [§1532]

Caveat emptor is still applied in some states, but the number grows smaller each year. Most states now hold that the seller must disclose all known material defects to the buyer. [**Johnson v. Davis**, 480 So. 2d 625 (Fla. 1985)] Many states have statutes requiring sellers to give buyers a written statement disclosing facts about the property.

(1) Off-site conditions [§1533]

Sometimes courts have required sellers to reveal the existence of off-site conditions that might affect market value, like hazardous waste nearby, a noisy neighbor, or crimes in the neighborhood. The breadth of the duty to disclose off-site conditions is not yet settled, and it constitutes a worry for real estate lawyers who may be liable for malpractice for giving the wrong advice to client sellers.

c. Real estate brokers [§1534]

If the seller has a duty to disclose, a real estate broker also has a duty to disclose to a buyer material defects known to the broker but unknown to and unobservable by the buyer. California requires real estate brokers for the seller to conduct a diligent inspection of the property and reveal discovered defects to the buyer. [**Easton v. Strassburger**, 152 Cal. App. 3d 90 (1984)] This case has not been followed in some other jurisdictions, where the listing agent is under no duty to inspect. [**Kubinsky v. Van Zandt Realtors**, 811 S.W.2d 711 (Tex. 1991)]

7. Remedies for Breach of Contract [§1535]

Unless a contrary intention is clearly manifested, payment of the purchase price and delivery of the deed are dependent promises. Neither party can place the other in default unless he himself *tenders his own performance* and *demands* that the other party perform. Thus, to place the seller in default, the buyer must, on closing day, tender payment and demand title from the seller. [**Century 21 All Western Real Estate & Investments, Inc. v. Webb**, 645 P.2d 52 (Utah 1982)] Unless the contract contains a "time is of the essence" provision, the seller has a reasonable period of time thereafter within which to tender performance. If one party breaches the contract, the remedies of the other party are *rescission, specific performance*, and *damages*.

a. Remedies of the buyer

(1) Rescission [§1536]

On breach by the seller, the buyer may rescind the contract and recover her down payment. However, if, as is customary, the seller has agreed only to furnish title at date of closing (law day), the buyer *cannot rescind prior to closing* on the ground that seller does not have title. The seller may be able to acquire title before closing and hence be able to perform. [**Luette v. Bank of Italy National Trust & Savings Association**, 42 F.2d 9 (9th Cir. 1930)] If before closing the buyer notifies the seller that title is defective and the buyer therefore rescinds the contract, the buyer—not the seller—is in breach. The seller is entitled to attempt to make his title good before closing. [**Cohen v. Kranz**, 12 N.Y.2d 242 (1963)]

(2) Specific performance [§1537]

Land is considered unique, making money damages for failure to convey land inadequate. Therefore, the buyer has a right to specific performance if the seller breaches the contract. Specific performance is an *equitable* remedy, however, and there are equitable defenses available to the defendant. If the defendant would suffer undue hardship, or if circumstances have so changed that specific performance would be inequitable, specific performance will be denied. [**Estate of Younge v. Huysmans**, *supra*, §1500]

(a) Abatement in price [§1538]

Although the buyer is entitled to specific performance, a court will not ordinarily require the seller to cure a defect in title. Where there is a defect and the buyer wants the property, the buyer's only remedy is to ask for an abatement in price. If the seller cannot perform fully, *e.g.*, because of an easement across the premises, or a deficiency in acreage contracted for, the buyer is entitled to specific performance with abatement in the agreed price compensating for the deficiency. [**Bartos v. Czerwinski**, 34 N.W.2d 566 (Mich. 1948)]

(3) Damages [§1539]

If the buyer chooses, the buyer can sue the seller *at law* for money damages rather than for specific performance.

(a) Benefit of bargain [§1540]

In most states, the buyer seeking damages is entitled to the difference between the contract price and the market value of the land on the date performance is due. This is known as the "benefit of the bargain" rule, because it gives the buyer the benefit of the bargain. [**Beard v. S/E Joint Venture**, 581 A.2d 1275 (Md. 1990); **Donovan v. Bachstadt**, 453 A.2d 160 (N.J. 1982)]

> **Example:** On July 1, V contracts to sell Blackacre to P for $20,000. Closing is to take place on October 1. Oil is discovered under the land in September. The land is worth $45,000 on October 1. V sells Blackacre to a bona fide purchaser (*i.e.*, one who pays value and takes without notice of any defect) on September 15 for $35,000. P is entitled to recover $25,000 as damages from V. [**Smith v. Warr**, 564 P.2d 771 (Utah 1977)]

(b) Exception—good faith of seller [§1541]

Note that in the preceding example, V is a "bad person" who intentionally breached the contract. But suppose that V does not act in bad faith. Suppose that the deal falls through because V's title is unmarketable. A deed in V's chain of title, unbeknownst to V, is a forgery. Is it fair to stick V for $25,000 in damages? About half the states say no, and follow this exception to the general rule: If the seller acts in good faith, the buyer is limited to recovery of any money paid to the seller, plus interest and expenses in examining the title ("money out of pocket"). In other words, where the seller is not acting in bad faith, the buyer is entitled only to be restored to her original position (as in rescission). [**Kramer v. Mobley**, 216 S.W.2d 930 (Ky. 1949)]

	BUYER'S REMEDIES FOR BREACH OF CONTRACT **gilbert**	
RESCISSION	If the seller breaches, the buyer may *rescind* the contract and *recover any down payment*, but usually the seller doesn't agree to furnish title until closing, so the buyer cannot rescind until then.
SPECIFIC PERFORMANCE	The buyer has the right to *specific performance* because land is unique, but a court generally will not force a seller to cure a title defect; instead it will order specific performance *with an abatement* in price due to title defect.
DAMAGES	In most states, the buyer may sue for the difference between the *contract price and the market value* of the property on the date performance is due (benefit of bargain damages).

b.   Remedies of the seller

(1)   Rescission [§1542]

On breach by the buyer, the seller can rescind the contract.

(2)   Specific performance [§1543]

A seller, like a buyer, is entitled to demand specific performance on the other party's breach of contract. If there is a defect in the seller's title that is insubstantial and not material, the seller can enforce the contract specifically with an abatement in the purchase price to compensate the buyer for the deficiency.

(a)   Defenses [§1544]

There may be a new trend to deny specific performance to the seller when the seller can easily resell and damages at law are adequate. [**Centex Homes Corp. v. Boag,** 320 A.2d 194 (N.J. 1974)—denying specific performance to seller of condominium unit]

(3)   Damages [§1545]

If the seller prefers to keep the land, the seller can do so and still sue the buyer for money damages—the difference between the contract price and the market price when performance is due. If, *e.g.*, the seller contracts to sell land for $20,000, and the market price is $15,000 on the date of closing, the seller is entitled to $5,000 in damages if the buyer does not perform. (If the value has increased or stayed the same, the seller can recover only nominal damages—*e.g.*, one dollar—for the breach.)

(a)   Liquidated damages [§1546]

The contract may provide that the seller can keep the down payment.

If the parties intended this provision to be an agreement for liquidated damages, it is enforceable if the amount stipulated does not greatly exceed the injury that will be suffered. Generally, if the amount of down payment bears some *reasonable relationship* to the *actual* damages the seller sustains as a result of the buyer's breach (*e.g.*, any decline in value; costs of reselling property, if any; loss of other prospects; loss of interest on expected purchase price, etc.), such a provision for liquidated damages will be upheld. [**Lynch v. Andrew**, *supra*, §1504; **Mahoney v. Tingley**, 529 P.2d 1068 (Wash. 1975)] Compare installment land contracts, *infra*, §1692, with ordinary contracts of sale.

SELLER'S REMEDIES FOR BREACH OF CONTRACT	gilbert
RESCISSION	If the buyer breaches, the seller may *rescind*.
SPECIFIC PERFORMANCE	The seller usually can get *specific performance*, but there is a trend to deny specific performance if the seller can easily resell and sue at law for damages.
DAMAGES	The seller can sue for the difference between the *contract price and the market price* when performance is due; alternatively, the seller may keep the down payment as *liquidated damages* if the parties so intended and the down payment amount bears some reasonable relationship to the actual damages sustained.

8. Equitable Conversion [§1547]

The doctrine of equitable conversion may be invoked to solve problems resulting from the two-step method of conveyancing: First there is the contract of sale, and second, some weeks later, the closing. During this period, various problems may arise that turn on who has "title" to the real property. The doctrine of equitable conversion was invented to treat the buyer as having title for certain purposes prior to the date set for closing.

a. Statement of doctrine [§1548]

The doctrine of equitable conversion is based on the idea that because either party can demand specific performance of the land sale contract, equity *regards as done that which ought to be done*. Thus, the buyer is regarded in equity as the owner of the land; the seller has a security interest for payment of the purchase price, not unlike a mortgage. Sometimes it is added that the seller holds the legal title in trust for the buyer as security for the debt owed the seller. [**Cannefax v. Clement**, 818 P.2d 546 (Utah 1991); **Griggs Land Co. v. Smith**, 89 P. 477 (Wash. 1907)]

e.g. **Example:** On July 1, O contracts to sell Blackacre to A for $5,000, closing to take place on September 1. As of July 1, in equity A is regarded as the owner of Blackacre; O is regarded as having a debt of $5,000 owed him and a security interest in Blackacre to protect the debt.

EXAM TIP	gilbert

The doctrine of equitable conversion was applied rather rigorously by the English courts to govern all relationships between buyer and seller during the period before closing. In this country, however, there is much divergence of view about its application; many courts say they apply equitable conversion only to carry out the presumed intent of the parties and to do equity. Hence, they might apply it in one context and not in another. Therefore, in addition to learning the doctrine, you should learn *which types of cases* it is usually applied to.

b. Devolution on death

(1) Early history [§1549]

The doctrine of equitable conversion originated in cases having to do with devolution of interests on death of one of the parties to a contract for sale of land. In England, real property descended to the primogenitary heir (eldest son); personal property was distributed to the next of kin (all of the children equally). If the seller's interest were real property, it descended to the heir. The courts, however, held that the seller's interest was personal property, which descended to all of the children equally. The doctrine of equitable conversion was the device invented to accomplish this result. Having invented the doctrine in this context, the English courts extended it logically to other contexts as well.

(2) Modern law [§1550]

Equitable conversion is widely applied in the United States to questions of both testate and intestate devolution, *i.e.*, to distribution of property both with and without a will. The seller's interest is treated as personal property secured by a lien; the buyer's interest is treated as real property.

---

e.g. **Example:** O, owner of Blackacre, executes a will devising "real property" to A and "personal property" to B. Subsequently, O contracts to sell Blackacre to C for $5,000. Before closing, O dies. Applying the doctrine of equitable conversion, O's interest in Blackacre is treated as personal property, and hence B is entitled to the $5,000 when paid. [**Shay v. Penrose**, 185 N.E.2d 218 (Ill. 1962)] Likewise, if C defaults and cannot pay the $5,000 on closing, B is entitled to Blackacre. Equitable conversion took place the moment the contract was signed; hence, at O's death, his interest, which passed under his will, was personal property. [**Clapp v. Tower**, 93 N.W. 862 (N.D. 1903)]

---

c. **Right to possession [§1551]**

Although the buyer has *equitable* title, she does *not* have the right to *possession*, which follows *legal* title. The contract, especially an installment sale contract, may put the buyer into possession. If it does, the buyer may not commit waste that would impair the security of the seller. In questions of waste, the seller under an installment land contract is treated as having a security interest in the property similar to a mortgage.

d. **Risk of loss [§1552]**

Suppose that before the date set for closing, the property is destroyed or damaged by fire, flood, or other cause not the fault of either party. Who has the risk of loss? The parties may cover this matter in their contract, but if they do not the court will apply a rule.

(1) Majority—buyer has risk of loss [§1553]

The majority of courts follows the old English rule enunciated in **Paine v. Meller,** 6 Ves. 349 (Ch. 1801), which applied equitable conversion and put the risk of loss on the buyer. By virtue of equitable conversion, the buyer owns the land, and the seller has only a security interest. If the buyer refuses to take the damaged property, the seller can sue for specific performance at the contract price or sue for damages. The amount of damage is the loss in value of the property due to the fire or other cause. [**Bleckley v. Langston,** 143 S.E.2d 671 (Ga. 1965)]

(a) Unmarketable title [§1554]

If the seller's title is unmarketable, and the seller cannot obtain specific performance, equitable conversion will not take place, and the risk of loss will not shift to the buyer. To shift the loss to the buyer, the seller must prove that he is entitled to specific performance. [**Sanford v. Breidenbach,** 173 N.E.2d 702 (Ohio 1960)]

(b) Insurance [§1555]

If the risk of loss is on the buyer, should the buyer be entitled, in the event of loss, to the proceeds of the seller's insurance policy? The English rule was that the insurance policy is a personal contract of indemnity, and hence the seller is entitled to the insurance proceeds and does not have to credit them against the purchase price. American courts have looked on this rule with marked disfavor. Most reject it completely on the ground that it gives the seller a windfall: He pockets both the insurance proceeds and the purchase price through specific performance. These courts require the seller to credit the insurance proceeds against the purchase price in an action for specific performance. They usually say the seller holds the insurance proceeds in a constructive trust for the buyer. [**Gilles v. Sprout,** 196 N.W.2d 612 (Minn. 1972)] A few states follow the English rule, but have created two exceptions that cover most cases that arise: (i) if the seller is required by the contract *to keep the property insured* for the benefit of the buyer, or (ii) if the buyer is required by the contract *to pay the premiums* on the seller's policy, the insurance proceeds are credited against the purchase price. [**Raplee v. Piper,** 3 N.Y.2d 179 (1957)]

EXAM TIP | gilbert

Remember that the majority rule is that even though the risk of loss is on the buyer, if the property is damaged or destroyed, the seller *must credit* any fire or casualty *insurance proceeds* he receives *against the purchase price* the buyer is required to pay.

---

(2) Minority—seller has risk of loss [§1556]

A minority of courts follows the so-called Massachusetts rule, which puts the risk of loss on the seller. These courts reject equitable conversion in this context. They imply a *condition in the contract* that (i) *if the loss is substantial,* and (ii) *the terms of the agreement show that the building constituted an important part of the subject matter* of the contract, the contract is not binding. If the building is destroyed, the buyer can rescind and recover any earnest money. [**Bryant v. Willison Real Estate Co.,** 350 S.E.2d 748 (W. Va. 1986)]

(a) Specific performance with abatement [§1557]

If the damage is *insubstantial,* the buyer can get specific performance with an abatement in the purchase price for the amount of damage. But where the damage is *substantial,* the Massachusetts theory is that the contract is not binding. Nonetheless, courts purporting to follow the Massachusetts rule have decreed specific performance to the buyer with abatement in the purchase price—not by the amount of actual damages, but by the amount of insurance received by the seller. [**Skelly Oil Co. v. Ashmore,** 365 S.W.2d 582 (Mo. 1963)] This result is hardly distinguishable from the majority view that the buyer has the risk of loss, but the seller holds any insurance proceeds as trustee for the buyer.

(b) Buyer's insurance [§1558]

Buyers sometimes take out insurance to protect themselves when they sign a contract to purchase real property. This is a common practice, particularly when commercial property is purchased. If the building is destroyed, the buyer is paid by the insurance company. A seller who has the risk of loss usually *cannot* reach the proceeds of the buyer's insurance. This accords with the common understanding of the parties that, although the continuation of the seller's insurance during the contract period may be for the protection of the buyer, the buyer's purchase of insurance is solely to protect the buyer. [**Sanford v. Breidenbach**, *supra,* §1554; *but see* **Holscher v. James**, 860 P.2d 646 (Idaho 1993)—holding seller was third-party beneficiary of buyer's insurance]

(3) Party in possession has risk of loss [§1559]

Some courts have held that the *party in possession* has the risk of loss. If the seller is still in possession, he bears the risk; if the buyer has gone into possession, she bears the risk. The Uniform Vendor and Purchaser Risk Act (adopted in California, Illinois, Michigan, New York, and a few other states) adopts this position.

e. Application to options [§1560]

In the United States, equitable conversion does not apply to an option to purchase *until* the option is exercised. *Rationale:* An option is specifically enforceable only by the buyer (optionee) and not by the seller (optionor). Equitable conversion applies only where there is a mutually specifically enforceable contract.

Example: O gives A a 90-day option to buy Whiteacre for $30,000. Within the 90-day period, O dies, leaving a will executed two years previously that devises B a life estate in Whiteacre. At O's death, equitable conversion has not occurred. At her death, O has legal title to Whiteacre subject to an option, and B takes a life estate in Whiteacre subject to that option. If A exercises the option, O's interest is converted into money, and at that time equitable conversion takes place and B takes a life estate in the $30,000. [**Eddington v. Turner**, 38 A.2d 738 (Del. 1944)]

---

9. The Closing [§1561]

At the closing, a third party (either a lawyer or escrow agent) is usually in charge. A check for the purchase price is handed by the buyer to the party in charge; a deed executed by the seller is also handed over. Any mortgage given to the seller or to a third-party lender is executed by the buyer and handed to the party in charge. The party in charge makes various agreed-upon adjustments in the amount owed, such as proration of taxes, utility bills, and mortgage payments to the date of closing. The party in charge then records the deed and any mortgage. Finally, the party in charge hands a check to the seller. The deal is closed.

B. The Deed

1. Formalities

a. Statute of Frauds [§1562]

To transfer an interest in land, the Statute of Frauds requires a writing signed by the party to be bound. The writing is usually in the form of a deed, but it may be an informal instrument. A letter evidencing a present intent to presently vest title in the grantee is sufficient. [**Metzger v. Miller,** 291 F. 780 (N.D. Cal. 1923)—letters saying "house is now yours," coupled with grantee moving in, evidenced intent to pass title]

(1) Executed parol gift [§1563]

A parol gift of land has sometimes been upheld in spite of the Statute of Frauds. To take a parol gift out of the Statute of Frauds, the grantee must take possession in reliance on the gift and *make valuable improvements* so that a substantial injustice would result from rigorously applying the Statute of Frauds. The doctrine of executed parol gift bears substantial similarity to the doctrine of part performance of a contract (*supra*, §1506). [**Hayes v. Hayes,** 148 N.W. 125 (Minn. 1914)]

(2) Signed by grantor only [§1564]

The writing must be signed by the party to be bound—the *grantor*. It is neither necessary nor customary that the *grantee* sign the deed. If a deed contains covenants by the grantee (*e.g.*, to use the property only for residential purposes), the grantee is bound by the covenants, even though he does not sign the deed, if the grantee *accepts* the deed.

(a) Forged deed [§1565]

No interest passes under a forged deed. Unless estoppel comes into play because of the purported grantor's acts, the deed is not legally effective at all. [**Martin v. Carter,** 400 A.2d 326 (D.C. 1979)]

EXAM TIP   gilbert

Watch for a situation in which a joint owner attempts to convey property by forging the signature(s) of the other owner(s). Such a conveyance would be *valid* as to the interest of the *owner whose signature is genuine* but *void* as to the *other owner(s)*. Thus, if one joint tenant executes a deed for the entire property with his own signature and the forged signature of the other joint tenant, the conveyance works a severance; the buyer would hold as a tenant in common with the joint tenant whose signature was forged.

(b) Distinguish—deed procured by fraud [§1566]

A forged deed is a nullity, and is not valid for any purpose. Neither the donee nor a subsequent bona fide purchaser who believes the forged deed is good takes anything. On the other hand, a deed signed by the grantor but *procured by fraud* is not void, only voidable. The deed is not good (can be voided) against a fraudulent grantee, but it is good against a subsequent bona fide purchaser. In the case of a deed delivered by fraud, the grantor has put the instrument into the chain of commerce, by which a subsequent bona fide purchaser can be harmed. The grantor must take the risk if she delivers the deed, and she must suffer against a subsequent bona fide purchaser. If, however, the deed is forged, and the grantor did not put the instrument in the chain of commerce so that another can be harmed, the grantor is protected. In the case of a forged deed, a subsequent bona fide purchaser takes the risk of forgery. Sometimes it is hard to tell the difference between forgery and fraud. [**McCoy v. Love,** 382 So. 2d 647 (Fla. 1979)]

(3) Acknowledgment [§1567]

Acknowledgment by the grantor in front of a notary public or attestation by witnesses is usually not necessary for an effective deed. However, acknowledgment or attestation is desirable for two reasons:

(a) Recordation [§1568]

Acknowledgment or witnessing is usually required for recordation of a deed. In most states, an unacknowledged deed cannot be recorded (*see infra*, §§1734 *et seq.*).

(b) Authentication [§1569]

In most states, an acknowledged or witnessed deed is self-authenticating, meaning that it can be admitted into evidence in any legal action even though no one can testify to its execution or delivery. An unacknowledged or unwitnessed deed may not be admitted into evidence without direct testimony regarding its execution. In addition, proof of delivery of the deed may be required, and this may be difficult if there were no witnesses.

(4) Seal [§1570]

At common law, a "deed" was defined as an instrument under seal. Today a seal is not required for a valid transfer, and unsealed instruments are commonly called deeds.

(5) Signature of spouse [§1571]

The spouse may have property rights accruing from marriage, such as dower, curtesy, homestead, or community property rights in the property. To release these, the spouse must join the deed.

b. Words of grant [§1572]

Any words indicating an intent to make a transfer will suffice. Words of grant include "I give, grant, bargain and sell, convey, quitclaim, assign." Only one word of grant is necessary, but deeds often contain many of the technical terms used at common law, which are no longer necessary for an effective deed.

(1) Modern deeds [§1573]

At common law there were numerous kinds of deeds, each adapted for a particular set of circumstances. Common law deeds included a "bargain and sale deed," a "covenant to stand seised," a "feoffment," and a "lease and release," among others. Today these deeds are no longer used. Modern deeds are of two types: (i) *warranty deeds*, by which the grantor warrants title, and (ii) *quitclaim deeds*, by which the grantor does not warrant title. (*See infra*, §§1632-1636.)

c. Consideration [§1574]

Consideration is *not* necessary to transfer land; a person can *give* land away. [**Chase Federal Savings & Loan Association v. Schreiber**, 479 So. 2d 90 (Fla. 1985)] It is neither necessary nor customary to recite the true consideration, if any, in the deed. The purchaser usually wants to keep the purchase price secret. However, it is customary to recite that the deed is given "for one dollar and other good and valuable consideration." This rebuts any implication of a resulting use or trust in favor of the grantor and raises a presumption that the grantee is a purchaser, not a donee, and hence entitled to protection under the recording acts (*see infra*, §§1742 *et seq.*).

d. Parts of the deed

(1) Granting clause [§1575]

The initial clause in a deed, setting forth the parties, the consideration, words of grant, the description of the land and its appurtenances, is known as the granting clause.

(2) Habendum clause [§1576]

The habendum clause is usually introduced by the words "to have and to hold" ("habendum et tenendum" in Latin). This ordinarily follows the granting clause and in feudal times was very important because it contained the name of the person (lord) from whom the land was held, the services due, and the kind of estate held. After feudalism declined and trusts arose, any declaration of trust was inserted in the habendum clause (*e.g.*, "to have and to hold to the use of B for life, then to the use of B's children"). If no trust is intended, the habendum clause in a modern deed will say that the grantee holds for his own use, thus negating a trust.

(a) Inconsistency [§1577]

If the habendum is inconsistent with the granting clause, they will be reconciled, if possible. It was sometimes said, in older cases, that a granting clause will prevail over a habendum in case of conflict, on the theory that the grantor could not cut back on the interest earlier conveyed. But modern courts usually find a means of reconciling the conflict by looking "within the four corners of an instrument" (*i.e.*, looking at all the terms of the document itself) to ascertain intent. [**First National Bank v. Townsend**, 555 P.2d 477 (Or. 1976)] e.g. **Example:** An elderly couple executed a deed to their land. The granting clause said "to our son, George," the consideration being that "George is to take care of the grantors as long as they live." The habendum clause said "to have and to hold the land to George and his wife Mae and their heirs and assigns." Looking at all parts of the deed, the court inferred that the deed was made in consideration of both George and Mae looking after the old couple, because the wife would be performing the household duties. Thus, the court held that the habendum clause controlled, and the conveyance was to George and Mae by the entirety, and not to George alone. [**Grayson v. Holloway,** 313 S.W.2d 555 (Tenn. 1958)]

(b) Not used in statutory forms [§1578]
The habendum clause is superfluous today and is omitted from all statutory forms of deeds.

(3) Grantor's covenants [§1579]
A final paragraph of the deed may include covenants of warranty by the grantor. (*See infra*, §§1631 *et seq.*)

(4) Signature and acknowledgment [§1580]
The grantor's signature and acknowledgment before a notary come at the end of the deed.

e. Description of the grantee [§1581]
If the instrument names a grantee, the grantee must be described with sufficient particularity so that it can be determined who is to take the grant. If the named grantee is a nonexistent or unascertained person, the deed may be invalid either for uncertainty or for failure to make delivery. [**United States v. Stubbs,** 776 F.2d 1472 (10th Cir. 1985)]

(1) Sufficient description required [§1582]
The grantee need not be actually named, as long as a sufficient description is given. A grant to the "wife" or "oldest living child" of a named person is valid.

(2) Grantee's name left blank [§1583]
A grantee is an essential part of a deed. If the grantee's name is left blank in the deed, some older cases held that the deed is a legal nullity. Under this view, the intended grantee can only sue in equity for specific performance of the contract to sell.

(a) Implied authority [§1584]
A majority of modern cases hold that if the grantee's name is blank,

the intended grantee is the agent of the grantor with implied authority to fill in his own or another name. The deed is a nullity when executed, but when the name is filled in, the instrument becomes operative as a deed. [**Board of Education v. Hughes,** 136 N.W. 1095 (Minn. 1912)]

1) Death of grantor [§1585]

Although the death of a principal usually terminates the power of the agent to act, if the grantor dies before the agent fills in the grantee's name, the agent can fill in the grantee's name after the grantor's death even in the case of a gratuitous transfer. Thus, courts bend the rules to make a deed in blank effective—and why not when they hold a blank check valid? [**Womack v. Stegner,** 293 S.W.2d 124 (Tex. 1956)]

2. Description of Land Conveyed

a. Admission of extrinsic evidence [§1586]

The property passing under a deed can be described by: metes and bounds (meaning "measurements and boundaries"); reference to a government survey, a recorded plat, or adjacent properties; a street and number system; or the name of the property. If the description in a deed furnishes any means of identification of the property involved, the description is sufficient. Extrinsic evidence is usually admissible to clear up any ambiguity. [**Bybee v. Hageman,** 66 Ill. 519 (1873)]

(1) Part of larger tract [§1587]

A conveyance of "one acre off the western end of my 30-acre tract" (the 30-acre tract being adequately described) would probably fail for uncertainty. "Off the western end" is too vague to tell *which* acre, and the admission of parol evidence to clear up the ambiguity here would probably be held to violate the Statute of Frauds. [**Asotin County Port District v. Clarkston Community Corp.,** 472 P.2d 554 (Wash. 1970)] However, if there is an *underlying contract* for sale, written or oral, which specified the particular acre, the grantee may bring a suit in equity to change the deed to comply with the contract.

(2) No ambiguity—extrinsic evidence not admissible [§1588]

If the description of a deed is not ambiguous—such as "the northeast quarter of the northeast quarter" or "the west 50 feet of lot 13"—extrinsic evidence, such as action of the parties in locating fences or oral agreements, is not admissible to contradict the deed. Such evidence is admissible only to show a mutual mistake in the description in a suit to reform the deed to carry out the parties' original intent. [**Walters v. Tucker,** 281 S.W.2d 843 (Mo. 1955)]

b. Canons of construction [§1589]

Where there is a mistake or inconsistency in the description, as where the deed leaves in doubt the exact location of a boundary line or gives two different locations for the line, canons of construction are applied to ascertain the parties' intent. These canons are designed to give effect to what the parties most likely intended, but they yield to any clear manifestation of the parties' intent. The order is: *original survey monuments* prevail over *natural monuments*, which prevail over *artificial monuments*, which prevail over *maps*, which prevail over *courses*, which prevail over *distances*, which prevail over a *name*, which prevails over *quantity*. [**Doman v. Brogan**, 592 A.2d 104 (Pa. 1991); **Pritchard v. Rebori**, 186 S.W. 121 (Tenn. 1916)]

(1) Survey monuments [§1590]

A survey monument is a specially placed stake or some natural object used in marking the lines and corners of a survey. When land is conveyed by reference to a survey, the survey monuments prevail over a less certain description if the original survey monuments can be found.

(2) Natural and artificial monuments [§1591]

A description based on natural or artificial monuments prevails over a description based on maps, courses and distances, or quantity. Thus, a call from "Point X to the old oak tree" prevails over a call from "Point X north 150 feet." *Rationale:* Property is normally bought in reliance on what can be seen, not on paper calculations. Furthermore, people cannot measure distances very accurately with the naked eye.

(a) Natural vs. artificial monuments [§1592]

Natural monuments (*e.g.*, tree, river) are regarded as more reliable than artificial, easily moved monuments (*e.g.*, surveyor's stake, fence). Hence, natural monuments prevail over artificial monuments if they are of greater permanence.

(3) Maps [§1593]

If a survey map has been made of the property, but the marks of the original survey have disappeared or were never made, the survey map describing courses and distances can be used to establish boundaries. A description based on a survey map prevails over a description by courses and distances or quantity.

(4) Courses and distances [§1594]

A description by courses and distances gives a starting point and the direction and length of the lines to be run. Courses (*e.g.*, angles) prevail over distances. If the parcel will not close as described, but will close by following the courses and lengthening or shortening the distances, this will be done. It is assumed that an angle, which fixes the shape of the lot, is more obvious to the parties than length.

Original survey monuments

prevail over

Natural monuments

prevail over

Artificial monuments

prevail over

Maps

prevail over

Courses

prevail over

Distances

prevail over

Name

prevails over

Quantity

(5) Name or quantity [§1595]

All the foregoing prevail over descriptions by name (*e.g.*, "Walker's Island") or quantity (*e.g.*, "being 300 acres"). As between these two, description by name prevails over description by quantity. Quantity is regarded as the least reliable description.

c. Streets and railways as boundaries [§1596]

If land is described as being bounded by a public or private right of way—or if the land conveyed is otherwise described but actually is bounded by such right of way—there is a rebuttable *presumption that the title of the grantee extends to the center of the right of way* (assuming the grantor owns to the center) or to the full width of it if the grantor owns the width of it and retains no land on the other side. [**Smith v. Hadad**, 314 N.E.2d 435 (Mass. 1974); **Parr v. Worley**, 599 P.2d 382 (N.M. 1979)]

(1) Rationale

This accords with (i) the presumed intention of the parties that the grantor not retain a narrow strip underlying the right of way; and (ii) the greater public convenience in having the land underlying the right of way owned by the abutters.

d. Water boundaries [§1597]

A description of a tract so framed as to have a water boundary carries title to the appurtenant land under water if owned by the grantor. A grantee of land abutting water normally expects access to the water; therefore, the deed is construed to give him the land under the water.

C. Delivery of the Deed

1. In General [§1598]

A deed is not effective to transfer an interest in land until it has been delivered by the grantor. "Delivery" requires words or conduct of the grantor that shows an *intent to make the deed operative* and to *pass an interest immediately* to the grantee. In other words, the conduct must show an intent to make the deed legally effective now. The usual method of delivery is handing over the deed from the grantor to the grantee, but handing over a deed without the concurrent intent is not an effective delivery. On the other hand, if the grantor intends to make delivery, manual transfer is not necessary. The crucial issue is intent—not what physically happens to the deed. Nonetheless, physical transfer of the deed is compelling evidence of intent.

e.g. **Example—no intent, but manual transfer:** O executes an instrument conveying Blackacre to A, and hands the instrument to A "for safekeeping." Even though it is handed to the named grantee, this is not a valid delivery. There is no evidence that O intended the instrument to have any present operative effect. [**Martinez v. Martinez,** 678 P.2d 1163 (N.M. 1984)]

Example—intent, but no transfer: O executes an instrument conveying Whiteacre to B. O attempts to give the instrument to B personally, but is unable to find B. Nevertheless, O quits possession of Whiteacre, tells other people B owns the land, and thereafter treats B as the owner thereof. Most courts would hold that there has been a sufficient delivery. [**McMahon v. Dorsey,** 91 N.W.2d 893 (Mich. 1958)]

a. Presumptions [§1599]

Courts have laid down, and usually follow, presumptions with respect to whether delivery had occurred. Delivery is presumed if: (i) the deed is *handed* to the grantee, (ii) the deed is *acknowledged* by the grantor before a notary, or (iii) the deed is *recorded*. [**LeMehaute v. LeMehaute,** 585 S.W.2d 276 (Mo. 1979)] No delivery is presumed if the grantor retains possession of the deed. However, these are presumptions only, and can be rebutted by any type of extrinsic evidence—including the grantor's conduct or statements made after the alleged delivery.

(1) Deeds effective at death [§1600]

In a surprising number of cases, grantors—wishing to avoid probate and lawyers—execute a deed of land in favor of a beneficiary and put the deed away in a safe deposit box. The deed is intended as a substitute for a will. If the grantor intended the deed to be legally effective *before* death, it is a validly delivered deed (creating a springing executory interest or remainder in the grantee). On the other hand, if the grantor did not intend the deed to be effective *until* death, the deed is not delivered during life and is no good as a deed. If not executed with the formalities required of wills, the document cannot be probated as a will either— and the grantee does not get the land. The cases involving this situation are hard to predict, but if it appears that the grantor never formed a definite crystallized intention to do a legally effective act and did not believe himself bound by the deed, there has been no delivery. [**Wiggill v. Cheney,** 597 P.2d 1351 (Utah 1979)] On the other hand, if the grantor tells third persons "that he had deeded that land to Pat," and the evidence suggests that the grantor kept the deed merely for safekeeping, a delivery probably has been made. The grantee's case is helped if the deed is kept in the grantor's safe deposit box to which the *grantee* has access. [**McMahon v. Dorsey,** *supra*]

b. Cancellation of delivery ineffective [§1601]

After there has been an effective delivery of a deed in fee simple, the title has passed to the grantee and a return of the deed to the grantor has no effect as a cancellation or reconveyance. The Statute of Frauds requires a *writing* to move title back to the grantor.

> **(e.g.) Example:** O hands a deed to grantee A, intending to make delivery. O changes her mind and asks A for the deed back. A gives the deed back to O. A still owns the land.

EXAM TIP	gilbert

Keep in mind that title passes *upon delivery*. It cannot be canceled or taken back once delivered. Thus, if a fact pattern on an exam has the grantee returning a deed to the grantor, remember this has no effect; it is not a cancellation or a reconveyance. To return title to the grantor, the grantee must *draw up a new deed and deliver it* to the grantor.

---

2. Conditional Delivery to Grantee

a. Written condition [§1602]

Where a deed contains a provision that it is to take effect only upon the happening of a condition precedent, it is possible to interpret it in one of two ways: (i) the provision may mean there is *no delivery* and the *deed is not effective at all until the condition happens*; or (ii) the provision may mean that the grantor intends the deed *to be legally effective now, but passing only an interest that is subject to a condition precedent*. Under the first construction the deed is a nullity, because it has not been delivered. Under the second, the grantee receives a valid springing executory interest (compare a common law conveyance "to my daughter upon her marriage," which created a springing executory interest in the daughter, *supra*, §455). This is a very subtle distinction, which produces litigation. But most litigation involves deeds used as will substitutes.

(1) Will substitutes [§1603]

A deed can be intended to operate as a substitute for a will. A will must be probated, with attendant costs of probate administration including lawyers' fees. A deed, *if effective*, avoids those costs. The will substitute cases usually involve one of three sets of facts: (i) where the deed is absolute on its face but the grantor retains possession of the deed (discussed *supra*, §1600); (ii) where a written condition in a deed handed to the grantee provides that the deed is not effective until the grantor's death or that the deed is revocable (*see* below); or (iii) where the deed is handed to an escrow agent with oral instructions to deliver the deed to the grantee at the grantor's death (discussed *infra*, §1609).

(a) Conditions relating to death of grantor [§1604]

Where the deed is handed to the grantee, and a written provision in the deed says the deed is on condition, the particular words of condition may be crucial in determining intent to deliver. If the deed says, "O conveys to A, reserving a life estate in O," there is no problem. The deed is delivered. If, however, the deed says, "this deed shall be effective only upon my death," the cases are split. Some hold that, although these words may be intended to be the equivalent of reserving a life estate, the word "effective" suggests the instrument is not to be effective at all until death. Under this reading, the instrument can be given effect only if executed as a will. [**Butler v. Sherwood,** 233 N.Y. 655 (1922)] Other cases hold the deed is validly delivered, creating a springing executory interest in the grantee. The word "effective" is construed to mean "effective to transfer possession"; it does not indicate an intent not to create a legal future interest. [**Abbott v. Holway,** *supra,* §455]

1) Surviving grantor [§1605]

If the deed says, "O conveys to A if A survives O," this looks very much like a will, except a will can be revoked and this deed, if effective, cannot be. Most cases take the position that, inasmuch as the condition of survivorship is not within O's control, O intends to presently create a contingent executory interest (or contingent remainder) in A. The deed is thus held good. [**Abbott v. Holway,** *supra*]

(b) Grantor retains power to revoke [§1606]

If the grantor retains the power to revoke the deed, the courts are split over whether the delivery is effective. Some courts hold the deed is void either on the theory that the grantor must surrender dominion and control in order to make an effective delivery, or on the theory that the deed is a testamentary instrument and is void as a deed. Neither reason is persuasive (*see* below). Some courts will give effect to the deed as creating a present interest in the grantee that can be revoked.

(c) Criticism [§1607]

In the will substitute cases, much confusion results from the courts' failure to make a consistent policy analysis. The fact that the deed is a will substitute ought to be irrelevant. Many other will substitutes are legally permitted when a *written instrument* is signed by the grantor: life insurance, joint bank accounts, inter vivos revocable trusts, and designation of beneficiaries on government bonds, pension plans, IRAs, Keogh plans, and savings accounts. If these inter vivos instruments may serve as will substitutes, there is no reason why a delivered deed should not be valid as a will substitute. The written provisions of a deed are as reliable as provisions of these other written instruments. Where the grantor *signs* a deed *with written conditions,* and *hands it over* to the grantee, experience indicates that the grantor intends the deed to be legally effective (otherwise, why would he do this?). The signed written instrument is reliable evidence; dangerous parol evidence is not necessary to give it effect. Thus, all deeds manually delivered with written conditions intended as will substitutes should be valid. Also, inasmuch as the death beneficiary named in other will substitutes can be revoked, there is no reason why a deed with the written power to revoke should be invalid. As with a life insurance beneficiary designation, the grantor intends to be bound unless he changes his mind. Nonetheless, so long as courts say the grantor must put the deed beyond his control for an effective delivery, no lawyer should use a deed as a will substitute. A revocable inter vivos trust, valid everywhere, is the preferred route. Thus, instead of executing a revocable deed in favor of A to be effective at O's death, O should execute a trust instrument providing, "O hereby declares he holds Blackacre in trust for O for life, and upon O's death, Blackacre is to go to A. O retains the right to revoke this trust at any time." This is a valid revocable trust. O can subsequently change his mind, revoke the trust, and get title to Blackacre back, if he desires.

b. Oral condition [§1608]

Although there is little reason in policy to refuse to give effect to written conditions in a deed, the policy of the Statute of Frauds is offended by oral conditions. Where the grantor hands over to the grantee a deed absolute on its face, with a contemporaneous oral understanding that the deed shall not take effect until some condition is performed, the general rule is that the delivery is valid and the oral condition is void. Courts do not like oral conditions contradicting a written instrument because of the possibilities of fraud and fabrication of evidence and the resulting uncertainty of real estate titles.

Example: O delivers to A a deed absolute on its face. O and A have an oral understanding that the deed is to be effective only if A survives O. A now owns the land. The delivery is good; the oral condition is void. **[Sweeney v. Sweeney,** 11 A.2d 806 (Conn. 1940)]

3. Deed Given to Third-Party Custodian (Escrow Agent) [§1609]

Although generally a deed delivered directly to a grantee cannot have oral conditions attached, a deed can be delivered in escrow with oral conditions attached. However, the rules regarding effective escrows may differ depending on whether the escrow is *donative* or *commercial*.

a. Donative escrow [§1610]

A donative escrow is one where the grantor is giving the land to the grantee, but desires to postpone the grantee's right to possession until a later date, usually the grantor's death. Typically, a donative escrow involves this situation:

O executes a deed naming A as grantee; O hands the deed to X, a trusted friend, and says, "Deliver this deed to A at my death." When O hands the deed to X, O has made an effective delivery, X becomes the agent of O and A, and O cannot recall the deed. X must deliver the deed to A at O's death. [**Stone v. Duvall**, 77 Ill. 475 (1875)]

(1) Grantee's rights [§1611]

At the time of the delivery in escrow, the grantee (A, in above example) receives a future interest in the property—properly classified as a springing executory interest but sometimes classified as a remainder. (For more on the grantee's rights, *see* the discussion of the relation-back doctrine, *infra*, §§1619 *et seq.*)

(2) Writing not required [§1612]

The instructions to the custodian X can be *oral* or *written*. The Statute of Frauds is to some extent violated by oral instructions, but courts have believed that the testimony of X, a disinterested party, is sufficiently reliable so as to justify not applying the Statute. Also, in donative transfers in escrow (unlike commercial escrows), the oral instructions are usually inferable from the deed, the surrounding circumstances, and experience—*i.e.*, the grantee ordinarily is a natural object of the grantor's bounty, the custodian a trusted friend, and experience indicates that the usual instruction is to deliver on the death of the grantor. Because of these considerations, the escrow agent's testimony is permitted to substitute for written instructions.

(3) Effect of grantor's reserving power to revoke [§1613]

If, in the escrow instructions, the grantor retains the power to recall the deed, the escrow is invalid. No delivery occurs—regardless of whether the power of revocation is ever exercised. The courts reason that the grantor must give up control to have an effective delivery in escrow. If the grantor can recall the deed, the escrow agent is *solely the grantor's agent*, and no delivery takes place when the deed is put in escrow because it is not beyond the grantor's control. [**Rosengrant v. Rosengrant**, 629 P.2d 800 (Okla. 1981); **Johnson v. Johnson**, 54 A. 378 (R.I. 1903)]

(a) Criticism [§1614]

A revocable escrow is invalid not for any reason of policy, but only because of unreasoning adherence to the ancient dogma that the grantor must surrender control to effect a delivery. The fact that a revocable donative escrow operates very much like a will is not objectionable in policy (*see supra*, §1607). Inasmuch as revocable trusts are permitted, there is no policy reason why revocable escrows should not be permitted. If the escrow custodian were a "trustee," the revocable transfer would be permissible. The ban on revocable escrows discriminates against persons (usually poorer persons) who do not consult lawyers and try to arrange their affairs by themselves. Lawyers will advise a revocable trust.

b. Commercial escrow [§1615]

A commercial escrow is a common and useful arrangement in buying and selling land. Typically, the seller hands a deed naming the buyer as grantee to an escrow agent with instructions to hand the deed to the grantee when and if, before a fixed date, the grantee hands over a cashier's check for the purchase price. This arrangement protects both the buyer and the seller: Money and title change hands at the same time. [**Ferguson v. Caspar,** 359 A.2d 17 (D.C. 1976)]

(1) Oral instructions [§1616]

Where the escrow agent is given written instructions, the grantor is bound by the delivery to the agent. On the other hand, where the grantor deposits the deed in escrow under *oral instructions*, most courts hold that the grantor may countermand the instructions and recall the deed while still in the escrow agent's hands, *unless there is a written contract of sale.*

Example: O orally agrees to sell Blackacre to A. O executes a deed in A's favor and hands the deed to Bank with *oral* instructions to deliver the deed to A if A pays $10,000 within 30 days. Ten days later, O has a better offer for Blackacre from B. O tells Bank not to deliver the deed to A. A brings $10,000 to Bank one week later. A has no enforceable contract right (Statute of Frauds), and A is not entitled to the deed. O still owns Blackacre.

(a) Rationale

O can revoke because the oral escrow instructions violate the Statute of Frauds. The purchase price is an indispensable part of a contract of sale. From the mere deposit of a deed into escrow, one cannot infer what is the purchase price. Because there is no underlying written contract of sale on which to sue, A has no rights against O.

1) Distinguish—donative escrows [§1617]

In donative escrows, the oral instructions can reasonably be inferred from the facts (delivery on death is almost always the instruction), so relying on the escrow agent's testimony is not dangerous. In commercial escrows, the price cannot be inferred from experience, and it is dangerous to let it depend on the agent's testimony.

(b) Minority contra [§1618]

A minority of courts consider an underlying written contract unnecessary, and will enforce an oral commercial escrow without one.

The textwriters also favor this minority view. *Rationale:* The deed is not a contract of sale but rather a conveyance, and delivery is merely a question of the grantor's intent, which can be proved by parol evidence.

c. Relation-back doctrine [§1619]

In escrow cases, courts often talk about the "first delivery" and the "second delivery." Suppose O executes a deed to A and puts it in escrow with X. The first delivery is when O hands the deed to X; the second delivery is when X hands the deed to A. When a valid delivery in escrow (either donative or commercial) has occurred, it is clear that neither the grantor nor the grantee has full title until the second delivery. Nonetheless, under some rules, legal rights depend on who has "title." To do justice, courts have invented the relation-back doctrine: Although title does not pass to the grantee until the second delivery, upon that delivery title will "relate back" to the first delivery so that the law assumes that it *passed at the first delivery.* The relation-back doctrine is a fiction applied only "where equity and justice require."

(1) Application [§1620]

Assume a valid delivery by O to X of a deed to Blackacre, naming A as grantee, to deliver to A on the occurrence of some condition. The relation-back doctrine applies in the following cases:

(a) Death of grantor [§1621]

Assume O dies after the first delivery. Only a will can pass title at death. To avoid this rule, the relation-back doctrine says title passed during O's life at the first delivery. O's heirs take subject to the grantee's rights.

(b) Incompetency of grantor [§1622]

Assume O becomes incompetent after the first delivery and cannot convey title. Under the relation-back doctrine, title passed at the first delivery, when O was competent.

(c) Creditor of grantor attaches [§1623]

Assume a creditor of O attaches Blackacre after the first delivery. The relation-back doctrine says O did not own Blackacre at the time of attachment, so A prevails over the creditor. *Rationale:* O's creditor should have no greater right than O with respect to the property.

(2) Not applicable as against subsequent bona fide purchaser [§1624]

The relation-back doctrine does *not* apply where the grantor subsequently executes and delivers a deed or mortgage to a bona fide purchaser or mortgagee. If the subsequent purchaser has no knowledge of the deed in escrow, the subsequent purchaser prevails. The person who claims to be a subsequent bona fide purchaser has the burden of showing that he had no notice of the prior escrow and that he gave valuable consideration. [**Hood v. Webster,** 271 N.Y. 57 (1936)]

4. Estoppel of Grantor [§1625]

Although delivery of a deed is required to make it effective, in some cases the grantor may be estopped to deny delivery even though no delivery was intended. These cases involve the grantor's entrusting the deed to another and the other breaching the trust so that a bona fide purchaser—a person without notice of the fact of nondelivery—acquires the land.

a. Delivery to grantee [§1626]

When the grantor gives possession of a deed voluntarily to the grantee (*e.g.,* to examine it), and the grantee violates the grantor's confidence and conveys the land to a bona fide purchaser, the grantor may be estopped to deny delivery. The grantor may be deemed negligent in so entrusting the deed. A rule applied in many situations where there are two honest persons and one dishonest one is: As between two innocent persons (grantor and bona fide purchaser), the one who could have prevented the loss to the other should bear it. Because the grantor could have prevented the loss to the subsequent purchaser by not entrusting the grantee with a deed, the grantor must bear the loss.

b. Delivery in escrow [§1627]

Suppose that the grantor puts a deed into escrow and the grantee wrongfully obtains possession of the deed from the escrow agent. Then the grantee sells the land to a bona fide purchaser who has no knowledge of the fraud. Is the grantor estopped from proving no delivery? The cases are split.

(1) Grantor not estopped [§1628]

Some cases hold that the grantor is not estopped, because the grantor did not intend delivery, and hence the grantor prevails against the bona fide purchaser.

(a) Exception—grantor's knowledge [§1629]

Under this view, however, if the grantee wrongfully obtains possession of the deed and records it, *and the grantor has knowledge of these facts*, the grantor will be estopped against a bona fide purchaser unless the grantor acts to expunge the deed from the record within a reasonable time.

 Example: O delivers a deed to X naming A as grantee. O instructs X to deliver the deed on payment of $10,000. X delivers the deed to A without receiving the $10,000. A records. O is informed of these facts and does nothing. One year later, A conveys to B, a bona fide purchaser who has no notice of O's claim. O is estopped to prove nondelivery, and B prevails. [**Clevenger v. Moore,** 298 P. 248 (Okla. 1931)—grantor estopped when she sat by while grantee recorded deed and went into possession for three months before selling to a bona fide purchaser]

(2) Grantor is estopped [§1630]

Other cases hold that the grantor is estopped against a bona fide purchaser. *Rationale:* Where the custodian is chosen by the grantor, he is the grantor's agent, and the grantor is bound by the acts of his agent. Also, inasmuch as the grantor could have prevented the loss to the bona fide purchaser by selecting a more trustworthy agent, the grantor should suffer the loss. [**Micklethwait v. Fulton,** 196 N.E. 166 (Ohio 1935)]

D. Warranties of Title

1. Covenants of Title [§1631]

Normally, the extent of the seller's liabilities for some defect in title is governed by the covenants of title contained in the deed. If the deed contains no covenants of title, the seller is not liable if title fails. No covenants of title are implied in the deed.

EXAM TIP   **gilbert**

Be careful not to confuse *covenants for title* with *real covenants* (written promises to do or not do something on the land). They are completely different. Real covenants do not relate to title. (*See supra,* §§1188 *et seq.*)

---

a. Types of deeds [§1632]

Various types of deeds are used in the several states to convey interests in property. Some warrant title, some do not. Although some jurisdictions have peculiar local terminology, under standard classification deeds can be divided into three types, depending on the warranties included. These types are: general warranty deeds, special warranty deeds, and quitclaim deeds.

(1) General warranty deed [§1633]

A general warranty deed normally contains the usual covenants (*infra,* §§1637-1643). It warrants title against defects arising *before* as well as *during* the time the grantor had title.

(2) Special warranty deed [§1634]

A special warranty deed also normally contains the usual covenants listed below; however, the warranties cover only defects arising *during the grantor's* tenure, and not defects arising prior to that time. Hence, the grantor guarantees only that *he* has done nothing to make title defective.

---

e.g. **Example:** O, owner of Blackacre, gives A a mortgage on Blackacre. O then forges a release of the mortgage, which is recorded. O then conveys to B by quitclaim deed. B then conveys to C by a special warranty deed. A still holds a valid mortgage on the property. B is not liable to C for the mortgage because B did nothing to make title defective. If B had given C a general warranty deed, B would be liable.

---

(3) Quitclaim deed [§1635]

A quitclaim deed warrants nothing. The grantor merely transfers whatever right, title, or interest he has, if any. A quitclaim deed is useful in clearing an apparent defect in title, where the grantor is not pursuing the claim.

(4) Statutory warranty deeds [§1636]

Statutes in a number of states provide for shortened forms of deeds, and in many cases, specific words of conveyance are deemed to include certain enumerated covenants. For example, the words "grant," "bargain," "convey," or "sell" often, by statute, presumptively connote general warranties of title.

b. Covenants for title in warranty deeds [§1637]

A warranty deed will contain all or most of the following six covenants:

(1) Covenant of seisin [§1638]

The grantor covenants that he owns the estate or interest that he purports to convey.

(2) Covenant of right to convey [§1639]

The grantor covenants that he has the power to make the conveyance. This covenant is satisfied if the grantor has title and is under no disability, or if he is acting as trustee or agent for the owner.

(3) Covenant against encumbrances [§1640]

The grantor covenants that there are no easements, covenants, mortgages, liens, or other encumbrances on the property.

(4) Covenant of quiet enjoyment [§1641]

The grantor covenants that the grantee will not be disturbed in possession or enjoyment of the property by a third party's lawful assertion of superior title.

(5) Covenant of warranty [§1642]

The grantor covenants that he will defend on behalf of the grantee any lawful claims existing at the date of conveyance, and will compensate the grantee for any loss sustained by the assertion of superior title. For all practical purposes, this covenant and the covenant of quiet enjoyment amount to the same thing.

(6) Covenant of further assurances [§1643]

The grantor covenants to perform whatever acts are reasonably necessary to perfect the purchaser's title, if it turns out to be imperfect. This covenant is not much used in the United States, and is often omitted from deeds. It is called a "usual covenant," but in fact it is rather unusual.

c. Merger of contract into deed [§1644]

When the seller and buyer sign a contract for the sale of land, the contract may call for a marketable title or the seller may make various promises with respect to title (*see supra*, §1517). Once the buyer accepts the deed, the usual rule is that the buyer can sue only on the covenants in the deed. Acceptance of the deed discharges the seller from his obligations under the contract. The contract is said to "merge" into the deed. *Rationale:* When the buyer accepts the deed, it is assumed the buyer accepts the deed as containing terms in compliance with the sales contract. The buyer cannot thereafter sue on the contract (although the buyer can sue on an express collateral undertaking not contained in the contract, such as a promise by the seller that "I will have the door fixed"). The merger rule is designed to carry out the assumed intention of the parties. [**Reed v. Hassell,** 340 A.2d 157 (Del. 1975)]

(1) New trend [§1645]

The merger doctrine is now in disfavor because it may not carry out the buyer's intent. It is not applied where a buyer reasonably expects a seller to carry out his contract obligations after the buyer accepts a deed. The usual way of avoiding the merger doctrine is to say that the particular obligation of the seller is an independent obligation not merged (or satisfied) by the deed.

2. Breach of Covenants

a. Covenants of seisin, of right to convey, and against encumbrances [§1646]

These covenants are called *present covenants*. This means that they are breached *when made*, if at all. At the time a covenant of seisin is made, *e.g.*, either the grantor has or does not have title. If he has title, the covenant is not, and can never be, breached. If he does not have title, the covenant is breached when made. Similarly, at the time a covenant against encumbrances is made, either an encumbrance exists (in which case the covenant is broken), or it does not exist (in which case the covenant can never be broken).

(1) What constitutes breach [§1647]

The covenant of seisin is breached if the grantor does not own the interest he purports to convey. The covenant against encumbrances is breached if there is an encumbrance on the property at the time the covenant is made. No eviction or disturbance of the grantee's possession is required to establish a breach.

(a) Grantee's knowledge of defect [§1648]

The usual rule is that covenants of seisin and against encumbrances are breached even though the grantee knew of the defect in title or of the encumbrance. Knowledge of the defect may be the very reason for insisting on a covenant against it. If the grantor does not expressly exclude a defect from the covenants, the grantor is liable for the defect, whether it is known or unknown.

1) Minority views [§1649]

A minority of jurisdictions holds a covenant against encumbrances is not breached if the buyer had actual or constructive knowledge of an *open and visible* encumbrance, such as a railroad easement. The theory is that the parties must have contemplated the continued existence of the encumbrance when they struck their bargain. This theory is not applied to an "invisible" encumbrance such as a mortgage or lien, and it is sometimes limited to public highways and public utility easements. [**Leach v. Gunnarson,** 619 P.2d 263 (Or. 1980)]

(2) Public land use controls [§1650]

The covenant against encumbrances is breached if there is a *private* encumbrance on title, such as an easement or a mortgage. It is not, however, breached by the existence of *public* land use controls, such as zoning ordinances and building codes. Moreover, it is not breached by a latent violation of a public land use control, which the public authorities may never discover or enforce. The buyer assumes the burden of complying with public controls. [**Frimberger v. Anzellotti,** 594 A.2d 1029 (Conn. 1991)]

(3) When breach occurs [§1651]

If there is a breach, it occurs *at the time of the conveyance.* The grantee has an immediate cause of action, and the statute of limitations begins to run immediately. *Note:* The statute of limitations (usually four to six years) begins to run when the present covenant is made. Thus, present covenants offer protection to the grantee only for a limited period of time and cannot be sued upon many years later.

(4) Whether the covenant "runs" [§1652]

If a covenant for title can be enforced against the covenantor by a transferee of the covenantee, it is said to "run with the land." The majority rule is that *present* covenants do *not* run with the land and *cannot* be enforced by remote grantees. At the time of breach, the covenant becomes a chose in action (*i.e.*, a personal right to sue for breach) in the grantee and the *chose in action is not impliedly assigned.* [**Babb v. Weemer,** 225 Cal. App. 2d 546 (1964)]

Example: A purports to convey Blackacre to B by a deed containing a covenant of seisin. In fact, O owns Blackacre. Therefore, the covenant of seisin is breached, and B has a chose in action (a right to sue A). B subsequently purports to convey Blackacre to C. The chose in action is not assigned to C, and C cannot sue A. *Criticism:* The rule developed at a time when choses in action were not assignable, a rule now repudiated. Today there is no reason why the chose in action should not be impliedly assigned from B to C. It is C, after all, who will be in possession when O shows up and who needs the protection of the warranty.

(a) Minority rule [§1653]

In some states, the chose in action is impliedly assigned by the original grantee to a subsequent grantee; thus, in the preceding example, C could sue A. [**Schofield v. Iowa Homestead Co.,** 32 Iowa 317 (1871); **Rockafellor v. Gray,** 191 N.W. 107 (Iowa 1922)]

b. Covenants of quiet enjoyment, warranty, and further assurances [§1654]

These covenants are *future covenants*. This means the covenant is not breached until the grantee is actually or constructively *evicted* sometime in the future.

(1) What constitutes breach [§1655]

A covenant of quiet enjoyment or warranty is breached only when the covenantee is evicted or disturbed in possession. The mere existence of a superior title does not constitute a breach of the covenant, and the grantee has no cause of action if she is not disturbed in some way. [**Brown v. Lober,** 389 N.E.2d 1188 (Ill. 1979)]

(a) Constructive eviction [§1656]

Actual eviction is not necessary for a breach of a future covenant. Constructive eviction will suffice. *Example:* The grantee is constructively evicted if she must buy the superior title to prevent eviction or is enjoined from using the property in violation of a restrictive covenant on the property. If the grantee's right to possession is interfered with by a paramount owner of some interest in the property, the grantee is constructively evicted.

(b) Defending lawsuits [§1657]

A covenantor has the duty of defending against *lawful* superior claims,

COMPARISON OF COVENANTS FOR TITLE IN WARRANTY DEEDS

gilbert

COVENANT	PROMISE	PRESENT OR FUTURE?
COVENANT OF SEISIN	Grantor *owns the estate or interest* he purports to convey	*Present* (*i.e.*, breached when made, if at all)
COVENANT OF RIGHT TO CONVEY	Grantor has the *power to make the conveyance* (*i.e.*, grantor has title and is under no disability or is acting as trustee or agent for the owner)	*Present*
COVENANT AGAINST ENCUMBRANCES	There are *no easements, covenants, mortgages, liens, or other encumbrances* on the property	*Present*
COVENANT OF QUIET ENJOYMENT	The grantee will *not be disturbed* in possession or enjoyment of the property by *a third party's lawful assertion of superior title*	*Future* (*i.e.*, covenant not breached until the grantee is actually or constructively evicted)
COVENANT OF WARRANTY	*Grantor will defend* on behalf of the grantee any lawful claims existing at the date of conveyance *and will compensate* the grantee for any loss sustained by the assertion of superior title	*Future*
COVENANT OF FURTHER ASSURANCES	*Grantor will perform* whatever acts are reasonably necessary *to perfect the purchaser's title* if it turns out to be imperfect	*Future*

but he has no duty to defend title against a wrongful claim by a third party. Refusal to defend against unlawful claims does not breach the covenant. The burden is thus put on the grantee to defend all claims; she can recover against the covenantor only if she loses. If she wins, she may be out a large sum of money in legal fees, but she cannot recover these from the covenantor. If the grantee loses, she can recover from the covenantor damages plus legal fees. The covenantor is not bound by the result of the lawsuit, however, unless the covenantee gives the covenantor notice of a lawsuit brought by an adverse claimant and requests the covenantor to defend it. Thus, in any litigation by a third party claiming paramount title, a covenantee should notify the covenantor and give him a chance to defend. If the covenantee does so, the covenantor will be bound by the result.

(2) When breach occurs [§1658]

A future covenant is not breached, and the statute of limitations does not begin to run, until the covenantee is disturbed in possession. This may be many years after the covenant is made. After the statute of limitations has run on present covenants (which are breached, if at all, when made), the grantee of a general warranty deed is protected only by the future covenants. If the grantee then discovers some defect in title, the grantee must wait until eviction to sue. (In the meantime, the covenantor may die, and the covenantee may not be able to sue anyone on later eviction.)

(3) Whether covenant runs [§1659]

A future covenant runs with the land if there is *privity of estate* between the original grantor-covenantor and the remote grantee. In this context, "privity of estate" means that the covenantor conveyed either *title or possession* to his grantee, who conveyed it to the remote grantee. The covenant attaches to the fee simple estate or the possessory estate and runs with it to subsequent grantees.

(a) No estate transferred [§1660]

If the grantor did not convey either title or possession, there is no "estate" (neither "fee simple estate" nor "possessory estate") to which the covenant can attach. In that case, in theory the covenant will not run. There must be an "estate" with which the covenant runs—or so goes the ancient metaphor.

> **Example:** Blackacre is unoccupied forest land owned by O. In 1994, A executes and delivers a deed of Blackacre to B with a covenant of warranty. In 1996, B quitclaims her interest in Blackacre to C. In 1999, C attempts to enter Blackacre but is prevented from doing so by O. C can recover from A only if there is privity of estate between them. However, because A had neither title nor possession, there is no privity and C cannot recover from A.

(b) Criticism [§1661]

The requirement of having an "estate" for the covenant to run with is purely metaphorical and makes no sense. Inasmuch as C can sue A if Blackacre is a house occupied successively by B and C, no reason appears why C cannot sue A if Blackacre is unpossessed land. Endowed with great powers of imagination in finding an "estate," some modern courts have found that A does indeed transfer an "interest" to B. The interest may be B's right, under the doctrine of estoppel by deed (*see infra*, §1671), to receive any title to Blackacre that A might subsequently acquire. Or the "interest" transferred by A may be the "constructive possession" of the land which arises when the grantor has apparent record title. Thus does legal fiction come to the rescue of a metaphor taken too literally. [**Solberg v. Robinson,** 147 N.W. 87 (S.D. 1914)]

c. Damages for breach [§1662]

The basic remedy for breach of contract is an award of damages, and the basic principle used in ascertaining those damages is that the injured party should be put into as good a position as she would have been had the contract been performed. In other words, the injured party is entitled to the benefit of the bargain. This principle has never been applied consistently to damages for breach of covenants of title. Courts have developed different rules, largely because of the expectations of the parties, notions of fairness, and the perceived difficulty of establishing the market value of land.

(1) Basic limitation [§1663]

Except in a few New England states, the grantee cannot recover more than the covenantor received as consideration. The amount received by the covenantor (in most cases the purchase price) sets the maximum liability of the covenantor. When land increases sharply in value, or the grantee improves it, the loss to the grantee on eviction several years after purchase may be far greater than the amount of the purchase price. Under this maximum liability rule, the grantee is certainly not in as good a position as she would be if the covenant had not been breached. Nonetheless, courts, believing that it would be unfair or not in accordance with the covenantor's expectations, refuse to require the covenantor to reimburse the grantee for her improvements or capital appreciation lost. If the covenantor had to pay the value of the land at the time of recovery (giving the grantee the benefit of the bargain), the resulting liability might be huge and wipe out a covenantor who received a small amount for the land.

(a) Gifts and exchanges [§1664]

If the land is a gift by the covenantor to the grantee, some courts allow no recovery for breach. Others allow the grantee to recover the market value of the land at the time the covenant is made. In case of exchange of land, the maximum liability is the market value of the land given up by the grantee.

(b) Interest [§1665]

Interest on the purchase price may be awarded to the grantee, but there is a conflict as to whether interest should be given from the date the covenant is made or only from time of eviction. Where the grantee has been in possession, some courts deny interest on the theory that possession of the land is the equivalent of interest on the purchase price. It unjustly enriches the grantee to give her both possession and interest. Other courts give the grantee interest on the theory that the grantee in possession is liable to the paramount owner for the fair rental value of the land, and interest is an approximate compensation for that liability. Of course, the paramount owner may not sue within the period of the statute of limitations, and under this solution, the grantee may end up with interest and no liability to the paramount owner. [**Hilliker v. Rueger,** 228 N.Y. 11 (1920)]

(2) Present covenants

(a) Covenant of seisin [§1666]

If title to the entire tract fails, the grantee is entitled to recover the full purchase price. If the grantee recovers, the grantee must reconvey her possessory interest to the covenantor. The grantee may decide not to sue on the covenant of seisin and to stay in possession until evicted, when she can sue on the covenant of general warranty. If the grantee stays in possession long enough, she may acquire title by adverse possession.

EXAM TIP   **gilbert**

Watch out for fact patterns in which the grantor sells an unimproved lot (*e.g.,* for $50,000), the grantee builds a house on the lot (*e.g.,* for $200,000), and a few years later the true owner of the lot comes forward. Although the grantor has breached the covenant of seisin, remember the grantee will bear a substantial loss here because in most states the grantee's recovery is *limited to the amount he paid* the grantor.

---

1) Partial breach [§1667]

If title to only part of the land fails, the grantee is entitled to recover as damages a proportionate part of the purchase price commensurate with the value of the land to which title fails. [**Knudson v. Weeks,** 394 F. Supp. 963 (D. Okla. 1975); **Hillsboro Cove, Inc. v. Archibald,** 322 So. 2d 585 (Fla. 1975)] Or, if the portion to which the grantee received title is not a usable parcel of land, the grantee can rescind and recover the entire purchase price. The grantee must give up possession of the portion to which title failed in order to recover more than nominal damages. [*But see* **Hilliker v. Rueger**, *supra*—grantee can recover damages and remain in possession (which seems unfair to the covenantor, for possession is a valuable right that can ripen into title)]

(b) Covenant against encumbrances [§1668]

Where a covenant against encumbrances is breached by the existence of a restrictive covenant or easement or other encumbrance not removable by the grantee, damages are the difference in value, at the date of sale, of the land with the encumbrance and the value of the land without it (subject to the maximum liability stated above). If, however, the grantee has the right to remove the encumbrance for a specific amount, such as paying off a mortgage, the measure of damages is the amount spent to remove the encumbrance. If the grantee does not remove a removable encumbrance, the grantee is entitled only to nominal damages unless she can prove actual damage by selling the property for less than market value. This rule is designed to induce the grantee to pay off the mortgage and establish damages clearly, thus avoiding speculative damages. [**McGuckin v. Milbank**, 152 N.Y. 297 (1897)]

(3) Future covenants [§1669]

For breach of a future covenant, which usually takes place some years after the covenant is made, the grantee is entitled to recover the consideration paid, or the amount spent in buying up a paramount claim, if reasonable. The grantee is not entitled to the value of the land at the time of eviction. Of course, the amount of the purchase price is the maximum liability of the covenantor.

(a) Suit by remote grantee [§1670]

When a remote grantee sues the covenantor, the courts have split on the measure of damages. The question arises whether the remote grantee should recover the amount received by the covenantor or, if she pays less, the amount paid by the remote grantee. One view is to give the remote grantee her actual damages (what she paid), but not exceeding the amount received by the covenantor. [**Taylor v. Wallace**, 37 P. 963 (Colo. 1894)] Another view takes the position that, because the basic measure of damages deprives the remote grantee of the value of the land at the time of eviction, the remote grantee should recover the amount received by the covenantor even though the consideration paid by the remote grantee was less. The covenantor is stripped of his profit, which goes to compensate in a rough way the grantee, who is unfairly treated by the basic rule set forth *supra* at §1663.

Example: Blackacre is owned by O. A conveys Blackacre to B by general warranty deed for $10,000. Subsequently, B conveys Blackacre to C by general warranty deed for $5,000. O ousts C. C can sue B for $5,000, or C can sue A. Under the first view set forth above, C can recover only $5,000 from A. Under the second view, C can recover $10,000 from A.

---

3. Estoppel by Deed [§1671]

Where a grantor purports to convey an estate in property that he does not then own, if the grantor subsequently acquires title, the title passes by operation of law to the grantee under the earlier deed. By executing a deed without title, the grantor is deemed impliedly to have covenanted that, when he obtains title, he will immediately convey it to the grantee. The doctrine of estoppel gives the grantee the thing bargained for, the land itself—and not merely damages.

Example: A, having no title (or a defective title), purports to convey a good title to B. Subsequently, A receives a good title from O. Under the doctrine of estoppel by deed, A is estopped to assert that he had no title at the time of his deed to B and therefore B did not take any title. Rather, A's after-acquired title inures to the benefit of B, and B owns the property. [**Robben v. Obering,** 279 F.2d 381 (7th Cir. 1960); **Schwenn v. Kaye,** 155 Cal. App. 3d 949 (1984)]

---

a. Application [§1672]

Originally, the doctrine of estoppel developed as an outgrowth of the covenants for title in a warranty deed. If A executed a warranty deed without title, A would be liable to B on the covenants of warranty. But if A later obtained title, it would avoid unnecessary litigation, and give B what B bargained for, to hold that A's title inured to B, rather than to force B to sue A for specific performance. Although originally applied to warranty deeds only, the doctrine has been applied in modern cases to quitclaim deeds that expressly purport to convey a fee simple. It is a doctrine to carry out probable intent, and if the parties thought the grantor was conveying title, the doctrine will be applied to carry any after-acquired title to the grantee.

b. Subsequent purchasers from grantor [§1673]

Whether estoppel by deed applies, so that the grantee prevails over subsequent purchasers from the grantor, is discussed in connection with the recording system, *infra*, §§1770-1772.

E. Warranties of Quality

1. Builder's Liability [§1674]

At common law, the builder of houses had no liability to the buyer, absent an express warranty. Caveat emptor was the rule. In the last 30 years, influenced by the development of implied warranties in sales of personal property and in leases, the law has changed. In almost all jurisdictions, courts now imply a *warranty of quality* in the sale of new homes. The builder impliedly warrants that the building is free from defective materials and is constructed in a sound and workmanlike manner. *Rationale:* The builder's greater ability to prevent defects, the home buyer's reliance on the builder's skill, the unequal bargaining power of the parties, and the importance to society of soundly constructed housing justify imposing on the builder liability for defects. [**Petersen v. Hubschman Construction Co.,** 389 N.E.2d 1154 (Ill. 1979); **Lempke v. Dagenais,** 547 A.2d 290 (N.H. 1988); **McDonald v. Mianecki,** 398 A.2d 1283 (N.J. 1979)] Important issues respecting the warranty remain to be worked out; the more important are mentioned below.

a. Tort or contract? [§1675]

The implied warranty of quality is a hybrid, resting on both tort and contract theory with confusing and inconsistent results. If tort theory is applied: the warranty is a duty imposed by public policy; it runs to all persons who buy the product; liability cannot be waived or disclaimed by a provision in the sales contract or conveyance; and the statute of limitations runs from the time of the discovery of the defect. On the other hand, if contract theory is applied: the implied warranty arises from the bargain; it runs only to those in privity of contract with the builder; it can be disclaimed by a provision in the conveyance; and the statute of limitations begins to run from the date of the conveyance. The courts have not consistently applied either theory; the implied warranty has developed more or less on an ad hoc basis.

b. Subsequent purchasers [§1676]

Subsequent purchasers of a house may have difficulty in recovering from the builder on a contract theory because of lack of privity of contract. On a tort theory, they may have difficulty recovering because both negligence liability and strict liability in tort are usually limited to physical injury and not mere economic loss. Nonetheless, because the builder is placing a defective house in the stream of commerce, and owes a duty of care to those who subsequently buy it, about half the courts that have considered the question have held that the builder has liability to subsequent purchasers regardless of any lack of privity. [**Richards v. Powercraft Homes, Inc.,** 678 P.2d 427 (Ariz. 1984); **Redarowicz v. Ohlendorf,** 441 N.E.2d 324 (Ill. 1982); **Oates v. Jag, Inc.,** 333 S.E.2d 222 (N.C. 1985)]

c. Disclaimer [§1677]

In a few cases, courts have permitted the implied warranty of quality to be disclaimed or waived by the buyer if the language of the contract is clear and unambiguous. [**Tyus v. Resta,** 476 A.2d 427 (Pa. 1984); **G-W-L, Inc. v. Robichaux,** 643 S.W.2d 392 (Tex. 1982)] The effect of the first buyer's disclaimer on the rights of a subsequent purchaser who does not know of the disclaimer is not settled.

d. Commercial buildings [§1678]

The cases so far have implied a warranty of quality *only* in the sale of housing, but in the future the warranty may be extended to sale of commercial buildings, just as the implied warranty of habitability has been extended from leases of rental housing to leases of commercial buildings (*see supra*, §882). At least one case has made a modest step in the direction of implying the warranty of quality in the case of a commercial building. [**Hodgson v. Chin,** 403 A.2d 942 (N.J. 1979)]

EXAM TIP	gilbert

The implied *warranty of quality* is an important warranty to remember when you see an exam fact pattern involving a new home that has substantial defects. But it is equally important to remember the *warranty's limitations*: It does *not* apply in the sale of commercial buildings or used homes; some courts allow the warranty to be disclaimed (although the disclaimer must be clear); and half the courts that have ruled on the issue have found that the warranty protection does not extend to subsequent purchasers.

2. Seller's Liability [§1679]

The seller of a used house who is not a builder has no liability based on an implied warranty of quality. Nonetheless, the seller is liable for misrepresentation and fraud. If the seller knowingly makes any false statement to the buyer as to some fact that materially affects the value of the premises to the buyer, and the buyer relies on the statement in purchasing, the buyer is entitled to relief. Similarly, the seller is liable for defective conditions that the seller has concealed. The traditional view is that the seller is not liable for failure to disclose defective conditions, but this view is changing in most states. Modern cases hold that the seller must disclose known defects that are not readily discoverable by the buyer, such as termites or roof leaks. [**Johnson v. Davis,** *supra,* §1532] The law in this area is moving in the direction of requiring the seller to divulge all known information that has a significant and measurable impact on market value.

F. The Mortgage

1. Why a Mortgage Is Used [§1680]

Most people do not have cash available to pay for the real property they are purchasing. They must go to a lender and borrow money. The lender—usually a bank or savings and loan association—has money to lend at the market rate of interest. If the borrower is an acceptable credit risk (has a job, pays bills on time, etc.), the lender will lend money to the borrower, to be paid back with interest over time. To secure the debt owed the lender, the borrower will give the lender a mortgage on the property. If the debt is not paid, the lender will "foreclose the mortgage." Foreclosing the mortgage means that the property will be sold, and from the proceeds the lender will be paid the amount of the debt and anything left will be given to the borrower. Mortgages are extremely useful in real estate transactions because they enable persons without capital to borrow capital from others and acquire real property for themselves. *Caveat:* In a brief synopsis such as is set forth here, only the general outline of mortgage law can be given. Although the outline is accurate, a detailed treatment would include numerous qualifications. Mortgage law is complex, and there are many local variations. The purpose of this synopsis is to give you information sufficient for an understanding of the mortgage problems that arise in a first-year property course.

2. Nature of the Mortgage Transaction [§1681]

The mortgage transaction consists of two documents: (i) the note and (ii) the mortgage. A *note* is a document that evidences the debt: "I, Borrower, promise to pay Lender $10,000 on June 1, 2005, with interest to be paid annually at 10% per annum." The note is a personal obligation of the borrower, and the lender can sue the borrower on the note if the borrower does not pay. The note is sometimes called the debtor's *bond.* The second document is the *mortgage.* It is the agreement that the land will be sold if the debt is not paid and the lender reimbursed from the proceeds of sale. The mortgage gives the lender *security.* In case of default on the note, the lender does not have recourse only against the general assets of the borrower—which may be few. The mortgage gives the lender recourse against the land. Thus, the lender's risk is limited; only if on foreclosure the land sells for less than the debt will the lender lose money. The mortgage ordinarily will be *recorded* in the county courthouse at the time it is given, which recordation will give the lender priority over subsequent purchasers of the land. Once the mortgage is recorded, any subsequent purchaser or creditor takes subject to the mortgage.

EXAM TIP   **gilbert**

Although we say two documents are involved in a mortgage transaction in order to emphasize the difference between the *note* and the *mortgage,* in many states, only one document is used. This one document contains **both** the note and the mortgage. You may encounter only one document on an exam, just be sure to recognize both elements.

---

3. Terminology [§1682]

Before discussing the law of mortgages, it is useful to define some of the common terms used in mortgage law.

a. Mortgagor [§1683]

The borrower or debtor is the mortgagor. Where a person buys land and gives a mortgage on the land to a lender, the buyer is the mortgagor.

b. Mortgagee [§1684]

The lender is the mortgagee.

c. Equity [§1685]

The borrower's interest in the land is called the equity (short for equity of redemption). This word came into common usage historically because it referred to the interest of the debtor protected by equity courts (*see infra*, §1693).

d. Deficiency judgment [§1686]
If, on foreclosure sale, the land does not bring enough to pay the debt, the lender can sue the borrower on the note for the deficiency. A judgment for this deficiency, collectible out of the general assets of the borrower, is called a deficiency judgment.

e. Purchase money mortgage [§1687]
A mortgage given to secure the purchase price of land is called a purchase money mortgage. If the borrower already owns the land and gives a mortgage to secure a debt, this mortgage is not a purchase money mortgage. If the debt is incurred to finance improvement of a house, the mortgage will be a *home improvement* mortgage.

f. Balloon payment mortgage [§1688]
A balloon payment mortgage is one that calls for periodic interest payments until the due date of the debt, when the *whole principal sum* must be paid at once. *Example:* Bank lends A $10,000, due in five years, with interest at 10% per year. At the end of each of the first four years, A must pay the bank $1,000 interest. At the end of the fifth year, A must pay the bank $1,000 plus $10,000 (the principal).

g. Amortized payment mortgage [§1689]
The typical home mortgage is not a balloon payment mortgage, but a mortgage for 25 or 30 years with even monthly payments over the period. The last monthly payment, in the same amount as the earlier ones, pays off the mortgage. There is no balloon payment at the end. The monthly payments are calculated so as to return principal as well as interest to the lender over the period of the mortgage.

h. Second mortgage [§1690]
More than one mortgage can be given on a tract of land. A mortgage given second in time, with notice of the earlier mortgage, is called a second mortgage. The second mortgagee's rights are *subject to* the rights of the first mortgagee. If the first mortgagee forecloses a mortgage debt of $20,000, *e.g.*, and the land sells for $15,000, all the proceeds go to the first mortgagee. The second mortgagee has a right to the proceeds only after the first mortgagee is paid off. As a result, second mortgages are riskier than first mortgages and command a higher interest rate.

i. Deed of trust [§1691]
In a large number of states, particularly in the South and West, the mortgage takes the form of a deed of trust. Instead of the borrower giving the lender a mortgage, the borrower gives the lender a deed of trust. By this arrangement the borrower transfers title to a third person *as trustee* for the lender to secure the debt. (The third person is often the nominee of the lender.) If the

debt is not paid, the trustee sells the land under a power of sale in the trust deed, pays off the debt, and pays over to the borrower anything left. The essential difference between a mortgage and a deed of trust relates to the power to sell the land on default. In some jurisdictions, the mortgagee must resort to *judicial foreclosure*, which is time-consuming and costly; a clause in the mortgage giving the mortgagee power to sell the land on default, without going through judicial proceedings, is void. In other jurisdictions, if the mortgage gives the mortgagee a *power of sale*, the power of sale is valid. The mortgagee can foreclose by his own public sale after notice to all parties, avoiding judicial foreclosure, but—at least in earlier times—the mortgagee could not bid on the property at the sale (thought to be self-dealing). To avoid judicial foreclosure and the rule that a mortgagee could not bid at his own sale, the deed of trust was invented. Under the deed of trust, on default by the buyer and request by the lender, the trustee can sell the land at a public sale out of court and the lender can bid at the trustee's sale.

(1) Note

Modern statutes now permit the mortgagee to bid at his own sale when he has a power of sale, and have largely eliminated the difference between a deed of trust and a mortgage with power of sale. In other respects, the rights of the borrower under a deed of trust are practically the same as under a mortgage.

j. Installment land contract [§1692]

An installment land contract is an agreement by the buyer to buy land and to pay for it over a period of years—maybe 10 or 20 years. In the contract, the seller agrees to deliver title at the end of the period. The buyer goes into possession, and the seller keeps title until the final payment. Keeping title is the seller's security. The installment land contract was once thought to have two particular advantages for a seller: (i) the seller can repossess on default without going through judicial foreclosure; and (ii) the seller can keep all payments made under the contract as damages on the buyer's default. However, the installment land contract functions as a mortgage, and courts more and more are extending the traditional rights of a mortgagor to the buyer under an installment land contract. The history of mortgage law is that equity stepped in to relieve borrowers from unconscionable contracts drafted by lenders and to give borrowers rights they could not contract away, and this history is now repeating itself with installment land contracts. [*See* **Skendzel v. Marshall**, 301 N.E.2d 641 (Ind. 1973)—holding installment land contract should be treated like a mortgage and judicial foreclosure required; forfeiture of payments is limited to situations where equitable (*i.e.*, where roughly equal to fair rental value); **Bean v. Walker**, 95 A.D.2d 70 (1983)—same; **Stonebraker v. Zinn**, 286 S.E.2d 911 (W. Va. 1982); *and see* **Union Bond & Trust Co. v. Blue Creek Redwood Co.**, 128 F. Supp. 709 (N.D. Cal. 1955)—buyer has right to make payments in default and continue contract, in effect giving buyer an equity of redemption; **Sebastian v. Floyd**, 585 S.W.2d 381 (Ky. 1979)]

4. History of the Mortgage [§1693]

To better secure the debts owed, money lenders in England by the seventeenth century had invented the ancestor of the modern mortgage. The lender insisted that the borrower convey the land *in fee simple* to the lender, *subject to a condition subsequent*: If the loan was repaid on the agreed date, the lender would reconvey the fee simple to the borrower. This condition subsequent was called a "proviso for redemption." The agreement was strictly enforced by the law courts, and if the borrower could not pay (redeem the land) *on the agreed date*, the land could never be redeemed. On default, the mortgagee was the absolute owner. Equity, however, viewed that result as excessively harsh on the borrower, who might, for good reason, be unable to present himself at the lender's office with the money on the due date. Equity intervened to give borrowers a right to redeem *at any time*, even years after the agreed date. Equity took the position that the borrower should be treated as the owner in equity, and the mortgage should be deemed no more than a device to secure the debt. This right to redeem was called "the equity of redemption." Because the right to redeem without limitation of time made it very difficult for the lender to sell the land upon default, equity gave the lender the right to *foreclose the right of redemption*. (Note that today we speak of "foreclosing the mortgage," but technically we mean "foreclosing the equity of redemption.") Foreclosure is a judicial proceeding that orders the property sold at public sale, the equity of redemption barred, the debt paid, and any excess proceeds given to the mortgagor.

a. Equitable mortgage [§1694]

Sometimes lenders try to avoid the protection equity has extended to borrowers by devious procedures. A lender, rather like the early English lenders, may insist on the borrower giving the lender a deed to the land in fee simple, with a lease back to the borrower with an option to repurchase. Or the lender may insist on a deed to the lender in fee simple absolute, and the lender promises to return the deed when the debt is paid. Courts have been astute to look through these forms to the *substance* of the transaction; when they find the parties intended the land to be security for a debt, they have declared the deed or other conveyance to be an *equitable mortgage—i.e.,* in equity, it will be *treated as a mortgage*. Extrinsic evidence is admissible to show the intent of the parties. [**Mid-State Investment Corp. v. O'Steen,** 133 So. 2d 455 (Fla. 1961); **Koenig v. Van Reken,** 279 N.W.2d 590 (Mich. 1979)]

EXAM TIP　　　　　　　　　　　　　　　　　　　　　**gilbert**

Equitable mortgages seem to fascinate some professors. Although the concept might seem obscure, don't be surprised to see an equitable mortgage issue arise in an exam fact pattern. Watch for facts where a landowner borrows money from a "friend" and repays (i) all of the loan and the friend refuses to reconvey, or (ii) part of the loan and the friend wants to take the property to satisfy the debt even though the value of the property exceeds the debt. Remember to mention that because the parties transferred the deed *only to serve as security* for an obligation, the court will treat the deed as a mortgage. Thus, the friend will have to reconvey if the loan has been paid or *follow normal foreclosure procedures* if the loan has not been repaid in full.

---

b. Statutory period of redemption [§1695]

In many states, by *statute* borrowers have a period of time *after judicial foreclosure* during which they can redeem from the purchaser at foreclosure sale. A two-year period is typical. These statutes were enacted to protect debtors by giving them more time to come up with the money and save their property. Do not confuse the *statutory right to redeem* the property from the purchaser at the foreclosure sale with the *judicially created equity of redemption*, which is cut off at the foreclosure sale.

5. Theory of the Mortgage [§1696]

Because the historical form of a mortgage purported to give title to the lender, with an equity of redemption in the borrower, the early American cases—from eastern states—treated legal title as being in the mortgagee. States adopting this theory are known as *title theory* states. Later cases—principally from the West—looked through form to substance and declared that legal title remained in the mortgagor and the mortgagee had merely a *lien* on the property to secure the debt. States adopting this theory are known as *lien theory* states. (Note that even in lien theory states, however, the mortgagor's interest is still known as "the equity.")

a. Difference in theories [§1697]

In almost all cases, these two theories do not lead to different results between the borrower and lender. Although courts may say they are title theory states, they in fact treat the mortgage as in substance a lien.

6. Transfer of the Mortgagor's Interest

a. Sale subject to the mortgage [§1698]

The mortgagor can transfer his interest ("the equity") *subject to the mortgage*. If the sale is "subject to the mortgage," the new buyer takes the land subject to the lien on it, but the new buyer is *not personally liable on the debt*. If the debt is not paid, the mortgagee can foreclose on the land, but the mortgagee cannot sue the new buyer on the debt. Thus, the mortgagee cannot get a deficiency judgment against the buyer who takes "subject to the mortgage." The original mortgagor remains liable on the debt, of course.

b. Sale with assumption of the mortgage [§1699]

The mortgagor can transfer his interest to a new buyer who assumes the mortgage. If the new buyer "assumes the mortgage," she becomes personally liable on the debt. The mortgagee can sue either the new buyer or the original mortgagor on the debt (as between them, the new buyer is primarily liable). Both are subject to a deficiency judgment if, upon foreclosure sale, the land does not bring a sum sufficient to discharge the debt. If the mortgagee elects to sue the original mortgagor on the debt, the mortgagor in turn can sue the new buyer, who assumed the mortgage, for the debt or foreclose upon the land.

	PURCHASE "SUBJECT TO" MORTGAGE	"ASSUMPTION" OF MORTGAGE
EXAMPLE	The buyer of a house agrees to buy the seller's house subject to the mortgage debt but does not assume the seller's mortgage debt	The buyer of a house agrees to assume the seller's mortgage debt
CAN THE MORTGAGEE SUE THE BUYER?	No	Yes
CAN THE MORTGAGEE FORECLOSE ON THE MORTGAGE LIEN AND SELL THE PROPERTY?	Yes	Yes

"SUBJECT TO" MORTGAGE VS. "ASSUMPTION OF" MORTGAGE — gilbert

c. **Due-on-sale clauses [§1700]**

Lenders often insert due-on-sale clauses in their mortgages. A due-on-sale clause provides that, at the mortgagee's election, the *entire mortgage debt is due on sale* of the mortgagor's interest. In other words, the mortgagee can accelerate the due date if the land is sold, requiring payment of the mortgage at that time. The purpose of this clause is twofold: (i) by requiring the lender's consent to assign the mortgage, the lender is protected against assignment to an unsatisfactory credit risk; and (ii) when the market interest rate rises, the clause permits the mortgagee to force the new buyer to refinance at a prevailing higher rate of interest. Federal law, preempting state law, holds that due-on-sale clauses are valid and enforceable. [**Fidelity Federal Savings & Loan Association v. de la Cuesta,** 458 U.S. 141 (1982); **McCausland v. Bankers Life Insurance Co.,** 757 P.2d 941 (Wash. 1988)]

7. **Default by the Mortgagor [§1701]**

On default by the mortgagor, the mortgagee can sue on the debt or foreclose on the mortgage. In a minority of states, the mortgagee must foreclose the mortgage and exhaust the security before suing on the debt. After either a judicial foreclosure or a sale under a power of sale in the mortgage, the mortgagee can get a deficiency judgment against the mortgagor for the difference between the amount of the debt and the amount realized from the sale. The mortgagor has been given various remedies against price inadequacy on foreclosure sale. The inadequacy may result from depressed real estate prices or from the fact that few bidders were at the sale. At many sales, the mortgagee is the only bidder.

FINANCING

Buyer finances purchase of land using the land as collateral. Usually done by giving lender a mortgage on the property, although it could be done with a deed of trust, installment land contract, absolute deed, or sale-leaseback.

DEFAULT

Mortgagor-borrower defaults. Mortgagee has right to foreclose. Up until the foreclosure sale, borrower may redeem by paying off mortgage and accrued interest (*equitable redemption*).

FORECLOSURE

Foreclosure must be by sale, usually judicial sale.

Proceeds distributed according to priority of security interests.

POST-FORECLOSURE

If the proceeds of the sale are insufficient to satisfy the debt, the mortgagee can bring a personal action against the borrower for deficiency.

Many states give the borrower a right to redeem for a fixed period (*e.g.*, two years) after fore-closure by paying the sale price (*statutory redemption*).

a. Legislation [§1702]

To protect the mortgagor in default, legislatures in some states have enacted various kinds of legislation.

(1) Fair market value limitations [§1703]

A statute may provide that the mortgagee can get a deficiency judgment only for the difference between the debt and the judicially determined fair market value of the property at foreclosure. This legislation is designed to protect the mortgagor from foreclosure sales in the time of depressed real estate prices.

(2) Anti-deficiency judgment [§1704]

A few states have legislation prohibiting the mortgagee from getting a deficiency judgment on purchase money mortgages. This legislation was usually enacted in the Great Depression, after persons had bought real estate in the 1920s in various promotion schemes.

(3) Statutory right of redemption [§1705]

The statutory right of redemption after foreclosure has been discussed *supra* (§1695). Under this statutory right, the mortgagor can in some states stay in possession until the redemption period has expired.

b. Judicial decisions [§1706]

Courts have set aside foreclosure sales for inadequacy of price where the price is so low as to shock the conscience of the court. And they may scrutinize the sale to make certain that proper notice was given and other safeguards complied with. [**Central Financial Services, Inc. v. Spears,** 425 So. 2d 403 (Miss. 1983)] Or the court may hold that a private foreclosure sale must use commercially reasonable methods for producing a fair price. [**Murphy v. Financial Development Corp.,** 495 A.2d 1245 (N.H. 1985)]

Chapter Eleven: Title Assurance

CONTENTS

Chapter Approach

Chapter Approach

Four methods of title assurance are used in the United States:

1. *Grantor's express warranties of title contained in deed*—this is the oldest method, inherited from the English (and discussed *supra*, §§1631 *et seq.*).

2. *System of recording land titles*—this involves an actual search of public records in the county recorder's office. Each state has some kind of recording system.

3. *Title registration* (sometimes called *Torrens system*)—this is available in only a few states and registers title to land, rather than evidence of title (as with recording statutes).

4. *Title insurance*—this method is increasing in use and insures good title, *i.e.*, insures the accuracy of the records by agreeing to defend the record title if litigated.

Title assurance questions often are found in fact situations where the landowner conveys the property to one person and later conveys it again to another. To determine the rights of the parties in this situation (or in any other title assurance question), consider:

1. The *language* of the recording act (race, notice, race-notice) or registration statute.

2. Whether any party has bona fide purchaser status (*i.e.*, a *purchaser or mortgagee* who had *no* actual, record, or inquiry *notice* at the time he gave *consideration*).

3. The effect of any *unrecorded or unregistered* instruments, any *errors* in recording or registration, and who bears the *costs* of those errors (grantor, grantee, title insurer).

A. Recording System

1. Common Law Rule—Prior in Time [§1707]

All states today have recording acts providing for recordation of documents affecting land title. These acts are designed to protect bona fide purchasers of land from secret unrecorded claims. Prior to these acts, the common law rule gave legal effect to conveyances in accordance with the time of execution. Thus, a grantee who was *prior in time* prevailed over one subsequent in time. For example, if O conveyed Blackacre to A, and later O conveyed Blackacre to B (who knew nothing of A's deed), A prevailed over B on the theory that O had conveyed title to A and had nothing left to convey to B. Under this rule, the purchase of land was risky, because B had no reliable way to assure that there was no prior deed. The recording acts now give B a way of discovering A's prior deed.

a. Exception in equity [§1708]

Equity, noting that the legal rule tended to encourage fraud, developed one important exception to the "prior in time" rule. If the prior interest was *equitable*, and therefore within the jurisdiction of the equity court, equity would not enforce it against a subsequent purchaser of a *legal* interest who did not know of the prior equitable interest and paid valuable consideration. Thus, suppose that O contracts to sell Blackacre to A; under the doctrine of equitable conversion, the contract gives A equitable title (*see supra*, §1547). Later O conveys legal title to Blackacre to B, and B is a purchaser for value who has no notice of A's equitable interest. The subsequent conveyance to B cuts off the prior equity in A. This was called the equitable doctrine of bona fide purchaser.

2. Recording Acts—In General [§1709]

In many cases, allowing the first grantee to prevail encouraged fraudulent acts by a grantor and imposed losses on innocent subsequent grantees. Consequently, as early as the Massachusetts Bay Colony in the seventeenth century, statutes were enacted in this country to require some sort of recordation to give "notice to the world" that title to property had been conveyed, and thus to put subsequent purchasers on guard. In general, such statutes set up a system that permits the recordation in each county of any deed (or other instrument affecting title) to property located in that county.

EXAM TIP   **gilbert**

Keep in mind that recordation is only an issue when there is *more than one grantee* contesting title. Recordation is not essential to the validity of a deed as between the grantor and the grantee. However, if a grantee does not record the instrument, he may lose out against other purchasers from his grantor.

---

3. Mechanics of Recording [§1710]

The following is a brief description of how the recording system works. Although a deed is used as an illustration, other instruments affecting title to land, such as mortgages, can also be recorded.

a. Filing copy [§1711]

The grantee or grantee's agent presents the deed to the county recorder, who stamps the date and time of filing thereon and makes a copy (usually a photocopy or microfilm). The recorder files this copy in an official "deed book," which contains copies of prior recorded deeds. After the official copy is made, the original deed is returned to the grantee.

b. Indexing [§1712]

The recorder *indexes* the deed by entering a notation in the "index book" showing in which deed book the deed can be found reproduced in full. Just as the card or online catalog is the key to finding books in a library, the index is used to find the deed in subsequent title searches. The usual index system includes an index for grantors and an index for grantees; tract indexes exist in a few localities.

(1) Grantor and grantee indexes [§1713]

Separate index volumes are maintained for grantors and grantees, enabling a title searcher to locate an instrument by searching under either the grantor's name or the grantee's name. In the grantor index, entries are made chronologically, as instruments are filed, under the name of the grantors, listed alphabetically. The entry will include first the grantor's name, then the name of the grantee, then a description of the property and the type of instrument, and finally a reference to the volume and page of the deed books where the recorder's copy of the instrument can be found. The grantee index will contain the identical information, except that it will be entered alphabetically under the name of the grantee.

(2) Tract index [§1714]

In urban areas where land has been platted and broken down into blocks and lots, the recording office may keep a tract index. Entries are made under block and lot number. All instruments are indexed on a page that deals only with the lot to which the instruments relate. This greatly simplifies title searches, for all the entries dealing with a specific parcel of land are kept together, rather than being found under the names of the many grantors and grantees who have previously owned the property.

c. Title search [§1715]

To understand the legal problems arising under the recording system, it is helpful to know how a title search is made. Suppose that O contracts to sell Blackacre to A. Prior to closing, a title search is made to assure A that O owns Blackacre and to determine if there are any encumbrances on O's title. How is this title search done?

(1) Tract index search [§1716]

If there is a tract index, the job is easy. The searcher looks at the page, indexed by block and lot, describing Blackacre, and at a glance can see prior recorded instruments conveying, mortgaging, or otherwise dealing with Blackacre.

(2) Grantor-grantee index search [§1717]

Where there are grantor and grantee indexes only, a title search is much more complicated. The title searcher first uses the grantee index to discover from whom each previous owner took title. Then the title searcher uses the grantor index to ascertain what transfers each owner made during his tenure on the land.

(a) Grantee index [§1718]

The searcher, S, goes first to the grantee index, and looks under O's name—starting at the present date and going backward—to find out who was O's grantor. (O's grantor was D.) When S finds the deed from D to O indexed under O's name in the grantee index, S then does not look any further under O's name but instead looks backward under D's name in the grantee index until S finds the deed by which D acquired title, which names the grantor. S repeats this process until a *"chain of title"* of previous owners for a period of years acceptable in the jurisdiction (usually 60 years or some other time well in excess of the period of the statute of limitations) has been established.

(b) Grantor index [§1719]

Now, having discovered the previous owners of Blackacre, S turns to the grantor index to determine whether any of these previous owners conveyed any interest in Blackacre before conveying the fee simple to the next owner. In the grantor index, S looks under each of the owner's names from the day title came into the owner until the day of recordation of a deed from the owner. (In some jurisdictions, S will have to search a longer period of time under each owner; *see infra*, §§1765 *et seq.*)

---

e.g. **Example:** A, owner of Blackacre, conveyed it to B in 1900. In 1930, B conveyed Blackacre to C. In 1955, C conveyed Blackacre to D. In 1975, D gave E Bank a mortgage on the property. In 1980, D conveyed Blackacre to O. O contracts to sell the land to A. Assume a title search back to 1900 is required. The title searcher, S, will look in the *grantee* index under O's name from the present back to 1980, when S finds the deed from D to O, then under D's name from 1980 to 1955, when S finds the deed from C to D, then under C's name from 1955 to 1930, then under B's name from 1930 backward. S will then look in the *grantor* index under B's name from 1900 to 1930, under C's name from 1930 to 1955, under D's name from 1955 to 1980, and under O's name from 1980 to the present. In this manner, S will pick up the mortgage to E Bank which is recorded in 1975 under D's name in the grantor index.

(c) Death of owner [§1720]

In the preceding example, we have assumed deeds from one owner to the next. But title can pass also by will or intestacy. Assume that in 1930 B died, devising Blackacre to C, and that in 1955 C died, leaving D as her sole heir. B's will can be found in the recorder's office or in the office of the probate court clerk; it will be indexed in a testators' or decedents' index, to which S must turn if S cannot find C's grantor in the index to deeds. D, who took title from C by intestate succession, has no recordable document signed by C. To perfect title, C's heir, D, will file in the recorder's office an affidavit of heirship, prepared by D, which will state that D is the sole heir of C. However, if D is lying and there are in fact two heirs, this affidavit cannot adversely affect another heir who is not disclosed thereon. The burden is on the subsequent purchaser to make sure that he has a deed from *all* persons who are C's heirs. Any heir who does not sign the deed retains his or her interest.

(3) Negligence in search [§1721]

A lawyer or abstractor who undertakes a title search owes a duty to the client to make a careful examination of the records. The title searcher is liable for negligence in this search. If the search is negligently made by an agent for the seller, who furnishes an abstract of title to the buyer, the buyer can sue the agent as a third-party beneficiary of the contract between seller and searcher. The search is made for the benefit of the buyer, not the seller, and the searcher can foresee the reliance by the buyer. [**First American Title Insurance Co. v. First Title Service Co.**, 457 So. 2d 467 (Fla. 1984); **Slate v. Boone County Abstract Co.**, 432 S.W.2d 305 (Mo. 1968)]

4. Types of Recording Acts [§1722]

There are three major types of recording acts: (i) "race," (ii) "notice," and (iii) "race-notice" statutes. (A fourth type, giving the purchaser a period of grace (such as 90 days) in which to record, was common in the last century but is largely outmoded today.)

a. "Race" statutes [§1723]

The earliest statutes were race statutes. Under a race statute, as between successive grantees to the same land, priority is determined solely by *who records first.* Whoever wins the race to record prevails over a person who has not recorded or who subsequently records. Notice is irrelevant.

Example: On January 1, O conveys Blackacre to A. A does not record. On February 1, O conveys Blackacre to B. B *knows* of the deed to A. B records. Then A records. B prevails over A because B recorded first. It is immaterial that B had actual notice of A's interest.

(1) Rationale

Determining who has actual notice depends on extrinsic evidence, which may be unreliable. To bar use of such evidence, race statutes protect whoever wins the race to the recorder's office. Thus, the title searcher may rely on the records to determine priorities. However, because it is deemed inequitable for a person with notice of a prior claim to prevail, very few states have race statutes today.

b. "Notice" statutes [§1724]

Notice statutes developed from race statutes. American courts, applying the early race statutes, thought that it was fraudulent and unfair for a second purchaser with notice of a prior claim (B in the example above) to prevail over the prior claim. The courts construed the race statutes to apply only to a subsequent purchaser for a valuable consideration without notice. This judicial construction became codified in time, and thus developed modern notice and race-notice statutes. Under a notice statute, a subsequent bona fide purchaser prevails over a prior grantee who fails to record. The subsequent purchaser wins under a notice statute if he has *no actual or constructive notice* of a prior claim at the time of the conveyance. A typical notice statute provides: "A conveyance of an estate in land (other than a lease for less than one year) shall not be valid against any subsequent purchaser for value, without notice thereof, unless the conveyance is recorded." About half the states have notice statutes.

Example: On January 1, O conveys Blackacre to A. A does not record. On February 1, O conveys Blackacre to B, who gives valuable consideration and has no notice of the deed from O to A. B prevails over A.

EXAM TIP   **gilbert**

Remember that under a notice statute, the subsequent bona fide purchaser is protected *regardless of whether she records at all*. Thus, if O conveys a parcel to A and A does not record, and O subsequently conveys the same parcel to B and B does not record, B will prevail over A even though their conduct is quite similar.

---

c. "Race-notice" statutes [§1725]

Race-notice statutes, like notice statutes, protect only subsequent purchasers *without notice* of the prior claim. But they do not protect all such subsequent purchasers. They protect a subsequent bona fide purchaser *only if he records before the prior grantee*. Under a race-notice statute, in order for a subsequent purchaser to win, he must *both* be without notice *and* win the race to record. A typical race-notice statute provides: "A conveyance of an estate in land (other than a lease for less than one year) shall not be valid against any subsequent purchaser for value, without notice thereof, *whose conveyance is first recorded.*" Race-notice statutes exist in about half the states.

Example: On January 1, O conveys Blackacre to A. A does not record. On February 1, O conveys Blackacre to B, a bona fide purchaser. On

February 3, A records. On February 15, B records. A prevails over B because B's conveyance was not first recorded. [**Simmons v. Stum**, 101 Ill. 454 (1882)]

EXAMPLES OF RECORDING STATUTES		**gilbert**
TYPE OF STATUTE	**TYPICAL LANGUAGE**	**EFFECT**
RACE	"No conveyance or mortgage of an interest in land is valid against any subsequent purchaser whose conveyance is first recorded."	Grantee *who records first* prevails.
NOTICE	"No conveyance or mortgage of an interest in land is valid against any subsequent purchaser for value without notice thereof, unless it is recorded."	Subsequent *bona fide purchaser* (*i.e.*, for value, without notice) prevails.
RACE-NOTICE	"No conveyance or mortgage of an interest in land is valid against any subsequent purchaser for value without notice thereof whose conveyance is first recorded."	Subsequent *bona fide purchaser* (*i.e.*, for value, without notice) *who records first* prevails.

5. Effect of Recordation

a. What recordation does [§1726]

Proper recordation gives the grantee the protection of the recording system. After recordation, all persons who thereafter take an interest in the land have constructive notice of the existence and contents of the recorded instrument, and no subsequent purchase without notice can arise. Also, in race-notice jurisdictions, because a grantee is not protected against prior unrecorded claims until he records, recordation protects the grantee from prior unrecorded claims as well as eliminates the possibility of a subsequent bona fide purchaser.

b. What recordation does not do

(1) Validate invalid deed [§1727]

Recordation is not necessary for a valid conveyance. A deed is valid between the grantor and grantee if it is delivered. Recordation raises a rebuttable *presumption* that the instrument has been validly delivered and that it is authentic (*see supra*, §1599), but if forged or not delivered, recordation will not validate it. [**Stone v. French**, 14 P. 530 (Kan. 1887)]

(a) Deed fraudulently procured [§1728]

Where a deed has been procured by fraud, the deed is void or voidable between the grantor and grantee. If the grantee conveys to a bona fide purchaser, the bona fide purchaser prevails over the grantor if the grantor was sufficiently negligent to create an estoppel. [**Hauck v. Crawford,** 62 N.W.2d 92 (S.D. 1953)]

(2) Protect against interests arising by operation of law [§1729]

Recordation does not protect a subsequent purchaser against prior interests that have arisen by *operation of law* (*e.g.*, dower rights, prescriptive and implied easements, title by adverse possession). Why not? The answer lies in a careful reading of the recording statute; it states that "a *conveyance* shall not be valid against a subsequent bona fide purchaser . . . ." Therefore, the statute applies only to *unrecorded conveyances*. Because interests arising by operation of law do not arise by conveyance, the recording acts do not apply, and subsequent purchasers take subject thereto.

Example: A adversely possesses Blackacre for the period of the statute of limitations. O, the record owner, then conveys Blackacre to B, a bona fide purchaser. Even though A's interest has never been recorded and a look at the premises would reveal nothing of A's claim, A prevails against B. [**Mugaas v. Smith,** 206 P.2d 332 (Wash. 1949)]

c.   Effect of failure to record

(1) Prior-in-time rule [§1730]

If a person does not record and thereby come within the protection of the recording act, the common law rule of "prior in time, prior in effect" is applicable. [**Gregerson v. Jensen,** 669 P.2d 396 (Utah 1983)]

(2) Power to defeat left in grantor [§1731]

If a person does not record, the person leaves in her grantor (and the grantor's heirs and devisees) the *power* to defeat the deed by executing a subsequent deed in favor of a bona fide purchaser. This is the logical and necessary consequence of the recording acts. This can be dramatically seen from the following illustration.

Example: O, prior to death, executes a deed of Blackacre to A, who does not record. O dies, leaving H as O's heir. (H does not prevail over A because H has not given valuable consideration.) H conveys to B, a bona fide purchaser, who records. B prevails over A. [**Earle v. Fiske,** 103 Mass. 491 (1870)] Even though A had title at O's death, and therefore no title passed to H, the title *shown on the records* was in O at O's death. Relying on the record, a bona fide purchaser can buy from O's heir and defeat A. Thus, although O had no title, the recording system gives O and O's heir the *power* to convey to a bona fide purchaser until A records her deed. Any other result would render the recording system useless because the records could not be relied upon.

(3) Suit against double-dealing grantor [§1732]

If a person fails to record and loses title to a subsequent purchaser, the person may sue her grantor who conveyed twice, and recover under the theory of unjust enrichment the amount that the grantor received from the subsequent purchaser. The grantor, exercising the power left in him by the unrecorded deed, is selling the prior purchaser's property, and the grantor holds the proceeds as constructive trustee for the prior purchaser. (*See* Remedies Summary.) [**Patterson v. Bryant,** 5 S.E.2d 849 (N.C. 1939)]

6. Requirements for Recordation

a. What can be recorded [§1733]

Practically every kind of deed, mortgage, contract to convey, or other instrument creating or affecting an interest in land can be recorded. A judgment or decree affecting title to property can also be recorded. And, even before judgment, where a pending lawsuit may affect title to property, any party to the action can record a lis pendens (notice of pending action) which will effectively put third parties on notice of all claims pending in the lawsuit.

b. Acknowledgments [§1734]

Most recording statutes provide that, to be recorded, a deed must be acknowledged by the grantor before a notary public. This requirement offers protection against forgery. In a few states, an instrument must be witnessed *as well as* acknowledged before a notary to be recorded. In a few states, an instrument must be witnessed *or* acknowledged.

c. What constitutes "recordation" [§1735]

The fact that an instrument has been copied and entered in the recorder's office does not necessarily mean that the instrument has been "recorded." The instrument must be entered in the recorder's books in a manner complying with the applicable statute or judicial decisions.

(1) Failure to index [§1736]

Occasionally, a clerk in the recorder's office fails to index the instrument properly. Is the grantee of such an instrument protected against a subsequent bona fide purchaser? The cases are split: One view protects the grantee, on the theory that, by delivering the deed for recordation, the grantee has done all that she could reasonably be expected to do to give "notice to the world" of her interest. The other view protects the subsequent bona fide purchaser on the theory that only a properly indexed instrument imparts sufficient constructive notice to a subsequent purchaser. [**Mortensen v. Lingo,** 99 F. Supp. 585 (D. Alaska 1951)] The latter is believed to be the better view, because as a practical matter until an instrument has been properly filed **and** indexed, there is no reasonable way to locate it. Further, the grantee of the prior instrument could have prevented the harm to the subsequent purchaser by seeing that the instrument was properly recorded. Accordingly, under the rule that as between two innocent persons, the one who could prevent the loss to another loses, the grantee, rather than the subsequent bona fide purchaser, should bear the loss.

(a) Indexing under misspelled name [§1737]

If an instrument is indexed under a misspelled name of the party (say, "Eliot" instead of the correct name, "Elliott"), does it give constructive notice? Some older cases applied the doctrine of *idem sonans* (if the name as written sounds the same as the pronunciation of the correct name, it refers to the correct person), and held that recorded names pronounced substantially the same as the correct ones gave constructive notice to subsequent purchasers. This doctrine seems to have fallen into disfavor, particularly in populous states or where the recording index has been computerized, and recent cases hold that the instrument does not give constructive notice unless it identifies the party by her correct name. [**Orr v. Byers,** 198 Cal. App. 3d 666 (1988)]

1) Diminutives [§1738]

Some cases from less-populated states have held that instruments identifying a party by a diminutive ("Bob" instead of "Robert") give constructive notice. Thus, under these cases the title searcher must search under diminutives. The searcher may also be required to look at instruments reciting an erroneous middle initial.

EXAM TIP | **gilbert**

If you see an instrument improperly indexed in an exam question, be sure to note the traditional rule that such recording was held **valid** if the name as written sounds the same as the correct name, but then note that because of the volume of extra names that would have to be checked in more populous states, most modern courts **reject** the traditional view and hold that the misindexing is not effective.

(b) Mother Hubbard clauses [§1739]

A Mother Hubbard clause is a provision in a deed that attempts to sweep within it other parcels not specifically described. For example, O gives A a mortgage on Blackacre "and all other land I own in Henry County." O also owns Whiteacre in Henry County.

In the grantor index, this mortgage will be entered in the "description of the land" index as a mortgage on Blackacre. Generally, Mother Hubbard clauses are not valid against subsequent purchasers of the undescribed land, and a bona fide purchaser of Whiteacre would not take subject to the mortgage. The reason is that because the mortgage will be indexed only as affecting Blackacre, it is an undue burden to require a title searcher to read all conveyances of other lots by an owner of the subject lot to see whether the conveyances affect the subject lot. [**Luthi v. Evans**, 576 P.2d 1064 (Kan. 1978)]

(2) Recording unacknowledged instrument

(a) No acknowledgment [§1740]

As noted above, the recording acts generally provide that to record any instrument it must first be acknowledged by the grantor before a notary. What happens if the recorder, by oversight, records a deed that has *not been acknowledged*? Because an unacknowledged deed does not qualify for recordation, it does *not* give constructive notice to subsequent purchasers. Unless the subsequent purchaser has actual or inquiry notice of the earlier deed, the subsequent purchaser prevails.

(b) Defective acknowledgment [§1741]

Where the recorded instrument has been acknowledged but the acknowledgment is defective for some reason *not apparent on the face* of the instrument, the better view is that the recordation imparts constructive notice. However, there is contrary authority holding that if an instrument is defectively acknowledged, it is not entitled to be recorded and hence cannot impart constructive notice. It has even been held that under a race-notice statute, if an instrument in the chain of title bears a defective acknowledgment, *no later instrument* in the chain can be deemed properly recorded so as to defeat a prior unrecorded claim.

Example (race-notice statute): O conveys Blackacre to A, who does not record. O later conveys to B by a deed that appears to bear a valid acknowledgment, but which is in fact defective (because O did not appear personally before the notary). B records this deed, and then sells to C, who records. Thereafter, A records his prior deed. *Held:* A prevails—because even though C recorded first, C's title is derivative of B's, and the defective acknowledgment in B's deed means that B's deed has never been "recorded." [**Messersmith v. Smith**, 60 N.W.2d 276 (N.D. 1953)]

1) Criticism

A hidden defect in an acknowledgment should not make the

deed unreliable. For the recording system to work efficiently, purchasers must be able to rely on what *appears* to be a perfectly recorded document.

7. Who Is Protected by Recording Acts

a. In general [§1742]

Only a bona fide purchaser ("BFP") is entitled to protection under notice and race-notice statutes. To attain this status, a person must: (i) be a *purchaser* (or mortgagee, or creditor if the statute so allows), (ii) who takes *without notice* (including actual, record, or inquiry notice) of the prior instrument, and (iii) gives a *valuable consideration*. If a person does not meet these requirements, he is not protected by the recording acts. The common law rule of first in time prevails. In a race jurisdiction, notice is irrelevant, but a race statute protects only subsequent purchasers for a valuable consideration who win the race to record.

EXAM TIP   **gilbert**

In determining who is a bona fide purchaser for purposes of protection of the recording statutes, remember that the purchaser must be without notice *at the time of conveyance*. It does not matter if she learns of an adverse claim after the conveyance but before recording.

---

b. Purchasers

(1) Purchasers and mortgagees [§1743]

All recording acts protect purchasers of the fee simple or any other interest in the property. Some recording acts expressly apply to mortgagees as well as to purchasers. But even if the statute does not expressly apply to mortgagees, mortgagees are treated as purchasers under judicial decisions because mortgagees take a security interest in the property in exchange for value.

(a) "Shelter rule" [§1744]

A person who takes *from* a BFP will prevail over any interest over which the BFP would have prevailed. This is true even where such person had actual knowledge of the prior unrecorded interest.

Example: O conveys to A, who fails to record. O then conveys to B, a BFP, who records. B then conveys to C, who has *actual knowledge* of the O to A deed. Inasmuch as B prevails over A, B's assignee, C, prevails over A. This is true whether C is a donee or purchaser. C is "sheltered" by the BFP.

---

1) Rationale

If the rule were otherwise, a BFP would not receive the full protection of the recording statute. The statute has the purpose of giving a BFP the value of the bargain, which includes the right to enjoy, convey, or devise his interest. Accordingly, the transferee from a BFP is not protected only if he is meritorious. The transferee is protected, whether or not meritorious, in order to give the BFP his expectations arising from his reliance on the records.

(2) Donees [§1745]

Generally, donees do not come within the protection of the recording system because they do not give value. It is considered unfair to take property away from A and give it to B if B does not give consideration for the property. It has been held, however, that where the recording statute is broadly worded to include "any class of persons with any kind of rights," donees are entitled to the protection of the recording system. [**Eastwood v. Shedd,** 442 P.2d 423 (Colo. 1968)]

EXAM TIP **gilbert**

Don't forget that unless the recording statute says otherwise, recording acts generally do **not protect donees**. Thus, if a fact pattern on an exam is asking about which of two subsequent donees would prevail, apply the common law rule ("prior in time") to the facts, not the recording statute.

---

(3) Creditors [§1746]

The recording acts vary considerably in the protection afforded creditors. Thus, the acts, as well as the judicial interpretations, must be examined carefully.

(a) Creditors not protected [§1747]

Some acts do not mention creditors nor extend protection to "all persons," and under such acts, a creditor can claim protection, if at all, only when he *purchases* the debtor-owner's interest *at a judicial sale* following an action to enforce the debt.

(b) Act extends to "creditors" or "all persons" [§1748]

In some states, the recording act protects "all creditors" or "all persons" against an unrecorded instrument. However, because creditors do not ordinarily rely on the record when extending credit, courts have held that, in spite of the statutory language, general creditors are *not* protected. Only *judgment or lien creditors* are protected. Bear in mind that the recording act protects judgment or lien creditors only against prior interests arising under instruments *capable of being recorded* (*see supra*, §1729). If the recording act is inapplicable in determining priorities, because the prior interest arises by operation of law, a court of equity may follow whatever rule of priority it deems equitable.

> **e.g.** **Example:** Seller deeds land to Buyer, taking back a note for the purchase price. Buyer promises that he will execute and record a mortgage on the property to secure the note, but Buyer does not do so (thereby acting fraudulently). A constructive trust arises on the land in favor of Seller at the time of the fraud. Subsequently, creditors of Buyer obtain judgments which become liens on the property. The recording act provides that an unrecorded conveyance (or mortgage) shall not be valid against creditors, but the recording act is inapplicable because the constructive trust arose by operation of law. The court can do what it regards as fair. It has been held that a subsequent creditor will be protected against a defrauded seller if and only if the creditor shows he affirmatively relied on the records at the time he extended credit. [**Osin v. Johnson,** 243 F.2d 653 (D.C. Cir. 1957)]

(c) Purchaser at execution sale [§1749]

A purchaser at a creditor's execution sale who does not have notice of a prior unrecorded instrument takes free of any claim under the instrument. If a judgment creditor is protected under the recording act from time of judgment, and after judgment a prior unrecorded deed is recorded, the purchaser at the execution sale is protected because he is sheltered under the creditor.

c. Without notice [§1750]

To be protected by a notice or race-notice statute, a subsequent purchaser must be without notice. "Without notice" means, in its most comprehensive sense, that the purchaser has no *actual, record,* or *inquiry* notice of the prior claim *at the time he paid consideration* and received his interest in the land.

(1) Actual notice [§1751]

If a subsequent grantee actually knows of the prior instrument, he has actual notice and is not a BFP. Proof of actual notice depends on extrinsic evidence.

(2) Record notice [§1752]

If an instrument is properly recorded, any subsequent purchaser has record notice and is therefore not a BFP. Record notice is one form of "constructive notice," *i.e.*, notice that the law imputes to the purchaser whether or not he actually knows.

(3) Inquiry notice [§1753]

Inquiry notice is another form of constructive notice. Under certain circumstances, a purchaser is required by law to make reasonable inquiries. He is charged with notice of whatever the inquiry would reveal, even though he made no inquiry. In a few states, such as Massachusetts, inquiry notice is irrelevant because the court has quite literally interpreted the recording act, which protects subsequent purchasers unless they have "actual notice" or record notice. [**Toupin v. Peabody,** 39 N.E. 280 (Mass. 1895)]

(a) Inquiry from quitclaim deed [§1754]

Although some courts hold that a purchaser under a quitclaim deed must make inquiry concerning possible unrecorded prior conveyances because a quitclaim deed is a suspicious circumstance, in a majority of states, a grantee under a quitclaim deed is treated the same as a grantee under a warranty deed. No inference is made that a quitclaim deed is given because the grantor had some doubt about the validity of his title. [**Winkler v. Miller,** 6 N.W. 698 (Iowa 1880)]

(b) Inquiry from possession [§1755]

Suppose that O conveys Blackacre to A, who does not record but goes into possession of Blackacre. O then conveys Blackacre to B. To be a bona fide purchaser, must B inquire of the possessor (A) as to A's possible claim to Blackacre?

1) Majority view [§1756]

B, the subsequent purchaser, is charged with knowledge of whatever an inspection of the property would have disclosed. Hence, B is on constructive notice of A's possession and what would be uncovered by inquiring of A. [**Wineberg v. Moore,** 194 F. Supp. 12 (N.D. Cal. 1961); **Cohen v. Thomas & Son Transfer Line, Inc.,** 586 P.2d 39 (Colo. 1978); **Waldorff Insurance & Bonding, Inc. v. Eglin National Bank,** 453 So. 2d 1383 (Fla. 1984); **Galley v. Ward,** 60 N.H. 331 (1880); **Miller v. Green,** 58 N.W.2d 704 (Wis. 1953)]

2) Minority views [§1757]

There are a number of minority views imposing a lesser inquiry burden on B. These views usually rest on language in the applicable recording act, especially language saying an unrecorded deed is void against persons having "actual notice." Some courts hold that B must make inquiry of A only if B *actually knows* A is in possession. [**Brinkman v. Jones,** 44 Wis. 498 (1878)—construing unusual statute applying to mortgages only, which provides unrecorded mortgage is invalid against person with actual notice] Another view is that if A's possession is *consistent* with record title, B does not have to make inquiry. Thus, suppose that T devises Blackacre to A for life, remainder to B. B then conveys her remainder to A, which conveyance is not recorded. B subsequently conveys her remainder to C. A's possession (as a life tenant) is consistent with A's record title of a life estate. Hence, C does not have to inquire of A to determine if he claims more than a life estate. [*But see* **Toland v. Corey**, 24 P. 190 (Utah 1890)—rejecting this view]

(c) **Inquiry from neighborhood [§1758]**

Deeds out from a common grantor (subdivider) to buyers of other lots in a residential subdivision may contain express written restrictions on land retained by the common grantor and later sold to a subsequent purchaser without any restrictions. Or, under the doctrine of implied reciprocal negative easements (*see supra*, §1230), a negative restriction on use may be imposed *by implication* on a lot in a subdivision, where there is a uniform scheme for development of the subdivision, even though the deed to that lot may contain no restrictions. If the restriction is not contained in a deed in the direct chain of title of the subject lot, the only way a purchaser can find such a restriction is to read all the deeds to other lots from the common grantor. Must a purchaser do this? Some courts have held that the purchaser has constructive notice of the contents of these other deeds out (discussed *infra*, §1776). At least one court has held that if, from the looks of the neighborhood, a purchaser should reasonably conclude that a restriction on use of the subject lot might exist, the purchaser is put on inquiry notice of the contents of other deeds out from the common grantor. These deeds may show a scheme from which a restriction will be implied on the purchaser's lot. [**Sanborn v. McLean**, *supra*, §1263]

Example: CG, owner of a subdivision of 20 lots, conveys lots 1 through 19 to various purchasers. Each deed restricts the lot to residential use only. Single-family houses are built on these lots. Under the doctrine of implied reciprocal negative easements, there is a scheme whereby lot 20 is impliedly restricted to residential use. CG conveys lot 20 to A. If A is a purchaser without notice, A will not take subject to the restriction. However, if the looks of the neighborhood should reasonably put A on inquiry, A must read the deeds from CG of lots 1 through 19 and, finding a scheme of residential development, take the risk that a court will imply a restriction on lot 20.

(d) **Inquiry into unrecorded instruments [§1759]**

If a recorded instrument refers *expressly* to an unrecorded instrument, in most states the purchaser has an obligation to make inquiry into the contents of the instrument. The purchaser has constructive notice of its contents. [**Harper v. Paradise**, 210 S.E.2d 710 (Ga. 1974);

Guerin v. Sunburst Oil & Gas Co., 218 P. 949 (Mont. 1923); *but see* **Tramontozzi v. D'Amicis,** 183 N.E. 295 (Mass. 1962)—no inquiry required in Massachusetts because recording act requires *actual* notice]

INQUIRY NOTICE—A SUMMARY | **gilbert**

SOME KEY POINTS TO REMEMBER ABOUT INQUIRY NOTICE:

- ☑ A few states don't recognize inquiry notice.

- ☑ A few states imply inquiry notice from a quitclaim deed.

- ☑ Some courts imply inquiry notice of restrictions in deeds from a common grantor if a uniform scheme for development of the subdivision is obvious from the neighborhood.

- ☑ Most states imply inquiry notice from the fact that a third party is in possession of the property, even if the purchaser did not inspect.

- ☑ Most states imply inquiry notice if a recorded instrument expressly refers to an unrecorded instrument.

---

d. Valuable consideration [§1760]

To be protected under the recording acts, a purchaser must give valuable consideration. A valuable consideration must be more than merely nominal, but it does not have to equal the market value of the property. It must be sufficient for a court to deem it equitable to deprive the prior purchaser of the land. "Love and affection" is *not* a valuable consideration, but labor and materials spent on repairing property may be. [**Horton v. Kyburz,** 53 Cal. 2d 59 (1959)]

EXAM TIP | **gilbert**

Remember that a purchaser is protected by a recording statute only from the time *consideration is paid*. Thus, even if the deed was delivered and recorded before the consideration was paid, a purchaser will *not prevail* over deeds recorded subsequently but before the consideration was paid.

---

(1) Distinguish—contract law [§1761]

The test of valuable consideration is different from that of contract law, where any consideration—even a peppercorn—suffices to make a contract enforceable. Here the law is trying to differentiate between a donee (not protected) and a purchaser (protected), and thus the consideration must be of substantial monetary value so that it is equitable to deprive another person of the land. [**Allaben v. Shelbourne,** 212 S.W.2d 719 (Mo. 1948)—one dollar is not valuable consideration; this case casts doubt on **Strong v. Whybark,** 102 S.W. 968 (Mo. 1907)—where five dollars was valuable consideration]

(2) Antecedent debts [§1762]

A person who receives a deed or mortgage as *security* for a preexisting debt has not given valuable consideration at the time the deed or mortgage is executed. The person is not at that time a bona fide purchaser for value. [**George M. McDonald & Co. v. Johns,** 114 P. 175 (Wash. 1911); **Gabel v. Drewrys, Ltd.,** 68 So. 2d 372 (Fla. 1953)]

Example: O becomes indebted to A. O conveys Blackacre to B, who does not record. O then gives A a mortgage on Blackacre to secure the indebtedness, and A records. B prevails over A.

(a) Creditor gives new consideration [§1763]

If the creditor gives new valuable consideration, usually in the form of worsening his legal position, this will be sufficient consideration. Thus, in the preceding example, if A extends the time of payment of the debt when he takes the mortgage, he gives valuable consideration. Or if a debtor conveys the property to the creditor in *satisfaction* of the debt, so that a suit cannot thereafter be brought on the debt, the creditor has given valuable consideration.

(3) Partial payment [§1764]

Where the purchaser has paid only part of the purchase price and has given a note to the grantor for the balance, most courts protect the purchaser only to the extent of payment made. Depending on the equities, the court will either give the subsequent purchaser a lien on the land for the amount paid *or* give the prior grantee a lien to the extent of the balance still owed the grantor by the subsequent purchaser. Under the first alternative, the subsequent purchaser loses the land, but he receives his money back. [**Daniels v. Anderson,** 642 N.E.2d 128 (Ill. 1994); **Durst v. Daugherty,** 17 S.W. 388 (Tex. 1891)] In a minority of states, a purchaser who gives cash and notes in payment of the purchase price is fully protected as a subsequent bona fide purchaser. [**Lewis v. Superior Court,** 30 Cal. App. 4th 1850 (1994)]

8. Chain of Title Problems [§1765]

Even though an instrument has actually been recorded and indexed in the recording office, the instrument might not be recorded in such a way as to give notice to subsequent purchasers. The deed may not be in the "chain of title." To give notice to subsequent purchasers, a deed must be in the "chain of title," as the term is defined in the jurisdiction. (*Note:* The problems that are discussed below do not arise if the jurisdiction has a tract index. They arise only where grantor and grantee indexes are used.)

a. Chain of title defined [§1766]

The "chain of title" includes, and is coextensive with, those documents of which the purchaser has constructive notice. In all jurisdictions using a grantor-grantee index system, a purchaser is charged with notice of those conveyances of the property by her grantor *recorded after the grantor acquired the property from his predecessor in title and recorded before a deed is recorded conveying title from that grantor to another.* Likewise, the purchaser is charged with notice of conveyances made by the various predecessors in title during similar periods of ownership. This is the standard title search, and all documents found in a standard title search are in the chain of title.

(1) Extended chain [§1767]

As noted below, in some jurisdictions "chain of title" is defined to include, in addition to the above conveyances, other conveyances that can be picked up by a more extensive record search.

(2) "Wild deeds" [§1768]

A "wild deed" is a recorded deed to the property which is not recorded within the chain of title. Sometimes the term "wild deed" is used in a narrower sense, meaning a recorded deed from a grantor who is not connected to the chain of title.

b. Grantor not connected to chain of title [§1769]

If a deed entered on the records has a grantor unconnected to the chain of title, such a deed is not recorded within the chain and does not give constructive notice.

Example: O conveys to A, who does not record. A conveys to B, who promptly records his deed from A. O conveys to C, a BFP, who records. *Result:* C prevails over B. The A to B deed is not connected to the chain of title; the O to A link is missing. There is no feasible way for C to discover the A to B deed; therefore, C prevails. [**Board of Education v. Hughes,** *supra,* §1584]

---

c. Deeds recorded before grantor obtained title—estoppel by deed [§1770]

Must a purchaser search the index under the name of a grantor prior to the date title came into the grantor to see if the grantor gave an earlier deed to the property to which the doctrine of estoppel by deed (*supra,* §1671) applies? Or to put the question another way, does a recorded deed from a grantor who has no title, but who afterwards obtains title, give constructive notice to a subsequent purchaser from the same grantor? Suppose that on June 1, O owns Blackacre, but on that day, A conveys Blackacre by warranty deed to B, who promptly records. On July 2, O conveys Blackacre to A, and this deed is also promptly recorded. Under the doctrine of estoppel by deed, title moves from O to A to B on July 2. No problems will arise if A does not convey the land to a subsequent purchaser. But, suppose that on August 3, A conveys Blackacre to C, a bona fide purchaser who has no actual notice of the prior A to B deed. Will estoppel by deed apply against a subsequent bona fide purchaser? Now who prevails?

(1) Majority—limited search required [§1771]

Most courts hold that C prevails over B on the theory that a deed from A to B, recorded prior to the time title came to A, is not in the chain of title. *Rationale:* It would put an excessive burden on the title searcher to require a search of the index under each grantor's name *prior* to the date the grantor acquired title. [**Sabo v. Horvath**, 559 P.2d 1038 (Alaska 1976); **Ryczkowski v. Chelsea Title & Guaranty Co.**, 449 P.2d 261 (Nev. 1969)]

(2) Minority—extended search required [§1772]

A minority of courts protect B over C. *Rationale:* Under the doctrine of estoppel by deed, if a grantor who does not have title later acquires it, it passes by operation of law immediately to the grantee. When A acquires title from O, title is transferred automatically to B by virtue of the estoppel arising from A's earlier deed to B. Therefore, A had nothing left to transfer to C. [**Ayer v. Philadelphia & Boston Face Brick Co.**, 34 N.E. 177 (Mass. 1893)] Under this theory, C must search title prior to the time each grantor acquired title to ascertain whether an estoppel applies against the grantor.

d. Deeds recorded late [§1773]

Must a purchaser search the index under the name of a grantor *after* the recordation of a deed by that grantor transferring title? Or to put the question another way, does a deed recorded after the grantor is shown by the record to have parted with title give constructive notice? Suppose that on January 1, O conveys to A, who does not then record. On February 2, O conveys to B, a donee, who records. B, being a donee, does not prevail over A. On March 3, A records. On April 4, B conveys to C, who has no actual notice of A's deed. C records. Who prevails?

(1) Limited search required [§1774]

In most states, C prevails over A. *Rationale:* If A prevails, the title searcher would have to look in the indexes under the name of each grantor in the chain of title to the present date (not just to the date of the first recorded deed from each grantor) to see if there was a deed executed before the first recorded deed but recorded later. This puts an excessive burden on the title searcher. [**Morse v. Curtis**, 2 N.E. 929 (Mass. 1885)] In jurisdictions following this rule, the title searcher looks under O's name in the grantor index only to February 2. The searcher looks under B's name after that date and does not find the O to A deed, recorded on March 3, and does not take subject to it.

(2) Extended search required [§1775]

In a minority of states (including California and New York), A's deed gives notice to subsequent purchasers, although recorded after B's deed. In these states, the title searcher must search *to the present date* under the name of *each person who ever owned* the property to pick up deeds recorded late. As this extended search would greatly increase the cost of conveyancing, title searchers in practice often ignore the law and take the risk.

e. Deeds from common grantor of adjacent lots [§1776]

Must a purchaser look at deeds to other lots from a grantor who owned the subject lot? Or to put the question another way, and narrow it somewhat, does a deed by a subdivider to another lot in a subdivision give constructive notice of any covenants or easements reserved over the neighboring lots? Suppose that subdivider O is developing a residential subdivision. O sells lot 1 to A and the deed provides that lot 1 is restricted to residential use. The deed also provides that "O on behalf of himself, his heirs and assigns, promises to use his remaining lots (2, 3, etc.) for residential purposes only." Then O sells lot 2 to B. The deed to B contains no restrictions. B wishes to erect a gasoline station. Is B bound by the restrictions on lot 2 in the O to A deed, of which he had no actual notice? The courts are split: Some hold that because the burden of title search would be excessive, deeds out to other lots from the common grantor are *not* in B's chain of title, and B is not bound by them. [**Buffalo Academy of the Sacred Heart v. Boehm Bros.**, *supra*, §1262; **Witter v. Taggart,** 78 N.Y.2d 234 (1991)] Others charge B with reading all deeds out from a common grantor, not just the deeds to his particular tract. Under this view, B has constructive notice and is bound by the restriction. [**Guillette v. Daly Dry Wall, Inc.**, *supra*, §1262]

9. Defects in the Recording System [§1777]

The recording system has numerous defects and has been much criticized.

a. Criticisms [§1778]

The recording system has been primarily criticized for the following reasons:

(1) Public records contain incomplete information [§1779]

Even with good record title, a person can be defeated as a result of a defect of fact or law not ascertainable from the recorded documents. Among such defects are: forged deed; deed with faulty acknowledgment by the notary public; deed by grantor who is described as single but who is in fact married and whose spouse has dower or community property rights; claims of heirs who have been omitted from affidavit of heirship and whose claims are not barred; will produced for probate after conveyance by heirs at law; claimants of title who supposedly have been barred by tax sale, foreclosure, or execution sale but who have not been barred because of lack of jurisdiction of court; statutory liens and implied easements and servitudes not required to be of record; notice imputed from possession but not discovered by the purchaser yet considered notice by the courts; and claims arising from adverse possession.

(2) Public records are inefficiently organized [§1780]

Grantor-grantee indexes are antiquated, inefficient, and can be searched only with great difficulty and expense. A tract index is needed.

(3) Expense [§1781]

Every time a piece of property is sold, a record search back to the inception of title is required. This record search by a different title searcher each time a new sale or mortgage occurs is wasteful and costly.

b. Remedies [§1782]

The following remedies have been proposed to cure the defects in the recording system:

(1) Title standards [§1783]

Title standards deal with the very exacting examiner. They are adopted by the local or state bar association and provide, in effect, that specified kinds of defects should not be challenged. They determine risks that are reasonable to take, but title standards are merely a form of "gentlemen's agreement," not binding on the courts or lawyers. Title standards have been promulgated by bar associations in half the states.

(2) Curative acts [§1784]

A curative act is like a short statute of limitations, curing some ancient irregularity of record. For example, a curative act may provide that an unacknowledged deed that has been of record for 10 years is deemed properly recorded. Curative acts have been enacted in many states, but they cure only specified defects and are of limited usefulness in clearing title.

(3) Tract index [§1785]

A tract index solves most of the problems relating to whether an instrument is in the chain of title (*see supra*, §1765), but it does not solve problems of inquiry notice (*see supra*, §1753) or of whether an instrument has been effectively recorded and indexed (*see supra*, §1736). Tract indexes exist in very few states, and even then are usually limited to certain counties within the state.

(4) Marketable title acts [§1786]

Marketable title acts, adopted in 18 states, attempt to limit record searches to a specified number of years—typically 20, 30, or 40 years. (For explanation here, a 30-year period will be assumed.) Under a 30-year marketable title act, if a good record chain of title is found based on a "root of title" more than 30 years old, any claims arising prior to the root of title (with some exceptions) are nullified. If there were no exceptions, a title searcher in 2006 would have to search back only to a root of title more than 30 years old (*i.e.*, a deed executed before 1976). Hence, if A conveyed a fee simple to Blackacre to B in 1973, that deed would be the root of title. All interests created prior to 1973 by whatever manner—deed, inheritance, or adverse possession—are deemed void. If A's claim rested on an earlier forged deed, say from F to A in 1969, that fact is irrelevant. If A is an interloper with no interest in the property, A's deed, no more than 30 years old, may be a root of title in some states. [**City of Miami v. St. Joe Paper Co.**, 364 So. 2d 439 (Fla. 1978)]

(a) Root of title updated [§1787]

The root of title may change as the years go by. *Remember:* The root is a conveyance more than 30 years old at the date of the search. If Blackacre is conveyed in 2011, and the records show a deed from B to C in 1979, that deed—and not the 1973 deed from A to B—is the root of title.

(b) Pre-root interests [§1788]

A pre-root interest is valid if it is referred to in the root of title or in a post-root instrument. Thus, in the 2006 search in the example above, if the 1973 deed from A to B said "subject to an easement in D created in 1934," D's easement would remain valid. On the other hand, if the search took place in 2011 and D's easement was not mentioned in the B to C deed (the new root of title), D's easement is extinguished.

1) Rerecording [§1789]

Pre-root interests can be preserved by being rerecorded within the 30-year period. Thus, it is wise to rerecord all claims every 30 years.

2) Exceptions [§1790]

Marketable title acts usually contain a number of exceptions for pre-root interests. These may include public easements, observable easements, utility easements, restrictive covenants, and mineral interests. These exceptions impair the usefulness of the marketable title act, for the title searcher must go beyond the root of title to ascertain the existence of these interests.

(c) Possession [§1791]

Under most of the marketable title acts, rights of a possessor are not barred. Thus, a purchaser should make a physical inspection of the land.

(d) Constitutionality [§1792]

Marketable title acts have been held constitutional on the ground that the social usefulness outweighs the impairment of old private rights. They operate like a statute of limitations, barring enforcement of a right unless the right is rerecorded within the period of the search. [**City of Miami v. St. Joe Paper Co.**, *supra*; **Presbytery of Southeast Iowa v. Harris**, 226 N.W.2d 232 (Iowa 1975)]

1) Rerecording requirement [§1793]

A statute providing that a mineral interest that has not been used for 20 years is extinguished unless the owner rerecords the interest within two years has been held valid by the Supreme Court. [**Texaco, Inc. v. Short**, *supra*, §393] Such a statute is similar to a marketable title act but is aimed only at eliminating dormant mineral interests.

B. Title Registration

1. In General [§1794]

Title registration is a system of title assurance entirely separate from the recording system. It is sometimes known as the "Torrens system" (after Sir Richard Torrens, who invented it). The basic principle of title registration is to register *title* to land, instead of recording *evidence* of title (as under the recording system). Title registration is built around three ideas: (i) getting title adjudicated by a court, then keeping it up to date by (ii) installing a tract index, and (iii) making the public records conclusive. At one time this system was available in 19 states, but about half of them have since repealed their Torrens acts. Today, only Hawaii, Illinois, Massachusetts, Minnesota, and Ohio substantially use title registration systems.

EXAM TIP gilbert

The key difference between the system of title registration (Torrens system) and the recording system is that the system of title registration actually registers *title* to land, whereas the recording system merely records *evidence of title*. Thus, the method for determining who has title in a Torrens system is much simpler because a searcher need only look in the tract index for the name of the owner.

---

2. How Title Registration Works

a. Initial registration [§1795]

First, a judicial proceeding in rem is started by the owner to clear away all past claims and adjudicate present title. A title searcher is appointed by the court to investigate the records and report to the court. Notice is given to all interested parties, after which the court approves the report of the situation of the title. The court issues a *certificate of title* binding, with few exceptions, on all the world. The certificate is issued in duplicate; the official copy stays in the recorder's office. A duplicate copy is given to the owner. The certificate states who owns title and also lists as "memorials" all encumbrances (mortgages, covenants, easements, etc.) to which the title is subject. [**State v. Johnson**, 179 S.E.2d 371 (N.C. 1971)]

b. Tract index [§1796]

Once a certificate of title is issued, it is indexed in a tract index. Thereafter, anyone wishing to see the state of the title will look up the lot number in the tract index and see, on the face of the certificate of title, who has title and memorials of all encumbrances on the lot. The searcher can then go to the books containing the originals or copies of all documents listed as memorials and examine them. Title search is vastly simplified.

c. Subsequent transfer [§1797]

Suppose that O has the title to Blackacre registered in her name. The certificate of title shows O as fee owner and also lists all mortgages, liens, easements, etc. Suppose that O wants to convey title to A. O delivers to A her duplicate certificate of title together with a deed to Blackacre. A submits the certificate to the recorder, who cancels O's certificate on the books, registers a new official certificate in favor of A, and delivers to A a new duplicate certificate. If A should later grant a mortgage to B, B would present her mortgage and A's duplicate certificate to the recorder, and the recorder would issue a new official certificate showing B's mortgage. Thus, the certificate is kept up to date.

d. Indemnity fund [§1798]

If any person's rights to the land are cut off without notice in the initial registration proceeding, she is paid from an indemnity fund established from title registration fees. If, subsequently, any person is harmed through the recorder's mistake (*e.g.*, omission of an encumbrance on a new certificate), she is likewise entitled to indemnification from the fund.

e. Records conclusive [§1799]

With few exceptions, the title certificate is conclusive. The certificate of title *is* title. Exceptions may include tax and mechanic's liens and public easements, which do not have to be entered on the certificate.

(1) Adverse possession [§1800]

Title to registered land *cannot* be claimed by adverse possession where the possession begins after the title is registered. The certificate of title is conclusive.

3. Defects in Conclusiveness [§1801]

Although by making the certificate conclusive title registration in theory offers great protection to the buyer, in practice this protection is less conclusive than it appears. Motivated by a desire to do equity, courts have resisted the idea that the certificate is conclusive and have lessened its reliability. The following are the major attacks that can be made on the conclusiveness of the certificate.

a. Defect in initial registration

(1) No notice given [§1802]

The Constitution requires that a person be given notice and hearing before being deprived of property. Reasonable efforts must be made to give notice reasonably calculated to reach the owner. If notice is not given, the court lacks jurisdiction, and its decree can be attacked afterward. A person in possession of the land at the time of the initial registration is easily located, and it has been held that he must be given personal notice of the registration proceedings. If not so notified, the possessor can set aside the decree in a suit against the original registrant. Whether the unnotified possessor can set aside the decree against a bona fide purchaser from the original registrant has not been decided.

(2) Fraud [§1803]

If the initial registration was procured by fraud or forgery, the decree can probably be set aside against the original registrant. If not, the person defrauded can have a constructive trust imposed on the person who fraudulently registered the title, if he still owns it. [**State Street Bank & Trust Co. v. Beale,** 227 N.E.2d 924 (Mass. 1967)] Whether the initial registration can be set aside for fraud after the title has come into the hands of a bona fide purchaser has not been decided.

(a) Subsequent transfer [§1804]

If fraud is involved in a subsequent transfer of title (*e.g.*, the registered owner entrusts his duplicate certificate to a person who forges a deed and acquires a new official certificate), the new certificate is valid if relied on by a subsequent bona fide purchaser. The person who registers title, or buys registered title, voluntarily enters into the Torrens system and can lose title unwillingly because of the conclusiveness of the certificate. (This cannot be said of a person who loses title by fraud or forgery in the initial registration.) [**Eliason v. Wilborn,** 281 U.S. 457 (1930)]

b. Bona fide purchasers [§1805]

Courts have introduced into the title registration system the idea that the title certificate protects only subsequent bona fide purchasers who rely on it. This, of course, is a basic principle of the recording system, but it is not part of the title registration statute. Applying this principle, courts have held that a person with *actual* notice of an unregistered interest (*e.g.*, a lease) does not prevail over it. [**Killam v. March,** 55 N.E.2d 945 (Mass. 1944); **Butler v. Haley Greystone Corp.,** 198 N.E.2d 635 (Mass. 1964)] Similarly, a person who does not make adequate inquiry into the validity of a signature on a deed is not in good faith and is not protected by the issuance of a certificate. These decisions are reminiscent of early courts that construed the race recording statutes (also designed to make the records conclusive) not to apply to a person with notice of prior claim. The battle between an efficient title transfer system decreed by the legislature and judicial notions of fairness (the concept of bona fide purchaser) continues.

(1) Possession as constructive notice [§1806]

The majority holds that possession does not give constructive notice to a person who purchases relying on a title certificate.

Example: O registers title in his name. Then, O deeds the property to A, but does not give A the certificate of title. A takes possession and records her deed in the grantor-grantee index. Later, O deeds the property to B, a bona fide purchaser who does not know A is on the land. O gives B the certificate of title. B prevails over A. The earlier recording of A's deed is not constructive notice, where B has been given the certificate of title. [**Abrahamson v. Sundman,** 218 N.W. 246 (Minn. 1928)]

C. Title Insurance

1. In General [§1807]

Title insurance is available in almost all states, but it is used more in some states than in others. There are two types of title insurance systems in general use.

a. Lawyer-title policies [§1808]

Suppose that A wants to buy Blackacre from O. A hires a lawyer to search the record. In addition to giving A an opinion as to the title, the lawyer furnishes an abstract of the record to a title insurance company. On the basis of this abstract, rather than its own independent investigation, the company insures title. This system keeps the lawyer in the picture as a title examiner.

b. Title-plant policies [§1809]

Some title insurance companies maintain duplicate records of all instruments in the county recording office. They have a separate title plant, with a tract index, and carry out their own independent title search. The lawyer does not search title for them. The employment of this kind of title insurance eliminates the lawyer from the title examination process.

2. Who Is Insured [§1810]

Title insurance can be taken out either by the owner of the property or by the mortgage lender. The insurance protects only the *person who owns the policy*. The policy does not run with the land to subsequent purchasers.

3. Extent of Coverage

a. Record title insured [§1811]

The title insurance company or its agent ordinarily conducts a search of record title only and does not go outside the records nor inspect the premises. Accordingly, the standard policy insures only a *good record title* as of the policy's date. In essence, the policy insures only the accuracy of the records, and agrees to defend the record title if litigated.

(1) What is record title [§1812]

"Record title" is generally coextensive with instruments properly recorded within the insured's "chain of title" as defined in the particular jurisdiction (*see supra*, §1766). An instrument not in the insured's chain of title is not insured against. Thus, a deed to a neighboring lot from a common grantor which purports to affect the insured lot is not insured against if the deed is outside the chain of title.

(2) Duty to disclose [§1813]

Most courts have held that, where a title insurance company undertakes to conduct a search of title, the company has a *duty to disclose* to the purchaser specific impediments to title. Thus, the title insurance company's obligations go beyond that of an insurer, which has no duty to disclose the risks it is taking. For example, where the policy states that "rights of way for existing roads" are not insured, and the existing road is 15 feet, but a lawsuit has been filed claiming a 40-foot right of way, which lawsuit is not brought to the purchaser's attention by the company, the company is liable. The purchaser's expectations include both *search and disclosure*. Where the company has the duty of searching and disclosing, it is liable for negligence in not making a careful search. [**White v. Western Title Insurance Co.**, 40 Cal. 3d 870 (1985); **Walker Rogge, Inc. v. Chelsea Title & Guaranty Co.**, 562 A.2d 208 (N.J. 1989)] A minority holds that the insurance company is not an abstracter and has no duty to disclose defects it discovers.

(a) Who can sue [§1814]

When the insurance company has the duty of disclosing the results of its searching, and does so, the company is liable for negligence not only to the insured but also to third parties who show foreseeable reliance on the disclosure. [**Transamerica Title Insurance Co. v. Johnson**, 693 P.2d 697 (Wash. 1985)]

(3) Giving legal advice [§1815]

If the title insurance company goes beyond insuring the purchaser against loss, and advises the purchaser as to the legal marketability of title, the company is giving legal advice and assumes responsibility therefor. If the legal advice is wrong and the company is negligent in giving such advice, the company is liable in damages (not limited to the amount of insurance liability stated in the policy).

b. Exclusions [§1816]

The standard title insurance policy does not insure against loss arising from the following defects, among others:

(1) Liens imposed by law but not shown on the public records [§1817]

This exception may include various statutory liens, such as a mechanic's or builder's lien. It also may include street assessments assessed to abutters, which by law become liens on the abutting property, without recordation.

Example: On January 1, the city council authorizes improvements to Green Street, to be assessed against the abutters and to become liens on their property as of July 1. In March, the title insurance company issues a policy to A, who buys a lot abutting Green Street. Because the lien does not arise until after the policy is issued, the company has no liability on the policy. [**Metropolitan Life Insurance Co. v. Union Trust Co.**, 283 N.Y. 33 (1940)]

---

(2) Claims of parties in possession not shown on the public records [§1818]

The insurance company does not physically inspect the property, and therefore does not insure against claims by adverse possession or possessory claims that could be found by inspection of the premises. [**Bothin v. California Title Insurance & Trust Co.**, 153 Cal. 718 (1908)]

(3) Boundary disputes [§1819]

The insurance company does not survey the property, and therefore does not insure against encroachments and boundary disputes that would be disclosed by a correct survey or inspection of the premises.

(4) Easements or servitudes not shown on the public records [§1820]

Implied easements or covenants and easements by necessity or by prescription are not covered by the policy.

(5) Zoning or building ordinances [§1821]

The policy does not insure against any law or government regulation restricting the use of land. This includes building codes, zoning ordinances, and subdivision regulations.

(6) Hazardous wastes [§1822]

The policy does not insure against hazardous wastes being found on the property. [**Lick Mill Creek Apartments v. Chicago Title Insurance Co.**, 231 Cal. App. 3d 1654 (1991)]

4. Amount of Liability

a. Maximum liability [§1823]

The maximum liability of the company is the amount set in the policy. Ordinarily, this is the purchase price of the property. Unless there is an inflation clause in the policy, the policy does not insure the present value of the property where such value exceeds the amount set in the policy.

b. General rule of liability [§1824]

The company is liable for the difference in value of the property with and without the defect, up to the maximum set by the policy. Values at the date of issuance of the policy are usually held to control.

---

e.g. **Example:** O sells Blackacre to A for $9,000. A takes out a title insurance policy for $7,000, which insures against any easements on Blackacre. Subsequently, A discovers that B has an easement over Blackacre. The true market value of Blackacre without the easement is $15,000 on the date of issuance of the policy (A bought at a great bargain). The value of Blackacre with the easement on the date of issuance of the policy is $5,000. A has been damaged $10,000, and can collect the maximum $7,000 under the policy. [**Beaullieu v. Atlanta Title & Trust Co.,** 4 S.E.2d 78 (Ga. 1939)]

Review Questions and Answers

Review Questions

1. Mabel and Ichabod are both licensed to hunt on Oprah's land. Mabel has a fox under pursuit.

    a. Ichabod overtakes Mabel and shoots the fox first. Can Ichabod keep the fox? _____

    b. Mabel captures an ordinary red fox and pens it in her yard. The fox escapes. Eric, who does not know the fox has been captured by Mabel, captures the fox. Can Eric keep the fox? _____

2. Lopez owns Greenacre, which is at a lower elevation than the surrounding property. In order to prevent flooding, Lopez constructs a dike which diverts surface runoff onto the adjacent land. In a state following the common enemy doctrine, can the adjoining property owners recover from Lopez for damage to their land? _____

3. Victoria Farms owns a parcel of land adjacent to Running River. May Victoria Farms properly take river water to irrigate its farmland that is not adjacent to the river and does not adjoin the parcel on the river? _____

4. Professor Marcia Law says, "A person who by an innocent mistake takes a chattel belonging to another and improves it with her labor is entitled to ownership of the chattel, but she must compensate the previous owner for the value of the chattel before improvement." Is this correct? _____

5. Ima Lukkin finds a ring owned by Opal Essent on property owned by Anna Mossity. Anna has never seen the ring before, but claims it as owner of the locus where the ring is found.

    a. If Ima finds the ring in Anna's private home while a guest there, is Ima entitled to the ring, as against Anna? _____

    b. If Ima finds the ring on the wash basin in the women's room of Anna's store, is Ima entitled to the ring, as against Anna? _____

    c. If Ima finds the ring in the ground while digging on Anna's farm, is Ima entitled to the ring, as against Anna? _____

    d. Ima finds the ring on the floor of Anna's shop. She gives the ring to Anna to look at and Anna refuses to give it back. Is Ima entitled to the full value of the ring from Anna? _____

6. Amy occupies Greenacre in the belief that it is Brownacre, which she has purchased from Jade. The statute of limitations for ejectment is 10 years.

    a.   Is Amy's possession hostile for purposes of adverse possession?   _____

    b.   If Amy occupies Greenacre for three years, then "sells" it to Charlie, who occupies it for seven years, is the owner barred from ejecting Charlie?   _____

7. Shinji plants a hedge on what he believes to be the true boundary between his property and that of his neighbor, Kim. In fact, the hedge is 20 feet inside Kim's property. If Shinji occupies the land inside the hedge for the requisite period of adverse possession, does he obtain title to the 20-foot strip?   _____

8. Without Mary Achee's permission, Juan During occupies a lake cabin owned by Mary each summer for 21 years; the cabin is unoccupied during the remainder of the year. The statutory period for adverse possession is 20 years.

    a.   Does Juan now have title to the cabin?   _____

    b.   Would the result be the same if Mary occupied the cabin for two weeks each winter during this period?   _____

9. Helen occupies Whiteacre openly, continuously, and hostilely to the true owner, Isaac, for 10 years. Thereafter, she conveys the property to Jane, who occupies Whiteacre under the deed for eight years. Jane leaves the property to move to Mexico, and Karl—learning of Jane's intentions from Jane's friend Lulu—moves in on the day of Jane's departure and continues in open, continuous, and hostile possession for three years.

    a.   If the statutory period for adverse possession is 20 years, does Karl have title to Whiteacre?   _____

    b.   Would the result be different if Jane had told Karl of her departure and invited him to occupy Whiteacre?   _____

10. Portia purports to convey a 40-acre tract of land, known in the community as "Birnham Woods," to MacDuff. Portia does not own Birnham Woods. Birnham Woods is forest land, not occupied by anyone. MacDuff occupies 15 of the 40 acres and continues in possession for the statutory period for adverse possession. Does MacDuff have title to all of the property described in the deed?   _____

11. Jack brings his watch to the Ace Watch Repair Co. for repair, taking back a claim check. Jack puts the claim check in his law school locker, from which it is stolen by Paul. Paul presents the claim check to Ace and receives the watch. Is Ace liable to Jack?   _____

12. In each of the following cases, is there a valid gift? Dolly, in bed ill and dying, is in a room with Bea and Sally.

    a.   Dolly says: "Sally, I want to give Bea my insurance policy in the bureau there, so please get it and give it to her." Sally, however, leaves the insurance policy where it is. Dolly dies. Does Bea own the policy?   _____

    b.   Dolly says: "Bea, I want to give you my little jewelry box here on the table and the diamond ring and bracelet locked in it. Here is the key." Bea takes the key, but the box stays where it is. Dolly dies. Does Bea own the diamond ring and bracelet?   _____

    c.   Dolly says: "Sally, I want to give Bea my jewelry in this box when I die. Take the box and give it to Bea on my death, but if I change my mind, return the box to me." Sally takes the box and hides it in her house. Dolly dies without changing her mind. Does Bea own the jewelry box—

        (1)   if Sally is deemed to be Dolly's agent?   _____

        (2)   if Sally is deemed to be a trustee?   _____

    d.   Dolly says: "Bea, I want you to have the proceeds in my savings account; the passbook is in my safe deposit box." Dolly then gives Bea the key to the box. Is Bea entitled to the savings account on Dolly's death?   _____

13. Are the following accurate statements of law?

    a.   The tenant of a freehold has seisin; the tenant of a nonfreehold estate does not hold seisin.   _____

    b.   Words of purchase indicate that consideration has been paid for the property.   _____

    c.   A future interest, unlike a present possessory interest, is not a presently existing interest.   _____

14. Antonia conveys Blackacre to Pedro "so long as Blackacre is used for agricultural purposes."

    a.   If Blackacre is used for industrial purposes, and the next day Pedro conveys "to Maria and her heirs," does Antonia have any rights against Maria?   _____

    b.   If the conveyance from Antonia to Pedro had concluded, "and if Blackacre is used for nonagricultural purposes, Antonia has a right of entry," would Maria have a fee simple determinable?   _____

15. In 1983, Margie Nalia conveys Blackacre to Fay Lanx "upon condition that Blackacre never be used for commercial purposes, and if it is so used, Margie has

a right to reenter." Two years later, Manny Curist, an adverse possessor, occupies the property and constructs a beauty salon. The adverse possession period is 20 years.

a. If Manny continues in possession until 2007, does he have good title against Margie? _____

b. Would Manny have a good title against Margie if the conveyance had been "to Fay Lanx so long as Blackacre is not used for commercial purposes"? _____

16. Oscar devises property "to my wife, Emmy, so long as she does not marry, and if she does marry, to Ching." If Emmy marries, will she lose the property? _____

17. Nicole devises Brownacre "to Olivia and the heirs of her body."

a. At common law, would this create a fee tail in Olivia, which she could devise to her cousin, cutting out her oldest son and heir? _____

b. Under modern law, can Olivia convey a fee simple absolute in Brownacre? _____

c. If the devise had been "to Olivia and the heirs of her body, but if she dies without surviving issue, to Penelope and her heirs," can Olivia convey a fee simple absolute today? _____

18. Indicate whether each of the following acts would probably constitute waste by a life tenant.

a. Life tenant replaces outmoded pipes with the same type of tubing, even though improved pipes are available at the same cost. _____

b. Life tenant plows under a vineyard and converts the property to industrial use, substantially increasing the value of the property. _____

19. Sid Com devises his summer cabin "to Hedda Steam, but if Hedda attempts to transfer the property without the consent of Bea Purr, then to Ella Quince." Hedda subsequently sells the cabin without Bea's consent.

a. Is Hedda's conveyance valid? _____

b. Would the result be the same if a condominium were involved, and the consent of the condominium board of directors were required? _____

20. Ashley, owner of Blackacre, conveys Blackacre to Bill for life. Bill subsequently leases Blackacre to Casey for a 25-year term, which is greater than Bill's life expectancy.

a. Do Ashley and Bill have reversions in Blackacre? _____

b.   Will Casey's leasehold continue if Bill dies within the 25-year period? _____

21. Diana conveys Blackacre "to School Board so long as it uses the land for school purposes, then to Mercy Hospital."

a.   Does Mercy Hospital have a possibility of reverter? _____

b.   Suppose there were no gift over to Mercy Hospital. After the conveyance, Diana conveys her interest in Blackacre to Elizabeth. Does Elizabeth have a possibility of reverter? _____

c.   Suppose the conveyance had been "to School Board, but if it ceases to use the land for school purposes, Diana has a right to reenter." Subsequent to the conveyance, Diana conveys her right of entry to Elizabeth. Does Elizabeth have a right of entry? _____

22. Sonia, a fee simple owner, conveys Greenacre to Lucy for life, then to Ellis if he reaches 21. Ellis is age 19. Does Sonia have a reversion? _____

23. Jason conveys Whiteacre "to Arnie for life, then to Bob and his heirs, but if Bob dies before Arnie, to Arnie's children who survive Arnie and their heirs." Arnie has a child, Carolyn. No other child is born to Arnie. Bob dies intestate. Carolyn dies intestate. Then Arnie dies. Does Jason own Whiteacre? _____

24. Grace conveys her house "to Henry for life, then to Ian, but if Ian predeceases Henry, then to Ian's children who survive Henry." Ian has one child, Jennifer, alive.

a.   Does Ian have a contingent remainder? _____

b.   Does Jennifer have a contingent remainder? _____

c.   Suppose the conveyance were "to Henry for life, remainder to Ian's heirs." Ian is alive. Do Ian's heirs have a vested remainder? _____

25. Victoria devises property "to Edward for life, then to Edward's children, and if Edward dies without children surviving him, to James." At Victoria's death, Edward has a son, George, alive.

a.   Does George have a vested remainder? _____

b.   Does James have a contingent remainder? _____

c.   Suppose Victoria had devised the property "to Edward for life, then to Edward's children who survive Edward, and if Edward dies without children surviving him, to James." Does James have a contingent remainder? _____

d.   Suppose that James dies while Edward and George are alive. Is James's interest destroyed? _____

26. Leonardo conveys Whiteacre to Veronica and her heirs at such time as Veronica "becomes a lawyer." Veronica is two years old.

    a. Prior to the Statute of Uses (1536), would Veronica have a legal interest in Whiteacre? _____

    b. Would the result be different after the Statute of Uses? _____

    c. Suppose the conveyance after the Statute of Uses had been "to Winston and his heirs, but at such time as Veronica becomes a lawyer, to Veronica and her heirs." Does Veronica have any interest in Whiteacre? _____

27. Rose conveys Greenacre "to my husband, Joseph, for life, remainder to my children and their heirs." At the time of the conveyance Rose has no children, and before any are born Rose transfers to Joseph "all my right, title, and interest in Greenacre." The jurisdiction has not abolished destructibility of contingent remainders.

    a. Do Rose's children have any interest in Greenacre? _____

    b. Would the result be different if Rose had a child, John, when the conveyance was made? _____

    c. If Rose had no child, would Rose's unborn children have any interest in the land if the jurisdiction has abolished destructibility of contingent remainders? _____

28. Jorge conveys Whiteacre "to Xavier in trust for the life of Peregrina to pay the income to Peregrina, remainder to Peregrina's heirs." The jurisdiction applies the Rule in Shelley's Case.

    a. Does the Rule in Shelley's Case apply? _____

    b. Would the result be different if the conveyance were "to Xavier in trust for the life of Peregrina to pay the income to Peregrina, and upon her death to convey the principal to Peregrina's heirs"? _____

29. Quinn conveys property "to Xavier in trust for Quinn for life, then to the heirs of Quinn." Subsequently Quinn seeks to terminate the trust, alleging that he owns all the equitable interest in the trust, is also the settlor, and therefore can terminate the trust. Can Quinn terminate the trust? _____

30. Do any of the following devises violate the Rule Against Perpetuities?

    a. T devises property "to the first child of A to become a lawyer." A's eldest child, B, is in law school. _____

    b. T devises property "to A for life, then to A's children who reach 25." A has no children living. _____

c. T devises land "to Library Board, but when it ceases to use the land for a library, to A and his heirs." _____

d. T devises land "to Library Board so long as used for library purposes, then to A and his heirs." _____

e. T devises property "to A for life, then to A's widow for life, then to A's issue." _____

f. T devises property "to A for life, then to A's widow for life, then to A's children." _____

31. Ann conveys Blackacre "to Ann, Ben, and Chelsea as joint tenants."

   a. Would this create a joint tenancy between the three at common law? _____

   b. Would this create a joint tenancy between Ben and Chelsea at common law? _____

   c. If Ben died, would Ann and Chelsea hold equal shares as tenants in common? _____

   d. Would the conveyance create a joint tenancy under modern law if the conveyance were "to Ann, Ben, and Chelsea"? _____

32. Don conveys Blackacre to Estelle, Fred, and Grant as joint tenants.

   a. Thereafter Estelle dies, devising to Harvey "all my interest" in Blackacre. Does Harvey take Estelle's interest? _____

   b. If thereafter Fred mortgages his interest in the property, then dies, does Grant hold Fred's share? _____

33. Shana Maidel and Che Getz buy property together, taking title "as joint tenants with right of survivorship." Shana contributes two-thirds of the purchase price.

   a. Has a joint tenancy been created? _____

   b. If Shana brings an action in partition, is she entitled to two-thirds of the selling price? _____

34. Sally Forth devises lakefront property to her daughter Marian Haste and Marian's husband, Art Fuldodger, as tenants by the entirety. Thereafter, Art accumulates substantial debts. Can Art's creditors reach the lakefront property to satisfy the debts? _____

35. Nina Diamonds and Jack O'Hartz purchase several hundred acres of farmland as tenants in common. Nina remains in the city and conducts her law practice while Jack moves onto the land, cultivates it, and produces a crop which he sells.

   a. Is Nina entitled to a share in the sales proceeds? _____

b. Is Nina entitled to one-half of the fair rental value of the farm? _____

c. Would your answer to b. be different if Jack had rented the land to Ace, who farmed it and paid $100 rent to Jack? _____

d. Suppose Jack discovers a uranium deposit under the farm, whereupon he excavates the ore and sells it. Is he liable to Nina for a portion of the sales proceeds? _____

e. Can Jack obtain a contribution from Nina for his costs in improving and enlarging various buildings upon the property? _____

36. Steven purchases Lazy Acres while married to Tricia. Subsequently Steven sells Lazy Acres to Uranus, a bona fide purchaser with no knowledge that Steven is married. Then Steven dies. The jurisdiction has common law dower.

a. Does Tricia have dower in Lazy Acres? _____

b. Suppose Steven had not sold Lazy Acres. Under a statutory elective share would Tricia's interest be greater than her dower interest? _____

37. Bjorn leases space in a shopping center to Christopher for 100 years.

a. At common law is this a valid lease? _____

b. Would the result be different if the lease to Christopher were "until the war is over"? _____

c. Would the result be different if the lease were an oral lease for two years, and Christopher occupied the space after paying one month's rent? _____

38. Dannielle rents an apartment to Eliza "at a rental of $250 per month payable on the 15th."

a. Does this create a month-to-month tenancy? _____

b. Suppose Dannielle decides to terminate Eliza's lease and on April 17th notifies Eliza to quit the premises on May 17th. Can Dannielle require Eliza to vacate the premises on May 17th? _____

39. L leases an office to T from year to year. At the end of the second year, T moves out without giving L any notice. Can L hold T for another year's rent? _____

40. L leases land to T "for as long as T may desire."

a. Does this create a tenancy at will? _____

b. Would the result be different if the lease were to T "for as long as L may desire"? _____

c.	Can T assign the lease to A?	_____

41.	L leases his farm to T for five years. When the five-year period expires, T remains on the farm.

a.	Can L elect to treat T as a tenant for a further five-year period?	_____

b.	Must L give T notice before evicting him from the farm?	_____

42.	L places a sign in the window of her home, advertising a basement apartment for rent. A, a black student, asks to rent the apartment but L refuses to do so because of A's color.

a.	Can A obtain damages or injunctive relief against L?	_____

b.	Would the result be different if L refused to rent to A because A was a woman?	_____

43.	L leases a warehouse to T. Shortly after T moves in, L informs T that L plans to use a 10-square-foot area in one corner of the building for his own storage and proceeds to close off this area.

a.	Does T's obligation to pay rent thereby abate?	_____

b.	Would the result be different if the corner space were occupied by a third party, B, under a valid claim of title to the building?	_____

44.	L rents an apartment to T. When T occupies the apartment, T discovers that he is temporarily without hot water while the water heater is being repaired.

a.	Can T move out and refuse to pay rent, on grounds of constructive eviction?	_____

b.	Assuming T claims constructive eviction, can T remain in the apartment and claim an offset against rent for the lack of hot water?	_____

c.	Would the result be different if the absence of hot water were a chronic problem and T claimed a breach by L of his duty to provide habitable quarters?	_____

45.	After occupying the apartment for several months, T discovers shorts in several electrical outlets. The lease does not expressly require L to make repairs on the apartment.

a.	Can T obtain an injunction requiring L to repair the faulty wiring?	_____

b.	Can T elect either to make the repairs herself and deduct them from the rent, or to have the rent reduced to the fair market value of the premises "as is"?	_____

c. Would the result be the same in most courts if the lease contained an express waiver by T of any rights against L for failure to make repairs? _____

d. Suppose T is a month-to-month tenant and reports the violation of the housing code to public authorities. L thereupon sues to evict T. Assuming L gave T the requisite notice to quit, does T have any defense to the action? _____

46. L rents an apartment to T. The first night on the premises, T steps out on the balcony, the balcony collapses, and T is injured.

a. Is L liable to T in tort under common law rules? _____

b. Would the result be different if it were T's girlfriend, A, who was injured? _____

c. Is L liable to T in tort if there is an implied warranty of habitability? _____

47. L rents to T a warehouse for storage of high explosives.

a. Shortly after the lease is signed, a substantial part of the warehouse is destroyed by a tornado. Will this terminate the lease? _____

b. Would the lease be terminated if, sometime after signing, the area were rezoned so as to prohibit storage of high explosives? _____

c. Suppose that the lease is terminated and T wants to remove special fireproof divider panels in the warehouse which T has installed. Can T remove them? _____

48. L rents her house on a month-to-month tenancy to T, who moves his furnishings and other belongings onto the premises. T pays his rent during the first three months, but fails to pay in the fourth month.

a. Can L thereupon enter the house and seize T's belongings to hold until the rent is paid? _____

b. If the rental agreement required T to pay two months' rent in advance as a security deposit, can L retain this amount when T fails to pay the fourth month's rent? _____

c. Can L enter the house and forcibly eject T? _____

d. Suppose L brings an unlawful detainer action against T. Can T defend on the ground that L has violated an implied covenant to repair, for which T has spent the rental owed? _____

49. L leases an office to T for three years, with rent payable on a monthly basis. The terms of the agreement provide that the breach of any covenant therein by T allows L to declare a forfeiture. T fails to pay rent during the term of the lease.

a. If L declares a forfeiture, is T liable for the remaining rent for the term (as well as arrearages)? _____

b. If T abandons the office after one year, can L leave the office vacant and sue T for rentals due? _____

50. L leases his summer cabin to T for five years. After one year, T transfers her entire interest in the cabin to A, who pays no rent to L.

a. Can L sue either T or A for the rent due? _____

b. Would the result be different if T had transferred possession to A for three years? _____

c. Would L be able to sue A if T had transferred possession to A for three years and A assumed all of the covenants in the L-T lease? _____

d. Is T's three-year transfer to A invalid if the L-T lease contains a covenant not to assign? _____

51. Professor Claire Voyant tells her students that "affirmative easements are much more widely recognized than negative easements, which are usually limited to those recognized in early English law."

a. Is Professor Voyant correct? _____

b. Voyant also comments that "in doubtful cases, courts incline toward finding an easement to be in gross rather than appurtenant, because an easement in gross benefits the owner personally." Is this an accurate statement? _____

52. Alexis, owner of two adjoining lots, Lots 1 and 2, sells Lot 1 to Blake.

a. If the deed to Blake conveys "Lot 1, excepting the 15-foot strip thereof bordering Lot 2 to be used as an irrigation ditch by Alexis," would this probably be held to except a fee rather than an easement? _____

b. Would the result be different if the deed had reserved the 15-foot strip for an irrigation ditch to be used by Claudia (another adjacent landowner)? _____

c. Suppose that Lot 2 is situated on higher ground than Lot 1. If the deed is silent on the subject, can Alexis claim drainage rights across Blake's property? _____

d. Prior to the sale of Lot 1, Alexis constructs an access road from Lot 2 to the public highway, and part of the access road crosses a corner of Lot 1. If the deed to Blake makes no mention of the road, does Alexis continue to have an easement across Lot 1? _____

e. Would the results in c. or d. be different if Blake conveys Lot 1 to Kirby? _____

53. Emma Lation purchases Greenacre from Dilly Gence, who tells Emma that there is a path across adjoining property to a public park (which Dilly has been using for 15 years).

   a. If Emma continues to use the path for an additional five years, and the period of limitations is 20 years, does she acquire an easement to reach the park? _____

   b. Would the result be different if the owner of the adjacent property posts a "no trespassing" sign at the boundary of Greenacre? _____

   c. Would the result be different if Greenacre were landlocked after being separated from the adjoining property, and the path gave it access to a public road? _____

54. In his deed to Blackacre, Gregory is given an easement across the adjoining land of the grantor, Heather, "for right of way purposes." Gregory proceeds to construct a factory on Blackacre and moves trucks in and out over Heather's land 24 hours a day.

   a. Can Heather enjoin such travel over her property? _____

   b. Suppose that Heather grants Gregory the use of an existing road across her property as an express easement. Gregory constructs buildings on Blackacre to make use of the road. Heather later decides to build on the existing right of way. Can she move the road elsewhere on the property? _____

   c. If Gregory sells Blackacre to Irene, does Irene have an easement across Heather's property? _____

   d. If Heather gives Jamie an easement to maintain a billboard on Heather's property, can Jamie assign it? _____

55. Shirley Eugeste is granted the right to use an access road across Romana Clay's land to reach a public street. If Shirley fails to use the road for 20 years, is her easement extinguished? _____

56. Professor Polly Onymous notes that "a primary difference between a real covenant and an equitable servitude is that the remedy for breach of a real covenant is damages and the remedy for breach of an equitable servitude is an injunction." Is this correct? _____

57. Quick covenants with his neighbor, Ralph, not to remove trees on the common boundary of their properties unless Ralph agrees thereto. Thereafter, Quick sells the property to Tricia, who uproots the trees. Can Ralph sue Tricia for damages? _____

58. Minna Skewel sells Blackacre to Millie Grazie, and Millie covenants not to use the property for commercial purposes of any kind. Millie later conveys a life estate in

Blackacre to I.C. Phydeaux, who enters upon the property and opens a veterinary hospital.

a. Can Minna sue I.C. for damages? _____

b. If I.C. had occupied Blackacre as an adverse possessor, would Minna be able to get damages from him? _____

59. Yetta grants Zelda an easement of way across Yetta's property in town, and Zelda covenants to keep the right of way in good repair.

a. If Yetta never uses the road, can her assigns enforce the covenant against Zelda? _____

b. Would the result be the same if Zelda had covenanted instead to keep Yetta's mountain cabin in good repair? _____

60. Anthony, a restaurant owner, contracts with Bolla Co. to use only Bolla products on the premises. Anthony then sells the restaurant to Catherine, who knows of the contract.

a. In the majority of courts, can Bolla enjoin Catherine from using a competitor's products? _____

b. Assuming the burden of the covenant runs, can Anthony be held liable for Catherine's refusal to purchase Bolla products? _____

61. Delta Land Co. develops a tract of 300 lots, called Washington Park. In the first 280 deeds, the grantees all agree to use their lots for single-family dwellings only, and Delta's representatives assure each grantee that Washington Park will be developed only for residential single-family dwellings. Erin, who has notice of the prior deeds, offers to purchase the remaining 20 lots at a premium price to erect an apartment complex.

a. If Delta conveys the lots to Erin with no covenants, can the neighbors prevent Erin from building the apartment houses? _____

b. Suppose the earlier 280 deeds had also contained a promise by each grantee to plant trees on his lot, and Delta had conveyed the final 20 lots to Erin without a covenant. Can Erin be compelled to plant trees on her property? _____

c. Suppose Erin's deed had contained an express covenant not to build multi-family housing, but Erin nevertheless files plans to construct an apartment house. Can the prior grantees enjoin the construction in most courts? _____

d. Would the result in a. and c. be different if Delta had reserved the right to modify restrictions as to each lot? _____

62. Sherry D. Cantor, a residential developer of a large parcel called Eden Acres, sells Lot 1 to Phyllis Teen. In the deed to Lot 1, Phyllis promises that she will (i) use the property for residential purposes only, (ii) build a fence six feet in height along her side boundaries, and (iii) pay the Eden Acres Property Owners' Association $100 a year to maintain a swimming pool for use of all buyers into Eden Acres. These covenants are stated in the deed to be covenants running with land, binding upon assignees, and enforceable by other owners in Eden Acres and the Property Owners' Association. Sherry sells Lot 2 to Maude Lynn, and the remaining lots to other purchasers. The deeds to all of the other parcels contain covenants identical to those in Lot 1. Subsequently Phyllis sells Lot 1 to Coco Vann. Coco, who is in the chicken business, plans to build a chicken ranch on Lot 1, and refuses to build the side fences and to pay the $100 a year assessment.

   a.   If Coco builds the chicken ranch, can Maude recover damages from Coco?   _____

   b.   In most states, is Maude entitled to an injunction compelling Coco to build the fences?   _____

   c.   If the deed to Lot 1 creates a lien against the lot to enforce the covenant to pay money, can the Property Owners' Association enforce the lien against Coco in states that define privity of estate as a mutual relationship?   _____

63. Jason, a developer, sells all 50 lots in a residential tract to grantees, each deed containing a covenant to use the property only for residential purposes. Houses are erected on most lots. Kerry, one of the grantees, now wants to construct a store on his lot.

   a.   If property adjacent to Kerry's lot outside the subdivision is being used for commercial purposes, can a neighbor in the subdivision enjoin construction of the store?   _____

   b.   Would the result be the same if Kerry's lot were zoned for commercial use?   _____

64. Mary Thon purchases stock in a cooperative apartment house and leases an apartment in the building. When she attempts to do calisthenics in the morning, the directors inform her that no prolonged jumping or running is permitted in the apartment.

   a.   If Mary continues her exercises, can her lease be terminated?   _____

   b.   Suppose Mary decides to sell her stock and lease to Annie Mator. The corporation rules provide that a tenant cannot assign her stock or lease without approval of the directors. If the directors refuse to consent to the assignment, with no evidence of illegal discrimination, can Mary obtain judicial review of their decision?   _____

65. Maggie is a hog farmer. Nigel, a neighboring homeowner, objects to the odor and noise from the hogs.

a. If keeping hogs is permitted under the local zoning ordinance, does Maggie have a defense to a nuisance action? _____

b. If Maggie were raising hogs when Nigel first purchased his property, would Maggie have a defense? _____

c. Could Shu-mo seek relief from the nuisance if she were a relative house-sitting for Nigel? _____

66. Bella Kose sues to enjoin Qua Corp., a nearby industrial plant, from polluting the air with soot and noxious gas.

a. Will the importance of Qua Corp. to the community be considered in a nuisance action? _____

b. If Bella is denied an injunction, is it possible for her to obtain damages from Qua Corp.? _____

c. If Bella is denied an injunction, but awarded damages, has she received a share of the "gains from trade"? _____

67. Theo conveys one-half of Whiteacre to Underground Explorers, Inc., which proceeds to excavate a fish pond near the border of Theo's property.

a. If the fish pond causes Theo's surface soil to subside, is Underground Explorers liable for damages? _____

b. Would the result be different if Theo had a house bordering the fish pond, which collapsed when the pond was excavated? _____

c. Suppose Theo grants Underground Explorers the right to remove minerals from Theo's portion of Whiteacre. Underground Explorers does so, and in the process negligently pollutes a well on the property. Is Underground Explorers liable to Theo? _____

68. Axel is a homeowner in Main Street, U.S.A. The Main Street City Council passes a zoning ordinance permitting three types of "nonobjectionable" commercial uses (a nursery school, a grocery store, and a bank) in a residential area where Axel's property is located.

a. If Axel sues to challenge the validity of the ordinance, must Axel bear the burden of proving it invalid? _____

b. Can Axel successfully challenge the ordinance as an uncompensated "taking" of his property? _____

c. Suppose that Barry, who operates a funeral parlor and would like to locate in a residential district, challenges the ordinance as a denial of equal protection. Must the city show that the ordinance promotes a compelling state interest? _____

69. Scenic City has an ordinance requiring approval of all proposed construction by a board of architects, in order to insure that no ugly buildings are built. Dan's proposed building plan is rejected, and he challenges the ordinance as unconstitutional.

   a.   If the ordinance provides that the board may refuse a building permit to a building "not conforming to the character of the neighborhood," will Dan probably prevail? _____

   b.   Scenic City also has an ordinance providing that historic buildings cannot be torn down. Is this constitutional? _____

   c.   Emma, a real estate developer, plans to build a subdivision in the city. Can the city council require that Emma dedicate certain space for a public playground within the subdivision? _____

70. Snob Hills, a suburb next to Big City, has an ordinance that excludes apartments from the city. Lolly Gagging wants to erect apartments.

   a.   Is the exclusion of apartments constitutional? _____

   b.   If Lolly is a developer who lives in Big City, who has no present plans to build in Snob Hills and owns no land there, but is looking to the future, can Lolly sue Snob Hills in federal court? _____

71. Crystal operates a meat market in Tiny Township. A zoning ordinance is passed which prevents any commercial use of property in the area where Crystal's market is located. The ordinance provides that any existing commercial use must be terminated within 30 days.

   a.   Must Crystal move within 30 days? _____

   b.   Can Crystal succeed in an action for inverse condemnation? _____

72. Big City amends its zoning map so as to reclassify Gentry's land, previously in a residential district, to a light industry zone.

   a.   Can Hattie, Gentry's neighbor, enjoin the amendment if it does not conform to Big City's master plan? _____

   b.   If Hattie brings suit, does Big City have the burden of proof? _____

73. Luis owns a lot in Star Pines; the zoning ordinance permits construction only upon the 50% of each parcel farthest from the street. Luis's lot has drainage problems making construction away from the street extremely expensive.

   a.   Is it possible for Luis to get a permit to build closer to the street? _____

   b.   Would the result be different if many lots in the area had the same problem? _____

74. Momoko owns Blackacre, a tract in the country.

   a. If the government takes one foot of Blackacre, must it pay Momoko for damage to the remainder? _____

   b. If the state prohibits the use of Blackacre for any use except as a public park, is the state liable in inverse condemnation? _____

   c. Suppose Blackacre is wetlands, and the state prohibits development. Is the state liable in inverse condemnation? _____

75. Nina owns Greenacre, which is prime agricultural land at the edge of suburbia; it has great potential for development. For agricultural use only the land is worth $100 an acre; for subdivision use, $500 an acre. The land is presently zoned for agricultural use. The county condemns two acres of Greenacre for a fire station. It argues that it should pay Nina $200, and not $1,000, because the government could destroy the $800 difference by refusing to rezone Blackacre. Is this sound? _____

76. Lauren executes a written contract to sell her apartment house to Matthew, with title to pass upon closing in 60 days.

   a. The contract calls for Matthew to tender the purchase price on September 14. Matthew submits the price on September 15. Can Matthew enforce the contract? _____

   b. If the contract makes no provision therefor, is there a warranty that Lauren will convey marketable title to Matthew? _____

   c. Prior to closing, Matthew discovers that Nick is the record owner of the property but that Lauren can prove title by adverse possession. Can Matthew cancel the escrow? _____

   d. Suppose Matthew discovers that the apartment has been constructed with insufficient sewer outlets, in violation of local building codes, and that legal action has begun regarding this violation. Can Matthew back out of the deal? _____

77. Orville contracts to sell Woodacre to Paula. On the date of closing, Paula tenders the purchase price but Orville refuses to convey the property and further discloses that the land is subject to an easement held by Quashee Co., an adjoining landowner.

   a. Can Paula obtain specific performance of the agreement? _____

   b. If Orville tenders title to the property subject to the easement of Quashee Co., but Paula refuses to pay the purchase price, can Orville compel specific performance of the contract? _____

c. Suppose that by the date of closing, the title to Woodacre is found to be held by Ross rather than Orville. Between the date of contract of sale and date of closing, the property has increased $50,000 in value. If Orville did not know that title was in Ross, is Paula entitled to $50,000 in damages? _____

78. A.C. O'Troubles contracts to sell his house to Gloria Fying. Shortly before closing, the house is destroyed by flood.

    a. Assuming Gloria has not yet occupied the house, can A.C. obtain specific performance of the contract? _____

    b. If A.C. has insurance on the property, must he credit the proceeds against the purchase price if the buyer bears the risk of loss and A.C. obtains specific performance? _____

79. In return for $5,000 Felix gives Gary a 30-day option to purchase an office building which Felix owns. Felix dies four days later, leaving a will which devises all of his real property to Herbie and the remainder of his estate to Iris. If Gary decides to exercise the option, is Iris entitled to the purchase price? _____

80. Professor Vera Similitude states that acknowledgment or attestation of a deed is not required to make it effective, but should be done wherever possible. Is she correct? _____

81. Sarah Yayvo conveys Blackacre to "the heirs of my deceased friend, Ferdinand Hapsburg." Is this a valid deed? _____

82. Juan conveys to Pablo "that portion of Whiteacre bounded on the south by the fire road." If Juan also owns the land over which the fire road runs, does Pablo have title to any portion of the road? _____

83. Helen Highwater prepares a deed of her house to Moira Less and has the deed recorded. She does not hand over the deed to Moira.

    a. Will this, without more, establish delivery of the deed to Moira? _____

    b. Can Helen introduce evidence that, despite recording the deed, she had no intent to make a present transfer to Moira? _____

84. Hazel Nutt executes a deed conveying Blackacre to Phil Burt, "upon condition that title pass next January 10th."

    a. If Hazel hands the deed to Phil, has there been a valid delivery? _____

    b. Would the result probably be the same if the condition were stated orally by Hazel when she handed the deed to Phil? _____

85. Paula executes a deed conveying Whiteacre to Monica and hands the deed to Monica's friend, Bill, with instructions to give the deed to Monica. Can Paula recall the deed before Bill gives it to Monica? _____

86. On July 1, pursuant to an oral contract of sale, Scott hands Tamar a deed naming Mei-ling as grantee of his ski cabin and orally instructs Tamar to give the deed to Mei-ling "if Mei-ling pays $5,000 before October 30."

   a. On August 1, Scott seeks to recall the deed so that he can sell the cabin to Virginia. Can he do so? _____

   b. Suppose that on July 10, Mei-ling steals the deed from Tamar and sells the cabin to Walter, a bona fide purchaser. Does title pass to Walter? _____

87. Scarlett conveys her farm, Possum Acres (not to be confused with Tara), to Melanie by a general warranty deed. Unknown to the parties, Scarlett's title to the property was defective at the time Rhett bought it for her.

   a. Is Scarlett liable to Melanie for the defect? _____

   b. Would the result be different if the conveyance were by a special warranty or quitclaim deed? _____

   c. If the soil on Possum Acres is no longer arable, is Scarlett liable to Melanie under the warranty deed? _____

88. Montana has a terrible dislike of lawyers. A deed executed by Montana in 1990 and promptly recorded conveyed Blackacre "to my daughter Georgia and her heirs, but if any child of Georgia becomes a lawyer, to Dakota and his heirs." Georgia has a child, Virginia, in grammar school. In 2005, Georgia purports to convey Blackacre in fee simple absolute to Tennessee by a general warranty deed. Tennessee pays Georgia $10,000, the full value of Blackacre.

   a. In 2007, Virginia is admitted to the bar. Tennessee sues Georgia for breach of the covenant of seisin. Can he recover? _____

   b. In 2007, Dakota ousts Tennessee from the land and Tennessee sues Georgia for breach of the covenant of general warranty. Can Tennessee recover from Georgia? _____

89. Ned purports to convey his house in fee simple to Olive, but Ned actually is a life tenant of the property. Olive occupies the house for 20 years until her death, devising the house to Phil.

   a. Can Phil sue Ned for breach of covenant? _____

   b. Would the result be different if Ned had a fee simple title to the house, but it was subject to a mortgage? _____

   c. In either case, would Ned be liable if Olive knew of the title defects and sued promptly? _____

d. Suppose that Quinn brings a quiet title action against Phil, establishes paramount title to the house, and ejects Phil. Can Phil sue Ned for breach of covenant? _____

90. Mario sells Blackacre to Eduardo, giving him a general warranty deed. Eduardo is subsequently evicted by Alicia in a quiet title action.

   a. If Eduardo successfully sues Mario for a breach of a covenant of quiet enjoyment, can Eduardo recover the amount he paid for Blackacre? _____

   b. Assuming Eduardo made improvements to Blackacre, can Eduardo recover the fair market value of the property at the time of eviction if it exceeds the purchase price paid? _____

91. Bella Theball conveys her truck farm to Al Eluya as a gift, but Al does not record the deed. Bella dies intestate, and her heirs sell the truck farm to Perry Stroyka, a bona fide purchaser without notice of the gift to Al.

   a. If Perry records immediately, will he prevail over Al in a quiet title action? _____

   b. Would the result be different in a "notice" state, if Perry likewise had failed to record? _____

   c. Would the result be different if Bella's heirs conveyed the property to Perry as a gift? _____

   d. If Bella's heirs had decided instead to keep the farm, would they prevail over Al in a quiet title suit? _____

92. Isaiah conveys Blackacre to John on June 1, and John records on June 15. On June 10, Isaiah conveys Blackacre to Kathy, a bona fide purchaser without knowledge of the deed to John. Kathy records on June 18.

   a. Will John prevail over Kathy in a "notice" jurisdiction? _____

   b. Will John prevail over Kathy in a "race-notice" or "race" jurisdiction? _____

93. Lucy is the grantee of property under a deed from Manuel, who had previously conveyed the same land to Nellie.

   a. If Manuel tells Lucy that he previously conveyed to Nellie, but that Nellie's title is unenforceable because not recorded, does this prevent Lucy from being a subsequent BFP? _____

   b. Would the result be the same if Manuel had told Lucy nothing, but Nellie had moved onto the property? _____

   c. Suppose Manuel had deeded the property to Lucy as security for a preexisting debt he owed Lucy. Would Lucy be a BFP? _____

d.   Would Lucy be a BFP if Lucy had obtained the property for less than its market value?

94.   Olivia conveys Whiteacre to Pedro, who immediately presents the deed to the recorder for filing. Unknown to Pedro, the deed is not indexed under Olivia's name in the recorder's office. Olivia subsequently sells Whiteacre to Quincy, a bona fide purchaser.

a.   Will Pedro prevail over Quincy?

b.   If Pedro's deed is properly recorded but contains no acknowledgment, will Pedro prevail over Quincy?

95.   Ramon conveys Blackacre to Sarah, who does not record. Sarah conveys Blackacre to Tim, who promptly records his deed from Sarah. Ramon then conveys to Ursula, a BFP, who records. Does Ursula prevail over Tim?

96.   Vincent resides on Whiteacre, which is owned by his father, Wilbur. Vincent deeds Whiteacre to Yvonne on March 10, and Yvonne records immediately. On March 25, Wilbur dies, devising Whiteacre to Vincent. Vincent then sells Whiteacre to Zachary, a BFP who knew nothing of the Vincent-Yvonne conveyance.

a.   In most states does Yvonne prevail over Zachary?

b.   Would Yvonne prevail against Vincent if Vincent had not sold the property to Zachary?

97.   On January 1, Abe mortgages Greenacre to Bob, who does not then record. On February 1, Abe mortgages Greenacre to Carol, who knows of Bob's mortgage. Carol records. Bob, learning of Carol's mortgage, records his mortgage on February 8. On March 1, Carol assigns her mortgage to Diana, a BFP. Does Diana prevail over Bob in most states?

98.   Evelyn, the owner of adjoining hillside parcels 1 and 2, conveys the upper parcel, number 1, to Felipe with a covenant by Evelyn that she, her heirs and assigns will not use parcel 2 to obstruct the view that parcel 1 commands over parcel 2. Evelyn later conveys parcel 2 to Gene, without mention of any restriction. Does Gene take parcel 2 subject to Felipe's rights?

99.   Harry conveys Brownacre to Iva, who registers title under the Torrens system. Thereafter, Jenna enters the property and remains in adverse possession throughout the requisite 20-year period. Has Jenna established title to Brownacre?

100.   Title Insurance Company insures title to Kenny's house in the amount of $50,000. Subsequently Kenny finds that his title is defective; the property is now worth $75,000. Can Kenny recover $50,000?

Answers to Review Questions

1.a. **YES**   The person who takes prior possession of the fox wins. A person must capture a wild animal, or mortally wound it, to take possession; mere pursuit is not enough. [§7]

b. **YES**   Although Mabel captured the fox, and thus took possession, she lost possession when the fox escaped. [§14]

2. **DEPENDS**   States following the common enemy doctrine allow diversion of surface waters onto adjacent land, but most require that Lopez's diversion be reasonable, avoiding disproportionate damage to his neighbors. [§28]

3. **DEPENDS**   In a natural flow jurisdiction, Victoria Farms can use water only on riparian land. In some reasonable use jurisdictions, Victoria Farms can use water on nonriparian lands if this does not harm other riparians. In prior appropriation jurisdictions, Victoria Farms can use the water on nonriparian land. [§§34, 38, 40]

4. **NO**   The innocent improver acquires title only if there is so great a disparity between the original and improved values of the chattel that it would be unfair to award it to the owner. If the owner gets the chattel, the innocent improver may be awarded the value of her labor where an injustice would otherwise result. [§46]

5.a. **NO**   The prior possessor usually wins. As against a guest, Anna has a prior constructive possession of all objects in her home, even though unaware of them. [§69]

b. **PROBABLY NOT**   The ring has probably been mislaid by the owner intentionally placing it there. She has left it in the custody (possession) of the owner of the store. [§74]

c. **NO**   Unless classified as treasure trove, property found under the surface of the soil is in the prior possession of the owner of the locus, even though the owner is unaware of it. A ring is not treasure trove. [§§67-68]

d. **YES**   Anna is not in prior possession. The ring has been lost, not mislaid, and is awarded to the finder. [§§72-74]

6.a. **YES**   Even though acting on a mistaken belief, Amy has a good faith belief that the land is hers and she intends to claim the land as her own. If she stays in possession long enough, she wins under either the objective or subjective test of claim of title. [§§97-100]

b. **YES**   Charlie can tack Amy's possession on to his own if he is in privity of estate with Amy. Even though Amy had no color of title to Greenacre, voluntary transfer of *possession* of Greenacre by Amy to Charlie puts Charlie in privity of estate with Amy. Thus, together they have held adversely for 10 years. [§§124-125]

7.	**SPLIT OF AUTHORITY**	Some courts say Shinji is not an adverse possessor if he would not have occupied the 20-foot strip if he had known it was not his. If he would not have occupied it had he known of the mistake, he does not have a hostile intent. Most courts reject this subjective view of hostile intent and find that Shinji acted hostilely when, believing the 20-foot strip was his, he performed objective acts claiming ownership. [§§106-108]
8.a.	**YES**	Juan has title by adverse possession if summer occupancy is the use an average owner would make of the property, which appears to be true in this case. [§122]
b.	**NO**	Mary's use tends to show that an average owner would use the property in the winter time (as well as in the summer). It also interrupts possession by the adverse possessor. Either will defeat Juan's attempt to gain title by adverse possession. [§122]
9.a.	**NO**	Privity of estate is present between Helen and Jane, but not between Jane and Karl. Hence, Karl's possession cannot be tacked onto Jane's, and a new 20-year period begins with Karl's possession. [§§124, 125]
b.	**YES**	An oral, voluntary transfer of possession is sufficient for privity of estate and tacking between successive adverse possessors. Hence, a total of 21 years in possession by Helen, Jane, and Karl gives Karl title to the property. [§125]
10.	**YES**	Where possession is under color of title, the adverse possessor is deemed to occupy all of the land described in the instrument, provided the land described is viewed in the community as one tract, possession is taken of a significant part, and no one is in possession of the part not actually occupied. [§138]
11.	**YES**	A voluntary bailee has strict liability for delivering the goods to the wrong person. [§200]
12.a.	**NO**	The insurance policy has not been delivered, either actually, constructively, or symbolically. [§§209, 212-216]
b.	**NO**	Constructive delivery (by a key) is not allowed when the object is capable of manual delivery. Dolly could easily hand over the box. [§212]
c.(1)	**NO**	A revocable escrow is invalid, because the donor has not surrendered control of the object. [§223]
(2)	**YES**	A revocable trust is valid. [§225]

d.	**YES**	Constructive delivery is allowed where a person is dying and is physically unable to go to the bank. [§§213-214]
13.a.	**YES**	A person is seised of land only if he has a freehold estate in possession. [§251]
b.	**NO**	Words of purchase state the name of the person or persons who are given an estate by grant or devise. For example, in a grant "to A and her heirs," the words "to A" are words of purchase, and the words "and her heirs" are words of limitation. [§257]
c.	**NO**	A future interest is a presently existing interest, but the holder is not entitled presently to possession. It can be passed by will or intestacy, and usually can be seized by creditors. [§366]
14.a.	**YES**	The fee simple determinable has ended, and Antonia, as owner, has the right to possession. [§§279-280]
b.	**NO**	The deed can be construed as creating either a determinable fee or a fee simple subject to condition subsequent. If construed as the former, the fee simple terminated upon industrial use. If construed as the latter (the preferred construction), Maria has a fee simple subject to Antonia's right of entry, which is now exercisable. [§291]
15.a.	**SPLIT OF AUTHORITY**	Some courts hold that the statute of limitations does not begin to run on Margie until she exercises her right of entry. Other courts hold the statute runs from the time of breach of condition. Also, the equitable doctrine of laches may run against Margie if her failure to assert her right would cause damage to Manny. (*See* Remedies Summary.) [§293]
b.	**YES**	When the fee simple determinable ends in 1984, title automatically reverts to Margie. Since 1984 Manny has been an adverse possessor. [§§87, 285, 383]
16.	**DEPENDS**	If the *intent* of Oscar is to give Emmy support only until she marries and becomes supported by her second husband, the condition restraining marriage is valid. If the intent of Oscar is to penalize Emmy for marrying, the restraint is void and Emmy has a fee simple absolute. A fee simple determinable upon remarriage has often been held indicative of an intent to support, not to penalize, and thus the restraint is probably valid. [§§294-295]
17.a.	**NO**	This would create a fee tail in Olivia, but she could not devise it by will. It was inherited by her eldest son and heir. [§§301, 304-305]
b.	**SPLIT OF AUTHORITY**	In some states the fee tail remains, and the fee tail tenant can convey a fee simple absolute by deed. In other states, the language in Nicole's will would create a fee simple in Olivia. But in still other states, the language in Nicole's devise would create a life estate in Olivia, remainder to her issue. In these states Olivia could not convey a fee simple. [§§315-319]

c.	**SPLIT OF AUTHORITY**	Where the fee tail remains, Olivia can bar the entail and remainder in Penelope by conveying a fee simple. Where the fee tail is abolished, Olivia can convey a fee simple absolute only in those states which construe the language in Nicole's will as giving Olivia a fee simple absolute. [§§315-319]
18.a.	**NO**	Life tenant's obligation is to maintain the property, not to make permanent improvements. [§331]
b.	**DEPENDS**	This is voluntary waste, but because it is *ameliorating*, the holder of the remainder may not have an action for damages if the property value is increased and the grantor had no intent to pass the vineyard itself to the remainderman. The answer depends on the grantor's intent. [§§333, 336]
19.a.	**YES**	The purported restraint on alienation is void, and Hedda can freely transfer the cabin to whomever she pleases. [§§344, 346]
b.	**NO**	A reasonable restraint on the transfer of a condominium unit is valid, provided it is not used to violate civil rights laws (*i.e.,* to discriminate because of race, religion, etc). [§§355, 816-834]
20.a.	**YES**	Ashley has a reversion, which becomes possessory upon Bill's death. Bill has a reversion, which becomes possessory, if at all, upon the expiration of 25 years within Bill's lifetime. [§§369, 378]
b.	**NO**	Bill cannot convey a larger estate than he has. Therefore, the leasehold will expire at Bill's death or after 25 years, whichever happens first. [§378]
21.a.	**NO**	A possibility of reverter cannot be created in a transferee. It is an interest retained by the *grantor* if created by deed, or retained by the *testator's heirs* if created by a will. Mercy Hospital has an executory interest, which is not subject to the Rule Against Perpetuities because all interests in Blackacre are given to charities. [§§384, 546]
b.	**SPLIT OF AUTHORITY**	In most jurisdictions a possibility of reverter is alienable, but in some it is not. In the latter, the conveyance to Elizabeth is void. [§§385-386]
c.	**SPLIT OF AUTHORITY**	Jurisdictions go three ways. In some, the right of entry is alienable (thus Elizabeth has it). In others, the right of entry cannot be alienated (thus Diana still has it). In still others, the mere attempt to alienate the right of entry destroys it (thus the School Board has a fee simple absolute). [§§391-392]
22.	**YES**	The property will revert to Sonia on Lucy's death if Ellis dies before reaching 21. [§421]
23.	**NO**	Jason does not have a reversion in Whiteacre because a vested remainder subject to divestment was given to Bob. Because Bob's interest was never divested (*i.e.,* no child of Arnie's survived him), Bob's heirs now own Whiteacre. [§410]

24.a. **NO**   Ian's interest is a vested remainder subject to divestment (*i.e.,* by Ian's failing to survive Henry). [§§410-411]

b. **NO**   Jennifer has an executory interest, which can become possessory only by *divesting* Ian's vested remainder. [§§375, 411, 456]

c. **NO**   Ian's heirs cannot be ascertained until his death. Hence the remainder is contingent because the takers are unascertained. [§419]

25.a. **YES**   George's remainder is vested subject to open up and let in other children, and also subject to complete divestment if Edward dies without children surviving him. [§413]

b. **NO**   James has an executory interest because his interest can vest only by divesting George's vested remainder. [§§375, 411, 456]

c. **YES**   James has a contingent remainder because his interest *can* become possessory *without divesting* anyone. If George had a vested remainder, as in the principal hypothetical, James could take possession only by divesting George, and thus would have an executory interest. However, here George has a contingent remainder. [§§374, 427]

d. **NO**   James's interest in both the principal hypothetical and in c. is transmissible at his death to his heirs. It is not contingent upon surviving anyone. [§432]

26.a. **NO**   Because Leonardo has not made present livery of seisin to Veronica, Veronica has no legal freehold interest. Before 1536, a freehold could not be created at law to spring out in the future. [§§442, 444]

b. **YES**   If, in the hundred or so years after the Statute of Uses, Leonardo would have to raise a use upon which the Statute operated. If he had used a feoffment to uses, a bargain and sale deed, or a covenant to stand seised, Veronica would have a legal *springing* executory interest that may divest the *transferor* (Leonardo). Under modern law, a springing executory interest can be created by any kind of deed or by will. [§§448-451, 458]

c. **YES**   Veronica has a *shifting* executory interest that may divest a *transferee* (Winston). [§456]

27.a. **NO**   The children have a contingent remainder, which is destroyed by merger of Joseph's life estate into Rose's reversion. [§§465, 471]

b. **YES**   John has a vested remainder in fee simple subject to open. Rose has no reversion. A vested remainder cannot be destroyed by merger. [§475]

c. **YES**   If destructibility of contingent remainders is abolished, Joseph has the life estate and reversion, subject to the indestructible interest in Rose's children. If Rose has a child, that child will take the property on Joseph's death. [§482]

28.a. **NO** Peregrina's life estate is equitable; the remainder in Peregrina's heirs is legal. Hence the Rule does not apply. [§§376, 484, 501]

b. **YES** Peregrina has an equitable life estate. Her heirs have an equitable remainder, which by the Rule in Shelley's Case is given to Peregrina. These merge and Peregrina has the equitable fee simple. [§§376, 501]

29. **DEPENDS** Under the Doctrine of Worthier Title, the remainder in Quinn's heirs is void, and Quinn has a reversion. If the Doctrine applies, Quinn has all the equitable interests in the trust and can terminate the trust. There is a rebuttable presumption that the Doctrine applies, but it can be overcome by contrary evidence of intent. In some states, the Doctrine has been abolished. In these states, Quinn cannot terminate the trust. [§§508, 516, 519]

30.a. **YES** The devise is void. B might die tomorrow, and the first child of A to become a lawyer might be an afterborn child. The first child of A to become a lawyer might become a lawyer more than 21 years after the death of A and B. [§528]

b. **YES** The devise to A's children is void. All of A's children will not necessarily reach age 25 within 21 years after A's death. A might die leaving a child under the age of four. [§§535, 537]

c. **YES** The executory interest to A violates the Rule because it might become possessory centuries hence. It is struck out. The Library Board has a fee simple absolute. [§547]

d. **YES** The executory interest to A violates the Rule and is struck out. The Library Board has a determinable fee, and T has a possibility of reverter. [§544]

e. **YES** This is the unborn widow case. The remainder in A's issue will not necessarily vest at the death of A and all of A's living issue. It may vest in afterborn issue at the death of A's widow, a woman not necessarily now alive. [§541]

f. **NO** The remainder in A's children will *vest in interest*, if at all, at A's death. No children can be born to A after that time. (In e., above, the remainder to A's *issue* cannot vest in interest until the widow dies because the class of *issue* will not close until then. *Remember:* "Children" includes only one generation; "issue" includes all descendants.) [§§409, 537]

31.a. **NO** Because Ann had an interest in Blackacre when the conveyance took place, there is no unity of time and title between Ann and her co-tenants. [§§592-594]

b. **YES** The common law presumed a joint tenancy so Ben and Chelsea take their two-thirds share as joint tenants between themselves; they hold with Ann as tenants in common. [§§597, 601]

c.	**NO**	Chelsea would have Ben's one-third share plus her own, giving her two-thirds. Ann now holds one-third interest with Chelsea as tenants in common. [§§586, 589]
d.	**NO**	Under modern law, the presumption is that a tenancy in common is created unless a joint tenancy is expressly stated (or in some states, unless an express right of survivorship is stated). [§§603, 606]
32.a.	**NO**	The attempted testamentary disposition is ineffective; the surviving joint tenants have the whole, relieved of Estelle's participation. [§590]
b.	**SPLIT OF AUTHORITY**	In "title theory" states, Fred has transferred title to his interest to the mortgagee, thus severing the joint tenancy. In "lien theory" states, Fred has given the mortgagee only a lien on his interest, and the joint tenancy is not severed. Fred owns Blackacre. (The lien states divide over whether Fred owns Blackacre subject to the mortgage or not.) [§§618-620]
33.a.	**YES**	Joint tenants must have equal shares. This is presumed by taking title as joint tenants, regardless of who pays the consideration. [§598]
b.	**MAYBE**	Partition is an equitable proceeding, and the presumption that joint tenants are entitled to equal shares on partition can be overcome by evidence that Shana did not intend a gift to Che and that this was a business venture. [§697]
34.	**SPLIT OF AUTHORITY**	In most states, the creditors of the husband cannot reach the property because the husband cannot alienate his interest without his wife's consent. In a few states, the husband's creditors can reach the husband's interest; however, they cannot deprive the wife of her interest in the property, including the right of survivorship. [§§649-651]
35.a.	**NO**	Nina is not entitled to share in the proceeds, nor is she liable for any net loss from farming. [§677]
b.	**SPLIT OF AUTHORITY**	In a majority of states, Nina is not entitled to one-half of the reasonable rental value unless Jack has ousted her (*i.e.*, refused to admit her in possession). In a minority of states, Jack must pay Nina one-half of the reasonable rental value. [§§664-671]
c.	**YES**	Jack must pay Nina one-half of any rent he receives from third parties. [§672]
d.	**YES**	Jack must pay one-half of the net amount received to Nina. [§§675-676]
e.	**NO**	A co-tenant cannot require other co-tenants to contribute for improvements to the property. However, upon partition Jack will receive whatever increase in value of the property is attributable to his improvements. [§686]
36.a.	**YES**	The dower attached immediately upon Steven's purchase of the land, and cannot be defeated by a subsequent transfer by Steven to a BFP. [§711]

| b. | **YES** | The statutory elective share gives the surviving spouse a fractional share (usually one-half or one-third) in fee simple of property owned by the decedent spouse at death. Dower is only a *life estate* in one-third of Lazy Acres. [§§714-715, 718] |

37.a. **YES**   A lease at common law can be for any number of years. [§770]

    b. **NO**   Most courts would consider this a tenancy for years, even though the termination date is indefinite. This classification comes closest to carrying out the parties' intention. [§771]

    c. **YES**   The lease would be unenforceable as a tenancy for years because of failure to comply with the Statute of Frauds. However, Christopher's entry plus payment of rent would create a *periodic* tenancy (the period being the same period for which rent is calculated in the invalid lease). [§§785, 801, 806]

38.a. **YES**   The period is determined by the rental period in the agreement. [§779]

    b. **DEPENDS**   By common law, the lease has to be terminated at the end of a rental period. However, statutes may give landlord or tenant the right to terminate on any day with 30 days' notice. [§§786-791]

39. **YES**   A periodic tenant must give notice to terminate the tenancy. A tenant for a term does not have to give notice. [§§774, 789]

40.a. **SPLIT OF AUTHORITY**   Some courts hold that T has a life estate determinable upon T's death. Others say that T is a tenant at will. [§§796-798]

    b. **YES**   This would probably create a tenancy at will, terminable by either L or T at any time. [§797]

    c. **NO**   A tenancy at will is personal, and any attempted assignment by the tenant terminates the tenancy. [§800]

41.a. **NO**   Where the term exceeds one year, the tenant can be held over to a new term up to a maximum of one year. [§812]

    b. **NO**   Assuming there is a tenancy at sufferance (*i.e.*, no implied consent by L to holdover for a period), L can evict T without prior notice. Notice is required to evict a periodic tenant, but not a tenant for years, which T is. [§§774, 809]

42.a. **YES**   The 1968 Fair Housing Act exempts L from its terms ("Mrs. Murphy" exception), but the 1866 Civil Rights Act gives A relief. [§§825-826]

    b. **YES**   The 1866 Civil Rights Act has no application to sex discrimination. [§818]

43.a. **YES**   Actual eviction by L from any portion of the premises causes T's rent obligation to abate entirely while L occupies the corner space. [§851]

b. **YES**   Here, T's rent would only abate proportionately to the space occupied by B. T would remain liable for rent on the remainder of the building. [§853]

44.a. **NO**   Because the lack of hot water is only temporary, there is probably insufficient interference with T's use and enjoyment to establish constructive eviction. The result would be contra if the problem occurred repeatedly or the delays were extended. [§§855, 858]

b. **NO**   The general rule is that T must vacate the premises before he can claim constructive eviction. [§862]

c. **YES**   In this situation, the absence of hot water could result in constructive eviction or breach of an implied covenant of habitability. If a breach of a covenant of habitability is found, T could elect to stay in the apartment and abate the rent. [§§880, 886]

45.a. **NO**   If there is no express covenant to repair, T cannot compel L to make repairs. Under an implied warranty of habitability, damages, and not an injunction, is the standard remedy. [§§891-893, 899-901]

b. **PROBABLY YES**   Modern cases give T the right to have her rent abated when the implied covenant of habitability is breached. In some states, T can use a reasonable portion of the rent money to make repairs. [§§901-905]

c. **SPLIT OF AUTHORITY**   Some courts uphold a waiver, unless unconscionable or against public policy. (Waiver of electrical defects, which make the house dangerous for habitation, might be against public policy.) Other courts hold that a waiver of the implied covenant of habitability in urban residential leases is void. [§§887, 910]

d. **YES**   Recent cases and statutes give T a defense of retaliatory eviction—which may permit T to remain in the apartment until L can show sound business reasons for the eviction. [§§907, 921-929]

46.a. **DEPENDS**   If L knew or should have known of the defective balcony, and did not warn T, L is liable in tort. Otherwise L is not liable. [§933]

b. **NO**   Common law says L is not liable to T's visitors if L warns T. [§934]

c. **DEPENDS**   Modern cases are holding L liable where L breaches a duty of repair (*i.e.*, negligence). [§§947-949]

47.a. **YES**   Statutes in almost all states would permit termination by T unless the lease required him to make substantial repairs. [§§968, 977-980]

b. **DEPENDS**   If T cannot make any other reasonable use of the warehouse, and if the zoning change was unforeseeable, the lease may be terminated because of illegality of use or frustration of purpose. However, upon the particular facts, T may have assumed the risk. [§§975-978]

c. **YES**   Under the modern trend, T has the right to remove such fixtures (and this might also be true under the earlier rule respecting "trade fixtures"). However, removal must occur within a reasonable time (if not prior to T's termination of the lease), and T must pay for any damage to the warehouse caused by the removal. [§§985-987]

48.a. **NO**   Even where L has a statutory lien on such property, L must first obtain a court order before seizing. Any seizure without a court order is unconstitutional. [§§989-991]

b. **NO**   L can retain only the amount necessary to cover rental due, costs of eviction, etc. [§§993, 995]

c. **NO (MAJORITY)**   A few states still permit such self-help remedies, but the growing trend is strongly contra, even where the lease provides that L can use self-help. [§§1020-1025]

d. **YES**   Up until recent years, this defense was not permitted in unlawful detainer actions, but the modern cases permit this defense. [§§1011, 1017-1018]

49.a. **NO**   Because forfeiture terminates the lease, T is not liable for future rent unless some other valid lease provision binds him to pay notwithstanding termination of the lease. [§§1002, 1006-1007]

b. **SPLIT OF AUTHORITY**   The old rule is that L can stand by and do nothing. However, the modern trend is to require L to mitigate damages by reletting. [§§1030-1032]

50.a. **YES**   L can sue T on the contract. L can sue A, assignee, because there is privity of estate between L and A. [§§1035-1037, 1047]

b. **YES**   This is a sublease, not an assignment, and L can sue T but not A for the rent. A sublessee is not in privity of estate with L. [§§1038, 1055]

c. **YES**   L is a third-party beneficiary of A's promise to T. [§1056]

d. **NO**   Such a transfer is a sublease, and the covenant, strictly construed, only prohibits assignment. [§1058]

51.a. **YES**   Negative easements are generally limited to the four common law types: light, air, support, and stream flow. But equitable servitudes, analogous to negative easements, are very common. [§§1084-1086, 1185]

b. **NO**   Courts favor easements appurtenant because they benefit land and increase its economic value, and the owner of an easement appurtenant is more easily located than is the owner of an easement in gross. [§§1087-1092]

52.a. **NO**   Although the description of the strip is quite definite, indicating a fee simple, the deed says "to be used," indicating an easement. [§1108]

b. **YES**   Most courts would not permit reservation of an easement in favor of a third party. A few courts would permit such an easement by reservation. [§§1113-1116]

c. **NO**   Alexis has reserved no rights. An easement will be implied only if there is a quasi-easement (existing visible use) the parties intended to continue. Drainage does not appear to qualify as a quasi-easement. [§§1117-1122]

d. **DEPENDS**   If Lot 2 were landlocked, Alexis would have an implied easement by necessity. If the road is merely convenient access to the highway, there is a split of authority. Some courts would deny Alexis an implied easement by reservation, but the majority would give her an implied easement by reservation on the basis of a quasi-easement if a replacement road would be costly and the facts indicated that the parties intended the use to continue. [§§1125-1128]

e. **NO**   If an implied easement exists in either case, it is valid against a subsequent purchaser of the servient estate, even if she is without notice. An implied easement does not arise from a recordable document, and is not within the recording system. [§§1093, 1728]

53.a. **YES**   Assuming the use by Dilly and Emma was hostile, open, notorious, and continuous, a prescriptive easement can be acquired over the path. Tacking is permitted. [§§1136-1144]

b. **SPLIT OF AUTHORITY**   Some courts, following the "lost grant" theory, hold that a sign indicates non-acquiescence, negating an implied lost grant. Others hold that the owner of the servient estate can break the running of a prescriptive easement only by erecting a permanent obstruction to bar further use of the path. [§§1134-1135, 1145]

c. **YES**   If Greenacre was formerly a part of a parcel containing the adjoining property, and if when separated from it Greenacre was landlocked, Greenacre would have a way of necessity over the adjoining parcel. (If Greenacre was not landlocked by separation from the adjoining parcel, no way of necessity exists over it; if Greenacre did not have a way of necessity, Emma would have to rely upon prescription—or bargain her way out.) [§1127]

54.a. **DEPENDS**   The amount of Gregory's use of the easement depends upon the burden to Heather's property contemplated when Blackacre was sold and the reasonableness of any change in use of the property and easement. [§§1150-1152]

b. **NO**   If the easement was specifically described in the deed, Heather cannot move it elsewhere for her own convenience. [§1158]

c.	**YES**	The easement is appurtenant and hence is transferred with the land. [§1168]
d.	**YES**	Although this is an easement in gross, it is of a commercial character and thus would be held assignable by most courts. [§§1169-1170]
55.	**NO**	Mere nonuse of an easement does not extinguish the easement regardless of how long the nonuse continues. [§1176]
56.	**YES**	The remedy available is a primary difference. Another difference is that privity may be required for a covenant to run at law but not in equity. [§§1189-1192, 1222-1228]
57.	**NO**	There must be privity of estate between Quick and Ralph in order for the burden of the covenant (on Quick's land) to run at law. There is no privity here, in any of the meanings of that term. [§§1201-1207]
58.a.	**NO**	Vertical privity of estate is necessary in order for the burden to run, allowing Minna to sue I.C. at law. Here, I.C. is not in vertical privity of estate because he did not succeed to Millie's entire estate. [§§1209-1211]
b.	**NO**	No privity of estate between Millie and I.C. exists. [§§1209-1210]
59.a.	**YES**	Both the benefit and burden touch and concern the land, because good repair enhances the value of the property (whether or not Yetta makes use of same). [§§1245, 1250]
b.	**NO**	Here, the covenant calls for performance on Yetta's mountain cabin, and assigns of the land in town cannot enforce this covenant because it does not touch and concern the land in town. [§1251]
60.a.	**NO**	The benefit is in gross; therefore, according to most courts, the burden will not run. [§§1255-1259]
b.	**NO**	Anthony has no control over the restaurant following the sale, and a cessation of his liability will be implied. [§1217]
61.a.	**SPLIT OF AUTHORITY**	Most courts would hold that Delta's common scheme of single-family dwellings creates an implied reciprocal negative servitude on the remaining 20 lots, which Erin has notice of, and which the subdivision neighbors can enforce. But some courts (California and Massachusetts are examples) will not imply a restrictive covenant on Erin's lots. In these jurisdictions, she can build the apartment houses. [§§1230-1235]
b.	**NO**	Only *negative* reciprocal servitudes will be implied; courts will not imply affirmative promises. [§1234]
c.	**YES**	The prior grantees can enforce the covenant either on the ground that an implied reciprocal servitude on the 20 lots arose when the subdivision was first

developed or on third-party beneficiary rationale. (California would not permit prior grantees to enforce unless they were expressly granted that right.) [§§1230-1236, 1243]

d. SPLIT OF AUTHORITY

This may negate any "common scheme," so that a restriction will not be implied in a. It also may establish that the benefit of the covenant runs to Delta and not to the neighbors (so that Delta alone can enforce the covenant). But there are cases contra. [§1237]

62.a. SPLIT OF AUTHORITY

If Sherry was in horizontal privity of estate with Phyllis, Maude can recover damages from Coco. Under the majority view, a grantor-grantee relationship provides privity, and Maude would win. Under the tenurial or mutual interest view, there is no privity. (Maude could get an injunction, because privity is not required in equity.) [§§1201-1207, 1226]

b. YES

In most states, equity will enforce an express affirmative covenant against a subsequent purchaser. In a few, equity will enforce only a negative covenant against a subsequent purchaser. [§§1223-1224, 1250-1254]

c. YES

The Association can sue in equity to enforce the express lien, even though an action at law for damages will not lie. [§§1214, 1252-1253]

63.a. YES

An injunction will be granted if the benefits of the restriction can still be achieved for the other lots in the subdivision. An injunction will be denied only if the *entire* 50-lot tract is now unsuitable for residential purposes. [§1277]

b. YES

A cumulative zoning ordinance is not in conflict with the private restriction because residences are permitted in commercial zones. (A zoning ordinance prohibiting residences in commercial zones might be held to override the private restriction.) [§1381]

64.a. DEPENDS

The corporation can establish reasonable rules of conduct, and terminate leases upon violation. If alternative facilities (gym, etc.) are available, and Mary is clearly disturbing surrounding tenants, the restriction may be reasonable. [§§1309-1310]

b. SPLIT OF AUTHORITY

Some courts refuse to review a refusal to consent provided it is not based on discriminatory grounds. Others will review the reasonableness of the refusal. [§1307]

65.a. NO

The fact that the use is authorized by zoning ordinances is not controlling in an action for private nuisance. [§1326]

b. DEPENDS

Plaintiff's coming to the nuisance is one factor, but not the sole controlling factor, in determining whether relief for a nuisance will be granted. [§1328]

c. NO

The complainant must have a property interest affected by the nuisance, unless she suffers bodily harm from the activity (which is unlikely here). [§1312]

66.a.	**YES**	The utility of the conduct is an important factor. The character of the neighborhood, the importance of Qua Corp. to the economy, the severity of the damage to Bella, and the available means of controlling pollutants are probably determinative. [§§1315, 1327]
b.	**YES**	If the pollution is found to be a nuisance but the activity is too important to be enjoined, a court may refuse an injunction and award damages to Bella. [§§1329-1330, 1350-1351]
c.	**NO**	If damages are given Bella, all the gains from trade are given to Qua Corp. [§1350]
67.a.	**YES**	Underground Explorers has strict liability for damage to neighboring land by withdrawing lateral support. [§1359]
b.	**MAYBE**	Some courts extend the duty of absolute support of adjoining land to buildings thereon. However, the majority holds the excavator liable only for negligence in excavating the pond, where the building slips because of the weight of the building. The question then is whether Underground Explorers was negligent. [§§1361-1362]
c.	**YES**	Because Underground Explorers was negligent in removing minerals, it is liable for damaging the neighbor's well. [§1364]
68.a.	**YES**	There is a presumption of validity that the ordinance is an exercise of the state's police power. [§1385]
b.	**NO**	Axel is not deprived of all reasonable use (he has residential and three commercial uses available). However, Axel might have an argument that the ordinance violates the enabling act or is a denial of substantive due process or equal protection. [§§1383, 1388, 1392, 1473]
c.	**NO**	Because this does not involve a suspect classification, the standard of review is whether the ordinance bears a rational relationship to a permissible state objective. [§1392]
69.a.	**NO**	The modern trend is to uphold such architectural review boards where the applicable standard is the "existing character of the neighborhood." [§1432]
b.	**YES**	If the existing use gives the owner a reasonable return on his investment, the ordinance will be upheld, according to most recent cases. [§1440]
c.	**MAYBE**	City must show that the permit conditions bear a rough proportionality to the negative impact of the development on the public. [§1481]
70.a.	**MAYBE**	Some cases hold that the complete exclusion of apartments from a suburban city is unconstitutional. [§§1449-1452]

b. **NO**   Lolly has no standing in federal court because she has no personal stake in the matter and the injury is too speculative. [§1456]

71.a. **NO**   Amortization ordinances have been upheld in most states if they are reasonable as applied. A 30-day period appears to be too short a time, even if Crystal's only investment is in the business. If she owns the nonconforming building, a 30-day period is clearly too short for amortization. [§§1404-1406]

b. **YES**   Because Crystal is not a nuisance and has no reasonable return on her investment under the ordinance, she is entitled to damages. [§§1472-1473, 1483]

72.a. **YES**   Any amendments that do not comply with the master plan may be attacked as "spot zoning." [§1412]

b. **SPLIT OF AUTHORITY**   The older cases held that a zoning amendment is presumptively valid, but some new cases put the burden of proof on the city to justify a zoning amendment. [§§1413-1415]

73.a. **YES**   Luis may obtain a variance allowing him to build closer to the street. [§§1416-1417]

b. **YES**   The hardship required for a variance must be unique and not general to the area. The proper remedy would be an amendment, not a variance. [§1417]

74.a. **YES**   This is known as severance damages. [§1492]

b. **YES**   The requirement that Momoko admit the public on her property, if she uses it at all, is a taking. Momoko has no reasonable private use left in Blackacre. [§§1469, 1473]

c. **NO**   Recent cases uphold wetlands zoning on the theory that existing uses permitted are reasonable and development is harmful. [§1442]

75. **NO**   Even though the government can regulate out value by refusing to rezone, fairness requires that it pay the market value (including speculative value about the probabilities of rezoning) on the date of condemnation. [§§1485, 1489-1491]

76.a. **YES**   Unless a "time is of the essence" clause is in the contract, this probably constitutes performance within a reasonable period. [§§1515-1516]

b. **YES**   There is an implied warranty that the seller will furnish marketable title at the closing. [§1517]

c. **SPLIT OF AUTHORITY**   Unless the contract specified marketable record title, most courts hold that the seller can prove title by adverse possession. [§1522]

d. **YES**   Building code violations usually do not make title unmarketable, but a legal action commenced to enforce the building code does. [§§1519, 1529, 1536]

77.a.	**YES**	If the value of Quashee's easement can be calculated (so that a proper abatement in the purchase price can be made), Paula is entitled to specific performance. [§§1537-1538]
b.	**DEPENDS**	If the easement is a substantial defect, specific performance is not available to the seller. If insubstantial, then the seller is entitled to specific performance with a reduction in purchase price for the easement. [§1543]
c.	**SPLIT OF AUTHORITY**	Where the seller's breach is unintentional (not known when the contract is signed), the courts are split. Many states would give the buyer $50,000, but others would give Paula only monies paid to Orville plus out-of-pocket costs (title search, etc.). *Compare:* If Orville knew all along that title was in Ross, Paula would get $50,000 in most states. [§§1539-1541]
78.a.	**SPLIT OF AUTHORITY**	In most states, Gloria is deemed to have title through equitable conversion and she bears the risk of loss. Hence, A.C. can enforce the contract. Other states follow the Massachusetts rule and put the risk of loss on the seller, or have a statute putting risk of loss on the party in possession. In these states, A.C. cannot get specific performance. [§§1548, 1552-1559]
b.	**YES**	Most courts require the seller to credit the insurance proceeds against the purchase price if the buyer bears the risk of loss. [§1555]
79.	**NO**	Felix, at death, had title subject to an option, and this title passes to Herbie, not Iris. Because the option is not exercised until after Felix's death, equitable conversion does not take place. [§1560]
80.	**YES**	While not necessary for an effective deed, acknowledgment or attestation may be required for recordation and is always helpful in authenticating the deed. [§§1567-1569]
81.	**YES**	Because Ferdinand is dead his heirs can be determined, and delivery can be made. If Ferdinand were alive, the deed might be void for uncertainty or for want of delivery (because Ferdinand's heirs are not presently ascertainable). [§1581]
82.	**YES**	Pablo presumptively takes title to the northern half of the road. [§1596]
83.a.	**YES**	If Helen demonstrates an intent that the deed have present operative effect, handing over the deed is not required to make delivery. Recordation raises a presumption of delivery. [§1599]
b.	**YES**	The presumption is rebuttable by evidence of the grantor's intent not to make delivery. [§1599]
84.a.	**YES**	Where the condition is stated in writing, there has been a valid delivery of a deed creating a future interest in the grantee. [§1602]

b. **NO**   Most courts would not admit parol evidence of Hazel's statement to show that delivery was subject to a condition. [§1608]

85. **NO**   Unless Bill is acting *solely* as Paula's agent (which does not appear to be the case here), there is a valid delivery to Bill for Monica when Bill receives the deed, and it cannot be recalled. [§§1610, 1613]

86.a. **SPLIT OF AUTHORITY**   When the escrow instructions are oral, some courts allow Scott to recall the deed, unless there is an underlying *written* contract of sale. Other courts do not require a written contract and enforce the escrow if Scott had the requisite intent to transfer on July 1. [§§1615-1618]

b. **SPLIT OF AUTHORITY**   If Scott had no knowledge of the theft and conveyance to Walter, some courts hold that no title passes to Mei-ling until the conditions of escrow are met, and hence Walter loses. Other courts hold that a bona fide purchaser prevails because Scott made it possible to defraud a person by placing the deed in escrow; therefore, Scott is estopped to plead no delivery. [§§1627-1630]

87.a. **YES**   A general warranty deed protects against defects arising before, as well as during, the grantor's tenure on the land. [§1633]

b. **YES**   A special warranty deed warrants only against defects arising while the warrantor has title. A quitclaim deed warrants nothing. [§§1634-1635]

c. **NO**   The usual covenants of title in a warranty deed do not include a covenant of fitness for intended use. For Scarlett to be liable, an express covenant of fitness would have to be included in the deed. [§§1631, 1637-1643]

88.a. **NO**   Dakota's executory interest violates the Rule Against Perpetuities and is void. Georgia has fee simple absolute and conveys same to Tennessee. Therefore, under common law, Tennessee cannot sue for breach of title warranty. If a court were to apply the wait-and-see doctrine, Virginia has been admitted to the bar in her lifetime and the gift to her is good. Georgia is liable for the breach of the covenant of seisin, unless the statute of limitations has run. [§§528, 547, 555, 1638]

b. **NO**   Tennessee should call the police or sue to eject Dakota. It's not Georgia's problem that Dakota used force to enter the land. [§1657]

89.a. **NO**   Phil has not been evicted, and cannot sue on a future covenant. A covenant of seisin is breached when made; the cause of action on this covenant is barred by the statute of limitations. [§§1651, 1658]

b. **NO**   A covenant against encumbrances is breached when made; the statute of limitations has run. [§1651]

c. **YES**   If Olive files within the limitations period, she can hold Ned for damages even though she knew of the defects. [§1648]

| d. | **YES** | Phil can sue on the covenants of quiet enjoyment and general warranty, which are breached when Phil is evicted. These future covenants run with the land to Olive's successor, Phil. [§§1654-1659] |

90.a. **YES**   Because Eduardo is the covenantee, he is entitled to his purchase price. If Eduardo had been a remote grantee, there is a split of authority. Some courts would give the remote grantee the amount received by Mario, which might be more than the remote grantee paid; others would limit the remote grantee to his purchase price or the amount received by Mario, whichever is less. [§§1662-1663, 1670]

b. **NO**   The maximum Eduardo can recover is the amount he paid Mario. [§1663]

91.a. **YES**   By recording, Perry prevails under all types of recording acts. [§1731]

b. **NO**   In a "notice" state, Perry still prevails because Al failed to record. In a "race-notice" or "race" state, however, Al would prevail. [§§1722-1725]

c. **YES**   Recording acts protect only subsequent purchasers (not donees); therefore the common law rule of prior in time gives the land to the first grantee in time, Al. [§1707, 1745]

d. **NO**   The heirs stand in Bella's shoes. Recordation is not required to establish the validity of a deed as between grantor and grantee. [§1709]

92.a. **NO**   Kathy had no notice on June 10 (the time of conveyance) and thus prevails over John. [§1724]

b. **YES**   John prevails in both, because he has recorded before Kathy. [§§1723, 1725]

93.a. **YES**   Regardless of enforceability, the prior conveyance is known to Lucy. [§1751]

b. **SPLIT OF AUTHORITY**   Most courts would charge Lucy with inquiry notice of the possessor's claim, and Nellie would prevail. A minority would not require Lucy to inspect the premises, and if she did not, she would prevail over Nellie. [§§1755-1757]

c. **NO**   A conveyance as security for an antecedent debt of the grantor is not a conveyance for valuable consideration. [§1762]

d. **YES**   The consideration paid by the subsequent purchaser must be of substantial pecuniary value, but need not be the full market value of the property. [§1760]

94.a. **SPLIT OF AUTHORITY**   The better view allows Quincy to prevail, on the ground that he lacked constructive notice. However, some courts protect Pedro on the theory that indexing is not part of recordation. [§1736]

b. **NO**   If the deed was not acknowledged, it cannot be recorded and does not give constructive notice to subsequent purchasers. Quincy prevails. [§1740]

| 95. | **YES** | Tim's recorded deed does not give constructive notice because its grantor was not connected to the chain of title. It is "wild." Ursula, who has no notice of it, prevails. [§§1765, 1768] |

96.a. **NO** Most courts protect the subsequent BFP, Zachary, on the theory that the Vincent-Yvonne conveyance is not in the chain of title because it was recorded prior to the date Vincent obtained title. A minority is contra, and applies the theory of estoppel by deed against the subsequent purchaser. [§§1770-1772]

b. **YES** As between Vincent and Yvonne, all courts protect Yvonne using the theory of estoppel by deed. [§1770]

97. **YES** Most courts protect Diana on the theory that Bob's deed, recorded after Carol's recordation, does not give notice to Carol's assignee. A minority protect Bob on the theory that his mortgage is recorded, and with an extended search Diana can find it. [§§1773-1775]

98. **SPLIT OF AUTHORITY** Some courts hold that the deed to Felipe is not in the chain of title of parcel 2, and, hence, Gene is a BFP who prevails. Other courts hold that Gene has constructive notice of the contents of deeds to other lots from a common grantor to other persons. Under this latter view, Felipe prevails. [§1776]

99. **NO** Title to registered land cannot be claimed by adverse possession where such possession begins after title is registered. [§1800]

100. **YES** Kenny can recover actual market loss up to the limit of the policy. [§§1823-1824]

Exam Questions and Answers

EXAM QUESTION I

Fourteen years ago, Olivia, owner of Blackacre, an 80-acre parcel of land, executed, delivered, and recorded a deed transferring two acres of Blackacre to Lincoln County. The relevant language of this deed stated:

> Olivia hereby grants two acres of Blackacre, located in the corner and adjacent to the road, to Lincoln County so long as the site is used as a highway weighing station. If the site ceases to be used as a highway weighing station, then Olivia has a right to reenter and retake the parcel.

Ten years later, Olivia executed a deed to Blackacre and delivered it to Alan. This deed described Blackacre as it had been described in the deed by which Olivia had acquired Blackacre. It made no mention of the deed to Lincoln County. A year later, Olivia died intestate survived by Bob, her sole heir.

The two-acre parcel conveyed to Lincoln County was continually used as a highway weighing station until last year, when Lincoln County removed the weighing equipment and sold its interest in the land to Gloria. Alan learned of the County's action before Gloria took possession. Alan removed the fences which had separated the two-acre parcel from Alan's land and fenced the outside boundaries of Blackacre so as to include the two-acre parcel with his land.

What are the potential claims each party may have to the two-acre parcel? Discuss.

EXAM QUESTION II

Dan and Earl pooled their life savings and purchased Greenacre. The deed named the grantees as "Dan, Earl, Felicia, and Georgia, as joint tenants and not as tenants in common."

Subsequently Dan died. The administrator of his estate brought an action against Earl, Felicia, and Georgia for the purpose of determining the respective interests in the property, if any, of the estate and the three defendants. Harry intervened claiming an interest in the property.

At the trial, Harry established by competent evidence that Dan wanted to borrow $10,000 from Harry but had no security other than Dan's interest in Greenacre; that Dan would not grant a mortgage of Greenacre because he did not want Georgia to know about the loan; that after considerable negotiation, Dan executed a deed purporting to grant all of his interest in Greenacre to Harry; that Dan then handed the deed to a mutual friend with instructions to give it to Harry after Dan's death; and that Harry then loaned Dan the $10,000.

What are the respective interests of Earl, Felicia, Georgia, and Harry in Greenacre? Discuss.

EXAM QUESTION III

Teresa, who owned a neighborhood grocery store and a large apartment house, leased a fourth floor apartment to Masaaki for five years at a monthly rental of $150. The lease was on a standard printed form containing language requiring the landlord to maintain all common areas in a "safe and sanitary condition" and making all terms of the lease binding on the successors and assigns of both parties. The following two clauses were added in handwriting:

27. Landlord agrees to leave Tenant a pint of milk and a newspaper every morning except Sunday.

28. Landlord will repaint the kitchen and bathroom during the second year of the lease and replace the kitchen sink with a new one within the first six months of the lease.

When Masaaki and Teresa signed the lease, a doorman and a garage attendant were on duty 24 hours a day. All entrances not under their direct observation were kept securely locked and were checked periodically by a guard from dusk to dawn.

A year later, Teresa sold and conveyed the apartment house to Jack. The following year, Jack sold and conveyed the apartment house to Karl. Masaaki has not received any milk or newspapers since the sale by Teresa. The repainting has never been done, and the sink has not been replaced.

Since Karl became the owner, conditions have deteriorated. Karl discharged the garage attendant and there has been no doorman on duty except in the afternoon and early evening. The 100-watt light bulbs in the hallways have been replaced with 25-watt bulbs. The locks on the doors from the fire escapes have fallen into disrepair. The responsibility for checking doors has been left to the local police, who are overburdened because of numerous thefts and violent crimes in the neighborhood. Recently, Masaaki was robbed and severely beaten in the hall just outside his apartment.

At the time of their respective purchases of the apartment house, Jack and Karl were aware of the printed form lease which Teresa used, but they had no knowledge of the two clauses added to Masaaki's lease.

A. What are Masaaki's rights against Jack? Discuss.

B. What are Masaaki's rights against Karl? Discuss.

EXAM QUESTION IV

In accordance with a written contract of sale, Leon deeded some land to City. On the land was a small open bandstand used for summer concerts. The deed contained this language: "To have and to hold so long as City uses the land for park purposes, and should City at any time stop using said land for park purposes, said land shall revert to the heirs of Leon."

The deed was placed in escrow with Local Loan on the oral understanding that the city would deposit the purchase price within 60 days after the date of the deed. Before the deposit was made, the bandstand was destroyed by a fire of unknown origin. The city deposited the purchase price in time, but contended that it was entitled to a deduction because of the fire loss. Leon disagreed but authorized delivery of the deed and consented not to withdraw the money until they could negotiate the matter.

The city took the deed and recorded it at once, but, because of the loss of the bandstand, began using the land for storage of City Street Department trucks. Leon immediately wrote to the city objecting to the use of the land and advising the city that he would instruct Local Loan to return the purchase price to the city if the city would immediately give up possession of the land and reconvey it to Leon. Three days later, before the city had taken any further action, Leon died.

The city then caused the execution and recordation of a deed of the land to Leon, removed all of the trucks from the land, and requested Leon's executor to instruct Local Loan to release the escrowed funds to the city.

Leon's executor wants to know whether he should comply with the city's request and whether the city would have a valid claim to either the land or the funds if he did not. What should he be advised? Discuss.

EXAM QUESTION V

For many years prior to June 13, 2003, Moe operated a tavern on property owned by him at 13 Exeter Street, in the city of Columbus. On June 13, 2003, Moe broke his leg and closed the tavern but did not remove any of the merchandise or fixtures. He reopened the tavern on September 10, 2003.

Effective July 1, 2003, Columbus adopted a zoning ordinance restricting use of property on Exeter Street to single-family dwellings but providing for continuation of any existing nonconforming uses by the owner or successors in title subject to the following provision:

> No nonconforming use, once abandoned, shall be reinstituted. For the purpose of this section, "abandoned" is defined as cessation of the nonconforming use for six months or more.

On March 15, 2005, Moe executed and delivered a deed to 13 Exeter Street to Dr. Nell to pay a past due bill for medical services she had rendered to him. Dr. Nell allowed Moe to continue to operate the tavern and did not immediately record her deed.

On September 15, 2005, Moe, for valuable consideration, executed and delivered a conveyance of "all my right, title, and interest" in 13 Exeter Street to Olga, who had no knowledge of Dr. Nell's deed. Dr. Nell recorded her deed on October 1, 2005, and Olga recorded her deed two days later.

Olga operated the tavern continuously from September 15, 2006 to January 10, 2007, when she closed the tavern because her liquor license was then suspended for nine months by the state board of liquor control.

A. Who should prevail in a quiet title action between Nell and Olga? Discuss.

B. If Olga prevails, will she be legally entitled to reopen the premises as a tavern when the suspension of her liquor license terminates? Discuss.

EXAM QUESTION VI

Three years ago, Alice Elliott, Betty and Bill Nku, Charlotte Roos, and Donna and David Bull owned the four first-floor apartment units in Fragrant Harmony Condominium. They want to create a smoke-free environment. At the suggestion of Donna Bull, they hire Grace Van Owen to draw up a suitable agreement, which they execute on March 2 of that year. The agreement reads:

> This Agreement, executed on March 2, WITNESSETH: Alice Eliot, Betty and Bill Nku, Charlotte Roos, and Donna and David Bull, being the owners respectively of Units 1A, 1B, 1C, and 1D in Fragrant Harmony Condominium, hereby promise on behalf of ourselves, our heirs and assigns, that smoking will not be permitted in Units 1A, 1B, 1C, and 1D of Fragrant Harmony Condominium. It is our intention to create a first floor in the condominium free of tobacco smoke and odor. It is further agreed and understood that this covenant is for the benefit of each of said units, and shall run with said units, and shall be binding upon our heirs, assigns, and all successors in interest.

This agreement is signed and notarized by Alice Elliott, Betty and Bill Nku, Charlotte Roos, and Donna and David Bull. It was recorded and indexed in the recorder's office under the parties' names as typed in the agreement (*i.e.,* with Alice Elliott's name misspelled).

Two years later, Patti Puffer and Sid Schnorer, unmarried cohabitants, bought Unit 1A from Alice Elliott. They took title as joint tenants with right of survivorship. Before the closing, the seller sent a title report to Sid at his office. The report stated that title in fee simple to Unit 1A was in Alice Elliott, subject to a mortgage and to covenants with the condominium association. The title report also mentioned that there was on record an "agreement by Alice Elliott, Betty and Bill Nku, Charlotte Roos, and Donna and David

Bull relating to Unit 1A." Sid filed the title report with other papers relating to the sale. The title report was never brought to Patti's attention.

In January of this year, Patti Puffer and Sid Schnorer bought Unit 1B from Betty and Bill Nku, taking title as joint tenants with right of survivorship. Soon thereafter, Patti and Sid broke down the wall between Units 1A and 1B and combined the units into one apartment.

After Patti and Sid moved into their remodeled Unit 1A-1B, Charlotte Roos smelled tobacco smoke in the hall. Tracing it to its source, she found Patti in Unit 1A-1B, happily puffing away on Gauloise cigarettes. Charlotte remonstrated, telling Patti that smoking was not permitted in Units 1A and 1B. Patti told Charlotte to get the heck out of her apartment and stay out.

An ill wind blows through the first floor of Fragrant Harmony Condominium. Patti smokes constantly, in the hall, in her apartment, and on her patios. Charlotte and the Bulls say that the smoke has permeated the fabric on the hall walls and their window curtains. The tobacco smoke from Patti's patios wafts over to theirs.

A. Charlotte and the Bulls come to you for advice. What remedies do they have and what obstacles, if any, might stand in their way?

B. Sid, who does not smoke, decides that he cannot stand Patti's smoking anymore. She refuses to quit. In July of this year, Sid moves out, saying "You're giving me cancer. I can't stay with you." Sid demands rent from Patti. She refuses, saying "Come back, darling, come back anytime. I love you, but I just can't give up the weed." What are Sid's rights against Patti?

EXAM QUESTION VII

Easement

Terry owned the tract of land described above, consisting of lots 1-6. Seventeen years ago, he sold lots 1-5. The deeds to lots 1-5 imposed an easement over the northerly 15 feet of lots 1-5 for the use and benefit of lots 2-6. This easement provides the only access to lots 2-6. The deeds to lots 1-5 also contained the following restriction: "To preserve high quality, this lot is conveyed on the condition it be used solely for residential purposes, and any other use may be enjoined and shall be cause for forfeiture." Residences were immediately built on lots 1-4. Lot 5 remained vacant. Terry sold lot 6 the following year without any use restrictions in the deed conveying it, and a residence was built on that lot.

Three years ago, Brian, a rock music promoter, purchased lot 6 and since then has operated a discotheque in the house on that lot. A few months later, Victor purchased lot 5 and built a family home, but experienced frequent noise disturbance from Brian's club.

All of the deeds were recorded.

Two years ago, a zoning ordinance was enacted and lots 1-6 were zoned "Single-Family Residential."

Brian's club prospered. Last year, by quitclaim deed, Brian acquired from Christina, who owned 60 acres of rural land surrounding the tract on the north, west and south, a one-acre parcel adjoining lot 6 on the west for use as a parking lot. Brian now plans to use a few rooms in the residence on lot 6 for a mortuary featuring rock funerals. Last month, despite Victor's appearance and objections, the county commissioners, stating that Christina's adjacent land was a likely shopping center site, rezoned lot 6 and the parking lot to "commercial." This would permit their use for mortuaries and discotheques. As Victor left the meeting, he told Brian that he would use every means legally available to prevent or hinder Brian's discotheque and mortuary operation on lot 6 and the parking lot.

Brian consults you before investing any more money in lot 6 or paving the parking lot. He wants to know what legal actions Victor and the owners of lots 1-4 might reasonably be anticipated to take, what defenses he might reasonably assert, what his chances of success are, and whether there is any other legal proceeding he might take to obtain alternate access to the parking lot. Discuss.

ANSWER TO EXAM QUESTION I

Alan's claim: Alan will claim that he owns the two-acre parcel of Blackacre based on the deed conveyed by Olivia. At issue is the interest created by the language in the deed to Lincoln County and whether the interest is alienable.

The interest that Olivia conveyed to Lincoln County in the two-acre parcel was either a fee simple determinable or a fee simple subject to condition subsequent. A fee simple is a present estate that has potentially infinite duration. If the fee simple is defeasible on the happening of some event, it may be a (i) fee simple determinable, (ii) fee simple subject to condition subsequent, or (iii) fee simple subject to executory limitation. A fee simple determinable is a present estate that automatically ends upon the happening of a stated event (*e.g.*, "for so long as," "until," "while"). A fee simple subject to condition subsequent does not end automatically but may be cut short upon the happening of a stated event (*e.g.*, "but if," "upon condition," "provided, however"). A fee simple subject to executory limitation is similar to a fee simple determinable in that it is automatically divested upon the happening of a stated event, but the forfeited interest passes to a third person rather than the grantor (*see* below).

Upon their divestment, fee simple estates may be followed by future interests. A future interest is a present interest that may or may not become possessory in the future. Future interests may be created in a grantee (*e.g.*, a remainder) or retained by the grantor and his heirs. If the interest is retained by the grantor, it must be a reversion, right of entry, or possibility of reverter. If the grantor fails to give away her entire estate in the conveyance, her interest is a reversion, because the property will revert back to the grantor when the lesser estate ends. Reversions generally follow fee tail or life estates. A right of entry exists when the grantor retains the right to cut short the estate she conveyed. Generally, a right of entry follows a fee simple subject to condition subsequent. A possibility of reverter arises when the grantor carves out for herself a determinable estate, which means that the property "possibly" may revert back to the grantor if an estate ends. Generally, a possibility of reverter follows a fee simple determinable.

Here, Olivia conveyed the two-acre parcel to Lincoln County for so long as it was used as a weighing station and if it ceased to be used as a weighing station, then she retained a right to reenter. The conveyance is ambiguous because the language "so long as," usually indicates a fee simple determinable, but the retained right of entry points to a fee simple subject to condition subsequent. In cases of ambiguity, courts usually interpret the interest to be a fee simple subject to condition subsequent, so as to require an affirmative action of forfeiture and also to permit more equitable defenses to be asserted.

If a court interprets the conveyance as a fee simple determinable, Olivia's interest is a possibility of reverter. On the other hand, if a court determines that the deed conveys a fee simple subject to condition subsequent (which it is more likely to conclude, as explained above), Olivia's interest is a right of entry. Regardless of the interpretation, Olivia's future interest is valid and is not subject to the Rule Against Perpetuities. The

Rule Against Perpetuities provides that no interest is good unless it must vest, if at all, not later than 21 years after some life in being at the creation of the interest ("measuring life"). Because the Rule focuses on what might happen, if there is any possibility that an interest will vest too remotely, the interest is void. The Rule applies only to contingent remainders and executory interests. Thus, the reversionary interest Olivia retained was not subject to the Rule Against Perpetuities.

If a court interprets the conveyance as a fee simple subject to condition subsequent, the condition upon which Olivia could exercise her right of entry is the termination of the continued use of the parcel as a highway weighing station. This condition occurred last year, after Olivia had conveyed Blackacre to Alan by deed. Thus, whether Alan has a claim to the two-acre parcel depends upon whether Olivia's interest is alienable.

Alan will argue that when Olivia conveyed the deed to him, describing Blackacre as it was described in Olivia's original deed (*i.e.*, without mentioning the deed to Lincoln County), it included the two-acre parcel on which the weighing station sat. Thus, Olivia must have intended to convey to him whatever interest she had in the parcel. Under modern law and in most states, both the possibility of reverter and the right of entry are transferable inter vivos. Thus, Alan may argue that he took Olivia's reversionary interest in the two-acre parcel by the deed conveying Blackacre and that when the County ceased using the parcel as a weighing station, title either reverted directly to him or he had a right of entry, which he exercised by removing the fences around the two-acre parcel.

Bob's claim: Bob will claim that he owns the two-acre parcel of Blackacre based on inheritance. At issue is whether Alan's deed included Olivia's reversionary interest.

Where a description in a deed is ambiguous, extrinsic evidence is allowed to show the intent of the parties. The deed to Alan is ambiguous because it purports to convey a fee simple estate to Alan in a two-acre parcel that Olivia did not own. Thus, Bob should be allowed to bring in evidence of the parties' true intent. He would then argue that Olivia did not intend to convey her reversionary interest to Alan because the deed did not mention that interest. It appears that Olivia merely erroneously copied the description of her land from her original deed and failed to account for the deed that she gave to the county. An intent to convey her reversionary interest should not be implied from such an error. Moreover, Alan could not reasonably have expected that he was obtaining an interest in the two-acre parcel because of the obvious presence of the weighing station on the land at the time of the conveyance. Thus, Olivia did not convey her reversionary interest in the two-acre parcel to Alan and still held the interest when she died. Therefore, the interest descended to Bob, as Olivia's sole heir, on her death.

Alternatively, Bob could argue that the possibility of reverter or right of entry retained by Olivia could not be transferred inter vivos. Although as discussed above, today most states allow inter vivos transfers of such interests, at common law and in some states, these interests are inalienable, or the possibility of reverter is and the right of entry is not. Thus, Bob may have an argument that Olivia could not convey her interest by deed and, hence, she still held her interest when she died. Therefore, the interest descended to Bob, as Olivia's sole heir, on her death.

Gloria's claim: Gloria will claim that she owns the two-acre parcel of Blackacre because she purchased it from Lincoln County. At issue is the effect of attempting to convey a right of entry.

As discussed above, while in most states today, a right of entry or possibility of reverter is alienable, in a few states the mere attempt to convey a right of entry destroys it. Thus, Gloria could argue that Olivia's conveyance created a fee simple subject to condition subsequent (*see* above) so that the reversionary interest retained by Olivia was a right of entry and that Olivia's attempt to convey it to Alan resulted in its destruction. If the future interest was destroyed, Lincoln County's interest would be enlarged to a fee simple absolute. A fee simple absolute is an estate of potentially infinite duration that cannot be divested and will not end on the happening of any event. It is completely alienable. Thus, when Lincoln County sold its interest in Blackacre to Gloria, Gloria became the owner of the fee simple absolute.

ANSWER TO EXAM QUESTION II

Interests created by deed: The first issue is whether the deed from the owner of Greenacre created a joint tenancy or a tenancy in common in Dan, Earl, Felicia, and Georgia. In almost all states, a joint tenancy can be created by appropriate language indicating an intent to create a joint tenancy; the language here is appropriate to create a joint tenancy. In a few states, it is necessary to state expressly that the tenants have the right of survivorship, which is not done here, and in these states, the parties would hold as tenants in common.

If a joint tenancy is created, Harry will lose unless the joint tenancy was severed by the escrow transaction. If a tenancy in common is created, Earl, Felicia, and Georgia have no rights in Dan's one-fourth share of Greenacre and Harry's rights depend upon how the escrow transaction is dealt with.

The escrow transaction: This is a very strange escrow transaction because the facts indicate a *commercial negotiation* took place between Dan and Harry, but the deed was put into escrow with oral instructions to deliver upon Dan's death, which are the common instructions in a *donative escrow*. A donative escrow is a substitute for a will. But rather clearly there was no donative intent here; a bargain of some kind was intended. What was it? Parol evidence is admissible to show the conditions of delivery where a deed is put into escrow. Harry's rights depend upon how this escrow transaction is characterized.

The escrow can be viewed as an arrangement to give Harry security for a loan; hence the deed in escrow was in essence a mortgage, executed in exchange for a loan. Courts can look through the form of a deed to substance and declare that the deed, though absolute on its face, is really intended to be a mortgage and will be so treated by the court. If this is done, then the mortgage (deed) is held by the escrow agent as security until Dan dies, and then is to be given to Harry. This seems the most likely intent of the parties.

If this is a mortgage, a Statute of Frauds problem arises. Where there is a commercial escrow with oral instructions to the escrow agent, the escrow may fail unless there is an underlying written contract. It is too dangerous to permit the escrow agent to fill in essential terms, such as price, by oral testimony. Here, however, extrinsic evidence that $10,000 was loaned (*e.g.,* by cancelled check) may be reliable; and part performance (handing over of the $10,000) may take the underlying agreement out of the Statute of Frauds. (If this were a donative escrow, no written instructions or agreement would be necessary, and the escrow would be valid, but there seems to be no donative intent here.)

There is also a question of delivery. If the grantor had a conditional right of recall (upon repayment of the loan, for instance), some cases would hold that the grantor lacks the necessary intent to convey a present interest unconditionally when the deed is put into escrow. For delivery to occur, the deed must pass beyond control of the grantor. If the grantor can get the deed (mortgage) back upon payment of money, it is arguable that there is no delivery because of the grantor's control. But, if this is viewed as a mortgage, this is specious, because it is the nature of a mortgage that it is released upon payment of money.

If delivery did not occur during Dan's life, so as to pass title to Harry, delivery by the friend at Dan's death is too late. The joint tenancy must be severed during life, not at death.

Effect on joint tenancy: If the escrow transaction is ineffective because of the Statute of Frauds or lack of delivery, Dan did not sever the joint tenancy during life and the three survivors now own Greenacre. If the escrow is valid, the rights of Earl, Felicia, and Georgia depend upon whether the escrow severed the joint tenancy. If not severed during Dan's life, they now own the property free of the mortgage.

If the escrow was in reality a mortgage, and treated as such, the escrow severed the joint tenancy only if the ***title theory*** of mortgages is followed, *i.e.,* that the mortgagee takes title, thereby breaking the four unities. If the ***lien theory*** is followed, no severance occurred because the mortgage is only a lien upon Dan's title, which disappears at Dan's death (the four unities of time, title, interest, and possession are not destroyed during Dan's life).

Conclusion: The court will probably hold that a joint tenancy was created, that the deed in escrow was in substance a mortgage, and that the mortgage did not effect a severance of the joint tenancy. If the court is in a "title theory" state, it may avoid that theory by holding that the escrow fails for lack of delivery or violates the Statute of Frauds. Therefore, Earl, Felicia, and Georgia own Greenacre free of the mortgage.

This result seems equitable and carries out the expectations of the joint tenants. Harry is little deserving of sympathy because he entered a secretive oral escrow transaction that disguises or confuses the truth. He could have easily protected himself in a mortgage transaction by having Dan convey his interest to a straw person (thus severing the joint tenancy), who after mortgaging to Harry, conveyed the equity back to Dan. Harry has caused the confusion, and brought the loss on himself. He is asking equitable relief and is not totally blameless himself.

ANSWER TO EXAM QUESTION III

A. Masaaki vs. Jack

There are three claims that Masaaki may raise against Jack:

1. Failure to deliver milk and newspapers

Jack is not liable on the covenant to deliver milk and newspapers. At issue is whether the burden of Teresa's promise to deliver the milk and newspaper every morning runs with the landlord's reversion, so that Teresa's assignee, Jack, is liable for it. For a covenant to run with the land, the parties must *intend* that it run, they must be in *privity* of estate, the covenant must *touch and concern* the land, and the defendant must have *notice*. There is privity of estate because Jack succeeded to Teresa's reversion by assignment, but there are problems with the other three requirements.

Intent: Although the lease expressly stated all terms of the lease were binding on assigns, it does not necessarily follow that the first of the two clauses added was intended to bind assignees. The printed statement might apply only to printed terms, and not to added clauses. The covenantor, Teresa, was a grocer who would conveniently leave milk and newspapers for tenants, and because of this the parties might not have intended that this added covenant run to assignees. This argument is buttressed by the fact that deliveries were not to occur on Sunday, if it can be shown that Teresa's grocery was closed on Sunday.

Touch and concern: The promise is to do a physical act on the leased premises. Ordinarily this type of promise, such as a promise to repaint, repair, or furnish heat, touches and concerns because it is directly related to the enjoyment of the premises. Here, however, it is probable that the promise by Teresa was intended to be a personal obligation of Teresa, not touching and concerning the land.

Notice: Jack had no notice of the added clauses and therefore, as assignee, is not subject to them unless notice is *implied*. This five-year lease should have been recorded, but was not. The question does not state whether the copy in the landlord's office, as well as the copy given the tenant, contained the added clauses. The purchaser should make inquiry of the prior landlord, and be deemed to have constructive notice of the leases as they appear in the landlord's office. He may be required to make inquiry of tenants as well, because they are in possession, but the cases differ on whether a purchaser can be a BFP without inquiring of tenants. Here, the apartment house was "large," and inquiry might be an unreasonable burden.

Therefore, Jack is not liable on the covenant to deliver milk and newspapers because it was a personal promise by Teresa.

2. **Failure to paint rooms**

Jack may be held liable on the covenant to repaint the kitchen and bathroom if he had notice. At issue is whether the burden of the covenant to repaint the rooms during the second year of the lease runs to Jack. The above analysis is applicable to the running of this covenant, except: There seems to be no argument that the parties intended this covenant to be a personal one which would overcome the express language in the lease; and the covenant touches and concerns because it affects the use and enjoyment of the premises.

If the notice problem can be hurdled, Masaaki can sue Jack on the covenant to repaint. It was breached while Jack was the landlord. Masaaki can receive damages from Jack.

3. **Failure to replace sink**

Jack is not liable on the covenant to replace the kitchen sink. This covenant was to be performed within the first six months, before Jack took title. This covenant was breached while Teresa owned the building, and became a chose in action in Masaaki. There was no longer any covenant to run with the land. One cannot sue a successor upon an obligation that falls due and is breached during the tenure of a predecessor.

B. **Masaaki vs. Karl**

1. **Failure to deliver milk and newspapers**

Karl is not liable on this covenant for the same reasons Jack is not.

2. **Failure to paint rooms and replace sink**

Karl is not liable for failure to paint and replace the sink because these obligations fell due and were breached during the tenure of predecessors. Karl is not liable for Jack's failure to repaint during the second year nor for Teresa's failure to replace the sink during the first six months.

3. Deterioration

Karl is liable to Masaaki for breach of the express obligation to maintain security and of the legal duty to maintain common areas in a safe condition.

Express obligation in lease: The express obligation in the lease to maintain common areas in a safe and sanitary condition affects the use and enjoyment of the property, and touches and concerns. The lease provision binding successors and assigns clearly applies to printed covenants in the leases. Karl had notice of the form lease containing this provision. Therefore, it runs with the land and Karl can be sued on this covenant. If the present conditions are found not to be "safe and sanitary" (a jury question), Karl is liable for damages, and may be enjoined to perform an express covenant. If the covenants are deemed dependent, Masaaki can rescind the lease. Karl also is liable for personal injuries suffered by Masaaki if (a jury believes) they resulted from Karl's breach of covenant.

Duty with respect to common areas: A landlord has a duty to maintain common areas, and must take precautions against the foreseeable acts of third parties. This liability is based on tort, not on breach of contract. Whether Masaaki's personal injuries were foreseeable (numerous crimes and thefts in neighborhood) and whether Karl's precautions were reasonable are questions for the jury, but there is a good case against Karl here, and the modern trend is in Masaaki's favor.

Implied warranty: Many recent cases have implied a continuing warranty of habitability in urban residential leases. If this were done, Masaaki might be able to recover for breach if the apartment house violated the city housing code or fell below some other applicable standard of habitability. Using this theory, Masaaki would have the remedies of damages and rescission.

Covenant of quiet enjoyment: The landlord covenants quiet enjoyment of the premises, which appears to be breached here by failure of the landlord to make the premises safe and by letting them deteriorate substantially below the level at the time of signing the lease. Breach of this covenant may constitute constructive eviction, which permits a tenant to rescind the lease and move out within a reasonable time.

Conclusion: Using one or more of the above theories, Masaaki can rescind the lease, recover damages (rent abatement) from Karl, and recover damages for personal injuries from Karl.

ANSWER TO EXAM QUESTION IV

Estates created by deed: The deed executed by Leon granted the city a fee simple determinable, with a purported executory interest in the heirs of Leon. It is an executory interest because it is a future interest following a fee simple, and is created in transferees described as "heirs." The executory interest violates the Rule Against Perpetuities because it is possible for it to become possessory long after lives in being plus 21 years. The executory interest is therefore struck out. This does not increase the determinable fee in the city. Because Leon has not granted the entire fee simple, Leon has a possibility of reverter. Upon cessation of park use by the city, title automatically reverts to Leon.

Deed placed in escrow: The deed was placed in escrow with oral instructions to deliver upon deposit of the purchase price within 60 days. There was an underlying written contract of sale; therefore the Statute of Frauds is satisfied. The contract is specifically enforceable, and the escrow is valid.

Bandstand destroyed by fire: Whether the city is entitled to a portion of the escrowed funds as damages (abatement in purchase price) depends upon whether the risk of loss is on the seller or the buyer in the particular jurisdiction. When the property is destroyed while the deed is in escrow, the majority of courts hold that the risk of loss is on the buyer. Because the contract is specifically enforceable, the doctrine of equitable conversion applies, and the buyer is treated as the owner of the property subject to the seller's lien for the purchase price. If this doctrine is followed, the risk of loss is on the city and it is not entitled to a deduction in the purchase price.

Some courts do not apply equitable conversion, and put the risk of loss on the seller by implying a condition in the contract that the contract is not binding if the building is destroyed. Others put the risk of loss on the seller until the buyer takes possession. Under these views, an abatement would be granted if the damage is slight and easily ascertainable and rescission by the seller would be inequitable. It appears here that destruction of a small open bandstand is slight and damages are probably easily ascertainable, and that it would be inequitable to deprive the city of its bargain (*i.e.,* force it either to rescind or take specific performance without abatement). This gives specific relief to the buyer, with damages in the same suit for seller's failure to perform.

Delivery out of escrow: The city took title when the deed was delivered out of escrow with Leon's and the city's consent. By accepting the deed, the city has lost its right to rescind the contract, and the city's only claim now is for abatement in purchase price.

Termination of determinable fee: Upon the city's cessation of park use, the determinable fee will automatically terminate and Leon will have title. Was storage of city trucks cessation of park use? It may be that temporary storage of trucks will not be deemed indicative of intent to cease using the land for a park. The facts are not clear as to whether such use was temporary or as to the extent of land used for storage.

Leon's offer: Leon offered to return the purchase price to the city if the city reconveyed. This is an offer to purchase, which probably expired at Leon's death. Generally, offers cannot be accepted after the death of the offeror; however, because Leon's executor could easily perform, it is not clear that the rule ought to be applied.

Execution of deed from the city to Leon: After Leon's death, the city executed and recorded a deed to Leon. This deed is probably a nullity because Leon is dead and there is no grantee, or it may be invalid for want of delivery. Moreover, if the city's determinable fee has ended, the city has no title to convey. Assuming, however, that the determinable fee has not ended, and that the deed is not a nullity, the city can bring an action to cancel the deed on the ground of failure of consideration (inability of executor to be bound by Leon's offer).

Therefore, the executor should not agree to release the funds because Leon owned the funds (perhaps minus partial abatement). Moreover, Leon's estate owns the land if the city's determinable fee has ended.

ANSWER TO EXAM QUESTION V

A. Nell vs. Olga

This is the situation:
Moe to Nell, who does not record.
Moe to Olga, for valuable consideration,
    without actual notice of Moe-Nell deed;
    deed then not recorded.
Nell records her deed.
Olga records her deed.

Who prevails in a quiet title action depends upon whether the jurisdiction has a race, notice, or race-notice statute.

Race statute: If the jurisdiction has a race statute, the person who records first wins. Nell recorded first. Therefore, Nell wins.

Notice statute: Under a notice statute, a subsequent purchaser for valuable consideration without notice prevails over a prior unrecorded instrument. In this case, Olga is a purchaser for value subsequent in time and prevails over Nell if Olga has no notice of the deed to Nell.

Olga has no record notice because the Moe-Nell deed is not recorded. Nor does she have actual knowledge. The only question is: Does she have inquiry notice? She does not have inquiry notice from Nell's possession because Nell is not in possession; the record owner, Moe, is in possession. However, the facts do not state what kind of deed this is from Moe to Olga. It looks like a quitclaim deed because it says "all my right, title, and interest," and nothing is said about warranties. If the deed is a quitclaim deed, some courts hold that it does not put the grantee on inquiry notice; others hold that it does put the grantee on inquiry notice.

If Olga is put on inquiry by the quitclaim deed, she still prevails because nothing could be learned from a reasonable inquiry. The conveyance from Moe to Nell is a secret conveyance, and Olga has no reason to suspect that Nell has an interest. Thus, Olga wins.

Race-notice statute: Under a race-notice statute, a subsequent BFP is protected only if she records before the previous instrument is recorded. Olga is protected only if she records before Nell. She did not. Therefore, Nell, prior in time, wins.

Note: It is irrelevant whether Nell pays valuable consideration or not. She is prior in time. It is the subsequent purchaser (Olga) who must pay valuable consideration to be protected. Therefore, the fact that the deed to Nell was to satisfy an antecedent debt is a red herring; Nell would win even if the deed were a gift.

B. Operation of tavern

Even if Olga prevails in the quiet title action, she may not be able to reopen the premises as a tavern when her liquor license suspension is over. The first issue is whether Moe abandoned the use when he closed the tavern for three months after breaking his leg. Moe operated a tavern long before the zoning ordinance took effect, and it was a nonconforming use when the ordinance took effect. It could be argued that it was not a nonconforming use on July 1, 2003, because it was not in use on that day as a tavern. But this argument is very weak. A use is not abandoned unless there is intent to abandon it. A temporary closing while Moe's leg was mending shows no intent to abandon. Similarly, if Moe had closed the tavern for a summer vacation in 2003, there would be no intent to abandon the use. Moreover, even under the ordinance definition of abandonment, which does not mention intent, there has been no abandonment because the use did not cease for six months. Therefore, the use was a nonconforming use on July 1, 2003.

Nonconforming uses can continue in existence after the zoning ordinance is enacted, unless abandoned. The next issue is whether Olga abandoned the use when her liquor license was suspended for nine months. This could go either way. Olga would argue that she did not *intend* to abandon, and that an "intent" requirement should be read into the ordinance. She will argue that if the intent requirement is not read into the ordinance, it is of dubious constitutionality; it may be a taking of her property without compensation. She will argue that she is in the same situation as a person who closed the tavern because of illness for nine months, or because a windstorm took the roof off, which could not be replaced for nine months.

On the other hand, the city will argue that intention is irrelevant, only objective acts count under the ordinance, and that the ordinance is constitutional without an intent requirement. Even if the ordinance would be unconstitutional as applied to persons who had to close involuntarily, the ordinance is not unconstitutional as applied to Olga because the suspension and resulting closure were self-inflicted.

Here, the court may be influenced by the degree of wrongdoing by Olga and the reason for the suspension. If the city's arguments are accepted, the state liquor board has the power to put a tavern owner out of business by suspending the license for six months. The legislature may not have intended to give the board that power, but only the power of temporary suspension. Thus, the zoning ordinance might be interpreted in such a manner as to withhold that power from the board. On the other hand, nonconforming uses are not favored and ordinances continuing them are strictly construed. It is difficult to predict the outcome of this case.

ANSWER TO EXAM QUESTION VI

A.   Charlotte and the Bulls' rights against Patti and Sid

Charlotte and the Bulls may be able to obtain damages from Patti for smoking on the premises or may be able to enjoin her smoking. At issue is whether they can establish a covenant or equitable servitude binding on Patti.

Real covenant: A covenant is a written promise to do or not to do something on the land. Real covenants run with the land at law, which means that subsequent owners of the land may enforce or be burdened by the covenant. For the burden on the property to run with the land to subsequent owners, the law requires that: (i) the agreeing parties must have intended that the successors in interest be bound by the terms of the covenant; (ii) a subsequent purchaser of the burdened land must have notice of the covenant; (iii) there must be horizontal and vertical privity of estate between the original promisor and promisee; and (iv) the covenant must touch and concern the land. For the benefit on the property to run with the land, so that the successor in interest is able to enforce the covenant, the successor must meet the same requirements discussed above, with the exceptions of notice and horizontal privity. The remedy for breach of a covenant is damages.

Intent: Charlotte and the Bulls would have no problem showing intent to create a covenant. Intent may be inferred by the circumstances surrounding the creation of the covenant or it may be evidenced by the language in the covenant. Here, the parties clearly intended the burden of the no-smoking agreement to run to subsequent owners, as evidenced by the language "this covenant . . . shall run with said units, and shall be binding upon our heirs, assigns, and all successors in interest."

Notice: Charlotte and the Bulls may have a problem showing that Patti had notice of the covenant. There are three types of notice: (i) actual, (ii) record, and (iii) inquiry. Actual notice is what the purchaser actually knows. Record notice is notice that the law imputes to the purchaser, *i.e.*, notice obtained from a prior recorded deed. Inquiry notice, recognized in some jurisdictions, is notice that the purchaser would have by inquiring into the property (*e.g.*, by visiting it to determine who is occupying the land). Here, Patti and Sid may not have record notice with respect to Unit 1A. The agreement is recorded under the incorrect name of "Eliot," not under the record owner, "Elliott." The jurisdictions split on whether proper indexing is required to effectively (and legally) record an instrument. The better view is that it is required and, thus, it could be argued that Patti and Sid did not have record notice.

Sid, however, had actual notice from the title report that an agreement existed concerning Unit 1A. This gave Sid inquiry notice as to its contents. However, notice to Sid will not constitute notice to Patti unless Sid is found to have been acting as Patti's agent, and nothing in the facts indicates that that is the case here.

With respect to Unit 1B, Patti and Sid had record notice of the agreement because the document was recorded under the correct names of the sellers. Moreover, because the recorded document purports to restrict Unit 1A in addition to Unit 1B, this would put Patti and Sid on inquiry notice that Unit 1A was also subject to the covenant. However, because Patti and Sid purchased Unit 1B after they purchased Unit 1A, this inquiry notice came too late to be binding concerning Unit 1A.

Privity: Charlotte and the Bulls might have a problem establishing privity. Under the majority view, horizontal privity is present only when one of the original parties to the promise succeeded to an estate previously owned by the other party (*e.g.*, grantor-grantee) and the conveyance is contained in the covenant. However, under a minority view, horizontal privity is present when the original promisor and promisee both have an interest in the property independent of the covenant (*e.g.*, grantor-grantee, landlord-tenant, mortgagor-mortgagee). Here, there was no grantor-grantee relationship between the original parties, but they did have mutual interests in the whole condominium property. They were co-tenants of the common spaces, such as halls, and they were all burdened and benefited by the mutual covenants with the condominium association, of which they were members. Thus, there is no horizontal privity under the majority view but there is horizontal privity under the minority view.

Vertical privity exists when the successor in interest holds the entire durational estate held by the original promisor or promisee. Here, Patti and Sid, as subsequent purchasers of Units 1A and 1B, succeeded to the entire durational estates held by Alice Elliott and the Nkus, respectively. Thus, there is vertical privity.

Touch and concern: Charlotte and the Bulls may have trouble showing the "touch and concern" requirement. "Touch and concern" means that the covenant either benefits or burdens the parties in their physical use and enjoyment of the property, or enhances the value of the benefited land. This requirement is the court's policy control, under which it may stop the running of a covenant if its social utility is outweighed by the burden imposed.

Here, it should first be pointed out that the covenant only prohibits smoking *in the units*. It does not expressly prohibit smoking in the hall, and it likely cannot be interpreted as such because it would place a restriction on the common areas over which all tenants (including those who are not parties to the covenant) share ownership. Moreover, the covenant may or may not prohibit smoking on the patio, depending on whether the patio is considered "in the unit." And because Patti probably did not have notice of the covenant as to Unit 1A, it probably does not apply to that unit. Thus, the question is whether the benefits of a covenant to refrain from smoking inside Unit 1B outweigh the burdens that the covenant imposes. This is a close call.

Because the covenant prohibits activity, it is a negative covenant. Negative covenants relating to the physical use of land have been held to touch and concern the land. The benefit of the covenant here, of course, is to live on a floor free from the smell and health risks of cigarette smoke. This might enhance the value of Charlotte's unit and the Bulls' unit. Moreover, as there is evidence that the smell of Patti's cigarettes has permeated Charlotte's and the Bulls' curtains, they clearly could obtain some benefit from a smoke-free environment. However, because smoking would be allowed in the common areas and unit 1A anyway (and perhaps also on Patti's patio), Charlotte and the Bulls might not get much benefit from enforcing the covenant as to Unit 1B. Moreover, the burden on Patti is heavy. She would not be allowed to indulge in a quiet, legal habit in the privacy of her own home in perpetuity. Thus, it is not clear whether a court would find that the covenant touches and concerns the land here.

Equitable servitude: Charlotte and the Bulls could try to argue that the agreement between the original tenants of 1A, 1B, 1C, and 1D was an equitable servitude. An equitable servitude is similar to a restrictive covenant except that it does not require privity between the parties and the remedy is different. If a successor in interest wants damages, she must seek to enforce the promise as a real covenant; but if she wants an injunction, she must seek to enforce the promise as an equitable servitude. The party seeking to enforce an equitable servitude need only prove that (i) the contracting parties intended that the servitude be enforceable by and against assignees, (ii) the servitude touches and concerns the property, and (iii) the assignee has notice of the servitude. Here, Charlotte and the Bulls would still have a problem proving notice and the touch and concern elements, as explained above.

B. **Sid's rights against Patti**

Sid may seek to collect his share of the reasonable rental value of the property or to partition the property. At issue are the rights of a co-tenant out of possession.

Under the majority rule, if one co-tenant is in exclusive possession of the property, she does not have to pay rent to the nonpossessing co-tenant. However, if the exclusively possessing co-tenant ousts the other co-tenant from the property (i.e., affirmatively deprives the other tenant of the right to possess the property), she must pay the ousted co-tenant his share of the reasonable rental value of the property.

This value, sometimes referred to as "mesne profits," is the reasonable value of the use of the land. In a minority of jurisdictions, the co-tenant out of possession has a right to his share of the reasonable rental value without ouster from the co-tenant in exclusive possession. Here, Sid is out of possession of the premises, but it is unclear whether he was ousted. Patti did not kick Sid out or bar him from the premises; indeed, she has told Sid that he may return at any time. The only thing that she did to keep Sid out of the premises is continue to smoke. Arguably, given the health risks of second-hand smoke, this is enough to constitute ouster, but this point is unsettled. Thus, if the jurisdiction does not require ouster, Sid may be entitled to his share of the reasonable rental value of the condominium unit, but if the jurisdiction requires ouster, it is uncertain whether Sid may recover any rent.

In any case, Sid may also seek partition of Unit 1A-1B. Partition, which may be sought by any joint tenant or tenant in common, is a judicial remedy that terminates the co-tenancy and divides the common property. Partition may be "in kind" or "by sale." Partition in kind is a physical partition of the property into separate tracts of land of equal value. Each party then owns his proportion of the land in fee simple. If physical partition is impracticable or not in the parties' best interests, the court may order a partition by sale. In a partition sale, the entire tract is sold and the proceeds are divided equally among the co-tenants. Here, if a court grants a partition in kind, Patti and Sid will each own a portion of the condominium unit equal in value to the other. On the other hand, if a court grants a partition by sale, Unit 1A-1B will be sold and Patti and Sid will equally split the proceeds. In either case, the joint tenancy will be terminated.

ANSWER TO EXAM QUESTION VII

1. **Use restriction**

Condition vs. covenant: The first issue is whether the residential use restriction can be enforced against Brian. The language in the deeds to lots 1-5 is ambiguous; it speaks of "condition," and says "shall be cause for forfeiture," indicating a right of entry in Terry, but also says "may be enjoined," indicating a covenant. A right of entry is not expressly retained, but it will be implied if the language of condition is clear enough. If a right of entry is retained, Terry has the right to enforce the right of entry, not the neighbors. Where there is an ambiguity, the court prefers a covenant construction, to avoid forfeiture, and the neighbors will urge that this is a covenant.

Creation of covenant: Nowhere is there in writing a restriction imposed on lot 6; the restrictions are imposed on lots 1-5. Therefore, the Statute of Frauds is not complied with, and a real covenant is not created on lot 6. However, in equity, in many but not all states a covenant (equitable servitude) will be implied on lot 6 if the common grantor showed by a scheme an intent to restrict all six lots. Here it looks like a scheme: the first 5 lots sold were restricted. If so, lot 6 is bound by an implied negative reciprocal servitude.

Does the burden run to Brian? If a court will imply a negative restriction on lot 6, it will be enforced in equity against Brian if the parties so intend, if the burden touches and concerns the land, and if Brian had notice (privity is irrelevant because the case is in equity, and cannot go into law because of the Statute of Frauds). As for intent, the parties did not say it runs to "assigns," but no technical words are necessary; the court will probably infer intent because of the nature of the covenant (to preserve high quality residential use). The restriction touches and concerns the use of the burdened tract. The real problem is *notice*. If Brian had no notice, he is not bound by the servitude.

Brian would have record notice if in the jurisdiction all deeds out from a common grantor (Terry) are in Brian's chain of title (*i.e.,* give constructive notice to purchasers of other lots in the subdivision). Courts are split on this issue.

Brian might be put on inquiry in some jurisdictions by the lay of the land, seeing residences on lots 1-4 (but lot 5 was vacant). If Brian should reasonably be put on inquiry, he would have to read the deeds of lots 1-4, and would be held to know of the implied reciprocal negative servitude.

Does the benefit run to Victor? The benefit of an equitable servitude may be enforced by a successor to the promisee if the parties so intend and the covenant touches and concerns the land. Here, Victor purchased lot 5 from Terry, the promisee. The requirements of intent and touch and concern are met with respect to the benefit end if they are met with respect to the burden end (above). Therefore, Victor may enforce the benefit.

Is the servitude enforceable by owners of lots 1-4? Yes, either as third-party beneficiaries of the implied promise Brian made at the time of purchase or as beneficiaries of a restriction implied on lot 6 at the time of sale of lots 1-4. Prior purchasers in a subdivision can almost always enforce an implied servitude. The scheme shows the intent of the subdivider to give them this right.

Defenses: Brian may argue that conditions have so changed in the neighborhood that the purpose of the restriction cannot be carried out and it would be inequitable to enforce it. The zoning change to commercial is some evidence that conditions have changed with respect to lot 6, but most courts will not allow this defense unless the conditions have changed in the whole restricted area, and lots 1-5 are still zoned residential, indicating that residential purposes can still be achieved there. Therefore, this defense probably will not help Brian.

If the zoning ordinance is cumulative, it does not conflict with the private covenant, and the most restrictive use (private covenant) controls. If residences are prohibited in a commercial zone, Brian has a nonconforming use and can stay. Therefore, Brian has small chance of succeeding in an argument that the rezoning lifted the private restrictions.

2. Easement

Brian can use the easement for access to any development reasonably to be expected by the parties. At issue is the scope of the easement. The scope of an easement depends on the parties' intent, which the court will ascertain based on how the easement was created, what changes are reasonably foreseeable by the parties, and what changes are necessary to achieve the easement's purpose under modern conditions. Here, the neighbors will argue that because lot 6 is restricted to residential use (above), the easement cannot be used for access to a commercial establishment. That is beyond the scope intended by the parties. If the court finds that lot 6 is not burdened by a restrictive covenant, then it is not likely to find excessive use of the easement here. But if the court finds that lot 6 was burdened, though the burden does not run to Brian for some reason (probably lack of notice), the court might find the use to reach commercial establishments to be excessive use beyond the intent of the parties (road was to service residences). If this is excessive use, Brian can be enjoined from using the easement for access by commercial customers.

Brian has also extended the benefit of the easement to a nondominant parcel, the one-acre parking lot. This is not permitted, and can be enjoined.

If Brian cannot get access to the parking lot by way of the easement, the one-acre parking lot has an easement by necessity over Christina's 60 acres to reach a public road. It was landlocked by the conveyance from Christina, so Christina's land is burdened by the easement. There can be no easement by necessity over the 15-foot strip to reach the parking lot because Terry did not landlock the one-acre tract.

3. Nuisance

The next issue is whether Victor and the owners of lots 1-4 have an action against Brian for nuisance. A nuisance is an unprivileged interference with a person's use and enjoyment of his land, for which the plaintiff may be awarded an injunction or damages. Mortuaries are very often held to be nuisances in residential areas, and the mortuary use could probably be enjoined by the neighbors. Brian's defense is that it is permitted by the zoning ordinance. This action might make the use presumptively not a nuisance, but is not conclusive.

The neighbors may also sue in nuisance against the discotheque. The court will weigh the gravity of the harm against the social utility. An important factor is that Brian came into an established residential area and began his discotheque; his action is harming prior uses. There are not enough facts (amount of noise, traffic, etc.) to make a final determination.

4. **Zoning change**

The final issue is whether Victor and the owners of lots 1-4 can set aside the rezoning. An amendment to a zoning ordinance (rezoning) that is not in accordance with the comprehensive plan is spot zoning, which is unlawful. Here, whether the neighbors can attack the commercial rezoning as spot zoning depends upon evidence not available here—principally, how much land was rezoned and what evidence there is of a comprehensive plan. The plan does not have to be in writing, but can consist of policies adhered to by the planning commission. If the neighbors succeeded, this would hurt Brian's defense to the nuisance action, and prevent mortuary use, not permitted in a residential zone. The discotheque would not violate the zoning ordinance, however, as it was a nonconforming use established before passage of the zoning ordinance.

5. **Conclusion**

In most states, the neighbors can get the discotheque enjoined for violation of the restrictive covenant, but in some, a strict view of the Statute of Frauds or a narrow view of what gives notice would bar the neighbors.

The neighbors can enjoin use of the easement to reach the parking lot.

The neighbors can prevent mortuary use either by suing for nuisance or by setting aside the rezoning. They might get an injunction against the discotheque as well, on grounds of nuisance.

Table of Cases

Hayes v. Hayes - §1563

Hecht v. Superior Court - §55

Henderson v. First National Bank of Dewitt - §143

Hendricks v. Stalnaker - §1313

Henley v. Continental Cablevision - §1164

Hessen v. Iowa Automobile Mutual Insurance Co. - §232

Hester v. Sawyers - §1139

Hewitt v. Hewitt - §743

Hickerson v. Bender - §1177

Hickey v. Green - §1509

Hidden Harbour Estates, Inc. v. Basso - §1294

Hidden Harbour Estates, Inc. v. Norman - §1295

Higgins v. Lodge - §240

Highland Construction, Inc. v. Paquette - §1124

Hilder v. St. Peter - §§893, 903, 904

Hill v. Community of Damien of Molokai - §§1266, 1267

Hilliker v. Rueger - §§1665, 1667

Hills Development Co. v. Township of Bernards - §1452

Hillsboro Cove, Inc. v. Archibald - §1667

Hillview Associates v. Bloomquist - §923

Hinkley v. State - §142

Hobson v. George Humphreys, Inc. - §828

Hocks v. Jeremiah - §214

Hodgson v. Chin - §1678

Hoffmann v. Kinealy - §1406

Holbrook v. Holbrook - §611

Holbrook v. Taylor - §1099

Holscher v. James - §1558

Holy Properties, Ltd. v. Kenneth Cole Productions, Inc. - §1031

Hood v. Webster - §1624

Hopkins the Florist, Inc. v. Fleming - §1178

Horse Pond Fish & Game Club, Inc. v. Cormier - §353

Horton v. Kyburz - §1760

Houston, In re Estate of - §430

Howard v. Kunto - §§86, 122, 125

Howard v. Spragins - §574

Huntington Branch, NAACP v. Town of Huntington - §1455

Hurley v. City of Niagara Falls - §77

Hurlocker v. Medina - §1127

I

Illinois & St. Louis Railroad & Coal Co. v. Cobb - §165

Illinois Central Railroad v. Illinois - §42

Imperial Colliery Co. v. Fout - §923

In re - see name of party

In re Estate of - see name of party

In re Marriage of - see name of party

Indiana State Bar Association, State ex rel. v. Indiana Real Estate Association - §1497

Ingalls v. Hobbs - §875

Ink v. City of Canton - §389

Innes v. Potter - §222

International News Service v. Associated Press - §53

Irons v. Smallpiece - §209

Isle Royale Mining Co. v. Hertin - §46

J

Jaber v. Miller - §1044

Jack Spring, Inc. v. Little - §1017

Jackson v. O'Connell - §614

Jacobs v. Morand - §858

Jacque v. Steenberg Homes, Inc. - §175

Jancik v. Department of Housing & Urban Development - §822

Jarvis v. Gillespie - §92

Javins v. First National Realty Corp.- §§887, 893, 896

Jee v. Audley - §540

Jenad, Inc. v. Village of Scarsdale - §1460

Joaquin v. Shiloh Orchards - §113

Johnson, State v. - §1795

Johnson v. Calvert - §56

Johnson v. City of Wheat Ridge - §293

Johnson v. Davis - §§1532, 1679

Johnson v. Hendrickson - §696

Johnson v. Johnson - §1613

Johnson v. M'Intosh - §4

Johnson v. O'Brien - §933

Johnson v. Whiton - §255

Joint Tribal Council of the Passamaquoddy Tribe v. Morton - §5

Jones v. Alfred H. Mayer Co. - §817

Jones v. Green - §606

Jones v. Northwest Real Estate Co. - §1270

Jones v. Taylor - §815

Jordan v. Talbot - §§992, 1025

Joslin v. Pine River Development Corp. - §1269

Just v. Marinette County - §§1442, 1476

Justice Court Mutual Housing Cooperative, Inc. v. Sandow - §1310

K

Kaiser Aetna v. United States - §1469

Kanelos v. Kettler - §948

Karches v. City of Cincinnati - §1484

Kasten Construction Co. v. Maple Ridge Construction Co. - §1515

Keeble v. Hickeringill - §11

Kelo v. City of New London - §1466

Kendall v. Ernest Pestana, Inc. - §§1060, 1061

Kennedy v. Kidd - §966

Keppell v. Bailey - §1203

Kern, In re Estate of - §510

Keystone Bituminous Coal Association v. DeBenedictis - §1478

Killam v. March - §1805

King, In re Marriage of - §702

Mid-State Investment Corp. v. O'Steen - **§1694**

Milheim v. Baxter - **§869**

Miller v. Green - **§1756**

Miller v. Lutheran Conference & Camp Association -
  §§1165, 1170

Miller v. Riegler - **§596**

Miller, State ex rel. v. Manders - **§1461**

Minjak Co. v. Randolph - **§857**

Miss Porter's School, Inc. v. Town Plan & Zoning
  Commission - **§1412**

Mitchell v. Castellaw - **§§1092, 1126**

Mohawk Containers, Inc. v. Hancock - **§1276**

Monroe v. Rawlings - **§§93, 122**

Montoya v. Barreras - **§1277**

Moore v. City of East Cleveland - **§§1389, 1448**

Moore v. Phillips - **§334**

Moore v. Regents of the University of California - **§54**

Morgan v. High Penn Oil Co. - **§1321**

Morgan v. Wiser - **§64**

Morone v. Morone - **§742**

Morse v. Aldrich - **§1204**

Morse v. Curtis - **§1774**

Mortensen v. Lingo - **§1736**

Moseley v. Bishop - **§1206**

Moudry v. Parkos - **§789**

Mountain Brow Lodge No. 82 v. Toscano - **§357**

Mowatt v. 1540 Lake Shore Drive Corp. - **§1307**

Mugaas v. Smith - **§1729**

Murphy v. Financial Development Corp. - **§1706**

Myron W. McIntyre, Ltd. v. Chanler Holding Corp. - **§933**

N

Nahrstedt v. Lakeside Village Condominium Association -
  §1294

National Audubon Society v. Superior Court - **§42**

Neal v. Craig Brown, Inc. - **§1038**

Nectow v. City of Cambridge - **§1385**

Neponsit Property Owners' Association v. Emigrant
  Industrial Savings Bank - **§§1214, 1242, 1252,
  1257**

New Jersey Coalition Against War in the Middle East v.
  J.M.B. Realty Corp. - **§179**

Newman v. Bost - **§213**

Newman v. Chase - **§652**

Newman v. Dore - **§720**

Nicholson v. Connecticut Half-Way House, Inc. - **§1324**

Niernberg v. Feld - **§1514**

Nitschke v. Doggett - **§797**

Noble v. Murphy - **§1294**

Nogarr, People v. - **§620**

Nollan v. California Coastal Commission - **§§1481, 1482**

Nome 2000 v. Fagerstrom - **§122**

Noone v. Price - **§§1360, 1361**

Northwest Real Estate Co. v. Serio - **§351**

O

O'Brien v. O'Brien - **§706**

O'Buck v. Cottonwood Village Condominium Association
  - **§1295**

O'Callaghan v. Waller & Beckwith Realty Co. - **§952**

O'Connor v. Clark - **§236**

O'Keeffe v. Snyder - **§145**

Oak's Oil Service, Inc. v. Massachusetts Bay Transportation Authority - **§392**

Oates v. Jag, Inc. - **§1676**

Oceanside, City of v. McKenna - **§1300**

Ochoa v. Rogers - **§47**

Old Line Life Insurance Co. v. Hawn - **§985**

Oldfield v. Stoeco Homes, Inc. - **§291**

Olivas v. Olivas - **§668**

Oppelt, In re Estate of - **§1519**

Orr v. Byers - **§1737**

Osin v. Johnson - **§1748**

Otero v. Pacheco - **§1122**

Othen v. Rosier - **§1128**

PQ

PA Northwestern Distributors, Inc. v. Zoning Hearing
  Board - **§1406**

Pacific Gamble Robinson Co. v. Lapp - **§739**

Page County Appliance Center, Inc. v. Honeywell, Inc. -
  §1313

Paine v. Meller - **§1553**

Painter v. Painter - **§702**

Pakenham's Case - **§1208**

Palazzolo v. Rhode Island - **§§1474, 1480**

Palmer v. Flint - **§609**

Palmer v. Palmer - **§§1130, 1132**

Palmer v. 309 East 87th Street Co. - **§1061**

Paradine v. Jane - **§972**

Park Place Home Brokers v. P-K Mobile Home Park -
  §832

Parker & Edgarton v. Foote - **§1187**

Parr v. Worley - **§1596**

Pasadena, City of v. California-Michigan Land & Water
  Co. - **§1161**

Patterson v. Bryant - **§1732**

Patterson v. Reigle - **§98**

Pearson v. Gardner - **§1510**

Pearson, In re Estate of - **§556**

Peet v. Roth Hotel Co. - **§§191, 196**

Pendergrast v. Aiken - **§28**

Pendoley v. Ferreira - **§1316**

Penn Bowling Recreation Center, Inc. v. Hot Shoppes,
  Inc. - **§1157**

Penn Central Transportation Co. v. City of New York -
  §§1440, 1480

Pennell v. City of San Jose - **§960**

Tri-State Hotel Co. v. Sphinx Investment Co. - **§1518**
Trustees of Columbia College v. Thacher - **§1277**
Tucker v. Badoian - **§28**
Tulk v. Moxhay - **§1220**
Turner v. Brocato - **§1231**
Tuttle, People *ex rel.* v. Walton - **§1015**
Tygard v. McComb - **§224**
Tyus v. Resta - **§1677**

U

Umphres v. J.R. Mayer Enterprises - **§1160**
Union Bond & Trust Co. v. Blue Creek Redwood Co. -
 §1692
Union National Bank of Lowell v. Nesmith - **§1181**
United States v. - *see* name of party
United States Jaycees v. McClure - **§177**
United States National Bank v. Homeland, Inc. - **§1032**
University Club v. Deakin - **§871**
Urbaitis v. Commonwealth Edison - **§1109**
Uston v. Resorts International Hotel, Inc. - **§178**

V

Vadney, *In re* Estate of - **§612**
Valatie, Village of v. Smith - **§1405**
Vanna White v. Samsung Electronics America, Inc. - **§51**
Van Sandt v. Royster - **§1122**
Van Valkenburgh v. Lutz - **§95**
Vasquez v. Glassboro Service Association - **§1024**
Vickers v. Township Committee - **§1449**
Village Board v. Jarrold - **§1418**
Village of - *see* name of village

WX

Waldorff Insurance & Bonding, Inc. v. Eglin National
 Bank - **§1756**
Waldrop v. Town of Brevard - **§1183**
Walker Rogge, Inc. v. Chelsea Title & Guaranty Co. -
 §1813
Wallach v. Riverside Bank - **§1517**
Walls v. Oxford Management Co. - **§944**
Walters v. Tucker - **§1588**
Ward v. Mattuschek - **§1500**
Warshawsky v. American Automotive Products Co. -
 §976

Waschak v. Moffat - **§1312**
Watts v. Watts - **§744**
Wayne, County of v. Hathcock - **§1466**
Weisner v. 791 Park Avenue Corp. - **§§355, 1307**
Welke v. City of Davenport - **§161**
Welton v. Gallagher - **§209**
Westchester, County of v. Town of Greenwich - **§1313**
Westchester Day School v. Village of Mamaroneck - **§1437**
Western Land Co. v. Truskolaski - **§1277**
Westville, Borough of v. Whitney Home Builders, Inc. -
 §35
Wetherbee v. Green - **§46**
Wheeler v. Schad - **§1205**
Whetzel v. Jess Fisher Management Co. - **§948**
White v. Brown - **§327**
White v. Smyth - **§676**
White v. Western Title Insurance Co. - **§1813**
Whitinsville Plaza, Inc. v. Kotseas - **§1249**
Wiggill v. Cheney - **§1600**
Wiley v. Tom Howell & Associates - **§1503**
Willard v. First Church of Christ, Scientist - **§1116**
Williams v. Melby - **§950**
Willow River Power Co., United States v. - **§43**
Winchester v. City of Stevens Point - **§163**
Wineberg v. Moore - **§1756**
Winkler v. Miller - **§1754**
Winston Towers 200 Association v. Saverio - **§1295**
Witter v. Taggart - **§1776**
Wolinsky v. Kadison - **§1301**
Womack v. Hyche - **§771**
Womack v. Stegner - **§1585**
Wood v. Board of County Commissioners - **§283**
Wright v. Bloom - **§630**

Y

Yee v. City of Escondido - **§1471**
Young v. Garwacki - **§950**
Young v. Hichens - **§§8, 9**
Younge, Estate of v. Huysmans - **§§1500, 1537**

Z

Zimmerman v. Shreeve - **§167**
Zylka v. City of Crystal - **§1422**

Index

Index

absolute, **§256**

"and his heirs," **§§258-260**

creation, **§§257-260**

restraints on. *See* Alienation

transferability, **§§261-277**

FEE SIMPLE CONDITIONAL, §298

FEE SIMPLE DETERMINABLE, §§279-285, 399

automatic termination, **§280**

creation, **§§282-283**

possibility of reverter, **§285**. *See also* Possibility of reverter

remainder following, **§399**

Rule Against Perpetuities, **§544**

transferability, **§284**

FEE SIMPLE SUBJECT TO CONDITION SUBSEQUENT, §§286-291

creation, **§§288-290**

determinable fee, distinguished from, **§§291-295**

right of entry, **§290**. *See also* Right of entry

FEE SIMPLE SUBJECT TO EXECUTORY LIMITATION, §296

FEE TAIL, §§297-320

FEUDALISM, §§241-245

FINDERS, §§57-77

abandoned property, **§§75-76**

employee, **§65**

equitable division, **§76**

general rule, **§57**

lost-mislaid distinction, **§72**

multiple finders, **§76**

object under soil, **§67**

"possession" defined, **§61**

"prior possessor" rule, **§§57-62**

private home, **§§69-70**

public place, **§§71-74**

treasure trove, **§68**

trespasser, **§§60, 64**

FIRST IN TIME RULE, §2

See also Capture, rule of

FIXTURES, §§982-987

See also Landlord and tenant

FOUR UNITIES RULE

See Co-tenancies

FREE RIDER PROBLEM, §1338

See also Nuisance

FREEHOLD ESTATES, §§251, 256-329

FUTURE INTERESTS

See also Executory interests; Possibility of reverter; Remainders; Reversion; Right of entry

defined, **§366**

in grantee, **§§373-375**

in grantor, **§§368-372**

Notes

Notes

Notes

Notes

Notes

Notes

Notes

Notes

Notes

Notes

Notes